Honda Civic Automotive Repair Manual

by Mike Stubblefield, Robert Maddox and John H Haynes

Member of the Guild of Motoring Writers

Models covered:
All Honda Civic, CRX and Wagon models
1984 through 1990

ABCDE
FGHIJ
KLMNO
PQRST

Haynes Publishing Group
Sparkford Nr Yeovil
Somerset BA22 7JJ England

Haynes Publications, Inc
861 Lawrence Drive
Newbury Park
California 91320 USA

Acknowledgement

We are grateful to the Champion Spark Plug Company who supplied the illustrations of various spark plug conditions.

© Haynes Publishing Group 1990

A book in the **Haynes Automotive Repair Manual Series**

Printed by J.H. Haynes & Co., Ltd. Sparkford Nr. Yeovil, Somerset BA22 7JJ, England

ISBN 1 85010 722 X

Library of Congress Catalog Card Number 90-83971

Contents

1989 Honda CRX Si

1989 Honda Civic Si Hatchback

1989 Honda Civic DX Four-door sedan

1989 Honda Civic 4WD Wagon

About this manual

Its purpose

The purpose of this manual is to help you get the best value from your vehicle. It can do so in several ways. It can help you decide what work must be done, even if you choose to have it done by a dealer service department or a repair shop; it provides information and procedures for routine maintenance and servicing; and it offers diagnostic and repair procedures to follow when trouble occurs.

We hope you use the manual to tackle the work yourself. For many simpler jobs, doing it yourself may be quicker than arranging an appointment to get the vehicle into a shop and making the trips to leave it and pick it up. More importantly, a lot of money can be saved by avoiding the expense the shop must pass on to you to cover its labor and overhead costs. An added benefit is the sense of satisfaction and accomplishment that you feel after doing the job yourself.

Using the manual

The manual is divided into Chapters. Each Chapter is divided into numbered Sections, which are headed in bold type between horizontal lines. Each Section consists of consecutively numbered paragraphs.

At the beginning of each numbered Section you will be referred to any illustrations which apply to the procedures in that Section. The reference numbers used in illustration captions pinpoint the pertinent Section and the Step within that Section. That is, illustration 3.2 means the illustration refers to Section 3 and Step (or paragraph) 2 within that Section.

Procedures, once described in the text, are not normally repeated. When it's necessary to refer to another Chapter, the reference will be given as Chapter and Section number. Cross references given without use of the word "Chapter" apply to Sections and/or paragraphs in the same Chapter. For example, "see Section 8" means in the same Chapter.

References to the left or right side of the vehicle assume you are sitting in the driver's seat, facing forward.

Even though we have prepared this manual with extreme care, neither the publisher nor the author can accept responsibility for any errors in, or omissions from, the information given.

NOTE

A **Note** provides information necessary to properly complete a procedure or information which will make the procedure easier to understand.

CAUTION

A **Caution** provides a special procedure or special steps which must be taken while completing the procedure where the **Caution** is found. Not heeding a **Caution** can result in damage to the assembly being worked on.

WARNING

A **Warning** provides a special procedure or special steps which must be taken while completing the procedure where the **Warning** is found. Not heeding a **Warning** can result in personal injury.

Introduction to the Honda Civic, CRX and Wagon

These models are available in two and four-door sedan, station wagon and hatchback body styles.

The transversely mounted inline four-cylinder engines used in these models are equipped with a carburetor or electronic fuel injection.

The engine drives the front wheels through either a five-speed manual or four-speed automatic transaxle via independent driveaxles. On four-wheel drive models, a transfer case, located on the transaxle, and a driveshaft are used to provide drive to the rear differential. On early models, a solid live axle is used at the rear. On later models, independent driveaxles are used.

Independent suspension, featuring strut damper units and either torsion bars (early models) or coil springs (later models), is used at the front wheels. On early models, the rear of the vehicle is suspended by a solid axle and strut/coil spring assemblies. On later models, independent suspension is used, featuring either strut/coil spring assemblies or separate coil springs and shock absorbers.

The power assisted rack and pinion steering unit is mounted behind the engine.

The brakes are disc at the front with either drum or discs at the rear, depending on model, with power assist standard.

Vehicle identification numbers

Modifications are a continuing and unpublicized process in vehicle manufacturing. Since spare parts manuals and lists are compiled on a numerical basis, the individual vehicle numbers are essential to correctly identify the component required.

Vehicle Identification Number (VIN)

This very important identification number is stamped on the firewall in the engine compartment and on a plate attached to the dashboard inside the windshield on the driver's side of the vehicle **(see illustration)**. The VIN also appears on the Vehicle Certificate of Title and Registration. It contains information such as where and when the vehicle was manufactured, the model year and the body style.

Engine number

On early models, the engine number is stamped into the right rear side of the engine block and is also on a plate on the left side of the radiator support. On later models, the engine number is stamped into the right front side of the engine block.

Transaxle number

The transaxle number is on a label or plate on the top or front surface of the transaxle.

Certification label

The certification label is located on the left front door pillar. It contains the name of the manufacturer, the month and year of production, the Gross Vehicle Weight Rating (GVWR) and the certification statement.

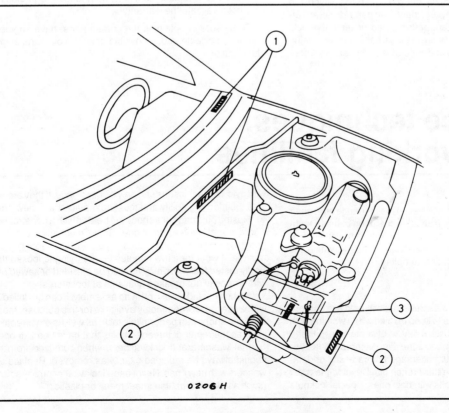

Vehicle identification number locations (early model shown)

1   Vehicle identification number
2   Engine number
3   Transaxle number

0206H

Buying parts

Replacement parts are available from many sources, which generally fall into one of two categories – authorized dealer parts departments and independent retail auto parts stores. Our advice concerning these parts is as follows:

Retail auto parts stores: Good auto parts stores will stock frequently needed components which wear out relatively fast, such as clutch components, exhaust systems, brake parts, tune-up parts, etc. These stores often supply new or reconditioned parts on an exchange basis, which can save a considerable amount of money. Discount auto parts stores are often very good places to buy materials and parts needed for general vehicle maintenance such as oil, grease, filters, spark plugs, belts, touch-up paint, bulbs, etc. They also usually sell tools and general accessories, have con-venient hours, charge lower prices and can often be found not far from home.

Authorized dealer parts department: This is the best source for parts which are unique to the vehicle and not generally available else-where (such as major engine parts, transmission parts, trim pieces, etc.).

Warranty information: If the vehicle is still covered under warranty, be sure that any replacement parts purchased – regardless of the source – do not invalidate the warranty!

To be sure of obtaining the correct parts, have engine and chassis numbers available and, if possible, take the old parts along for positive identification.

Maintenance techniques, tools and working facilities

Maintenance techniques

There are a number of techniques involved in maintenance and repair that will be referred to throughout this manual. Application of these techniques will enable the home mechanic to be more efficient, better organized and capable of performing the various tasks properly, which will ensure that the repair job is thorough and complete.

Fasteners

Fasteners are nuts, bolts, studs and screws used to hold two or more parts together. There are a few things to keep in mind when working with fasteners. Almost all of them use a locking device of some type, either a lockwasher, locknut, locking tab or thread adhesive. All threaded fasteners should be clean and straight, with undamaged threads and undamaged corners on the hex head where the wrench fits. Develop the habit of replacing all damaged nuts and bolts with new ones. Special locknuts with nylon or fiber inserts can only be used once. If they are removed, they lose their locking ability and must be replaced with new ones.

Rusted nuts and bolts should be treated with a penetrating fluid to ease removal and prevent breakage. Some mechanics use turpentine in a spout-type oil can, which works quite well. After applying the rust penetrant, let it work for a few minutes before trying to loosen the nut or bolt. Badly rusted fasteners may have to be chiseled or sawed off or removed with a special nut breaker, available at tool stores.

If a bolt or stud breaks off in an assembly, it can be drilled and removed with a special tool commonly available for this purpose. Most automotive machine shops can perform this task, as well as other repair procedures, such as the repair of threaded holes that have been stripped out.

Flat washers and lockwashers, when removed from an assembly, should always be replaced exactly as removed. Replace any damaged washers with new ones. Never use a lockwasher on any soft metal surface (such as aluminum), thin sheet metal or plastic.

Fastener sizes

For a number of reasons, automobile manufacturers are making wider and wider use of metric fasteners. Therefore, it is important to be able to tell the difference between standard (sometimes called U.S. or SAE) and metric hardware, since they cannot be interchanged.

All bolts, whether standard or metric, are sized according to diameter, thread pitch and length. For example, a standard 1/2 – 13 x 1 bolt is 1/2 inch in diameter, has 13 threads per inch and is 1 inch long. An M12 – 1.75 x 25 metric bolt is 12 mm in diameter, has a thread pitch of 1.75 mm (the distance between threads) and is 25 mm long. The two bolts are nearly identical, and easily confused, but they are not interchangeable.

In addition to the differences in diameter, thread pitch and length, metric and standard bolts can also be distinguished by examining the bolt heads. To begin with, the distance across the flats on a standard bolt head is measured in inches, while the same dimension on a metric bolt is sized in millimeters (the same is true for nuts). As a result, a standard wrench should not be used on a metric bolt and a metric wrench should not be used on a standard bolt. Also, most standard bolts have slashes radiating out from the center of the head to denote the grade or strength of the bolt, which is an indication of the amount of torque that can be applied to it. The greater the number of slashes, the greater the strength of the bolt. Grades 0 through 5 are commonly used on automobiles. Metric bolts have a property class (grade) number, rather than a slash, molded into their heads to indicate bolt strength. In this case, the higher the number, the stronger the bolt. Property class numbers 8.8, 9.8 and 10.9 are commonly used on automobiles.

Strength markings can also be used to distinguish standard hex nuts from metric hex nuts. Many standard nuts have dots stamped into one side, while metric nuts are marked with a number. The greater the number of dots, or the higher the number, the greater the strength of the nut.

Metric studs are also marked on their ends according to property class (grade). Larger studs are numbered (the same as metric bolts), while smaller studs carry a geometric code to denote grade.

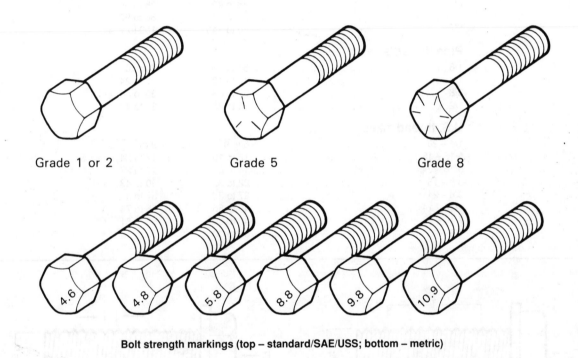

Grade 1 or 2   Grade 5   Grade 8

4.6   4.8   5.8   8.8   9.8   10.9

Bolt strength markings (top – standard/SAE/USS; bottom – metric)

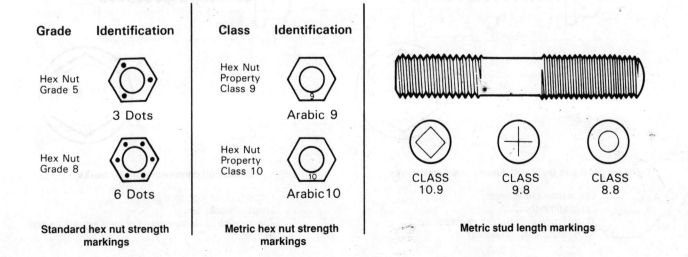

Grade	Identification
Hex Nut Grade 5	3 Dots
Hex Nut Grade 8	6 Dots

Standard hex nut strength markings

Class	Identification
Hex Nut Property Class 9	Arabic 9
Hex Nut Property Class 10	Arabic 10

Metric hex nut strength markings

CLASS 10.9   CLASS 9.8   CLASS 8.8

Metric stud length markings

It should be noted that many fasteners, especially Grades 0 through 2, have no distinguishing marks on them. When such is the case, the only way to determine whether it is standard or metric is to measure the thread pitch or compare it to a known fastener of the same size.

Standard fasteners are often referred to as SAE, as opposed to metric. However, it should be noted that SAE technically refers to a non-metric *fine thread* fastener only. Coarse thread non-metric fasteners are referred to as USS sizes.

Since fasteners of the same size (both standard and metric) may have different strength ratings, be sure to reinstall any bolts, studs or nuts removed from your vehicle in their original locations. Also, when replacing a fastener with a new one, make sure that the new one has a strength rating equal to or greater than the original.

Tightening sequences and procedures

Most threaded fasteners should be tightened to a specific torque value (torque is the twisting force applied to a threaded component such as a nut or bolt). Overtightening the fastener can weaken it and cause it to break, while undertightening can cause it to eventually come loose. Bolts, screws and studs, depending on the material they are made of and their thread diameters, have specific torque values, many of which are noted in the Specifications at the beginning of each Chapter. Be sure to follow the torque recommendations closely. For fasteners not assigned a specific torque, a general torque value chart is presented here as a guide. These torque values are for dry (unlubricated) fasteners threaded into steel or cast iron (not aluminum). As was previously mentioned, the size and grade of a fastener determine the amount of torque that can safely be

Metric thread sizes	Ft-lbs	Nm
M-6	6 to 9	9 to 12
M-8	14 to 21	19 to 28
M-10	28 to 40	38 to 54
M-12	50 to 71	68 to 96
M-14	80 to 140	109 to 154

Pipe thread sizes		
1/8	5 to 8	7 to 10
1/4	12 to 18	17 to 24
3/8	22 to 33	30 to 44
1/2	25 to 35	34 to 47

U.S. thread sizes		
1/4 – 20	6 to 9	9 to 12
5/16 – 18	12 to 18	17 to 24
5/16 – 24	14 to 20	19 to 27
3/8 – 16	22 to 32	30 to 43
3/8 – 24	27 to 38	37 to 51
7/16 – 14	40 to 55	55 to 74
7/16 – 20	40 to 60	55 to 81
1/2 – 13	55 to 80	75 to 108

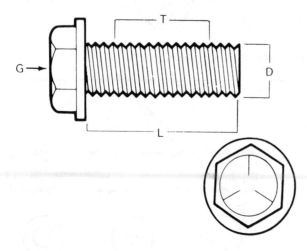

Standard (SAE and USS) bolt dimensions/grade marks

- G   Grade marks (bolt length)
- L   Length (in inches)
- T   Thread pitch (number of threads per inch)
- D   Nominal diameter (in inches)

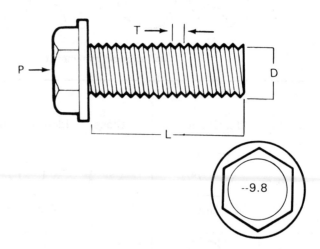

Metric bolt dimensions/grade marks

- P   Property class (bolt strength)
- L   Length (in millimeters)
- T   Thread pitch (distance between threads in millimeters)
- D   Diameter

applied to it. The figures listed here are approximate for Grade 2 and Grade 3 fasteners. Higher grades can tolerate higher torque values.

Fasteners laid out in a pattern, such as cylinder head bolts, oil pan bolts, differential cover bolts, etc., must be loosened or tightened in sequence to avoid warping the component. This sequence will normally be shown in the appropriate Chapter. If a specific pattern is not given, the following procedures can be used to prevent warping.

Initially, the bolts or nuts should be assembled finger-tight only. Next, they should be tightened one full turn each, in a criss-cross or diagonal pattern. After each one has been tightened one full turn, return to the first one and tighten them all one-half turn, following the same pattern. Finally, tighten each of them one-quarter turn at a time until each fastener has been tightened to the proper torque. To loosen and remove the fasteners, the procedure would be reversed.

Component disassembly

Component disassembly should be done with care and purpose to help ensure that the parts go back together properly. Always keep track of the sequence in which parts are removed. Make note of special characteristics or marks on parts that can be installed more than one way, such as a grooved thrust washer on a shaft. It is a good idea to lay the disassembled parts out on a clean surface in the order that they were removed. It may also be helpful to make sketches or take instant photos of components before removal.

When removing fasteners from a component, keep track of their locations. Sometimes threading a bolt back in a part, or putting the washers and nut back on a stud, can prevent mix-ups later. If nuts and bolts cannot be returned to their original locations, they should be kept in a compartmented box or a series of small boxes. A cupcake or muffin tin is ideal for this purpose, since each cavity can hold the bolts and nuts from a particular area (i.e. oil pan bolts, valve cover bolts, engine mount bolts, etc.). A pan of this type is especially helpful when working on assemblies with very small parts, such as the carburetor, alternator, valve train or interior dash and trim pieces. The cavities can be marked with paint or tape to identify the contents.

Whenever wiring looms, harnesses or connectors are separated, it is a good idea to identify the two halves with numbered pieces of masking tape so they can be easily reconnected.

Gasket sealing surfaces

Throughout any vehicle, gaskets are used to seal the mating surfaces between two parts and keep lubricants, fluids, vacuum or pressure contained in an assembly.

Many times these gaskets are coated with a liquid or paste-type gasket sealing compound before assembly. Age, heat and pressure can sometimes cause the two parts to stick together so tightly that they are very difficult to separate. Often, the assembly can be loosened by striking it with a soft-face hammer near the mating surfaces. A regular hammer can be used if a block of wood is placed between the hammer and the part. Do not hammer on cast parts or parts that could be easily damaged. With any particularly stubborn part, always recheck to make sure that every fastener has been removed.

Avoid using a screwdriver or bar to pry apart an assembly, as they can easily mar the gasket sealing surfaces of the parts, which must remain smooth. If prying is absolutely necessary, use an old broom handle, but keep in mind that extra clean up will be necessary if the wood splinters.

After the parts are separated, the old gasket must be carefully scraped off and the gasket surfaces cleaned. Stubborn gasket material can be soaked with rust penetrant or treated with a special chemical to soften it so it can be easily scraped off. A scraper can be fashioned from a piece of copper tubing by flattening and sharpening one end. Copper is recommended because it is usually softer than the surfaces to be scraped, which reduces the chance of gouging the part. Some gaskets can be removed with a wire brush, but regardless of the method used, the mating surfaces must be left clean and smooth. If for some reason the gasket surface is gouged, then a gasket sealer thick enough to fill scratches will have to be used during reassembly of the components. For most applications, a non-drying (or semi-drying) gasket sealer should be used.

Hose removal tips

Warning: *If the vehicle is equipped with air conditioning, do not disconnect any of the A/C hoses without first having the system depressurized by a dealer service department or a service station.*

Hose removal precautions closely parallel gasket removal precautions. Avoid scratching or gouging the surface that the hose mates against or the connection may leak. This is especially true for radiator hoses. Because of various chemical reactions, the rubber in hoses can bond itself to the metal spigot that the hose fits over. To remove a hose, first loosen the hose clamps that secure it to the spigot. Then, with slip-joint pliers, grab the hose at the clamp and rotate it around the spigot. Work it back and forth until it is completely free, then pull it off. Silicone or other lubricants will ease removal if they can be applied between the hose and the outside of the spigot. Apply the same lubricant to the inside of the hose and the outside of the spigot to simplify installation.

As a last resort (and if the hose is to be replaced with a new one anyway), the rubber can be slit with a knife and the hose peeled from the spigot. If this must be done, be careful that the metal connection is not damaged.

If a hose clamp is broken or damaged, do not reuse it. Wire-type clamps usually weaken with age, so it is a good idea to replace them with screw-type clamps whenever a hose is removed.

Tools

A selection of good tools is a basic requirement for anyone who plans to maintain and repair his or her own vehicle. For the owner who has few tools, the initial investment might seem high, but when compared to the spiraling costs of professional auto maintenance and repair, it is a wise one.

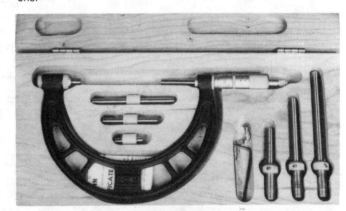

Micrometer set

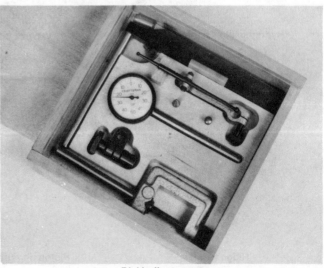

Dial indicator set

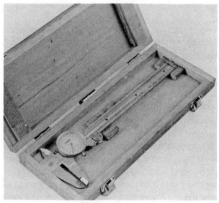

Dial caliper

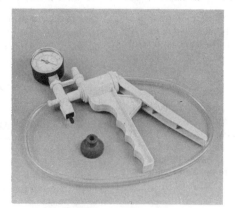

Hand-operated vacuum pump

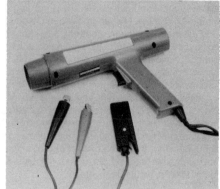

Timing light

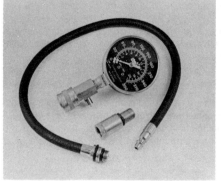

Compression gauge with spark plug
hole adapter

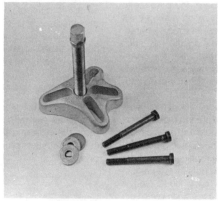

Damper/steering wheel puller

General purpose puller

Hydraulic lifter removal tool

Valve spring compressor

Valve spring compressor

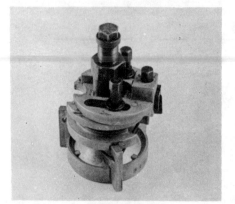

Ridge reamer

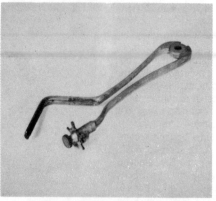

Piston ring groove cleaning tool

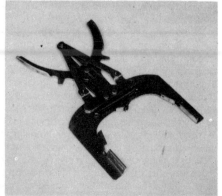

Ring removal/installation tool

Ring compressor

Cylinder hone

Brake hold-down spring tool

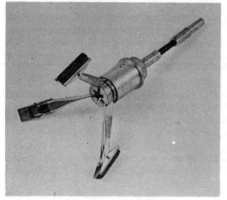
Brake cylinder hone

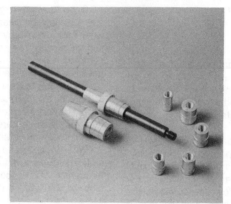
Clutch plate alignment tool

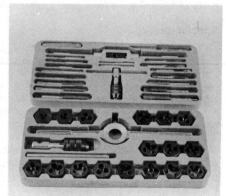
Tap and die set

To help the owner decide which tools are needed to perform the tasks detailed in this manual, the following tool lists are offered: *Maintenance and minor repair, Repair/overhaul and Special.*

The newcomer to practical mechanics should start off with the maintenance and minor repair tool kit, which is adequate for the simpler jobs performed on a vehicle. Then, as confidence and experience grow, the owner can tackle more difficult tasks, buying additional tools as they are needed. Eventually the basic kit will be expanded into the repair and overhaul tool set. Over a period of time, the experienced do-it-yourselfer will assemble a tool set complete enough for most repair and overhaul procedures and will add tools from the special category when it is felt that the expense is justified by the frequency of use.

Maintenance and minor repair tool kit

The tools in this list should be considered the minimum required for performance of routine maintenance, servicing and minor repair work. We recommend the purchase of combination wrenches (box-end and open-end combined in one wrench). While more expensive than open end wrenches, they offer the advantages of both types of wrench.

Combination wrench set (1/4-inch to 1 inch or 6 mm to 19 mm)
Adjustable wrench, 8 inch
Spark plug wrench with rubber insert
Spark plug gap adjusting tool
Feeler gauge set
Brake bleeder wrench
Standard screwdriver (5/16-inch x 6 inch)
Phillips screwdriver (No. 2 x 6 inch)
Combination pliers – 6 inch
Hacksaw and assortment of blades
Tire pressure gauge
Grease gun
Oil can
Fine emery cloth
Wire brush

Battery post and cable cleaning tool
Oil filter wrench
Funnel (medium size)
Safety goggles
Jackstands(2)
Drain pan

Note: *If basic tune-ups are going to be part of routine maintenance, it will be necessary to purchase a good quality stroboscopic timing light and combination tachometer/dwell meter. Although they are included in the list of special tools, it is mentioned here because they are absolutely necessary for tuning most vehicles properly.*

Repair and overhaul tool set

These tools are essential for anyone who plans to perform major repairs and are in addition to those in the maintenance and minor repair tool kit. Included is a comprehensive set of sockets which, though expensive, are invaluable because of their versatility, especially when various extensions and drives are available. We recommend the 1/2-inch drive over the 3/8-inch drive. Although the larger drive is bulky and more expensive, it has the capacity of accepting a very wide range of large sockets. Ideally, however, the mechanic should have a 3/8-inch drive set and a 1/2-inch drive set.

Socket set(s)
Reversible ratchet
Extension – 10 inch
Universal joint
Torque wrench (same size drive as sockets)
Ball peen hammer – 8 ounce
Soft-face hammer (plastic/rubber)
Standard screwdriver (1/4-inch x 6 inch)
Standard screwdriver (stubby – 5/16-inch)
Phillips screwdriver (No. 3 x 8 inch)
Phillips screwdriver (stubby – No. 2)

Pliers – vise grip
Pliers – lineman's
Pliers – needle nose
Pliers – snap-ring (internal and external)
Cold chisel – 1/2-inch
Scribe
Scraper (made from flattened copper tubing)
Centerpunch
Pin punches (1/16, 1/8, 3/16-inch)
Steel rule/straightedge – 12 inch
Allen wrench set (1/8 to 3/8-inch or 4 mm to 10 mm)
A selection of files
Wire brush (large)
Jackstands (second set)
Jack (scissor or hydraulic type)

Note: Another tool which is often useful is an electric drill with a chuck capacity of 3/8-inch and a set of good quality drill bits.

Special tools

The tools in this list include those which are not used regularly, are expensive to buy, or which need to be used in accordance with their manufacturer's instructions. Unless these tools will be used frequently, it is not very economical to purchase many of them. A consideration would be to split the cost and use between yourself and a friend or friends. In addition, most of these tools can be obtained from a tool rental shop on a temporary basis.

This list primarily contains only those tools and instruments widely available to the public, and not those special tools produced by the vehicle manufacturer for distribution to dealer service departments. Occasionally, references to the manufacturer's special tools are included in the text of this manual. Generally, an alternative method of doing the job without the special tool is offered. However, sometimes there is no alternative to their use. Where this is the case, and the tool cannot be purchased or borrowed, the work should be turned over to the dealer service department or an automotive repair shop.

Valve spring compressor
Piston ring groove cleaning tool
Piston ring compressor
Piston ring installation tool
Cylinder compression gauge
Cylinder ridge reamer
Cylinder surfacing hone
Cylinder bore gauge
Micrometers and/or dial calipers
Hydraulic lifter removal tool
Balljoint separator
Universal-type puller
Impact screwdriver
Dial indicator set
Stroboscopic timing light (inductive pick-up)
Hand operated vacuum/pressure pump
Tachometer/dwell meter
Universal electrical multimeter
Cable hoist
Brake spring removal and installation tools
Floor jack

Buying tools

For the do-it-yourselfer who is just starting to get involved in vehicle maintenance and repair, there are a number of options available when purchasing tools. If maintenance and minor repair is the extent of the work to be done, the purchase of individual tools is satisfactory. If, on the other hand, extensive work is planned, it would be a good idea to purchase a modest tool set from one of the large retail chain stores. A set can usually be bought at a substantial savings over the individual tool prices, and they often come with a tool box. As additional tools are needed, add–on sets, individual tools and a larger tool box can be purchased to expand the tool selection. Building a tool set gradually allows the cost of the tools to be spread over a longer period of time and gives the mechanic the freedom to choose only those tools that will actually be used.

Tool stores will often be the only source of some of the special tools that are needed, but regardless of where tools are bought, try to avoid cheap ones, especially when buying screwdrivers and sockets, because they won't last very long. The expense involved in replacing cheap tools will eventually be greater than the initial cost of quality tools.

Care and maintenance of tools

Good tools are expensive, so it makes sense to treat them with respect. Keep them clean and in usable condition and store them properly when not in use. Always wipe off any dirt, grease or metal chips before putting them away. Never leave tools lying around in the work area. Upon completion of a job, always check closely under the hood for tools that may have been left there so they won't get lost during a test drive.

Some tools, such as screwdrivers, pliers, wrenches and sockets, can be hung on a panel mounted on the garage or workshop wall, while others should be kept in a tool box or tray. Measuring instruments, gauges, meters, etc. must be carefully stored where they cannot be damaged by weather or impact from other tools.

When tools are used with care and stored properly, they will last a very long time. Even with the best of care, though, tools will wear out if used frequently. When a tool is damaged or worn out, replace it. Subsequent jobs will be safer and more enjoyable if you do.

Working facilities

Not to be overlooked when discussing tools is the workshop. If anything more than routine maintenance is to be carried out, some sort of suitable work area is essential.

It is understood, and appreciated, that many home mechanics do not have a good workshop or garage available, and end up removing an engine or doing major repairs outside. It is recommended, however, that the overhaul or repair be completed under the cover of a roof.

A clean, flat workbench or table of comfortable working height is an absolute necessity. The workbench should be equipped with a vise that has a jaw opening of at least four inches.

As mentioned previously, some clean, dry storage space is also required for tools, as well as the lubricants, fluids, cleaning solvents, etc. which soon become necessary.

Sometimes waste oil and fluids, drained from the engine or cooling system during normal maintenance or repairs, present a disposal problem. To avoid pouring them on the ground or into a sewage system, pour the used fluids into large containers, seal them with caps and take them to an authorized disposal site or recycling center. Plastic jugs, such as old antifreeze containers, are ideal for this purpose.

Always keep a supply of old newspapers and clean rags available. Old towels are excellent for mopping up spills. Many mechanics use rolls of paper towels for most work because they are readily available and disposable. To help keep the area under the vehicle clean, a large cardboard box can be cut open and flattened to protect the garage or shop floor.

Whenever working over a painted surface, such as when leaning over a fender to service something under the hood, always cover it with an old blanket or bedspread to protect the finish. Vinyl covered pads, made especially for this purpose, are available at auto parts stores.

Booster battery (jump) starting

Observe these precautions when using a booster battery to start a vehicle:

a) Before connecting the booster battery, make sure the ignition switch is in the Off position.

b) Turn off the lights, heater and other electrical loads.

c) Your eyes should be shielded. Safety goggles are a good idea.

d) Make sure the booster battery is the same voltage as the dead one in the vehicle.

e) The two vehicles MUST NOT TOUCH each other!

f) Make sure the transmission is in Neutral (manual) or Park (automatic).

g) If the booster battery is not a maintenance-free type, remove the vent caps and lay a cloth over the vent holes.

Connect the red jumper cable to the positive (+) terminals of each battery.

Connect one end of the black jumper cable to the negative (–) terminal of the booster battery. The other end of this cable should be connected to a good ground on the vehicle to be started, such as a bolt or bracket on the engine block **(see illustration)**. Make sure the cable will not come into contact with the fan, drivebelts or other moving parts of the engine.

Start the engine using the booster battery, then, with the engine running at idle speed, disconnect the jumper cables in the reverse order of connection.

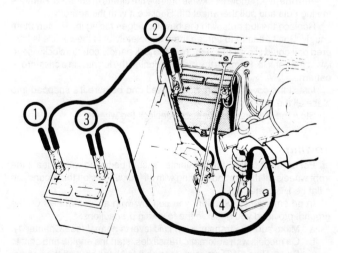

Make the booster battery cable connections in the numerical order shown (note that the negative cable of the booster battery is NOT attached to the negative terminal of the dead battery)

Jacking and towing

Jacking

Warning: *The jack supplied with the vehicle should only be used for changing a tire or placing jackstands under the frame. Never work under the vehicle or start the engine while this jack is being used as the only means of support.*

The vehicle should be on level ground. Place the shift lever in Park, if you have an automatic, or Reverse if you have a manual transaxle. Block the wheel diagonally opposite the wheel being changed. Set the parking brake.

Remove the spare tire and jack from stowage. Remove the wheel cover and trim ring (if so equipped) with the tapered end of the lug nut wrench by inserting and twisting the handle and then prying against the back of the wheel cover. Loosen, but do not remove, the lug nuts (one-half turn is sufficient).

Place the scissors-type jack under the side of the vehicle and adjust the jack height until it is sitting directly below the jacking point nearest the wheel to be changed. There is a front and rear jacking point on each side of the vehicle **(see illustration)**.

Turn the jack handle clockwise until the tire clears the ground. Remove the lug nuts and pull the wheel off. Replace it with the spare.

Replace the lug nuts with the beveled edges facing in. Tighten them snugly. Don't attempt to tighten them completely until the vehicle is lowered or it could slip off the jack. Turn the jack handle counterclockwise to lower the vehicle. Remove the jack and tighten the lug nuts in a criss-cross pattern.

Install the cover and trim ring, if used and be sure it's snapped into place all the way around.

Stow the tire, jack and wrench. Unblock the wheels.

Towing

For greatest safety, these vehicles should be towed with at least the front wheels off the ground (towing with all four wheels off the ground, on a flat bed, is preferred).

In an emergency situation, you can tow with all four wheels on the ground, provided you observe the following precautions:

a   Make sure the transmission fluid level is normal (see Chapter 1).

b   On models with automatic transaxles, start the engine and shift to D4 (or D on 4WD models), then shift to N and shut off the engine. **Note:** *If the engine does not run or the transaxle cannot be shifted while the engine is running, the vehicle must be transported on flat bed equipment.*

c   While towing, do not exceed 35 mph or tow for distances more than 50 miles.

On 4WD models, before towing the vehicle with the front wheels raised off the ground, place the transaxle in Neutral and manually disengage the 4WD system to prevent the raised wheels from turning.

Equipment specifically designed for towing should be used. It should be attached to the main structural members of the vehicle, not the bumpers or brackets.

Safety is a major consideration when towing and all applicable state and local laws must be obeyed. Safety chains must be used at all times.

While towing, the parking brake should be released and the transmission must be in Neutral. The steering must be unlocked (ignition switch in the Off position). Remember that power steering and power brakes will not work with the engine off.

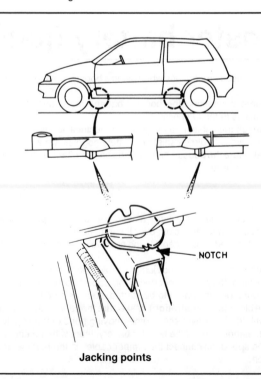

Jacking points

Automotive chemicals and lubricants

A number of automotive chemicals and lubricants are available for use during vehicle maintenance and repair. They include a wide variety of products ranging from cleaning solvents and degreasers to lubricants and protective sprays for rubber, plastic and vinyl.

Cleaners

Carburetor cleaner and choke cleaner is a strong solvent for gum, varnish and carbon. Most carburetor cleaners leave a dry-type lubricant film which will not harden or gum up. Because of this film it is not recommended for use on electrical components.

Brake system cleaner is used to remove grease and brake fluid from the brake system, where clean surfaces are absolutely necessary. It leaves no residue and often eliminates brake squeal caused by contaminants.

Electrical cleaner removes oxidation, corrosion and carbon deposits from electrical contacts, restoring full current flow. It can also be used to clean spark plugs, carburetor jets, voltage regulators and other parts where an oil-free surface is desired.

Demoisturants remove water and moisture from electrical components such as alternators, voltage regulators, electrical connectors and fuse blocks. They are non-conductive, non-corrosive and non-flammable.

Degreasers are heavy-duty solvents used to remove grease from the outside of the engine and from chassis components. They can be sprayed or brushed on and, depending on the type, are rinsed off either with water or solvent.

Lubricants

Motor oil is the lubricant formulated for use in engines. It normally contains a wide variety of additives to prevent corrosion and reduce foaming and wear. Motor oil comes in various weights (viscosity ratings) from 5 to 80. The recommended weight of the oil depends on the season, temperature and the demands on the engine. Light oil is used in cold climates and under light load conditions. Heavy oil is used in hot climates and where high loads are encountered. Multi-viscosity oils are designed to have characteristics of both light and heavy oils and are available in a number of weights from 5W-20 to 20W-50.

Gear oil is designed to be used in differentials, manual transmissions and other areas where high-temperature lubrication is required.

Chassis and wheel bearing grease is a heavy grease used where increased loads and friction are encountered, such as for wheel bearings, balljoints, tie-rod ends and universal joints.

High-temperature wheel bearing grease is designed to withstand the extreme temperatures encountered by wheel bearings in disc brake equipped vehicles. It usually contains molybdenum disulfide (moly), which is a dry-type lubricant.

White grease is a heavy grease for metal-to-metal applications where water is a problem. White grease stays soft under both low and high temperatures (usually from −100 to +190-degrees F), and will not wash off or dilute in the presence of water.

Assembly lube is a special extreme pressure lubricant, usually containing moly, used to lubricate high-load parts (such as main and rod bearings and cam lobes) for initial start-up of a new engine. The assembly lube lubricates the parts without being squeezed out or washed away until the engine oiling system begins to function.

Silicone lubricants are used to protect rubber, plastic, vinyl and nylon parts.

Graphite lubricants are used where oils cannot be used due to contamination problems, such as in locks. The dry graphite will lubricate metal parts while remaining uncontaminated by dirt, water, oil or acids. It is electrically conductive and will not foul electrical contacts in locks such as the ignition switch.

Moly penetrants loosen and lubricate frozen, rusted and corroded fasteners and prevent future rusting or freezing.

Heat-sink grease is a special electrically non-conductive grease that is used for mounting electronic ignition modules where it is essential that heat is transferred away from the module.

Sealants

RTV sealant is one of the most widely used gasket compounds. Made from silicone, RTV is air curing, it seals, bonds, waterproofs, fills surface irregularities, remains flexible, doesn't shrink, is relatively easy to remove, and is used as a supplementary sealer with almost all low and medium temperature gaskets.

Anaerobic sealant is much like RTV in that it can be used either to seal gaskets or to form gaskets by itself. It remains flexible, is solvent resistant and fills surface imperfections. The difference between an anaerobic sealant and an RTV-type sealant is in the curing. RTV cures when exposed to air, while an anaerobic sealant cures only in the absence of air. This means that an anaerobic sealant cures only after the assembly of parts, sealing them together.

Thread and pipe sealant is used for sealing hydraulic and pneumatic fittings and vacuum lines. It is usually made from a teflon compound, and comes in a spray, a paint-on liquid and as a wrap-around tape.

Chemicals

Anti-seize compound prevents seizing, galling, cold welding, rust and corrosion in fasteners. High-temperature anti-seize, usually made with copper and graphite lubricants, is used for exhaust system and exhaust manifold bolts.

Anaerobic locking compounds are used to keep fasteners from vibrating or working loose and cure only after installation, in the absence of air. Medium strength locking compound is used for small nuts, bolts and screws that may be removed later. High-strength locking compound is for large nuts, bolts and studs which aren't removed on a regular basis.

Oil additives range from viscosity index improvers to chemical treatments that claim to reduce internal engine friction. It should be noted that most oil manufacturers caution against using additives with their oils.

Gas additives perform several functions, depending on their chemical makeup. They usually contain solvents that help dissolve gum and varnish that build up on carburetor, fuel injection and intake parts. They also serve to break down carbon deposits that form on the inside surfaces of the combustion chambers. Some additives contain upper cylinder lubricants for valves and piston rings, and others contain chemicals to remove condensation from the gas tank.

Miscellaneous

Brake fluid is specially formulated hydraulic fluid that can withstand the heat and pressure encountered in brake systems. Care must be taken so this fluid does not come in contact with painted surfaces or plastics. An opened container should always be resealed to prevent contamination by water or dirt.

Weatherstrip adhesive is used to bond weatherstripping around doors, windows and trunk lids. It is sometimes used to attach trim pieces.

Undercoating is a petroleum-based, tar-like substance that is designed to protect metal surfaces on the underside of the vehicle from corrosion. It also acts as a sound-deadening agent by insulating the bottom of the vehicle.

Waxes and polishes are used to help protect painted and plated surfaces from the weather. Different types of paint may require the use of different types of wax and polish. Some polishes utilize a chemical or abrasive cleaner to help remove the top layer of oxidized (dull) paint on older vehicles. In recent years many non-wax polishes that contain a wide variety of chemicals such as polymers and silicones have been introduced. These non-wax polishes are usually easier to apply and last longer than conventional waxes and polishes.

Safety first!

Regardless of how enthusiastic you may be about getting on with the job at hand, take the time to ensure that your safety is not jeopardized. A moment's lack of attention can result in an accident, as can failure to observe certain simple safety precautions. The possibility of an accident will always exist, and the following points should not be considered a comprehensive list of all dangers. Rather, they are intended to make you aware of the risks and to encourage a safety conscious approach to all work you carry out on your vehicle.

Essential DOs and DON'Ts

DON'T rely on a jack when working under the vehicle. Always use approved jackstands to support the weight of the vehicle and place them under the recommended lift or support points.

DON'T attempt to loosen extremely tight fasteners (i.e. wheel lug nuts) while the vehicle is on a jack – it may fall.

DON'T start the engine without first making sure that the transmission is in Neutral (or Park where applicable) and the parking brake is set.

DON'T remove the radiator cap from a hot cooling system – let it cool or cover it with a cloth and release the pressure gradually.

DON'T attempt to drain the engine oil until you are sure it has cooled to the point that it will not burn you.

DON'T touch any part of the engine or exhaust system until it has cooled sufficiently to avoid burns.

DON'T siphon toxic liquids such as gasoline, antifreeze and brake fluid by mouth, or allow them to remain on your skin.

DON'T inhale brake lining dust – it is potentially hazardous (see *Asbestos* below)

DON'T allow spilled oil or grease to remain on the floor – wipe it up before someone slips on it.

DON'T use loose fitting wrenches or other tools which may slip and cause injury.

DON'T push on wrenches when loosening or tightening nuts or bolts. Always try to pull the wrench toward you. If the situation calls for pushing the wrench away, push with an open hand to avoid scraped knuckles if the wrench should slip.

DON'T attempt to lift a heavy component alone – get someone to help you.

DON'T rush or take unsafe shortcuts to finish a job.

DON'T allow children or animals in or around the vehicle while you are working on it.

DO wear eye protection when using power tools such as a drill, sander, bench grinder, etc. and when working under a vehicle.

DO keep loose clothing and long hair well out of the way of moving parts.

DO make sure that any hoist used has a safe working load rating adequate for the job.

DO get someone to check on you periodically when working alone on a vehicle.

DO carry out work in a logical sequence and make sure that everything is correctly assembled and tightened.

DO keep chemicals and fluids tightly capped and out of the reach of children and pets.

DO remember that your vehicle's safety affects that of yourself and others. If in doubt on any point, get professional advice.

Asbestos

Certain friction, insulating, sealing, and other products – such as brake linings, brake bands, clutch linings, torque converters, gaskets, etc. – contain asbestos. *Extreme care must be taken to avoid inhalation of dust from such products, since it is hazardous to health.* If in doubt, assume that they *do* contain asbestos.

Fire

Remember at all times that gasoline is highly flammable. Never smoke or have any kind of open flame around when working on a vehicle. But the risk does not end there. A spark caused by an electrical short circuit, by two metal surfaces contacting each other, or even by static electricity built up in your body under certain conditions, can ignite gasoline vapors, which in a confined space are highly explosive. Do not, under any circumstances, use gasoline for cleaning parts. Use an approved safety solvent.

Always disconnect the battery ground (–) cable *at the battery* before working on any part of the fuel system or electrical system. Never risk spilling fuel on a hot engine or exhaust component.

It is strongly recommended that a fire extinguisher suitable for use on fuel and electrical fires be kept handy in the garage or workshop at all times. Never try to extinguish a fuel or electrical fire with water.

Fumes

Certain fumes are highly toxic and can quickly cause unconsciousness and even death if inhaled to any extent. Gasoline vapor falls into this category, as do the vapors from some cleaning solvents. Any draining or pouring of such volatile fluids should be done in a well ventilated area.

When using cleaning fluids and solvents, read the instructions on the container carefully. Never use materials from unmarked containers.

Never run the engine in an enclosed space, such as a garage. Exhaust fumes contain carbon monoxide, which is extremely poisonous. If you need to run the engine, always do so in the open air, or at least have the rear of the vehicle outside the work area.

If you are fortunate enough to have the use of an inspection pit, never drain or pour gasoline and never run the engine while the vehicle is over the pit. The fumes, being heavier than air, will concentrate in the pit with possibly lethal results.

The battery

Never create a spark or allow a bare light bulb near a battery. They normally give off a certain amount of hydrogen gas, which is highly explosive.

Always disconnect the battery ground (–) cable *at the battery* before working on the fuel or electrical systems.

If possible, loosen the filler caps or cover when charging the battery from an external source (this does not apply to sealed or maintenancefree batteries). Do not charge at an excessive rate or the battery may burst.

Take care when adding water to a non maintenance–free battery and when carrying a battery. The electrolyte, even when diluted, is very corrosive and should not be allowed to contact clothing or skin.

Always wear eye protection when cleaning the battery to prevent the caustic deposits from entering your eyes.

Household current

When using an electric power tool, inspection light, etc., which operates on household current, always make sure that the tool is correctly connected to its plug and that, where necessary, it is properly grounded. Do not use such items in damp conditions and, again, do not create a spark or apply excessive heat in the vicinity of fuel or fuel vapor.

Secondary ignition system voltage

A severe electric shock can result from touching certain parts of the ignition system (such as the spark plug wires) when the engine is running or being cranked, particularly if components are damp or the insulation is defective. In the case of an electronic ignition system, the secondary system voltage is much higher and could prove fatal.

Conversion factors

Length (distance)

Inches (in)	X	25.4	= Millimetres (mm)	X	0.0394	= Inches (in)
Feet (ft)	X	0.305	= Metres (m)	X	3.281	= Feet (ft)
Miles	X	1.609	= Kilometres (km)	X	0.621	= Miles

Volume (capacity)

Cubic inches (cu in; in^3)	X	16.387	= Cubic centimetres (cc; cm^3)	X	0.061	= Cubic inches (cu in; in^3)
Imperial pints (Imp pt)	X	0.568	= Litres (l)	X	1.76	= Imperial pints (Imp pt)
Imperial quarts (Imp qt)	X	1.137	= Litres (l)	X	0.88	= Imperial quarts (Imp qt)
Imperial quarts (Imp qt)	X	1.201	= US quarts (US qt)	X	0.833	= Imperial quarts (Imp qt)
US quarts (US qt)	X	0.946	= Litres (l)	X	1.057	= US quarts (US qt)
Imperial gallons (Imp gal)	X	4.546	= Litres (l)	X	0.22	= Imperial gallons (Imp gal)
Imperial gallons (Imp gal)	X	1.201	= US gallons (US gal)	X	0.833	= Imperial gallons (Imp gal)
US gallons (US gal)	X	3.785	= Litres (l)	X	0.264	= US gallons (US gal)

Mass (weight)

Ounces (oz)	X	28.35	= Grams (g)	X	0.035	= Ounces (oz)
Pounds (lb)	X	0.454	= Kilograms (kg)	X	2.205	= Pounds (lb)

Force

Ounces-force (ozf; oz)	X	0.278	= Newtons (N)	X	3.6	= Ounces-force (ozf; oz)
Pounds-force (lbf; lb)	X	4.448	= Newtons (N)	X	0.225	= Pounds-force (lbf; lb)
Newtons (N)	X	0.1	= Kilograms-force (kgf; kg)	X	9.81	= Newtons (N)

Pressure

Pounds-force per square inch (psi; lbf/in^2; lb/in^2)	X	0.070	= Kilograms-force per square centimetre (kgf/cm^2; kg/cm^2)	X	14.223	= Pounds-force per square inch (psi; lbf/in^2; lb/in^2)
Pounds-force per square inch (psi; lbf/in^2; lb/in^2)	X	0.068	= Atmospheres (atm)	X	14.696	= Pounds-force per square inch (psi; lbf/in^2; lb/in^2)
Pounds-force per square inch (psi; lbf/in^2; lb/in^2)	X	0.069	= Bars	X	14.5	= Pounds-force per square inch (psi; lbf/in^2; lb/in^2)
Pounds-force per square inch (psi; lbf/in^2; lb/in^2)	X	6.895	= Kilopascals (kPa)	X	0.145	= Pounds-force per square inch (psi; lbf/in^2; lb/in^2)
Kilopascals (kPa)	X	0.01	= Kilograms-force per square centimetre (kgf/cm^2; kg/cm^2)	X	98.1	= Kilopascals (kPa)

Torque (moment of force)

Pounds-force inches (lbf in; lb in)	X	1.152	= Kilograms-force centimetre (kgf cm; kg cm)	X	0.868	= Pounds-force inches (lbf in; lb in)
Pounds-force inches (lbf in; lb in)	X	0.113	= Newton metres (Nm)	X	8.85	= Pounds-force inches (lbf in; lb in)
Pounds-force inches (lbf in; lb in)	X	0.083	= Pounds-force feet (lbf ft; lb ft)	X	12	= Pounds-force inches (lbf in; lb in)
Pounds-force feet (lbf ft; lb ft)	X	0.138	= Kilograms-force metres (kgf m; kg m)	X	7.233	= Pounds-force feet (lbf ft; lb ft)
Pounds-force feet (lbf ft; lb ft)	X	1.356	= Newton metres (Nm)	X	0.738	= Pounds-force feet (lbf ft; lb ft)
Newton metres (Nm)	X	0.102	= Kilograms-force metres (kgf m; kg m)	X	9.804	= Newton metres (Nm)

Power

Horsepower (hp)	X	745.7	= Watts (W)	X	0.0013	= Horsepower (hp)

Velocity (speed)

Miles per hour (miles/hr; mph)	X	1.609	= Kilometres per hour (km/hr; kph)	X	0.621	= Miles per hour (miles/hr; mph)

Fuel consumption*

Miles per gallon, Imperial (mpg)	X	0.354	= Kilometres per litre (km/l)	X	2.825	= Miles per gallon, Imperial (mpg)
Miles per gallon, US (mpg)	X	0.425	= Kilometres per litre (km/l)	X	2.352	= Miles per gallon, US (mpg)

Temperature

Degrees Fahrenheit = (°C x 1.8) + 32   Degrees Celsius (Degrees Centigrade; °C) = (°F - 32) x 0.56

*It is common practice to convert from miles per gallon (mpg) to litres/100 kilometres (l/100km), where mpg (Imperial) x l/100 km = 282 and mpg (US) x l/100 km = 235

Troubleshooting

Contents

This section provides an easy reference guide to the more common problems which may occur during the operation of your vehicle. These problems and their possible causes are grouped under headings denoting various components or systems, such as Engine, Cooling system, etc. They also refer you to the chapter and/or section which deals with the problem.

Remember that successful troubleshooting is not a mysterious black art practiced only by professional mechanics. It is simply the result of the right knowledge combined with an intelligent, systematic approach to the problem. Always work by a process of elimination, starting with the simplest solution and working through to the most complex – and never overlook the obvious. Anyone can run the gas tank dry or leave the lights on overnight, so don't assume that you are exempt from such oversights.

Finally, always establish a clear idea of why a problem has occurred and take steps to ensure that it doesn't happen again. If the electrical system fails because of a poor connection, check the other connections in the system to make sure that they don't fail as well. If a particular fuse continues to blow, find out why – don't just replace one fuse after another. Remember, failure of a small component can often be indicative of potential failure or incorrect functioning of a more important component or system.

Engine and performance

1 Engine will not rotate when attempting to start

1 Battery terminal connections loose or corroded (Chapter 1).
2 Battery discharged or faulty (Chapter 1).
3 Automatic transmission not completely engaged in Park (Chapter 7) or clutch not completely depressed (Chapter 8).
4 Broken, loose or disconnected wiring in the starting circuit (Chapters 5 and 12).
5 Starter motor pinion jammed in flywheel ring gear (Chapter 5).
6 Starter solenoid faulty (Chapter 5).
7 Starter motor faulty (Chapter 5).
8 Ignition switch faulty (Chapter 12).
9 Starter pinion or flywheel teeth worn or broken (Chapter 5).

2 Engine rotates but will not start

1 Fuel tank empty.
2 Battery discharged (engine rotates slowly) (Chapter 5).
3 Battery terminal connections loose or corroded (Chapter 1).
4 Carburetor flooded and/or fuel level in carburetor incorrect. This will usually be accompanied by a strong fuel odor from under the hood. Wait a few minutes, depress the accelerator pedal all the way to the floor and attempt to start the engine.
5 Choke control inoperative (Chapter 4).
6 Fuel not reaching the carburetor. With the engine off, open the hood and remove the air cleaner. Observe the top of the carburetor (manually move the choke plate back if necessary). Have an assistant depress the accelerator pedal and check that fuel spurts into the carburetor. If not, check the fuel filter (Chapter 1), fuel lines and fuel pump (Chapter 4).
7 Excessive fuel leaking past the carburetor inlet needle, or, on fuel-injected models, leaking fuel injector(s), faulty fuel pump, pressure regulator, etc. (Chapter 4); faulty idle mixture adjuster sensor (Chapter 6).
8 Fuel not reaching the fuel injectors (fuel-injected models) (Chapter 4).
9 Ignition components damp or damaged (Chapter 5).
10 Worn, faulty or incorrectly gapped spark plugs (Chapter 1).
11 Broken, loose or disconnected wiring in the starting circuit (Chapter 5).
12 Loose distributor is changing ignition timing (Chapter 5).
13 Broken, loose or disconnected wires at the ignition coil or faulty coil (Chapter 5).

3 Engine hard to start when cold

1 Battery discharged or low (Chapter 1).
2 Carburetor flooded (see Section 2).
3 Malfunctioning fuel system (Chapter 4).
4 On fuel-injected models, idle mixture adjuster sensor malfunctioning (Chapter 6).
5 Carburetor choke malfunctioning (Chapter 4).
6 Excessive fuel leaking past the carburetor inlet needle, or, on fuel-injected models, injector(s) leaking (Chapter 4).
7 Distributor rotor carbon tracked (Chapter 5).

4 Engine hard to start when hot

1 Air filter clogged (Chapter 1).
2 Carburetor flooded (see Section 2).
3 Fuel not reaching the carburetor or fuel injection system (Chapter 4).
4 Corroded battery connections, especially ground (Chapter 1).

5 Starter motor noisy or excessively rough in engagement

1 Pinion or flywheel gear teeth worn or broken (Chapter 5).
2 Starter motor mounting bolts loose or missing (Chapter 5).

6 Engine starts but stops immediately

1 Loose or faulty electrical connections at distributor, coil or alternator (Chapter 5).
2 Insufficient fuel reaching the carburetor or fuel injector(s) (Chapters 1 and 4). On carbureted models, disconnect the fuel line. Place a container under the disconnected fuel line and observe the flow of fuel from the line. If little or none flows, check the fuel pump fuse and fuel pump. Also check for blockage in the fuel lines.
3 Vacuum leak at the gasket between the carburetor or throttle body and the engine. Make sure all mounting nuts and bolts are tightened completely and make sure all vacuum hoses are connected correctly and in good condition (Chapter 4).

7 Oil puddle under engine

1 Oil pan gasket and/or oil pan drain bolt washer leaking (Chapter 2).
2 Oil pressure sending unit leaking (Chapter 2).
3 Valve covers leaking (Chapter 2).
4 Engine oil seals leaking (Chapter 2).
5 Oil pump housing leaking (Chapter 2).

8 Engine lopes while idling or idles erratically

1 Vacuum leakage. Check the mounting bolts/nuts at the carburetor/throttle body and intake manifold for tightness. Make sure all vacuum hoses are connected and in good condition. Use a stethoscope or a length of fuel hose held against your ear to listen for vacuum leaks while the engine is running. A hissing sound will be heard. Check the carburetor/throttle body and intake manifold gasket surfaces.
2 Leaking EGR valve (Chapter 6).
3 Air filter clogged (Chapter 1).
4 Fuel pump not delivering sufficient fuel to the carburetor or fuel injection system (Chapter 4).

5 Leaking head gasket (Chapter 2).
6 Timing belt and/or pulleys worn (Chapter 2).
7 Camshaft lobes worn (Chapter 2).
8 Carburetor or fuel-injection system malfunctioning (Chapter 4).

9 Engine misses at idle speed

1 Spark plugs worn or not gapped properly (Chapter 1).
2 Faulty spark plug wires (Chapter 1).
3 Vacuum leaks. Check as described in Section 8.
4 Incorrect ignition timing (Chapter 1).
5 Uneven or low compression (Chapter 2).
6 Idle speed incorrect (Chapter 4)
7 Carburetor or fuel-injection system malfunctioning (Chapter 4).
8 Sticking or faulty emissions system components (Chapter 6).

10 Engine misses throughout driving speed range

1 Fuel filter clogged and/or impurities in the fuel system (Chapter 1).
2 Low fuel output at the fuel injector(s) or injector(s) clogged (Chapter 4).
3 Carburetor malfunctioning (Chapter 4).
4 Faulty or incorrectly gapped spark plugs (Chapter 1).
5 Incorrect ignition timing (Chapter 5).
6 Cracked distributor cap, disconnected distributor wires or damaged distributor components (Chapters 1 and 5).
7 Leaking spark plug wires (Chapters 1 or 5).
8 Faulty emission system components (Chapter 6).
9 Low or uneven cylinder compression pressures (Chapter 2).
10 Weak or faulty ignition system (Chapter 5).
11 Vacuum leaks. Check as described in Section 8.

11 Engine stumbles on acceleration

1 Spark plugs fouled (Chapter 1).
2 Carburetor or fuel injection system needs adjustment or repair (Chapter 4).
3 Fuel filter clogged (Chapters 1 and 4).
4 Incorrect ignition timing (Chapter 5).
5 Vacuum leak(s). Check as described in Section 8.
6 Faulty spark plug wire(s) or other ignition system components.

12 Engine surges while holding accelerator steady

1 Vacuum leak(s). Check as described in Section 8.
2 Fuel pump faulty (Chapter 4).
3 Loose fuel injector wire harness connectors (Chapter 4).
4 Defective ECU (Chapter 6).

13 Engine stalls

1 Idle speed incorrect (Chapter 1).
2 Fuel filter clogged and/or water and impurities in the fuel system (Chapters 1 and 4).
3 Distributor components damp or damaged (Chapter 5).
4 Faulty emissions system components (Chapter 6).
5 Faulty or incorrectly gapped spark plugs (Chapter 1).
6 Faulty spark plug wires (Chapter 1).

7 Vacuum leak at the carburetor/throttle body, intake manifold or vacuum hoses. Check as described in Section 8.
8 Valve clearances incorrectly set (Chapter 1).
9 Fault in the carburetor or fuel-injection system.

14 Engine lacks power

1 Incorrect ignition timing (Chapter 5).
2 Excessive play in distributor shaft (Chapter 5).
3 Worn rotor, distributor cap or wires (Chapters 1 and 5).
4 Faulty or incorrectly gapped spark plugs (Chapter 1).
5 Carburetor or fuel injection system out of adjustment or excessively worn (Chapter 4).
6 Faulty coil (Chapter 5).
7 Brakes binding (Chapter 9).
8 Automatic transaxle fluid level incorrect (Chapter 1).
9 Clutch slipping (Chapter 8).
10 Fuel filter clogged and/or impurities in the fuel system (Chapters 1 and 4).
11 Emission control system not functioning properly (Chapter 6).
12 Low or uneven cylinder compression pressures (Chapter 2).

15 Engine backfires

1 Emission control system not functioning properly (Chapter 6).
2 Ignition timing incorrect (Chapter 5).
3 Faulty secondary ignition system (cracked spark plug insulator, faulty plug wires, distributor cap and/or rotor) (Chapters 1 and 5).
4 Carburetor or fuel injection system in need of adjustment or worn excessively (Chapter 4).
5 Vacuum leaks. Check as described in Section 8.
6 Valve clearances incorrectly set and/or valves sticking or burned (Chapter 1).

16 Pinging or knocking engine sounds during acceleration or uphill

1 Incorrect grade of fuel.
2 Ignition timing incorrect (Chapter 5).
3 Carburetor or fuel injection system in need of adjustment or overhaul (Chapter 4).
4 Improper or damaged spark plugs or wires (Chapter 1).
5 Worn or damaged distributor components (Chapter 5).
6 Faulty emission system (Chapter 6).
7 Vacuum leaks. Check as described in Section 8.
8 Carbon build-up in cylinders.

17 Engine runs with oil pressure light on

1 Low oil level or oil diluted (Chapter 1).
2 Idle rpm below specification (Chapter 1).
3 Short in wiring circuit (Chapter 12).
4 Faulty oil pressure sender (Chapter 2).
5 Worn engine bearings and/or oil pump (Chapter 2).

18 Engine diesels (continues to run) after switching off

1 Idle speed too high (Chapter 1).
2 Vacuum leak(s). Check as described in Section 8.
3 Excessive engine operating temperature (Chapter 3).

4   Ignition timing not correctly adjusted.
5   Carburetor in need of overhaul.
6   Thermo-controlled air cleaner heat valve stuck (Chapter 6).

Engine electrical system

19   Battery will not hold a charge

1   Alternator drivebelt defective or not adjusted properly (Chapter 1).
2   Battery electrolyte level low (Chapter 1).
3   Battery terminals loose or corroded (Chapter 1).
4   Alternator not charging properly (Chapter 5).
5   Loose, broken or faulty wiring in the charging circuit (Chapter 5).
6   Short in vehicle wiring (Chapter 12).
7   Internally defective battery (Chapters 1 and 5).

20   Alternator light fails to go out

1   Faulty alternator or charging circuit (Chapter 5).
2   Alternator drivebelt defective or out of adjustment (Chapter 1).
3   Alternator voltage regulator inoperative (Chapter 5).

21   Alternator light fails to come on when key is turned on

1   Warning light bulb defective (Chapter 12).
2   Fault in the printed circuit, dash wiring or bulb holder (Chapter 12).

Fuel system

22   Excessive fuel consumption

1   Dirty or clogged air filter element (Chapter 1).
2   Incorrectly set ignition timing (Chapter 5).
3   Emissions system not functioning properly (Chapter 6).
4   Carburetor or fuel injection system internal parts excessively worn or damaged (Chapter 4).
5   Low tire pressure or incorrect tire size (Chapter 1).

23   Fuel leakage and/or fuel odor

1   Leaking fuel feed or return line (Chapters 1 and 4).
2   Tank overfilled.
3   Evaporative canister filter clogged (Chapters 1 and 6).
4   Carburetor malfunctioning or fuel injector internal parts excessively worn (Chapter 4)

Cooling system

24   Overheating

1   Insufficient coolant in system (Chapter 1).
2   Water pump drivebelt defective or out of adjustment (Chapter 1).
3   Radiator core blocked or grille restricted (Chapter 3).
4   Thermostat faulty (Chapter 3).
5   Electric cooling fan blades broken or cracked (Chapter 3).
6   Radiator cap not maintaining proper pressure (Chapter 3).
7   Ignition timing incorrect (Chapter 5).

25   Overcooling

1   Faulty thermostat (Chapter 3).
2   Inaccurate temperature gauge sending unit (Chapter 3)

26   External coolant leakage

1   Deteriorated/damaged hoses; loose clamps (Chapters 1 and 3).
2   Water pump seal defective (Chapter 3).
3   Leakage from radiator, coolant reservoir or heater core (Chapter 3).
4   Engine drain or water jacket core plug(s) leaking (Chapter 2).

27   Internal coolant leakage

1   Leaking cylinder head gasket (Chapter 2).
2   Cracked cylinder bore or cylinder head (Chapter 2).

28   Coolant loss

1   Too much coolant in system (Chapter 1).
2   Coolant boiling away because of overheating (Chapter 3).
3   Internal or external leakage (Chapter 3).
4   Faulty radiator cap (Chapter 3).

29   Poor coolant circulation

1   Inoperative water pump (Chapter 3).
2   Restriction in cooling system (Chapters 1 and 3).
3   Water pump drivebelt defective/out of adjustment (Chapter 1).
4   Thermostat sticking (Chapter 3).

Clutch

30   Pedal travels to floor – no pressure or very little resistance

1   Broken clutch cable (Chapter 8).
2   Broken release bearing or fork (Chapter 8).

31   Unable to select gears

1   Faulty transaxle (Chapter 7).
2   Faulty clutch disc (Chapter 8).
3   Fork and bearing not assembled properly (Chapter 8).
4   Faulty pressure plate (Chapter 8).
5   Pressure plate-to-flywheel bolts loose (Chapter 8).

32   Clutch slips (engine speed increases with no increase in vehicle speed)

1   Clutch plate worn (Chapter 8).
2   Clutch plate is oil soaked by leaking rear main seal (Chapter 8).
3   Clutch plate not seated. It may take 30 or 40 normal starts for a new one to seat.
4   Warped pressure plate or flywheel (Chapter 8).
5   Weak diaphragm spring (Chapter 8).
6   Clutch plate overheated. Allow to cool.

33 Grabbing (chattering) as clutch is engaged

1   Oil on clutch plate lining, burned or glazed facings (Chapter 8).
2   Worn or loose engine or transaxle mounts (Chapters 2 and 7).
3   Worn splines on clutch plate hub (Chapter 8).
4   Warped pressure plate or flywheel (Chapter 8).
5   Burned or smeared resin on flywheel or pressure plate (Chapter 8).

34 Transaxle rattling (clicking)

1   Release fork loose (Chapter 8).
2   Clutch plate damper spring failure (Chapter 8).
3   Low engine idle speed (Chapter 1).

35 Noise in clutch area

1   Fork shaft improperly installed (Chapter 8).
2   Faulty bearing (Chapter 8).

36 Clutch pedal stays on floor

1   Broken clutch cable (Chapter 8).
2   Broken release bearing or fork (Chapter 8).

37 High pedal effort

1   Clutch cable or linkage binding (Chapter 8).
2   Pressure plate faulty (Chapter 8).

Manual transaxle

38 Knocking noise at low speeds

1   Worn driveaxle constant velocity (CV) joints (Chapter 8).
2   Worn side gear shaft counterbore in differential case (Chapter 7A).

39 Noise most pronounced when turning

   Differential gear noise (Chapter 7A).

40 Clunk on acceleration or deceleration

1   Loose engine or transaxle mounts (Chapters 2 and 7A).
2   Worn differential pinion shaft in case.
3   Worn side gear shaft counterbore in differential case (Chapter 7A).
4   Worn or damaged driveaxle inboard CV joints (Chapter 8).

41 Clicking noise in turns

   Worn or damaged outboard CV joint (Chapter 8).

42 Vibration

1   Rough wheel bearing (Chapters 1 and 10).
2   Damaged driveaxle (Chapter 8).
3   Out of round tires (Chapter 1).
4   Tire out of balance (Chapters 1 and 10).
5   Worn CV joint (Chapter 8).

43 Noisy in neutral with engine running

1   Damaged input gear bearing (Chapter 7A).
2   Damaged clutch release bearing (Chapter 8).

44 Noisy in one particular gear

1   Damaged or worn constant mesh gears (Chapter 7A).
2   Damaged or worn synchronizers (Chapter 7A).
3   Bent reverse fork (Chapter 7A).
4   Damaged fourth speed gear or output gear (Chapter 7A).
5   Worn or damaged reverse idler gear or idler bushing (Chapter 7A).

45 Noisy in all gears

1   Insufficient lubricant (Chapter 7A).
2   Damaged or worn bearings (Chapter 7A).
3   Worn or damaged input gear shaft and/or output gear shaft (Chapter 7A).

46 Slips out of gear

1   Worn or improperly adjusted linkage (Chapter 7A).
2   Transaxle loose on engine (Chapter 7A).
3   Shift linkage does not work freely, binds (Chapter 7A).
4   Input gear bearing retainer broken or loose (Chapter 7A).
5   Dirt between clutch cover and engine housing (Chapter 7A).
6   Worn shift fork (Chapter 7A).

47 Leaks lubricant

1   Side gear shaft seals worn (Chapter 8).
2   Excessive amount of lubricant in transaxle (Chapters 1 and 7A).
3   Loose or broken input gear shaft bearing retainer (Chapter 7A).
4   Input gear bearing retainer O-ring and/or lip seal damaged (Chapter 7A).

48 Locked in gear

1   Shift linkage worn or damaged (Chapter 7A).
2   Internal transaxle damage (Chapter 7A).

Automatic transaxle

Note: *Due to the complexity of the automatic transaxle, it is difficult for the home mechanic to properly diagnose and service this component. For problems other than the following, the vehicle should be taken to a dealer or transmission shop.*

49   Fluid leakage

1   Automatic transmission fluid is a deep red color. Fluid leaks should not be confused with engine oil, which can easily be blown onto the transaxle by air flow.
2   To pinpoint a leak, first remove all built-up dirt and grime from the transaxle housing with degreasing agents and/or steam cleaning. Then drive the vehicle at low speeds so air flow will not blow the leak far from its source. Raise the vehicle and determine where the leak is coming from. Common areas of leakage are:
   a) Pan (Chapters 1 and 7)
   b) Dipstick tube (Chapters 1 and 7)
   c) Transaxle oil lines (Chapter 7)
   d) Speedometer driven gear assembly or speed sensor (Chapter 7)

50   Transaxle fluid brown or has a burned smell

Transaxle fluid burned (Chapter 1).

51   General shift mechanism problems

1   Chapter 7, Part B, deals with checking and adjusting the shift linkage on automatic transaxles. Common problems which may be attributed to poorly adjusted linkage are:
   a) Engine starting in gears other than Park or Neutral.
   b) Indicator on shifter pointing to a gear other than the one actually being used.
   c) Vehicle moves when in Park.
2   Refer to Chapter 7B for the shift linkage adjustment procedure.

52   Transaxle will not downshift with accelerator pedal pressed to the floor

Throttle valve cable out of adjustment (Chapter 7B).

53   Engine will start in gears other than Park or Neutral

Neutral start switch malfunctioning (Chapter 7B).

54   Transaxle slips, shifts roughly, is noisy or has no drive in forward or reverse gears

There are many probable causes for the above problems, but the home mechanic should be concerned with only one possibility – fluid level. Before taking the vehicle to a repair shop, check the level and condition of the fluid as described in Chapter 1. Correct the fluid level as necessary or change the fluid and filter if needed. If the problem persists, have a professional diagnose the cause.

Driveaxles

55   Clicking noise in turns

Worn or damaged outboard CV joint (Chapter 8).

56   Shudder or vibration during acceleration

1   Excessive toe-in (Chapter 10).
2   Incorrect spring heights (Chapter 10).
3   Worn or damaged inboard or outboard CV joints (Chapter 8).
4   Sticking inboard CV joint assembly (Chapter 8).

57   Vibration at highway speeds

1   Out of balance front wheels and/or tires (Chapters 1 and 10).
2   Out of round front tires (Chapters 1 and 10).
3   Worn CV joint(s) (Chapter 8).

Brakes

Note: *Before assuming that a brake problem exists, make sure that:*
   a) The tires are in good condition and properly inflated (Chapter 1).
   b) The front end alignment is correct (Chapter 10).
   c) The vehicle is not loaded with weight in an unequal manner.

58   Vehicle pulls to one side during braking

1   Incorrect tire pressures (Chapter 1).
2   Front end out of line (have the front end aligned).
3   Front, or rear, tires not matched to one another.
4   Restricted brake lines or hoses (Chapter 9).
5   Malfunctioning drum brake or caliper assembly (Chapter 9).
6   Loose suspension parts (Chapter 10).
7   Loose calipers (Chapter 9).
8   Excessive wear of brake shoe or pad material or disc/drum on one side.

59   Noise (high-pitched squeal when the brakes are applied)

Front and/or rear disc brake pads worn out. The noise comes from the wear sensor rubbing against the disc (does not apply to all vehicles). Replace pads with new ones immediately (Chapter 9).

60   Brake roughness or chatter (pedal pulsates)

1   Excessive lateral runout (Chapter 9).
2   Uneven pad wear (Chapter 9).
3   Defective rotor (Chapter 9).

61   Excessive brake pedal effort required to stop vehicle

1   Malfunctioning power brake booster (Chapter 9).
2   Partial system failure (Chapter 9).
3   Excessively worn pads or shoes (Chapter 9).
4   Piston in caliper or wheel cylinder stuck or sluggish (Chapter 9).
5   Brake pads or shoes contaminated with oil or grease (Chapter 9).
6   New pads or shoes installed and not yet seated. It will take a while for the new material to seat against the rotor or drum.

62   Excessive brake pedal travel

1   Partial brake system failure (Chapter 9).
2   Insufficient fluid in master cylinder (Chapters 1 and 9).
3   Air trapped in system (Chapters 1 and 9).

63   Dragging brakes

1   Incorrect adjustment of brake light switch (Chapter 9).
2   Master cylinder pistons not returning correctly (Chapter 9).
3   Restricted brakes lines or hoses (Chapters 1 and 9).
4   Incorrect parking brake adjustment (Chapter 9).

64   Grabbing or uneven braking action

1   Malfunction of proportioning valve (Chapter 9).
2   Malfunction of power brake booster unit (Chapter 9).
3   Binding brake pedal mechanism (Chapter 9).

65   Brake pedal feels spongy when depressed

1   Air in hydraulic lines (Chapter 9).
2   Master cylinder mounting bolts loose (Chapter 9).
3   Master cylinder defective (Chapter 9).

66   Brake pedal travels to the floor with little resistance

1   Little or no fluid in the master cylinder reservoir caused by leaking caliper piston(s) (Chapter 9).
2   Loose, damaged or disconnected brake lines (Chapter 9).

67   Parking brake does not hold

Parking brake linkage improperly adjusted (Chapters 1 and 9).

Suspension and steering systems

Note: *Before attempting to diagnose the suspension and steering systems, perform the following preliminary checks:*
   a)   Tires for wrong pressure and uneven wear.
   b)   Steering universal joints from the column to the steering gear for loose connectors or wear.
   c)   Front and rear suspension and the steering gear assembly for loose or damaged parts.
   d)   Out-of-round or out-of-balance tires, bent rims and loose and/or rough wheel bearings.

68   Vehicle pulls to one side

1   Mismatched or uneven tires (Chapter 10).
2   Broken or sagging springs (Chapter 10).
3   Wheel alignment (Chapter 10).
4   Front brake dragging (Chapter 9).

69   Abnormal or excessive tire wear

1   Wheel alignment (Chapter 10).
2   Sagging or broken springs (Chapter 10).

3   Tire out of balance (Chapter 10).
4   Worn strut damper (Chapter 10).
5   Overloaded vehicle.
6   Tires not rotated regularly.

70   Wheel makes a thumping noise

1   Blister or bump on tire (Chapter 10).
2   Improper strut damper action (Chapter 10).

71   Shimmy, shake or vibration

1   Tire or wheel out-of-balance or out-of-round (Chapter 10).
2   Loose or worn wheel bearings (Chapters 1, 8 and 10).
3   Worn tie-rod ends (Chapter 10).
4   Worn lower balljoints (Chapters 1 and 10).
5   Excessive wheel runout (Chapter 10).
6   Blister or bump on tire (Chapter 10).

72   Hard steering

1   Lack of lubrication at balljoints, tie-rod ends and steering gear assembly (Chapter 10).
2   Front wheel alignment (Chapter 10).
3   Low tire pressure(s) (Chapters 1 and 10).

73   Poor returnability of steering to center

1   Lack of lubrication at balljoints and tie-rod ends (Chapter 10).
2   Binding in balljoints (Chapter 10).
3   Binding in steering column (Chapter 10).
4   Lack of lubricant in steering gear assembly (Chapter 10).
5   Front wheel alignment (Chapter 10).
6   Steering or suspension components damaged (Chapter 10).

74   Abnormal noise at the front end

1   Lack of lubrication at balljoints and tie-rod ends (Chapters 1 and 10).
2   Damaged strut mounting (Chapter 10).
3   Worn control arm bushings or tie-rod ends (Chapter 10).
4   Loose stabilizer bar (Chapter 10).
5   Loose wheel nuts (Chapters 1 and 10).
6   Loose suspension bolts (Chapter 10).

75   Wander or poor steering stability

1   Mismatched or uneven tires (Chapter 10).
2   Lack of lubrication at balljoints and tie-rod ends (Chapters 1 and 10).
3   Worn strut assemblies (Chapter 10).
4   Loose stabilizer bar (Chapter 10).
5   Broken or sagging springs (Chapter 10).
6   Wheel alignment (Chapter 10).

76   Erratic steering when braking

1   Wheel bearings worn (Chapter 10).
2   Broken or sagging springs (Chapter 10).
3   Leaking wheel cylinder or caliper (Chapter 10).
4   Warped rotors or drums (Chapter 10).

77   Excessive pitching and/or rolling around corners or during braking

1   Loose stabilizer bar (Chapter 10).
2   Worn strut dampers or mountings (Chapter 10).
3   Broken or sagging springs (Chapter 10).
4   Overloaded vehicle.

78   Suspension bottoms

1   Overloaded vehicle.
2   Worn strut dampers (Chapter 10).
3   Incorrect, broken or sagging springs (Chapter 10).

79   Cupped tires

1   Front wheel or rear wheel alignment (Chapter 10).
2   Worn strut dampers (Chapter 10).
3   Wheel bearings worn (Chapter 10).
4   Excessive tire or wheel runout (Chapter 10).
5   Worn balljoints (Chapter 10).

80   Excessive tire wear on outside edge

1   Inflation pressures incorrect (Chapter 1).
2   Excessive speed in turns.
3   Front end alignment incorrect (excessive toe-in). Have professionally aligned.
4   Suspension arm bent or twisted (Chapter 10).

81   Excessive tire wear on inside edge

1   Inflation pressures incorrect (Chapter 1).
2   Front end alignment incorrect (toe-out). Have professionally aligned.
3   Loose or damaged steering components (Chapter 10).

82   Tire tread worn in one place

1   Tires out of balance.
2   Damaged or buckled wheel. Inspect and replace if necessary.
3   Defective tire (Chapter 1).

Chapter 1   Tune-up and routine maintenance

Contents

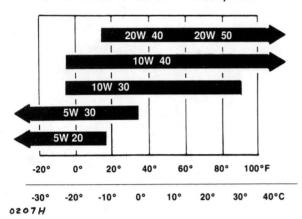

Manual transaxle lubricant viscosity chart

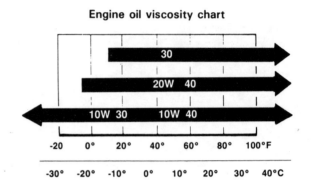

Engine oil viscosity chart

0207H

Recommended SAE viscosity grades for engine oils and manual transaxle lubricants

For best fuel economy and cold starting, select the lowest SAE viscosity grade oil for the expected temperature range

---

Specifications

Recommended lubricants and fluids

Engine oil	
Type	API grade SG/CC multigrade and fuel efficient oil
Viscosity	See accompanying chart
Automatic transaxle fluid type	Dexron II automatic transmission fluid
Manual transaxle	
Lubricant type	API grade SF or SG engine oil
Viscosity	See accompanying chart
Rear differential lubricant (4WD models)	
Above 41-degrees F (5-degrees C)	Hypoid gear oil (API GL5) SAE90
Below 41-degrees F (5-degrees C)	Hypoid gear oil (API GL5) SAE80
Brake fluid type	DOT 3 brake fluid
Power steering fluid type	Honda power steering fluid

Ignition system

Spark plug type and gap	Refer to the Vehicle Emission Control Information label in the engine compartment
Spark plug wire resistance	Less than 25,000 ohms
Ignition timing	Refer to the Vehicle Emission Control Information label in the engine compartment
Engine firing order	1-3-4-2

Thermostat rating

Starts to open	172-degrees F (78-degrees C)
Fully open	194-degrees F (90-degrees C)

Drivebelt deflection

Power steering pump	5/16 to 1/2-inch (9 to 12 mm)
Alternator	1/4-inch (6 mm)
Air conditioning compressor	3/8 to 1/2-inch (10 to 12 mm)

Clutch cable release arm freeplay

1984 through 1987	0.16 to 0.20 inch (4.0 to 5.0 mm)
1988 on	0.12 to 0.16 inch (3.0 to 4.0 mm)

Brakes

Disc brake pad lining thickness (minimum) . . . . 1/8-inch (3.0 mm)
Drum brake shoe lining thickness (minimum) . . . . 1/8-inch (3.0 mm)
Parking brake adjustment
    1984 through 1987 . . . . 4 to 8 clicks
    1988 on . . . . 6 to 10 clicks

Suspension and steering

Steering wheel freeplay limit . . . . 0.39 inch (10.0 mm)
Balljoint allowable movement
    1984 and 1985 . . . . Not available
    1986 on . . . . None

Valve clearances (engine cold)

12 and 16-valve engines
    Intake and auxiliary valves . . . . 0.007 to 0.009 in (0.17 to 0.22 mm)
    Exhaust valve
        Carbureted 12-valve (HF) engine . . . . 0.007 to 0.009 in (0.17 to 0.22 mm)
        All others . . . . 0.009 to 0.011 in (0.22 to 0.27 mm)
8-valve engine
    Intake valve . . . . 0.005 to 0.007 in (0.12 to 0.17 mm)
    Exhaust valve . . . . 0.007 to 0.009 in (0.17 to 0.22 mm)

Throttle cable deflection . . . . 3/16 to 3/8 in (4 to 10 mm)

Capacities

Engine oil . . . . 3.7 qt (3.5 liter)
Automatic transaxle
    2WD models
        1984 and 1985 . . . . 3.0 qt (2.8 liter)
        1986 on . . . . 2.5 qt (2.4 liter)
    4WD Wagon models . . . . 3.4 qt (3.2 liter)
Manual transaxle
    2WD models
        1984 through 1987 . . . . 2.4 qt (2.3 liter)
        1988 on . . . . 1.9 qt (1.8 liter)
    4WD Wagon models . . . . 2.4 qt (2.3 liter)
Rear differential lubricant (4WD only) . . . . 0.7 qt.(0.68 liter)
Coolant . . . . 5.5 qt (5.3 liter) (approximately)

Torque specifications
Ft-lbs (unless otherwise indicated)

Automatic transaxle drain plug 29
Manual transaxle drain and fill plugs . . . . 30 to 40
Wheel lug nuts 80
Fuel filter (fuel-injected models)
    Banjo bolt 16
    Service bolt . . . . 108 in-lbs
    Clamp bolt . . . . 108 in-lbs

---

1   Introduction

This chapter is designed to help the home mechanic maintain the Honda Civic, CRX and Wagon for peak performance, economy, safety and long life.

On the following pages is a master maintenance schedule, followed by Sections dealing specifically with each item on the schedule. Visual checks, adjustments, component replacement and other helpful items are included. Refer to the accompanying photos of the engine compartment and the underside of the vehicle for the location of various components.

Servicing your Civic, CRX or Wagon in accordance with the mileage/time maintenance schedule and the following Sections will provide it with a planned maintenance program that should result in a long and reliable service life. This is a comprehensive plan, so maintaining some items but not others at the specified service intervals will not produce the same results.

As you service your Civic, CRX or Wagon, you will discover that many of the procedures can – and should – be grouped together because of the nature of the particular procedure you're performing or because of the close proximity of two otherwise unrelated components to one another.

For example, if the vehicle is raised for chassis lubrication, you should inspect the exhaust, suspension, steering and fuel systems while you're under the vehicle. When you're rotating the tires, it makes good sense to check the brakes and wheel bearings since the wheels are already removed.

Finally, let's suppose you have to borrow or rent a torque wrench. Even if you only need to tighten the spark plugs, you might as well check the torque of as many critical fasteners as time allows.

The first step of this maintenance program is to prepare yourself before the actual work begins. Read through all sections pertinent to the procedures you're planning to do, then make a list of and gather together all the parts and tools you will need to do the job. If it looks as if you might run into problems during a particular segment of some procedure, seek advice from your local parts store or dealer service department.

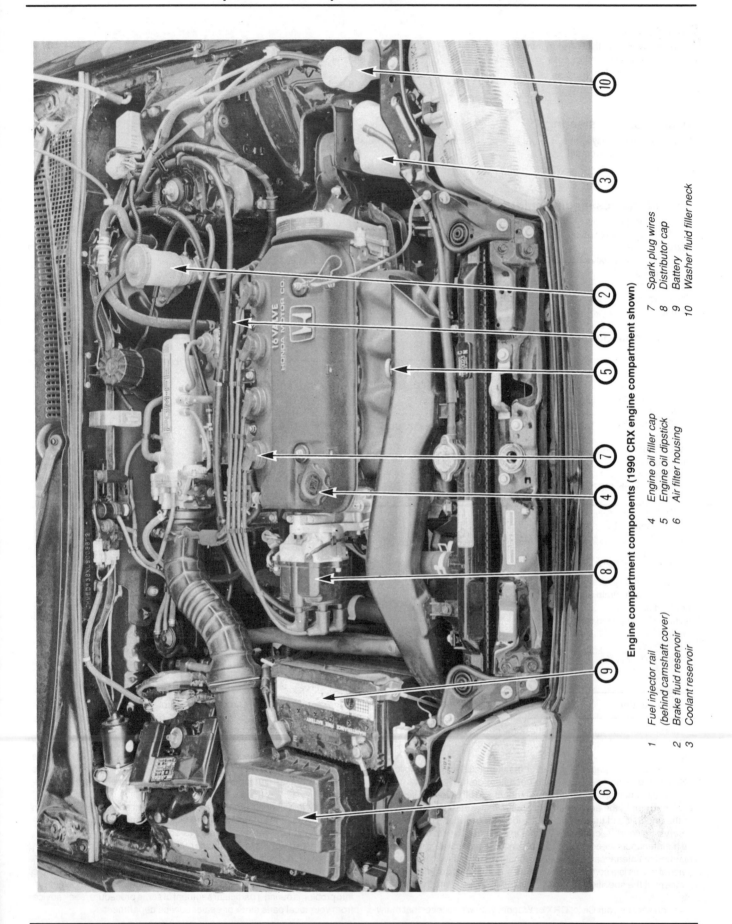

Engine compartment components (1990 CRX engine compartment shown)

1   Fuel injector rail
    (behind camshaft cover)
2   Brake fluid reservoir
3   Coolant reservoir

4   Engine oil filler cap
5   Engine oil dipstick
6   Air filter housing

7   Spark plug wires
8   Distributor cap
9   Battery
10 Washer fluid filler neck

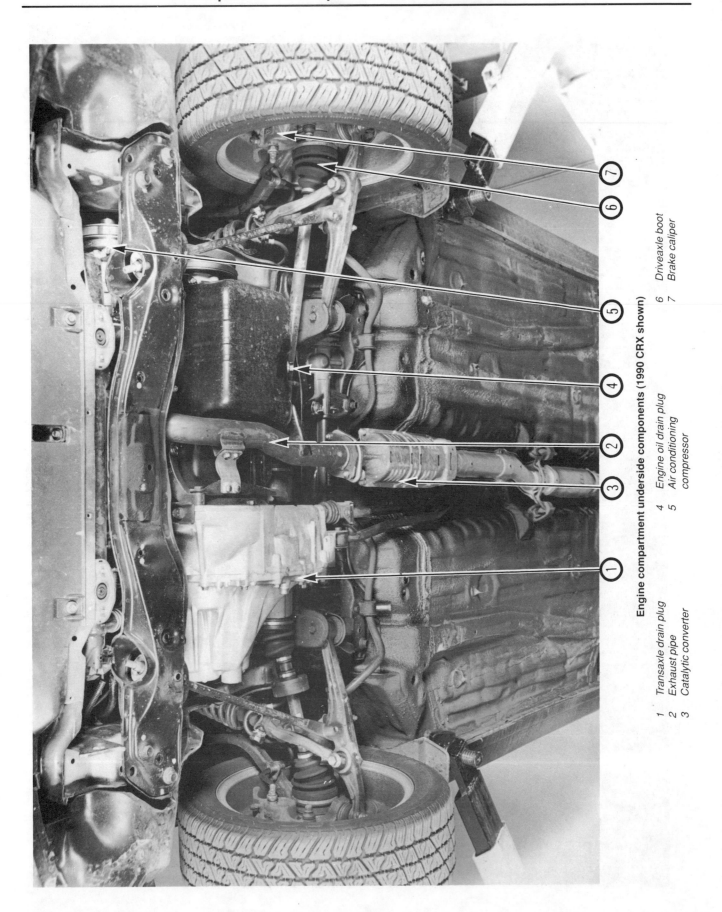

Engine compartment underside components (1990 CRX shown)

1 Transaxle drain plug
2 Exhaust pipe
3 Catalytic converter
4 Engine oil drain plug
5 Air conditioning compressor
6 Driveaxle boot
7 Brake caliper

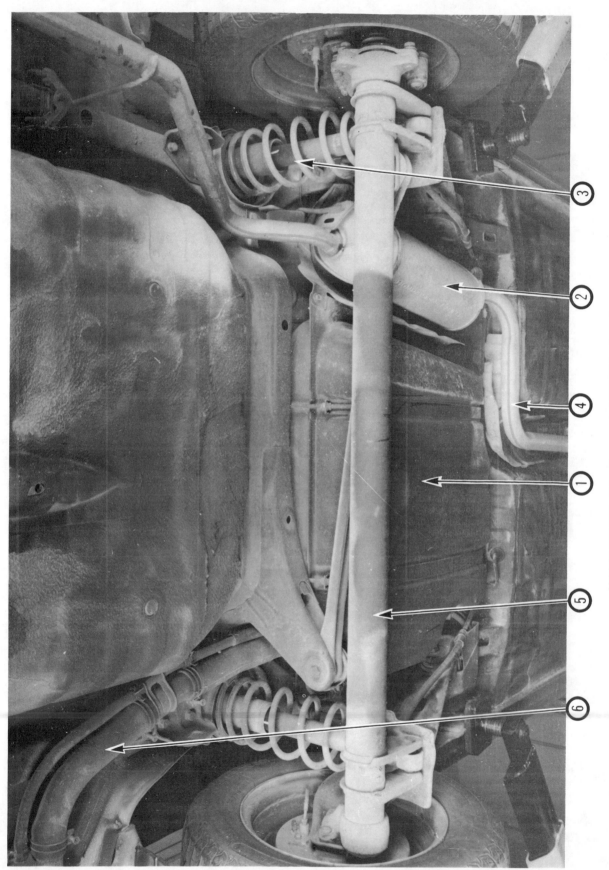

Vehicle rear underside components (1986 Civic shown)

1   Fuel tank
2   Muffler
3   Strut/spring assembly
4   Exhaust pipe
5   Axle housing
6   Fuel tank filler neck

2 Honda Civic, CRX and Wagon Maintenance schedule

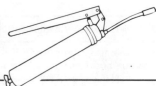

The maintenance intervals in this manual are provided with the assumption that you, not the dealer, will be doing the work. These are the minimum maintenance intervals recommended by the factory for Civics, CRX's and Wagons that are driven daily. If you wish to keep your vehicle in peak condition at all times, you may wish to perform some of these procedures even more often. Because frequent maintenance enhances the efficiency, performance and resale value of your car, we encourage you to do so. If you drive in dusty areas, tow a trailer, idle or drive at low speeds for extended periods or drive for short distances (less than four miles) in below freezing temperatures, shorter intervals are also recommended.

When your vehicle is new, it should be serviced by a factory authorized dealer service department to protect the factory warranty. In many cases, the initial maintenance check is done at no cost to the owner.

Every 250 miles or weekly, whichever comes first

Check the engine oil level (Section 4)
Check the engine coolant level (Section 4)
Check the windshield washer fluid level (Section 4)
Check the brake fluid level (Section 4)
Check the tires and tire pressures (Section 5)

Every 3000 miles or 3 months, whichever comes first

All items listed above plus:
Check the power steering fluid level (Section 6)
Check the automatic transaxle fluid level (Section 7)
Change the engine oil and oil filter (Section 8)

Every 7500 miles or 6 months, whichever comes first

All items listed above plus:
Inspect and replace, if necessary, the windshield wiper blades (Section 9)
Check and adjust, if necessary, the clutch release arm freeplay (Section 16)
Check and service the battery (Section 10)
Check and adjust, if necessary, the engine drivebelts (Section 11)
Inspect and replace, if necessary, all underhood hoses (Section 12)
Check the cooling system (Section 13)
Rotate the tires (Section 14)
Check the front disc brake pads (Section 15)
Check the rear disc pads – 1990 CRX (Section 15)

Every 15,000 miles or 12 months, whichever comes first

All items listed above plus:
Adjust the valve clearances (Section 20)
Inspect the brake system (Section 15)*
Replace the air filter (Section 17)
Inspect the fuel system (Section 21)
Check and replace, if necessary, the spark plugs (Section 18)

Inspect and replace, if necessary, the spark plug wires, distributor cap and rotor (Section 19)
Change the automatic transaxle fluid (1984 and 1985 models) (Section 31)**
Check the manual transaxle lubricant level (Section 22)*
Check the rear differential lubricant level – 4WD only (Section 23)*
Inspect the suspension and steering components (Section 24)*
Check the driveaxle boots (Section 25)

Every 30,000 miles or 24 months, whichever comes first

All items listed above plus:
Check the operation of the carburetor choke system (Section 26)
Check and replace, if necessary, the PCV valve (Section 27)
Service the cooling system (drain, flush and refill) (Section 28)
Inspect the exhaust system (Section 29)
Replace the brake fluid (Section 30)
Change the automatic transaxle fluid (1986 through 1990 models) (Section 31)**
Change the manual transaxle lubricant (Section 32)
Change the rear differential lubricant – 4WD only (Section 33)

Every 60,000 miles or 24 months, whichever comes first

All items listed above plus:
Replace the fuel filter (Section 40)
Check and adjust, if necessary, the engine ignition timing (Section 34)
Check and adjust, if necessary, the engine idle speed (Section 37)
Inspect the evaporative emissions control system (Section 38)
Check the Exhaust Gas Recirculation (EGR) system (Section 39)
Check the operation of the thermostatic air cleaner (Section 35)
Check the operation of the throttle linkage (Section 36)

*This item is affected by "severe" operating conditions as described below. If your vehicle is operated under "severe" conditions, perform all maintenance indicated with a * at 3000-mile/three-month intervals. Severe conditions are indicated if you mainly operate your vehicle under one or more of the following conditions:*
In dusty areas
Towing a trailer
Idling for extended periods and/or low speed operation
Operating when outside temperatures remain below freezing and when most trips are less than four miles
** If operated under one or more of the following conditions, change the automatic transaxle fluid and filter every 7500 miles (1984 and 1985 models) or 15,000 miles (1986 through 1990 models):
In heavy city traffic where the outside temperature regularly reaches 90-degrees F (32-degrees C) or higher
In hilly or mountainous terrain

3   Tune-up general information

The term tune-up is used in this manual to represent a combination of individual operations rather than one specific procedure.

If, from the time the vehicle is new, the routine maintenance schedule is followed closely and frequent checks are made of fluid levels and high wear items, as suggested throughout this manual, the engine will be kept in relatively good running condition and the need for additional work will be minimized.

More likely than not, however, there will be times when the engine is running poorly due to lack of regular maintenance. This is even more likely if a used vehicle, which has not received regular and frequent maintenance checks, is purchased. In such cases, an engine tune-up will be needed outside of the regular routine maintenance intervals.

The first step in any tune-up or engine diagnosis to help correct a poor running engine would be a cylinder compression check. A check of the engine compression (Chapter 2 Part B) will give valuable information regarding the overall performance of many internal components and should be used as a basis for tune-up and repair procedures. If, for instance, a compression check indicates serious internal engine wear, a conventional tune-up will not help the running condition of the engine and would be a waste of time and money. Because of its importance, compression checking should be performed by someone with the proper compression testing gauge and the knowledge to use it properly.

The following series of operations are those most often needed to bring a generally poor running engine back into a proper state of tune.

Minor tune-up

Clean, inspect and test the battery (Section 10)
Check all engine related fluids (Section 4)
Check and adjust the drivebelts (Section 11)
Replace the spark plugs (Section 18)
Inspect the distributor cap and rotor (Section 19)
Inspect the spark plug and coil wires (Section 19)
Check and adjust the idle speed (Section 37)
Check the air filter (Section 17)
Check the cooling system (Section 13)
Check all underhood hoses (Section 12)

Major tune-up

All items listed under minor tune-up, plus . . .
Check the EGR system (Section 39)

Check the ignition system (Chapter 5)
Check the charging system (Chapter 5)
Check the fuel system (Section 21)
Replace the air filter (Section 17)
Replace the distributor cap and rotor (Section 19)
Replace the spark plug wires (Section 19)

4   Fluid level checks

1   Fluids are an essential part of the lubrication, cooling, brake, clutch and other systems. Because these fluids gradually become depleted and/or contaminated during normal operation of the vehicle, they must be periodically replenished. See Recommended lubricants, fluids and capacities at the beginning of this Chapter before adding fluid to any of the following components. **Note:** *The vehicle must be on level ground before fluid levels can be checked.*

Engine oil

Refer to illustrations 4.2, 4.4, 4.6a and 4.6b
2   The engine oil level is checked with a dipstick located at the front side of the engine **(see illustration)**. The dipstick extends through a metal tube from which it protrudes down into the engine oil pan.
3   The oil level should be checked before the vehicle has been driven, or about 15 minutes after the engine has been shut off. If the oil is checked immediately after driving the vehicle, some of the oil will remain in the upper engine components, producing an inaccurate reading on the dipstick.
4   Pull the dipstick from the tube and wipe all the oil from the end with a clean rag or paper towel. Insert the clean dipstick all the way back into its metal tube and pull it out again. Observe the oil at the end of the dipstick. At its highest point, the level should be between the upper and lower holes **(see illustration)**.
5   It takes one quart of oil to raise the level from the lower hole to the upper hole on the dipstick. Do not allow the level to drop below the lower hole or oil starvation may cause engine damage. Conversely, overfilling the engine (adding oil above the upper hole) may cause oil fouled spark plugs, oil leaks or oil seal failures.
6   Remove the threaded cap from the camshaft cover to add oil **(see illustrations)**. Use an oil can spout or funnel to prevent spills. After adding the oil, install the filler cap hand tight. Start the engine and look carefully for any small leaks around the oil filter or drain plug. Stop the engine and

4.2   **The engine oil dipstick (arrow) is located at the front side of the engine, behind the radiator**

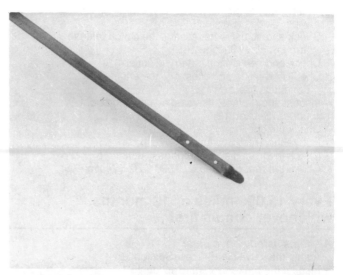

4.4   **The oil level should be between the two holes (or marks) in the dipstick – if it isn't, add enough oil to bring the level to or near the upper hole (it takes one quart to raise the level from the lower to the upper hole)**

4.6a The oil filler cap is located on the camshaft cover – to prevent dirt from contaminating the engine, always make sure the area around this opening is clean before removing the cap; the cap either unscrews counterclockwise, as shown here . . .

4.6b . . . or is rotated 1/4-turn counterclockwise and lifted off

check the oil level again after it has had sufficient time to drain from the upper block and cylinder head galleys.

7   Checking the oil level is an important preventive maintenance step. A continually dropping oil level indicates oil leakage through damaged seals, from loose connections, or past worn rings or valve guides. If the oil looks milky in color or has water droplets in it, a cylinder head gasket may be blown. The engine should be checked immediately. The condition of the oil should also be checked. Each time you check the oil level, slide your thumb and index finger up the dipstick before wiping off the oil. If you see small dirt or metal particles clinging to the dipstick, the oil should be changed (see Section 8).

Engine coolant

Refer to illustration 4.9

8   All vehicles covered by this manual are equipped with a pressurized coolant recovery system. A white coolant reservoir located at the front of the engine compartment is connected by a hose to the base of the coolant filler cap. If the coolant heats up during engine operation, coolant can escape through a pressurized filler cap, then through a connecting hose into the reservoir. As the engine cools, the coolant is automatically drawn back into the cooling system to maintain the correct level.

9   The coolant level should be checked regularly. It must be between the Max and Min lines on the reservoir. The level will vary with the temperature of the engine. When the engine is cold, the coolant level should be at or slightly above the Min mark on the reservoir. Once the engine has warmed up, the level should be at or near the Max mark. If it isn't, allow the fluid in the tank to cool, then remove the cap from the reservoir **(see illustration)** and add coolant to bring the level up to the Max line. Use only ethylene/glycol type coolant and water in the mixture ratio recommended by your owner's manual. Do not use supplemental inhibitors or additives. If only a small amount of coolant is required to bring the system up to the proper level, water can be used. However, repeated additions of water will dilute the recommended antifreeze and water solution. In order to maintain the proper ratio of antifreeze and water, it is advisable to top up the coolant level with the correct mixture. Refer to your owner's manual for the recommended ratio.

10   If the coolant level drops within a short time after replenishment, there may be a leak in the system. Inspect the radiator, hoses, engine coolant filler cap, drain plugs, air bleeder plugs and water pump. If no leak is evident, have the radiator cap pressure tested by your dealer. **Warning:** *Never remove the radiator cap or the coolant recovery reservoir cap when the engine is running or has just been shut down, because the cooling system*

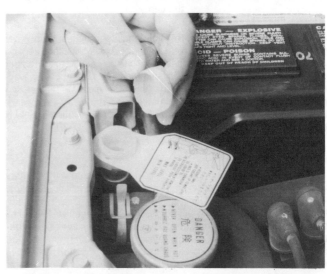

4.9 Make sure the coolant level in the reservoir is between the Max and Min lines (on some models, they must be viewed below the battery using a flashlight) – if it's below the Min line, add a sufficient quantity of the specified mixture of antifreeze and water (carbureted engine shown)

is hot. Escaping steam and scalding liquid could cause serious injury.

11   If it is necessary to open the radiator cap, wait until the system has cooled completely, then wrap a thick cloth around the cap and turn it to the first stop. If any steam escapes, wait until the system has cooled further, then remove the cap.

12   When checking the coolant level, always note its condition. It should be relatively clear. If it is brown or rust colored, the system should be drained, flushed and refilled. Even if the coolant appears to be normal, the corrosion inhibitors wear out with use, so it must be replaced at the specified intervals.

13   Do not allow antifreeze to come in contact with your skin or painted surfaces of the vehicle. Flush contacted areas immediately with plenty of water.

Windshield washer fluid

Refer to illustration 4.14

14   Fluid for the windshield (and rear window on some models) washer system is stored in a plastic reservoir which is located at the front of the

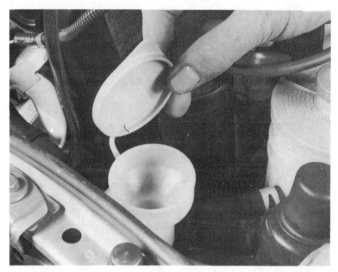

4.14   The windshield washer fluid reservoir is located at the front of the engine compartment – fluid can be added after flipping up the cap

4.15   Remove the cell caps to check the water level in the battery – if the level is low, add distilled water only

engine compartment (see illustration). In milder climates, plain water can be used to top up the reservoir, but the reservoir should be kept no more than 2/3 full to allow for expansion should the water freeze. In colder climates, the use of a specially designed windshield washer fluid, available at your dealer and any auto parts store, will help lower the freezing point of the fluid. Mix the solution with water in accordance with the manufacturer's directions on the container. Do not use regular antifreeze. It will damage the vehicle's paint.

Battery electrolyte

Refer to illustration 4.15

15   Most vehicles covered by this manual are equipped with a battery which is permanently sealed (except for vent holes) and has no filler caps. Water doesn't have to be added to these batteries at any time. If a conventional battery is installed on your vehicle, check the electrolyte level of all six battery cells. It must be between the upper and lower levels (see illustration). If the level is low, unsnap or unscrew the filler/vent cap and add distilled water. Install and securely retighten the cap. Caution: *Overfilling the cells may cause electrolyte to spill over during periods of heavy charging, causing corrosion or damage.*

Brake fluid

Refer to illustration 4.17

16   The brake master cylinder is mounted on the front of the power booster unit in the engine compartment.

17   To check the fluid level of the brake master cylinder reservoir, simply look at the MAX and MIN marks on the reservoir (see illustration). The level should be between the two marks.

18   If the level is low, wipe the top of the reservoir cover with a clean rag to prevent contamination of the brake system before lifting the cap.

19   Add only the specified brake fluid to the brake reservoir (refer to Recommended lubricants and fluids at the front of this chapter or to your owner's manual). Mixing different types of brake fluid can damage the system. Fill the brake master cylinder reservoir only to about 3/4-inch below the Max line – this brings the fluid to the correct level when you put the cap back on. Warning: *Use caution when filling the reservoir – brake fluid can harm your eyes and damage painted surfaces. Do not use brake fluid that has been opened for more than one year or has been left open. Brake fluid absorbs moisture from the air. Excess moisture can cause a dangerous loss of braking.*

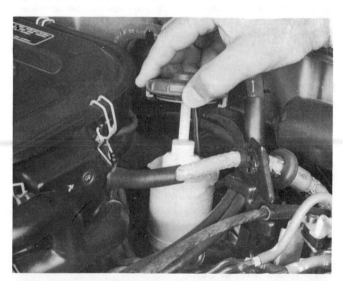

4.17   The brake fluid level should be kept between the Max and Min marks on the translucent plastic reservoir – lift up the cap to add fluid

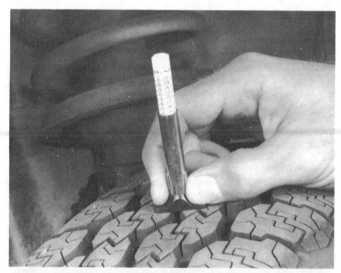

5.2   Use a tire tread depth indicator to monitor tire wear – they are available at auto parts stores and service stations and cost very little

Condition	Probable cause	Corrective action	Condition	Probable cause	Corrective action
Shoulder wear	● Underinflation (both sides wear) ● Incorrect wheel camber (one side wear) ● Hard cornering ● Lack of rotation	● Measure and adjust pressure. ● Repair or replace axle and suspension parts. ● Reduce speed. ● Rotate tires.	Feathered edge Toe wear	● Incorrect toe	● Adjust toe-in.
Center wear	● Overinflation ● Lack of rotation	● Measure and adjust pressure. ● Rotate tires.	Uneven wear	● Incorrect camber or caster ● Malfunctioning suspension ● Unbalanced wheel ● Out-of-round brake drum ● Lack of rotation	● Repair or replace axle and suspension parts. ● Repair or replace suspension parts. ● Balance or replace. ● Turn or replace. ● Rotate tires.

5.3   This chart will help you determine the condition of the tires, the probable cause(s) of abnormal wear and the corrective action necessary

20   While the reservoir cap is removed, inspect the master cylinder reservoir for contamination. If deposits, dirt particles or water droplets are present, the fluid should be replaced (see Section 30).

21   After filling the reservoir to the proper level, make sure the lid is properly seated to prevent fluid leakage and/or system pressure loss.

22   The brake fluid in the master cylinder will drop slightly as the brake linings at each wheel wear down during normal operation. If the master cylinder requires repeated replenishing to keep it at the proper level, this is an indication of leakage in the brake system, which should be corrected immediately. Check all brake lines and connections, along with the wheel cylinders and booster (see Section 15 for more information).

23   If, upon checking the master cylinder fluid level, you discover an empty or nearly empty reservoir, the brake system should be bled (see Chapter 9).

5   Tire and tire pressure checks

Refer to illustrations 5.2, 5.3, 5.4a, 5.4b and 5.8

1   Periodic inspection of the tires may spare you from the inconvenience of being stranded with a flat tire. It can also provide you with vital information regarding possible problems in the steering and suspension systems before major damage occurs.

2   Normal tread wear can be monitored with a simple, inexpensive device known as a tread depth indicator **(see illustration)**. When the tread depth reaches the specified minimum, replace the tire(s).

3   Note any abnormal tread wear **(see illustration)**. Tread pattern irregularities such as cupping, flat spots and more wear on one side than the other are indications of front end alignment and/or balance problems. If any of these conditions are noted, take the vehicle to a tire shop or service station to correct the problem.

4   Look closely for cuts, punctures and embedded nails or tacks. Sometimes a tire will hold its air pressure for a short time or leak down very slowly even after a nail has embedded itself into the tread. If a slow leak persists, check the valve core to make sure it is tight **(see illustration)**. Examine the tread for an object that may have embedded itself into the tire or for a "plug" that may have begun to leak (radial tire punctures are repaired with a plug that is installed in a puncture). If a puncture is suspected, it can be

5.4a   If a tire loses air on a steady basis, check the valve core first to make sure it's snug (special inexpensive wrenches are commonly available at auto parts stores)

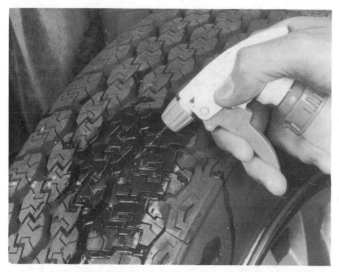

5.4b If the valve core is tight, raise the corner of the vehicle with the low tire and spray a soapy water solution onto the tread as the tire is turned slowly – leaks will cause small bubbles to appear

5.8 To extend the life of the tires, check the air pressure at least once a week with an accurate gauge (don't forget the spare!)

easily verified by spraying a solution of soapy water onto the puncture area **(see illustration)**. The soapy solution will bubble if there is a leak. Unless the puncture is inordinately large, a tire shop or gas station can usually repair the punctured tire.

5   Carefully inspect the inboard sidewall of each tire for evidence of brake fluid leakage. If you see any, inspect the brakes immediately.

6   Correct tire air pressure adds miles to the lifespan of the tires, improves mileage and enhances overall ride quality. Tire pressure cannot be accurately estimated by looking at a tire, particularly if it is a radial. A tire pressure gauge is therefore essential. Keep an accurate gauge in the glovebox. The pressure gauges fitted to the the nozzles of air hoses at gas stations are often inaccurate.

7   Always check tire pressure when the tires are cold. "Cold," in this case, means the vehicle has not been driven over a mile in the three hours preceding a tire pressure check. A pressure rise of four to eight pounds is not uncommon once the tires are warm.

8   Unscrew the valve cap protruding from the wheel or hubcap and push the gauge firmly onto the valve **(see illustration)**. Note the reading on the gauge and compare this figure to the recommended tire pressure shown on the tire placard on the left door jamb. Be sure to reinstall the valve cap to

keep dirt and moisture out of the valve stem mechanism. Check all four tires and, if necessary, add enough air to bring them up to the recommended pressure levels.

9   Don't forget to keep the spare tire inflated to the specified pressure (consult your owner's manual). Note that the air pressure specified for the compact spare is significantly higher than the pressure of the regular tires.

---

6   Power steering fluid level check

Refer to illustration 6.4a and 6.4b

1   Unlike manual steering, the power steering system relies on fluid which may, over a period of time, require replenishing.

2   The fluid reservoir for the power steering pump on 1984 through 1987 models is attached to the pump at the drivebelt end of the engine. On 1988 and later models, it's located at the left front corner of the engine compartment.

3   For the check, the front wheels should be pointed straight ahead and the engine should be off.

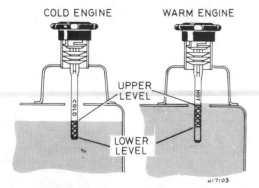

6.4a On 1984 through 1987 models, the power steering fluid dipstick is marked on both sides – if the fluid is warm (after the vehicle has been driven several miles), the level should be in the crosshatched area (between the upper and lower levels) on the HOT side – if the fluid is cold, the level should be in the crosshatched area on the COLD side

6.4b On 1988 and later models, the power steering fluid reservoir is translucent so the fluid level can be checked without removing the cap – keep the level between the two lines (arrows)

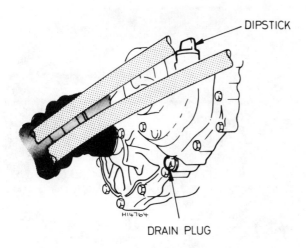

DIPSTICK

DRAIN PLUG

7.3 The automatic transaxle dipstick screws into the transaxle case (2WD model shown)

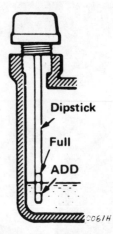

Dipstick

Full

ADD

7.5 Unscrew and remove the dipstick, wipe it off and insert it without screwing it in – the fluid level should be between the Full and Add marks

4   On 1984 through 1987 models, the level is checked with a dipstick attached to the inside of the filler cap (see illustration). On 1988 and later models, the reservoir is translucent plastic and the fluid level can be checked visually (see illustration).

5   If additional fluid is required, pour the specified type directly into the reservoir, using a funnel to prevent spills.

6   If the reservoir requires frequent fluid additions, all power steering hoses, hose connections, the power steering pump and the rack and pinion assembly should be carefully checked for leaks.

7   Automatic transaxle fluid level check

Refer to illustrations 7.3 and 7.5

1   The level of the automatic transaxle fluid should be carefully maintained. Low fluid level can lead to slipping or loss of drive, while overfilling can cause foaming, loss of fluid and transaxle damage.

2   The transaxle fluid level should only be checked when the engine is off.

3   Remove the dipstick (see illustration). Check the level of the fluid on the dipstick and note its condition.

4   Wipe the fluid from the dipstick with a clean rag and reinsert it, but don't screw it in.

5   Pull the dipstick out again and note the fluid level (see illustration). The level should be between the Full and Add marks on the dipstick. If the level is low, add the specified automatic transmission fluid through the dipstick opening with a funnel.

6   Add just enough of the specified fluid to fill the transaxle to the proper level. It takes about one pint to raise the level from the Add mark to the Full mark, so add the fluid a little at a time and keep checking the level until it is correct.

7   The condition of the fluid should also be checked along with the level. If the fluid at the end of the dipstick is black or a dark reddish-brown color, or if it emits a burned smell, the fluid should be changed (see Section 31). If you are in doubt about the condition of the fluid, purchase some new fluid and compare the two for color and smell.

8   Engine oil and oil filter change

Refer to illustrations 8.2, 8.7, 8.12 and 8.14

1   Frequent oil changes are the best preventive maintenance the home mechanic can give the engine, because aging oil becomes diluted and contaminated, which leads to premature engine wear.

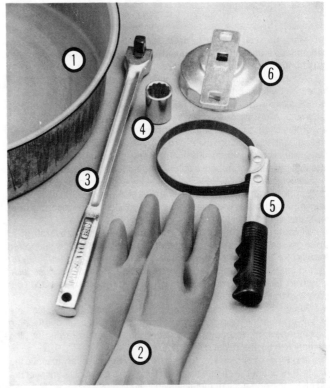

8.2 These tools are required when changing the engine oil and filter

1   *Drain pan – It should be fairly shallow in depth, but wide to prevent spills*

2   *Rubber gloves – When removing the drain plug and filter, you will get oil on your hands (the gloves will prevent burns)*

3   *Breaker bar – Sometimes the oil drain plug is tight and a long breaker bar is needed to loosen it*

4   *Socket – To be used with the breaker bar or a ratchet (must be the correct size to fit the drain plug – six-point preferred)*

5   *Filter wrench – This is a metal band-type wrench, which requires clearance around the filter to be effective*

6   *Filter wrench – This type fits on the bottom of the filter and can be turned with a ratchet or breaker bar (different size wrenches are available for different types of filters)*

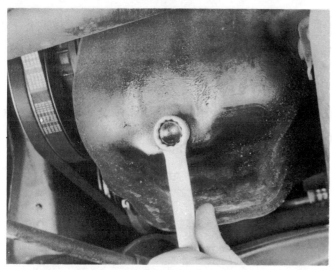

8.7   Use the proper size box-end wrench or six-point socket to remove the oil drain plug without rounding off its corners

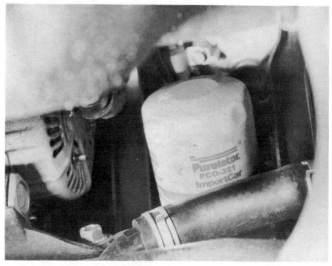

8.12   The oil filter is usually on very tight and will require a special wrench for removal – DO NOT use the wrench to tighten the new filter (view is from beneath the driver's side of the vehicle)

2   Make sure you have all the necessary tools before you begin this procedure **(see illustration)**. You should also have plenty of rags or newspapers handy for mopping up any spills.

3   Access to the underside of the vehicle is greatly improved if the vehicle can be lifted on a hoist, driven onto ramps or supported by jackstands. **Warning:** *Do not work under a vehicle which is supported only by a bumper, hydraulic or scissors-type jack.*

4   If this is your first oil change, get under the vehicle and familiarize yourself with the locations of the oil drain plug and the oil filter. The engine and exhaust components will be warm during the actual work, so try to anticipate any potential problems before the engine and accessories are hot.

5   Park the vehicle on a level spot. Start the engine and allow it to reach its normal operating temperature. Warm oil and sludge will flow out more easily. Turn off the engine when it's warmed up. Remove the filler cap from the camshaft cover.

6   Raise the vehicle and support it securely on jackstands. **Warning:** *To avoid personal injury, never get beneath the vehicle when it is supported by only by a jack. The jack provided with your vehicle is designed solely for raising the vehicle to remove and replace the wheels. Always use jackstands to support the vehicle when it becomes necessary to place your body underneath the vehicle.*

7   Being careful not to touch the hot exhaust components, place the drain pan under the drain plug in the bottom of the pan and remove the plug **(see illustration)**. You may want to wear gloves while unscrewing the plug the final few turns if the engine is hot.

8   Allow the old oil to drain into the pan. It may be necessary to move the pan farther under the engine as the oil flow slows to a trickle. Inspect the old oil for the presence of metal shavings and chips.

9   After all the oil has drained, wipe off the drain plug with a clean rag. Even minute metal particles clinging to the plug would immediately contaminate the new oil.

10   Clean the area around the drain plug opening, reinstall the plug and tighten it securely, but do not strip the threads.

11   Move the drain pan into position under the oil filter.

12   Loosen the oil filter **(see illustration)** by turning it counterclockwise with the filter wrench. Any standard filter wrench will work. Sometimes the oil filter is screwed on so tightly that it cannot be loosened. If this situation occurs, punch a metal bar or long screwdriver directly through the side of the canister and use it as a T-bar to turn the filter. Be prepared for oil to spurt out of the canister as it is punctured. Once the filter is loose, use your hands to unscrew it from the block. Just as the filter is detached from the block, immediately tilt the open end up to prevent the oil inside the filter from spilling out. **Warning:** *The engine exhaust manifold may still be hot, so be careful.*

8.14   Lubricate the oil filter gasket with clean engine oil before installing the filter on the engine

13   With a clean rag, wipe off the mounting surface on the block. If a residue of old oil is allowed to remain, it will smoke when the block is heated up. It will also prevent the new filter from seating properly. Also make sure that the none of the old gasket remains stuck to the mounting surface. It can be removed with a scraper if necessary.

14   Compare the old filter with the new one to make sure they are the same type. Smear some clean engine oil on the rubber gasket of the new filter and screw it into place **(see illustration)**. Because overtightening the filter will damage the gasket, do not use a filter wrench to tighten the filter. Tighten it by hand until the gasket contacts the seating surface. Then seat the filter by giving it an additional 3/4-turn.

15   Remove all tools, rags, etc. from under the vehicle, being careful not to spill the oil in the drain pan, then lower the vehicle.

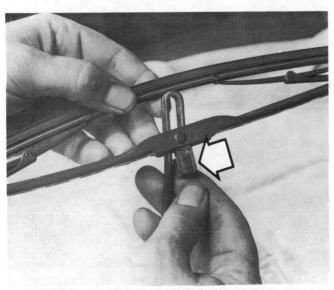

9.6   Press in on the lock tab (arrow) and push the blade assembly out of the hook at the end to remove it

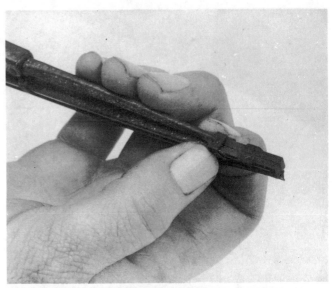

9.7   Squeeze the blade element tabs, pull the element out of the metal frame and remove it

9.8   Install the metal retainers in the new wiper element before inserting it into the frame

16   Add new oil to the engine through the oil filler cap in the camshaft cover. Use a spout or funnel to prevent oil from spilling onto the top of the engine. Pour three quarts of fresh oil into the engine. Wait a few minutes to allow the oil to drain into the pan, then check the level on the oil dipstick (see Section 4 if necessary). If the oil level is at or near the upper hole on the dipstick, install the filler cap hand tight, start the engine and allow the new oil to circulate.

17   Allow the engine to run for about a minute. While the engine is running, look under the vehicle and check for leaks at the oil pan drain plug and around the oil filter. If either is leaking, stop the engine and tighten the plug or filter slightly.

18   Wait a few minutes to allow the oil to trickle down into the pan, then recheck the level on the dipstick and, if necessary, add enough oil to bring the level to the upper hole.

19   During the first few trips after an oil change, make it a point to check frequently for leaks and proper oil level.

20   The old oil drained from the engine cannot be reused in its present state and should be discarded. Oil reclamation centers, auto repair shops and gas stations will normally accept the oil, which can be refined and used again. After the oil has cooled, it can be drained into a suitable container (capped plastic jugs, topped bottles, milk cartons, etc.) for transport to one of these disposal sites.

9   Windshield wiper blade inspection and replacement

Refer to illustrations 9.6, 9.7 and 9.8

1   The windshield wiper and blade assembly should be inspected periodically for damage, loose components and cracked or worn blade elements.

2   Road film can build up on the wiper blades and affect their efficiency, so they should be washed regularly with a mild detergent solution.

3   The action of the wiping mechanism can loosen bolts, nuts and fasteners, so they should be checked and tightened, as necessary, at the same time the wiper blades are checked.

4   If the wiper blade elements are cracked, worn or warped, or no longer clean adequately, they should be replaced with new ones.

5   Lift the arm assembly away from the glass for clearance.

6   Press in on the lock tab and push the blade assembly down the wiper arm, out of the hook at the end **(see illustration)**.

7   Squeeze the blade element tabs tightly and pull the element out of the metal frame **(see illustration)**.

8   Remove the metal retainers from the element and install them in the new element **(see illustration)**.

9   Insert the element into the frame and push it until the element tabs lock.

10   Place the metal arm assembly in the hook on the wiper arm and press it into place until the lock tab snaps into place.

10   Battery check and maintenance

Refer to illustrations 10.1, 10.6a, 10.6b, 10.7a and 10.7b

1   A routine preventive maintenance program for the battery in your vehicle is the only way to ensure quick and reliable starts. But before performing any battery maintenance, make sure that you have the proper

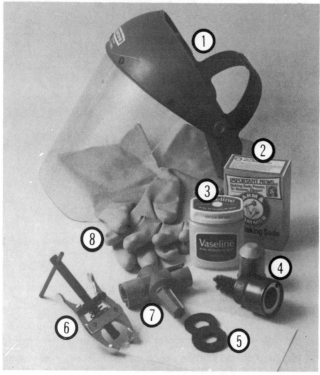

10.1   Tools and materials required for battery maintenance

1   *Face shield/safety goggles – When removing corrosion with a brush, the acidic particles can easily fly up into your eyes*
2   *Baking soda – A solution of baking soda and water can be used to neutralize corrosion*
3   *Petroleum jelly – A layer of this on the battery posts will help prevent corrosion*
4   *Battery post/cable cleaner – This wire brush cleaning tool will remove all traces of corrosion from the battery posts and cable clamps*
5   *Treated felt washers – Placing one of these on each post, directly under the cable clamps, will help prevent corrosion*
6   *Puller – Sometimes the cable clamps are very difficult to pull off the posts, even after the nut/bolt has been completely loosened. This tool pulls the clamp straight up and off the post without damage.*
7   *Battery post/cable cleaner – Here is another cleaning tool which is a slightly different version of number 4 above, but it does the same thing*
8   *Rubber gloves – Another safety item to consider when servicing the battery; remember that's acid inside the battery!*

10.6a   Battery terminal corrosion usually appears as light, fluffy powder

10.6b   Removing the cable from a battery post with a wrench – sometimes a special battery pliers is required for this procedure if corrosion has caused deterioration of the nut hex (always remove the ground cable first and hook it up last!)

equipment necessary to work safely around the battery (see illustration).
2   There are also several precautions that should be taken whenever battery maintenance is performed. Before servicing the battery, always turn the engine and all accessories off and disconnect the cable from the negative terminal of the battery.
3   The battery produces hydrogen gas, which is both flammable and explosive. Never create a spark, smoke or light a match around the battery. Always charge the battery in a ventilated area.
4   Electrolyte contains poisonous and corrosive sulfuric acid. Do not allow it to get in your eyes, on your skin on on your clothes. Never ingest it. Wear protective safety glasses when working near the battery. Keep children away from the battery.
5   Note the external condition of the battery. If the positive terminal and cable clamp on your vehicle's battery is equipped with a rubber protector, make sure that it's not torn or damaged. It should completely cover the terminal. Look for any corroded or loose connections, cracks in the case or cover or loose hold-down clamps. Also check the entire length of each cable for cracks and frayed conductors.
6   If corrosion, which looks like white, fluffy deposits (see illustration) is evident, particularly around the terminals, the battery should be removed for cleaning. Loosen the cable clamp nuts with a wrench, being careful to remove the negative cable first, and slide them off the terminals (see illustration). Then disconnect the hold-down clamp nuts, remove the clamp and lift the battery from the engine compartment.
7   Clean the cable clamps thoroughly with a battery brush or a terminal cleaner and a solution of warm water and baking soda (see illustration). Wash the terminals and the top of the battery case with the same solution but make sure that the solution doesn't get into the battery. When cleaning the cables, terminals and battery top, wear safety goggles and rubber gloves to prevent any solution from coming in contact with your eyes or hands. Wear old clothes too – even diluted, sulfuric acid splashed onto clothes will burn holes in them. If the terminals have been extensively corroded, clean them up with a terminal cleaner (see illustration). Thoroughly wash all cleaned areas with plain water.
8   Before reinstalling the battery in the engine compartment, inspect the plastic battery carrier. If it's dirty or covered with corrosion, remove it and clean it in the same solution of warm water and baking soda. Inspect the

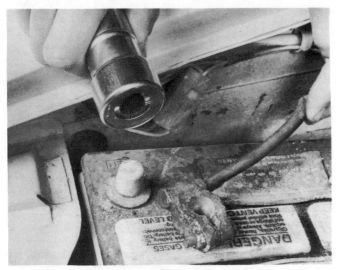

10.7a Regardless of the type of tool used on the battery posts, a clean, shiny surface should be the result

10.7b When cleaning the cable clamps, all corrosion must be removed (the inside of the clamp is tapered to match the taper on the post, so don't remove too much material)

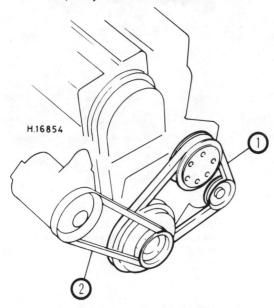

H.16854

① ②

11.2 Typical drivebelt layout

1   Alternator and water pump belt
2   Power steering pump belt

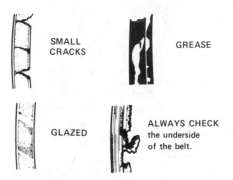

SMALL CRACKS   GREASE

GLAZED   ALWAYS CHECK
the underside
of the belt.

11.3a Here are some of the more common problems associated with V-belts – check the belts very carefully to prevent an untimely breakdown

metal brackets which support the carrier to make sure that they are not covered with corrosion. If they are, wash them off. If corrosion is extensive, sand the brackets down to bare metal and spray them with a zinc-based primer (available in spray cans at auto paint and body supply stores).

9   Reinstall the battery carrier and the battery back into the engine compartment. Make sure that no parts or wires are laying on the carrier during installation of the battery.

10   Install a pair of specially treated felt washers around the terminals (available at auto parts stores), then coat the terminals and the cable clamps with petroleum jelly or grease to prevent further corrosion. Install the cable clamps and tighten the nuts, being careful to install the negative cable last.

11   Install the hold-down clamp and nuts. Tighten the nuts only enough to hold the battery firmly in place. Overtightening these nuts can crack the battery case.

12   Further information on the battery, charging and jump starting can be found in Chapter 5 and at the front of this manual.

11   Drivebelt check, adjustment and replacement

Refer to illustrations 11.2, 11.3a, 11.3b, 11.4, 11.6, 11.7 and 11.10

Check

1   The alternator and air conditioning compressor drivebelts are either V-belts or V-ribbed belts. Sometimes referred to as "fan" belts, the drivebelts are located at the left end of the engine. The good condition and proper adjustment of the belts is critical to the operation of the engine. Because of their composition and the high stresses to which they are subjected, drivebelts stretch and deteriorate as they get older. They must therefore be periodically inspected.

2   The number of belts used on a particular vehicle depends on the accessories installed. One belt transmits power from the crankshaft to the alternator and water pump **(see illustration)**. If your vehicle is equipped with power steering or air conditioning, the power steering pump and/or A/C compressor is driven by another belt or belts.

3   With the engine off, open the hood and locate the drivebelts at the left end of the engine. With a flashlight, check each belt: On V-belts, check for cracks and separation of the belt plies **(see illustration)**. On V-ribbed belts, check for separation of the adhesive rubber on both sides of the core, core separation from the belt side, a severed core, separation of the ribs from the adhesive rubber, cracking or separation of the ribs, and torn

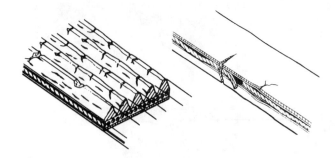

11.3b   Check V-ribbed belts for signs of wear like these – if the belt looks worn, replace it

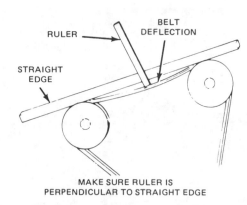

MAKE SURE RULER IS
PERPENDICULAR TO STRAIGHT EDGE

11.4   Measuring drivebelt deflection with a straightedge and ruler

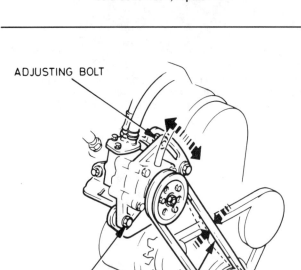

11.6   Typical power steering pump drivebelt adjustment details

A Drivebelt deflection

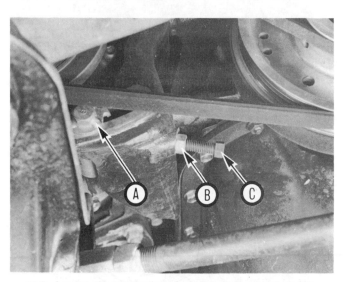

11.7   Loosen the nut on the other side of the pivot bolt (A), loosen the locknut (B), then adjust the belt tension with the adjusting bolt (C) – after adjustment, be sure to tighten the locknuts

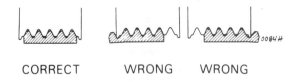

CORRECT   WRONG   WRONG

11.10   When installing a V-ribbed belt, make sure it is centered on the pulley – it must not overlap either edge of the pulley

or worn ribs or cracks in the inner ridges of the ribs **(see illustration)**. On both belt types, check for fraying and glazing, which gives the belt a shiny appearance. Both sides of the belt should be inspected, which means you will have to twist the belt to check the underside. Use your fingers to feel the belt where you can't see it. If any of the above conditions are evident, replace the belt (go to Step 8).

4   The tightness of each belt is checked by pushing on it at a distance halfway between the pulleys **(see illustration)**. Apply about 10 pounds of force with your thumb and see how much the belt moves down (deflects). Refer to the Specifications listed in this Chapter for the amount of deflection allowed in each belt.

Adjustment

5   If adjustment is necessary, it is done by moving the belt-driven accessory on the bracket.

6   For some components, there will be an adjusting bolt and a pivot bolt **(see illustration)**. Both must be loosened slightly to enable you to move the component. After the two bolts have been loosened, move the component away from the engine (to tighten the belt) or toward the engine (to loosen the belt). After adjustment, tighten the bolts securely.

7   On some components, loosen the pivot bolt and locknut on the adjusting bolt. Turn the adjusting bolt to tension the belt **(see illustration)**.

Replacement

8   To replace a belt, follow the above procedures for drivebelt adjustment but slip the belt off the crankshaft pulley and remove it. If you are replacing the alternator belt, you will have to remove the air conditioning compressor belt first because of the way they are arranged on the crankshaft pulley. Because of this and because belts tend to wear out more or less together, it is a good idea to replace both belts at the same time. Mark each belt and its appropriate pulley groove so the replacement belts can be installed in their proper positions.

9   Take the old belts to the parts store in order to make a direct comparison for length, width and design.

10   After replacing a V-ribbed drivebelt, make sure it fits properly in the ribbed grooves in the pulleys **(see illustration)**. It is essential that the belt be properly centered.

11   Adjust the belt(s) in accordance with the procedure outlined above.

12   Underhood hose check and replacement

Caution: *Replacement of air conditioning hoses must be left to a dealer service department or air conditioning shop that has the equipment to de-pressurize the system safely. Never remove air conditioning components or hoses until the system has been depressurized.*

General

1   High temperatures in the engine compartment can cause the deterioration of the rubber and plastic hoses used for engine, accessory and emission systems operation. Periodic inspection should be made for cracks, loose clamps, material hardening and leaks.

2   Information specific to the cooling system hoses can be found in Section 13.

3   Some, but not all, hoses are secured to the fittings with clamps. Where clamps are used, check to be sure they haven't lost their tension, allowing the hose to leak. If clamps aren't used, make sure the hose has not expanded and/or hardened where it slips over the fitting, allowing it to leak.

Vacuum hoses

4   It's quite common for vacuum hoses, especially those in the emissions system, to be color coded or identified by colored stripes molded into them. Various systems require hoses with different wall thicknesses, collapse resistance and temperature resistance. When replacing hoses, be sure the new ones are made of the same material.

5   Often the only effective way to check a hose is to remove it completely from the vehicle. If more than one hose is removed, be sure to label the hoses and fittings to ensure correct installation.

6   When checking vacuum hoses, be sure to include any plastic T-fittings in the check. Inspect the fittings for cracks and the hose where it fits over the fitting for distortion, which could cause leakage.

7   A small piece of vacuum hose (1/4-inch inside diameter) can be used as a stethoscope to detect vacuum leaks. Hold one end of the hose to your ear and probe around vacuum hoses and fittings, listening for the "hissing" sound characteristic of a vacuum leak. **Warning:** *When probing with the vacuum hose stethoscope, be very careful not to come into contact with moving engine components such as the drivebelts, cooling fan, etc.*

Fuel hose

Warning: *There are certain precautions which must be taken when inspecting or servicing fuel system components. Work in a well ventilated area and do not allow open flames (cigarettes, appliance pilot lights, etc.) or bare light bulbs near the work area. Mop up any spills immediately and do not store fuel-soaked rags where they could ignite. On vehicles equipped with fuel injection, the fuel system is under pressure, so if any fuel lines are to be disconnected, the pressure in the system must be relieved first (see Chapter 4 for more information).*

8   Check all rubber fuel lines for deterioration and chafing. Check especially for cracks in areas where the hose bends and just before fittings, such as where a hose attaches to the fuel filter.

9   High quality fuel line, usually identified by the word Fluroelastomer printed on the hose, should be used for fuel line replacement. Never, under any circumstances, use unreinforced vacuum line, clear plastic tubing or water hose for fuel lines.

10   Spring-type clamps are commonly used on fuel lines. These clamps often lose their tension over a period of time, and can be "sprung" during removal. Replace all spring-type clamps with screw clamps whenever a hose is replaced.

Metal lines

11   Sections of metal line are often used for fuel line between the fuel pump and fuel injection unit. Check carefully to be sure the line has not been bent or crimped and that cracks have not started in the line.

12   If a section of metal fuel line must be replaced, only seamless steel tubing should be used, since copper and aluminum tubing don't have the strength necessary to withstand normal engine vibration.

13   Check the metal brake lines where they enter the master cylinder and brake proportioning unit (if used) for cracks in the lines or loose fittings. Any sign of brake fluid leakage calls for an immediate thorough inspection of the brake system.

13   Cooling system check

Refer to illustration 13.4

1   Many major engine failures can be attributed to a faulty cooling system. If the vehicle is equipped with an automatic transmission, the cooling system also cools the transmission fluid and thus plays an important role in prolonging transmission life.

2   The cooling system should be checked with the engine cold. Do this before the vehicle is driven for the day or after the engine has been shut off for at least three hours.

3   Remove the radiator cap by turning it to the left until it reaches a stop. If you hear a hissing sound (indicating there is still pressure in the system), wait until it stops. Now press down on the cap with the palm of your hand and continue turning to the left until the cap can be removed. Thoroughly clean the cap, inside and out, with clean water. Also clean the filler neck on the radiator. All traces of corrosion should be removed. The coolant inside the radiator should be relatively transparent. If it's rust colored, the system should be drained and refilled (Section 28). If the coolant level isn't up to the top, add additional antifreeze/coolant mixture (see Section 4).

4   Carefully check the large upper and lower radiator hoses along with the smaller diameter heater hoses which run from the engine to the firewall. Inspect each hose along its entire length, replacing any hose which is cracked, swollen or shows signs of deterioration. Cracks may become more apparent if the hose is squeezed **(see illustration)**. Regardless of condition, it's a good idea to replace hoses with new ones every two years.

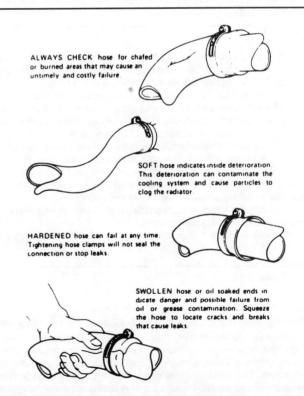

ALWAYS CHECK hose for chafed or burned areas that may cause an untimely and costly failure.

SOFT hose indicates inside deterioration. This deterioration can contaminate the cooling system and cause particles to clog the radiator.

HARDENED hose can fail at any time. Tightening hose clamps will not seal the connection or stop leaks.

SWOLLEN hose or oil soaked ends indicate danger and possible failure from oil or grease contamination. Squeeze the hose to locate cracks and breaks that cause leaks.

13.4   Hoses, like drivebelts, have a habit of failing at the worst possible time – to prevent the inconvenience of a blown radiator or heater hose, inspect them carefully as shown here

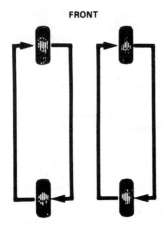

14.2   The recommended tire rotation pattern for these models

15.6   You will find an inspection hole like this in each caliper – placing a steel ruler across the hole should enable you to determine the thickness of the remaining pad material

5   Make sure that all hose connections are tight. A leak in the cooling system will usually show up as white or rust colored deposits on the areas adjoining the leak. If wire-type clamps are used at the ends of the hoses, it may be a good idea to replace them with more secure screw-type clamps.
6   Use compressed air or a soft brush to remove bugs, leaves, etc. from the front of the radiator or air conditioning condenser. Be careful not to damage the delicate cooling fins or cut yourself on them.
7   Every other inspection, or at the first indication of cooling system problems, have the cap and system pressure tested. If you don't have a pressure tester, most gas stations and repair shops will do this for a minimal charge.

---

14   Tire rotation

Refer to illustration 14.2
1   The tires should be rotated at the specified intervals and whenever uneven wear is noticed. Since the vehicle will be raised and the tires removed anyway, check the brakes (Section 15) at this time.
2   Radial tires must be rotated in a specific pattern **(see illustration)**.
3   Refer to the information in Jacking and towing at the front of this manual for the proper procedures to follow when raising the vehicle and changing a tire. If the brakes are to be checked, do not apply the parking brake as stated. Make sure the tires are blocked to prevent the vehicle from rolling.
4   Preferably, the entire vehicle should be raised at the same time. This can be done on a hoist or by jacking up each corner and then lowering the vehicle onto jackstands placed under the frame rails. Always use four jackstands and make sure the vehicle is firmly supported.
5   After rotation, check and adjust the tire pressures as necessary and be sure to check the lug nut tightness.
6   For further information on the wheels and tires, refer to Chapter 10.

---

15   Brake check

Refer to illustrations 15.6, 15.9, 15.14 and 15.16
Note: *For detailed photographs of the brake system, refer to Chapter 9.*
1   In addition to the specified intervals, the brakes should be inspected every time the wheels are removed or whenever a defect is suspected.
2   Any of the following symptoms could indicate a potential brake system defect: The vehicle pulls to one side when the brake pedal is depressed; the brakes make squealing or dragging noises when applied; brake travel is excessive; the pedal pulsates; brake fluid leaks, usually onto the inside of the tire or wheel.
3   Loosen the wheel lug nuts.
4   Raise the vehicle and place it securely on jackstands.

5   Remove the wheels (see Jacking and towing at the front of this book, or your owner's manual, if necessary).

Disc brakes

Note: *Most models have disc brakes on the front only; however, some later CRX models have disc brakes at the rear also.*
6   There are two pads – an outer and an inner – in each caliper. The pads are visible through an inspection hole in each caliper **(see illustration)**.
7   Check the pad thickness by looking at each end of the caliper and through the inspection hole in the caliper body. If the lining material is less than the specified thickness, replace the pads. **Note:** *Keep in mind that the lining material is riveted or bonded to a metal backing plate and the metal portion is not included in this measurement.*
8   If it is difficult to determine the exact thickness of the remaining pad material by the above method, or if you are at all concerned about the condition of the pads, remove the caliper(s), then remove the pads from the calipers for further inspection (see Chapter 9).

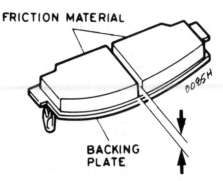

15.9   If a more precise measurement of pad thickness is necessary, remove the pads and measure the remaining friction material – spraying the pad with brake cleaner will help you determine where the friction material ends and the steel backing plate begins

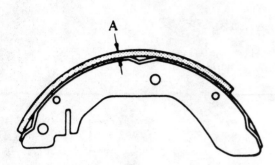

15.14 If the lining is bonded to the brake shoe, measure the lining thickness from the outer surface to the metal shoe, as shown here; if the lining is riveted to the shoe, measure from the lining outer surface to the rivet head

15.16 Use a small screwdriver to carefully peel back the rubber boots (arrow) on both sides of the wheel cylinder – if there's any brake fluid behind the boots, the wheel cylinders must be replaced (trailing brake shoe pulled down for clarity)

9   Once the pads are removed from the calipers, clean them with brake cleaner and remeasure them with a small steel pocket ruler or a vernier caliper **(see illustration)**.
10   Measure the disc thickness with a micrometer to make sure that it still has service life remaining. If any disc is thinner than the specified minimum thickness, replace it (see Chapter 9). Even if the disc has service life remaining, check its condition. Look for scoring, gouging and burned spots. If these conditions exist, remove the disc and have it resurfaced (see Chapter 9).
11   Before installing the wheels, check all brake lines and hoses for damage, wear, deformation, cracks, corrosion, leakage, bends and twists, particularly in the vicinity of the rubber hoses at the calipers. Check the clamps for tightness and the connections for leakage. Make sure all hoses and lines are clear of sharp edges, moving parts and the exhaust system. If any of the above conditions are noted, repair, reroute or replace the lines and/or fittings as necessary (see Chapter 9).

Rear drum brakes

Note: *Some later CRX models are equipped with disc brakes at the rear. See the disc brake procedure above for these models.*
12   Refer to Chapter 9 and remove the rear brake drums.
13   **Warning:** *Brake dust produced by lining wear and deposited on brake components contains asbestos, which is hazardous to your health. DO NOT blow it out with compressed air and DO NOT inhale it! DO NOT use gasoline or solvents to remove the dust. Brake system cleaner should be used to flush the dust into a drain pan. After the brake components are wiped clean with a damp rag, dispose of the contaminated rag(s) and solvent in a covered and labelled container. Try to use non-asbestos replacement parts whenever possible.*
14   Note the thickness of the lining material on the rear brake shoes **(see illustration)** and look for signs of contamination by brake fluid and grease. If the lining material is within 1/16-inch of the recessed rivets or metal shoes, replace the brake shoes with new ones. The shoes should also be replaced if they are cracked, glazed (shiny lining surfaces) or contaminated with brake fluid or grease. See Chapter 9 for the replacement procedure.
15   Check the shoe return and hold-down springs and the adjusting mechanism to make sure they're installed correctly and in good condition. Deteriorated or distorted springs, if not replaced, could allow the linings to drag and wear prematurely.
16   Check the wheel cylinders for leakage by carefully peeling back the rubber boots **(see illustration)**. If brake fluid is noted behind the boots, the wheel cylinders must be replaced (see Chapter 9).
17   Check the drums for cracks, score marks, deep scratches and hard spots, which will appear as small discolored areas. If imperfections cannot

be removed with emery cloth, the drums must be resurfaced by an automotive machine shop (see Chapter 9 for more detailed information).
18   Refer to Chapter 9 and install the brake drums.
19   Install the wheels and snug the wheel lug nuts finger tight.
20   Remove the jackstands and lower the vehicle.
21   Tighten the wheel lug nuts to the specified torque.

Brake booster check

22   Sit in the driver's seat and perform the following sequence of tests.
23   With the engine stopped, depress the brake pedal several times- the travel distance should not change.
24   With the brake fully depressed, start the engine – the pedal should move down a little when the engine starts.
25   Depress the brake, stop the engine and hold the pedal in for about 30 seconds – the pedal should neither sink nor rise.
26   Restart the engine, run it for about a minute and turn it off. Then firmly depress the brake several times – the pedal travel should decrease with each application.
27   If your brakes do not operate as described above when the preceding tests are performed, the brake booster is either in need of repair or has failed. Refer to Chapter 9 for the removal procedure.

Parking brake

28   Slowly pull up on the parking brake and count the number of clicks you hear until the handle is up as far as it will go. The adjustment is correct if you hear the number of clicks listed in this Chapter's Specifications. If you hear more or fewer clicks, it's time to adjust the parking brake (see Chapter 9).
29   An alternative method of checking the parking brake is to park the vehicle on a steep hill with the parking brake set and the transmission in Neutral. If the parking brake cannot prevent the vehicle from rolling, it is in need of adjustment (see Chapter 9).

16   Clutch release arm freeplay check and adjustment

Refer to illustrations 16.2 and 16.3

1   Raise the vehicle and support it securely on jackstands.

16.2   **Move the clutch release arm up and down and measure the freeplay (view is from beneath the driver's side of the vehicle)**

16.3   **Turn the knurled knob (arrow) (it is easier to reach from the engine compartment) to adjust the clutch release arm freeplay**

2   Move the clutch release arm up and down and measure the freeplay **(see illustration)**.
3   If the freeplay is not as specified, turn the knurled knob at the top of the bracket to adjust the freeplay **(see illustration)**. Turn the knob counterclockwise to increase the freeplay and clockwise to decrease it. Operate the clutch several times and recheck the freeplay, adjusting as necessary.

17   Air and PCV filter replacement

Refer to illustrations 17.3, 17.4, 17.9a and 17.9b

1   At the specified intervals, the air filter and (if equipped) PCV filter should be replaced with new ones. The engine air cleaner also supplies filtered air to the PCV system.
2   The filter is located on top of the carburetor or in a housing next to the engine.
3   On carburetor-equipped models, remove the wing nut(s) on top of the filter housing, release the clips on the side of the filter housing and lift off the air cleaner cover for access to the filter element **(see illustration)**.
4   On fuel injection-equipped models, remove the nuts and lift off the air cleaner cover (early models) or disengage the clips and pull the cover back (later models) for access to the element **(see illustration)**.
5   While the air cleaner cover is off, be careful not to drop anything down into the carburetor or air cleaner assembly.
6   Lift the air filter element out of the housing and wipe out the inside of the air cleaner housing with a clean rag. Be sure to note how it's installed so the new filter can be installed in the same way.
7   Place the new filter in the air cleaner housing. Make sure it seats properly in the bottom of the housing. Check the new filter to see if it's marked to indicate how it should be installed.
8   On carbureted models, the PCV filter is located in a housing on the side of the air cleaner housing. **Note:** *Fuel-injected models are not equipped with a PCV filter.*
9   Remove the housing screws and lift out the old filter **(see illustrations)**.
10   Install the new PCV filter.
11   Install the air cleaner cover and any hoses which were disconnected.

17.3   **Removing the air filter (carbureted models)**

17.4   **Removing the air filter (fuel-injected models)**

17.9a Remove the two screws that retain the PCV filter housing to the air filter housing

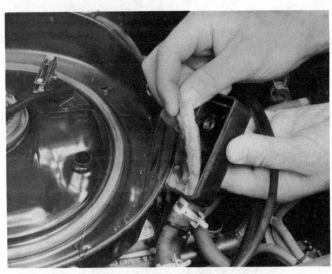

17.9b Remove the filter retainer and carefully lift the filter out of the PCV filter housing

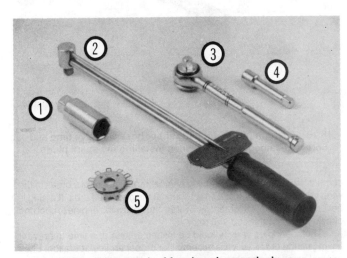

18.1 Tools required for changing spark plugs

1 *Spark plug socket* – This will have special padding inside to protect the spark plug's porcelain insulator
2 *Torque wrench* – Although not mandatory, using this tool is the best way to ensure the plugs are tightened properly
3 *Ratchet* – Standard hand tool to fit the spark plug socket
4 *Extension* – Depending on model and accessories, you may need special extensions and universal joints to reach one or more of the plugs
5 *Spark plug gap gauge* – This gauge for checking the gap comes in a variety of styles. Make sure the gap for your engine is included.

---

18 Spark plug check and replacement

Refer to illustrations 18.1, 18.4a, 18.4b, 18.6 and 18.10

1 Spark plug replacement requires a spark plug socket which fits onto a ratchet wrench. This socket is lined with a rubber grommet to protect the porcelain insulator of the spark plug and to hold the plug while you insert it into the spark plug hole. You will also need a wire-type feeler gauge to check and adjust the spark plug gap and a torque wrench to tighten the

new plugs to the specified torque **(see illustration)**.
2 If you are replacing the plugs, purchase the new plugs, adjust them to the proper gap and then replace each plug one at a time. **Note:** *When buying new spark plugs, it's essential that you obtain the correct plugs for your specific vehicle. This information can be found on the Vehicle Emissions Control Information (VECI) label located on the underside of the hood or in the owner's manual. If these two sources specify different plugs, purchase the spark plug type specified on the VECI label because that information is provided specifically for your engine.*
3 Inspect each of the new plugs for defects. If there are any signs of cracks in the porcelain insulator of a plug, don't use it.
4 Check the electrode gaps of the new plugs. Check the gap by inserting the wire gauge of the proper thickness between the electrodes at the tip of the plug **(see illustration)**. The gap between the electrodes should be identical to that specified on the VECI label. If the gap is incorrect, use

18.4a Spark plug manufacturers recommend using a wire type gauge when checking the gap – if the wire does not slide between the electrodes with a slight drag, adjustment is required

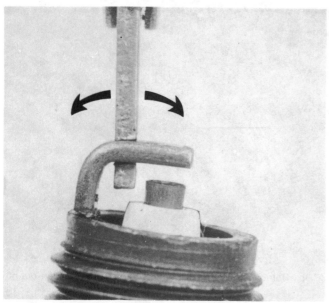

18.4b To change the gap, bend the *side* electrode only, as indicated by the arrows, and be very careful not to crack or chip the porcelain insulator surrounding the center electrode

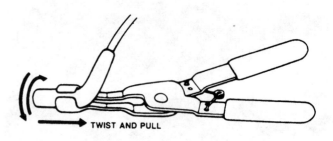

18.6 When removing the spark plug wires, pull only on the boot and twist it back-and-forth

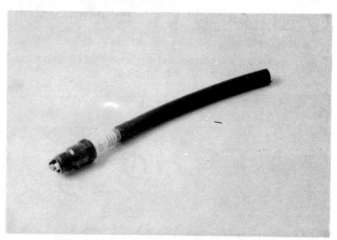

18.10 A length of 3/16-inch ID rubber hose will save time and prevent damaged threads when installing the spark plugs

the notched adjuster on the feeler gauge body to bend the curved side electrode slightly **(see illustration)**.

5   If the side electrode is not exactly over the center electrode, use the notched adjuster to align them. **Caution:** *If the gap of a new plug must be adjusted, bend only the base of the ground electrode. Do not touch the tip.*

Removal

6   To prevent the possibility of mixing up spark plug wires, work on one spark plug at a time. Remove the wire and boot from one spark plug. Grasp the boot – not the cable – as shown, give it a half twisting motion and pull straight out **(see illustration)**.

7   If compressed air is available, blow any dirt or foreign material away from the spark plug area before proceeding (a common bicycle pump will also work).

8   Remove the spark plug.

9   Whether you are replacing the plugs at this time or intend to reuse the old plugs, compare each old spark plug with those shown in the accompanying color photos to determine the overall running condition of the engine.

Installation

10   It's often difficult to insert spark plugs into their holes without cross-threading them. To avoid this possibility, fit a short piece of 3/16-inch ID rubber hose over the end of the spark plug **(see illustration)**. The flexible hose acts as a universal joint to help align the plug with the plug hole. Should the plug begin to cross-thread, the hose will slip on the spark plug, preventing thread damage. Tighten the plug securely.

11   Attach the plug wire to the new spark plug, again using a twisting motion on the boot until it is firmly seated on the end of the spark plug.

12   Follow the above procedure for the remaining spark plugs, replacing them one at a time to prevent mixing up the spark plug wires.

19   Spark plug wire, distributor cap and rotor check and replacement

Refer to illustrations 19.11 and 19.12

1   The spark plug wires should be checked whenever new spark plugs are installed.

2   Begin this procedure by making a visual check of the spark plug wires while the engine is running. In a darkened garage (make sure there is ventilation) start the engine and observe each plug wire. Be careful not to come into contact with any moving engine parts. If there is a break in the wire, you will see arcing or a small spark at the damaged area. If arcing is noticed, make a note to obtain new wires, then allow the engine to cool and check the distributor cap and rotor.

3   The spark plug wires should be inspected one at a time to prevent mixing up the order, which is essential for proper engine operation. Each original plug wire should be numbered to help identify its location. If the number is illegible, a piece of tape can be marked with the correct number and wrapped around the plug wire.

4   Disconnect the plug wire from the spark plug. A removal tool can be used for this purpose or you can grasp the rubber boot, twist the boot half a turn and pull the boot free. Do not pull on the wire itself.

5   Check inside the boot for corrosion, which will look like a white crusty powder.

6   Push the wire and boot back onto the end of the spark plug. It should fit tightly onto the end of the plug. If it doesn't, remove the wire and use pliers to carefully crimp the metal connector inside the wire boot until the fit is snug.

7   Using a clean rag, wipe the entire length of the wire to remove built-up dirt and grease. Once the wire is clean, check for burns, cracks and other damage. Do not bend the wire sharply, because the conductor might break.

8   Disconnect the wire from the distributor. Again, pull only on the rubber boot. Check for corrosion and a tight fit. Replace the wire in the distributor.

9   Inspect the remaining spark plug wires, making sure that each one is securely fastened at the distributor and spark plug when the check is complete.

10   If new spark plug wires are required, purchase a set for your specific engine model. Pre-cut wire sets with the boots already installed are available. Remove and replace the wires one at a time to avoid mix-ups in the firing order.

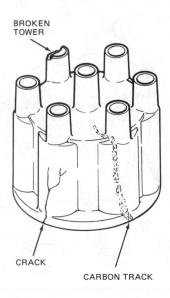

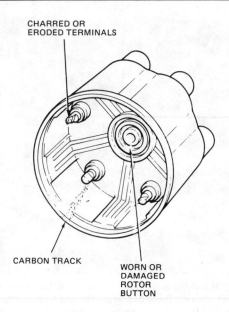

19.11   Shown here are some of the common defects to look for when inspecting the distributor cap (if in doubt about its condition, install a new one)

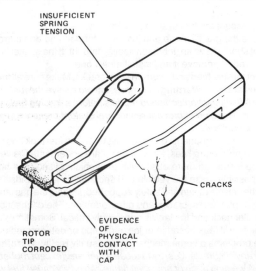

19.12   The ignition rotor should be checked for wear and corrosion as indicated here (if in doubt about its condition, buy a new one)

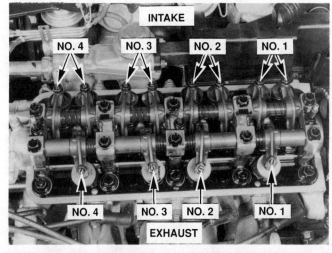

20.5   Valve adjustment screw locations and numbering – twelve-valve (two intake valves per cylinder) engine shown

11   Detach the distributor cap by removing the two cap retaining bolts. Look inside it for cracks, carbon tracks and worn, burned or loose contacts **(see illustration)**.

12   Pull the rotor off the distributor shaft and examine it for cracks and carbon tracks **(see illustration)**. Replace the cap and rotor if any damage or defects are noted.

13   It is common practice to install a new cap and rotor whenever new spark plug wires are installed, but if you wish to continue using the old cap, check the resistance between the spark plug wires and the cap first. If the indicated resistance is more than the maximum value listed in this Chapter's Specifications, replace the cap and/or wires.

14   When installing a new cap, remove the wires from the old cap one at a time and attach them to the new cap in the exact same location – do not simultaneously remove all the wires from the old cap or firing order mix-ups may occur.

20   Valve clearance check and adjustment

Refer to illustrations 20.5 and 20.6

1   The valve clearances are checked and adjusted with the engine cold.

2   On carbureted models, remove the air cleaner assembly (see Chapter 4).

3   Remove the camshaft cover (see Chapter 2A).

4   Using the procedure in Chapter 2A, position the number one piston (the one closest to the drivebelt end of the engine) at Top Dead Center (TDC).

5   With the engine in this position, the number one cylinder valve adjustment can be checked and adjusted **(see illustration)**.

20.6   To adjust a valve clearance, loosen the adjuster nut with a wrench and back off the adjuster screw with a screwdriver; carefully tighten the adjuster screw until you feel a slight drag when withdrawing the feeler gauge, then tighten the adjuster nut while still holding the adjuster screw with a screwdriver (adjusting an exhaust valve is shown)

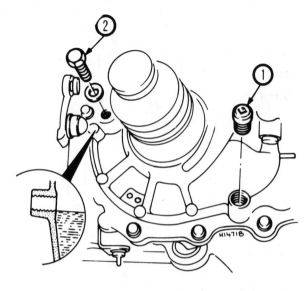

22.1   The manual transaxle drain (1) and fill (2) plugs are located on the right side of the transaxle case

6   Start with the intake valve clearance. **Note:** *Most models have two intake valves per cylinder (12-valve and 16-valve engines); on these models, the adjustment procedure and clearance are the same for both valves.* Insert a feeler gauge of the thickness listed in this Chapter's Specifications between the intake valve stem and the adjusting screw. Withdraw it; you should feel a slight drag. If there's no drag or a heavy drag, loosen the adjuster nut and back off the adjuster screw **(see illustration)**. Carefully tighten the adjuster screw until you can feel a slight drag on the feeler gauge as you withdraw it.

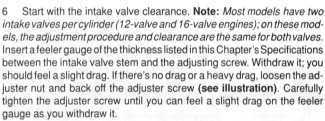

7   Hold the adjuster screw with a screwdriver (to keep it from turning) and tighten the locknut. Recheck the clearance to make sure it hasn't changed.
8   Adjust the number one exhaust valve using the same procedure you used for the intake valve(s). **Note:** *16-valve engines have two exhaust valves per cylinder; on these models, the adjustment procedure and clearance are the same for both valves.* Be sure to use a feeler gauge of the specified thickness. If your vehicle is equipped with auxiliary valves (smaller valves, adjacent to the exhaust valves), also adjust the number one auxiliary valve using the same procedure. Note that the auxiliary valves have a different clearance than exhaust valves.
9   Using the procedure in Chapter 2A, position the number three piston at TDC. Check and adjust the number three cylinder valve clearances.
10   Position the number four piston at TDC. Check and adjust the number four cylinder valves.
11   Position the number two piston at TDC. Check and adjust the number two cylinder valves.
12   Install the camshaft cover and the air cleaner assembly.

21   Fuel system check

Warning: *Certain precautions should be observed when inspecting or servicing the fuel system components. Work in a well ventilated area and do not allow open flames (cigarettes, appliance pilot lights, etc.) near the work area. Mop up spills immediately and do not store fuel soaked rags where they could ignite. It is a good idea to keep a dry chemical (Class B) fire extinguisher near the work area any time the fuel system is being serviced.*

1   If you smell gasoline while driving or after the vehicle has been sitting

in the sun, inspect the fuel system immediately.
2   Remove the gas filler cap and inspect it for damage and corrosion. The gasket should have an unbroken sealing imprint. If the gasket is damaged or corroded, remove it and install a new one.
3   Inspect the fuel feed and return lines for cracks. Make sure all fuel line connections are tight. **Warning:** *It is necessary to relieve the fuel system pressure on fuel-injection equipped models before servicing fuel system components. The correct procedures for fuel system pressure relief are outlined in Chapter 4.*
4   Since some components of the fuel system – the fuel tank and part of the fuel feed and return lines, for example – are underneath the vehicle, they can be inspected more easily with the vehicle raised on a hoist. If that's not possible, raise the vehicle and secure it on jackstands.
5   With the vehicle raised and safely supported, inspect the gas tank and filler neck for punctures, cracks and other damage. The connection between the filler neck and the tank is particularly critical. Sometimes a rubber filler neck will leak because of loose clamps or deteriorated rubber. These are problems a home mechanic can usually rectify. **Warning:** *Do not, under any circumstances, try to repair a fuel tank (except rubber components). A welding torch or any open flame can easily cause fuel vapors inside the tank to explode.*
6   Carefully check all rubber hoses and metal lines leading away from the fuel tank. Check for loose connections, deteriorated hoses, crimped lines and other damage. Carefully inspect the lines from the tank to the fuel injection system or carburetor. Repair or replace damaged sections as necessary.

22   Manual transaxle lubricant level check

Refer to illustration 22.1

1   The manual transaxle does not have a dipstick. To check the fluid level, raise the vehicle and support it securely on jackstands. The fill plug is on the right side of the transaxle housing **(see illustration)**. Remove it. If the lubricant level is correct, it should be up to the lower edge of the hole.
2   If the transaxle needs more lubricant (if the level is not up to the hole), use a syringe, squeeze bottle or pump to add more. Stop filling the transaxle when the lubricant begins to run out the hole.
3   Install the plug and tighten it securely. Drive the vehicle a short distance, then check for leaks.

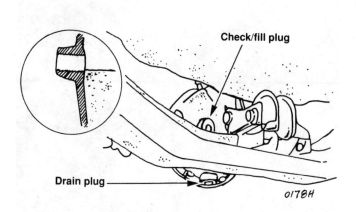

23.2   Locations of the check/fill and drain plugs on the rear differential

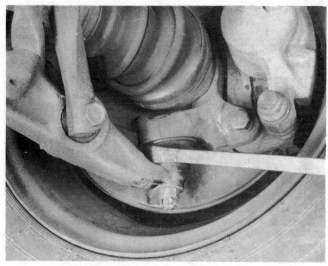

24.8   Pry between the balljoint and lower suspension arm to check for movement indicating balljoint wear

23   Rear differential (4WD models) lubricant level check

Refer to illustration 23.2

1   The rear differential on 4WD models has a check/fill plug which must be removed to check the lubricant level. If the vehicle is raised to gain access to the plug, be sure to support it safely on jackstands – DO NOT crawl under the vehicle when it's supported only by a jack.

2   Remove the check/fill plug from the differential **(see illustration)**.

3   The lubricant level should be at the bottom of the plug opening **(see illustration 23.2)**. If not, use a syringe to add the recommended lubricant until it just starts to run out of the opening.

4   Install the plug and tighten it securely.

24   Steering and suspension check

Refer to illustrations 24.8 and 24.9

Note: *For detailed illustrations of the steering and suspension components, refer to Chapter 10.*

With the wheels on the ground

1   With the vehicle stopped and the front wheels pointed straight ahead, rock the steering wheel gently back and forth. If freeplay is excessive, a front wheel bearing, main shaft yoke, intermediate shaft yoke, lower arm balljoint or steering system joint is worn or the steering gear is out of adjustment or damaged. Refer to Chapter 10 for the appropriate repair procedure.

2   Other symptoms, such as excessive vehicle body movement over rough roads, swaying (leaning) around corners and binding as the steering wheel is turned, may indicate faulty steering and/or suspension components.

3   Check the shock absorbers by pushing down and releasing the vehicle several times at each corner. If the vehicle does not come back to a level position within one or two bounces, the shocks/struts are worn and must be replaced. When bouncing the vehicle up and down, listen for squeaks and noises from the suspension components. Additional information on suspension components can be found in Chapter 10.

4   Note whether the vehicle looks canted to one side or corner. If is, try to level it by rocking it down. If this doesn't work, look for bad springs or worn or loose suspension parts.

5   Raise the vehicle with a floor jack and support it securely on jackstands. See Jacking and towing at the front of this book for the proper jacking points.

6   Check the tires for irregular wear patterns (see Section 5) and proper inflation.

Under the vehicle

Warning: *Do not climb under the vehicle unless it's supported securely on jackstands!*

7   Inspect the universal joint between the steering shaft and the steering gear housing. Check the steering gear housing for grease or fluid leakage. Make sure that the dust seals and boots are not damaged and that the boot clamps are not loose. Check the steering linkage for looseness or damage. Check the tie-rod ends for excessive play. Look for loose bolts, broken or disconnected parts and deteriorated rubber bushings on all suspension and steering components. While an assistant turns the steering wheel from side to side, check the steering components for free movement, chafing and binding. If the steering components do not seem to be reacting with the movement of the steering wheel, try to determine where the slack is located

8   Check the balljoints for wear by prying between each balljoint and lower suspension arm **(see illustration)** to ensure the balljoint has no play. If any balljoint does have play, replace it. Refer to Chapter 10 for the front balljoint replacement procedure.

9   Inspect the balljoint boots for tears and leaking grease **(see illustration)**. Replace the boots with new ones if they are damaged (see Chapter 10).

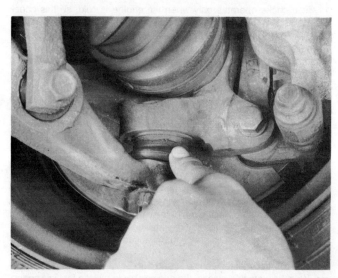

24.9   Push on the balljoint boot to check for tears and grease leaks

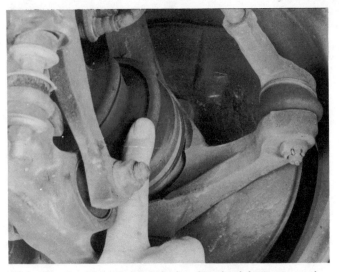

25.2   Flex the driveaxle boots by hand to check for tears, cracks and leaking grease

26.3   The carburetor choke plate is visible after removing the top cover of the air cleaner (air cleaner assembly shown removed for clarity)

25   Driveaxle boot check

Refer to illustration 25.2

1   The driveaxle boots are very important because they prevent dirt, water and foreign material from entering and damaging the constant velocity (CV) joints. Oil and grease can cause the boot material to deteriorate prematurely, so it's a good idea to wash the boots with soap and water.
2   Inspect the boots for tears and cracks as well as loose clamps **(see illustration)**. If there is any evidence of cracks or leaking grease, they must be replaced as described in Chapter 8.

26   Carburetor choke check

Refer to illustration 26.3

1   The choke operates only when the engine is cold, so this check should be performed before the engine has been started for the day.
2   Take off the top cover of the air cleaner assembly. It's held in place by a nut (or nuts) at the center and clips at the sides. If any vacuum hoses must be disconnected, make sure you tag the hoses for reinstallation in their original positions. Place the top cover and nuts aside, out of the way of moving engine components.
3   Look at the center of the air cleaner housing. You will notice a flat plate at the carburetor opening **(see illustration)**.
4   Press the accelerator pedal to the floor. The plate should close completely. Start the engine while you watch the plate at the carburetor. Don't position your face near the carburetor, as the engine could backfire, causing serious burns. When the engine starts, the choke plate should open slightly.
5   Allow the engine to continue running at an idle speed. As the engine warms up to operating temperature, the plate should slowly open, allowing more air to enter through the top of the carburetor.
6   After a few minutes, the choke plate should be fully open to the vertical position. Tap the accelerator to make sure the fast idle cam disengages.
7   You'll notice that the engine speed corresponds with the plate opening. With the plate fully closed, the engine should run at a fast idle speed. As the plate opens and the throttle is moved to disengage the fast idle cam, the engine speed will decrease.

27.2a   Squeeze the PCV hose gently with a pair of pliers – use a rag to protect the hose surface (carbureted engine shown)

8   Refer to Chapter 4 for specific information on adjusting and servicing the choke components.

27   Positive Crankcase Ventilation (PCV) valve check and replacement

Refer to illustrations 27.2a and 27.2b
Note: *for a detailed discussion of the PCV system, refer to Chapter 6*

1   The PCV valve is located in the crankcase breather chamber or in the hose which connects the crankcase breather chamber to the intake manifold.

Check

2   With the engine idling at normal operating temperature, squeeze the PCV hose located at the top of the engine gently shut with a pair of pliers, using a rag to protect the hose surface **(see illustrations)**. Pinch the hose

CARBON DEPOSITS

Symptoms: Dry sooty deposits indicate a rich mixture or weak ignition. Causes misfiring, hard starting and hesitation.

Recommendation: Check for a clogged air cleaner, high float level, sticky choke and worn ignition points. Use a spark plug with a longer core nose for greater anti-fouling protection.

OIL DEPOSITS

Symptoms: Oily coating caused by poor oil control. Oil is leaking past worn valve guides or piston rings into the combustion chamber. Causes hard starting, misfiring and hesition.

Recommendation: Correct the mechanical condition with necessary repairs and install new plugs.

TOO HOT

Symptoms: Blistered, white insulator, eroded electrode and absence of deposits. Results in shortened plug life.

Recommendation: Check for the correct plug heat range, over-advanced ignition timing, lean fuel mixture, intake manifold vacuum leaks and sticking valves. Check the coolant level and make sure the radiator is not clogged.

PREIGNITION

Symptoms: Melted electrodes. Insulators are white, but may be dirty due to misfiring or flying debris in the combustion chamber. Can lead to engine damage.

Recommendation: Check for the correct plug heat range, over-advanced ignition timing, lean fuel mixture, clogged cooling system and lack of lubrication.

HIGH SPEED GLAZING

Symptoms: Insulator has yellowish, glazed appearance. Indicates that combustion chamber temperatures have risen suddenly during hard acceleration. Normal deposits melt to form a conductive coating. Causes misfiring at high speeds.

Recommendation: Install new plugs. Consider using a colder plug if driving habits warrant.

GAP BRIDGING

Symptoms: Combustion deposits lodge between the electrodes. Heavy deposits accumulate and bridge the electrode gap. The plug ceases to fire, resulting in a dead cylinder.

Recommendation: Locate the faulty plug and remove the deposits from between the electrodes.

NORMAL

Symptoms: Brown to grayish-tan color and slight electrode wear. Correct heat range for engine and operating conditions.

Recommendation: When new spark plugs are installed, replace with plugs of the same heat range.

ASH DEPOSITS

Symptoms: Light brown deposits encrusted on the side or center electrodes or both. Derived from oil and/or fuel additives. Excessive amounts may mask the spark, causing misfiring and hesitation during acceleration.

Recommendation: If excessive deposits accumulate over a short time or low mileage, install new valve guide seals to prevent seepage of oil into the combustion chambers. Also try changing gasoline brands.

WORN

Symptoms: Rounded electrodes with a small amount of deposits on the firing end. Normal color. Causes hard starting in damp or cold weather and poor fuel economy.

Recommendation: Replace with new plugs of the same heat range.

DETONATION

Symptoms: Insulators may be cracked or chipped. Improper gap setting techniques can also result in a fractured insulator tip. Can lead to piston damage.

Recommendation: Make sure the fuel anti-knock values meet engine requirements. Use care when setting the gaps on new plugs. Avoid lugging the engine.

SPLASHED DEPOSITS

Symptoms: After long periods of misfiring, deposits can loosen when normal combustion temperature is restored by an overdue tune-up. At high speeds, deposits flake off the piston and are thrown against the hot insulator, causing misfiring.

Recommendation: Replace the plugs with new ones or clean and reinstall the originals.

MECHANICAL DAMAGE

Symptoms: May be caused by a foreign object in the combustion chamber or the piston striking an incorrect reach (too long) plug. Causes a dead cylinder and could result in piston damage.

Recommendation: Remove the foreign object from the engine and/or install the correct reach plug.

27.2b   Squeezing the PCV hose on a fuel-injected engine

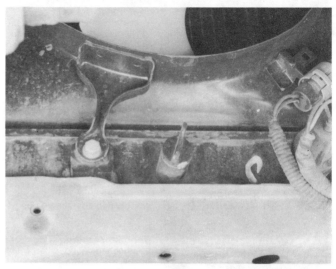

28.4   On most models you will have to remove a cover for access to the radiator drain fitting located at the bottom of the radiator – if possible before opening the valve, push a short section of 3/8-inch inner diameter plastic hose onto the plastic fitting to direct the coolant into the container

as gently as possible to avoid damaging the hose.

3   If the PCV valve is operating properly, it will make a clicking sound when the hose is pinched shut. If it doesn't, replace the valve.

4   Check the hoses between the intake manifold and breather chamber for plugging, deterioration and other damage. Replace hoses as necessary.

Replacement

5   Detach the hose or hoses and remove the valve, noting its installed position and direction.

6   When purchasing a replacement PCV valve, make sure it's for your particular vehicle and engine size. Compare the old valve with a new one to make sure they're the same.

7   Installation is the reverse of removal.

---

28   Cooling system servicing (draining, flushing and refilling)

Refer to illustrations 28.4 and 28.13

Warning: *Do not allow antifreeze to come in contact with your skin or painted surfaces of the vehicle. Rinse off spills immediately with plenty of water. Antifreeze is highly toxic if ingested. Never leave antifreeze lying around in an open container or in puddles on the floor; children and pets are attracted by it's sweet smell and may drink it. Check with local authorities about disposing of used antifreeze. Many communities have collection centers which will see that antifreeze is disposed of safely.*

Draining

1   Periodically, the cooling system should be drained, flushed and refilled to replenish the antifreeze mixture and prevent formation of rust and corrosion, which can impair the performance of the cooling system and cause engine damage. When the cooling system is serviced, all hoses and the radiator cap should be checked and replaced if necessary.

2   Apply the parking brake and block the wheels. If the vehicle has just been driven, wait several hours to allow the engine to cool down before beginning this procedure.

3   Once the engine is completely cool, remove the radiator cap.

4   Move a large container under the radiator drain fitting to catch the coolant. If the radiator drain fitting can accommodate a drain hose, attach a 3/8-inch inner diameter hose to the drain fitting to direct the coolant into the container (some models are already equipped with a hose), then open the drain fitting (a pair of pliers may be required to turn it) **(see illustration)**.

5   After the coolant stops flowing out of the radiator, move the container under the engine block drain plug on the front side of the engine. Loosen the plug and allow the coolant in the block to drain.

6   While the coolant is draining, check the condition of the radiator hoses, heater hoses and clamps (refer to Section 13 if necessary).

7   Replace any damaged clamps or hoses (refer to Chapter 3 for detailed replacement procedures).

Flushing

8   Once the system is completely drained, flush the radiator with fresh water from a garden hose until water runs clear at the drain. The flushing action of the water will remove sediments from the radiator but will not remove rust and scale from the engine and cooling tube surfaces.

9   These deposits can be removed by the chemical action of a cleaner. Follow the procedure outlined in the manufacturer's instructions. If the radiator is severely corroded, damaged or leaking, it should be removed (see Chapter 3) and taken to a radiator repair shop.

10   Remove the overflow hose from the coolant recovery reservoir. Drain the reservoir and flush it with clean water, then reconnect the hose.

Refilling

11   Close and tighten the radiator drain. Install and tighten the block drain plug.

12   Place the heater temperature control in the maximum heat position.

13   Loosen the coolant bleeder screw in the inlet housing **(see illustration)**.

14   Slowly add new coolant (a 50/50 mixture of water and antifreeze) to the radiator until bubble-free coolant flows from the bleeder screw. Tighten the screw and continue adding coolant to the radiator until it's full. Add coolant to the reservoir until the level is at the upper mark.

15   Leave the radiator cap off and run the engine in a well-ventilated area until the thermostat opens (coolant will begin flowing through the radiator and the upper radiator hose will become hot).

16   Turn the engine off and let it cool. Add more coolant mixture to bring the level back up to the lip on the radiator filler neck.

17   Squeeze the upper radiator hose to expel air, then add more coolant mixture if necessary. Replace the radiator cap.

18   Start the engine, allow it to reach normal operating temperature and check for leaks.

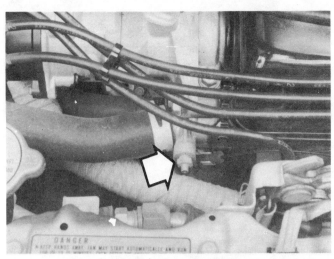

28.13   The coolant bleeder screw (arrow) is located on the inlet housing – the screw must be opened during the filling process to bleed air out of the system (carbureted engine shown)

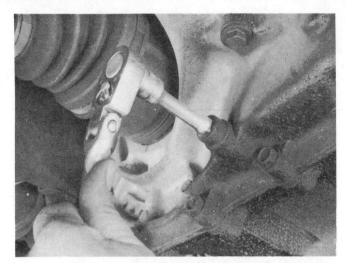

32.1   Use a 3/8-inch drive ratchet and extension to remove the manual transaxle drain plug

29   Exhaust system check

1   With the engine cold (at least three hours after the vehicle has been driven), check the complete exhaust system from its starting point at the engine to the end of the tailpipe. This should be done on a hoist where unrestricted access is available.

2   Check the pipes and connections for evidence of leaks, severe corrosion or damage. Make sure that all brackets and hangers are in good condition and tight.

3   At the same time, inspect the underside of the body for holes, corrosion, open seams, etc. which may allow exhaust gases to enter the passenger compartment. Seal all body openings with silicone sealer or body putty.

4   Rattles and other noises can often be traced to the exhaust system, especially the mounts and hangers. Try to move the pipes, muffler and catalytic converter. If the components can come in contact with the body or suspension parts, secure the exhaust system with new mounts.

5   Check the running condition of the engine by inspecting inside the end of the tailpipe. The exhaust deposits here are an indication of engine state-of-tune. If the pipe is black and sooty or coated with white deposits, the engine is in need of a tune-up, including a thorough fuel system inspection and adjustment.

30   Brake fluid replacement

1   Because brake fluid absorbs moisture which could ultimately cause corrosion of the brake components, and air which could make the braking system less effective, the fluid should be replaced at the specified intervals. This job can be accomplished for a nominal fee by a properly equipped brake shop using a pressure bleeder. The task can also be done by the home mechanic with the help of an assistant. To bleed the air and old fluid and replace it with fresh fluid from sealed containers, refer to the brake bleeding procedure in Chapter 9.

2   If there is any possibility that incorrect fluid has been used in the system, drain all the fluid and flush the system with alcohol. Replace all piston seals and cups, as they will be affected and could possibly fail under pressure.

31   Automatic transaxle fluid change

Note: *The fluid capacity of the 2WD and the 4WD transaxles is different. Be sure to refer to the specifications listed in this Chapter for the proper amount.*

1   At the specified time intervals, the automatic transaxle fluid should be drained and replaced.

2   Before beginning work, purchase the specified transmission fluid (see Recommended fluids and lubricants at the front of this chapter).

3   Other tools necessary for this job include jackstands to support the vehicle in a raised position, an appropriately-sized wrench, a drain pan capable of holding at least six pints, newspapers and clean rags.

4   The fluid should be drained immediately after the vehicle has been driven. Hot fluid is more effective than cold fluid at removing built up sediment. **Caution:** *Fluid temperature can exceed 350-degrees in a hot transaxle. Wear protective gloves.*

5   After the vehicle has been driven to warm up the fluid, raise it and place it on jackstands for access to the transaxle and differential drain plugs.

6   Move the necessary equipment under the vehicle, being careful not to touch any of the hot exhaust components.

7   Place the drain pan under the drain plug in the transaxle **(see illustration 7.3)** and remove the drain plug with the wrench. Be sure the drain pan is in position, as fluid will come out with some force. Once the fluid is drained, clean the drain plug and reinstall it securely.

8   Lower the vehicle.

9   With the engine off, unscrew and remove the dipstick, then add new fluid to the transaxle through the dipstick hole (see Recommended fluids and lubricants for the recommended fluid type and capacity). Use a funnel to prevent spills. It is best to add a little fluid at a time, continually checking the level with the dipstick (see Section 7). Allow the fluid time to drain into the pan.

10   Start the engine and shift the selector into all positions from P through 2, then shift into P and apply the parking brake.

11   Turn off the engine and check the fluid level. Add fluid to bring the level between the Add and Full marks.

32   Manual transaxle lubricant change

Refer to illustrations 32.1 and 32.3

Note: *The lubricant capacity of the 2WD and the 4WD transaxles is different. Be sure to refer to the Specifications listed in this Chapter for the proper amount.*

1   Raise the vehicle, support it securely on jackstands and position a drain pan under the drain plug **(see illustration)**. Remove the fill plug **(see illustration 22.1)**, then remove the drain plug and drain the lubricant. Check the lubricant for metal particles which indicate transaxle wear or damage.

2   Reinstall the drain plug and tighten it securely.

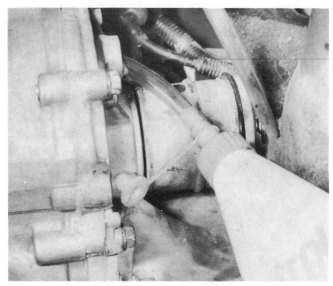

32.3   Use a squeeze bottle with a tube attached (shown) or a syringe or pump to fill the transaxle

3   Add new lubricant until it begins to run out of the filler hole **(see illustration)**. See *Recommended lubricants and fluids* for the specified lubricant type. Reinstall the fill plug and tighten it securely.

33   Rear differential (4WD models) lubricant change

1   Drive the vehicle for several miles to warm up the differential lubricant, then raise the vehicle and support it securely on jackstands.
2   Move a drain pan, rags, newspapers and a 3/8-inch drive breaker bar or ratchet with an extension under the vehicle.
3   With the drain pan under the differential, use the breaker bar or ratchet and extension to loosen the drain plug. It's the lower of the two plugs **(see illustration 23.2)**.
4   Once loosened, carefully unscrew it with your fingers until you can remove it from the case.
5   Allow all of the lubricant to drain into the pan, then replace the drain plug and tighten it securely.
6   Feel with your hands along the bottom of the drain pan for any metal bits that may have come out with the lubricant. If there are any, it's a sign of excessive wear, indicating that the internal components should be carefully inspected in the near future.
7   Remove the differential fill plug located above the drain plug. Using a hand pump, syringe or squeeze bottle with a tube attached, fill the differential with the correct grade of lubricant (see this Chapter's Specifications) until the level is just at the bottom of the plug hole.
8   Reinstall the plug and tighten it securely.
9   Lower the vehicle. Check for leaks at the drain plug after the first few miles of driving.

34   Ignition timing check and adjustment

Refer to illustrations 34.1 and 34.7
Note: *It is imperative that the procedures included on the Vehicle Emissions Control Information (VECI) label be followed when adjusting the ignition timing. The label will include all information concerning preliminary steps to be performed before adjusting the timing, as well as the timing specifications. If any information on the VECI differs from the procedure that follows, the VECI label is correct.*

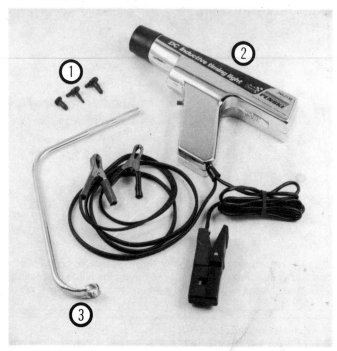

34.1   Tools needed to check and adjust the ignition timing

1 **Vacuum plugs** – *Vacuum hoses will, in most cases, have to be disconnected and plugged. Molded plugs in various shapes and sizes are available for this.*
2 **Inductive pick-up timing light** – *Flashes a bright concentrated beam of light when the number one spark plug fires. Connect the leads according to the instructions supplied with the light.*
3 **Distributor wrench** – *On some models, the hold-down bolt for the distributor is difficult to reach and turn with conventional wrenches or sockets. A special wrench like this must be used.*

1   With the ignition off, locate the VECI label under the hood and read through and perform all preliminary instructions concerning ignition timing. Several special tools will be needed for this procedure **(see illustration)**.
2   On 1986 and 1987 models, detach the hoses from the distributor vacuum advance unit and plug the hoses.
3   On 1988 and later models, you must connect a jumper wire between the two terminals (brown and green/white wires) of the ignition timing adjuster connector. On 1988 and 1989 models, this connector is at the left rear corner of the engine compartment; you must remove a yellow rubber cap from the connector before hooking up the jumper wire. On 1990 models, the connector is located under the right side of the dash.
4   With the ignition off, connect the inductive pick-up lead of the timing light to the number one spark plug (the one closest to the drivebelt end of the engine). Connect the battery leads of the timing light according to the manufacturer's instructions (they are normally attached to the vehicle's battery terminals).
5   The crankshaft pulley at the drivebelt end of the engine has four colored notches that represent different degrees of timing advance. Directly above the crankshaft pulley, on the timing belt cover, is a pointer. These notches and pointer are known as the timing marks.
6   Start the engine and point the timing light at the timing marks.
7   The appropriate notch on the pulley (refer to the VECI label) will appear stationary and be aligned with the pointer if the timing is correct. If an adjustment is required, loosen the adjusting bolt and rotate the distributor slightly until the timing is correct **(see illustration)**.
8   Tighten the adjusting bolt and recheck the timing.

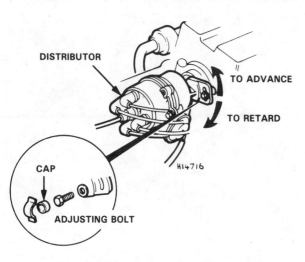

34.7   After loosening the adjusting bolt, rotate the
distributor to adjust the timing

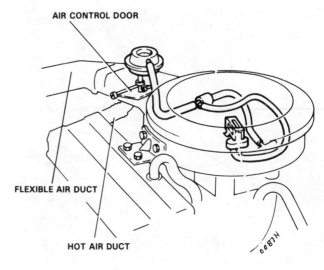

35.3   Typical thermostatic air cleaner details

9   Turn off the engine and remove the timing light.
10   Reconnect the vacuum advance hoses or remove the jumper wire.

35   Thermostatic air cleaner check (carbureted models)

Refer to illustration 35.3
1   Some engines are equipped with a thermostatically controlled air cleaner which draws air to the carburetor from different locations, depending on engine temperature.
2   This is a visual check. If access is limited, a small mirror may have to be used.
3   Locate the air control door inside the air cleaner assembly. It's inside the long snorkel of the metal air cleaner housing **(see illustration)**.
4   If there is a flexible air duct attached to the end of the snorkel, leading to an area behind the grille, disconnect it at the snorkel. This will enable you to look through the end of the snorkel and see the air control door inside.
5   The check should be done when the engine is cold. Start the engine and look through the snorkel at the air control door, which should move to a closed position. With the door closed, air cannot enter through the end of the snorkel, but instead enters the air cleaner through the hot air duct attached to the exhaust manifold and the heat stove passage.
6   As the engine warms up to operating temperature, the air control door should open to allow air through the snorkel end. Depending on outside temperature, this may take 10-to-15 minutes. To speed up this check you can reconnect the snorkel air duct, drive the vehicle, then check to see if the air control door is completely open.
7   If the thermo-controlled air cleaner isn't operating properly see Chapter 6 for more information.

36   Throttle linkage inspection

Refer to illustration 36.3
1   Inspect the throttle linkage for damage and missing parts and for binding and interference when the accelerator pedal is depressed.
2   Lubricate the various linkage pivot points with engine oil.
3   Push on the throttle cable with your fingers to check the deflection. It should deflect about 3/16 to 3/8-inch. If the deflection is incorrect, loosen the locknut and turn the adjusting nut as necessary to adjust the tension **(see illustration)**.
4   Tighten the locknut.

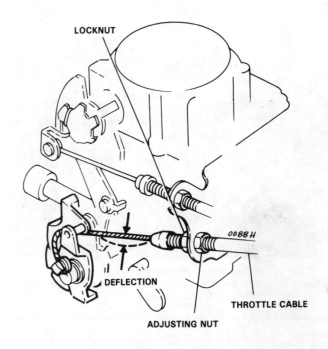

36.3   Throttle cable adjustment details

37   Idle speed check and adjustment

1   Engine idle speed is the speed at which the engine operates when no accelerator pedal pressure is applied, as when stopped at a traffic light. This speed is critical to the performance of the engine itself, as well as many subsystems.
2   Start the engine and allow it to warm up to normal operating temperature (the cooling fan should come on at least twice).
3   Stop the engine. Hook up a hand-held tachometer in accordance with the manufacturer's instructions.
4   Set the parking brake firmly and block the wheels to prevent the vehicle from rolling. Place the transaxle in Neutral (manual transaxle) or Park (automatic transaxle).

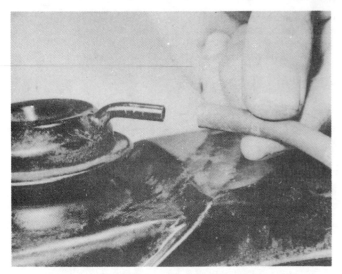

37.5   On carbureted models, detach the hose from the thermostatic air cleaner valve motor and plug the hose

37.6   On carbureted models, adjust the idle speed with the throttle stop screw (arrow)

37.8a   On 1985 through 1987 models, disconnect and plug the hose that connects the idle control solenoid valve to the intake manifold

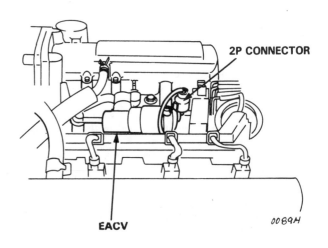

37.8b   On 1988 and later models, disconnect the 2P connector from the Electronic Air Control Valve (EACV)

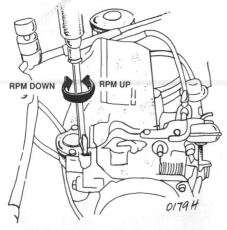

37.9a   Location of the idle speed adjustment screw on 1985 through 1987 fuel-injected models

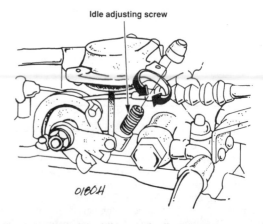

37.9b   Location of the idle speed adjustment screw on 1988 and later fuel-injected models

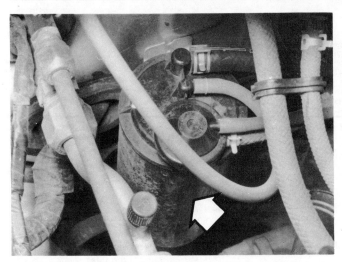

38.2   Inspect the charcoal canister (arrow) and hoses attached
to it for damage

39.2   To check the EGR valve, reach under it and push up on the
diaphragm with a finger – you should be able to push the
diaphragm up-and-down within the housing

Carbureted models

Refer to illustrations 37.5 and 37.6

5   Disconnect the hose from the thermostatic air cleaner valve motor and plug the hose **(see illustration)**.
6   Start the engine, note the idle speed rpm on the tachometer and compare it to that specified on the VECI label. If the idle speed is too low or too high, adjust it by turning the throttle stop screw **(see illustration)**.
7   Turn off the engine, disconnect the tachometer and connect the thermostatic air cleaner hose.

Fuel injected models

Refer to illustrations 37.8a, 37.8b, 37.9a and 37.9b

8   On 1985 through 1987 models, disconnect the hose (vacuum hose #10) that connects the idle control solenoid valve (located at the rear of the engine compartment on either the right or left side) to the intake manifold **(see illustration)**. On 1988 and later models disconnect the 2P connector from the Electronic Air Control Valve (EACV) **(see illustration)**.
9   Start the engine, note the idle speed on the tachometer and compare it to that specified on the VECI label. If the idle speed is too low or too high, adjust it by turning the adjusting screw located on the throttle body **(see illustrations)**.
10   Turn off the engine and disconnect the tachometer.
11   After adjustment, reconnect the idle control solenoid valve hose (1985 through 1987 models) or EACV connector (1988 and later models).

38   Evaporative emissions control system check

Refer to illustration 38.2

1   The function of the Fuel Evaporative Emission Control (EVAP) System is to store fuel vapors from the fuel tank in a charcoal canister until they can be routed to the intake manifold where they mix with incoming air before being burned in the cylinder combustion chambers.
2   The most common symptom of a faulty evaporative emissions system is a strong fuel odor in the engine compartment. If a fuel odor is detected, inspect the charcoal canister, located in the engine compartment, and the hoses attached to it **(see illustration)**.
3   The evaporative emissions control system is explained in more detail in Chapter 6.

39   Exhaust Gas Recirculation (EGR) system check (1984 through 1987 models only)

Refer to illustration 39.2

1   The EGR valve is usually located on the intake manifold, adjacent to

the carburetor or throttle body. Most of the time when a problem develops in this emissions system, it's due to a stuck or corroded EGR valve.
2   With the engine cold to prevent burns, push on the EGR valve diaphragm. Using moderate pressure, you should be able to press the diaphragm up-and-down within the housing **(see illustration)**.
3   If the diaphragm doesn't move or moves only with much effort, replace the EGR valve with a new one. If in doubt about the condition of the valve, compare the free movement of your EGR valve with a new valve.
4   Refer to Chapter 6 for more information on the EGR system.

40   Fuel filter replacement

Refer to illustrations 40.3, 40.5, 40.6, 40.7, 40.8, 40.9 and 40.13

1   This job should be done with the engine cold (after sitting at least three hours). Place an approved gasoline container under the fuel filter.

Carbureted models

2   These models are equipped with two filters: the main filter located under the vehicle adjacent to fuel tank and an auxiliary filter in the engine compartment.

Main filter

3   Raise the vehicle and support it securely on jackstands. Remove the fuel filter cover **(see illustration)**.

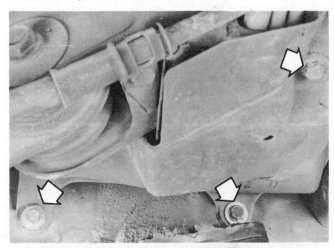

40.3   Remove the bolts (arrows) that retain the fuel filter cover to
the body

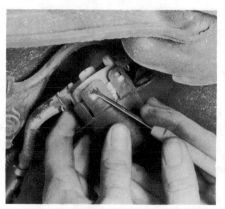

40.5   Remove the bolts (arrows) and lower the fuel filter and holder assembly

40.6   Pry the locking clips off the tabs while pushing the filter up out of the holder

40.7   Compress the fuel line clamps with pliers, then slide the clamps back on the hoses and disconnect the hoses from the filter

4   Use small locking pliers to clamp the fuel lines attached to the filter shut.

5   Remove the bolts and lower the fuel filter and holder assembly for access **(see illustration)**.

6   Pry back the locking clips and push the filter up out of the holder **(see illustration)**,

7   Use pliers to slide the fuel line clamps back and disconnect the fuel hoses from the filter **(see illustration)**.

8   Install the new filter by reversing the removal procedure. Make sure the arrow on the filter faces the front of the vehicle **(see illustration)**.

Auxiliary filter

9   Use small locking pliers to clamp the fuel lines attached to the filter shut. Slide the fuel line clamps back using pliers, grasp the fuel lines and disconnect them from the filter using a twisting motion **(see illustration)**.

10   Installation is the reverse of removal.

Fuel injected models

11   These models have one fuel filter, located in the engine compartment.

12   Place a shop towel or rag around the filter and depressurize the fuel system as described in Chapter 4.

13   Remove the banjo and service bolts, disconnect the fittings, remove the clamp and lift the filter from the engine compartment **(see illustration)**.

14   Installation is the reverse of removal. use new banjo and service bolt washers. Tighten the bolts to the torques listed in this Chapter's Specifications.

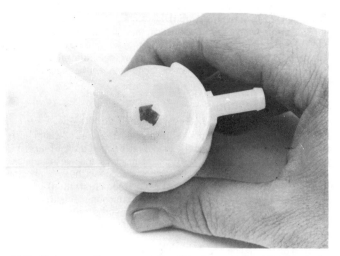

40.8   Make sure the arrow on the filter faces toward the front of the vehicle

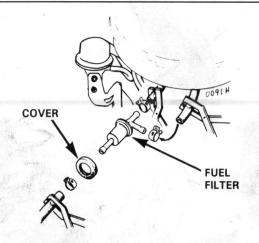

40.9   Typical auxiliary fuel filter (carburetor-equipped models) installation details

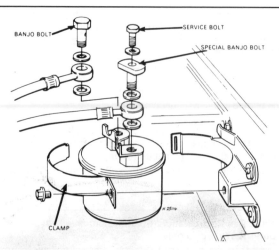

40.13   Fuel injection filter installation details (typical)

Chapter 2 Part A Engine

Contents

Specifications

General

Displacement	
1984	1300 cc (1342 cc or 82 c.i.)
1984 through 1987	1500 cc (1488 cc or 91 c.i.)
1988-on	1500 cc (1493 cc or 91 c.i.)
1989-on	1600 cc (1590 cc or 97 c.i.)
Cylinder numbers (drivebelt end-to-transaxle end)	1-2-3-4
Firing order	1-3-4-2

Camshaft and rocker arms

Camshaft endplay	
Standard	0.002 to 0.006 in (0.05 to 0.15 mm)
Service limit	0.02 in (0.5 mm)

Camshaft and rocker arms (continued)

Lobe height
  1984 through 1987
    Intake
      Auxiliary .... 1.7447 in (44.315 mm)
      1500 cc (main) .... 1.5894 in (40.370 mm)
      1300 cc (main) .... 1.5645 in (39.739 mm)
    Exhaust
      1500 cc .... 1.5274 in (38.796 mm)
      1300 cc .... 1.5654 in (39.762 mm)
  1988 on
    Intake
      4-speed M/T* .... 1.3728 in (34.868 mm)
      5-speed M/T and A/T* .... 1.4411 in (36.603 mm)
      CRX (8-valve engine) .... 1.7067 in (43.349 mm)
    Exhaust
      4-speed M/T* .... 1.3951 in (35.435 mm)
      5-speed M/T* .... 1.4467 in (36.747 mm)
      A/T* .... 1.4468 in (36.750 mm)
      CRX (8-valve engine) .... 1.4790 in (37.567 mm)
Camshaft journal-to-bearing (oil) clearance
  Standard .... 0.002 to 0.004 in (0.05 to 0.089 mm)
  Service limit .... 0.006 in (0.15 mm)
Camshaft runout
  Standard .... 0.001 in (0.03 mm)
  Service limit .... 0.002 in (0.06 mm)
Rocker arm-to-shaft (oil) clearance
  1984 through 1987
    Standard .... 0.0007 to 0.0021 in (0.018 to 0.054 mm)
    Service limit .... 0.003 in (0.08 mm)
  1988 on
    Standard
      Intake .... 0.0007 to 0.0020 in (0.017 to 0.050 mm)
      Exhaust .... 0.0007 to 0.0021 in (0.018 to 0.050 mm)
    Service limit (intake and exhaust) .... 0.003 in (0.08 mm)

Oil pump clearances

Standard
  Inner rotor-to-outer rotor .... 0.006 in (0.14 mm)
  Pump body-to-rotor
    Radial clearance .... 0.004 to 0.007 in (0.10 to 0.175 mm)
    Side clearance .... 0.001 to 0.003 in (0.03 to 0.08 mm)
Service limit
  Inner rotor-to-outer rotor .... 0.008 in (0.20 mm)
  Pump body-to-rotor
    Radial clearance .... 0.008 in (0.20 mm)
    Side clearance .... 0.006 in (0.15 mm)

Torque specifications

	Ft-lbs
Camshaft sprocket bolt	27
Camshaft cover crown nuts	7
Crankshaft (vibration) damper bolt	
1984 through 1987	83
1988-on	119
Cylinder head bolts	
Step 1	22
Step 2	49
Flywheel bolts (manual transaxle)	76
Driveplate bolts (automatic transaxle)	54
Exhaust manifold-to-cylinder head bolts	22
Exhaust manifold-to-header pipe self-locking nuts	33
Exhaust manifold bracket bolts	20
Intake manifold bracket bolts	16
Intake manifold part A-to-part B nuts	17
Intake manifold-to-cylinder head bolts	16
Oil pan bolts	9
Oil pick-up tube bolts	17
Oil pump-to-engine block bolts/nuts	9

M/T designates manual transaxle; A/T designates automatic transaxle.

1   General information

This Part of Chapter 2 is devoted to in-vehicle repair procedures for the engine. All information concerning engine removal and installation and engine block and cylinder head overhaul can be found in Part B of this Chapter.

The following repair procedures are based on the assumption the engine is installed in the vehicle. If the engine has been removed from the vehicle and mounted on a stand, many of the steps outlined in this Part of Chapter 2 will not apply.

The Specifications included in this Part of Chapter 2 apply only to the procedures contained in this Part. Part B of Chapter 2 contains the Specifications necessary for cylinder head and engine block rebuilding.

The engines covered in this manual came with one of three basic SOHC (Single Overhead Cam) cylinder head designs. The first design was produced from 1984 on and was available with fuel injection or a carburetor. It has two intake valves and one exhaust valve per cylinder, plus a small auxiliary valve on carbureted models. The engine is usually marked 12 VALVE on the camshaft cover. The second design was also available with fuel injection or a carburetor and has two intake and two exhaust valves per cylinder, but no auxiliary valve. The third design has one intake and one exhaust valve per cylinder. To maintain consistency and reduce confusion, the various engines will be referred to as "8-valve", "12-valve" and "16-valve".

2   Repair operations possible with the engine in the vehicle

Many major repair operations can be accomplished without removing the engine from the vehicle.

Clean the engine compartment and the exterior of the engine with some type of degreaser before any work is done. It will make the job easier and help keep dirt out of the internal areas of the engine.

Depending on the components involved, it may be helpful to remove the hood to improve access to the engine as repairs are performed (refer to Chapter 11 if necessary). Cover the fenders to prevent damage to the paint. Special pads are available, but an old bedspread or blanket will also work.

3.6   Make a mark (arrow) on the distributor body adjacent to the number one spark plug wire terminal

If vacuum, exhaust, oil or coolant leaks develop, indicating a need for gasket or seal replacement, the repairs can generally be made with the engine in the vehicle. The intake and exhaust manifold gaskets, camshaft cover gasket, oil pan gasket, crankshaft oil seals and cylinder head gasket are all accessible with the engine in place.

Exterior engine components, such as the intake and exhaust manifolds, the oil pan, the oil pump, the water pump, the starter motor, the alternator, the distributor and the fuel system components can be removed for repair with the engine in place.

Since the cylinder head can be removed without pulling the engine, camshaft and valve component servicing can also be accomplished with the engine in the vehicle. Replacement of the timing belt and sprockets is also possible with the engine in the vehicle.

In extreme cases caused by a lack of necessary equipment, repair or replacement of piston rings, pistons, connecting rods and rod bearings is possible with the engine in the vehicle. However, this practice is not recommended because of the cleaning and preparation work that must be done to the components involved.

3   Top Dead Center (TDC) for number one piston – locating

Refer to illustrations 3.6 and 3.9

Note: *The following procedure is based on the assumption the distributor is correctly installed. If you're trying to locate TDC to install the distributor correctly, piston position must be determined by feeling for compression at the number one spark plug hole, then aligning the ignition timing marks as described in step 8.*

1   Top Dead Center (TDC) is the highest point in the cylinder each piston reaches as it travels up-and-down when the crankshaft turns. Each piston reaches TDC on the compression stroke and again on the exhaust stroke, but TDC generally refers to piston position on the compression stroke.

2   Positioning the piston(s) at TDC is an essential part of many procedures such as rocker arm removal, camshaft and timing belt/sprocket removal and distributor removal.

3   Before beginning this procedure, be sure to place the transmission in Neutral and apply the parking brake or block the rear wheels. Also, disable the ignition system by detaching the coil wire from the center terminal of the distributor cap and grounding it on the block with a jumper wire. Remove the spark plugs (see Chapter 1).

4   To bring any piston to TDC, the crankshaft must be turned using one of the methods outlined below. When looking at the drivebelt end of the engine, normal crankshaft rotation is counterclockwise.

   a) The preferred method is to turn the crankshaft with a socket and ratchet attached to the bolt threaded into the front of the crankshaft.

   b) A remote starter switch, which may save some time, can also be used. Follow the instructions included with the switch. Once the piston is close to TDC, use a socket and ratchet as described in the previous Paragraph.

   c) If an assistant is available to turn the ignition switch to the Start position in short bursts, you can get the piston close to TDC without a remote starter switch. Make sure your assistant is out of the vehicle, away from the ignition switch, then use a socket and ratchet as described in Paragraph a) to complete the procedure.

5   Note the position of the terminal for the number one spark plug wire on the distributor cap. If the terminal isn't marked, follow the plug wire from the number one cylinder spark plug to the cap.

6   Use a felt-tip pen or chalk to make a mark on the distributor body directly adjacent to the terminal **(see illustration).**

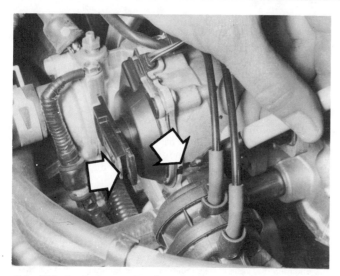

3.9 With the timing marks aligned, the rotor should point at the mark you made on the distributor body (arrows)

4.4 Remove the crown nuts (arrows) and any wires, hoses or brackets attached to the camshaft cover (Multi-Point Fuel Injected engine shown)

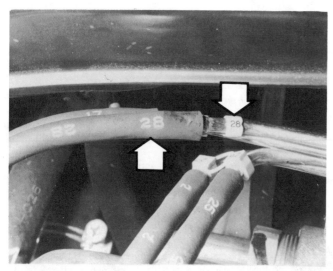

5.4 Check each wire, cable and hose connection to see if it's numbered (arrows); if not, number it yourself with tape and a felt-tip marker prior to disassembly

7 Detach the cap from the distributor (see Chapter 1 if necessary) and set it aside.
8 Turn the crankshaft (see Paragraph 4 above) until the TDC mark on the crankshaft drivebelt pulley is aligned with the pointer on the engine timing cover. On most engines, the TDC mark is painted white, but at any rate it always stands alone, separated from the ignition timing marks on the pulley.
9 Look at the distributor rotor – it should be pointing directly at the mark you made on the distributor body. If it is, go to Step 12 (see illustration).
10 If the rotor is 180-degrees off, the number one piston is at TDC on the exhaust stroke.
11 To get the piston to TDC on the compression stroke, turn the crankshaft one complete turn (360-degrees) counterclockwise. The rotor should now be pointing at the mark on the distributor. When the rotor is pointing at the number one spark plug wire terminal in the distributor cap and the ignition timing marks are aligned, the number one piston is at TDC on the compression stroke.

12 After the number one piston has been positioned at TDC on the compression stroke, TDC for any of the remaining pistons can be located by turning the crankshaft and following the firing order. Mark the remaining spark plug wire terminal locations on the distributor body just like you did for the number one terminal, then number the marks to correspond with the cylinder numbers. As you turn the crankshaft, the rotor will also turn. When it's pointing directly at one of the marks on the distributor, the piston for that particular cylinder is at TDC on the compression stroke.

4 Camshaft cover – removal and installation

Refer to illustration 4.4
1 Disconnect the negative cable from the battery.
2 Remove the air cleaner assembly (see Chapter 4).
3 Detach the crankcase ventilation tubes from the camshaft cover.
4 Remove any wires and/or brackets from the camshaft cover (see illustration).
5 Remove the upper timing belt cover (see Section 7).
6 Remove the crown nuts, washers and grommets, then lift the camshaft cover off the engine. If it's stuck, DO NOT pry between the cover and cylinder head or oil leaks will develop. Instead, tap the cover with a soft-face hammer to jar it loose.
7 Thoroughly clean the cover and cylinder head gasket mating surfaces to remove all traces of old gasket material.
8 Using a new gasket, reinstall the cover and tighten the crown nuts to the torque listed in this Chapter's specifications.
9 Reinstall the remaining parts in the reverse order of removal.
10 Run the engine and check for oil leaks at the cover.

5 Intake manifold – removal and installation

Refer to illustrations 5.4, 5.5 and 5.6
1 Remove the air cleaner assembly and, on fuel injected models, relieve the fuel pressure (see Chapter 4).
2 Disconnect the negative cable from the battery.
3 Drain the cooling system (see Chapter 1).
4 Label, then disconnect all wires, control cables and hoses connecting the intake manifold to the vehicle (see illustration).

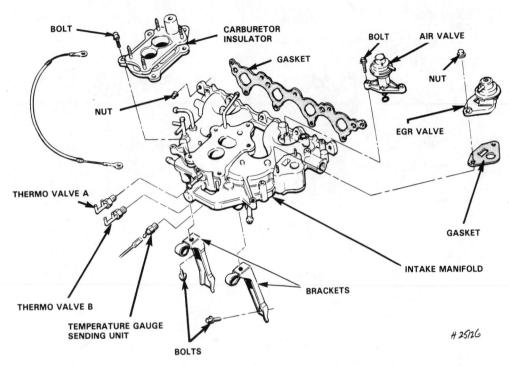

5.5   Exploded view of a typical intake manifold – carbureted models

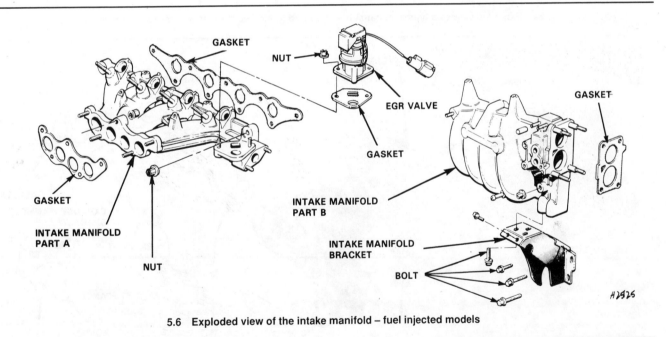

5.6   Exploded view of the intake manifold – fuel injected models

5   On carbureted models, remove the two bolts that secure the manifold to the brackets and all the intake manifold-to-cylinder head nuts **(see illustration)**. Detach the manifold from the engine.

6   Fuel injected models have a two-piece manifold **(see illustration)**. Remove the bracket-to-manifold bolts, unscrew the nuts and detach part B of the manifold.

7   Remove the intake manifold-to-cylinder head nuts and detach part A of the manifold.

8   Thoroughly clean the gasket mating surfaces on the manifold (or manifold parts) and the cylinder head to remove all traces of old gasket material. If a new manifold is being installed, transfer all detachable parts **(see illustration 5.5 or 5.6)** to the new manifold.

9   Using a new gasket, reinstall the manifold (or, on fuel injected models, part A of the manifold). Tighten the nuts from the center out, following a spiral pattern, in several steps to the torque listed in this Chapter's specifications.

10   On fuel injected models, reinstall part B of the manifold using a new gasket. Tighten the nuts from the center out to the torque listed in this Chapter's specifications.

11   Reinstall the remaining parts in the reverse order of removal. Tighten the intake manifold bracket bolts to the torque listed in this Chapter's specifications.

12   Refill the radiator.

13   Run the engine and check for leaks and proper operation.

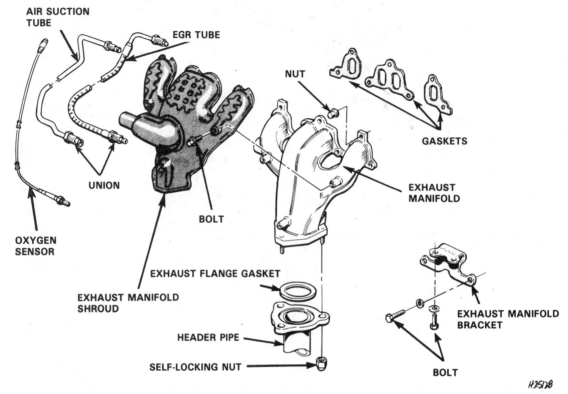

6.3a   Exploded view of a typical exhaust manifold and related components – carbureted models

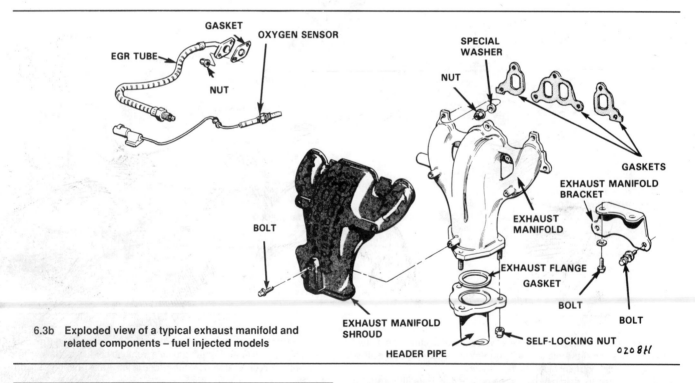

6.3b   Exploded view of a typical exhaust manifold and related components – fuel injected models

6   Exhaust manifold – removal and installation

Refer to illustrations 6.3a and 6.3b

Warning: *The engine must be completely cool before beginning this procedure.*

1   Disconnect the negative cable from the battery.

2   Unplug the oxygen sensor wire harness. If you're installing a new manifold, remove the sensor (see Chapter 6).

3   Remove the three bolts that secure the exhaust manifold shroud to the manifold, then detach the shroud, EGR tube and air suction tube (if equipped) from the manifold **(see illustrations)**.

4   Apply penetrating oil to the exhaust manifold mounting nuts/bolts.

5   Raise the vehicle and support it securely on jackstands.

6   Working underneath the vehicle, apply penetrating oil to the two exhaust manifold-to-bracket bolts and the three self-locking nuts on the header pipe flange.

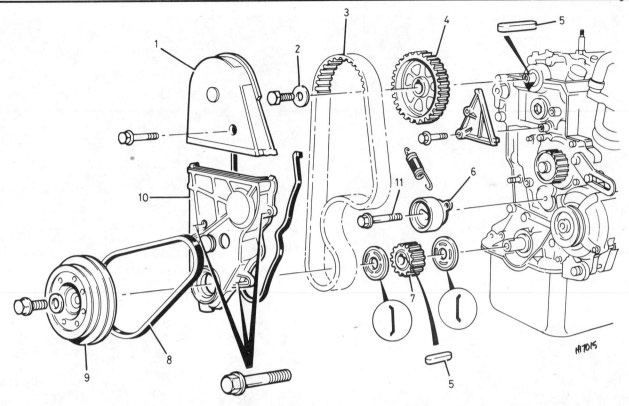

7.9a   Timing belt and related components – exploded view

1	Upper timing belt cover	4	Camshaft sprocket	7	Crankshaft sprocket
2	Washer	5	Woodruff key	8	Alternator drivebelt
3	Timing belt	6	Belt tensioner	9	Crankshaft drivebelt pulley

10	Lower timing belt cover
11	Timing belt tensioner adjustment bolt

7   Remove the self-locking nuts and separate the header pipe from the exhaust manifold.

8   Remove the exhaust manifold-to-bracket bolts.

9   Lower the vehicle.

10   Remove the nuts and detach the manifold and gaskets.

11   Use a scraper to remove all traces of old gasket material and carbon deposits from the manifold and cylinder head mating surfaces. If the gasket was leaking, have the manifold checked for warpage at an automotive machine shop and resurfaced if necessary.

12   Position new gaskets on the cylinder head.

13   Install the manifold and thread the mounting nuts into place.

14   Working from the center out, tighten the nuts to the torque listed in this Chapter's specifications in three or four equal steps.

15   Reinstall the remaining parts in the reverse order of removal. Be sure to use new self-locking nuts, a new exhaust flange gasket and a new EGR tube flange gasket (fuel injected models). Tighten all fasteners to the torque listed in this Chapter's specifications.

16   Run the engine and check for exhaust leaks.

---

7   Timing belt and sprockets – removal, inspection and installation

Removal

Refer to illustrations 7.9a, 7.9b, 7.9c, 7.14, 7.15, 7.16, 7.17a, 7.17b, 7.17c, 7.18a and 7.18b

1   Disconnect the negative cable from the battery.

2   Place blocks behind the rear wheels and set the parking brake.

3   Loosen the lug nuts on the left front wheel and raise the front of the vehicle. Support the front of the vehicle securely on jackstands.

4   Remove the left front wheel for easier access to the end of the crankshaft.

5   Support the engine with a floor jack. Place a block of wood between the jack pad and the oil pan to avoid damaging the pan.

6   Remove the left engine mount (see Section 17).

7   Remove the spark plugs and drivebelts (see Chapter 1).

8   Position the number one piston at Top Dead Center (see Section 3).

9   Remove the tensioner seal/bolts and detach the upper timing belt cover **(see illustrations)**. Note the gasket under the cover **(see illustration)** – it doesn't have to be removed or replaced unless it's damaged.

10   Remove the alternator and bracket (see Chapter 5).

7.9b   Remove the bolts (arrows) to detach the upper timing belt cover

7.9c When removing the upper timing belt cover, note the gasket under the cover – it doesn't have to be removed or replaced unless it's damaged

7.14   Remove the water pump pulley bolts (arrows), then slip off the pulley

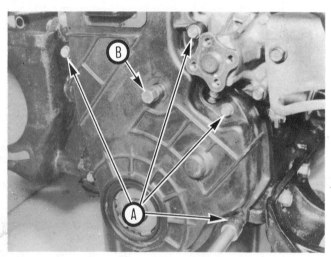

7.15   To remove the lower timing belt cover, unscrew the mounting bolts (A) – use the timing belt tensioner bolt (B) to adjust the timing belt tension

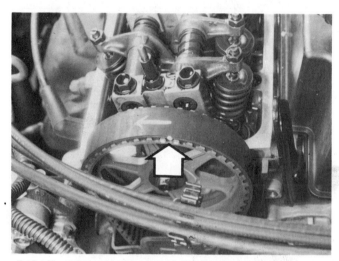

7.16   If you intend to reuse the belt, make an arrow to indicate direction of rotation and match marks (arrow) to align the sprockets with the belt

7.17a   Remove the outer belt guide – note that the curved outer edge faces away from the belt (belt removed for clarity)

7.17b   It's not necessary to remove the crankshaft sprocket unless you intend to replace the oil seal

7.17c   After removing the sprocket, slide off the inner belt guide; note that the curved edge faces away from the timing belt

7.18a   Remove the camshaft sprocket bolt (lower arrow) – when reinstalling the sprocket, the dot (upper arrow) or UP mark should be at the top (twelve o'clock position)

7.18b   After you have detached the camshaft sprocket, remove the Woodruff key (arrow) from the camshaft

7.19   Check the belt adjustment idler pulley for rough rotation and bearing play

11   Unbolt the power steering pump without disconnecting the hoses and set it aside (see Chapter 10).

12   On air conditioned vehicles, detach the wires and unbolt the air conditioning compressor. Set it aside without disconnecting the refrigerant hoses (see Chapter 3).

13   To keep the crankshaft pulley from turning, have an assistant hold a large screwdriver wedged in the ring gear teeth on the flywheel. Loosen the pulley-to-crankshaft bolt with a socket and breaker bar. Slip the pulley off the crankshaft.

14   Remove the bolts and detach the water pump pulley (see illustration).

15   Remove the lower timing belt cover (see illustration).

16   If you intend to reuse the timing belt, use white paint or chalk to make match marks to align the sprockets with the belt and an arrow to indicate the direction of rotation (see illustration).

17   Loosen the timing belt tensioner bolt (see illustration 7.15), remove the outer belt guide (see illustration) and slip the belt off. Note the way the belt guide is facing for proper reinstallation. If you're replacing the crankshaft oil seal, slip the sprocket and inner belt guide off the crankshaft (see illustrations).

18   If you're replacing the camshaft or camshaft oil seal, slip a large screwdriver through the camshaft sprocket to keep it from rotating and remove the bolt, then pull off the sprocket (see illustration). Also remove the Woodruff key (see illustration).

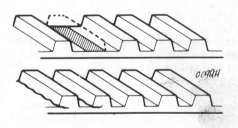

7.20a   Check the timing belt for cracked and missing teeth

Inspection

Refer to illustrations 7.19, 7.20a, 7.20b and 7.20c

19   Rotate the belt adjustment idler pulley by hand and move it from side-to-side, checking for play and rough rotation (see illustration). Replace it if roughness or play is detected.

20   Check the timing belt for wear (especially on the thrust side of the teeth), cracks, splits, fraying and oil contamination (see illustrations).

7.20b   If the belt is cracked or worn, check the pulleys for nicks and burrs

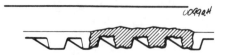

7.20c   Wear on one side of the belt indicates pulley misalignment

7.22   There are two index grooves on the rear face of the camshaft sprocket – both must be parallel to the cylinder head gasket surface (arrow)

8.2   Use a seal removal tool or screwdriver to pry the crankshaft front oil seal out of the bore

Replace the belt if any of these conditions are noted. **Note:** *Unless the engine has very low mileage, it's common practice to replace the timing belt with a new one every time it's removed. Don't reinstall the original belt unless it's in like-new condition. Never reinstall a belt in questionable condition.*

Installation

Refer to illustration 7.22

21   If you removed the sprockets, reinstall them. Don't forget the Woodruff key for the camshaft sprocket and the inner belt guide for the crankshaft sprocket (you can leave the outer guide off for now). Tighten the camshaft sprocket bolt to the torque listed in this Chapter's specifications.

22   Before installing the timing belt, make sure the dot or "UP" mark on the camshaft sprocket is at the top **(see illustration 7.18a)** and the two index marks are in line with the cylinder head surface **(see illustration)**. **Note:** *On later engines, the marks are located on the outside of the sprocket.*

23   Temporarily reinstall the crankshaft pulley and bolt and turn the crankshaft (if it was disturbed) until the timing marks on the drivebelt pulley and the pointer on the timing cover are aligned (see Section 3).

24   Install the timing belt with slight tension between the sprockets on the front (radiator) side. With the belt tensioner bolt loose, slowly rotate the crankshaft counterclockwise for a distance of three teeth on the camshaft sprocket. This puts tension on the belt.

25   Tighten the belt tensioner bolt.

26   Carefully turn the crankshaft through two revolutions and recheck the timing marks and camshaft sprocket index marks for proper alignment. If the crankshaft binds or seems to hit something, do not force it, as the valves may be hitting the pistons. If this happens, valve timing is incorrect. Remove the belt and go back to Step 22.

27   Remove the crankshaft pulley bolt.

28   Reinstall the remaining parts in the reverse order of removal. Tighten the crankshaft pulley bolt to the torque listed in this Chapter's specifications.

29   Run the engine and check for proper operation.

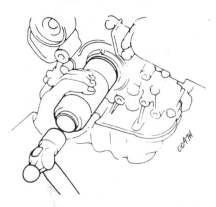

8.4   Lubricate the seal lip and carefully tap the new seal into place with a large socket or piece of pipe and a hammer

8   Crankshaft front oil seal – replacement

Refer to illustrations 8.2 and 8.4

1   Remove the timing belt and crankshaft sprocket (see Section 7).

2   Note how far the seal is seated in the bore, then carefully pry it out with a screwdriver or seal removal tool **(see illustration)**. Don't scratch the housing bore or damage the crankshaft in the process (if the crankshaft is damaged, the new seal will end up leaking). If a screwdriver is used, wrap electrician's tape around the tip so it won't nick the crankshaft.

3   Clean the bore in the housing and coat the outer edge of the new seal with engine oil or multi-purpose grease. Apply moly-base grease to the seal lip.

4   Using a socket with an outside diameter slightly smaller than the outside diameter of the seal, carefully drive the new seal into place with a hammer **(see illustration)**. Make sure it's installed squarely and driven in

9.2   Insert a small screwdriver between the seal lip and camshaft (arrow) to remove the seal

9.4   If a seal driver isn't available, use a hammer and section of pipe or a large socket to tap the new seal into place

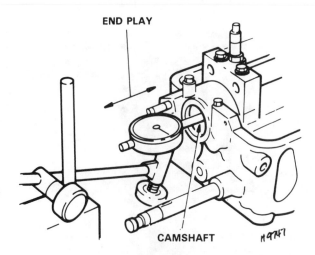

10.3   To check camshaft end play, mount a dial indicator as shown and move the camshaft forward and backward (arrows)

10.4a   Loosen the rocker arm shaft pedestal bolts (arrows), . . .

to the same depth as the original. If a socket isn't available, a short section of large diameter pipe will also work. Check the seal after installation to make sure the garter spring didn't pop out of place.
5   Reinstall the crankshaft sprocket and timing belt (see Section 7).
6   Run the engine and check for oil leaks at the front seal.

9   Camshaft oil seal – replacement

Refer to illustrations 9.2 and 9.4
1   Remove the timing belt and camshaft sprocket (see Section 7).
2   Note how far the seal is seated in the bore, then carefully pry it out with a seal removal tool or a small screwdriver **(see illustration)**. Don't scratch the bore or damage the camshaft in the process (if the camshaft is damaged, the new seal will end up leaking). If a screwdriver is used, wrap electrician's tape around the tip so it won't nick the camshaft.
3   Clean the bore and coat the outer edge of the new seal with engine oil or multi-purpose grease. Apply moly-base grease to the seal lip.
4   Using a socket with an outside diameter slightly smaller than the outside diameter of the seal, carefully drive the new seal into place with a hammer **(see illustration)**. Make sure it's installed squarely and driven in

to the same depth as the original. If a socket isn't available, a short section of pipe will also work.
5   Reinstall the camshaft sprocket and timing belt (see Section 7).
6   Run the engine and check for oil leaks at the camshaft seal.

10   Camshaft and rocker arms – removal, inspection and installation

Removal
Refer to illustrations 10.3, 10.4a, 10.4b and 10.5
1   Remove the camshaft cover (see Section 4) and the timing belt and camshaft sprocket (see Section 7).
2   Remove the distributor (see Chapter 5).
3   Loosen the valve adjustment locknuts and back off the adjustment screws until they no longer hold the valves open (see Chapter 1). Measure the camshaft end play with a dial indicator **(see illustration)**. If it's greater than the specified maximum, the camshaft and/or the cylinder head is excessively worn and will have to be replaced.
4   Loosen each rocker arm shaft pedestal bolts 1/4-turn at a time following a criss-cross pattern **(see illustration)**. Once all the bolts are loose, lift

10.4b   . . . then lift off the rocker arm assembly – leave the pedestal bolts in place to hold the assembly together while it's removed from the cylinder head

10.5   Once the rocker arm assembly is removed, the camshaft can be lifted out

10.6   Check the camshaft lobes for pitting, wear and score marks – if scoring is excessive, as is the case here, replace the camshaft

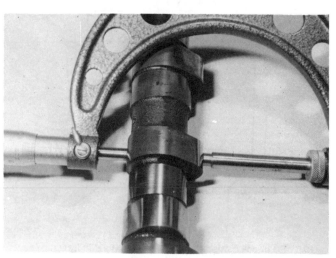

10.7   Measuring camshaft lobe height

10.8a   Lay a strip of Plastigage on each camshaft journal

10.8b   Rocker arm shaft pedestal bolt tightening sequence

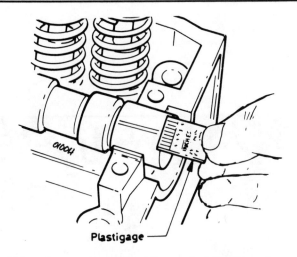

10.8c Compare the width of the crushed Plastigage to the scale on the envelope to determine the oil clearance

10.9a The rocker arms, springs and pedestals will slide off the shaft after removal of the pedestal bolts

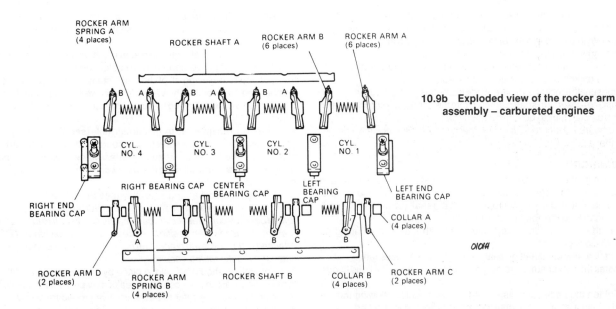

10.9b Exploded view of the rocker arm assembly – carbureted engines

the rocker arm assembly off the engine as a unit **(see illustration)**. Leave the bolts in their holes to hold the rocker arm assembly components together.

5   Lift the camshaft out of the cylinder head **(see illustration)** and clean it with solvent.

Inspection

Refer to illustrations 10.6, 10.7, 10.8a, 10.8b, 10.8c, 10.9a, 10.9b and 10.10

6   Visually examine the camshaft lobes **(see illustration)** and bearing journals. Look for wear, pitting, score marks, galling and evidence of overheating (blue, discolored areas). Also look for flaking away of the hardened surface layer of each lobe.

7   Using a micrometer, measure the height of each camshaft lobe **(see illustration)**. If any measurements are less than specified, replace the camshaft.

8   Check the oil clearance for each camshaft journal as follows:
   a) Clean the bearing caps and camshaft journals with lacquer thinner or acetone and a clean cloth.
   b) Carefully lay the camshaft in place in the head. Don't use any lubrication. **Note:** *Do not rotate the camshaft during this procedure.*
   c) Lay a strip of Plastigage on each journal **(see illustration)**.
   d) Set the rocker arm assembly in place and install the pedestal bolts finger-tight.
   e) Tighten the bolts to the specified torque in 1/4-turn increments, following the recommended sequence **(see illustration)**.
   f) Remove the bolts as described in Step 4 and lift off the rocker arm assembly.
   g) Compare the width of the crushed Plastigage on each journal (at it's widest point) to the scale on the Plastigage envelope **(see illustration)**.
   h) If the clearance is greater than specified, the camshaft and/or cylinder head is excessively worn and will have to be replaced.
   i) Scrape off the Plastigage with your fingernail or the edge of a credit card – don't nick or scratch the journals or bearing caps.

9   Slip the bolts out of the rocker arm assembly and slide the components off the shafts. Store all the components in order so they can be reinstalled in the same locations **(see illustrations)**.

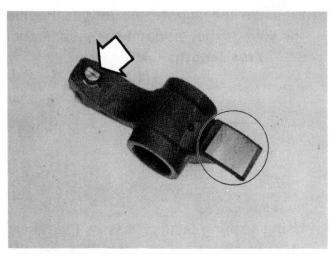

10.10   Check the camshaft contact face and the ends of the adjusting screws for wear and damage

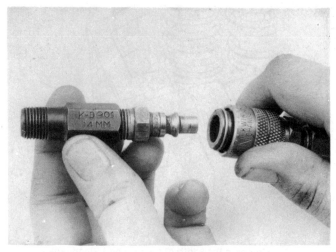

11.4   This is what the air hose adapter that threads into the spark plug hole looks like – they're commonly available from auto parts stores

10   Visually inspect the rocker arms **(see illustration)** and shafts for wear. Check the rocker arm-to-camshaft contact faces and the shaft bores. Also note the condition of the adjustment screws and locknuts, the cap bearing surfaces and the springs and bushings.

11   Use a micrometer to measure the rocker shaft diameter at the points where the rocker arms ride. Record the results.

12   Measure the rocker arm bore inside diameters and record the results. Subtract the rocker arm shaft diameter from the corresponding rocker arm bore inside diameter to determine the oil clearance.

13   Compare the clearances to the Specifications. Replace any components that are worn.

Installation

14   Lubricate the rocker arm components, camshaft lobes, journals and seal contact surfaces with engine assembly lube or moly-base grease. Reassemble the rocker arm components on the shafts and install the pedestal bolts to hold the components in place.

15   Lay the camshaft in the cylinder head with the keyway facing up (twelve o'clock position).

16   Install a new camshaft oil seal (see Section 9 if necessary).

17   Install the rocker arm assembly and tighten the pedestal bolts finger-tight.

18   Tighten the pedestal bolts in 1/4-turn increments, following the sequence in illustration 10.8b, until the specified torque is reached.

19   Install the Woodruff key in the end of the camshaft and slip the timing belt sprocket into position. Tighten the sprocket bolt to the torque listed in this Chapter's Specifications. Slip a pry bar or large screwdriver through a hole in the sprocket to keep it from turning. Make sure the alignment hole is at the top and the index marks on each side are parallel to the cylinder head **(see illustration 7.22)**.

20   Reinstall the timing belt and the remaining components in the reverse order of removal.

---

11   Valve springs, retainers and seals – replacement

Refer to illustrations 11.4, 11.9 and 11.17

Note: *This procedure does not apply to the 16-Valve engine. Broken valve springs and defective valve stem seals can be replaced without removing the cylinder head. Two special tools and a compressed air source are normally required to perform this operation, so read through this Section carefully and rent or buy the tools before beginning the job. If compressed air isn't available, a length of nylon rope can be used to keep the valves from falling into the cylinder during this procedure.*

1   Refer to Section 4 and remove the camshaft cover from the cylinder head.

2   Remove the spark plug from the cylinder which has the defective component. If all of the valve stem seals are being replaced, all of the spark plugs should be removed.

3   Turn the crankshaft until the piston in the affected cylinder is at TDC (top dead center) on the compression stroke (refer to Section 3 for instructions). If you're replacing all of the valve stem seals, begin with cylinder number one and work on the valves for one cylinder at a time. Move from cylinder-to-cylinder following the firing order sequence (see the Specifications).

4   Thread an adapter into the spark plug hole **(see illustration)** and connect an air hose from a compressed air source to it. Most auto parts stores can supply the air hose adapter. **Note:** *Many cylinder compression gauges utilize a screw-in fitting that may work with your air hose quick-disconnect fitting.*

5   Remove the rocker arm assembly (see Section 10).

6   Apply compressed air to the cylinder. **Warning:** *The piston may be forced down by compressed air, causing the crankshaft to turn suddenly. If the wrench used when positioning the number one piston at TDC is still attached to the bolt in the crankshaft nose, it could cause damage or injury when the crankshaft moves.*

7   The valves should be held in place by the air pressure. If the valve faces or seats are in poor condition, leaks may prevent air pressure from retaining the valves – refer to the alternative procedure below.

8   If you don't have access to compressed air, an alternative method can be used. Position the piston at a point just before TDC on the compression stroke, then feed a long piece of nylon rope through the spark plug hole until it fills the combustion chamber. Be sure to leave the end of the rope hanging out of the engine so it can be removed easily. Use a large ratchet and socket to rotate the crankshaft in the normal direction of rotation (counterclockwise) until slight resistance is felt.

9   Stuff shop rags into the cylinder head holes above and below the valves to prevent parts and tools from falling into the engine, then use a valve spring compressor to compress the spring. Remove the keepers with small needle-nose pliers or a magnet **(see illustration)**. **Note:** *A couple of different types of tools are available for compressing the valve springs with the head in place. Obtain one that grips the lower spring coils and presses on the retainer as the knob is turned.*

10   Remove the spring retainer and valve spring(s), then remove the guide seal. **Note:** *If air pressure fails to hold the valve in the closed position during this operation, the valve face and/or seat is probably damaged. If so, the cylinder head will have to be removed for additional repair operations.*

11   Wrap a rubber band or tape around the top of the valve stem so the valve won't fall into the combustion chamber, then release the air pressure. **Note:** *If a rope was used instead of air pressure, turn the crankshaft slightly in the direction opposite normal rotation.*

11.9   Use a spring compressor (1) to release the spring pressure so the valve keepers (2) can be removed

11.17   Apply a small dab of grease to each keeper before installation to hold it in place on the valve stem until the

12   Inspect the valve stem for damage. Rotate the valve in the guide and check the end for eccentric movement, which would indicate the valve is bent.

13   Move the valve up-and-down in the guide and make sure it doesn't bind. If the valve stem binds, either the valve is bent or the guide is damaged. In either case, the head will have to be removed for repair.

14   Reapply air pressure to the cylinder to retain the valve in the closed position, then remove the tape or rubber band from the valve stem. If a rope was used instead of air pressure, rotate the crankshaft in the normal direction of rotation until slight resistance is felt.

15   Lubricate the valve stem with engine oil and install a new guide seal. **Note:** *Intake and exhaust seals are not interchangeable. Intake seals have a white spring and exhaust seals have a black spring.*

16   Install the spring in position over the valve. **Note:** *Place the ends of the valve springs with closely wound coils or paint marks against the cylinder head.*

17   Install the valve spring retainer. Compress the valve spring and carefully position the keepers in the groove. Apply a small dab of grease to the inside of each keeper to hold it in place if necessary **(see illustration)**.

18   Remove the pressure from the spring tool and make sure the keepers are seated.

19   Disconnect the air hose and remove the adapter from the spark plug hole. If a rope was used in place of air pressure, pull it out of the cylinder.

20   Refer to Section 10 and install the rocker arm assembly.

21   Install the spark plug(s) and hook up the wire(s).

22   Refer to Section 4 and install the camshaft cover.

23   Start and run the engine, then check for oil leaks and unusual sounds coming from the camshaft cover area.

12   Cylinder head – removal and installation

Note: *The engine must be completely cool before beginning this procedure.*

Removal

Refer to illustrations 12.10a, 12.10b, 12.12a and 12.12b

1   Disconnect the negative cable from the battery.

2   Drain the coolant from the engine block and radiator (see Chapter 1).

3   Drain the engine oil and remove the oil filter (see Chapter 1).

4   On fuel injected models, relieve the fuel system pressure (see Chapter 4).

5   Remove the intake manifold (see Section 5).

6   Remove the exhaust manifold (see Section 6).

7   Remove the timing belt and camshaft sprocket (see Section 7).

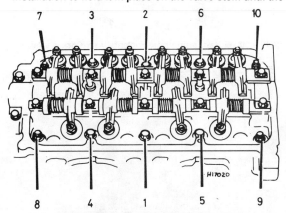

12.10a   Cylinder head bolt TIGHTENING sequence (1984 through 1987 models) – when loosening the bolts, reverse this sequence

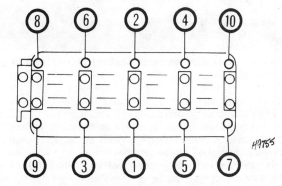

12.10b   Cylinder head bolt TIGHTENING sequence (1988 and later models) – when loosening the bolts, reverse this sequence

8   Remove the camshaft and rocker arm assembly.

9   Check the cylinder head. Label and remove any remaining items such as coolant fittings, tubes, cables, hoses and wires. At this point the head should be ready for removal.

10   Using a socket and breaker bar, loosen the cylinder head bolts in 1/4-turn increments until they can be removed by hand. Reverse the recommended tightening sequence **(see illustrations)** to avoid warping the head.

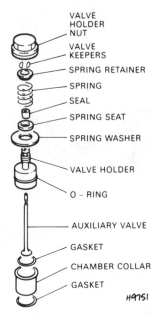

VALVE
HOLDER
NUT

VALVE
KEEPERS

SPRING RETAINER

SPRING

SEAL

SPRING SEAT

SPRING WASHER

VALVE HOLDER

O – RING

AUXILIARY VALVE

GASKET

CHAMBER COLLAR

GASKET

H9751

12.12a   Auxiliary valve components – exploded view

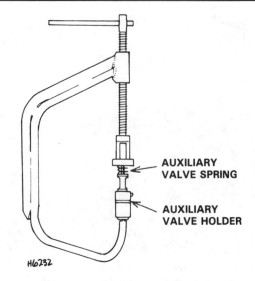

AUXILIARY
VALVE SPRING

AUXILIARY
VALVE HOLDER

H6232

12.12b   A valve spring compressor can be used to compress the spring and remove the keepers so the auxiliary valve assembly can be dismantled – spring compressors of this type can be rented

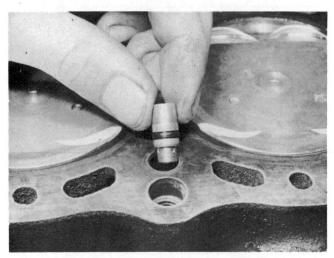

12.14   Remove the oil control jet from the block

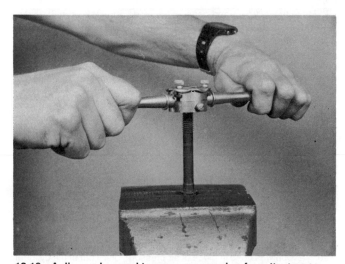

12.18   A die can be used to remove corrosion from the head bolt threads prior to installation

11   Lift the cylinder head off the engine block. If it's stuck, very carefully pry up at the ends, beyond the gasket surface.

12   Remove all external components from the head to allow for thorough cleaning and inspection. Some engines are equipped with auxiliary valves. They can be removed from the cylinder head after unscrewing the valve holder nut with a deep socket **(see illustration)**. The valve can be disassembled for seal replacement **(see illustration)**. If any components are worn, the entire assembly should be replaced. Always use a new gasket and O-ring when installing an auxiliary valve.

13   See Chapter 2, Part B, for cylinder head servicing procedures.

Installation

Refer to illustrations 12.14, 12.18 and 12.20

14   If equipped, remove the oil control jet **(see illustration)** and clean the orifices.

15   Use a gasket scraper to remove all traces of carbon and old gasket material from the cylinder head and block mating surfaces, then clean them with lacquer thinner or acetone. If there's oil on the mating surfaces when the head is installed, the gasket may not seal correctly and leaks could develop. When working on the block, stuff the cylinders with clean

shop rags to keep out debris. Use a vacuum cleaner to remove material that falls into the cylinders.

16   Check the block and head mating surfaces for nicks, deep scratches and other damage. If damage is slight, it can be removed with a file; if it's excessive, machining may be the only alternative.

17   Use a tap of the correct size to chase the threads in the head bolt holes, then clean the holes with compressed air – make sure that nothing remains in the holes. **Warning:** *Wear eye protection when using compressed air for cleaning.*

18   Mount each bolt in a vise and run a die down the threads to remove corrosion and restore the threads **(see illustration)**. Dirt, corrosion, sealant and damaged threads will affect torque readings.

19   Reinstall the oil control jet. Be sure to use a new O-ring.

20   Position the new gasket over the dowel pins in the block **(see illustration)**.

21   Carefully set the head on the block without disturbing the gasket.

22   Before installing the head bolts, apply a small amount of clean engine oil to the threads.

23   Install the bolts in their original locations and tighten them finger-tight. Following the recommended sequence **(see illustration 12.10a or 12.10b)**, tighten the bolts in two steps to the specified torque.

12.20   Position the new gasket over the dowel pins (arrows)

13.7a   Remove the front bolts (arrows) from the center crossmember, . . .

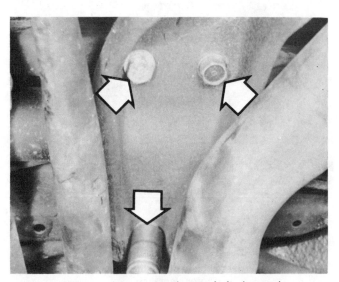

13.7b   . . . then remove the rear bolts (arrows)

13.14   Apply RTV sealant to the corners of the oil pan (arrows)

24   The remaining installation steps are the reverse of removal.
25   Check and adjust the valves as necessary (see Chapter 1).
26   Refill the cooling system, install a new oil filter and add oil to the engine (see Chapter 1).
27   Run the engine and check for leaks. Set the ignition timing (see Chapter 1) and road test the vehicle.

13   Oil pan – removal and installation

Refer to illustrations 13.7a, 13.7b, 13.14, 13.15a and 13.15b

1   Disconnect the negative cable from the battery.
2   Set the parking brake and place blocks behind the rear wheels.
3   Raise the front of the vehicle and support it securely on jackstands.
4   Remove the splash shields under the engine (if equipped).
5   Drain the engine oil and remove the oil filter (see Chapter 1). Remove the oil dipstick. On 4WD models, drain the transmission fluid.
6   Disconnect the front exhaust pipe from the engine and remove the clamp behind the engine to allow the pipe to hang down. **Note:** On 4WD models, remove the driveshaft (see Chapter 8).

7   Attach a hoist and lifting sling to the engine (see Chapter 2, Part B, Section 5) and raise the engine just enough to take the weight off the lower engine mount. Unbolt the lower engine mount (see Section 17), then remove the crossmember under the oil pan **(see illustrations)**.
8   On 4WD models, remove the left side cover and driven gear from the transfer case. Also, on all vehicles remove the engine-to-transaxle dust shield.
9   Remove the bolts and detach the oil pan. If it's stuck, pry it loose very carefully with a small screwdriver or putty knife. Don't damage the mating surfaces of the pan and block or oil leaks could develop.
10   Use a scraper to remove all traces of old gasket material and sealant from the block and oil pan. Clean the mating surfaces with lacquer thinner or acetone.
11   Make sure the threaded bolt holes in the block are clean.
12   Check the oil pan flange for distortion, particularly around the bolt holes. If necessary, place the pan on a block of wood and use a hammer to flatten and restore the gasket surface.
13   Check the oil pump pick-up tube assembly for cracks and a blocked screen. If the pick-up/screen must be removed, refer to Section 14.
14   Apply RTV sealant to the four oil pan corners **(see illustration). Note:** The oil pan must be installed within three minutes once the sealant has been applied.

13.15a   Be sure the oil pan gasket fits over the locating pins (arrow)

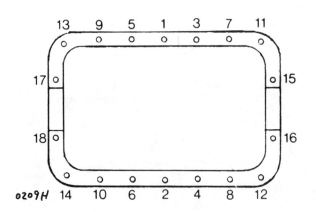

13.15b   Oil pan bolt tightening sequence

14.8   Remove the oil pump cover screws – they're extremely tight and may require an impact driver

14.9   Use a feeler gauge to check the inner rotor-to-outer rotor clearance

14.10   Use a feeler gauge to check the rotor side (end) clearance

14.11a   Use a feeler gauge to check the radial clearance between the housing and the outer rotor

14.11b Install the oil pump inner rotor with the dimple facing out

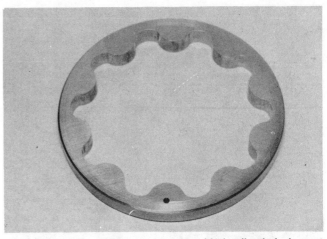

14.11c Install the oil pump outer rotor with the dimple facing out

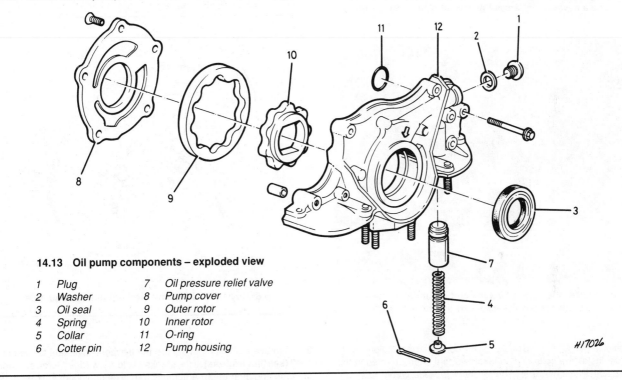

14.13 Oil pump components – exploded view

1	Plug	7	Oil pressure relief valve
2	Washer	8	Pump cover
3	Oil seal	9	Outer rotor
4	Spring	10	Inner rotor
5	Collar	11	O-ring
6	Cotter pin	12	Pump housing

H17026

15　Carefully position a new gasket (see illustration) and the oil pan on the engine block, then install the bolts. Follow the tightening sequence (see illustration) and tighten them to the specified torque in three or four steps.

16　The remainder of installation is the reverse of removal. Be sure to add oil and install a new oil filter.

17　Run the engine and check for oil pressure and leaks.

14　Oil pump – removal, inspection and installation

Refer to illustrations 14.8, 14.9, 14.10, 14.11a, 14.11b, 14.11c, 14.13 and 14.15

1　Drain the engine oil (see Chapter 1).

2　Position the number one piston at TDC on the compression stroke (see Section 3).

3　Remove the camshaft cover (see Section 4) and the timing belt upper cover.

4　Remove the drivebelts and the crankshaft drivebelt pulley and detach the timing belt lower cover.

5　Remove the timing belt (see Section 7) and crankshaft sprocket.

6　Remove the oil pan (see Section 13) and detach the oil pick-up tube and screen assembly (it's held in place with three bolts).

7　Unbolt the oil pump from the front of the block.

8　Remove the screws and lift off the pump cover (see illustration).

9　Measure the inner rotor-to-outer rotor clearance with feeler gauges (see illustration). Compare the results to the specifications listed in this Chapter.

10　Check the pump rotor side (end) clearance as well (see illustration).

11　Check the radial clearance between the housing and the outer rotor (see illustration). Be sure to assemble the inner rotor and outer rotor with the dimples facing out (see illustrations).

12　Replace the pump if the clearances are excessive or signs of wear or damage are visible.

13　Install a new oil seal in the pump housing until it bottoms in the bore (see illustration). Pack the pump cavity with petroleum jelly, apply thread locking compound to the screws and install the pump cover. Tighten the pump cover screws to the torque listed in this Chapter's Specifications.

14.15   Use a new O-ring (arrow) on the oil pick-up tube flange

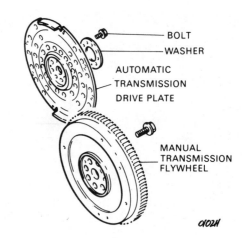

BOLT
WASHER
AUTOMATIC
TRANSMISSION
DRIVE PLATE

MANUAL
TRANSMISSION
FLYWHEEL

15.3a   Flywheel/driveplate components – exploded view

15.3b   Most models have twelve-point mounting bolts – a twelve-point socket is required

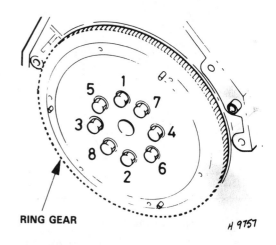

RING GEAR

15.8   Flywheel/driveplate bolt tightening sequence

14   Position a new O-ring and gasket on the pump and install it on the engine block. Install the bolts and tighten them to the torque listed in this Chapter's specifications. **Note:** *To prevent oil leakage, apply sealant to the bolt threads.*

15   Reinstall the oil pick-up tube and screen assembly. Be sure to use a new O-ring or gasket on the tube flange **(see illustration).**

16   Reinstall the timing belt and related components.

17   Check the oil level and add oil, if necessary. Start the engine and check for oil pressure and leaks.

18   Recheck the oil level.

15   Flywheel/driveplate – removal and installation

Refer to illustrations 15.3a, 15.3b and 15.8

1   Raise the vehicle and support it securely on jackstands, then refer to Chapter 7 and remove the transaxle. If it's leaking, now would be a very good time to replace the front pump seal/O-ring (automatic transaxle only).

2   Remove the pressure plate and clutch disc (see Chapter 8) (manual transaxle equipped vehicles). Now is a good time to check/replace the clutch components and pilot bearing.

3   Remove the bolts that secure the flywheel/driveplate to the crankshaft **(see illustrations).** If the crankshaft turns, wedge a large screwdriver in the ring gear teeth. Automatic transaxle equipped vehicles have a spacer washer between the bolts and driveplate.

4   Detach the flywheel/driveplate from the crankshaft. Since the flywheel is fairly heavy, be sure to support it while removing the last bolt.

5   Clean the flywheel to remove grease and oil. Inspect the clutch mating surface for cracks, rivet grooves, burned areas and score marks. Light scoring can be removed with emery cloth. Lay the flywheel on a flat surface and use a straightedge to check for warpage. Check for cracked and broken ring gear teeth.

6   Clean and inspect the mating surfaces of the flywheel/driveplate and the crankshaft. If the crankshaft rear seal is leaking, replace it before reinstalling the flywheel/driveplate.

7   Position the flywheel/driveplate against the crankshaft. Note that most engines have an alignment dowel to ensure correct installation. Before installing the bolts, apply thread locking compound to the threads. Be sure to install the spacer washer with the driveplate.

8   After installing the bolts finger-tight, wedge a screwdriver in the ring gear teeth to keep the flywheel/driveplate from turning. Tighten the bolts to the torque listed in this Chapter's specifications. Work up to the final torque in three steps and follow the tightening sequence **(see illustration).**

9   The remainder of installation is the reverse of the removal procedure.

16.3 Pry out the oil seal very carefully – don't damage the surface of the crankshaft or the new seal will leak

16.6   Use a hammer and punch to install the new seal and seat it in the bore

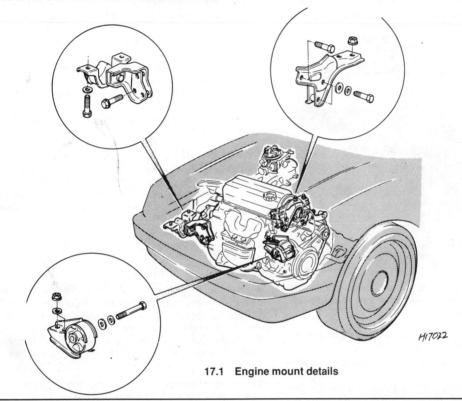

H17022

17.1   Engine mount details

---

16   Crankshaft rear oil seal – replacement

Refer to illustrations 16.3 and 16.6

1   Remove the transaxle (see Chapter 7).
2   Remove the flywheel/driveplate (see Section 15).
3   The old seal can be removed by gently prying it out with a screwdriver **(see illustration)**. Be sure to note how far it's recessed into the bore before removing it; the new seal must be driven in an equal amount. **Caution:** *Be very careful not to scratch or otherwise damage the crankshaft or the bore in the housing as oil leaks could develop.*
4   Clean the crankshaft and seal bore with lacquer thinner or acetone. Check the seal contact surface very carefully for scratches and nicks that could damage the new seal lip and cause oil leaks. If the crankshaft is damaged, try to remove the nicks and scratches with crocus cloth. If this doesn't work, the only alternative is a new or different crankshaft.
5   Lubricate the lips of the seal with moly-base grease. Also fill the spring

groove with grease.
6   Carefully work the seal lip over the end of the crankshaft and tap the new seal into place with a hammer and blunt punch until it's seated **(see illustration)**. Be very careful not to damage the seal or crankshaft.
7   Reinstall the flywheel/driveplate and transaxle, run the engine and check for oil leaks.

---

17   Engine mounts – check and replacement

Refer to illustrations 17.1, 17.9a, 17.9b and 17.12

1   The engine is attached to the chassis by three weight-bearing mounts **(see illustration)**. The engine mounts seldom require attention, but if they are broken or deteriorated, they should be replaced immediately or the added strain placed on the driveline components may cause damage or wear.

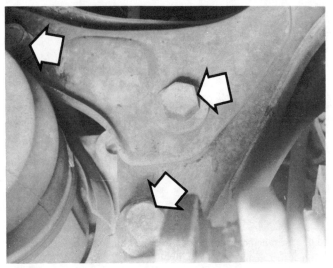

17.9a   Remove the three mount-to-bellhousing bolts (arrows)

17.9b   The side mount is located near the clutch cable

17.12   Remove the through-bolt (1), then the mounting bolts (2); some mounts have vertical through-bolts, others have horizontal ones

Check

2   During the check, the engine must be raised slightly to remove the weight from the mounts.

3   Raise the vehicle and support it securely on jackstands, then position a jack under the engine oil pan. Place a large block of wood between the jack head and the oil pan, then carefully raise the engine just enough to take the weight off the mounts. **Warning:** *DO NOT place any part of your body under the engine when it's supported only by a jack!*

4   Check the mounts to see if the rubber is cracked, hardened or sepa-

rated from the metal plates. Sometimes the rubber will split right down the center.

5   Check for relative movement between the mount plates and the engine or frame (use a large screwdriver or pry bar to attempt to move the mounts). If movement is noted, lower the engine and tighten the mount fasteners.

6   Rubber preservative should be applied to the mounts to slow deterioration.

Replacement

7   Disconnect the negative battery cable from the battery, then raise the vehicle and support it securely on jackstands (if not already done).

8   Support the engine with a floor jack under the oil pan. Place a block of wood between the jack head and the oil pan to protect the pan from damage. **Warning:** *DO NOT place any part of your body under the engine when its supported only by a jack!* **Note:** *When installing any of the mounts or the torque strut, use thread locking compound on the mounting nuts and/or bolts.*

Lower mounts – side and rear

9   Remove the bolts that attach the engine mounts to the bellhousing (rear mount) and transaxle (side mount) **(see illustrations)**.

10   On the rear mount, remove the upper retaining nut that secures the mount to the lower section that's bolted to the chassis.

11   On the side mount, remove the two bolts that attach the mount to the frame. Remove the entire mount from the chassis as a complete unit.

Upper mount

12   Remove the through-bolt that retains the upper mount to the chassis section of the engine mount **(see illustration)**.

13   Remove the upper mount retaining bolts and lift it out of the mounting bracket.

All mounts

14   Installation is the reverse of removal. Tighten the bolts securely.

Chapter 2 Part B
General engine overhaul procedures

Contents

Specifications

General

Displacement .... See Part A
Cylinder numbers .... See Part A
Firing order 1-3-4-2

Engine identification (first 3 or 5 characters in engine serial number)

EW1	1500 carbureted
EV1	1300 carbureted
EW3	1500 fuel-injected
D15A2	
CRX	1500 carbureted
Hatchback, sedan and wagon	1300 carbureted
D15A3	1500 fuel-injected
D15B1	1.5 liter DPFI
D15B2	1.5 liter DPFI
D15B6	1.5 liter MPFI
D16A6	1.6 liter MPFI

Cylinder compression (at 300 rpm/wide open throttle)

Nominal
Carbureted engines	
1300 cc only	171 psi
All others	164 psi
Fuel-injected engines	
Si only	156 psi
All others	185 psi

Minimum
Carbureted engines	
1300 cc only	142 psi
All others	135 psi
Fuel-injected engines	
Si only	128 psi
All others	135 psi
Maximum variation between cylinders	28 psi

Oil pressure (at normal operating temperature)

1984 through 1987	
At idle	21 psi minimum
At 3000 rpm	48 to 60 psi
1988	
At idle	24 psi minimum
At 3000 rpm	60 to 70 psi
1989-on	
At idle	10 psi minimum
At 3000 rpm	50 psi

Crankshaft and bearings

Crankshaft end play	
Standard	0.004 to 0.014 in (0.10 to 0.35 mm)
Service limit	0.018 in (0.45 mm)
Main bearing journal diameter	
1500	1.9676 to 1.9685 in (49.976 to 50.000 mm)
4WD, CRX Si, Civic 1.6 liter	2.1644 to 2.1654 in (54.976 to 55.000 mm)
All others	1.7707 to 1.7717 in (44.976 to 45.000 mm)
Main bearing journal taper/out-of-round	
Standard	0.0002 in (0.005 mm)
Service limit	0.0004 in (0.010 mm)
Main bearing oil clearance (standard)	
1300 and 1500	0.0009 to 0.0017 in (0.024 to 0.042 mm)
1988 (1.5 and 1.6 liter except 4WD)	0.0010 to 0.0017 in (0.024 to 0.042 mm)
1988 4WD only	
No. 1, 2, 4, 5 journals	0.0010 to 0.0017 (0.024 to 0.042 mm)
No. 3 journal	0.0012 to 0.0019 (0.030 to 0.048 mm)
1989-on (1.5 liter)	
No. 2, 3, 4 journals	0.0010 to 0.0017 (0.024 to 0.042 mm)
No. 1, 5 journals	0.0007 to 0.0014 (0.018 to 0.036 mm)
1989-on (1.6 liter)	
No. 1, 5 journals	0.0007 to 0.0014 (0.018 to 0.036 mm)
No. 2, 4 journals	0.0010 to 0.0017 (0.024 to 0.042 mm)
No. 3 journal	0.0012 to 0.0019 (0.030 to 0.048 mm)

Main bearing oil clearance (service limit – all main bearings)
    1984 through 1987 .... 0.003 in (0.007 mm)
    1988-on .... 0.002 in (0.005 mm)
Connecting rod journal diameter
    1500 .... 1.6526 to 1.6535 in (41.976 to 42.000 mm)
    4WD, CRX Si, Civic 1.6 liter .... 1.7707 to 1.7717 in (44.976 to 45.000 mm)
    All others .... 1.4951 to 1.4961 in (37.976 to 38.000 mm)
Connecting rod journal taper/out-of-round
    Standard
        1984 through 1987, 1988-on CRX .... 0.0002 in (0.005 mm)
        1988-on Wagons and Civics .... 0.0001 in (0.0025 mm)
    Service limit .... 0.0004 in (0.010 mm)
Connecting rod bearing oil clearance
    Standard .... 0.0008 to 0.0015 in (0.020 to 0.038 mm)
    Service limit
        1984 through 1987 .... 0.003 in (0.07 mm)
        1988-on .... 0.002 in (0.05 mm)
Connecting rod end play
    Standard .... 0.006 to 0.012 in (0.15 to 0.30 mm)
    Service limit .... 0.016 in (0.40 mm)

Engine block

Deck warpage limit .... 0.003 in (0.08 mm)
Bore diameter
    1984 through 1987
        Standard .... 2.9133 to 2.9142 in (74.00 to 74.02 mm)
        Service limit .... 2.9173 in (74.10 mm)
    1988-on
        Standard .... 2.9526 to 2.9535 in (75.00 to 75.02 mm)
        Service limit .... 2.9555 in (75.07 mm)
Piston-to-bore clearance
    Standard .... 0.0004 to 0.0016 in (0.010 to 0.040 mm)
    Service limit
        1984 through 1987 .... 0.003 in (0.07 mm)
        1988-on .... 0.002 in (0.05 mm)
Bore taper/out-of-round limit .... 0.002 in (0.05 mm)

Pistons and rings

Piston diameter (measured 5/8-inch [16 mm] above bottom edge of skirt)
    1984 and 1985
        Standard .... 2.9122 to 2.9133 in (73.97 to 73.99 mm)
        Service limit .... 2.912 in (73.96 mm)
    1986 and 1987
        CRX/CRX si
            Standard .... 2.9122 to 2.9129 in (73.97 to 73.99 mm)
            Service limit .... 2.912 in (73.96 mm)
        CRX HF
            Standard .... 2.9118 to 2.9123 in (73.958 to 73.99 mm)
            Service limit .... 2.911 in (73.95 mm)
        Civic Std., DX, GL, Si
            Standard .... 2.9122 to 2.9130 in (73.97 to 73.99 mm)
            Service limit .... 2.912 in (73.96 mm)
    1988 and 1989
        Standard .... 2.9520 to 2.9524 in (74.98 to 74.99 mm)
        Service limit .... 2.9517 in (74.97 mm)
    1990
        CRX/CRX Si, Wagon, Civic
            Standard .... 2.9520 to 2.9524 in (74.98 to 74.99 mm)
            Service limit .... 2.9517 in (74.97 mm)
        CRX HF (8-valve engine)
            Standard .... 2.9518 to 2.9526 in (74.97 to 74.99 mm)
            Service limit .... Not available
Piston ring side clearance
    Top ring
        Standard .... 0.0012 to 0.0024 in (0.030 to 0.060 mm)
        Service limit .... 0.005 in (0.13 mm)

Pistons and rings (continued)

Piston ring side clearance
  Second ring
    Standard . . . . 0.0012 to 0.0022 in (0.030 to 0.055 mm)
    Service limit . . . . 0.005 in (0.13 mm)
Piston ring end gap
  1984 through 1987
    Top and second ring
      Standard . . . . 0.006 to 0.014 in (0.15 to 0.35 mm)
      Service limit . . . . 0.024 in (0.60 mm)
    Oil control ring (fuel injected 1987 1300 engine only)
      Standard . . . . 0.012 to 0.035 in (0.30 to 0.90 mm)
      Service limit . . . . 0.040 in (1.1 mm)
    Oil control ring (all others)
      Standard . . . . 0.008 to 0.024 in (0.20 to 0.9 mm)
      Service limit . . . . 0.032 in (0.8 mm)
  1988
    Top ring
      Standard . . . . 0.006 to 0.014 in (0.15 to 0.35 mm)
      Service limit . . . . 0.020 in (0.60 mm)
    Second ring
      Standard . . . . 0.006 to 0.014 in (0.30 to 0.35 mm)
      Service limit . . . . 0.020 in (0.60 mm)
    Oil control ring
      Standard (wagon only) . . . . 0.008 to 0.024 in (0.20 to 0.60 mm)
      Standard (all others) . . . . 0.008 to 0.031 in (0.20 to 0.80 mm)
      Service limit (wagon only) . . . . 0.030 in (0.70 mm)
      Service limit (all others) . . . . 0.040 in (0.90 mm)
  1989-on (except 1990 wagon)
    Top ring
      Standard . . . . 0.006 to 0.012 in (0.15 to 0.30 mm)
      Service limit . . . . 0.020 in (0.60 mm)
    Second ring
      Standard . . . . 0.012 to 0.018 in (0.30 to 0.45 mm)
      Service limit . . . . 0.020 in (0.60 mm)
    Oil control ring
      Standard . . . . 0.008 to 0.031 in (0.20 to 0.8 mm)
      Service limit . . . . 0.040 in (0.9 mm)
  1990 (wagon only)
    Top ring
      Standard . . . . 0.006 to 0.014 in (0.15 to 0.35 mm)
      Service limit . . . . 0.020 in (0.60 mm)
    Second ring (DX)
      Standard . . . . 0.006 to 0.014 in (0.15 to 0.35 mm)
      Service limit . . . . 0.020 in (0.60 mm)
    Second ring (4WD)
      Standard . . . . 0.012 to 0.018 in (0.30 to 0.45 mm)
      Service limit . . . . 0.020 in (0.60 mm)
    Oil control ring
      Standard . . . . 0.008 to 0.031 in (0.20 to 0.80 mm)
      Service limit . . . . 0.035 in (0.9 mm)

Valves and springs

Valve stem diameter
  1984 through 1987
    Auxiliary valve
      Standard . . . . 0.2587 to 0.2593 in (6.572 to 6.587 mm)
      Service limit . . . . 0.257 in (6.54 mm)
    Intake valve
      Standard . . . . 0.2591 to 0.2594 in (6.58 to 6.59 mm)
      Service limit . . . . 0.258 in (6.55 mm)
    Exhaust valve
      Standard . . . . 0.2579 to 0.2583 in (6.58 to 6.59 mm)
      Service limit . . . . 0.257 in (6.52 mm)
  1988-on
    Intake valve
      Standard . . . . 0.2157 to 0.2161 in (5.48 to 5.49 mm)
      Service limit . . . . 0.2146 in (5.45 mm)

Exhaust valve
   Standard . . . .   0.2147 to 0.2150 in (5.45 to 5.46 mm)
   Service limit . . . .   0.2134 in (5.42 mm)
Valve stem-to-guide clearance
  1984 through 1987
   Auxiliary valve
     Standard . . . .   0.001 to 0.002 in (0.023 to 0.058 mm)
     Service limit . . . .   0.003 in (0.08 mm)
   Intake valve (1987 Civic only)
     Standard . . . .   0.002 to 0.004 in (0.04 to 0.10 mm)
     Service limit . . . .   0.006 in (0.16 mm)
   Intake valve (all others)
     Standard . . . .   0.001 to 0.002 in (0.02 to 0.05 mm)
     Service limit . . . .   0.003 in (0.08 mm)
   Exhaust valve (1987 Civic only)
     Standard . . . .   0.004 to 0.006 in (0.10 to 0.16 mm)
     Service limit . . . .   0.009 in (0.22 mm)
   Exhaust valve (all others)
     Standard . . . .   0.002 to 0.003 in (0.05 to 0.08 mm)
     Service limit . . . .   0.004 in (0.11 mm)
  1988-on
   Intake valve
     Standard . . . .   0.001 to 0.002 in (0.02 to 0.05 mm)
     Service limit . . . .   0.003 in (0.08 mm)
   Exhaust valve
     Standard . . . .   0.002 to 0.003 in (0.05 to 0.08 mm)
     Service limit . . . .   0.004 in (0.11 mm)
Valve spring installed height
  Auxiliary valve . . . .   0.980 in (25.00 mm)
  Intake valve
   1984 . . . .   1.690 in (43.0 mm)
   1985-on . . . .   Not available
  Exhaust valve
   1984 . . . .   1.690 in (43.0 mm)
   1985-on . . . .   Not available
Valve spring out-of-square limit . . . .   0.068 in (1.75 mm)
Valve spring free length
  1984 through 1987
   Auxiliary valve spring
     Standard . . . .   1.25 in (31.73 mm)
     Service limit . . . .   1.22 in (31.0 mm)
   Inner valve spring
     Standard . . . .   1.733 in (44.02 mm)
     Service limit . . . .   Not available
   Outer valve spring (CRX HF [1985], Civic 1300)
     Standard . . . .   1.93 in (49.1 mm)
     Service limit . . . .   1.89 in (48.1 mm)
   Outer valve spring (CRX HF [1986])
     Standard . . . .   1.699 in (43.15 mm)
     Service limit . . . .   1.66 in (42.1 mm)
   Outer valve spring (CRX Si)
     Standard . . . .   1.868 in (47.45 mm)
     Service limit . . . .   Not available
   Outer valve spring (all others)
     Standard . . . .   1.87 in (47.6 mm)
     Service limit . . . .   1.83 in (46.6 mm)
  1988-on
   Intake valve (CRX HF [8-valve engine])
     Standard . . . .   2.0260 in (51.46 mm)
     Service limit . . . .   1.9929 in (50.62 mm)
   Intake valve (all others)
     Standard . . . .   1.9126 in (48.58 mm)
     Service limit . . . .   1.8756 in (47.64 mm)
   Exhaust valve (CRX HF [8-valve engine])
     Standard . . . .   2.2157 in (56.28 mm)
     Service limit . . . .   2.1854 in (55.51 mm)
   Exhaust valve (all others)
     Standard . . . .   1.9366 in (49.19 mm)
     Service limit . . . .   1.9024 in (48.32 mm)

Valves and springs (continued)

Valve margin width
  1984 through 1987
    Intake valve
      Standard .... 0.041 to 0.053 in (1.05 to 1.35 mm)
      Service limit .... 0.039 in (1.00 mm)
    Exhaust valve
      Standard .... 0.065 to 0.077 in (1.65 to 1.95 mm)
      Service limit .... 0.057 in (1.45 mm)
  1988-on
    Intake valve
      Standard .... 0.033 to 0.045 in (0.85 to 1.15 mm)
      Service limit .... 0.026 in (0.65 mm)
    Exhaust valve
      Standard .... 0.041 to 0.053 in (1.05 to 1.35 mm)
      Service limit .... 0.037 in (0.95 mm)

Torque specifications*

	Ft-lbs
Connecting rod cap nuts	23
Main bearing cap bolts	
1984 through 1987	33
1988-on	
Separate caps and bridge	48
One-piece cap assembly	33

*.**Note:** *Refer to Part A for additional torque specifications.*

---

1   General information

Included in this portion of Chapter 2 are the general overhaul procedures for the cylinder head and internal engine components.

The information ranges from advice concerning preparation for an overhaul and the purchase of replacement parts to detailed, step-by-step procedures covering removal and installation of internal engine components and the inspection of parts.

The following Sections have been written based on the assumption the engine has been removed from the vehicle. For information concerning in-vehicle engine repairs, as well as removal and installation of the external components necessary for the overhaul, see Part A of this Chapter and Section 7 of this Part.

The Specifications included in this Part are only those necessary for the inspection and overhaul procedures which follow. Refer to Part A for additional Specifications.

---

2   Engine overhaul – general information

Refer to illustration 2.4

It's not always easy to determine when, or if, an engine should be completely overhauled, as a number of factors must be considered.

High mileage is not necessarily an indication an overhaul is needed, while low mileage doesn't preclude the need for an overhaul. Frequency of servicing is probably the most important consideration. An engine that has had regular and frequent oil and filter changes, as well as other required maintenance, will most likely give many thousands of miles of reliable service. Conversely, a neglected engine may require an overhaul very early in its life.

Excessive oil consumption is an indication that piston rings, valve seals and/or valve guides are in need of attention. Make sure oil leaks aren't responsible before deciding the rings and/or guides are bad. Perform a cylinder compression check to determine the extent of the work required (see Section 3).

Check the oil pressure with a gauge installed in place of the oil pressure sending unit **(see illustration)** and compare it to the Specifications. If it's extremely low, the bearings and/or oil pump are probably worn out.

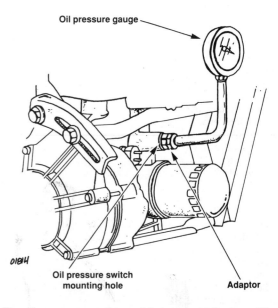

2.4   The oil pressure sending unit is located in the top of the oil filter housing – remove the sending unit to install a test gauge

Oil pressure gauge

Oil pressure switch mounting hole

Adaptor

01814

Loss of power, rough running, knocking or metallic engine noises, excessive valve train noise and high fuel consumption rates may also point to the need for an overhaul, especially if they're all present at the same time. If a complete tune-up doesn't remedy the situation, major mechanical work is the only solution.

An engine overhaul involves restoring the internal parts to the specifications of a new engine. During an overhaul, the piston rings are replaced and the cylinder walls are reconditioned (rebored and/or honed). If a rebore is done by an automotive machine shop, new oversize pistons must also be installed. The main and connecting rod bearings are generally replaced with new ones and, if necessary, the crankshaft may be reground to restore the journals. Generally, the valves are serviced as well, since they're usually in less-than-perfect condition at this point. While the engine is being overhauled, other components, such as the distributor, starter and

3.6 A compression gauge with a threaded fitting for the spark plug hole is preferred over the type that requires hand pressure to maintain the seal – be sure to open the throttle as far as possible during the compression check!

alternator, can be rebuilt as well. The end result should be a like new engine that will give many trouble free miles. **Note:** *Critical cooling system components such as the hoses, drivebelts, thermostat and water pump MUST be replaced with new parts when an engine is overhauled.* The radiator should be checked carefully to ensure it isn't clogged or leaking (see Chapter 3). Also, we don't recommend overhauling the oil pump – always install a new one when an engine is rebuilt.

Before beginning the engine overhaul, read through the entire procedure to familiarize yourself with the scope and requirements of the job. Overhauling an engine isn't difficult, but it is time consuming. Plan on the vehicle being tied up for a minimum of two weeks, especially if parts must be taken to an automotive machine shop for repair or reconditioning. Check on availability of parts and make sure all necessary special tools and equipment are obtained in advance. Most work can be done with typical hand tools, although a number of precision measuring tools are required for inspecting parts to determine if they must be replaced. Often an automotive machine shop will handle the inspection of parts and offer advice concerning reconditioning and replacement. **Note:** *Always wait until the engine has been completely disassembled and all components, especially the engine block, have been inspected before deciding what service and repair operations must be performed by an automotive machine shop.* Since the block's condition will be the major factor to consider when determining whether to overhaul the original engine or buy a rebuilt one, never purchase parts or have machine work done on other components until the block has been thoroughly inspected. As a general rule, time is the primary cost of an overhaul, so it doesn't pay to install worn or substandard parts.

As a final note, to ensure maximum life and minimum trouble from a rebuilt engine, everything must be assembled with care in a spotlessly clean environment.

3   Cylinder compression check

Refer to illustration 3.6

1   A compression check will tell you what mechanical condition the upper end (pistons, rings, valves, head gaskets) of the engine is in. Specifically, it can tell you if the compression is down due to leakage caused by worn piston rings, defective valves and seats or a blown head gasket. **Note:** *The engine must be at normal operating temperature and the battery must be fully charged for this check. Also, if the engine is equipped with a carburetor, the choke valve must be all the way open to get an accurate compression reading (if the engine's warm, the choke should be open).*

2   Begin by cleaning the area around the spark plugs before you remove them (compressed air should be used, if available, otherwise a small brush or even a bicycle tire pump will work). The idea is to prevent dirt from getting into the cylinders as the compression check is being done.
3   Remove all of the spark plugs from the engine (Chapter 1).
4   Block the throttle wide open.
5   Detach the coil wire from the center of the distributor cap and ground it on the engine block. Use a jumper wire with alligator clips on each end to ensure a good ground. On fuel injected vehicles, the fuel pump circuit should also be disabled (see Chapter 4).
6   Install the compression gauge in the number one spark plug hole **(see illustration)**.
7   Crank the engine over at least seven compression strokes and watch the gauge. The compression should build up quickly in a healthy engine. Low compression on the first stroke, followed by gradually increasing pressure on successive strokes, indicates worn piston rings. A low compression reading on the first stroke, which doesn't build up during successive strokes, indicates leaking valves or a blown head gasket (a cracked head could also be the cause). Deposits on the undersides of the valve heads can also cause low compression. Record the highest gauge reading obtained.
8   Repeat the procedure for the remaining cylinders and compare the results to the Specifications.
9   Add some engine oil (about three squirts from a plunger-type oil can) to each cylinder, through the spark plug hole, and repeat the test.
10   If the compression increases after the oil is added, the piston rings are definitely worn. If the compression doesn't increase significantly, the leakage is occurring at the valves or head gasket. Leakage past the valves may be caused by incorrect valve clearances, burned valve seats and/or faces or warped, cracked or bent valves.
11   If two adjacent cylinders have equally low compression, there's a strong possibility the head gasket between them is blown. The appearance of coolant in the combustion chambers or the crankcase would verify this condition.
12   If one cylinder is about 20 percent lower than the others, and the engine has a slightly rough idle, a worn lobe on the camshaft could be the cause.
13   If the compression is unusually high, the combustion chambers are probably coated with carbon deposits. If that's the case, the cylinder head should be removed and decarbonized.
14   If compression is way down or varies greatly between cylinders, it would be a good idea to have a leak-down test performed by an automotive repair shop. This test will pinpoint exactly where the leakage is occurring and how severe it is.

4   Engine removal – methods and precautions

If you've decided an engine must be removed for overhaul or major repair work, several preliminary steps should be taken.

Locating a place to work is extremely important. Adequate work space, along with storage space for the vehicle, will be needed. If a shop or garage isn't available, at the very least a flat, level, clean work surface made of concrete or asphalt is required.

Cleaning the engine compartment and engine before beginning the removal procedure will help keep tools clean and organized.

An engine hoist or A-frame will also be necessary. Make sure the equipment is rated in excess of the combined weight of the engine and accessories. Safety is of primary importance, considering the potential hazards involved in lifting the engine out of the vehicle.

If the engine is being removed by a novice, a helper should be available. Advice and aid from someone more experienced would also be helpful. There are many instances when one person cannot simultaneously perform all of the operations required when lifting an engine out of a vehicle.

Plan the operation ahead of time. Arrange for or obtain all of the tools and equipment you'll need prior to beginning the job. Some of the equipment necessary to perform engine removal and installation safely and with relative ease are (in addition to an engine hoist) a heavy duty floor jack,

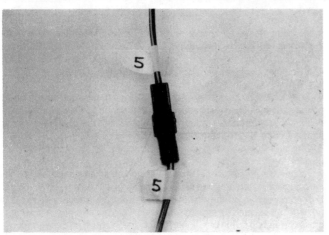

5.6   Label both ends of each wire (as well as each vacuum hose, coolant hose and fuel hose) before disconnecting it

complete sets of wrenches and sockets as described in the front of this manual, wood blocks and plenty of rags and cleaning solvent for mopping up spilled oil, coolant and gasoline. If the hoist must be rented, make sure you arrange for it in advance and perform all of the operations possible without it beforehand. This will save you money and time.

Assume the vehicle will be out of use for quite a while. A machine shop will be required to perform some of the work a do-it-yourselfer can't accomplish without special equipment. These shops often have a busy schedule, so it would be a good idea to consult them before removing the engine in order to accurately estimate the amount of time required to rebuild or repair components that may need work.

Always be extremely careful when removing and installing the engine. Serious injury can result from careless actions. Plan ahead, take your time and a job of this nature, although major, can be accomplished successfully.

---

5   Engine – removal and installation

Refer to illustrations 5.6, 5.14, 5.17 and 5.21
Note: *Read through the entire Section before beginning this procedure. The engine and transaxle are removed as a unit and then separated outside the vehicle.*

Removal

1   On fuel-injected models, relieve the fuel system pressure (see Chapter 4).
2   Disconnect the negative cable from the battery.
3   Place protective covers on the fenders and cowl and remove the hood (see Chapter 11).
4   Remove the air cleaner assembly (see Chapter 4).
5   Raise the vehicle and support it securely on jackstands. Drain the cooling system and engine oil and remove the drivebelts (see Chapter 1).
6   Clearly label, then disconnect all vacuum lines, coolant and emissions hoses, wiring harness connectors, ground straps and fuel lines. Masking tape and/or a touch up paint applicator work well for marking items **(see illustration)**. Take instant photos or sketch the locations of components and brackets.
7   Remove the cooling fan(s), shroud(s) and radiator (see Chapter 3).
8   Release the residual fuel pressure in the tank by removing the gas cap, then undo the fuel lines between the engine and body (see Chapter 4). Plug or cap all open fittings.
9   Disconnect the throttle linkage (and TV linkage and speed control cable, when equipped) from the engine (see Chapter 4). **Note:** *Be careful not to bend the cable when removing it from the linkage. Always replace a kinked cable with a new one.*
10   On power steering equipped vehicles, unbolt the power steering pump. If clearance allows, tie the pump aside without disconnecting the hoses. If necessary, remove the pump (see Chapter 10).
11   On air conditioned vehicles, unbolt the compressor and set it aside (see Chapter 3). Do not disconnect the refrigerant hoses.
12   Detach the exhaust pipe from the manifold (see Part A).
13   Detach the driveaxles (see Chapter 8), wire harness, shift linkage and speedometer cable from the transaxle (see Chapter 7). **Note:** *On 4WD vehicles, remove the shift control cable from the transfer case section of the transaxle unit. Also disconnect the axle shaft from the transaxle unit.*
14   Attach a lifting sling to the brackets on the engine. Position a hoist and connect the sling to it. Take up the slack until there's slight tension on the hoist **(see illustration)**.
15   Recheck to be sure nothing except the mounts are still connecting the engine/transaxle to the vehicle. Disconnect anything still remaining.
16   Support the transaxle with a floor jack. Place a block of wood on the jack head to prevent damage to the transaxle. Remove the through-bolts and nuts from the engine mounts and torque strut (see Part A). Unbolt the transaxle mount bracket (if equipped) from the transaxle (see Chapter 7). **Warning:** *DO NOT place any part of your body under the engine/transaxle when it's supported only by a hoist or other lifting device.*

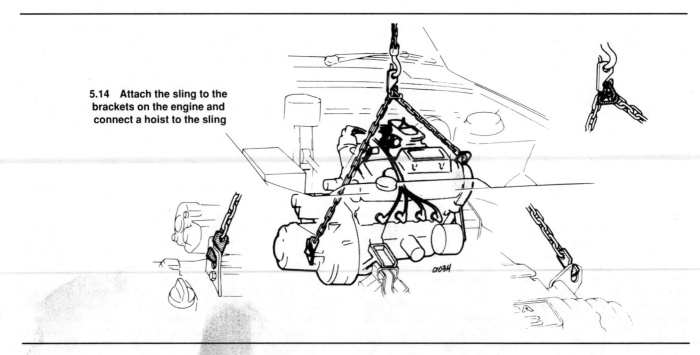

5.14   Attach the sling to the brackets on the engine and connect a hoist to the sling

5.17   Slowly lift the engine/transaxle assembly out of the vehicle

5.21   Remove the bolts and separate the engine and transaxle

17   Slowly lift the engine/transaxle out of the vehicle **(see illustration)**. It may be necessary to pry the mounts away from the frame brackets.
18   Move the engine/transaxle away from the vehicle and carefully lower the hoist until the transaxle is supported in a level position.
19   Remove the engine block-to-transaxle brace.
20   On automatic transaxle equipped models, detach the torque converter dust shield from the lower bellhousing. Remove the torque converter-to-driveplate fasteners (see Chapter 7) and push the converter back slightly into the bellhousing.
21   Remove the engine-to-transaxle bolts and separate the engine from the transaxle **(see illustration)**. The torque converter should remain in the transaxle.
22   Place the engine on the floor or remove the flywheel/driveplate and mount the engine on an engine stand.

Installation

23   Check the engine/transaxle mounts. If they're worn or damaged, replace them.
24   On manual transaxle equipped models, inspect the clutch components (see Chapter 8) and on automatic models inspect the converter seal and bushing.
25   On manual transaxle equipped vehicles, apply a dab of high-temperature grease to the pilot bearing.
26   On automatic transaxle equipped models, apply a dab of grease to the nose of the converter and the seal lips.
27   Carefully guide the transaxle into place, following the procedure outlined in Chapter 7. **Caution:** *Do not use the bolts to force the engine and transaxle into alignment. It may crack or damage major components.*
28   Install the engine-to-transaxle bolts and tighten them securely.
29   Attach the hoist to the engine and carefully lower the engine/transaxle assembly into the engine compartment.
30   Install the mount bolts and tighten them securely.
31   Reinstall the remaining components and fasteners in the reverse order of removal.
32   Add coolant, oil, power steering and transmission fluid as needed (see Chapter 1).
33   Run the engine and check for proper operation and leaks. Shut off the engine and recheck the fluid levels.

6   Engine rebuilding alternatives

The do-it-yourselfer is faced with a number of options when performing an engine overhaul. The decision to replace the engine block, piston/connecting rod assemblies and crankshaft depends on a number of factors,

with the number one consideration being the condition of the block. Other considerations are cost, access to machine shop facilities, parts availability, time required to complete the project and the extent of prior mechanical experience on the part of the do-it-yourselfer.

Some of the rebuilding alternatives include:

Individual parts – If the inspection procedures reveal the engine block and most engine components are in reusable condition, purchasing individual parts may be the most economical alternative. The block, crankshaft and piston/connecting rod assemblies should all be inspected carefully. Even if the block shows little wear, the cylinder bores should be surface honed.

Short block – A short block consists of an engine block with a crankshaft and piston/connecting rod assemblies already installed. All new bearings are incorporated and all clearances will be correct. The existing camshaft, valve train components, cylinder head and external parts can be bolted to the short block with little or no machine shop work necessary.

Long block – A long block consists of a short block plus an oil pump, oil pan, cylinder head, camshaft cover, camshaft and valve train components, timing belt and sprockets. All components are installed with new bearings, seals and gaskets incorporated throughout. The installation of manifolds and external parts is all that's necessary.

Give careful thought to which alternative is best for you and discuss the situation with local automotive machine shops, auto parts dealers and experienced rebuilders before ordering or purchasing replacement parts.

7   Engine overhaul – disassembly sequence

Refer to illustration 7.5

1   It's much easier to disassemble and work on the engine if it's mounted on a portable engine stand, which can often be obtained from an equipment rental yard. Before the engine is mounted on a stand, the flywheel/driveplate and rear oil seal should be removed from the engine.
2   If a stand isn't available, it's possible to disassemble the engine with it blocked up on the floor. Be extra careful not to tip or drop the engine when working without a stand.
3   If you're going to obtain a rebuilt engine, all external components must come off first, to be transferred to the replacement engine, just as they will if you're doing a complete engine overhaul yourself. These include:

Alternator and brackets
Emissions control components
Distributor, spark plug wires and spark plugs
Thermostat and housing cover
Water pump

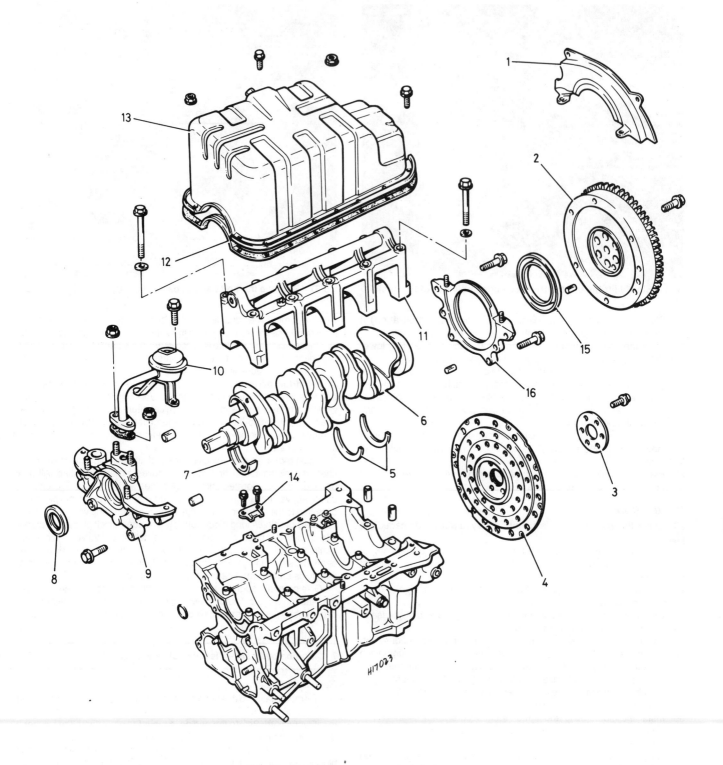

7.5 Engine components – exploded view

1	Flywheel cover (manual transaxle)	7	Main bearings	12	Oil pan gasket
2	Flywheel (manual transaxle)	8	Crankshaft front oil seal	13	Oil pan
3	Spacer washer	9	Oil pump	14	Oil deflector
4	Driveplate (automatic transaxle)	10	Oil pick-up tube/screen	15	Crankshaft rear oil seal
5	Thrust bearings	11	One-piece main bearing cap	16	Oil seal housing
6	Crankshaft		assembly (monobloc)		

Carburetor or EFI components
Intake/exhaust manifolds
Oil filter
Engine mounts
Clutch and flywheel/driveplate

Note: *When removing the external components from the engine, pay close attention to details that may be helpful or important during installation. Note the installed position of gaskets, seals, spacers, pins, brackets, washers, bolts and other small items.*

4   If you're obtaining a short block, which consists of the engine block, crankshaft, pistons and connecting rods all assembled, then the cylinder head, oil pan and oil pump will have to be removed as well. See Engine rebuilding alternatives for additional information regarding the different possibilities to be considered.

5   If you're planning a complete overhaul, the engine must be disassembled and the internal components removed in the following order **(see illustration)**.

Camshaft cover
Intake and exhaust manifolds
Timing belt covers
Timing belt and sprockets
Cylinder head
Oil pan
Oil pick-up tube/screen assembly
Oil pump
Piston/connecting rod assemblies
Rear main oil seal housing
Crankshaft and main bearings

6   Before beginning the disassembly and overhaul procedures, make sure the following items are available. Also, refer to Engine overhaul – reassembly sequence for a list of tools and materials needed for engine reassembly.

Common hand tools
Small cardboard boxes or plastic bags for storing parts
Gasket scraper
Ridge reamer
Vibration damper puller
Micrometers
Telescoping gauges
Dial indicator set
Valve spring compressor
Cylinder surfacing hone
Piston ring groove cleaning tool
Electric drill
Tap and die set
Wire brushes
Oil gallery brushes
Cleaning solvent

8   Cylinder head – disassembly

Refer to illustrations 8.1, 8.2, 8.3 and 8.4

Note: *New and rebuilt cylinder heads are commonly available for most engines at dealerships and auto parts stores. Due to the fact that some specialized tools are necessary for the disassembly and inspection procedures, and replacement parts may not be readily available, it may be more practical and economical for the home mechanic to purchase a replacement head rather than taking the time to disassemble, inspect and recondition the original.*

1   Cylinder head disassembly involves removal of the intake and exhaust valves and related components. If they're still in place, remove the auxiliary valves (if equipped), rocker arm assemblies and camshaft from the cylinder head **(see illustration)**. Refer to Part A for further information.

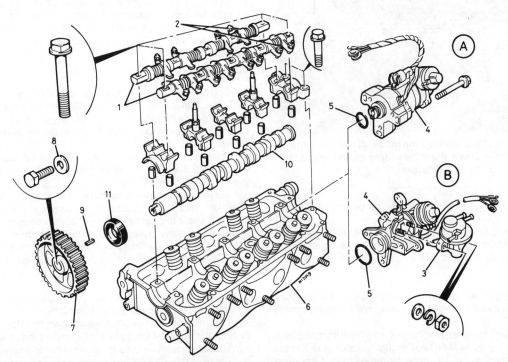

8.1 Cylinder head and related components – exploded view

1	Rocker arm assemblies	5	O-ring	8	Special washer	11	Oil seal
2	Valve adjusting screws	6	Cylinder head	9	Woodruff key	A	Fuel injected engine
3	Fuel pump	7	Camshaft sprocket	10	Camshaft	B	Carbureted engine
4	Distributor						

8.2   A small plastic bag, with an appropriate label, can be used to store the valve train components so they can be kept together and reinstalled in the correct location

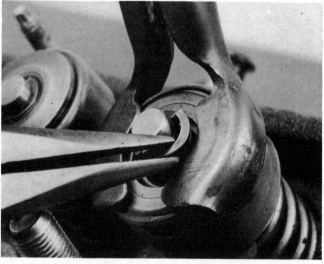

8.3   Use a valve spring compressor to compress the spring, then remove the keepers from the valve stem

8.4   If the valve won't pull through the guide, deburr the edge of the stem end and the area around the keeper groove with a file or whetstone

Label the parts or store them separately so they can be reinstalled in their original locations.

2   Before the valves are removed, arrange to label and store them, along with their related components, so they can be kept separate and re-installed in the same valve guides they are removed from **(see illustration)**.

3   Compress the springs on the first valve with a spring compressor and remove the keepers **(see illustration)**. Carefully release the valve spring compressor and remove the retainer, the spring and the spring seat (if used).

4   Pull the valve out of the head, then remove the oil seal from the guide. If the valve binds in the guide (won't pull through), push it back into the head and deburr the area around the keeper groove with a fine file or whetstone **(see illustration)**.

5   Repeat the procedure for the remaining valves. Remember to keep all the parts for each valve together so they can be reinstalled in the same locations.

6   Once the valves and related components have been removed and stored in an organized manner, the head should be thoroughly cleaned

and inspected. If a complete engine overhaul is being done, finish the engine disassembly procedures before beginning the cylinder head cleaning and inspection process.

---

9   Cylinder head – cleaning and inspection

Refer to illustrations 9.11, 9.13, 9.14, 9.15, 9.16 and 9.17

1   Thorough cleaning of the cylinder head and related valve train components, followed by a detailed inspection, will enable you to decide how much valve service work must be done during the engine overhaul. **Note:** *If the engine was severely overheated, the cylinder head is probably warped (see Step 12).*

Cleaning

2   Scrape all traces of old gasket material and sealant off the head gasket, intake manifold and exhaust manifold sealing surfaces. Be very careful not to gouge the cylinder head. Special gasket removal solvents that soften gaskets and make removal much easier are available at auto parts stores.

3   Remove all built up scale from the coolant passages.

4   Run a stiff wire brush through the various holes to remove deposits that may have formed in them.

5   Run an appropriate size tap into each of the threaded holes to remove corrosion and thread sealant that may be present. If compressed air is available, use it to clear the holes of debris produced by this operation. **Warning:** *Wear eye protection when using compressed air!*

6   Clean the cylinder head with solvent and dry it thoroughly. Compressed air will speed the drying process and ensure all holes and recessed areas are clean. **Note:** *Decarbonizing chemicals are available and may prove very useful when cleaning the cylinder head and valve train components. They are very caustic and should be used with caution. Be sure to follow the instructions on the container.*

7   Clean the rocker arms with solvent and dry them thoroughly (don't mix them up during the cleaning process). Compressed air will speed the drying process and can be used to clean out the oil passages.

8   Clean all the valve springs, spring seats, keepers and retainers with solvent and dry them thoroughly. Do the components from one valve at a time to avoid mixing up the parts.

9   Scrape off any heavy deposits that may have formed on the valves, then use a motorized wire brush to remove deposits from the valve heads and stems. **Warning:** *Wear eye protection. Again, make sure the valves don't get mixed up.*

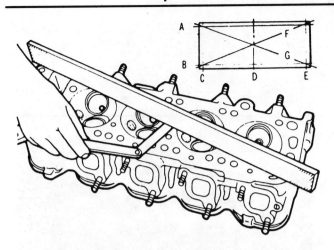

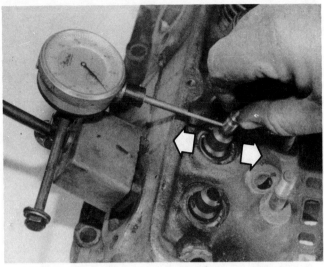

9.11 Check the cylinder head gasket surface for warpage by trying to slip a feeler gauge under the straightedge (see the Specifications for the maximum warpage allowed and use a feeler gauge of that thickness)

9.13 A dial indicator can be used to determine the valve stem-to-guide clearance (move the valve stem as indicated by the arrows)

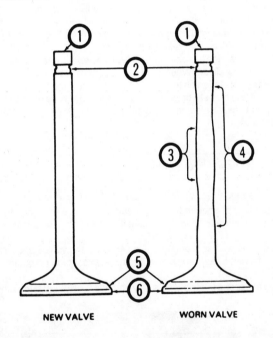

9.14 Check for valve wear at the points shown here

1	Valve tip	4	Stem (most worn area)
2	Keeper groove	5	Valve face
3	Stem (least worn area)	6	Margin

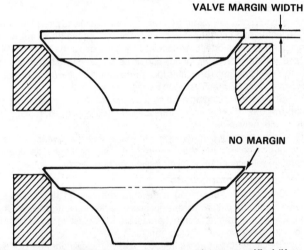

9.15 The margin width on each valve must be as specified (if no margin exists, the valve cannot be reused)

Inspection

Note: *Be sure to perform all of the following inspection procedures before concluding that machine shop work is required. Make a list of the items that need attention.*

Cylinder head

10   Inspect the head very carefully for cracks, evidence of coolant leakage and other damage. If cracks are found, check with an automotive machine shop concerning repair. If repair isn't possible, a new cylinder head should be obtained.

11   Using a precision straightedge and feeler gauge, check the head gasket mating surface for warpage **(see illustration)**. If the warpage exceeds the specified limit, it can be resurfaced at an automotive machine shop.

12   Examine the valve seats in each of the combustion chambers. If they're pitted, cracked or burned, the head will require valve service that's beyond the scope of the home mechanic.

13   Check the valve stem-to-guide clearance by measuring the lateral movement of the valve stem with a dial indicator attached securely to the head **(see illustration)**. The valve must be in the guide and approximately 1/16-inch off the seat. The total valve stem movement indicated by the gauge needle must be divided by two to obtain the actual clearance. After this is done, if there's still some doubt regarding the condition of the valve guides, they should be checked by an automotive machine shop (the cost should be minimal).

Valves

14   Carefully inspect each valve face for uneven wear, deformation, cracks, pits and burned areas **(see illustration)**. Check the valve stem for scuffing and galling and the neck for cracks. Rotate the valve and check for any obvious indication that it's bent. Look for pits and excessive wear on the end of the stem. The presence of any of these conditions indicates the need for valve service by an automotive machine shop.

15   Measure the margin width on each valve **(see illustration)**. Any valve with a margin narrower than specified will have to be replaced with a new one.

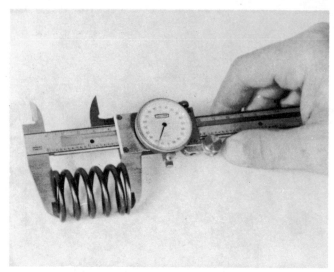

9.16   Measure the free length of each valve spring with a dial or vernier caliper

9.17   Check each valve spring for squareness

Valve components

16   Check each valve spring for wear (on the ends) and pits. Measure the free length and compare it to the Specifications **(see illustration)**. Any springs that are shorter than specified have sagged and should not be re-used. The tension of all springs should be checked with a special fixture before deciding they're suitable for use in a rebuilt engine (take the springs to an automotive machine shop for this check).

17   Stand each spring on a flat surface and check it for squareness **(see illustration)**. If any of the springs are distorted or sagged, replace all of them with new parts.

18   Check the spring retainers and keepers for obvious wear and cracks. Any questionable parts should be replaced with new ones, as extensive damage will occur if they fail during engine operation.

Rocker arm components

19   Check the rocker arm faces (the areas that contact the camshaft and valve stems) for pits, wear, galling, score marks and rough spots. Check the rocker arm-to-shaft contact areas and the adjusting screws as well. Look for cracks in each rocker arm.

20   Check the rocker arm shaft bolt holes in the cylinder head for damaged threads.

All components

21   Any damaged or excessively worn parts must be replaced with new ones.

22   If the inspection process indicates the valve components are in generally poor condition and worn beyond the specified limits, which is usually the case in an engine that's being overhauled, reassemble the valves in the cylinder head and refer to Section 10 for valve servicing recommendations.

10   Valves – servicing

1   Because of the complex nature of the job and the special tools and equipment needed, servicing of the valves, the valve seats and the valve guides, commonly known as a valve job, should be done by a professional.

2   The home mechanic can remove and disassemble the head, do the initial cleaning and inspection, then reassemble and deliver it to a dealer service department or an automotive machine shop for the actual service work. Doing the inspection will enable you to see what condition the head and valvetrain components are in and will ensure that you know what work and new parts are required when dealing with an automotive machine shop.

3   The shop will remove the valves and springs, recondition or replace the valves and valve seats, recondition the valve guides, check and re-place the valve springs, spring retainers and keepers (as necessary), replace the valve seals with new ones, reassemble the valve components and make sure the installed spring height is correct. The cylinder head gasket surface will also be resurfaced if it's warped.

4   After the valve job has been performed by a professional, the head will be in like new condition. When the head is returned, be sure to clean it again before installation on the engine to remove any metal particles and abrasive grit that may still be present from the valve service or head resurfacing operations. Use compressed air, if available, to blow out all the oil holes and passages.

11   Cylinder head – reassembly

Refer to illustrations 11.3a, 11.3b, 11.5a, 11.5b, 11.5c and 11.8

1   Regardless of whether or not the head was sent to an automotive repair shop for valve servicing, make sure it's clean before beginning reassembly.

2   If the head was sent out for valve servicing, the valves and related components will already be in place. Begin the reassembly procedure with Step 8.

3   Drop the spring seats over the valve guides **(see illustration)**, install

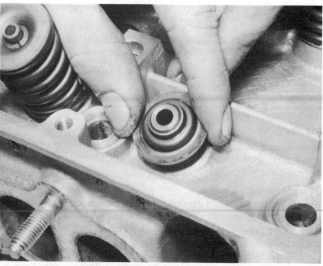

11.3a   Drop the spring seats over the valve guides

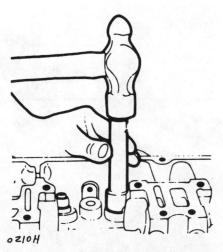

11.3b   Gently tap the valve seals into place with a seal installation tool or a deep socket and hammer

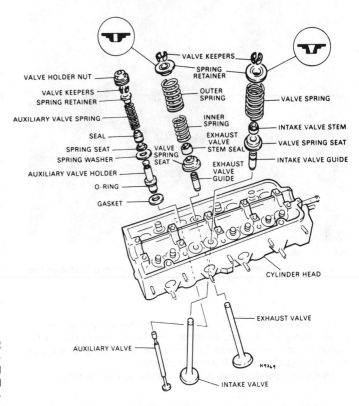

11.5a   Exploded view of a carbureted engine's cylinder head components – fuel injected models don't have auxiliary valves

new seals on each of the valve guides. Note that the intake and exhaust seals are not interchangeable. Intake seals have a white spring and exhaust seals have a black spring. Using a hammer and deep socket or seal installation tool, gently tap each seal into place until it's completely seated on the guide **(see illustration)**. Don't twist or cock the seals during installation or they won't seal properly on the valve stems.

4   Beginning at one end of the head, lubricate and install the first valve. Apply moly-base grease or clean engine oil to the valve stem.

5   Set the valve springs and retainers in place **(see illustrations)** (note that the intake and exhaust retainers are different and should not be interchanged). Exhaust valves have an inner and an outer spring.

6   Compress the springs with a valve spring compressor and carefully install the keepers in the groove, then slowly release the compressor and make sure the keepers seat properly. Apply a small dab of grease to each keeper to hold it in place if necessary.

7   Repeat the procedure for the remaining valves. Be sure to return the components to their original locations – don't mix them up!

8   Check the installed valve spring height with a ruler graduated in 1/32-inch increments or a dial caliper. If the head was sent out for service work, the installed height should be correct (but don't automatically assume it is). The measurement is taken from the top of each spring seat or

11.5b   Make sure each outer valve spring (right) is installed with the narrow pitch end (arrow) against the cylinder head

11.5c   Install the valve retainer over the springs and valve stem

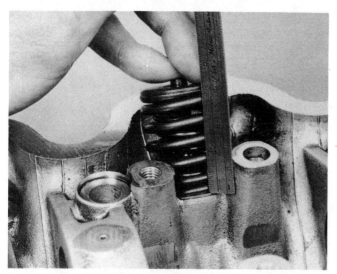

11.8   Double-check the height with the valve springs installed (do this for each valve)

12.1   A ridge reamer is required to remove the ridge from the top of the cylinder – do this before removing the pistons

shim(s) to the bottom of the retainer **(see illustration)**. If the height is greater than specified, shims can be added under the springs to correct it. **Caution:** *Don't, under any circumstances, shim the springs to the point where the installed height is less than specified.*

9   Install the camshaft and rocker arm assembly (see Part A).

12   Pistons/connecting rods – removal

Refer to illustrations 12.1, 12.3, 12.4a, 12.4b and 12.6
Note: *Prior to removing the piston/connecting rod assemblies, remove the cylinder head and oil pan by referring to the appropriate Sections in Part A.*

1   Use your fingernail to feel if a ridge has formed at the upper limit of ring travel (about 1/4-inch down from the top of each cylinder). If carbon deposits or cylinder wear have produced ridges, they must be completely removed with a special tool **(see illustration)**. Follow the manufacturer's instructions provided with the tool. Failure to remove the ridges before at-

tempting to remove the piston/connecting rod assemblies may result in piston breakage.

2   After the cylinder ridges have been removed, turn the engine upside-down so the crankshaft is facing up.

3   Before the connecting rods are removed, check the end play with feeler gauges. Slide them between the first connecting rod and the crankshaft throw until the play is removed **(see illustration)**. The end play is equal to the thickness of the feeler gauge(s). If the end play exceeds the service limit, new connecting rods will be required. If new rods (or a new crankshaft) are installed, the end play may fall under the specified minimum (if it does, the rods will have to be machined to restore it – consult an automotive machine shop for advice if necessary). Repeat the procedure for the remaining connecting rods.

4   Check the connecting rods and caps for identification marks **(see illustration)**. If they aren't plainly marked, use a small center punch to make the appropriate number of indentations **(see illustration)** on each rod and cap (1, 2, 3, etc., depending on the cylinder they're associated with).

12.3   Check the connecting rod end play with a feeler gauge as shown here

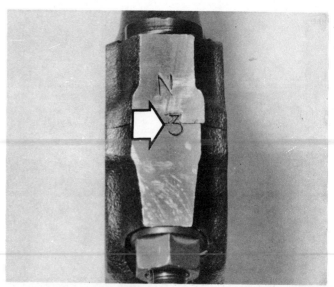

12.4a   DO NOT confuse the stamped numbers on the parting surface, such as this 3 (arrow), with cylinder numbers – this number indicates big-end bore size

12.4b To avoid confusion during reassembly, the connecting rods and caps should be marked with a center punch to indicate which cylinder they're installed in

12.6 To prevent damage to the crankshaft journals and cylinder walls, slip sections of hose over the rod bolts before removing the pistons

5   Loosen each of the connecting rod cap nuts 1/2-turn at a time until they can be removed by hand. Remove the number one connecting rod cap and bearing insert. Don't drop the bearing insert out of the cap.
6   Slip a short length of plastic or rubber hose over each connecting rod cap bolt to protect the crankshaft journal and cylinder wall as the piston is removed **(see illustration)**.
7   Remove the bearing insert and push the connecting rod/piston assembly out through the top of the engine. Use a wooden hammer handle to push on the upper bearing surface in the connecting rod. If resistance is felt, double-check to make sure all of the ridge was removed from the cylinder.
8   Repeat the procedure for the remaining cylinders.
9   After removal, reassemble the connecting rod caps and bearing inserts in their respective connecting rods and install the cap nuts finger-tight. Leaving the old bearing inserts in place until reassembly will help prevent the connecting rod bearing surfaces from being accidentally nicked or gouged.
10   Don't separate the pistons from the connecting rods (see Section 17 for additional information).

---

13   Crankshaft – removal

Refer to illustration 13.3

Note: *The crankshaft can be removed only after the engine has been removed from the vehicle. It's assumed the flywheel or driveplate, rear main oil seal housing, crankshaft pulley, timing belt/crankshaft sprocket, oil pan, oil pump, oil pick-up tube/screen assembly and piston/connecting rod assemblies have already been removed.*

1   Before the crankshaft is removed, check the end play. Mount a dial indicator with the stem in line with the crankshaft and just touching the end.
2   Push the crankshaft all the way to the rear and zero the dial indicator. Next, pry the crankshaft to the front as far as possible and check the reading on the dial indicator. The distance it moves is the end play. If it's greater than specified, check the crankshaft thrust surfaces for wear. If no wear is evident, new thrust bearings should correct the end play.
3   If a dial indicator isn't available, feeler gauges can be used. Gently pry or push the crankshaft all the way to the front of the engine. Slip feeler gauges between the crankshaft and the front face of the thrust bearing to determine the clearance **(see illustration)**.

4   **Note:** *Some engines have a one-piece main bearing cap assembly* **(see illustration 7.5)**, *while others have individual bearing caps with a bridge that ties them together. Regardless of the design, make sure the cap assembly or individual bearing caps are marked with a center punch so they can be reinstalled in their original relationship to the engine block. They must not be mixed up or turned around.* Loosen the main bearing cap assembly or bridge bolts 1/4-turn at a time each, working from the center out, until they can be removed by hand.
5   Detach the cap assembly from the block. If the engine has individual caps, lift off the bridge, then remove the caps. Note the locations of the dowel pins and, on engines with individual caps, the O-ring between the center bearing cap and the bridge. If necessary, gently tap the caps with a soft-face hammer to dislodge them from the engine block. Try not to drop the bearing inserts if they come out with the caps.
6   Carefully lift the crankshaft out of the engine. Reinstall the bearing inserts, the caps and bridge or cap assembly and bolts. Tighten the bolts finger-tight.

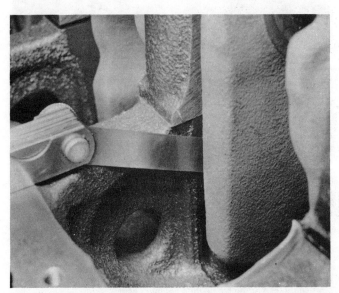

13.3 Feeler gauges can be used to check crankshaft end play at the center (number 3) main bearing

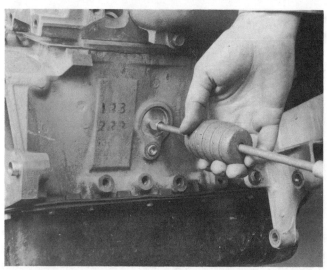

14.2   The core plugs should be removed with a puller – if they're driven into the block they may be impossible to retrieve

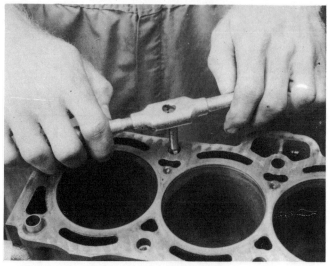

14.9   All threaded holes in the block – particularly the main bearing cap and cylinder head bolt holes – should be cleaned and restored with a tap (be sure to remove debris from the holes after this is done)

14.11   A large socket and an extension can be used to drive the new core plugs into the bores

14   Engine block – cleaning

Refer to illustrations 14.2, 14.9 and 14.11

Caution: *The core plugs (also known as freeze or soft plugs) may be difficult or impossible to retrieve if they're driven into the block coolant passages.*

1   Remove all external components before cleaning the block.
2   Drill a small hole in the center of each core plug and pull them out with an auto body type dent puller **(see illustration)**.
3   Using a gasket scraper, remove all traces of gasket material from the engine block. Be very careful not to nick or gouge the gasket sealing surfaces.
4   Remove the main bearing bridge and caps or cap assembly and separate the bearing inserts from the caps and the engine block. Tag the bearings, indicating which cylinder they were removed from and whether they were in the cap or the block, then set them aside.
5   Remove all threaded oil gallery plugs from the block. The plugs are usually very tight – they may have to be drilled out and the holes retapped.

Use new plugs when the engine is reassembled.
6   If the engine is extremely dirty it should be taken to an automotive machine shop to be steam cleaned or hot tanked.
7   After the block is returned, clean all oil holes and oil galleries one more time. Brushes specifically designed for this purpose are available at most auto parts stores. Flush the passages with warm water until the water runs clear, dry the block thoroughly and wipe all machined surfaces with a light, rust preventive oil. If you have access to compressed air, use it to speed the drying process and blow out all the oil holes and galleries. **Warning:** *Wear eye protection when using compressed air!*
8   If the block isn't extremely dirty or sludged up, you can do an adequate cleaning job with hot soapy water and a stiff brush. Take plenty of time and do a thorough job. Regardless of the cleaning method used, be sure to clean all oil holes and galleries very thoroughly, dry the block completely and coat all machined surfaces with light oil.
9   The threaded holes in the block must be clean to ensure accurate torque readings during reassembly. Run the proper size tap into each of the holes to remove rust, corrosion, thread sealant or sludge and restore damaged threads **(see illustration)**. If possible, use compressed air to clear the holes of debris produced by this operation. Now is a good time to clean the threads on the head bolts and the main bearing cap bolts as well.
10   Reinstall the main bearing caps and bridge or cap assembly and tighten the bolts finger-tight.
11   After coating the sealing surfaces of the new core plugs with Permatex no. 2 sealant, install them in the engine block **(see illustration)**. Make sure they're driven in straight and seated properly or leakage could result. Special tools are available for this purpose, but a large socket, with an outside diameter that will just slip into the core plug, a 1/2-inch drive extension and a hammer will work just as well.
12   Apply non-hardening sealant (such as Permatex no. 2 or Teflon pipe sealant) to the new oil gallery plugs and thread them into the holes in the block. Make sure they're tightened securely.
13   If the engine isn't going to be reassembled right away, cover it with a large plastic trash bag to keep it clean.

15   Engine block – inspection

Refer to illustrations 15.4a, 15.4b, 15.4c, 15.14a and 15.14b

1   Before the block is inspected, it should be cleaned as described in Section 14.
2   Visually check the block for cracks, rust and corrosion. Look for stripped threads in the threaded holes. It's also a good idea to have the

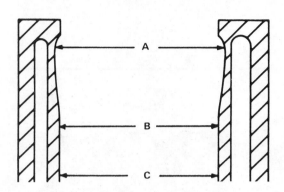

15.4a Measure the diameter of each cylinder just under the ridge area (A), at the center (B) and at the bottom (C)

15.4b The ability to "feel" when the telescoping gauge is at the correct point will be developed over time, so work slowly and repeat the check until you're satisfied the bore measurement is accurate

block checked for hidden cracks by an automotive machine shop with the special equipment to do this type of work. If defects are found, have the block repaired, if possible, or replaced.

3   Check the cylinder bores for scuffing and scoring.

4   Measure the diameter of each cylinder at the top (just under the ridge area), center and bottom of the cylinder bore, parallel to the crankshaft axis **(see illustrations)**. **Note:** *These measurements should not be made with the bare block mounted on an engine stand – the cylinders could be distorted and the measurements may be inaccurate.*

5   Next, measure each cylinder's diameter at the same three locations across the crankshaft axis. Compare the results to the Specifications.

6   If the required precision measuring tools aren't available, the piston-to-cylinder clearances can be obtained, though not quite as accurately, using feeler gauge stock. Feeler gauge stock comes in 12-inch lengths and various thicknesses and is generally available at auto parts stores. Purchase thicknesses equal to the Specified maximum and minimum piston clearances.

7   To check the clearance, select a feeler gauge and slip it into the cylinder along with the matching piston. The piston must be positioned exactly as it normally would be. The feeler gauge must be between the piston and cylinder on one of the thrust faces (90-degrees to the piston pin bore).

8   The piston should slip through the cylinder (with the feeler gauge in place) with moderate pressure.

9   If it falls through or slides through easily, the clearance is excessive and a new piston will be required. If the piston binds at the lower end of the cylinder and is loose toward the top, the cylinder is tapered. If tight spots are encountered as the piston/feeler gauge is rotated in the cylinder, the cylinder is out-of-round.

10   Repeat the procedure for the remaining pistons and cylinders.

11   If the cylinder walls are badly scuffed or scored, or if they're out-of-round or tapered beyond the limits given in the Specifications, have the engine block rebored and honed at an automotive machine shop. If a rebore is done, oversize pistons and rings will be required.

12   If the cylinders are in reasonably good condition and not worn to the outside of the limits, and if the piston-to-cylinder clearances can be maintained properly, then they don't have to be rebored. Honing is all that's necessary (Section 16).

13   Standard bore pistons installed at the factory come in three sizes: Standard, 0.25 mm oversize and 0.50 mm oversize. Measure the cylinder bore and consult the specifications listed in this Chapter for the various sizes.

14   Using a precision straightedge and feeler gauge, check the block deck (the surface that mates with the cylinder head) for distortion **(see illustrations)**. If it's distorted beyond the specified limit, have it resurfaced by an automotive machine shop.

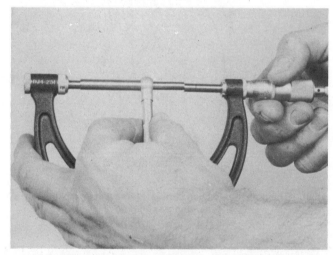

15.4c The gauge is then measured with a micrometer to determine the bore size

15.14a Check the block deck for warpage with a precision straightedge and feeler gauges

15.14b Lay the straightedge across the block, diagonally and from end-to-end when making the check

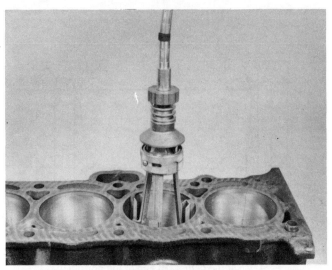

16.3a Lubricate the bore with plenty of oil and move the hone up-and-down in the cylinder at a pace which will produce a fine crosshatch pattern

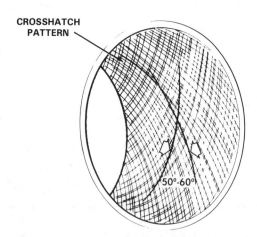

16.3b The crosshatch lines should intersect at approximately a 60-degree angle

16 Cylinder honing

Refer to illustrations 16.3a and 16.3b

1   Prior to engine reassembly, the cylinder bores must be honed so the new piston rings will seat correctly and provide the best possible combustion chamber seal. **Note:** *If you don't have the tools or don't want to tackle the honing operation, most automotive machine shops will do it for a reasonable fee.*

2   Before honing the cylinders, install the main bearing caps and bridge or cap assembly and tighten the bolts to the torque listed in this Chapter's specifications.

3   Two types of cylinder hones are commonly available – the flex hone or "bottle brush" type and the more traditional surfacing hone with spring-loaded stones. Both will do the job, but for the less experienced mechanic the "bottle brush" hone will probably be easier to use. You'll also need some kerosene or honing oil, rags and an electric drill. Proceed as follows:

   a) Mount the hone in the drill, compress the stones and slip it into the first cylinder **(see illustration)**. Be sure to wear safety goggles or a face shield!

   b) Lubricate the cylinder with plenty of honing oil or kerosene, turn on the drill and move the hone up-and-down in the cylinder at a pace that will produce a fine crosshatch pattern on the cylinder walls. Ideally, the crosshatch lines should intersect at approximately a 60-degree angle **(see illustration)**. Be sure to use plenty of lubri-

cant and don't take off any more material than absolutely necessary to produce the desired finish. **Note:** *Piston ring manufacturers may specify a smaller crosshatch angle than the traditional 60-degrees – read and follow any instructions included with the new rings.*

   c) Don't withdraw the hone from the cylinder while it's running. Instead, shut off the drill and continue moving the hone up-and-down in the cylinder until it comes to a complete stop, then compress the stones and withdraw the hone. If you're using a "bottle brush" type hone, stop the drill, then turn the chuck in the normal direction of rotation while withdrawing the hone from the cylinder.

   d) Wipe the oil out of the cylinder and repeat the procedure for the remaining cylinders.

4   After the honing job is complete, chamfer the top edges of the cylinder bores with a small file so the rings won't catch when the pistons are installed. Be very careful not to nick the cylinder walls with the end of the file.

5   The entire engine block must be washed again very thoroughly with warm, soapy water to remove all traces of the abrasive grit produced during the honing operation. **Note:** *The bores can be considered clean when a lint-free white cloth – dampened with clean engine oil- used to wipe them out doesn't pick up any more honing residue, which will show up as gray areas on the cloth.* Be sure to run a brush through all oil holes and galleries and flush them with running water.

6   After rinsing, dry the block and apply a coat of light rust preventive oil to all machined surfaces. Wrap the block in a plastic trash bag to keep it clean and set it aside until reassembly.

17 Pistons/connecting rods – inspection

Refer to illustrations 17.4a, 17.4b, 17.10 and 17.11

1   Before the inspection process can be carried out, the piston/connecting rod assemblies must be cleaned and the original piston rings removed from the pistons. **Note:** *Always use new piston rings when the engine is reassembled.*

2   Using a piston ring installation tool, carefully remove the rings from the pistons. Be careful not to nick or gouge the pistons in the process.

3   Scrape all traces of carbon off the top of the piston. A hand-held wire brush or a piece of fine emery cloth can be used once the majority of the deposits have been scraped away. Do not, under any circumstances, use a wire brush mounted in an electric drill to remove deposits from the pistons. The piston material is soft and may be eroded away by the wire brush.

17.4a   The piston ring grooves can be cleaned with a special tool, as shown here, . . .

17.4b   . . . or a section of a broken ring

4   Use a piston ring groove cleaning tool to remove carbon deposits from the ring grooves. If a tool isn't available, a piece broken off the old ring will do the job. Be very careful to remove only the carbon deposits – don't remove any metal and do not nick or scratch the sides of the ring grooves **(see illustrations)**.

5   Once the deposits have been removed, clean the piston/rod assemblies with solvent and dry them with compressed air (if available). Make sure the oil return holes in the back sides of the ring grooves are clear.

6   If the pistons and cylinder walls aren't damaged or worn excessively, and if the engine block is not rebored, new pistons won't be necessary. Normal piston wear appears as even vertical wear on the piston thrust surfaces and slight looseness of the top ring in its groove. New piston rings, however, should always be used when an engine is rebuilt.

7   Carefully inspect each piston for cracks around the skirt, at the pin bosses and at the ring lands.

8   Look for scoring and scuffing on the thrust faces of the skirt, holes in the piston crown and burned areas at the edge of the crown. If the skirt is scored or scuffed, the engine may have been suffering from overheating and/or abnormal combustion, which caused excessively high operating temperatures. The cooling and lubrication systems should be checked thoroughly. A hole in the piston crown is an indication that abnormal com-

bustion (preignition) was occurring. Burned areas at the edge of the piston crown are usually evidence of spark knock (detonation). If any of the above problems exist, the causes must be corrected or the damage will occur again. The causes may include intake air leaks, incorrect fuel/air mixture, incorrect ignition timing and EGR system malfunctions.

9   Corrosion of the piston, in the form of small pits, indicates coolant is leaking into the combustion chamber and/or the crankcase. Again, the cause must be corrected or the problem may persist in the rebuilt engine.

10   Measure the piston ring side clearance by laying a new piston ring in each ring groove and slipping a feeler gauge in beside it **(see illustration)**. Check the clearance at three or four locations around each groove. Be sure to use the correct ring for each groove – they are different. If the side clearance is greater than specified, new pistons will have to be used.

11   Check the piston-to-bore clearance by measuring the bore (see Section 15) and the piston diameter. Make sure the pistons and bores are correctly matched. Measure the piston across the skirt, at a 90-degree angle to and in-line with the piston pin, 5/8-inch (16 mm) up from the bottom of the skirt **(see illustration)**. Subtract the piston diameter from the bore diameter to obtain the clearance. If it's greater than specified, the block will have to be rebored and new pistons and rings installed.

12   Check the piston-to-rod clearance by twisting the piston and rod in op-

17.10   Check the ring side clearance with a feeler gauge at several points around the groove

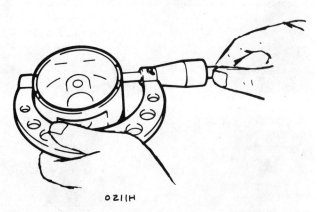

17.11   Measure the piston diameter at a 90-degree angle to the piston pin, 5/8-inch (16 mm) up from the bottom edge of the skirt

18.1   Clean the crankshaft oil passages with a wire or stiff plastic bristle brush and flush them out with solvent

18.3   Rubbing a penny lengthwise on each journal will give you a quick idea of its condition – if copper rubs off the penny and adheres to the crankshaft, the journals should be reground

posite directions. Any noticeable play indicates excessive wear, which must be corrected. The piston/connecting rod assemblies should be taken to an automotive machine shop to have the pistons and rods resized and new pins installed.

13   If the pistons must be removed from the connecting rods for any reason, they should be taken to an automotive machine shop. While they're there, have the connecting rods checked for bend and twist, since automotive machine shops have special equipment for this purpose. **Note:** *Unless new pistons and/or connecting rods must be installed, do not disassemble the pistons and connecting rods.*

14   Check the connecting rods for cracks and other damage. Temporarily remove the rod caps, lift out the old bearing inserts, wipe the rod and cap bearing surfaces clean and inspect them for nicks, gouges and scratches. After checking the rods, replace the old bearings, slip the caps into place and tighten the nuts finger-tight. **Note:** *If the engine is being rebuilt because of a connecting rod knock, be sure to install new rods.*

18   Crankshaft – inspection

Refer to illustrations 18.1, 18.3, 18.4 and 18.6

1   Clean the crankshaft with solvent and dry it with compressed air (if available). Be sure to clean the oil holes with a stiff brush **(see illustration)** and flush them with solvent.

2   Check the main and connecting rod bearing journals for uneven wear, scoring, pits and cracks.

3   Rub a penny across each journal several times **(see illustration)**. If a journal picks up copper from the penny, it's too rough and must be reground.

4   Remove all burrs from the crankshaft oil holes with a stone, file or scraper **(see illustration)**.

5   Check the rest of the crankshaft for cracks and other damage. It should be magnafluxed to reveal hidden cracks – an automotive machine

18.4   Chamfer the oil holes to remove sharp edges that might gouge or scratch the new bearings

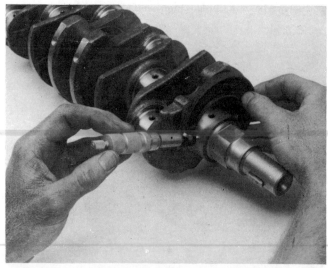

18.6   Measure the diameter of each crankshaft journal at several points to detect taper and out-of-round conditions

FATIGUE FAILURE   **IMPROPER SEATING**

SCRATCHED BY DIRT   **LACK OF OIL**

EXCESSIVE WEAR   **TAPERED JOURNAL**

A2903-1A

19.1   When inspecting the main and connecting rod bearings, look for these problems

shop will handle the procedure.

6   Using a micrometer, measure the diameter of the main and connecting rod journals **(see illustration)** and compare the results to the specifications at the beginning of this Chapter. By measuring the diameter at a number of points around each journal's circumference, you'll be able to determine whether or not the journal is out-of-round. Take the measurement at each end of the journal, near the crank throws, to determine if the journal is tapered.

7   If the crankshaft journals are damaged, tapered, out-of-round or worn beyond the limits given in the Specifications, have the crankshaft reground by an automotive machine shop. Be sure to use the correct size bearing inserts if the crankshaft is reconditioned.

8   Check the oil seal journals at each end of the crankshaft for wear and damage. If the seal has worn a groove in the journal, or if it's nicked or scratched, the new seal may leak when the engine is reassembled. In some cases, an automotive machine shop may be able to repair the journal by pressing on a thin sleeve.

If repair isn't feasible, a new or different crankshaft should be installed.

9   Refer to Section 19 and examine the main and rod bearing inserts.

---

19   Main and connecting rod bearings – inspection and selection

Inspection

Refer to illustration 19.1

1   Even though the main and connecting rod bearings should be re-

placed with new ones during the engine overhaul, the old bearings should be retained for close examination, as they may reveal valuable information about the condition of the engine **(see illustration)**.

2   Bearing failure occurs because of lack of lubrication, the presence of dirt or other foreign particles, overloading the engine and corrosion. Regardless of the cause of bearing failure, it must be corrected before the engine is reassembled to prevent it from happening again.

3   When examining the bearings, remove them from the engine block, the main bearing caps or cap assembly, the connecting rods and the rod caps and lay them out on a clean surface in the same general position as their location in the engine. This will enable you to match any bearing problems with the corresponding crankshaft journal.

4   Dirt and other foreign particles get into the engine in a variety of ways. It may be left in the engine during assembly, or it may pass through filters or the PCV system. It may get into the oil, and from there into the bearings. Metal chips from machining operations and normal engine wear are often present. Abrasives are sometimes left in engine components after reconditioning, especially when parts aren't thoroughly cleaned using the proper cleaning methods. Whatever the source, these foreign objects often end up embedded in the soft bearing material and are easily recognized. Large particles will not embed in the bearing and will score or gouge the bearing and journal. The best prevention for this cause of bearing failure is to clean all parts thoroughly and keep everything spotlessly clean during engine assembly. Frequent and regular engine oil and filter changes are also recommended.

5   Lack of lubrication (or lubrication breakdown) has a number of interrelated causes. Excessive heat (which thins the oil), overloading (which squeezes the oil from the bearing face) and oil leakage or throw off (from excessive bearing clearances, worn oil pump or high engine speeds) all contribute to lubrication breakdown. Blocked oil passages, which usually are the result of misaligned oil holes in a bearing shell, will also oil starve a bearing and destroy it. When lack of lubrication is the cause of bearing failure, the bearing material is wiped or extruded from the steel backing of the bearing. Temperatures may increase to the point where the steel backing turns blue from overheating.

6   Driving habits can have a definite effect on bearing life. Full throttle, low speed operation (lugging the engine) puts very high loads on bearings, which tends to squeeze out the oil film. These loads cause the bearings to flex, which produces fine cracks in the bearing face (fatigue failure). Eventually the bearing material will loosen in pieces and tear away from the steel backing. Short trip driving leads to corrosion of bearings because insufficient engine heat is produced to drive off the condensed water and corrosive gases. These products collect in the engine oil, forming acid and sludge. As the oil is carried to the engine bearings, the acid attacks and corrodes the bearing material.

7   Incorrect bearing installation during engine assembly will lead to bearing failure as well. Tight fitting bearings leave insufficient bearing oil clearance and will result in oil starvation. Dirt or foreign particles trapped behind a bearing insert result in high spots on the bearing, which lead to failure.

Selection

Refer to illustrations 19.10, 19.11, 19.12, 19.14, 19.15 and 19.16

8   If the original bearings are worn or damaged, or if the oil clearances are incorrect (Section 22 or 23), the following procedures should be used to select the correct new bearings for engine reassembly. However, if the crankshaft has been reground, new undersize bearings must be installed – the following procedure should not be used if undersize bearings are required! The automotive machine shop that reconditions the crankshaft will provide or help you select the correct size bearings. Regardless of how the bearing sizes are determined, use the oil clearance, measured with Plastigage, as a guide to ensure the bearings are the right size.

Main bearings

9   If you need to use a STANDARD size main bearing, install one that has the same color code as the original bearing. The color code is on the edge of the bearing.

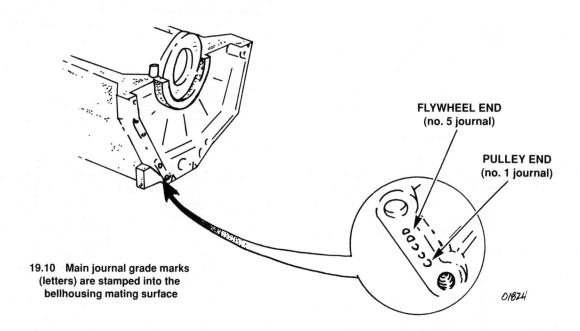

19.10   Main journal grade marks (letters) are stamped into the bellhousing mating surface

FLYWHEEL END
(no. 5 journal)

PULLEY END
(no. 1 journal)

Main Journal Code Locations (Numbers)

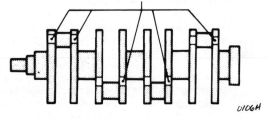

19.11   The main bearing journal grade numbers are stamped adjacent to their respective journals

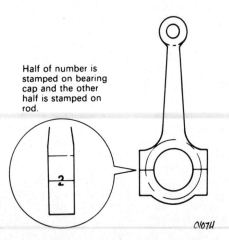

Half of number is stamped on bearing cap and the other half is stamped on rod.

19.14   The number stamped on the parting surface of the connecting rod and cap indicates the big-end bearing bore size – it does NOT indicate the cylinder number it came from

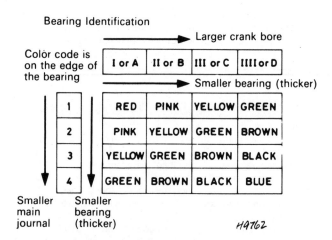

Bearing Identification

Color code is on the edge of the bearing

Larger crank bore →

Smaller bearing (thicker) →

	I or A	II or B	III or C	IIII or D
1	RED	PINK	YELLOW	GREEN
2	PINK	YELLOW	GREEN	BROWN
3	YELLOW	GREEN	BROWN	BLACK
4	GREEN	BROWN	BLACK	BLUE

Smaller main journal ↓

Smaller bearing (thicker) ↓

19.12   Find the correct main bearing color code by using the letter or Roman numeral on the block and the Arabic number on the crankshaft – example: C3 would be Brown

10   If the color code on the original main bearing has been obscured, locate the main journal grade marks stamped into the bellhousing or oil pan mating surface on the engine block **(see illustration)**.

11   Locate the main journal grade numbers on the crankshaft as well **(see illustration)**.

12   Use the accompanying chart to determine the correct bearings for each journal **(see illustration)**.

Connecting rod bearings

13   If you need to use a STANDARD size rod bearing, install one that has the same color code as the original.

14   If the color code has been obscured, locate the number stamped on each connecting rod cap **(see illustration)**. This code indicates the connecting rod big-end bearing bore size.

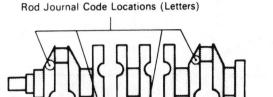

Rod Journal Code Locations (Letters)

0108H

19.15   The connecting rod bearing journal code letters are stamped adjacent to their respective journals

15   Locate the letters stamped on the crankshaft **(see illustration)**. These letters denote the size of their respective connecting rod journals.
16   Use the accompanying chart **(see illustration)** to determine the correct bearings for each journal.

All bearings

17   Remember, the oil clearance is the final judge when selecting new bearing sizes. If you have any questions or are unsure which bearings to use, get help from a dealer parts or service department.
18   **Note:** *If new connecting rod or main bearings are installed, after the engine is reassembled it must be run at idle speed until normal operating temperature is reached, then allowed to idle for an additional 15-minutes.*

20   Engine overhaul – reassembly sequence

1   Before beginning engine reassembly, make sure you have all the necessary new parts, gaskets and seals as well as the following items on hand:

Common hand tools
A 1/2-inch drive torque wrench
Piston ring installation tool
Piston ring compressor
Vibration damper installation tool
Short lengths of rubber or plastic hose
to fit over connecting rod bolts
Plastigage
Feeler gauges
A fine-tooth file
New engine oil
Engine assembly lube or moly-base grease
Gasket sealant
Thread locking compound

2   In order to save time and avoid problems, engine reassembly must be done in the following general order:

Crankshaft and main bearings
Piston rings
Piston/connecting rod assemblies
Rear main oil seal/housing
Oil pump
Oil pick-up tube/screen assembly
Oil pan
Cylinder head
Camshaft and rocker arms
Timing belt and sprockets
Timing belt covers
Intake and exhaust manifolds
Camshaft cover
Flywheel/driveplate

Bearing Identification

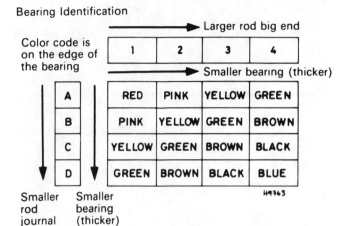

	1	2	3	4
A	RED	PINK	YELLOW	GREEN
B	PINK	YELLOW	GREEN	BROWN
C	YELLOW	GREEN	BROWN	BLACK
D	GREEN	BROWN	BLACK	BLUE

H9763

Color code is on the edge of the bearing — Larger rod big end — Smaller bearing (thicker)

Smaller rod journal   Smaller bearing (thicker)

19.16   Find the correct connecting rod bearing color code by using the letter on each crankshaft throw and the number on the respective connecting rod – example: D4 would be Blue

21   Piston rings – installation

Refer to illustrations 21.3, 21.4, 21.5, 21.9a, 21.9b and 21.12

1   Before installing the new piston rings, the ring end gaps must be checked. It's assumed the piston ring side clearance has been checked and verified correct (Section 17).
2   Lay out the piston/connecting rod assemblies and the new ring sets so the ring sets will be matched with the same piston and cylinder during the end gap measurement and engine assembly.
3   Insert the top (number one) ring into the first cylinder and square it up with the cylinder walls by pushing it in with the top of the piston **(see illustration)**. The ring should be near the bottom of the cylinder, at the lower limit of ring travel.

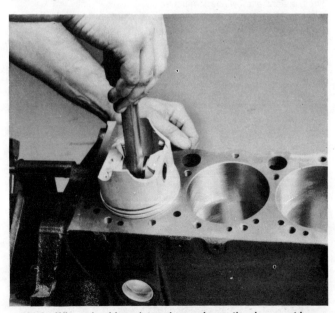

21.3   When checking piston ring end gap, the ring must be square in the cylinder bore (this is done by pushing the ring down with the top of a piston as shown)

21.4   With the ring square in the cylinder, measure the end gap with a feeler gauge

21.5   If the end gap is too small, clamp a file in a vise and file the ring ends – from the outside in only – to enlarge the gap slightly

4   To measure the end gap, slip feeler gauges between the ends of the ring until a gauge equal to the gap width is found **(see illustration)**. The feeler gauge should slide between the ring ends with a slight amount of drag. Compare the measurement to the Specifications. If the gap is larger or smaller than specified, double-check to make sure you have the correct rings before proceeding.

5   If the gap is too small, it must be enlarged or the ring ends may come in contact with each other during engine operation, which can cause serious damage to the engine. The end gap can be increased by filing the ring ends very carefully with a fine file. Mount the file in a vise equipped with soft jaws, slip the ring over the file with the ends contacting the file face and slowly move the ring to remove material from the ends. When performing this operation, file only from the outside in **(see illustration)**.

6   Excess end gap isn't critical unless it's greater than 0.040-inch. Again, double-check to make sure you have the correct rings for the engine.

7   Repeat the procedure for each ring that will be installed in the first cylinder and for each ring in the remaining cylinders. Remember to keep rings, pistons and cylinders matched up.

8   Once the ring end gaps have been checked/corrected, the rings can be installed on the pistons.

9   The oil control ring (lowest one on the piston) is installed first. It's usu-

ally composed of three separate components. Slip the spacer/expander into the groove **(see illustration)**. If an anti-rotation tang is used, make sure it's inserted into the drilled hole in the ring groove. Next, install the lower side rail. Don't use a piston ring installation tool on the oil ring side rails, as they may be damaged. Instead, place one end of the side rail into the groove between the spacer/expander and the ring land, hold it firmly in place and slide a finger around the piston while pushing the rail into the groove **(see illustration)**. Next, install the upper side rail in the same manner.

10   After the three oil ring components have been installed, check to make sure both the upper and lower side rails can be turned smoothly in the ring groove.

11   The number two (middle) ring is installed next. It's usually stamped with a mark which must face up, toward the top of the piston. **Note:** *Always follow the instructions printed on the ring package or box – different manufacturers may require different approaches. Do not mix up the top and middle rings, as they have different cross sections.*

12   Use a piston ring installation tool and make sure the identification mark is facing the top of the piston, then slip the ring into the middle groove on the piston **(see illustration)**. Don't expand the ring any more than necessary to slide it over the piston.

13   Install the number one (top) ring in the same manner. Make sure the

21.9a   Installing the spacer/expander in the oil control ring groove

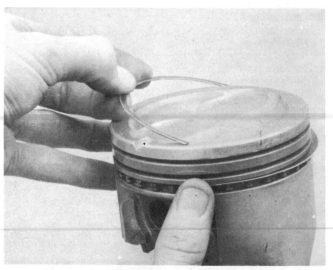

21.9b   DO NOT use a piston ring installation tool when installing the oil ring side rails

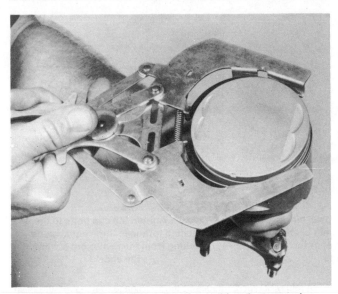

21.12   Install the compression rings with a ring expander

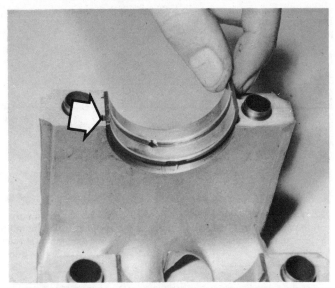

22.5   Make sure the bearing tang fits securely into the recess in the cap (arrow) – also, be sure to match the holes in the bearings with the oil holes in the caps and block

mark is facing up. Be careful not to confuse the number one and number two rings.

14   Repeat the procedure for the remaining pistons and rings.

22   Crankshaft – installation and main bearing oil clearance check

Refer to illustrations 22.5, 22.6a, 22.6b, 22.11, 22.12, 22.13 and 22.15

1   Crankshaft installation is the first step in engine reassembly. It's assumed at this point that the engine block and crankshaft have been cleaned, inspected and repaired or reconditioned.

2   Position the engine with the bottom facing up.

3   Remove the main bearing cap assembly or bridge and caps. If individual caps are used, lay them out in the proper order to ensure correct installation.

4   If they're still in place, remove the original bearing inserts from the block and caps or cap assembly. Wipe the bearing surfaces in the block and caps with a clean, lint-free cloth. They must be kept spotlessly clean.

Main bearing oil clearance check

5   Clean the back sides of the new main bearing inserts and lay one in each main bearing saddle in the block. Lay the other bearing from each set in the corresponding main bearing cap. Make sure the tang on the bearing insert fits into the recess in the block or cap **(see illustration)**. **Caution:** *The oil holes in the block or caps must line up with the oil hole in each bearing insert. Do not hammer the bearing into place and don't nick or gouge the bearing faces. No lubrication should be used at this time.*

6   The thrust bearings must be installed in the center main bearing cap and saddle **(see illustrations)**.

7   Clean the faces of the bearings in the block and the crankshaft main bearing journals with a clean, lint-free cloth.

8   Check or clean the oil holes in the crankshaft, as any dirt here can only go one way – straight through the new bearings.

9   Once you're certain the crankshaft is clean, carefully lay it in position in the main bearings.

10   Before the crankshaft can be permanently installed, the main bearing oil clearance must be checked.

11   Cut several pieces of the appropriate size Plastigage (they must be slightly shorter than the width of the main bearings) and place one piece on

22.6a   Place the lower thrust bearing in position at the center crankshaft journal with the oil grooves facing OUT, then rotate it into position in the block by turning the crankshaft

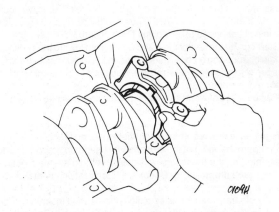

22.6b   Install the thrust bearing in the center main bearing cap with the oil grooves facing OUT

22.11   Lay the Plastigage strips (arrow) on the main bearing journals, parallel to the crankshaft centerline

22.12   Make sure the dowel pins are in place, then install the main bearing cap assembly (shown here) or the caps and bridge

22.13   Tighten the cap bolts to the specified torque in three equal steps, working from the center out toward the ends

22.15   Compare the width of the crushed Plastigage to the scale on the envelope to determine the main bearing oil clearance (always take the measurement at the widest point of the Plastigage); be sure to use the correct scale – inch and metric scales are included

each crankshaft main bearing journal, parallel with the journal axis **(see illustration)**.

12   Clean the faces of the bearings in the caps and install the one-piece cap assembly or the individual bearing caps in their respective positions (don't mix them up). Make sure the dowel pins are in place **(see illustration)**. Install the bridge and/or bolts. Don't disturb the Plastigage.

13   Starting with the center main and working out toward the ends, tighten the main bearing cap bolts, in three steps, to the torque listed in this Chapter's specifications **(see illustration)**. Don't rotate the crankshaft at any time during this operation.

14   Remove the bolts and carefully lift off the main bearing cap assembly or bridge and caps. Keep them in order. Don't disturb the Plastigage or rotate the crankshaft. If any of the main bearing caps are difficult to remove, tap them gently with a soft-face hammer to loosen them.

15   Compare the width of the crushed Plastigage on each journal to the scale printed on the Plastigage envelope to obtain the main bearing oil clearance **(see illustration)**. Check the Specifications to make sure it's correct.

16   If the clearance is not as specified, the bearing inserts may be the wrong size (which means different ones will be required). Before deciding different inserts are needed, make sure no dirt or oil was between the bearing inserts and the caps or block when the clearance was measured. If the Plastigage was wider at one end than the other, the journal may be tapered (refer to Section 18).

17   Carefully scrape all traces of the Plastigage material off the main bearing journals and/or the bearing faces. Use your fingernail or the edge of a credit card – don't nick or scratch the bearing faces.

Final crankshaft installation

Note: *If the engine has individual main bearing caps and a bridge, install the pistons and connecting rods first (Section 24), then install the main bearing caps and bridge.*

18   Carefully lift the crankshaft out of the engine.

19   Clean the bearing faces in the block, then apply a thin, uniform layer of moly-base grease or engine assembly lube to each of the bearing surfaces. Be sure to coat the grooved sides of the thrust bearings.

20   Make sure the crankshaft journals are clean, then lay the crankshaft back in place in the block.

21   Clean the faces of the bearings in the caps, then lubricate them.

22   Install the cap assembly or the caps and bridge. Be sure to install the thrust bearings. **Note:** *On engines with individual bearing caps and a bridge, install a new O-ring between the bridge and center main bearing cap.*

23   Install the bolts finger-tight.

24   Tighten the bearing cap bolts to the specified torque – work from the center out and approach the final torque in three steps.

25   On manual transaxle equipped models, install a new pilot bearing in the end of the crankshaft (see Chapter 8).

26   Rotate the crankshaft a number of times by hand to check for any obvious binding.

27   Check the crankshaft end play with a feeler gauge or a dial indicator as described in Section 13. The end play should be correct if the crankshaft thrust faces aren't worn or damaged and new thrust bearings have been installed.

28   Install the rear main oil seal and housing.

23   Rear main oil seal installation

1   The crankshaft must be installed first and the main bearing cap assembly or caps and bridge bolted in place, then the new seal should be installed in the housing and the housing bolted to the block.

2   Check the seal contact surface on the crankshaft very carefully for scratches and nicks that could damage the new seal lip and cause oil leaks. If the crankshaft is damaged, the only alternative is a new or different crankshaft.

3   The old seal can be removed from the housing by driving it out from the back side with a hammer and punch. Be sure to note how far it's recessed into the bore before removing it; the new seal will have to be recessed an equal amount. Be very careful not to scratch or otherwise damage the bore in the housing or oil leaks could develop.

4   Make sure the housing is clean, then apply a thin coat of engine oil to the outer edge of the new seal. The seal must be pressed squarely into the

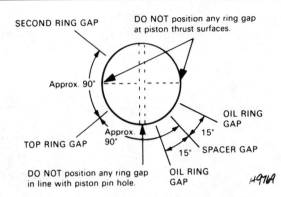

24.5   **Position the piston ring gaps as shown here before installing the piston/connecting rod assemblies in the engine**

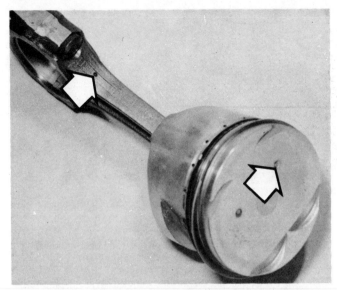

24.9   **When installing the pistons, the small holes (arrows) must face the intake manifold side; if there are arrows on top of the piston, they should face the drivebelt end of the engine**

24.11   **The piston can be tapped (gently) into the cylinder bore with the end of a wooden or plastic hammer handle**

bore, so hammering it into place isn't recommended. If you don't have access to a press, sandwich the housing and seal between two smooth pieces of wood and press the seal into place with the jaws of a large vise. The pieces of wood must be thick enough to distribute the force evenly around the entire circumference of the seal. Work slowly and make sure the seal enters the bore squarely. **Note:** *On 1988 and later models, the seal must be pressed in until there's a gap of 0.008 to 0.020-inch between the inner edge of the seal and the lip in the housing bore. Use a feeler gauge to confirm the width of the gap all the way around the edge. DO NOT bottom the seal against the lip in the bore.*

5   As a last resort, the seal can be tapped into the housing with a hammer. Use a block of wood to distribute the force evenly and make sure the seal is driven in squarely.

6   The seal lips must be lubricated with clean engine oil or moly-base grease before the seal/housing is slipped over the crankshaft and bolted to the block. Use a new gasket and RTV sealant.

7   Tighten the bolts in 1/4-turn increments until they're all secure.

24   Pistons/connecting rods – installation and rod bearing oil clearance check

Refer to illustrations 24.5, 24.9, 24.11, 24.13 and 24.17

1   Before installing the piston/connecting rod assemblies, the cylinder walls must be perfectly clean, the top edge of each cylinder must be chamfered, and the crankshaft must be in place. **Note:** *If the engine has individual main bearing caps and a bridge, install the pistons and connecting rods first, then install the main bearing caps and bridge.*

2   Remove the cap from the end of the number one connecting rod (refer to the marks made during removal). Remove the original bearing inserts and wipe the bearing surfaces of the connecting rod and cap with a clean, lint-free cloth. They must be kept spotlessly clean.

Connecting rod bearing oil clearance check

3   Clean the back side of the new upper bearing insert, then lay it in place in the connecting rod. Make sure the tang on the bearing fits into the recess in the rod. Don't hammer the bearing insert into place and be very careful not to nick or gouge the bearing face. Don't lubricate the bearing at this time.

4   Clean the back side of the other bearing insert and install it in the rod cap. Again, make sure the tang on the bearing fits into the recess in the cap, and don't apply any lubricant. It's critically important that the mating surfaces of the bearing and connecting rod are perfectly clean and oil free when they're assembled.

5   Position the piston ring gaps at intervals around the piston **(see illustration)**.

6   Slip a section of plastic or rubber hose over each connecting rod cap bolt.

7   Lubricate the piston and rings with clean engine oil and attach a piston ring compressor to the piston. Leave the skirt protruding about 1/4-inch to guide the piston into the cylinder. The rings must be compressed until

they're flush with the piston.

8   Rotate the crankshaft until the number one connecting rod journal is at BDC (bottom dead center) and apply a coat of engine oil to the cylinder walls.

9   With the mark or arrow on top of the piston facing the correct way **(see illustration)**, gently insert the piston/connecting rod assembly into the number one cylinder bore and rest the bottom edge of the ring compressor on the engine block.

10   Tap the top edge of the ring compressor to make sure it's contacting the block around its entire circumference.

11   Gently tap on the top of the piston with the end of a wooden or plastic hammer handle **(see illustration)** while guiding the end of the connecting rod into place on the crankshaft journal. The piston rings may try to pop out of the ring compressor just before entering the cylinder bore, so keep some downward pressure on the ring compressor. Work slowly – if any resistance is felt as the piston enters the cylinder, stop immediately! Find out what's hanging up and fix it before proceeding. Do not, for any reason, force the piston into the cylinder; you might break a ring and/or the piston.

12   Once the piston/connecting rod assembly is installed, the connecting rod bearing oil clearance must be checked before the rod cap is permanently bolted in place.

13   Cut a piece of the appropriate size Plastigage slightly shorter than the width of the connecting rod bearing and lay it in place on the number one

24.13   Lay the Plastigage strips on each rod bearing journal, parallel to the crankshaft centerline

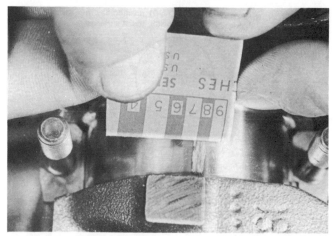

24.17   Measuring the width of the crushed Plastigage to determine the rod bearing oil clearance (be sure to use the correct scale – inch and metric scales are included)

connecting rod journal, parallel with the journal axis (see illustration).

14   Clean the connecting rod cap bearing face, remove the protective hoses from the connecting rod bolts and install the rod cap. Make sure the mating mark on the cap is on the same side as the mark on the connecting rod.

15   Install the nuts and tighten them to the specified torque, working up to it in three steps. **Note:** *Use a thin-wall socket to avoid erroneous torque readings that can result if the socket is wedged between the rod cap and nut. If the socket tends to wedge itself between the nut and the cap, lift up on it slightly until it no longer contacts the cap. Do not rotate the crankshaft at any time during this operation.*

16   Remove the nuts and detach the rod cap, being very careful not to disturb the Plastigage.

17   Compare the width of the crushed Plastigage to the scale printed on the Plastigage envelope to obtain the oil clearance (see illustration). Compare it to the Specifications to make sure the clearance is correct.

18   If the clearance is not as specified, the bearing inserts may be the wrong size (which means different ones will be required). Before deciding different inserts are needed, make sure no dirt or oil was between the bearing insert and the connecting rod or cap when the clearance was measured. Also, recheck the journal diameter. If the plastigage was wider at one end than the other, the journal may be tapered (see Section 18).

Final connecting rod installation

19   Carefully scrape all traces of Plastigage material off the rod journal and/or bearing face. Be very careful not to scratch the bearing – use your fingernail or the edge of a credit card.

20   Make sure the bearing faces are perfectly clean, then apply a uniform layer of clean moly-base grease or engine assembly lube to both of them. You'll have to push the piston into the cylinder to expose the face of the bearing insert in the connecting rod – be sure to slip the protective hoses over the rod bolts first.

21   Slide the connecting rod back into place on the journal, remove the protective hoses from the rod cap bolts, install the rod cap and tighten the nuts to the specified torque. Again, work up to the torque in three steps.

22   Repeat the entire procedure for the remaining pistons/connecting rods.

23   The important points to remember are . . .

   a) Keep the back sides of the bearing inserts and the insides of the connecting rods and caps perfectly clean when assembling them.

   b) Make sure you have the correct piston/rod assembly for each cylinder.

   c) The arrow on the piston must face the front (drivebelt end) of the engine; the dimples, if used, must face the intake manifold side.

   d) Lubricate the cylinder walls with clean oil.

   e) Lubricate the bearing faces when installing the rod caps after the oil clearance has been checked.

   f) Be sure the match marks on the connecting rod and cap line up.

24   After all the piston/connecting rod assemblies have been properly in-

stalled, rotate the crankshaft a number of times by hand to check for any obvious binding.

25   As a final step, the connecting rod end play must be checked. Refer to Section 12 for this procedure.

26   Compare the measured end play to the Specifications to make sure it's correct. If it was correct before disassembly and the original crankshaft and rods were reinstalled, it should still be right. If new rods or a new crankshaft were installed, the end play may be inadequate. If so, the rods will have to be removed and taken to an automotive machine shop for resizing.

27   If necessary, install the main bearing caps and bridge (see Section 22).

25   Initial start-up and break-in after overhaul

Warning: *Have a fire extinguisher handy when starting the engine for the first time.*

1   Once the engine has been installed in the vehicle, double-check the engine oil and coolant levels.

2   With the spark plugs out of the engine and the ignition system disabled (see Section 3), crank the engine until oil pressure registers on the gauge or the light goes out.

3   Install the spark plugs, hook up the plug wires and restore the ignition system functions (Section 3).

4   Start the engine. It may take a few moments for the fuel system to build up pressure, but the engine should start without a great deal of effort. **Note:** *If backfiring occurs through the carburetor or throttle body, recheck the valve timing and ignition timing.*

5   After the engine starts, it should be allowed to warm up to normal operating temperature. **Note:** *If new main or connecting rod bearings were installed, run the engine at idle speed until it reaches normal operating temperature, then continue to run it at idle for approximately 15-minutes. While the engine is warming up, make a thorough check for fuel, oil and coolant leaks.*

6   Shut the engine off and recheck the engine oil and coolant levels.

7   Drive the vehicle to an area with minimum traffic, accelerate at full throttle from 30 to 50 mph, then allow the vehicle to slow to 30 mph with the throttle closed. Repeat the procedure 10 or 12 times. This will load the piston rings and cause them to seat properly against the cylinder walls. Check again for oil and coolant leaks.

8   Drive the vehicle gently for the first 500 miles (no sustained high speeds) and keep a constant check on the oil level. It's not unusual for an engine to use oil during the break-in period.

9   At approximately 500 to 600 miles, change the oil and filter.

10   For the next few hundred miles, drive the vehicle normally. Do not pamper it or abuse it.

11   After 2000 miles, change the oil and filter again and consider the engine broken in.

Chapter 3   Cooling, heating and air conditioning systems

Contents

Specifications

General

Coolant capacity .... See Chapter 1
Drivebelt deflection .... See Chapter 1
Radiator pressure cap rating .... 11 to 15 psi

Torque specifications   Ft-lbs

Water pump pulley bolts 9
Thermostat housing bolts 9
Water pump attaching bolts 9

---

1   General information

Refer to illustrations 1.1, 1.2 and 1.3

Engine cooling system

All vehicles covered by this manual employ a pressurized engine cooling system with thermostatically controlled coolant circulation **(see illustration)**. An impeller type water pump mounted on the drivebelt end of the block pumps coolant through the engine. The coolant flows around each cylinder and toward the rear of the engine. Cast-in coolant passages direct coolant around the intake and exhaust ports, near the spark plug areas and in close proximity to the exhaust valve guides.

A wax pellet type thermostat is located in a housing near the drivebelt end of the engine **(see illustration)**. During warm up, the closed thermostat prevents coolant from circulating through the radiator. As the engine nears normal operating temperature, the thermostat opens and allows hot coolant to travel through the radiator, where it's cooled before returning to the engine.

The cooling system is sealed by a pressure type radiator cap, which raises the boiling point of the coolant and increases the cooling efficiency of the radiator. If the system pressure exceeds the cap pressure relief value, the excess pressure in the system forces the spring-loaded valve inside the cap off its seat and allows the coolant to escape through the overflow tube into a coolant reservoir. When the system cools, the excess coolant is automatically drawn from the reservoir back into the radiator **(see illustration)**.

The coolant reservoir does double duty as both the point at which fresh coolant is added to the cooling system to maintain the proper fluid level and as a holding tank for overheated coolant.

This type of cooling system is known as a closed design because coolant that escapes past the pressure cap is saved and reused.

Heating system

The heating system consists of a blower fan and heater core located in the heater box, the hoses connecting the heater core to the engine cooling system and the heater/air conditioning control head on the dashboard. Hot engine coolant is circulated through the heater core. When the heater mode is activated, a flap door opens to expose the heater box to the pas-senger compartment. A fan switch on the control head activates the blower motor, which forces air through the core, heating the air.

Air conditioning system

The air conditioning system consists of a condenser mounted in front of the radiator, an evaporator mounted adjacent to the heater core, a compressor mounted on the engine, a filter-drier (accumulator) which contains a high pressure relief valve and the plumbing connecting all of the above components.

A blower fan forces the warmer air of the passenger compartment through the evaporator core (sort of a radiator-in-reverse), transferring the heat from the air to the refrigerant. The liquid refrigerant boils off into low pressure vapor, taking the heat with it when it leaves the evaporator.

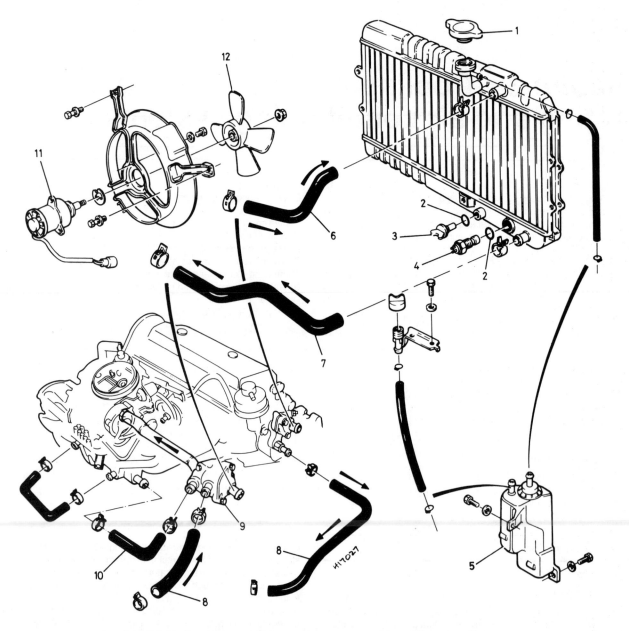

1.1   Principal components of the cooling system – carbureted engine shown

1	Radiator pressure cap	4	Thermo-switch	7	Lower radiator hose
2	O-rings	5	Coolant reservoir	8	Heater hoses
3	Drain plug	6	Upper radiator hose	9	Thermostat housing

10	Bypass inlet hose
11	Fan motor
12	Fan

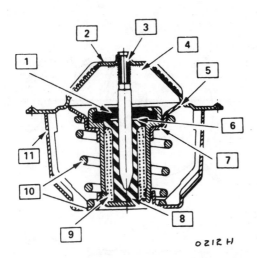

1.2 Pellet type thermostat – cutaway view

1 Flange seal	5 Valve seat	8 Rubber diaphragm
2 Flange	6 Teflon seal	9 Wax pellet
3 Piston	7 Valve	10 Coil spring
4 Nut		11 Frame

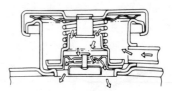

VACUUM RELIEF

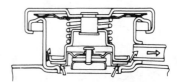

PRESSURE RELIEF

1.3 Pressure-type radiator cap

2 Antifreeze – general information

Warning: *Do not allow antifreeze to come in contact with your skin or painted surfaces of the vehicle. Rinse off spills immediately with plenty of water. Never leave anti-freeze lying around in an open container or in a puddle on the driveway or garage floor. Children and animals are attracted by its sweet smell and may drink it. Anti-freeze is toxic, so use good sense when disposing of it. Some communities maintain toxic material disposal sites and/or offer regular pick-up of hazardous materials. Anti-freeze is also combustible, so don't store or use it near open flames.*

The cooling system should be filled with a water/ethylene glycol-based antifreeze solution, which will prevent freezing down to at least -20-degrees F, or lower if local climate requires it. It also provides protection against corrosion and increases the coolant boiling point.

The cooling system should be drained, flushed and refilled at the specified intervals (see Chapter 1). Old or contaminated antifreeze solutions are likely to cause damage and encourage the formation of rust and scale in the system. Use distilled water with the antifreeze.

Before adding antifreeze, check all hose connections, because antifreeze tends to search out and leak through very minute openings. Engines don't normally consume coolant, so if the level goes down, find the cause and correct it.

The exact mixture of antifreeze-to-water which you should use depends on the relative weather conditions. The mixture should contain at least 50-percent antifreeze, but should never contain more than 70-percent antifreeze. Consult the mixture ratio chart on the antifreeze container before adding coolant. Hydrometers, used to test the coolant, are available at most auto parts stores. Use antifreeze which meets the vehicle manufacturer's specifications.

3 Thermostat – check and replacement

Warning: *Do not allow antifreeze to come in contact with your skin or painted surfaces of the vehicle. Rinse off spills immediately with plenty of water. Never leave anti-freeze lying around in an open container or in a puddle on the driveway or garage floor. Children and animals are attracted by its sweet smell and may drink it. Anti-freeze is toxic, so use good sense*

when disposing of it. Some communities maintain toxic material disposal sites and/or offer regular pick-up of hazardous materials. Anti-freeze is also combustible, so don't store or use it near open flames.

Do not remove the radiator cap, drain the coolant or replace the thermostat until the engine has cooled completely.

Check

1   Before assuming the thermostat is to blame for a cooling system problem, check the coolant level, drivebelt tension (Chapter 1) and temperature gauge (or light) operation.

2   If the engine seems to be taking a long time to warm up (based on heater output or temperature gauge operation), the thermostat is probably stuck open. Replace the thermostat with a new one.

3   If the engine runs hot, use your hand to check the temperature of the upper radiator hose. If the hose isn't hot, but the engine is, the thermostat is probably stuck closed, preventing the coolant inside the engine from escaping to the radiator. Replace the thermostat. **Caution:** *Don't drive the vehicle without a thermostat. The computer may stay in open loop, causing emissions and fuel economy to suffer.*

4   If the upper radiator hose is hot, it means the coolant is flowing and the thermostat is open. Consult the Troubleshooting Section at the front of this manual for cooling system diagnosis.

Replacement

Refer to illustrations 3.10 and 3.13

5   Disconnect the negative battery cable from the battery.

6   Drain the cooling system (see Chapter 1). If the coolant is relatively new or in good condition (see Chapter 1), save it and reuse it.

7   Follow the lower radiator hose to the engine to locate the thermostat housing.

8   Compress the hose clamp with pliers, then slide the clamp away from the thermostat housing. Detach the hose from the fitting. If it's stuck, grasp it near the end with a pair of adjustable pliers and twist it to break the seal, then pull it off. If the hose is old or deteriorated, cut it off and install a new one.

9   If the outer surface of the large fitting that mates with the hose is deteriorated (corroded, pitted, etc.) it may be damaged further by hose removal. If it is, the thermostat housing cover will have to be replaced.

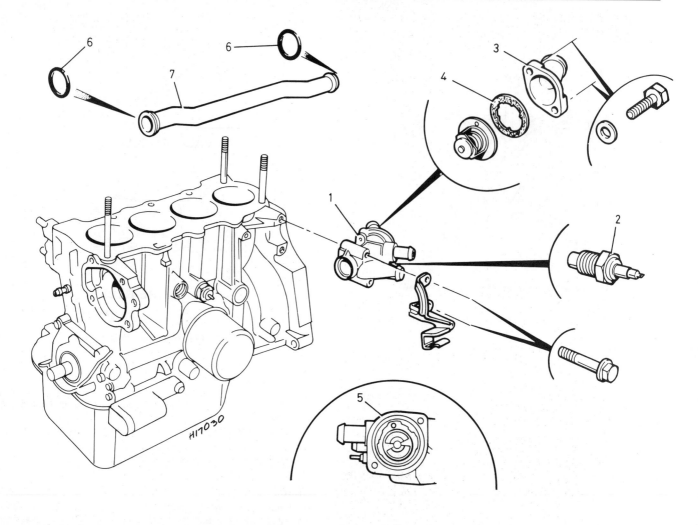

3.10 Thermostat and associated components – exploded view

1	Thermostat housing	4	Gasket	6	O-ring
2	Temperature gauge sending unit	5	Thermostat	7	Water pump inlet pipe
3	Thermostat housing cover				

10   Remove the bolts and detach the housing cover **(see illustration)**. If the cover is stuck, tap it with a soft-face hammer to jar it loose. Be prepared for some coolant to spill as the gasket seal is broken.

11   Note how it's installed (which end is facing out), then remove the thermostat.

12   Stuff a rag into the engine opening, then remove all traces of old gasket material and sealant from the housing and cover with a gasket scraper. Remove the rag from the opening and clean the gasket mating surfaces with lacquer thinner or acetone.

13   Install the new thermostat in the housing. Make sure the correct end faces out – the spring end is normally directed into the engine **(see illustration)**. Make sure the air bleed is at the top.

14   Apply a thin, uniform layer of RTV sealant to both sides of the new seal and position it on the housing.

15   Install the cover and bolts. Tighten the bolts to the torque listed in this Chapter's specifications.

16   Reattach the hose to the fitting. Use a new hose clamp and tighten it securely.

17   Refill the cooling system (Chapter 1).

18   Start the engine and allow it to reach normal operating temperature, then check for leaks and proper thermostat operation (as described in Steps 2 through 4).

3.13 Install the thermostat with the air bleed (arrow) at the top and the spring side toward the engine

4.2a   Slide the rubber boot back to expose the terminals of the thermal fan switch

4.2b   To test the fan circuit, disconnect the wires from the switch and use a jumper wire to connect them – to remove the switch, drain the cooling system and unscrew the switch (use Teflon tape or other sealant on the threads of the switch when installing it)

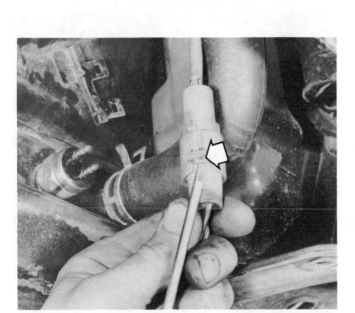

4.6   The fan motor electrical connector is located adjacent to the fan motor – lift up on the lock tab (arrow) and unplug it

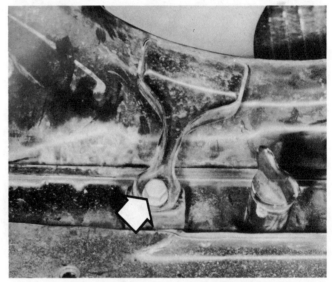

4.9a   Remove the bolt that secures the fan assembly to the lower section of the radiator

---

4   Engine cooling fan – check, removal and installation

Warning: *To avoid possible injury or damage, DO NOT operate the engine with a damaged fan. Do not attempt to repair fan blades – replace a damaged fan with a new one.*

Check

Refer to illustrations 4.2a and 4.2b

1   To test the motor, unplug the electrical connector at the motor and use jumper wires to connect the fan directly to the battery. If the fan still doesn't work, replace the motor.

2   If the motor tested OK, the fault lies in the thermal fan switch or the wiring which connects the components. To test the circuit, detach the wires from the fan switch, located at the bottom of the radiator **(see illustrations)**, and connect a jumper wire between the two wires. With the igni-

tion turned to the On position (but the engine off for safety) the fan should come on. If the fan now works, the fault lies in the thermal fan switch.

3   If the fan does not come on, carefully check all wiring and connections. If no obvious problems are found, further diagnosis should be done by a dealer service department or repair shop.

Removal and installation

Refer to illustrations 4.6, 4.9a and 4.9b

4   Disconnect the negative battery cable from the battery.

5   Remove the fan wire harness from the clips.

6   Lift up on the connector lock tabs and unplug the fan wire harness **(see illustration)**.

7   Remove the coolant reservoir (see Section 6).

8   Drain the coolant (see Chapter 1) and remove the upper and lower radiator hoses.

9   Remove the throttle body air duct (if equipped) for access, then unbolt the fan bracket and shroud assembly **(see illustrations)**. Carefully lift the

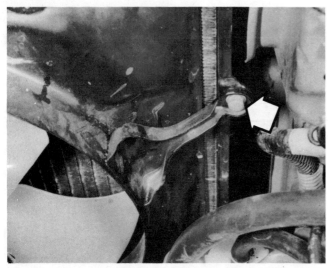

4.9b Remove the bolt from the side of the cooling fan assembly

5.6 Remove the bolts that retain the hood latch to the body, then place the latch off to the side

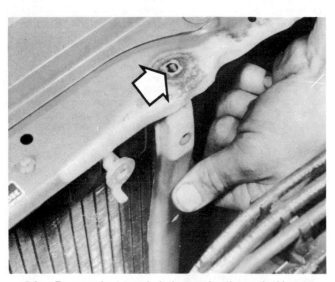

5.8a Remove the upper bolt that retains the vertical brace

5.8b The lower bolt that retains the brace is accessible from under the vehicle

fan shroud assembly out of the engine compartment, being very careful not to damage the radiator fins.
10   To detach the fan from the motor, remove the motor shaft clip.
11   To remove the bracket from the fan motor, remove the mounting nuts.
12   Installation is the reverse of removal.

5   Radiator – removal and installation

Refer to illustrations 5.6, 5.8a, 5.8b and 5.12

Warning: *Do not allow antifreeze to come in contact with your skin or painted surfaces of the vehicle. Rinse off spills immediately with plenty of water. Never leave anti-freeze lying around in an open container or in a puddle on the driveway or garage floor. Children and animals are attracted by its sweet smell and may drink it. Anti-freeze is toxic, so use good sense when disposing of it. Some communities maintain toxic material disposal sites and/or offer regular pick-up of hazardous materials. Anti-freeze is also combustible, so don't store or use it near open flames.*
Wait until the engine is completely cool before beginning this procedure.

Removal

1   Disconnect the negative battery cable from the battery.
2   Drain the cooling system (see Chapter 1). If the coolant is relatively new or in good condition, save it and reuse it.
3   Compress the hose clamps with pliers and slide them away from the radiator, then detach the radiator hoses from the fittings. If they're stuck, grasp each hose near the end with a pair of adjustable pliers and twist it to break the seal, then pull it off – be careful not to distort the radiator fittings! If the hoses are old or deteriorated, cut them off and install new ones.
4   Remove the distributor cap (see Chapter 1).
5   Disconnect the electrical connector for the cooling fan **(see illustration 4.6)**.
6   Remove the bolts that attach the hood latch to the body and place the latch to the side **(see illustration)**.
7   Remove the two bolts securing the radiator to the body and the bolt that retains the left hand hood lock.
8   Remove the bolts that retain the vertical brace located directly in front of the radiator **(see illustrations)**. The lower bolt must be reached from under the vehicle. Remove the brace.
9   Remove the fan assembly (see Section 4).

5.12   Lift the radiator out

6.2   Disconnect the coolant reservoir hose

10   If the vehicle is equipped with an automatic transaxle, disconnect the cooler lines from the radiator. Use a drip pan to catch spilled fluid.

11   Plug the cooler lines and fittings.

12   Carefully lift out the radiator **(see illustration)**. Don't spill coolant on the vehicle or scratch the paint.

13   With the radiator removed, it can be inspected for leaks and damage. If it needs repair, have a radiator shop or dealer service department perform the work, as special techniques are required.

14   Bugs and dirt can be removed from the radiator with compressed air and a soft brush. Don't bend the cooling fins as this is done.

15   Check the radiator mounts for deterioration and make sure there's nothing in them when the radiator is installed.

Installation

16   Installation is the reverse of the removal procedure. Be sure the rubber mounts are in place.

17   After installation, fill the cooling system with the proper mixture of antifreeze and water. Refer to Chapter 1 if necessary.

18   Start the engine and check for leaks. Allow the engine to reach normal operating temperature, indicated by the upper radiator hose becoming hot. Recheck the coolant level and add more if required.

19   If you're working on a vehicle equipped with an automatic transaxle, check and add fluid as needed (see Chapter 1).

---

6   Coolant reservoir – removal and installation

Refer to illustration 6.2

Warning: *Do not allow antifreeze to come in contact with your skin or painted surfaces of the vehicle. Rinse off spills immediately with plenty of water. Never leave anti-freeze lying around in an open container or in a puddle on the driveway or garage floor. Children and animals are attracted by its sweet smell and may drink it. Anti-freeze is toxic, so use good sense when disposing of it. Some communities maintain toxic material disposal sites and/or offer regular pick-up of hazardous materials. Anti-freeze is also combustible, so don't store or use it near open flames.*

1   The coolant reservoir is mounted adjacent to the radiator at the right front corner of the engine compartment.

2   Follow the coolant reservoir hose from the coolant reservoir to the top of the radiator neck. Detach the hose **(see illustration)**.

3   Remove the battery and the battery tray (see Chapter 5).

4   Remove the battery support (see Chapter 5).

5   Remove the bolts that retain the reservoir to the body **(see illustration 1.1)**. Lift the reservoir straight up to remove it.

6   Temporarily pour the coolant into a clean container. Wash out and inspect the reservoir for cracks and other damage. Replace it if it is damaged.

7   Installation is the reverse of removal. Refill the coolant reservoir. If the original coolant is in good condition (see Chapter 1), it can be reused.

---

7   Water pump – check

---

1   A failure in the water pump can cause serious engine damage due to overheating.

2   There are three ways to check the operation of the water pump while it's installed on the engine. If the pump is defective, it should be replaced with a new or rebuilt unit.

3   With the engine running at normal operating temperature, squeeze the upper radiator hose. If the water pump is working properly, a pressure surge should be felt as the hose is released. **Warning:** *Keep your hands away from the fan blades!*

4   Water pumps are equipped with weep or vent holes. If a failure occurs in the pump seal, coolant will leak from the hole. In most cases you'll need a flashlight and small mirror to find the hole on the water pump from underneath to check for leaks.

5   If the water pump shaft bearings fail there may be a howling sound at the front of the engine while it's running. Shaft wear can be felt if the water pump pulley is rocked up and down. Don't mistake drivebelt slippage, which causes a squealing sound, for water pump bearing failure.

---

8   Water pump – replacement

Refer to illustrations 8.7 and 8.11

Warning: *Do not allow antifreeze to come in contact with your skin or painted surfaces of the vehicle. Rinse off spills immediately with plenty of water. Never leave anti-freeze lying around in an open container or in a puddle on the driveway or garage floor. Children and animals are attracted by its sweet smell and may drink it. Anti-freeze is toxic, so use good sense when disposing of it. Some communities maintain toxic material disposal sites and/or offer regular pick-up of hazardous materials. Anti-freeze is also combustible, so don't store or use it near open flames. Wait until the engine is completely cool before beginning this procedure.*

8.7   Remove the water pump retaining bolts (arrows)

1   Disconnect the negative battery cable from the battery.
2   Drain the cooling system (see Chapter 1). If the coolant is relatively new or in good condition, save it and reuse it.
3   Remove the drivebelts (see Chapter 1).
4   Remove the air cleaner (see Chapter 1) and the camshaft cover (see Chapter 2A).
5   Remove the two bolts that retain the timing belt upper cover and lift off the cover (see Chapter 2, Part A).
6   Remove the lower timing belt cover and remove the timing belt (see Chapter 2, Part A).
7   Remove the water pump retaining bolts **(see illustration)** and remove the water pump from the engine.
8   Compare the new pump to the old one to make sure they're identical.
9   Remove all traces of old gasket sealer from the engine.
10   Clean the engine and new water pump mating surfaces with lacquer thinner or acetone.
11   Apply a thin layer of RTV sealant to the O-ring groove in the new pump, then carefully install a new O-ring to the pump **(see illustration)**.
12   Carefully attach the pump to the engine.
13   Install the bolts finger tight (if they also hold an accessory bracket in place, be sure to reposition the bracket at this time). Tighten them to the torque listed in this Chapter's Specifications, in 1/4-turn increments. Don't overtighten them or the pump may be distorted.

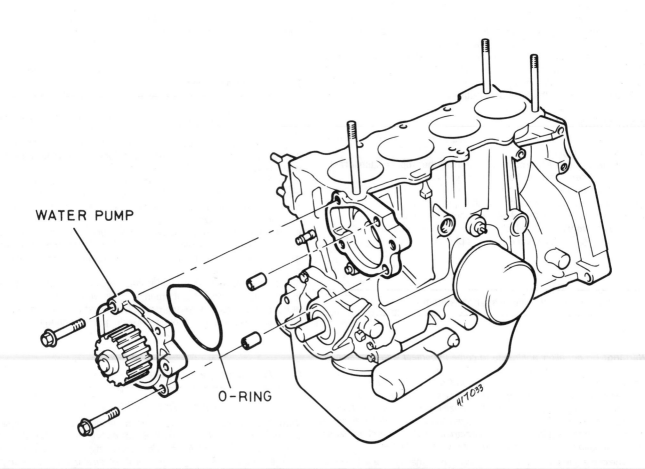

WATER PUMP

O-RING

8.11   Install a new O-ring to the pump, making sure it isn't twisted

14   Reinstall all parts removed for access to the pump.
15   Refill and bleed the cooling system and check the drivebelt tension (see Chapter 1). Run the engine and check for leaks.

9   Coolant temperature sending unit – check and replacement

Warning: *Do not allow antifreeze to come in contact with your skin or painted surfaces of the vehicle. Rinse off spills immediately with plenty of water. Never leave anti-freeze lying around or in an open container or in a puddle on the driveway or garage floor. Children and animals are attracted by its sweet smell and may drink it. Anti-freeze is toxic, so use good sense when disposing of it. Some communities maintain toxic material disposal sites and/or offer regular pick-up of hazardous materials. Anti-freeze is also combustible, so don't store or use it near open flames. Wait until the engine is completely cool before beginning this procedure.*

1   The coolant temperature indicator system is composed of a temperature gauge mounted in the instrument panel and a coolant temperature sending unit mounted on the engine. On some models, the sending unit is screwed into the thermostat housing **(see illustration 3.10)**. On others, it's mounted in the engine block, next to the thermostat housing. In either case, the sending unit has only one terminal, and only one wire leading to it. Some vehicles have more than one sending unit, but only one is used for the indicator system. **Warning:** *This vehicle is equipped with an electric cooling fan – stay clear of the fan blades, which can come on at any time.*
2   If an overheating indication occurs, check the coolant level in the system and then make sure the wiring between the gauge and the sending unit is secure and all fuses are intact.
3   Test the circuit by grounding the wire to the sending unit while the ignition is on (engine not running for safety). If the gauge deflects full scale, the circuit is okay. Replace the sending unit.
4   If the sending unit must be replaced, simply unscrew it from the engine and install the replacement. Use sealant on the threads. Make sure the engine is cool before removing the defective sending unit. There will be some coolant loss as the unit is removed, so be prepared to catch it. Check the level after the replacement has been installed.

10   Blower unit – removal and installation

Refer to illustrations 10.4 and 10.5

1   Disconnect the negative cable from the battery.
2   Remove the glove compartment and right lower dash panel (see Chapter 11).
3   The blower unit is located in the passenger compartment above the right front footwell.
4   Disconnect the cooling tube and the electrical connector from the blower unit, then remove the retaining screws **(see illustration)**. Lower the unit from under the dash.
5   If the motor is being replaced, transfer the fan to the new motor prior to installation **(see illustration)**.
6   Installation is the reverse of removal. Check for proper operation.

11   Heater core – removal and installation

Refer to illustration 11.6

1   Disconnect the negative cable from the battery.
2   Drain the cooling system (see Chapter 1).
3   Working in the engine compartment, disconnect the heater hoses from the heater control valve.
4   Remove the instrument panel and the center console (see Chapter 11).

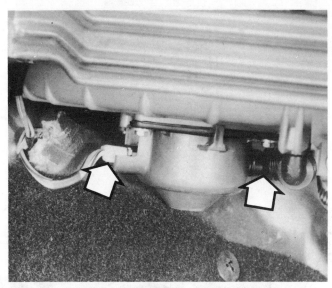

10.4   To remove the blower unit, detach the electrical connector and the cooling tube (arrows), then remove the mounting bolts

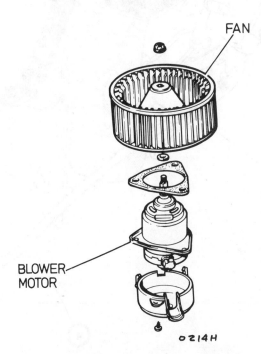

FAN

BLOWER MOTOR

O2I4H

10.5   Exploded view of the blower motor and related components

5   Remove the heater controls (see Section 12) and disconnect the heater hoses under the dash, where they connect to the heater core housing.
6   Label and detach the air ducts, wiring and controls still attached to the heating unit **(see illustration)**.
7   Unbolt the heating unit and detach it from the vehicle.
8   Remove the screws and clips and separate the two halves of the housing. Take out the old heater core and install the new unit.
9   Reassemble the heater unit and check the operation of the air control flaps. If any parts bind, correct the problem before installation.
10   Reinstall the remaining parts in the reverse order of removal.

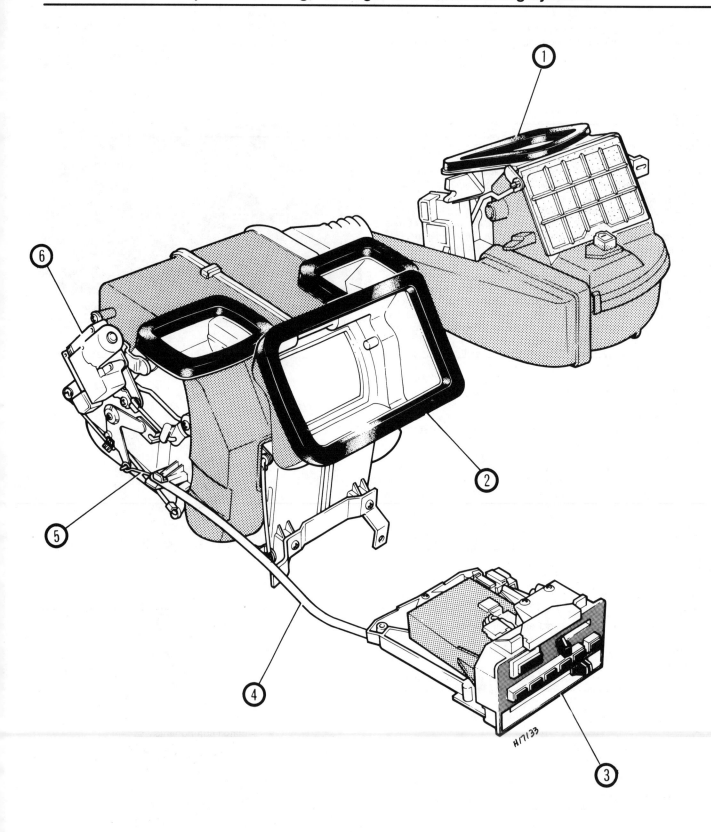

11.6   General view of the heater components (typical)

1	Blower housing	3	Heater controller	5	Heater valve cable
2	Heater housing	4	Air mix cable	6	Mode control motor

12   Air conditioner and heater control assembly – removal and installation

Refer to illustrations 12.3, 12.4, 12.5a, 12.5b, 12.5c, 12.5d and 12.8

Removal

1   Disconnect the negative cable from the battery.
2   Remove the radio (see Chapter 12).
3   Pull the knobs from the heater control assembly **(see illustration)** and pry off the faceplate with a small screwdriver.
4   Remove the mounting screws located on the front of the control assembly **(see illustration)**.
5   Pull the control out slightly. On some models it will be necessary to disconnect the cables at the operating ends before this is possible **(see illustrations)**. Before disconnecting the cables, mark the relationship of each cable to its cable clamp. This will ensure installation in the same position.

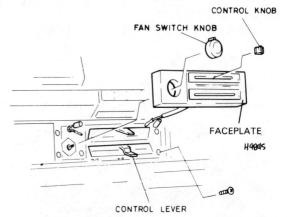

12.3   Pull off the knobs, then use a small screwdriver to pry off the faceplate

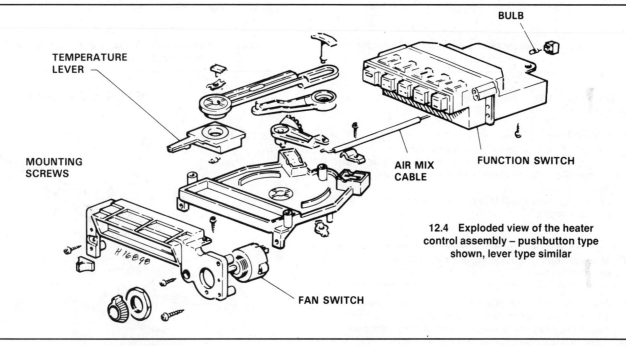

12.4   Exploded view of the heater control assembly – pushbutton type shown, lever type similar

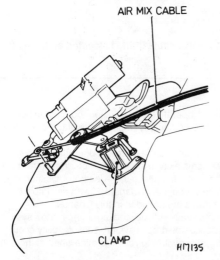

12.5a   The air mix cable (if equipped) is usually mounted on the left side of the heater housing

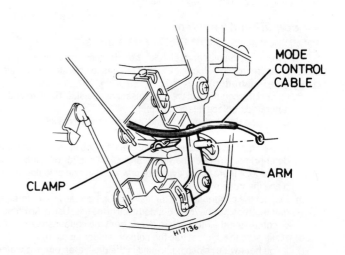

12.5b   The heater mode control cable (if equipped) is usually mounted on the right side of the heater housing

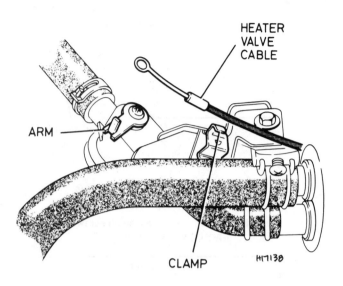

12.5c   The heater valve cable is located near the hose clamps

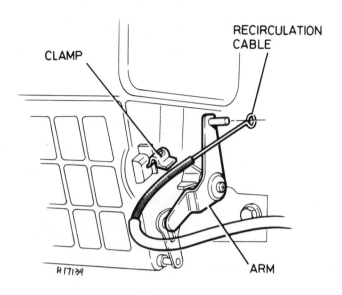

12.5d   The heater recirculation cable is located on the upper section of the heater unit

6   Detach the cables and wiring from the control assembly and lift the assembly from the dash.

Installation

7   To install the unit, reverse the above procedure.
8   To adjust the cables, align the marks you made earlier. Fasten the clips and check for stiffness or binding through the full range of operation **(see illustration)**.
9   Run the engine and check for proper functioning of the heater (and air conditioning, if equipped).

---

13   Air conditioning and heating system – check and maintenance

---

Warning: *The air conditioning system is under high pressure. Do not loosen any hose fittings or remove any components until after the system has been discharged by a dealer service department or an automotive air conditioning shop. Always wear eye protection when adding refrigerant or disconnecting air conditioning system fittings.*

Air conditioning system

Refer to illustrations 13.1a, 13.1b, 13.5, 13.6 and 13.9

1   The following maintenance checks should be performed on a regular basis to ensure that the air conditioner continues to operate at peak efficiency **(see illustration)**.
   a) Inspect the condition of the compressor drivebelt. If it is worn or deteriorated, replace it (see Chapter 1).
   b) Check the drivebelt tension and, if necessary, adjust it (see Chapter 1).
   c) Inspect the system hoses. Look for cracks, bubbles, hardening and deterioration. Inspect the hoses and all fittings for oil bubbles or seepage. If there is any evidence of wear, damage or leakage, replace the hose(s).
   d) Inspect the condenser fins for leaves, bugs and any other foreign material that may have embedded itself in the fins. Use a "fin comb" or compressed air to remove debris from the condenser.
   e) Make sure the system has the correct refrigerant charge.
   f) If you hear water sloshing around in the dash area or have water dripping on the carpet, slip the evaporator housing condensation drain tube off **(see illustration)** and insert a piece of wire into both the evaporator housing and the tube to clear any blockage.

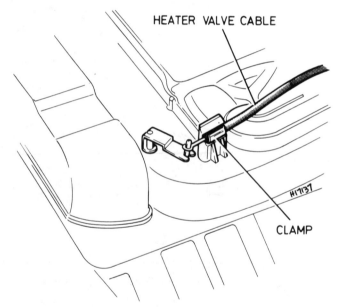

12.8   The heater valve cable fitting is located at the heater end

2   It's a good idea to operate the system for about ten minutes at least once a month. This is particularly important during the winter months because long term non-use can cause hardening, and subsequent failure, of the seals. Note that running the defroster operates the system.
3   Because of the complexity of the air conditioning system and the special equipment necessary to service it, in-depth troubleshooting and repairs are beyond the scope of this manual. However, simple component replacement procedures are provided in this Chapter.
4   The most common cause of poor cooling is simply a low system refrigerant charge. If a noticeable drop in system cooling ability occurs, one of the following quick checks will help you determine whether the refrigerant level is low.
5   With the air conditioning operating, inspect the sight glass **(see the accompanying illustration or illustration 14.3)**. If the refrigerant looks foamy, it's low. Charge the system (see below).

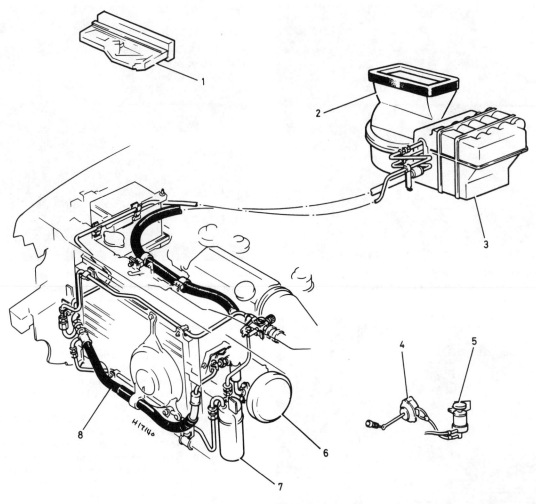

13.1a   General layout of the air conditioning system

1	Heater and air conditioning control panel	3	Evaporator	5	Idle control solenoid	7	Receiver/drier
2	Blower	4	Idle boost diaphragm	6	Compressor	8	Condenser

13.1b   The evaporator condensation drain tube (arrow) is located under the dash near the center of the vehicle

13.5   The sight glass on most models (arrow) is located in the left front corner of the engine compartment – on some models it's mounted in the top of the receiver/drier

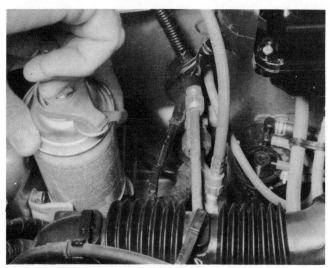

**13.6   Always connect the charging kit to the low pressure line –
it's the larger diameter of the two lines**

**13.9   Place a thermometer in the center dash vent to monitor the
temperature of the air entering the passenger compartment**

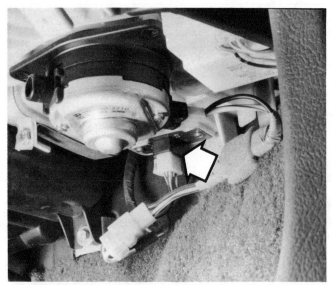

**13.11   The blower resistor (arrow) is located under the right side
of the dash, behind the blower motor**

Adding refrigerant

6   Buy an automotive "charging kit" at an automotive parts store. A charging kit includes a 14-ounce can of refrigerant, a can tap valve and a short section of hose which can be attached between the tap valve and the system low side service valve. **Warning:** *Do not connect the hose to the "high side" of the system!* **(see illustration)**. Because one can of refrigerant may not be sufficient to bring the system charge up to its proper level, it's a good idea to buy a few additional cans. Make sure the first can you add to the system contains red refrigerant dye. If the system is leaking, the red dye will leak out with the refrigerant and help you pinpoint the location of the leak.
Warning: *Wear eye protection while performing this Step.*
7   Hook up the charging kit in accordance with the manufacturer's instructions.
8   Warm up the engine and operate the system.
9   Place a thermometer in the center dashboard vent **(see illustration)** and add refrigerant until the indicated temperature is around 40 to 45-degrees F.

Heating system
Refer to illustration 13.11
10   If the air coming out of the heater vents isn't hot, the problem could stem from any of the following causes:
   a) The thermostat is stuck open, preventing the engine coolant from warming up enough to carry heat to the heater core. Replace the thermostat (see Section 3).
   b) A heater hose is blocked, preventing the flow of coolant through the heater core. Feel both heater hoses at the firewall. They should be hot. If one of them is cold, there is an obstruction in one of the hoses or in the heater core, or the heater control valve is shut. Detach the hoses and back flush the heater core with a water hose. If the heater core is clear but circulation is impeded, remove the two hoses and flush them out with a water hose.
   c) If flushing fails to remove the blockage from the heater core, the core must be replaced.
11   If the blower motor speed does not correspond to the setting selected on the blower switch, the problem could be a bad fuse, circuit, switch, blower motor resistor or motor.
   a) Before checking for an inoperative blower motor or circuit, always check the fuse first.
   b) Using a test light or voltmeter, check the voltage at the motor.
   c) Pull the heating/air conditioning control assembly (see Section 12) far enough from the dash to verify – with a test light or voltmeter – that current is reaching the blower switch on the control assembly. If the switch is not getting current, troubleshoot the circuit between the battery and the switch (see the wiring diagrams at the end of this manual).
   d) Locate the blower motor resistor below the glove box **(see illustration)**. Check the resistor to make sure that it is getting current from the blower switch.
      1) If the resistor is not getting current, check the wire.
      2) If the wire is good, replace the switch (see Section 12).
   e) Using a test light or voltmeter, verify that the blower motor is getting current. If the blower motor is not getting current, replace the resistor.
12   If there isn't any air coming out of the vents:
   a) Turn the ignition ON and activate the fan control. Place your ear at the heating/air conditioning register (vent) and listen. Most motors are audible. Can you hear the motor running?
   b) If you can't (and have already verified that the blower switch and the blower motor resistor are good), the blower motor itself is probably bad (see Section 10). **Note:** *You can determine the motor's condition by hooking up a fused jumper wire directly between battery voltage and the blower motor.*

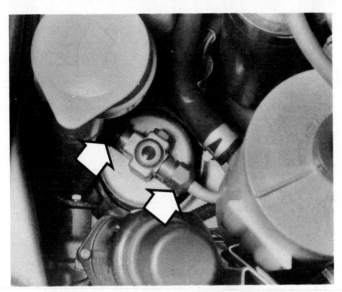

14.3   Using a flare-nut wrench, disconnect the refrigerant lines (arrows)

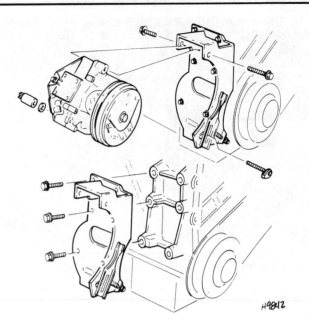

15.7   Mounting details of the air conditioning compressor (typical)

13   If the carpet under the heater core is damp, or if antifreeze vapor or steam is coming through the vents, the heater core is leaking. Remove it (see Section 11) and install a new unit (most radiator shops will not repair a leaking heater core).

14   Air conditioning receiver/drier – removal and installation

Refer to illustration 14.3

Warning: *For this operation, the system must be discharged by an air conditioning technician. Do not attempt to do this by yourself. The refrigerant is under high pressure and can cause serious injury and respiratory irritation.*

Removal

1   Have the refrigerant discharged by an air conditioning technician.
2   Disconnect the battery (see Chapter 5) and detach the left front fender liner. The receiver/drier is located near the left front corner of the engine compartment.
3   Disconnect the refrigerant lines **(see illustration)** from the receiver/drier and cap the open fittings to prevent dirt and moisture entry.
4   Remove the bolt and slip the receiver/drier from the engine compartment wall.

Installation

5   Installation is the reverse of removal.
6   Have the system evacuated, charged and leak tested by the shop that discharged it. If the receiver was replaced, have them add about 20cc (0.7 oz.) refrigeration oil.

15   Air conditioning compressor – removal and installation

Refer to illustration 15.7

Warning: *The air conditioning system is under high pressure. DO NOT disassemble any part of the system (hoses, compressor, line fittings, etc.) until after the system has been depressurized by a dealer service department or service station.*

Removal

1   Have the air conditioning system discharged (see Warning above).
2   Disconnect the negative battery cable from the battery and raise the front of the vehicle, supporting it securely on jackstands.
3   Working under the vehicle, unplug the electrical connector from the compressor clutch.
4   Remove the drivebelt (see Chapter 1).
5   Disconnect the refrigerant lines from the compressor. Plug the open fittings to prevent entry of dirt and moisture.
6   If equipped, remove the power steering pump (see Chapter 10) and any other components that may obstruct access to the compressor.
7   Unbolt the compressor from the mounting brackets **(see illustration)** and remove it from the vehicle.
8   If a new compressor is being installed, follow the directions with the compressor regarding the draining of excess oil prior to installation.
9   The clutch may have to be transferred from the original to the new compressor.

Installation

10   Installation is the reverse of removal. Replace all O-rings with new ones specifically made for A/C system use and lubricate them with refrigerant oil.
11   Have the system evacuated, recharged and leak tested by the shop that discharged it.

16   Air conditioning condenser – removal and installation

Refer to illustrations 16.4 and 16.5

Warning: *For this operation, the system must be discharged by an air conditioning technician. Do not attempt to do this by yourself. The refrigerant is under high pressure and can cause serious injury and respiratory irritation.*

Removal

1   Have the refrigerant discharged by an air conditioning technician.
2   Remove the radiator as described in Section 5.

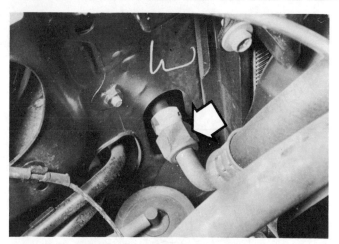

16.4   The upper fitting (arrow) can be reached from the engine compartment, adjacent to the left side of the radiator – use two wrenches to loosen it

3   Disconnect the negative cable from the battery.

4   Remove the grille (and hood on models with front-mounted hood hinges) for access (see Chapter 11) and disconnect the lower and upper fittings **(see illustration)**. Cap the open fittings immediately to keep moisture and dirt out of the system.

5   Remove the hood latch (if necessary) and condenser mounting bolts **(see illustration)** and lower the condenser out.

Installation

6   Install the condenser, brackets and bolts, making sure the rubber cushions fit on the mounting points properly.

7   Reconnect the refrigerant lines, using new O-rings where needed.

8   Reinstall the remaining parts in the reverse order of removal.

9   Have the system evacuated, charged and leak tested by the shop that discharged it.

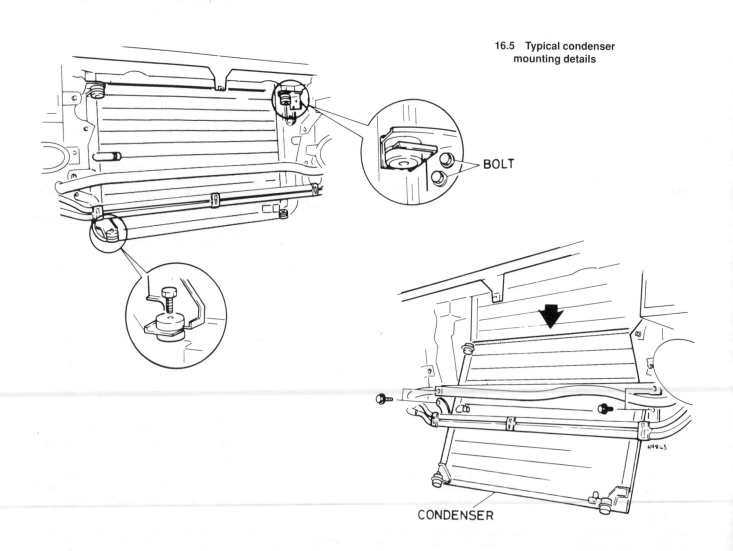

16.5   Typical condenser mounting details

BOLT

CONDENSER

Chapter 4 Fuel and exhaust systems

Contents

Specifications

General

Fuel pressure
   Carbureted models . . . . 2.7 to 3.8 psi
   Fuel-injected models . . . . 35 to 41 psi (with vacuum hose disconnected from pressure regulator)
Fuel injector resistance
   Multi-point fuel injection . . . . 1.5 to 2.5 ohms
   Dual-point fuel injection . . . . 6 to 10 ohms

Torque specifications

Ft-lbs (unless otherwise indicated)

Fuel injection service bolt	108 in-lbs
Carburetor mounting nuts	15
Throttle body mounting nuts	16
Fuel rail mounting nuts	108 in-lbs

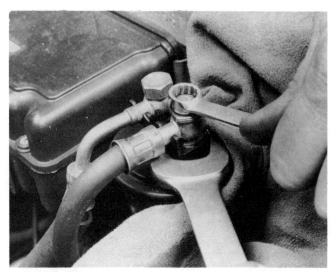

2.2   To relieve the fuel pressure on a fuel-injected vehicle, you'll need one wrench to loosen the service bolt on top of the fuel filter and another wrench to hold the special banjo bolt into which the service bolt is installed

3.17   Remove the service bolt from the top of the fuel filter and attach a fuel pressure gauge

1   General information

Some vehicles covered by this manual are equipped with a feedback carburetor. Others are equipped with an electronic fuel injection system. In 1984, all vehicles were equipped with a three-barrel feedback carburetor. In 1985, some models were again equipped with the three-barrel carburetor, while other models were equipped with an optional electronic fuel injection system. These vehicles were equipped with one of two types of fuel injection, depending on the model, year and engine size – multi-point fuel injection or dual-point fuel injection. The multi-point fuel injection uses timed impulses to sequentially inject the fuel directly into the intake port of each cylinder. The injectors are controlled by the Electronic Control Unit (ECU). The ECU monitors various engine parameters and delivers the exact amount fuel, in the correct sequence, into the intake ports. The dual-point fuel injection system uses two injectors mounted in the throttle body to disperse the fuel into the intake manifold.

Carbureted engines are equipped with a mechanical fuel pump. The pump is located on the cylinder head. 1985 through 1987 fuel-injected models are equipped with an electric fuel pump, mounted near the fuel tank behind the left rear wheel. The electric fuel pump on 1988 and later models is mounted in the fuel tank.

The exhaust system consists of a header pipe, a catalytic converter, an exhaust pipe and a muffler. Each of these components is replaceable. For further information regarding the catalytic converter, refer to Chapter 6.

2   Fuel pressure relief procedure (fuel-injected models)

Refer to illustration 2.2

Warning: *Gasoline is extremely flammable, so take extra precautions when you work on any part of the fuel system. Don't smoke or allow open flames or bare light bulbs near the work area, and don't work in a garage where a natural gas-type appliance (such as a water heater or clothes dryer) with a pilot light is present. If you spill any fuel on your skin, rinse it off immediately with soap and water. When you perform any kind of work on the fuel system, wear safety glasses and have a Class B type fire extinguisher on hand.*

1   Detach the cable from the negative battery terminal. Unscrew the fuel filler cap to relieve pressure built up in the fuel tank.

2   You'll need two wrenches for this procedure: One to loosen the service bolt at the top of the fuel filter and another to hold the special banjo bolt into which the service bolt is installed **(see illustration)**.

3   Place a shop rag over the service bolt.

4   While holding the special banjo bolt, slowly loosen the service bolt one complete turn.

5   Always replace the washer between the service bolt and the special banjo bolt whenever the service bolt is loosened to relieve fuel pressure. Tighten the service bolt to the torque listed in this Chapter's Specifications.

3   Fuel pump/fuel pressure – check

Warning: *Gasoline is extremely flammable, so take extra precautions when you work on any part of the fuel system. Don't smoke or allow open flames or bare light bulbs near the work area, and don't work in a garage where a natural gas-type appliance (such as a water heater or clothes dryer) with a pilot light is present. If you spill any fuel on your skin, rinse it off immediately with soap and water. When you perform any kind of work on the fuel system, wear safety glasses and have a Class B type fire extinguisher on hand.*

Carbureted models

Preliminary check

1   If you suspect insufficient fuel delivery, first inspect all fuel lines to ensure that the problem is not simply a leak in a line.

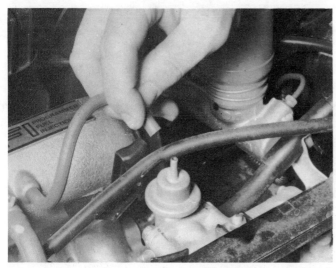

3.18a   Location of the pressure regulator on a multi-point fuel injection system

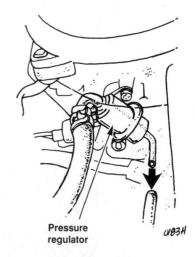

Pressure regulator

3.18b   Location of the fuel filter and the pressure regulator on a Dual Point fuel injection system

2   If there are no leaks evident in the fuel lines, inspect the fuel pump itself. The following checks will tell you if the fuel pump is leaking and whether it is pumping fuel.

3   Before performing the following checks, detach the cable from the negative terminal of the battery and remove the air cleaner housing (see Section 7).

Fuel pump output check

4   Hook up a remote starter switch in accordance with the manufacturer's instructions. If you don't have a remote starter switch, you will need an assistant to help you with this and the following procedure.

5   Trace the fuel outlet hose from the pump to the carburetor and detach it at the carburetor.

6   Attach the cable to the negative terminal of the battery.

7   Detach the wires from the primary terminals of the ignition coil (see Chapter 5).

8   Place a metal container under the open end of the fuel pump outlet hose.

9   Direct the fuel pump outlet hose into the container while cranking the engine for a few seconds with the remote starter (or while an assistant cranks the engine with the ignition key).

10   If fuel is emitted in well defined spurts, the pump is operating satisfactorily. If fuel dribbles or trickles out the hose, the pump is defective. Replace it (see Section 4).

Fuel pressure check

11   Disconnect the fuel line at the fuel filter in the engine compartment, and connect a fuel pressure gauge to the line.

12   Disconnect the fuel return line at the fuel pump and plug the return fitting with a suitable cap.

13   Start the engine and allow it to idle until pressure stabilizes, then turn the engine OFF.

14   The fuel pressure should be as listed in this Chapter's Specifications. If the pressure reading is incorrect, replace the fuel pump.

Fuel-injected models

Fuel pump operational check

Note: *On 1985 through 1987 models, the fuel pump is located underneath the vehicle, immediately ahead of the left rear wheel. On 1988 and later models, its located inside the fuel tank.*

15   Set the parking brake and have an assistant turn the ignition switch to the On position while you listen at the fuel pump. You should hear a whirring sound, lasting for a couple of seconds. Start the engine. The whirring sound should now be continuous (although harder to hear with the engine running). If there is no whirring sound, either the fuel pump or the fuel main relay circuit is defective.

Pressure check

Refer to illustrations 3.17, 3.18a and 3.18b

16   Relieve the fuel pressure (see Section 2).

17   Remove the service bolt from the top of the fuel filter and attach a fuel pressure gauge **(see illustration)**.

18   Start the engine. Detach the vacuum hose from the pressure regulator **(see illustrations)**. With the engine idling, measure the fuel pressure. It should be as listed in this Chapter's Specifications.

19   If the fuel pressure is not within specification, check the following:

   a) If the pressure is higher than specified, check for a faulty regulator (see Section 14) or a pinched or clogged fuel return hose or pipe.

   b) If the pressure is lower than specified:
      1) Inspect the fuel filter – make sure it's not clogged.
      2) Look for a pinched or clogged fuel hose between the fuel tank and the fuel pump.
      3) Check the pressure regulator for a malfunction (see Section 14).
      4) Look for leaks in the fuel line.
      5) Look for a pinched, broken or disconnected regulator vacuum hose.

20   If there are no problems with any of the above-listed components, check the fuel pump (see below).

Fuel pump check

21   If you suspect a problem with the fuel pump, verify the pump actually runs. Have an assistant turn the ignition switch to On – you should hear a brief whirring noise as the pump comes on and pressurizes the system. Have the assistant start the engine. This time you should hear a constant whirring sound from the pump (but it's more difficult to hear with the engine running).

22   If the pump does not come on (makes no sound), proceed to the next step.

23   Jack up the rear of the vehicle and place it securely on jackstands.

24   Remove the left rear wheel.

25   On 1985 through 1987 models, remove the fuel pump cover (see Section 4) and detach the black and black/yellow wires (make sure the ignition switch is turned off before disconnecting the wires). On 1988 and later models, the fuel pump connector is directly above the fuel tank, and access to it can be gained by removing the rear seat. The connector has the same designated color code (black and black/yellow wires in the connector.

26   Touch the positive probe of a voltmeter to the black/yellow wire and the negative probe to the black wire, then turn on the ignition switch and verify there is voltage available.

27   If voltage is available, replace the fuel pump (see Section 4).

28   If no voltage is available, check the main relay (see below).

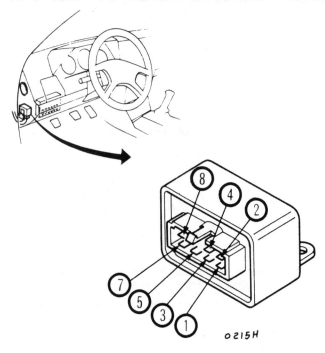

4.3   Detach the fuel lines from the fuel pump. Place rags under the lines to catch dripping fuel

3.29   The main relay is located under the dash near the fuse box – refer to the terminal number when testing the relay

Main relay check
Refer to illustration 3.29

29   To test the main relay, first remove it from its location next to the under-dash fuse panel **(see illustration)**.

30   Using a pair of jumper wires, connect the battery positive terminal to the no. 4 relay terminal, ground the no. 8 terminal, then check for continuity between the no. 5 and no. 7 terminals. If there's no continuity, replace the relay.

31   Connect the battery positive terminal to the no. 5 relay terminal, ground the no. 2 terminal and verify there's continuity between the no. 1 and no. 3 terminals. If there isn't, replace the relay.

32   Connect the battery positive terminal to the no. 3 relay terminal and ground the no. 8 terminal. Verify there's continuity between the no. 5 and no. 7 terminals. If there is no continuity, replace the relay.

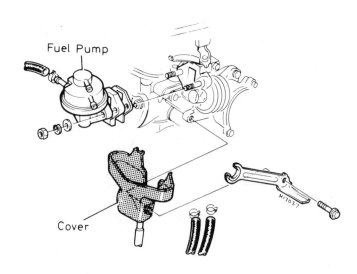

4.4   Fuel pump mounting details (carbureted models)

---

4   Fuel pump – removal and installation

Warning: *Gasoline is extremely flammable, so take extra precautions when you work on any part of the fuel system. Don't smoke or allow open flames or bare light bulbs near the work area, and don't work in a garage where a natural gas-type appliance (such as a water heater or clothes dryer) with a pilot light is present. If you spill any fuel on your skin, rinse it off immediately with soap and water. When you perform any kind of work on the fuel system, wear safety glasses and have a Class B type fire extinguisher on hand.*

Carbureted models
Refer to illustrations 4.3 and 4.4

1   Relieve the fuel pressure from the system by removing the cap from the fuel tank.

2   Disconnect the cable from the negative terminal of the battery.

3   Detach the fuel lines from the pump **(see illustration)**. Place rags under the fuel lines to catch any spilled fuel.

4   Remove the fuel pump cover and any brackets attached to the fuel pump assembly **(see illustration)**.

5   Remove the fuel pump mounting bolts and remove the fuel pump.

6   Remove all the old gasket material from the fuel pump flange.

7   Installation is the reverse of removal.

Fuel-injected models

1985 through 1987
Refer to illustrations 4.12 and 4.13

8   Detach the cable from the negative battery terminal

9   Relieve the fuel system pressure (see Section 2).

10   Loosen the lug nuts of the left rear wheel. Raise the rear of the vehicle and place it securely on jackstands.

11   Remove the left rear wheel (see Chapter 1).

12   Remove the fuel pump shield retaining bolts and detach the shield **(see illustration)**.

13   Unscrew the pulsation damper from the end of the pump **(see illustration)**. Be prepared for fuel spillage.

14   Detach the fuel line and electrical connector from the fuel pump.

15   Unbolt the pump from its mounting bracket and remove it.

16   Installation is the reverse of removal. Be sure to replace the sealing washer between the fuel hose and the pump **(see illustration 4.13)**.

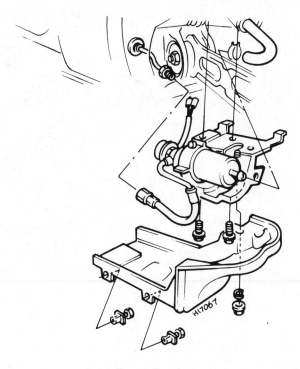

4.12   Details of the externally-mounted electric fuel pump

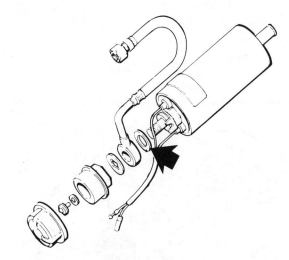

4.13   Whenever you remove the fuel pump, replace the sealing washer (arrow)

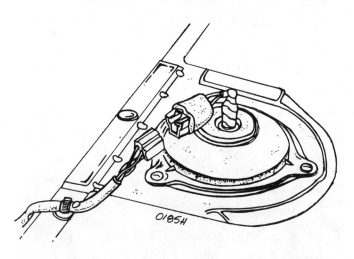

4.20   The electrical connector for the fuel pump is located under the rear seat

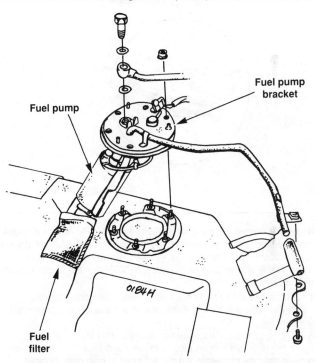

Fuel pump bracket

Fuel pump

Fuel filter

4.22   Carefully lift the fuel pump assembly out of the tank by angling it slightly

17   After you have installed the new pump, have an assistant turn the ignition switch to On two or three times while you watch for any leaks where the fuel lines are attached to the pump.

1988 through 1990

Refer to illustrations 4.20 and 4.22

18   Detach the cable from the negative battery terminal. Relieve the fuel pressure from the system (see Section 2).
19   Remove the rear seat.
20   Unplug the electrical connectors from the fuel pump and sending unit **(see illustration)**.
21   Remove the fuel tank from the vehicle (see Section 5).
22   Remove the mounting nuts from the fuel pump **(see illustration)**.
23   Remove the fuel pump from the tank.
24   Remove the sock filter from the end of the pump.

25   Detach the pump from its bracket.
26   Installation is the reverse of removal.

5   Fuel tank – removal and installation

Refer to illustrations 5.6 and 5.8
Warning: *Gasoline is extremely flammable, so take extra precautions when you work on any part of the fuel system. Don't smoke or allow open flames or bare light bulbs near the work area, and don't work in a garage where a natural gas-type appliance (such as a water heater or clothes dryer) with a pilot light is present. If you spill any fuel on your skin, rinse it off immediately with soap and water. When you perform any kind of work on the fuel system, wear safety glasses and have a Class B type fire extinguisher on hand.*

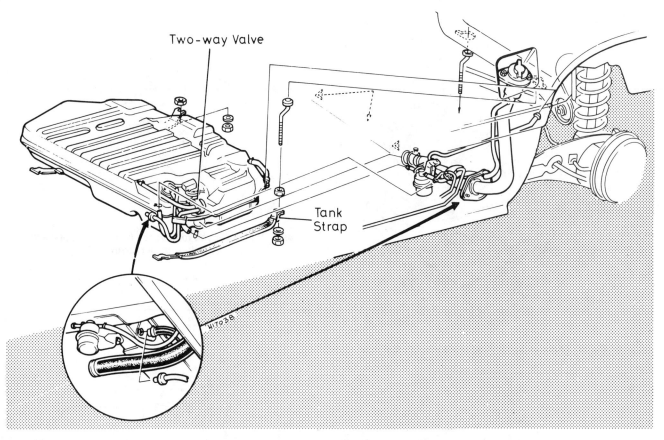

Two-way Valve

Tank
Strap

5.6   Fuel tank and related components (typical)

Note: *The following procedure is much easier to perform if the fuel tank is empty. Some tanks have a drain plug for this purpose. If the tank does not have a drain plug, the fuel can be siphoned from the tank using a siphoning kit, available at most auto parts stores. NEVER start the siphoning action with your mouth!*

1   Remove the fuel tank filler cap to relieve fuel tank pressure.
2   If the vehicle is fuel-injected, relieve the fuel system pressure (see Section 2).
3   Detach the cable from the negative terminal of the battery.
4   If the tank has a drain plug, remove it and drain the fuel into an approved gasoline container. If it doesn't have a drain plug, siphon the fuel into an approved gasoline container, using a siphoning kit (available at most auto parts stores).
5   Raise the vehicle and place it securely on jackstands.
6   Label, then disconnect the fuel lines and any hoses or brackets **(see illustration)**.
7   Support the fuel tank with a floor jack. Position a piece of wood between the jack head and the fuel tank to protect the tank.
8   Disconnect both fuel tank retaining straps and pivot them down until they are hanging out of the way **(see illustration)**.
9   Lower the tank enough to disconnect the electrical connectors and ground strap from the fuel pump and fuel gauge sending unit.
10   Remove the tank from the vehicle.
11   Installation is the reverse of removal.

---

6   Fuel tank cleaning and repair – general information

---

1   All repairs to the fuel tank or filler neck should be carried out by a professional who has experience in this critical and potentially dangerous

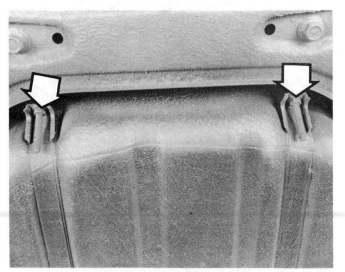

5.8   Remove the nuts (arrows) and drop the fuel tank retaining straps down

work. Even after cleaning and flushing of the fuel system, explosive fumes can remain and ignite during repair of the tank.
2   If the fuel tank is removed from the vehicle, it should not be placed in an area where sparks or open flames could ignite the fumes coming out of the tank. Be especially careful inside garages where a natural gas-type appliance is located, because the pilot light could cause an explosion.

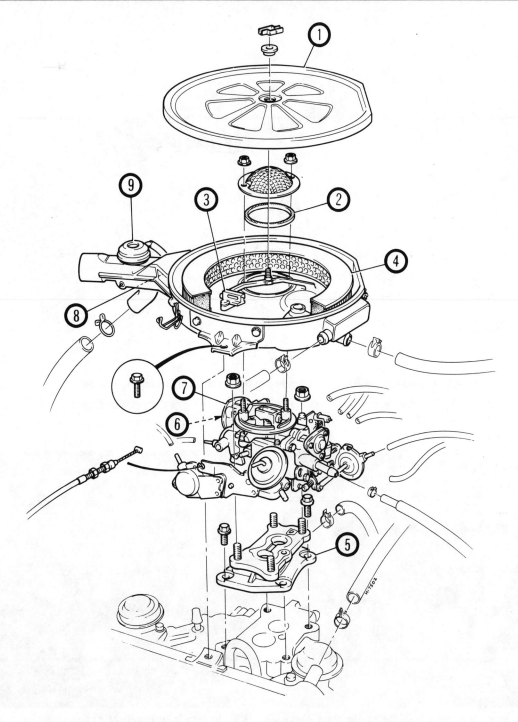

7.4 Exploded view of the air cleaner housing (carbureted models)

1	Air cleaner cover	3	Air bleed valve	5	Insulator	7	Automatic choke
2	Air cleaner insulator	4	Air filter element	6	Fast idle unloader	8	Air temperature sensor
						9	Intake air control diaphragm

---

7   Air cleaner housing – removal and installation

Carbureted models

Refer to illustration 7.4

1   Detach the cable from the negative battery terminal.
2   Remove the wing nut(s) from the air cleaner cover and detach the

cover and filter element (see Chapter 1).
3   Label, then detach all hoses attached to the air cleaner housing.
4   Remove the nuts that attach the air cleaner housing to the carburetor and the bolts that attach the housing bracket to the valve cover (**see illustration**). Remove the protective screen (if equipped) and lift off the air cleaner housing.
5   Installation is the reverse of removal.

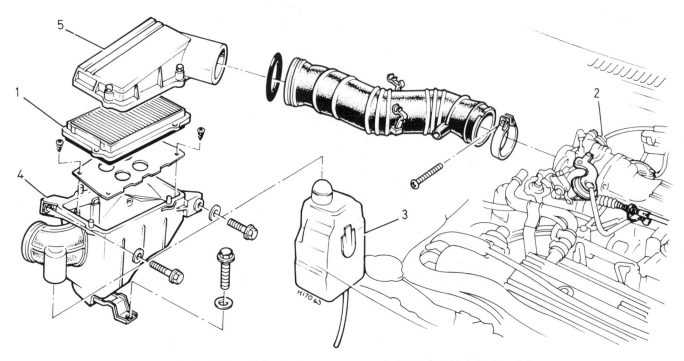

7.8   Exploded view of the air cleaner components (typical fuel-injected model)

1	Air filter element	3	Resonator	5	Air cleaner cover
2	Throttle body	4	Air cleaner housing		

8.3   To detach the accelerator cable from the throttle bracket on a carbureted model, push back the cable boot (A), loosen the cable adjustment locknut (B) until it's beyond the groove in the cable housing (C), then align the groove with the slot in the mounting bracket and pull out the cable

8.8   To detach the accelerator cable (arrow) from the firewall, rotate the grommet 90-degrees and pull it out of the firewall (be sure to use sealant when installing the grommet on the new cable or it may leak)

Fuel-injected models

Refer to illustration 7.8

6   Detach the cable from the negative battery terminal.
7   Remove the air cleaner cover and filter element (see Chapter 1).
8   Label, then detach all hoses from the air cleaner housing **(see illustration)**.
9   Remove the mounting fasteners and detach the housing.
10   Installation is the reverse of removal.

8   Accelerator cable – replacement

Carbureted models

Refer to illustrations 8.3, 8.8 and 8.10

1   Detach the cable from the negative battery terminal.
2   Remove the air cleaner assembly (see Section 7).
3   Push back the boot and loosen the locknut until it is beyond the groove in the accelerator cable housing **(see illustration)**.

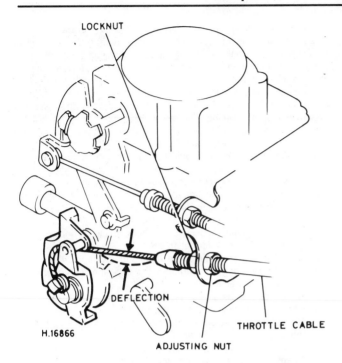

8.10 To adjust the accelerator cable on a carbureted model. loosen the locknut, turn it until the cable has about 3/16 to 3/8 inch deflection, then tighten the locknut

8.14 Rotate the throttle shaft until the cable is out of the guide groove in the bellcrank, then detach the cable end

4   Pull back the cable until the groove is aligned with the slot in the mounting bracket, then slide the cable out of the mounting bracket (see illustration 8.3).
5   Detach the cable end from the throttle link.
6   Working from underneath the dash, detach the other end of the cable from the accelerator pedal arm.
7   Detach the cable from all retaining bracket(s) on the camshaft cover and from any retaining clips that attach it to the transaxle throttle valve cable, if equipped.
8   Rotate the firewall cable grommet 90-degrees (see illustration), then pull the cable through the firewall from the engine side.
9   Installation is the reverse of removal. Be sure to apply sealant to the mating surface of the firewall cable grommet when installing the new cable.
10   To adjust the cable:
   a)   Verify that the accelerator cable operates smoothly. It must not bind or stick.
   b)   Start the engine and check the cable deflection at the throttle linkage (see illustration). It should be about 3/16 to 3/8-inch. If the deflection isn't within specifications, loosen the locknut, turn the adjusting nut until the deflection is within specifications and tighten the locknut.
   c)   After the cable is correctly adjusted, have an assistant help you verify that the throttle valve opens all the way when you push the accelerator pedal to the floor and that it returns to the idle position when you release the accelerator.

Fuel-injected models

Refer to illustrations 8.14 and 8.18

11   Detach the cable from the negative battery terminal.
12   Remove the fresh air duct between the throttle body and the air cleaner assembly (see Section 7).
13   Loosen the locknut and remove the accelerator cable from its bracket (see illustration 8.3).
14   Rotate the throttle shaft bellcrank until the cable is out of its guide groove in the bellcrank (see illustration) and detach the cable from the bellcrank.

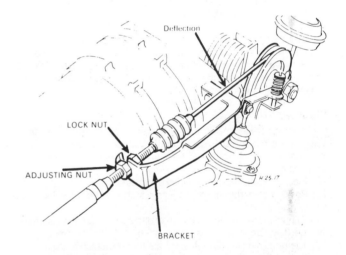

8.18 Lift up the cable to remove the slack, then turn the adjusting nut until the cable housing groove is 1/8-inch from the bracket

15   Working from underneath the dash, detach the cable from the accelerator pedal.
16   To free the cable from the firewall, rotate the rubber grommet (see illustration 8.8) about 90-degrees, pull the grommet from the firewall and pull the cable through the firewall from the engine compartment side.
17   Installation is the reverse of removal.
18   To adjust the cable (see illustration):
   a)   Lift up on the cable to remove any slack.
   b)   Turn the adjusting nut until the groove in the throttle cable housing is 1/8-inch from the cable bracket.
   c)   Tighten the locknut and check cable deflection at the throttle linkage. Deflection should be 3/8 to 1/2-inch. If deflection is not within specifications, loosen the locknut and turn the adjusting nut until the deflection is as specified.
   d)   After you have adjusted the throttle cable, have an assistant help you verify that the throttle valve opens all the way when you depress the accelerator pedal to the floor and that it returns to the idle position when you release the accelerator. Verify the cable operates smoothly. It must not bind or stick.

e) If the vehicle is equipped with an automatic transaxle, adjust the transaxle throttle valve cable (see Chapter 7B).
f) If the vehicle is equipped with cruise control, have the cruise control cable adjusted by a dealer service department or other repair shop.

9   Carburetor – removal and installation

Warning: *Gasoline is extremely flammable, so take extra precautions when you work on any part of the fuel system. Don't smoke or allow open flames or bare light bulbs near the work area, and don't work in a garage where a natural gas-type appliance (such as a water heater or clothes dryer) with a pilot light is present. If you spill any fuel on your skin, rinse it off immediately with soap and water. When you perform any kind of work on the fuel system, wear safety glasses and have a Class B type fire extinguisher on hand.*

Removal

1   Remove the fuel filler cap to relieve fuel tank pressure.
2   Remove the air cleaner from the carburetor. Be sure to label all vacuum hoses attached to the air cleaner housing.
3   Disconnect the throttle cable from the throttle lever (see Section 8).
4   If the vehicle is equipped with an automatic transaxle, disconnect the transaxle throttle valve cable from the throttle lever (see Chapter 7B).
5   Clearly label all vacuum hoses and fittings, then disconnect the hoses.
6   Disconnect the fuel line from the carburetor.
7   Label the wires and terminals, then unplug all electrical connectors.
8   Remove the mounting fasteners and detach the carburetor from the intake manifold. Remove the carburetor mounting gasket. Stuff a shop rag into the intake manifold openings.

Installation

9   Use a gasket scraper to remove all traces of gasket material and sealant from the intake manifold (and the carburetor, if it's being reinstalled), then remove the shop rag from the manifold openings. Clean the mating surfaces with lacquer thinner or acetone.
10   Place a new gasket on the intake manifold.
11   Position the carburetor on the gasket and install the mounting fasteners.
12   To prevent carburetor distortion or damage, tighten the fasteners to the specified torque in a criss-cross pattern, 1/4-turn at a time.
13   The remaining installation steps are the reverse of removal.
14   Check and, if necessary, adjust the idle speed (see Chapter 1).
15   If the vehicle is equipped with an automatic transaxle, refer to Chapter 7B for the throttle valve cable adjustment procedure.
16   Start the engine and check carefully for fuel leaks.

10   Carburetor diagnosis and overhaul – general information

Refer to illustration 10.5

Warning: *Gasoline is extremely flammable, so take extra precautions when you work on any part of the fuel system. Don't smoke or allow open flames or bare light bulbs near the work area, and don't work in a garage where a natural gas-type appliance (such as a water heater or clothes dryer) with a pilot light is present. If you spill any fuel on your skin, rinse it off immediately with soap and water. When you perform any kind of work on the fuel system, wear safety glasses and have a Class B type fire extinguisher on hand.*

Diagnosis

1   A thorough road test and check of carburetor adjustments should be done before any major carburetor service work. Specifications for some adjustments are listed on the Vehicle Emissions Control Information (VECI) label found in the engine compartment.

2   Carburetor problems usually show up as flooding, hard starting, stalling, severe backfiring and poor acceleration. A carburetor that's leaking fuel and/or covered with wet looking deposits definitely needs attention.
3   Some performance complaints directed at the carburetor are actually a result of loose, out-of-adjustment or malfunctioning engine or electrical components. Others develop when vacuum hoses leak, are disconnected or are incorrectly routed. The proper approach to analyzing carburetor problems should include the following items:

a) Inspect all vacuum hoses and actuators for leaks and correct installation (see Chapters 1 and 6).
b) Tighten the intake manifold and carburetor mounting nuts/bolts evenly and securely.
c) Perform a cylinder compression test (see Chapter 2).
d) Clean or replace the spark plugs as necessary (see Chapter 1).
e) Check the spark plug wires (see Chapter 1).
f) Inspect the ignition coil primary wires.
g) Check the ignition timing (follow the instructions printed on the Emissions Control Information label).
h) Check the fuel pump pressure/volume (see Chapter 4).
i) Check the air control diaphragm in the air cleaner for proper operation (see Chapter 1).
j) Check/replace the air filter element (see Chapter 1).
k) Check the PCV system (see Chapter 6).
l) Check/replace the fuel filter (see Chapter 1). Also, the strainer in the tank could be restricted.
m) Check for a plugged exhaust system.
n) Check EGR valve operation (see Chapter 6).
o) Check the choke – it should be completely open at normal engine operating temperature (see Chapter 1).
p) Check for fuel leaks and kinked or dented fuel lines (see Chapters 1 and 4).
q) Check accelerator pump operation with the engine off (remove the air cleaner cover and operate the throttle as you look into the carburetor throat – you should see a stream of gasoline enter the carburetor).
r) Check for incorrect fuel or bad gasoline.
s) Check the valve clearances (if applicable) and camshaft lobe lift (see Chapters 1 and 2)
t) Have a dealer service department or repair shop check the electronic engine and carburetor controls.

4   Diagnosing carburetor problems may require that the engine be started and run with the air cleaner off. While running the engine without the air cleaner, backfires are possible. This situation is likely to occur if the carburetor is malfunctioning, but just the removal of the air cleaner can lean the fuel/air mixture enough to produce an engine backfire. **Warning:** *Do not position any part of your body, especially your face, directly over the carburetor during inspection and servicing procedures. Wear eye protection!*

Overhaul

5   Once it's determined that the carburetor needs an overhaul **(see illustration)**, several options are available. If you're going to attempt to overhaul the carburetor yourself, first obtain a good quality carburetor rebuild kit (which will include all necessary gaskets, internal parts, instructions and a parts list). You'll also need some special solvent and a means of blowing out the internal passages of the carburetor with air.
6   An alternative is to obtain a new or rebuilt carburetor. They are readily available from dealers and auto parts stores. Make absolutely sure the exchange carburetor is identical to the original. A tag is usually attached to the top of the carburetor or a number is stamped on the float bowl. It will help determine the exact type of carburetor you have. When obtaining a rebuilt carburetor or a rebuild kit, make sure the kit or carburetor matches your application exactly. Seemingly insignificant differences can make a large difference in engine performance.
7   If you choose to overhaul your own carburetor, allow enough time to disassemble it carefully, soak the necessary parts in the cleaning solvent (usually for at least one-half day or according to the instructions listed on the carburetor cleaner) and reassemble it, which will usually take much longer than disassembly. When disassembling the carburetor, match each part with the illustration in the carburetor kit and lay the parts out in

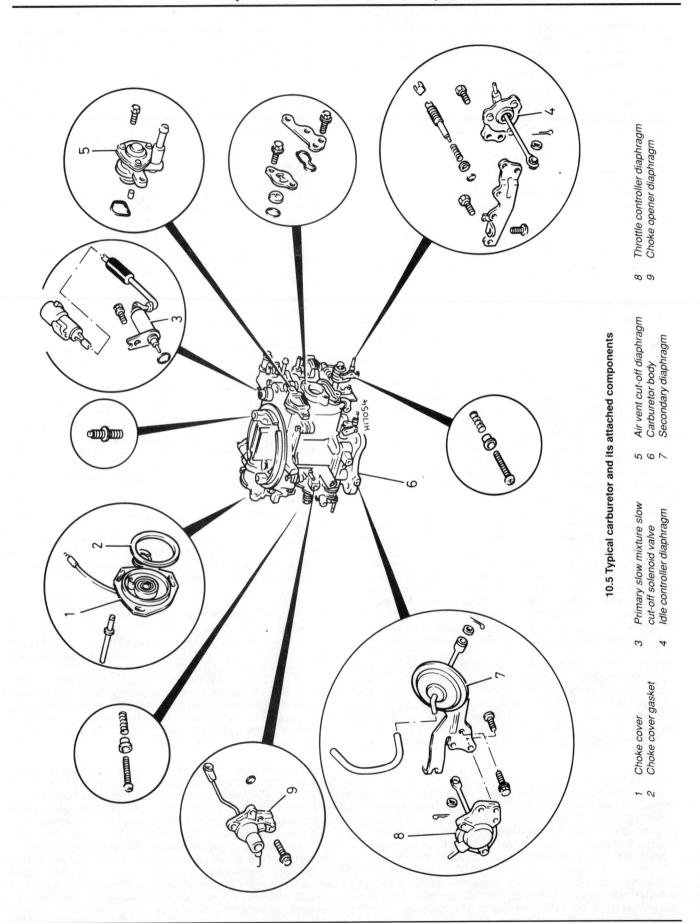

10.5 Typical carburetor and its attached components

1	Choke cover
2	Choke cover gasket
3	Primary slow mixture slow cut-off solenoid valve
4	Idle controller diaphragm
5	Air vent cut-off diaphragm
6	Carburetor body
7	Secondary diaphragm
8	Throttle controller diaphragm
9	Choke opener diaphragm

order on a clean work surface. Overhauls by inexperienced mechanics can result in an engine which runs poorly or not at all. To avoid this, use care and patience when disassembling the carburetor so you can reassemble it correctly.

8   Because carburetor designs are constantly modified by the manufacturer in order to meet increasingly more stringent emissions regulations, it isn't feasible to include a step-by-step overhaul of each type. You'll receive a detailed, well-illustrated set of instructions with most carburetor overhaul kits. They will apply in a more specific manner to the carburetor on your vehicle.

11   Fuel injection system – general information

Refer to illustration 11.1

The Programmed Fuel Injection (PGM-FI) system **(see illustration)** consists of three sub-systems: air intake, electronic control and fuel delivery. Although there are two variations of this system (multi-point fuel injection or dual-point fuel injection), they both operate in a similar manner.

Air intake system

The air intake system consists of the air cleaner, the air intake pipe, the throttle body, the idle control system, the fast idle mechanism and the intake manifold. A resonator in the air intake tube provides silencing as air is drawn into the system.

The throttle body on the multi-point system is a two-barrel, side-draft design with the primary air horn at the top. The lower portion of the throttle body is heated by engine coolant to prevent icing in cold weather. The throttle body on the dual-point system is a single-barrel, down-draft design, which also houses the two fuel injectors. On either system, a throttle sensor attached to the throttle shaft senses changes in throttle opening. To slow the movement of the throttle valve as it closes, a dashpot is added to vehicles equipped with a manual transaxle.

When the engine is idling, the air-fuel ratio is controlled by the idle control system, which consists of the Electronic Control Unit (ECU), the idle control, fast idle, automatic transaxle idle control and air conditioning idle control solenoid valves. The first three of these solenoid valves alter the amount of air bypassed into the air intake manifold. The air conditioning idle control solenoid valve opens the air conditioning idle control valve when the air conditioning system is turned on.

When the idle speed is low because of electrical or other loads on the engine, the idle control solenoid valve opens to allow extra air into the intake manifold. This additional air allows the idle speed to increase to its normal speed. The valve also reduces fast idle speed during warm-up, once the coolant temperature has surpassed 104-degrees F. Finally, to prevent rough running after the engine starts, the valve is opened during cranking and immediately after starting to provide additional air into the intake manifold.

The fast idle control solenoid valve also opens when the engine is cold to prevent erratic idling by passing additional air to the intake manifold to raise the idle speed. The fast idle control solenoid valve is energized by the coolant temperature and atmospheric pressure sensors. The valve is open below 105-degrees F at sea level and below 104-degrees F at high altitude.

When the automatic transaxle is in gear, the idle speed tends to go down. The automatic transaxle idle control solenoid valve compensates for this by sending more air to the intake in order to maintain the correct idle speed.

If the air conditioning system is on, the air conditioning idle control solenoid valve opens to increase air flow and maintain the normal idle speed.

In 1988, these four idle control valves were replaced by the Electronic Air Control Valve (EACV). Like the solenoid valves in the idle control system described above, this valve changes the amount of air bypassed into the intake manifold in response to changes in an electrical signal from the ECU.

After the engine starts, the EACV opens. The amount of air is increased to raise the idle speed about 150 to 250 rpm. When the coolant temperature is low, the EACV is opened to obtain the proper fast idle speed. The amount of bypassed air is controlled in relation to the coolant temperature. When the coolant temperature is below 122-degrees F, it also activates the fast idle valve to prevent the idle speed from dropping.

Electronic control system

The electronic control system consists of an eight-bit microprocessor (computer) and various sensors:

The crank angle sensor, which is an integral part of the distributor assembly, consists of two rotors (TDC and CYL) and a pickup for each rotor. The distributor is driven off the end of the camshaft, and the rotors are coupled to the distributor shaft, so they turn together as a unit as the cam rotates. The CYL pickup detects the position of the no. 1 cylinder as the base for sequential injection; the TDC pickup determines the injection timing for each cylinder. The TDC pickup also monitors engine speed to help determine the basic discharge duration for different operating conditions.

The Manifold Absolute Pressure (MAP) sensor converts manifold pressure readings into electrical voltage signals and sends them to the ECU. This data, along with the data from the TDC and CYL sensors, enables the ECU to determine the duration during which fuel is injected.

The atmospheric pressure (PA) sensor converts atmospheric pressures into voltage signals and sends them to the ECU. These signals enable the ECU to modify the basic fuel discharge duration to compensate for changes in the atmospheric pressure.

The coolant temperature (TW) sensor uses a temperature dependent diode (thermistor) to measure differences in the coolant temperature. The resistance of the thermistor decreases with a rise in coolant temperature. The ECU uses this input to increase or decrease the fuel discharge duration.

The intake air temperature (TA) sensor, which is located in the intake manifold, is also a thermistor. In operation, it's similar to the TW sensor but has a lower thermal capacity for quicker response time.

The throttle angle sensor is a variable resistor. The sensor is mounted on the end of the throttle valve shaft. As the throttle valve is rotated, the resistance varies, altering the output voltage to the control unit, which in turn alters the fuel discharge duration.

The oxygen sensor monitors the oxygen content in the exhaust gas and sends a variable voltage signal to the ECU, which alters the fuel discharge duration.

When the ignition key is turned to Start, the starter switch sends a signal to the ECU, which increases the amount of fuel injected, in accordance with the engine temperature. The amount of fuel injected is gradually reduced once the engine is started.

Fuel delivery system

The fuel delivery system consists of these components: The fuel pump, the pressure regulator, the fuel injectors (four on multi-point systems and two on dual point systems), the injector resistor (multi-point system only) and the main relay.

The fuel pump is an inline, direct drive type. Fuel is drawn through a filter into the pump, flows past the armature through the one-way valve, passes through another filter and is delivered to the injectors. A relief valve prevents excessive pressure build-up by opening in the event of a blockage in the discharge side and allowing fuel to flow from the high to the low pressure side.

The pressure regulator maintains a constant fuel pressure to the injectors. The spring chamber of the pressure regulator is connected to the intake manifold to constantly maintain the fuel pressure at 36 psi higher than the pressure in the manifold. When the difference between the fuel pressure and manifold pressure exceeds this figure, the diaphragm is pushed up and excess fuel is fed back to the fuel tank through the return line.

The injectors are solenoid-actuated, constant stroke, pintle types consisting of a solenoid, plunger, needle valve and housing. When current is applied to the solenoid coil, the needle valve raises and pressurized fuel fills the injector housing and squirts out the nozzle. The needle valve lift and the fuel pressure are constant, so the injection quantity is determined by the length of time the valve is open, i.e. the length of time during which current is supplied to the solenoid coils.

11.1   Fuel injection and emission components on a 16-valve engine equipped with multi-point fuel injection

1   Charcoal canister
2   Manifold Absolute Pressure (MAP) sensor
3   Throttle angle sensor (Located on backside of the throttle body)
4   Throttle body
5   Electronic Air Control Valve (EACV)
6   Throttle cable
7   Fuel pressure regulator
8   Intake air temperature sensor
9   Injector resistor
10 Oxygen sensor
11 Electronic ignition connector

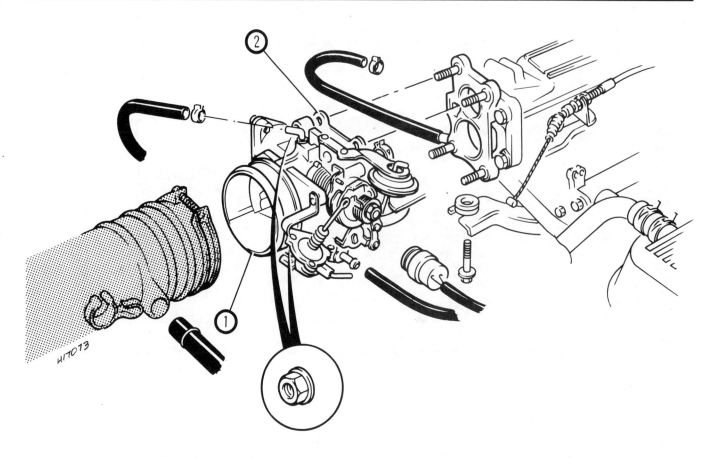

13.13   An exploded view of the throttle body (multi-point fuel injection system)

1   Throttle body   *2   Gasket*

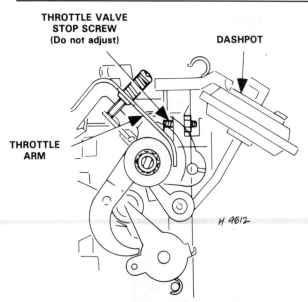

13.15   A typical dashpot assembly (1987 and earlier multi-point fuel injection systems)

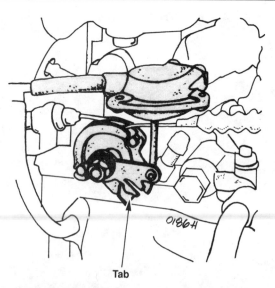

13.21   Bend this tab to adjust the engine rpm when the dashpot hose is disconnected (1988 and later dual-point system shown, multi-point system similar)

Because it determines opening and closing intervals – which in turn determine the air-fuel mixture ratio – injector timing must be quite accurate. To attain the best possible injector response, the current rise time, when voltage is being applied to each injector coil, must be as short as possible.

The number of windings in the coil has therefore been reduced to lower the inductance in the coil. However, this creates low coil resistance, which could compromise the durability of the coil. The flow of current in the coil is therefore restricted by a resistor installed in the injector wire harness.

The main relay, which is installed adjacent to the fuse box, is a direct coupler type which contains the relays for the electronic control unit power supply and the fuel pump power supply.

12 Fuel injection system – check

Note: *The following procedure is based on the assumption that the fuel pressure is adequate (see Section 3).*

Preliminary checks

1   Check the ground wire connections on the intake manifold for tightness. Check all wiring harness connectors that are related to the system. Loose connectors and poor grounds can cause many problems that resemble more serious malfunctions.
2   Check to see that the battery is fully charged, as the control unit and sensors depend on an accurate supply voltage in order to properly meter the fuel.
3   Check the air filter element – a dirty or partially blocked filter will severely impede performance and economy (see Chapter 1).
4   If a blown fuse is found, replace it and see if it blows again. If it does, search for a grounded wire in the harness to the fuel pump.
5   On multi-port systems check the air intake duct to the intake manifold for leaks, which will result in an excessively lean mixture. Also check the condition of all vacuum hoses connected to the intake manifold.
6   On multi-port systems, remove the air intake duct from the throttle body and check for dirt, carbon or other residue build-up. If it's dirty, clean it with carburetor cleaner and a toothbrush.
7   With the engine running, place a screwdriver against each injector, one at a time, and listen through the handle for a clicking sound, indicating operation.
8   The remainder of the system checks can be found in the following Sections.

13 Throttle body – component check, removal and installation

Throttle body

Check (multi-point fuel injection system only)

1   On top of the throttle body, locate the vacuum hose that goes to the canister. Detach it from the throttle body and attach a vacuum gauge in its place.
2   Start the engine and warm it to its normal operating temperature (wait until the cooling fan comes on twice). Verify the gauge indicates no vacuum.
3   Open the throttle slightly from idle and verify that the gauge indicates vacuum.
4   Stop the engine and verify the throttle cable and valve operate smoothly without binding or sticking.
5   If the throttle cable or valve binds or sticks, check for a build-up of sludge on the cable or throttle shaft.
6   If a build-up of sludge is evident, try removing it with carburetor cleaner or a similar solvent.
7   If cleaning fails to remedy the problem, replace the throttle body.

Replacement (multi-point and dual-point systems)
Refer to illustration 13.13

8   Detach the cable from the negative battery terminal. If you're working on a dual-point system, relieve the fuel system pressure (see Section 2).
9   If you are working on a multi-point system, remove the air duct that connects the air cleaner assembly to the throttle body. If you're working on a dual-point system, remove the air intake chamber.
10   Label, then detach, all vacuum hoses from the throttle body.
11   Detach the accelerator cable (see Section 8) and, if equipped, the transaxle throttle valve cable (see Chapter 7B).
12   Detach the coolant hoses from the throttle body (multi-point system only). If you're working on a dual-point system, detach the fuel hoses from the fuel pressure regulator and the throttle body.
13   Remove the four mounting nuts and detach the throttle body and gasket **(see illustration)**.
14   Installation is the reverse of removal. Be sure to adjust the accelerator cable (see Section 8) and, if equipped, the throttle valve cable (see Chapter 7B).

Throttle control (dashpot) system
1985 through 1987 models
Refer to illustration 13.15

15   The dashpot **(see illustration)** slows the closing of the throttle valve during gear shifting or deceleration.
16   Slowly open the throttle arm until the dashpot rod is raised up as far as it will go.
17   Release the throttle arm and measure the time until the throttle arm contacts the stop screw. This should take about 1/4 to two seconds.
   a) If the time is over two seconds, replace the dashpot check valve and re-check it.
   b) If the rod doesn't operate, check for binding in the linkage or a clogged check valve or vacuum line. If they're okay, replace the dashpot.

1988 and later models
Refer to illustration 13.21

18   Start the engine and allow it to warm up
19   Connect a tachometer in accordance with the manufacturer's instructions.
20   Disconnect the vacuum hose from the dashpot and check the engine speed. It should be approximately 2500 ± 500 rpm.
21   If the engine speed is too high, adjust it by bending the tab on the throttle arm **(see illustration)**.
22   If the engine speed didn't change when the hose was disconnected, connect a vacuum gauge to the hose and check for vacuum (the gauge should register vacuum). If the gauge doesn't indicate vacuum, check the hose for a blockage or cracks and repair it as necessary.
23   If the gauge does register vacuum, but the engine speed didn't change when the hose was disconnected in Step 20, replace the dashpot.
24   Check and, if necessary, adjust the idle speed (see Chapter 1).

14 Fuel pressure regulator – check and replacement

Warning: *Gasoline is extremely flammable, so take extra precautions when you work on any part of the fuel system. Don't smoke or allow open flames or bare light bulbs near the work area, and don't work in a garage where a natural gas-type appliance (such as a water heater or clothes dryer) with a pilot light is present. If you spill any fuel on your skin, rinse it off immediately with soap and water. When you perform any kind of work on the fuel system, wear safety glasses and have a Class B type fire extinguisher on hand.*

Check

1   Inspect the fuel system for pinched or broken vacuum hoses and fuel lines.
2   Connect a fuel pressure gauge following the procedure outlined in Section 3.
3   Start the engine and check the fuel pressure. Detach the vacuum hose from the regulator (see illustrations 3.18a and 3.18b) and verify the fuel pressure rises. If the fuel pressure doesn't rise, carefully pinch the fuel return line with a pair of pliers (place a rag over the hose first, so as not to damage it). If the pressure now rises, replace the fuel pressure regulator.

Replacement
Refer to illustrations 14.6a and 14.6b

4   Detach the cable from the negative battery terminal.
5   Relieve the system fuel pressure (see Section 2).

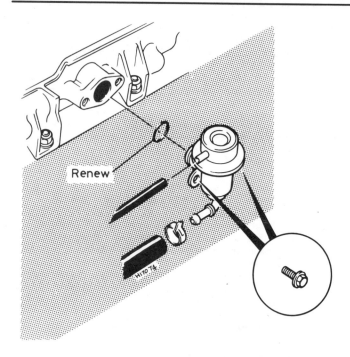

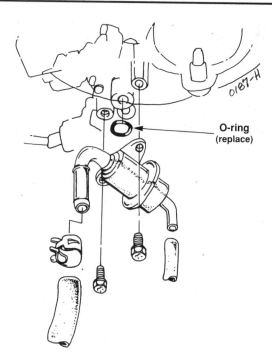

O-ring
(replace)

14.6a   To replace the fuel pressure regulator on a multi-port system, detach the vacuum hose and fuel return hose, then remove the two retaining bolts – be sure to replace the O-ring

14.6b   The fuel pressure regulator on the dual-point system is mounted on the side of the throttle body

6   Detach the vacuum hose and fuel return hose from the regulator **(see illustrations)**.

7   Remove the two bolts and detach the regulator.

8   Installation is the reverse of removal. Be sure to use a new O-ring. Apply clean engine oil to the O-ring and install it in its proper position. Be sure you don't damage the O-ring when you install the regulator.

15   Fuel injectors – check, removal and installation

Warning: *Gasoline is extremely flammable, so take extra precautions when you work on any part of the fuel system. Don't smoke or allow open flames or bare light bulbs near the work area, and don't work in a garage where a natural gas-type appliance (such as a water heater or clothes dry-er) with a pilot light is present. If you spill any fuel on your skin, rinse it off immediately with soap and water. When you perform any kind of work on the fuel system, wear safety glasses and have a Class B type fire extinguisher on hand.*

Multi-point fuel injection system
Check
Refer to illustrations 15.2 and 15.3

1   Start the engine and warm it to its normal operating temperature.

2   With the engine idling, unplug each injector one-at-a-time **(see illustration),** note the change in idle speed, then reconnect the injector. If the idle speed drop is almost the same for each cylinder, the injectors are operating correctly. If unplugging a particular injector fails to change the idle speed, proceed to the next step.

15.2   Before unplugging an injector connector, use a scribe (shown) or a small screwdriver to pry the spring clip loose

15.3   With the engine running, check for voltage at the injector electrical connector

15.10   Remove the nut (arrow) and detach the two ground cables from the intake manifold

3   Check the injector electrical connector with a high-impedance voltmeter **(see illustration)** or a special injector harness test light, available at some auto parts stores.

   a)   If the voltage fluctuates between zero and two volts, the injector is receiving proper voltage. Check the resistance of the injector (see Step 4).

   b)   If there is no voltage, check the injector resistor (see Section 16).

   c)   If the injector resistor is operating normally, check the wiring between the resistor and the injector and between the injector and the ECU for a short circuit, break in the wire or bad connection.

   d)   If there is voltage at the electrical connector, but the injector is malfunctioning, listen to the clicking sound of each injector with a stethoscope. If the suspect injector isn't making the same clicking sound as the other injectors, check its resistance (see below).

4   With the engine stopped, unplug the injector electrical connector and measure the resistance across the terminals of the injector. It should be as listed in this Chapter's Specifications. If the resistance is not as specified, replace the injector (see below).

Replacement

Refer to illustrations 15.10, 15.11, 15.12, 15.13 and 15.17

5   Detach the cable from the negative battery terminal.

6   Relieve the fuel pressure (see Section 2).

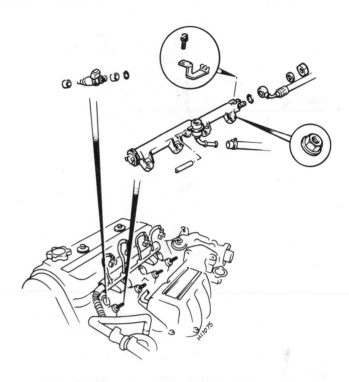

15.11   Fuel rail installation details

7   Remove the air cleaner assembly (see Section 7).

8   Unplug the injector connector(s) **(see illustration 15.2).**

9   Detach the vacuum hose and fuel return hose from the fuel pressure regulator (see Section 14).

10   Detach the two ground cables from the intake manifold **(see illustration)**.

11   Detach the fuel line from the fuel rail **(see illustration)**.

12   Remove the mounting nuts **(see illustration)** and detach the fuel rail and injectors.

13   Remove the injector(s) from the fuel rail and remove and discard the seal ring(s) **(see illustration)**. Note the location of the injector O-ring and cushion ring, then remove and discard them. **Note:** *Whether you're replacing an injector or a leaking O-ring, it's a good idea to remove all the injectors from the fuel rail and replace all the O-rings and cushion rings.*

15.12   Remove the fuel rail mounting nuts (arrows), then pull the fuel rail assembly and injectors off the manifold

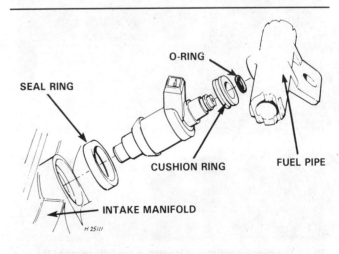

15.13   An exploded view of a multi-point injector assembly – note the relationship of the injector to the seal ring, cushion ring and O-ring to ensure proper reassembly

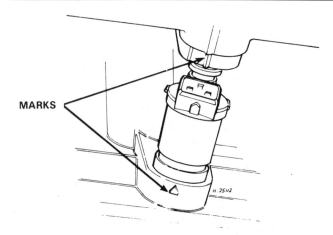

15.17   Be sure the mark on each injector connector is aligned with the mark on the intake manifold

14   Coat the new cushion ring(s) with clean engine oil and slide it/them onto the injector(s).
15   Coat the new O-ring(s) with clean engine oil and place it/them on the injector(s), then insert each injector into its corresponding bore in the fuel rail.
16   Coat the new seal ring(s) with clean engine oil and press it/them into the injector bore(s) in the intake manifold.
17   Install the injector and fuel rail assembly on the intake manifold. Make sure the centerline of the electrical connector on each injector is aligned with its corresponding mark on the intake manifold **(see illustration)**. Tighten the fuel rail mounting nuts to the torque listed in this Chapter's Specifications.
18   The remainder of installation is the reverse of removal.
19   After the injector/fuel rail assembly installation is complete, turn the ignition switch to On, but don't operate the starter (this activates the fuel pump for about two seconds, which builds up fuel pressure in the fuel lines and the fuel rail). Repeat this about two or three times, then check the fuel lines, rail and injectors for fuel leakage.

Dual-point fuel injection system
Check
20   Disconnect the electrical connectors from the main (upper) and auxiliary (lower) fuel injectors.

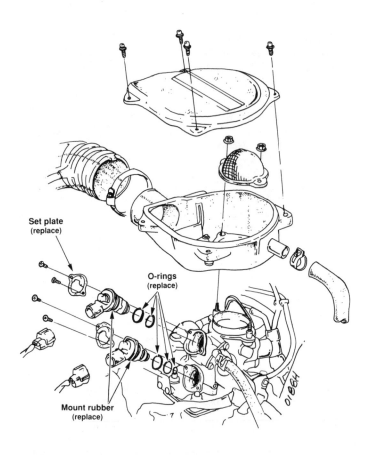

15.26   Fuel injector installation details (dual-point fuel injection system)

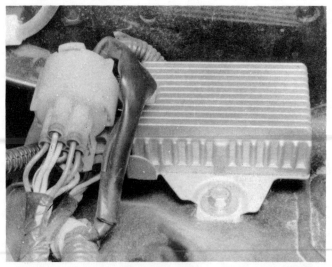

16.2   The injector resistor is located in the left corner of the engine compartment

16.4   To check the injector resistor, measure the resistance between the power supply terminal (A) and the other 4 terminals in the connector – resistance should be about 5 to 7 ohms

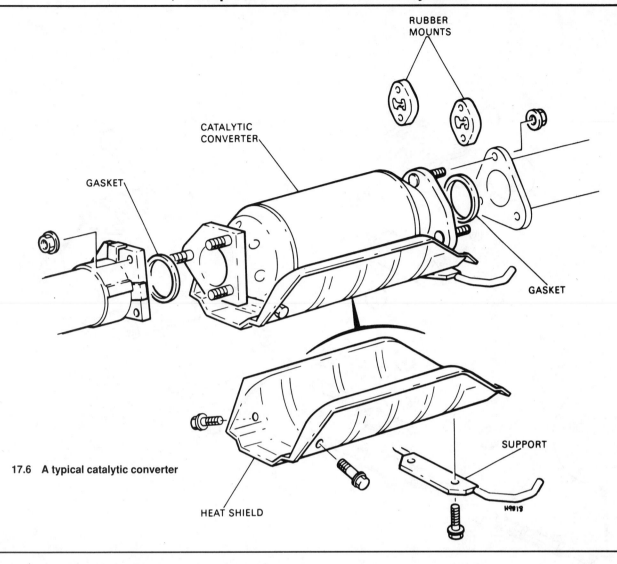

RUBBER
MOUNTS

CATALYTIC
CONVERTER

GASKET

GASKET

SUPPORT

17.6   **A typical catalytic converter**

HEAT SHIELD

21   Measure the resistance across the terminals of each injector and compare your readings to the values listed in this Chapter's Specifications. If the resistance of either injector is not as specified, replace it.
22   Any further checks should be performed by a dealer service department or other repair shop.

Replacement

Refer to illustration 15.26

23   Disconnect the cable from the negative terminal of the battery.
24   Remove the air intake chamber.
25   Disconnect the electrical connector(s) from the injector(s).
26   Remove the set plate screws **(see illustration)** and pull the injector(s) out of the throttle body.
27   Lubricate the new O-rings with clean engine oil and install them onto the injector(s). Insert the injector(s) into the throttle body and install the set plate screws.
28   The remainder of installation is the reverse of removal.

16   Injector resistor (multi-point system only) – check and replacement

Refer to illustrations 16.2 and 16.4

Check

1   Detach the cable from the negative battery terminal.

2   Locate the injector resistor **(see illustration)**. It's on the left side of the engine compartment.
3   Trace the wire harness from the resistor back to its connector and unplug it.
4   Check the resistance between the power supply terminal (A) and each of the other four terminals in the connector **(see illustration)**. Resistance for each of the four checks should be about 5 to 7 ohms.
5   If the indicated resistance isn't within specification, replace the resistor.

Replacement

6   Detach the cable from the negative battery terminal.
7   Disconnect the electrical connector from the injector resistor.
8   Remove the bolts that attach the resistor to the body and remove the unit.
9   Installation is the reverse of removal.

17   Exhaust system servicing – general information

Refer to illustrations 17.1a, 17.1b and 17.6

Warning: *Inspection and repair of exhaust system components should be done only after enough time has elapsed after driving the vehicle to allow the system components to cool completely. Also, when working under the vehicle, make sure it is securely supported on jackstands.*

1   The exhaust system **(see illustrations)** consists of the exhaust manifold(s), the catalytic converter, the muffler, the tailpipe and all connecting

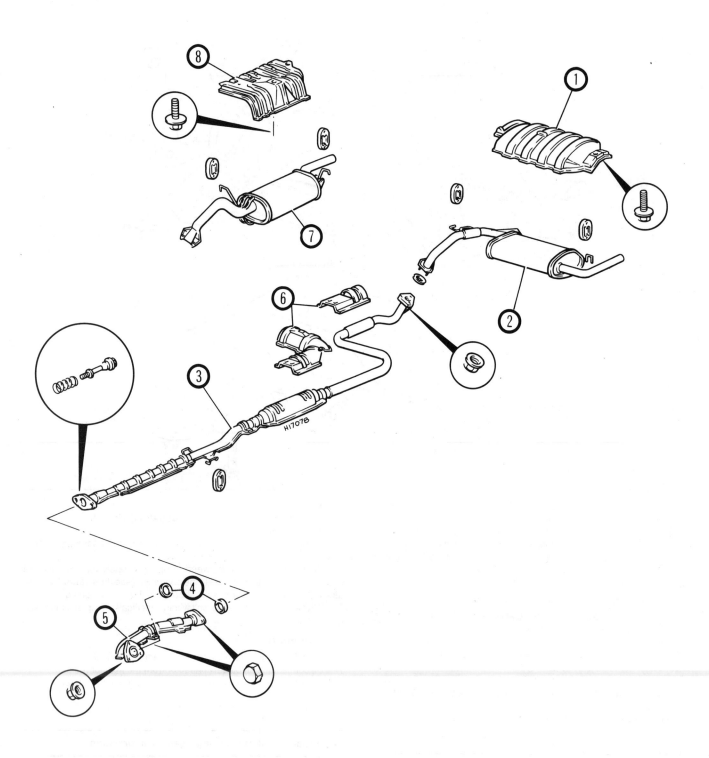

17.1a   Typical exhaust system (except CRX and Hatchback Si)

1	Fuel tank heat shield (Hatchback)	3	Exhaust pipe	6	Heat shield	8	Fuel tank heat shield (Sedan and Wagon)
2	Muffler (Hatchback)	4	Gasket	7	Muffler (Sedan and Wagon)		
		5	Header pipe				

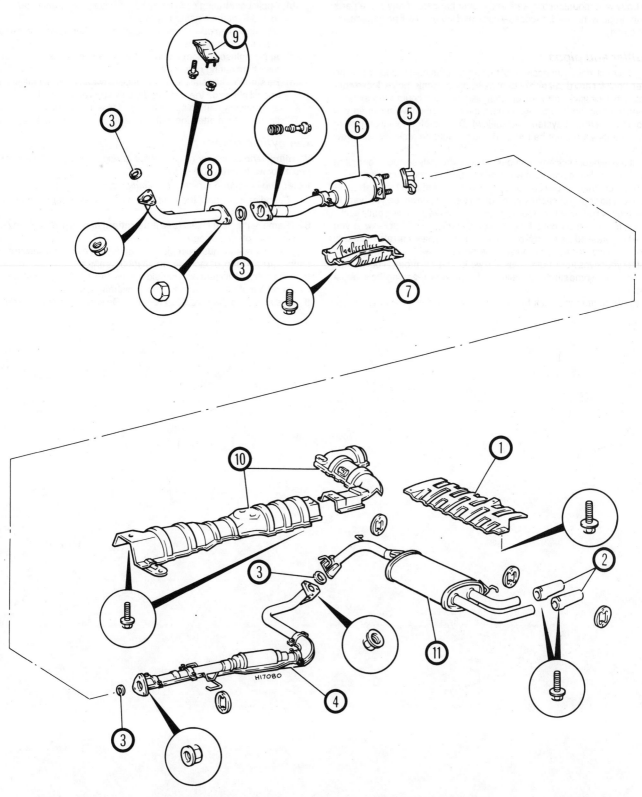

17.1b   Typical exhaust system fitted to CrX Si and Hatchback Si models

1	Fuel tank heat shield	4	Exhaust pipe	7	Lower converter cover	10	Heat shields
2	Exhaust tailpipes	5	Converter upper cover	8	Header pipe	11	Muffler
3	Gasket	6	Catalytic converter	9	Header pipe bracket	

pipes, brackets, hangers and clamps. The exhaust system is attached to the body with mounting brackets and rubber hangers. If any of the parts are improperly installed, excessive noise and vibration will be transmitted to the body.

Muffler and pipes

2   Conduct regular inspections of the exhaust system to keep it safe and quiet. Look for any damaged or bent parts, open seams, holes, loose connections, excessive corrosion or other defects which could allow exhaust fumes to enter the vehicle. Also check the catalytic converter when you inspect the exhaust system (see below). Deteriorated exhaust system components should not be repaired; they should be replaced with new parts.

3   If the exhaust system components are extremely corroded or rusted together, welding equipment will probably be required to remove them. The convenient way to accomplish this is to have a muffler repair shop remove the corroded sections with a cutting torch. If, however, you want to save money by doing it yourself (and you don't have a welding outfit with a cutting torch), simply cut off the old components with a hacksaw. If you have compressed air, special pneumatic cutting chisels can also be used. If you do decide to tackle the job at home, be sure to wear safety goggles to protect your eyes from metal chips and work gloves to protect your hands.

4   Here are some simple guidelines to follow when repairing the exhaust system:

   a) Work from the back to the front when removing exhaust system components.

   b) Apply penetrating oil to the exhaust system component fasteners to make them easier to remove.

   c) Use new gaskets, hangers and clamps when installing exhaust systems components.

   d) Apply anti-seize compound to the threads of all exhaust system fasteners during reassembly.

   e) Be sure to allow sufficient clearance between newly installed parts and all points on the underbody to avoid overheating the floor pan and possibly damaging the interior carpet and insulation. Pay particularly close attention to the catalytic converter and heat shield.

Catalytic converter

Warning: *The converter gets very hot during operation. Make sure it's cooled down before you touch it.*

Note: *See Chapter 6 for more information on the catalytic converter.*

5   Periodically, inspect the heat shield for cracks, dents and loose or missing fasteners.

6   Remove the heat shield **(see illustration)** and inspect the converter for cracks or other damage.

7   If the converter must be replaced, remove the mounting nuts from the flanges at each end, detach the rubber mounts and separate the converter from the exhaust system (you should be able to push the exhaust pipes at each end out of the way to clear the converter studs.

8   Installation is the reverse of removal. Be sure to use new gaskets.

Chapter 5   Engine electrical systems

Contents

Specifications

Ignition coil

Primary resistance
  1984 .... 1.24 to 1.46 ohms
  1985 .... 1.06 to 1.24 ohms
  1986 and 1987 (between terminals A and D) .... 1.2 to 1.5 ohms
  1988-on (between terminals A and D) .... 0.3 to 0.5 ohms
Secondary resistance
  1984 .... 8,000 to 12,000 ohms
  1985 .... 7,400 to 11,000 ohms
  1986 and 1987
    Between terminal A and tower .... 11,074 to 11,526 ohms.
    Between terminals B and D .... Approx 2,200 ohms
  1988-on (between terminal A and tower) .... 9,760 to 14,640 ohms

Radio condenser capacitance .... 0.47 ± 0.09 microfarads

Charging system
Alternator brush length (minimum) 1/4-inch

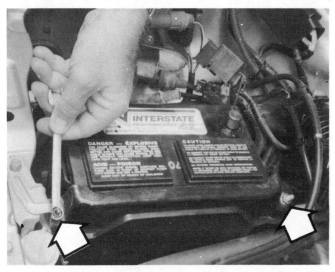

4.2   To remove the battery, detach the negative, then the positive cable clamps from their respective terminals, remove the two nuts (arrows) and detach the hold-down clamp

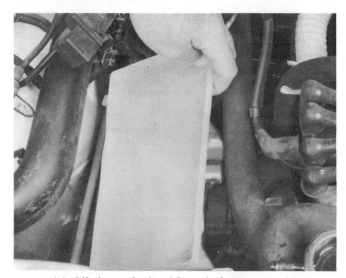

4.4   Lift the carrier (tray) from the battery support

1   General information

The engine electrical systems include all ignition, charging and starting components. Because of their engine-related functions, these components are discussed separately from chassis electrical devices such as the lights, the instruments, etc. (which are included in Chapter 12).

Always observe the following precautions when working on the electrical systems:

a) Be extremely careful when servicing engine electrical components. They are easily damaged if checked, connected or handled improperly.

b) Never leave the ignition switch on for long periods of time with the engine off.

c) Don't disconnect the battery cables while the engine is running.

d) Maintain correct polarity when connecting a battery cable from another vehicle during jump starting.

e) Always disconnect the negative cable first and hook it up last or the battery may be shorted by the tool being used to loosen the cable clamps.

It's also a good idea to review the safety-related information regarding the engine electrical systems located in the Safety First section near the front of this manual before beginning any operation included in this Chapter.

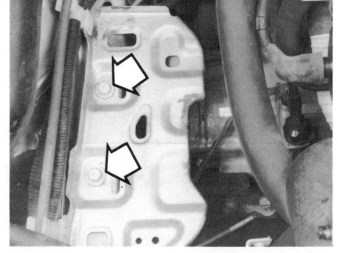

4.5   Remove the bolts that attach the support to the body. Two of the bolts are located under the plate

2   Battery – emergency jump starting

Refer to the Booster battery (jump) starting procedure at the front of this manual.

3   Battery cables – check and replacement

1   Periodically inspect the entire length of each battery cable for damage, cracked or burned insulation and corrosion. Poor battery cable connections can cause starting problems and decreased engine performance.

2   Check the cable-to-terminal connections at the ends of the cables for cracks, loose wire strands and corrosion. The presence of white, fluffy deposits under the insulation at the cable terminal connection is a sign that the cable is corroded and should be replaced. Check the terminals for distortion, missing mounting bolts and corrosion.

3   When removing the cables, always disconnect the negative cable first and hook it up last or the battery may be shorted by the tool used to loosen the cable clamps. Even if only the positive cable is being replaced, be sure to disconnect the negative cable from the battery first (see Chapter 1 for further information regarding battery cable removal).

4   Disconnect the old cables from the battery, then trace each of them to their opposite ends and detach them from the starter solenoid and ground terminals. Note the routing of each cable to ensure correct installation.

5   If you are replacing either or both of the old cables, take them with you when buying new cables. It is vitally important that you replace the cables with identical parts. Cables have characteristics that make them easy to identify: positive cables are usually red, larger in cross-section and have a larger diameter battery post clamp; ground cables are usually black, smaller in cross-section and have a slightly smaller diameter clamp for the negative post.

6   Clean the threads of the solenoid or ground connection with a wire brush to remove rust and corrosion. Apply a light coat of battery terminal corrosion inhibitor, or petroleum jelly, to the threads to prevent future corrosion.

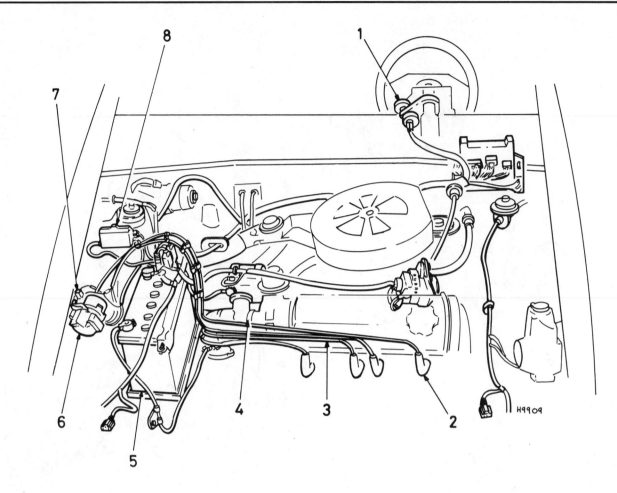

5.1   General layout of the ignition system components

1	*Ignition switch*	3	*Spark plug wires*	5	*Battery*	7	*Radio suppressor*
2	*Spark plug*	4	*Distributor*	6	*Ignition coil*	8	*Main fuse*

7   Attach the cable to the solenoid or ground connection and tighten the mounting nut/bolt securely.

8   Before connecting a new cable to the battery, make sure that it reaches the battery post without having to be stretched.

9   Connect the positive cable first, followed by the negative cable.

4   Battery – removal and installation

Refer to illustrations 4.2, 4.4 and 4.5

1   **Caution:** *Always disconnect the negative cable first and hook it up last or the battery may be shorted by the tool being used to loosen the cable clamps. Disconnect both cables from the battery terminals.*

2   Remove the battery hold-down clamp **(see illustration)**.

3   Lift out the battery. Be careful – it's heavy. **Note:** *Battery straps and handlers are available at most auto parts stores for a reasonable price. They make it easier to remove and carry the battery.*

4   While the battery is out, remove and inspect the carrier (tray) for corrosion **(see illustration)**.

5   If corrosion has leaked down to the battery support, remove the bolts

and lift the support out **(see illustration)**. Clean the deposits from the metal to prevent the support from further oxidation.

6   If you are replacing the battery, make sure you get one that's identical, with the same dimensions, amperage rating, cold cranking rating, etc.

7   Installation is the reverse of removal.

5   Ignition system – general information

Refer to illustrations 5.1, 5.2a and 5.2b

Warning: *Transistorized electronic ignition systems generate considerably higher voltage than conventional systems. Be extra careful when servicing these ignition systems.*

The electronic ignition system consists of the ignition switch, battery, coil, distributor, spark plug wires and spark plugs **(see illustration)**.

All distributors are driven by the camshaft. Distributors on early models employ centrifugal and vacuum advance systems; later model distributors are advanced and retarded by the Electronic Control Unit. Several distributors are used on the vehicles covered by this manual: Fuel injected models use a Toyo Denso distributor. Carbureted models may be equipped

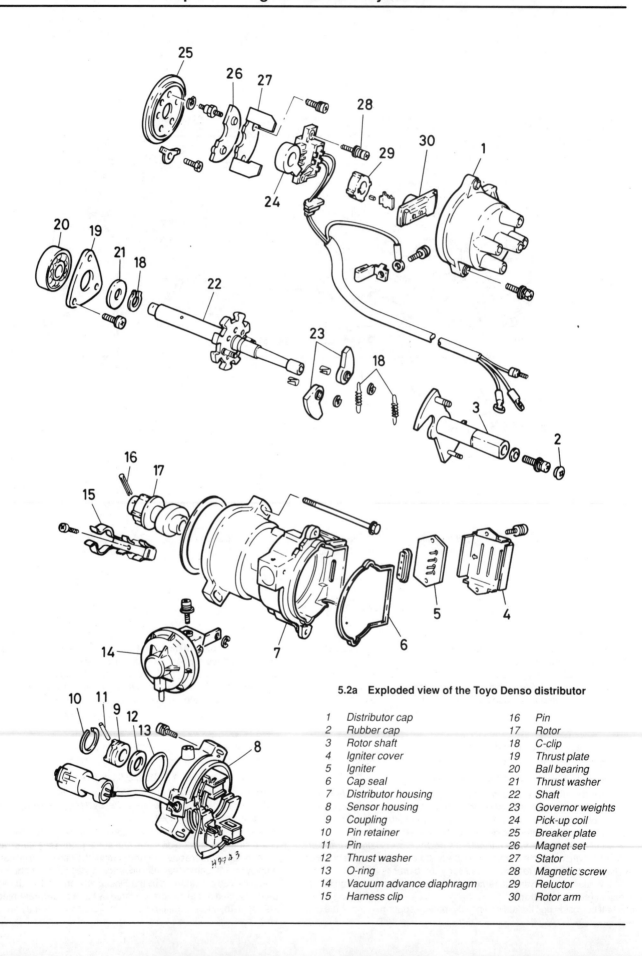

5.2a   Exploded view of the Toyo Denso distributor

1	Distributor cap	16	Pin
2	Rubber cap	17	Rotor
3	Rotor shaft	18	C-clip
4	Igniter cover	19	Thrust plate
5	Igniter	20	Ball bearing
6	Cap seal	21	Thrust washer
7	Distributor housing	22	Shaft
8	Sensor housing	23	Governor weights
9	Coupling	24	Pick-up coil
10	Pin retainer	25	Breaker plate
11	Pin	26	Magnet set
12	Thrust washer	27	Stator
13	O-ring	28	Magnetic screw
14	Vacuum advance diaphragm	29	Reluctor
15	Harness clip	30	Rotor arm

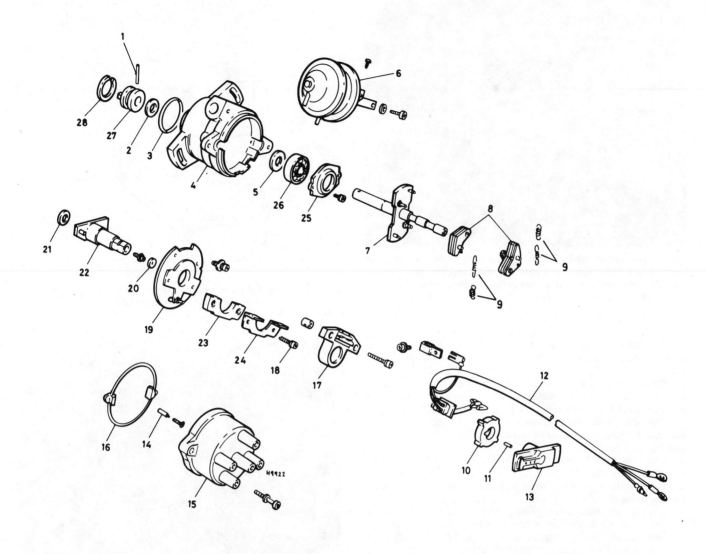

5.2b   Exploded view of the Hitachi distributor

1	Pin	8	Governor weights	15	Distributor cap	22	Rotor shaft
2	Thrust washer	9	Governor springs	16	O-ring	23	Magnet set
3	O-ring	10	Reluctor	17	Igniter/pick-up coil	24	Stator
4	Distributor housing	11	Pin	18	Magnetic screw	25	Thrust plate
5	Oil seal	12	Primary lead	19	Breaker plate	26	Ball bearing
6	Vacuum advance diaphragm	13	Rotor lead	20	Rubber cap	27	Coupling
7	Shaft	14	Carbon contact	21	Thrust washer	28	Pin retainer

with either a Hitachi or a Toyo Denso distributor. Both units are similar – the primary difference between the two is the physical location of the components such as the igniter, reluctor, stator, magnet, etc. For example, the igniter on the Hitachi is located inside the distributor, underneath the rotor **(see illustration)**; on the Toyo Denso, the igniter is located on the outside of the distributor housing **(see illustration)**. Fuel injected models (1988 through 1990) employ a crank angle sensor, which is located between the distributor and the cylinder head. These later models use a self diagnostic system to detect problems within the fuel injection and ignition system. Refer to Chapter 6 for the trouble codes that are particular to the ignition system.

6   Ignition system – check

Refer to illustration 6.3

Warning: *Because of the very high voltage generated by the ignition system, extreme care should be taken whenever an operation is performed involving ignition components. This not only includes the coils, control module and spark plug wires, but related items connected to the system as well, such as the plug connections, tachometer and any test equipment.*

6.3   To use a calibrated ignition tester, simply disconnect a spark plug wire, clip the tester to a convenient ground and operate the starter – if there's enough power to fire the plug, sparks will be visible between the electrode tip and the tester body

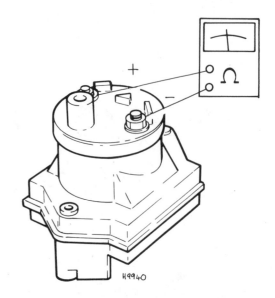

7.3a   Checking the resistance between the coil primary terminals (1984 models)

1   With the ignition switch turned to the "on" position, a "battery" light or an "oil pressure" light is a basic check for ignition and battery supply to the ECU.

2   Check all ignition wiring connections for tightness, cuts, corrosion or any other signs of a bad connection.

3   Use a spark tester to verify adequate secondary voltage (25,000 volts) at the spark plug **(see illustration)**. A faulty or poor connection at that plug could also result in a misfire. Also check for carbon deposits inside the spark plug boot.

4   Check for carbon tracking on the coil. If carbon tracking is evident, replace the coil and be sure the secondary wires related to that coil are clean and tight. Excessive wire resistance or faulty connections could cause damage to the coil.

5   Using an ohmmeter, check the resistance between the coil terminals. If an open is found (verified by an infinite reading), replace the coil.

6   Using an ohmmeter, check the resistance of the spark plug wires. Each wire should measure less than 30,000 ohms.

7   Additional checks should be performed by a dealer service department or an automotive repair shop.

---

7   Ignition coil – check and replacement

Check

1   Make sure the ignition switch is turned Off for the following checks.

2   Remove the rubber boot (cover) from the coil (if equipped) and detach the high tension lead from the secondary terminal (coil tower). Mark and disconnect the wires from the primary terminals.

1984 and 1985 models

Refer to illustrations 7.3a, 7.3b, 7.4a and 7.4b

3   Using an ohmmeter, touch the probes to the primary terminals of the coil **(see illustrations)**, measure the resistance and compare your reading to the value listed in this Chapter's Specifications.

4   Touch the probes to the secondary terminal and the positive primary terminal **(see illustrations)**, measure the resistance and compare your reading to the value listed in this Chapter's Specifications.

5   The above figures will vary somewhat with the temperature of the coil. The specified resistance values are for a coil temperature of about 70-degrees F.

7.3b   Checking the resistance between the coil primary terminals (1985 models)

6   If the coil fails either check, replace it.

1986 and 1987 models

Refer to illustrations 7.8 and 7.9

7   Unplug the primary and secondary connectors and the coil high tension lead.

8   Using an ohmmeter, touch the probes to primary terminals A and D **(see illustration)**, measure the resistance and compare your reading to the value listed in this Chapter's Specifications.

9   Touch the probes to terminal A and the secondary terminal (coil tower) **(see illustration)**, measure the resistance and compare your reading to the value listed in this Chapter's Specifications.

10   Touch the probes to terminals B and D **(see illustration 7.8)**, measure the resistance and compare your reading to the value listed in this Chapter's Specifications.

11   The above figures will vary somewhat with coil temperature. The specified resistance values are for a coil temperature of about 70-degrees.

12   If the coil passes all three checks, it's okay. Plug in the connectors. If it fails any of the above checks, replace it.

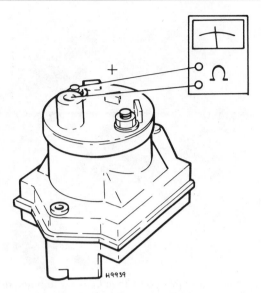

7.4a Checking the resistance between the coil positive terminal and the high tension terminal (1984 models)

7.4b Checking the resistance between the coil positive terminal and the high tension terminal (1985 models)

1988 and later models

13   Remove the distributor cap (see Chapter 1).

14   Remove the screws that attach the black/yellow and white/blue wires from the primary terminals of the coil (terminals A and B, respectively).

15   Using an ohmmeter, measure the resistance between the two terminals. Compare your reading with the value listed in this Chapter's Specifications.

16   Next, check the resistance between the secondary terminal (coil tower) and primary terminal A. Compare your reading with the value listed in this Chapter's Specifications. Replace the coil if they do not coincide.

Replacement

1984 and 1985 models

17   Detach the cable from the negative terminal of the battery.

18   Detach the wires from the primary terminals and unplug the coil high tension lead.

19   Loosen the clamp screw on the coil bracket and slide the coil out.

20   Installation is the reverse of removal.

1986 and 1987 models

21   Detach the cable from the negative terminal of the battery.

22   Using pieces of numbered tape, mark the positions of the primary wires. Unplug the primary connectors and detach the high tension lead from the coil.

23   Remove the two mounting bolts and detach the coil from its mounting bracket.

24   Installation is the reverse of removal.

1988 and later models

25   Detach the cable from the negative terminal of the battery. Remove the distributor cap (see Chapter 1).

26   Mark the positions of the black/yellow wire and the white/blue wire. Remove the two screws and disconnect the wires.

27   Remove the four mounting screws and lift the ignition coil out of the housing.

28   Installation is the reverse of removal.

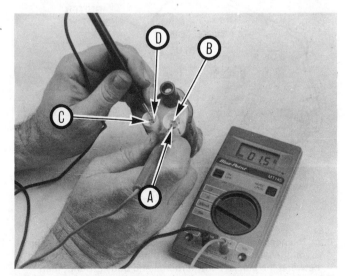

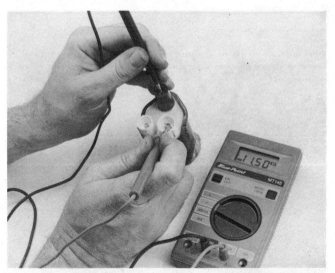

7.8 Checking the resistance between primary terminals A and D (1986 and 1987 models) (coil removed for clarity)

7.9 Checking the resistance between primary terminal A and the high tension terminal (1986 and 1987 models) (coil removed for clarity)

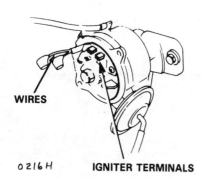

WIRES

0216H   **IGNITER TERMINALS**

8.2   To test the igniter on a Hitachi distributor, unplug the wires and check the resistance between the two igniter terminals

---

8   Igniter – check and replacement

Note: *If your distributor has a cover on the side like the one shown in illustration 8.7a, it's a Toyo Denso distributor. If not, it's a Hitachi.*

1984 through 1987 models – Hitachi distributor

Refer to illustration 8.2

1   Remove the distributor cap (see Chapter 1).
2   Unplug the wires from the igniter **(see illustration)**.
3   With the ignition switch turned to the On position, check the voltage between the blue wire and a good ground, then between the black/yellow wire and ground. There should be battery voltage for both checks. If not, there is a fault elsewhere in the ignition system.
4   With the wires still disconnected, check continuity in both directions between the two igniter terminals with an ohmmeter set on the R X 100 scale. There should be continuity in only one direction. If there is continuity in neither direction or both directions, replace the igniter (proceed to the next step).
5   Remove the two screws that secure the igniter to the distributor and lift out the igniter.

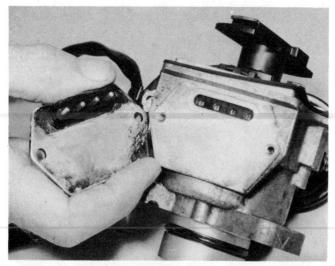

8.7b   . . . then unplug the igniter from the distributor base

---

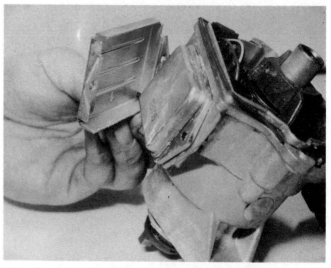

8.7a   To remove the igniter on a Toyo Denso distributor, remove the two screws and lift off the igniter cover . . .

6   Installation is the reverse of removal. Be sure to reconnect the igniter wires.

1984 through 1987 models – Toyo Denso distributor

Refer to illustrations 8.7a, 8.7b and 8.8

7   Remove the igniter cover and unplug the igniter unit from the distributor **(see illustrations)**.
8   With the ignition switch turned to the On position, check the voltage between the Blue 1 terminal and ground, then between the black/yellow terminal and ground **(see illustration)**. There should be battery voltage for both checks.
9   Connect a jumper wire between the Blue 2 and green terminals on the igniter unit **(see illustration 8.8)**. With the ohmmeter scale set to R X 100, check for continuity in both directions between the black/yellow and Blue 1 terminals. There should be continuity in only one direction.
10   Replace the igniter if it fails any of the above tests.

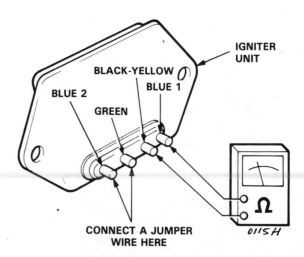

IGNITER UNIT

BLACK-YELLOW
BLUE 2   **BLUE 1**
GREEN

Ω

0115H

CONNECT A JUMPER WIRE HERE

8.8   To check the igniter on a Toyo Denso distributor, measure the voltage between the Blue 1 terminal and body ground and between the black/yellow terminal and body ground; then connect a jumper wire between the Blue 2 and green terminals and check for continuity in both directions between the black-yellow and Blue 1 terminals

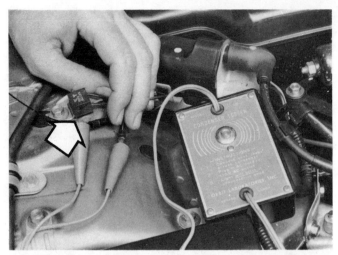

9.1   The radio condenser (arrow) is mounted on the shock tower at the right rear of the engine compartment – if you have a condenser checker, hook it up as shown and check the condenser; if you don't have one, remove the condenser and have it checked by a television repair shop

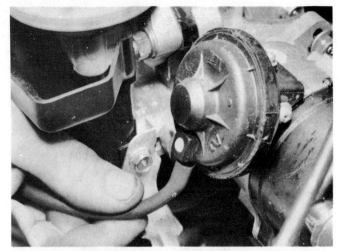

10.2   Disconnect the vacuum hose(s) from the vacuum advance diaphragm

1988 and later models

11   Use the self diagnostic system to determine if the ignition system is failing (see Chapter 6). On 1988 and 1989 models, the igniter must be checked by accessing the ECU diagnostic harness. Have the vehicle checked at a dealership service department to verify that the igniter is defective. On 1990 models, check the igniter directly at the distributor.

12   Check to make sure that fuse #32 (50 Amp), located in the dash fuse box is not blown.

13   Mark and disconnect the connectors from the igniter.

14   Check for voltage between the black/yellow wire and ground with the ignition On. There should be battery voltage. If not, there is an open circuit in the black/yellow wire somewhere between the igniter and the ignition switch.

15   Check for voltage between the white/blue wire and ground with the ignition On. There should be battery voltage. If not, there is an open circuit in the white/blue wire somewhere between the igniter and the ignition switch, or possibly a defective coil.

16   Using an ohmmeter, check for continuity between the white wire and ground. There should be continuity. If continuity does not exist, there is an open circuit in the white wire between the igniter and the PGM-FI (fuel injection system) ECU.

17   Check for continuity between the blue wire and ground. There should be continuity. If continuity does not exist, there is an open circuit in the blue wire between the igniter unit and the tachometer or the automatic transaxle control unit.

18   If all the continuity and voltage tests are normal and the vehicle still will not start – replace the igniter.

9   Radio condenser – check and replacement

Refer to illustration 9.1

Note: *The radio condenser is a device that reduces ignition noise in the radio. It is included in this Chapter because it can prevent the engine from running if it fails.*

1   If you own or have access to a condenser tester, check the capacitance of the condenser **(see illustration)** and compare your reading with the value listed in this Chapter's Specifications. If you don't have a condenser tester, or access to one, take the condenser to a television repair shop and have it tested.

2   If the indicated capacitance isn't within specification, replace the condenser.

10   Distributor – removal and installation

Removal

Refer to illustrations 10.2, 10.4, 10.6a and 10.6b

1   Detach the cable from the negative battery terminal.

2   Detach the vacuum hose(s) from the vacuum advance diaphragm on the distributor **(see illustration)**.

3   Detach the primary wires from the coil.

4   Look for a raised "1" on the distributor cap **(see illustration)**. This marks the location for the number one cylinder spark plug wire terminal. If the cap does not have a mark for the number one terminal, locate the number one spark plug and trace the wire back to the terminal on the cap.

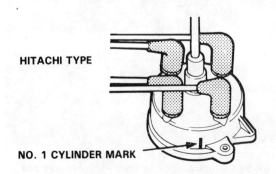
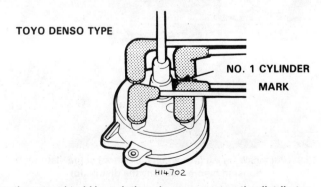

HITACHI TYPE

NO. 1 CYLINDER MARK

TOYO DENSO TYPE

NO. 1 CYLINDER MARK

H14702

10.4   Look for a raised number 1 on the distributor cap – that's where the rotor should be pointing when you remove the distributor

10.6a   Make one mark directly underneath the rotor tip . . .

10.6b   . . . and another between the distributor base and the cylinder head (arrow)

5   Remove the distributor cap (see Chapter 1) and turn the engine over until the rotor is pointing toward the number one spark plug terminal (see locating TDC procedure in Chapter 2).

6   Make a mark on the edge of the distributor base directly below the rotor tip and in line with it (if the rotor on your engine has more than one tip, use the center one for reference). Also, mark the distributor base and the cylinder head to ensure the distributor is installed correctly **(see illustrations)**.

7   Unplug the igniter wires (see Section 8).

8   Remove the distributor hold-down bolt(s) and pull out the distributor. **Caution:** *DO NOT turn the crankshaft while the distributor is out of the engine, or the alignment marks will be useless.*

Installation

Refer to illustrations 10.9 and 10.10

Note: *If the crankshaft has been moved while the distributor is out, the number one piston must be repositioned at TDC. This can be done by feeling for compression pressure at the number one plug hole as the crankshaft is turned. Once compression is felt, align the ignition timing zero mark with the pointer.*

9   Install a new O-ring on the distributor housing **(see illustration)**.

10   Insert the distributor into the cylinder head in exactly the same relationship to the head that it was when removed. **Note:** *The lugs on the end of the distributor and the corresponding grooves in the camshaft end are offset to eliminate the possibility of installing the distributor 180-degrees out of time* **(see illustration)**.

11   Recheck the alignment marks between the distributor base and the cylinder head to verify the distributor is in the same position it was in before removal. Also check the rotor to see if it's aligned with the mark you made on the distributor.

12   Loosely install the hold-down bolt(s).

13   Attach the igniter leads.

14   Install the distributor cap.

10.9   Put a new O-ring (arrow) on the bottom of the distributor housing before installing the distributor

10.10   The end of the camshaft has an offset groove which matches the lugs on the distributor shaft – this ensures you won't install the distributor 180-degrees out of phase

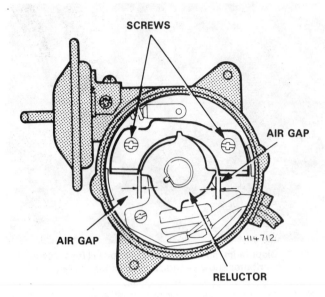

11.3a   On a Hitachi distributor, measure the air gaps at the two points indicated

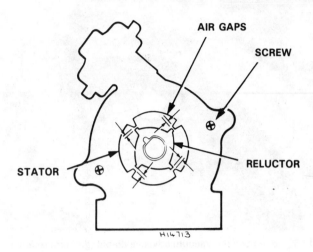

11.3b   On a Toyo Denso distributor, measure the air gaps at the four points indicated

15   Reattach the spark plug wires to the plugs (if removed).
16   Connect the cable to the negative terminal of the battery.
17   Check the ignition timing (see Chapter 1) and tighten the distributor hold-down bolt(s) securely.

11   Reluctor air gap (1984 through 1987 models only) – check and adjustment

Refer to illustrations 11.3a and 11.3b
Note: *Refer to Section 8 to determine which kind of distributor your vehicle has.*
1   Detach the cable from the negative battery terminal.
2   Remove the distributor cap and rotor (see Chapter 1).
3   Using a non-magnetic feeler gauge, verify the air gaps between the stator and reluctor are equal **(see illustrations)**.
   a) If your vehicle is equipped with a Hitachi distributor and the gaps aren't equal, loosen the screws **(see illustration 11.3a)** and move the stator until the air gaps are equal. Tighten the screws, then re-check the gaps to make sure they are still equal.
   b) If your vehicle is equipped with a Toyo Denso distributor and the gaps aren't equal, check for damage to the stator or reluctor. If any damage to the stator is evident, replace the distributor; if there is damage to the reluctor, replace it (see Section 12).

12   Reluctor (1984 through 1987 models only) – replacement

Refer to illustration 12.3
1   Detach the cable from the negative battery terminal.
2   Remove the distributor cap (see Chapter 1).
3   Remove the reluctor by prying it off with a pair of small screwdrivers **(see illustration)**. Be careful – using excessive force to pry off the reluctor may result in a damaged stator.
4   Installation is the reverse of removal. Make sure you install the new reluctor with the number or letter manufacturing code facing up and the gap in the pin facing away from the shaft.

13   Vacuum advance mechanism – check and replacement

Check
1   Detach the cable from the negative battery terminal.
2   Remove the distributor cap.
3   Detach the vacuum hose(s) from the vacuum advance diaphragm on the distributor and attach a vacuum pump to the fitting. If there are two hoses, attach the pump where the outer hose connects.
4   Turn the breaker plate right and left to check for freedom of movement.
5   Apply a gradual vacuum while watching the breaker plate. Verify the breaker plate operates smoothly – there should be no binding.
   a) If there's binding, find the source of the binding and free the breaker plate.
   b) If the vacuum pump gauge indicates a loss of vacuum, the diaphragm is defective and must be replaced.

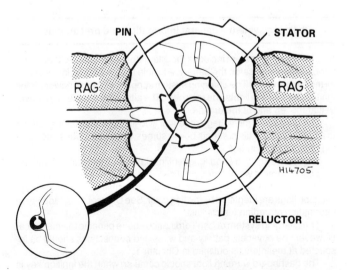

12.3   To remove the reluctor from the distributor shaft, pry it off with a pair of screwdrivers – be sure to use a couple of rags under the screwdrivers to protect the stator assembly from damage

13.6   To remove the vacuum advance diaphragm, first remove the C-clip (arrow) that attaches it to the breaker plate

13.7   Diaphragm mounting screws (arrows) (Toyo Denso distributor shown – Hitachi distributor similar)

Replacement

Refer to illustrations 13.6 and 13.7

6   Remove the C-clip from the vacuum advance diaphragm arm **(see illustration)**.
7   Remove the diaphragm mounting screws **(see illustration)**.
8   Detach the diaphragm arm, then pull the diaphragm out of the distributor.
9   Installation is the reverse of removal.

14   Centrifugal advance mechanism – check

1   Detach the vacuum hose(s) from the vacuum advance diaphragm and plug it (them).
2   Connect a timing light in accordance with the manufacturer's instructions.
3   Start the engine and increase the engine speed from idle to about 2500 RPM. The timing mark (T) should appear to move past the pointer toward the firewall, indicating an increase in ignition advance. If it doesn't, check the centrifugal advance mechanism for sticking or binding.

15   Charging system – general information and precautions

The charging system includes the alternator, an internal voltage regulator, a charge indicator, the battery, a fusible link and the wiring between all the components. The charging system supplies electrical power for the ignition system, the lights, the radio, etc. The alternator is driven by a drivebelt at the left end of the engine.

The purpose of the voltage regulator is to limit the alternator's voltage to a preset value. This prevents power surges, circuit overloads, etc., during peak voltage output.

The fusible link is a short length of insulated wire integral with the engine compartment wiring harness. The link is four wire gauges smaller in diameter than the circuit it protects. Production fusible links and their identification flags are identified by the flag color. See Chapter 12 for additional information regarding fusible links.

The charging system doesn't ordinarily require periodic maintenance. However, the drivebelt, battery and wires and connections should be inspected at the intervals outlined in Chapter 1.

The dashboard warning light should come on when the ignition key is turned to On, but it should go off immediately after the engine is started. If it remains on, there is a malfunction in the charging system (see Section 16). Some vehicles are also equipped with a voltmeter. If the voltmeter indicates abnormally high or low voltage, check the charging system (see Section 16).

Be very careful when making electrical circuit connections to a vehicle equipped with an alternator and note the following:

a) When reconnecting wires to the alternator from the battery, be sure to note the polarity.
b) Before using arc welding equipment to repair any part of the vehicle, disconnect the wires from the alternator and the battery terminals.
c) Never start the engine with a battery charger connected.
d) Always disconnect both battery leads before using a battery charger.
e) The alternator is turned by an engine drivebelt which could cause serious injury if your hands, hair or clothes become entangled in it with the engine running.
f) Because the alternator is connected directly to the battery, it could arc or cause a fire if overloaded or shorted out.
g) Wrap a plastic bag over the alternator and secure it with rubberbands before steam cleaning the engine.

16   Charging system – check

1   If a malfunction occurs in the charging circuit, don't automatically assume that the alternator is causing the problem. First check the following items:

a) Check the drivebelt tension and condition (Chapter 1). Replace it if it's worn or deteriorated.
b) Make sure the alternator mounting and adjustment bolts are tight.
c) Inspect the alternator wiring harness and the connectors at the alternator and voltage regulator. They must be in good condition and tight.
d) Check the fusible link (if equipped) located between the starter solenoid and the alternator. If it's burned, determine the cause, repair the circuit and replace the link (the vehicle won't start and/or the accessories won't work if the fusible link blows). Sometimes a fusible link may look good, but still be bad. If in doubt, remove it and check for continuity.
e) Start the engine and check the alternator for abnormal noises (a shrieking or squealing sound indicates a bad bearing).
f) Check the specific gravity of the battery electrolyte. If it's low, charge the battery (doesn't apply to maintenance free batteries).
g) Make sure the battery is fully charged (one bad cell in a battery can cause overcharging by the alternator).
h) Disconnect the battery cables (negative first, then positive). Inspect the battery posts and the cable clamps for corrosion. Clean them thoroughly if necessary (see Chapter 1). Reconnect the cable to the negative terminal.

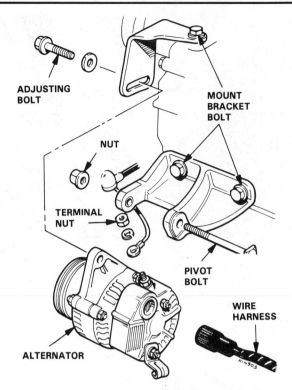

17.3   Alternator mounting details – typical

i)   With the key off, connect a test light between the negative battery post and the disconnected negative cable clamp.
   1)   If the test light does not come on, reattach the clamp and proceed to the next step.
   2)   If the test light comes on, there is a short (drain) in the electrical system of the vehicle. The short must be repaired before the charging system can be checked.
   3)   Disconnect the alternator wiring harness.
       (a)   If the light goes out, the alternator is bad.
       (b)   If the light stays on, pull each fuse until the light goes out (this will tell you which component is shorted).
2   Using a voltmeter, check the battery voltage with the engine off. If should be approximately 12-volts.
3   Start the engine and check the battery voltage again. It should now be approximately 14-to-15 volts.

4   Turn on the headlights. The voltage should drop, and then come back up, if the charging system is working properly.
5   If the voltage reading is more than the specified charging voltage, replace the voltage regulator (refer to Section 18). If the voltage is less, the alternator diode(s), stator or rectifier may be bad or the voltage regulator may be malfunctioning.

---

17   Alternator – removal and installation

Refer to illustration 17.3
1   Detach the cable from the negative terminal of the battery.
2   Mark and detach the electrical connectors from the alternator.
3   Loosen the alternator adjusting bolt and pivot bolt nut, then detach the drivebelt **(see illustration)**.
4   Remove the adjusting and pivot bolts and separate the alternator from the engine.
5   If you are replacing the alternator, take the old one with you when purchasing a replacement unit. Make sure the new/rebuilt unit looks identical to the old alternator. Look at the terminals – they should be the same in number, size and location as the terminals on the old alternator. Finally, look at the identification numbers – they will be stamped into the housing or printed on a tag attached to the housing. Make sure the numbers are the same on both alternators.
6   Many new/rebuilt alternators DO NOT have a pulley installed, so you may have to switch the pulley from the old unit to the new/rebuilt one. When buying an alternator, find out the shop's policy regarding pulleys – some shops will perform this service free of charge.
7   Installation is the reverse of removal.
8   After the alternator is installed, adjust the drivebelt tension (see Chapter 1).
9   Check the charging voltage to verify proper operation of the alternator (see Section 16).

---

18   Voltage regulator and alternator brushes – replacement

Refer to illustrations 18.2a, 18.2b, 18.2c, 18.3, 18.4a, 18.4b, 18.5 and 18.7
Note: *Don't attempt to overhaul the alternator. If replacing the brushes and regulator does not solve the alternator problem, take the alternator to a dealer and have it rebuilt or exchange it as a core for a rebuilt unit.*
1   Remove the alternator (see Section 17) and place it on a clean workbench.
2   Remove the three rear cover nuts, the nut and terminal insulator and the rear cover **(see illustrations)**.

18.2a   Remove the three nuts from the rear cover

18.2b   Take the nut, washer and terminal insulator off terminal B and remove the alternator rear cover

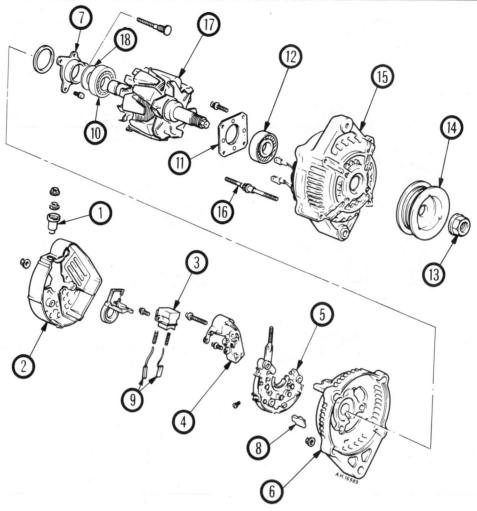

18.2c   Exploded view of the alternator

1	Terminal	6	Rear housing	11	Bearing retainer
2	Rear end cover	7	Bearing mount	12	Front bearing
3	Brush holder	8	Insulator sleeve	13	Pulley locknut
4	IC regulator	9	Brushes	14	Pulley
5	Diode (rectifier assembly)	10	Rear bearing		

15	Stator assembly/drive end housing
16	Stator through bolt
17	Rotor
18	Spacer ring

18.3   Once the rear cover is removed, remove the five screws (arrows) that retain the voltage regulator and the brush holder

18.4a   Remove the brush holder, . . .

18.4b   . . . then remove the regulator

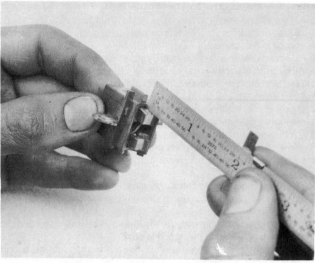

18.5   Measure the exposed length of the brushes and compare your measurements to the specified minimum length to determine whether they should be replaced

18.7   To install the brush holder, depress each brush with a small screwdriver to clear the shaft

3   Remove the five voltage regulator and brush holder retaining screws **(see illustration)**.
4   Remove the brush holder and the regulator from the rear end frame **(see illustrations)**. If you are only replacing the regulator, proceed to Step 8, install the new unit, reassemble the alternator and install it on the engine (see Section 17). If you are going to replace the brushes, proceed with the next Step.
5   Measure the exposed length of each brush **(see illustration)** and compare it to the specified minimum length. If the length of either brush is less than the specified minimum, replace the brushes.
6   Make sure that each brush moves smoothly in the brush holder.
7   Install the brush holder by depressing each brush with a small screwdriver to clear the shaft **(see illustration)**.
8   Install the voltage regulator and brush holder screws into the rear frame.
9   Install the rear cover and tighten the three nuts securely.
10   Install the terminal insulator and tighten it with the nut.
11   Install the alternator (see Section 17).

19   Starting system – general information and precautions

The sole function of the starting system is to turn over the engine quickly enough to allow it to start.

The starting system consists of the battery, the starter motor, the starter solenoid and the wires connecting them. The solenoid is mounted directly on the starter motor.

The solenoid/starter motor assembly is installed on the lower part of the engine, next to the transmission bellhousing.

When the ignition key is turned to the Start position, the starter solenoid is actuated through the starter control circuit. The starter solenoid then connects the battery to the starter. The battery supplies the electrical energy to the starter motor, which does the actual work of cranking the engine.

The starter motor on some vehicles equipped with manual transaxles can only be operated when the clutch pedal is depressed; the starter on all vehicles equipped with an automatic transaxles can only be operated when the selector lever is in Park or Neutral.

Always observe the following precautions when working on the starting system:

a) Excessive cranking of the starter motor can overheat it and cause serious damage. Never operate the starter motor for more than 15 seconds at a time without pausing to allow it to cool for at least two minutes.
b) The starter is connected directly to the battery and could arc or cause a fire if mishandled, overloaded or shorted out.
c) Always detach the cable from the negative terminal of the battery before working on the starting system.

20   Starter motor – in-vehicle check

Note: *Before diagnosing starter problems, make sure the battery is fully charged.*

1   If the starter motor does not turn at all when the switch is operated, make sure the shift lever is in Neutral or Park (automatic transmission) or the clutch pedal is depressed (manual transmission).
2   Make sure the battery is charged and all cables, both at the battery and starter solenoid terminals, are clean and secure.
3   If the starter motor spins but the engine is not cranking, the overrunning clutch in the starter motor is slipping and the starter motor must be replaced.
4   If, when the switch is actuated, the starter motor does not operate at all but the solenoid clicks, then the problem lies with either the battery, the

main solenoid contacts or the starter motor itself (or the engine is seized).

5   If the solenoid plunger cannot be heard when the switch is actuated, the battery is bad, the fusible link is burned (the circuit is open) or the solenoid itself is defective.

6   To check the solenoid, connect a jumper lead between the battery (+) and the ignition switch wire terminal (the small terminal) on the solenoid. If the starter motor now operates, the solenoid is OK and the problem is in the ignition switch, neutral start switch or the wiring.

7   If the starter motor still does not operate, remove the starter/solenoid assembly for disassembly, testing and repair.

8   If the starter motor cranks the engine at an abnormally slow speed, first make sure that the battery is charged and that all terminal connections are tight. If the engine is partially seized, or has the wrong viscosity oil in it, it will crank slowly.

9   Run the engine until normal operating temperature is reached, then disconnect the coil wire from the distributor cap and ground it on the engine.

10   Connect a voltmeter positive lead to the positive battery post and connect the negative lead to the negative post.

11   Crank the engine and take the voltmeter readings as soon as a steady figure is indicated. Do not allow the starter motor to turn for more than 15 seconds at a time. A reading of nine volts or more, with the starter motor turning at normal cranking speed, is normal. If the reading is nine volts or more but the cranking speed is slow, the motor is faulty. If the reading is less than nine volts and the cranking speed is slow, the solenoid contacts are probably burned, the starter motor is bad, the battery is discharged or there is a bad connection.

21   Starter motor – removal and installation

1   Detach the cable from the negative terminal of the battery.

2   Clearly label, then disconnect the wires from the terminals on the starter motor solenoid.

3   Remove the mounting bolts and detach the starter.

4   Installation is the reverse of removal.

22   Starter solenoid – removal and installation

1   Disconnect the cable from the negative terminal of the battery.

2   Remove the starter motor (see Section 21).

3   Disconnect the large wire from the solenoid to the starter motor terminal.

4   Remove the screws which secure the solenoid to the starter motor gear housing and detach the solenoid from the gear housing.

5   While the solenoid is removed, check the overrunning clutch by sliding it along its shaft. If it doesn't move freely, or if the clutch slips when you rotate the armature while holding the drive gear, replace the clutch assembly. If the gear is worn or damaged, replace the complete overrunning clutch assembly (the gear isn't available separately). If the starter gear teeth are damaged, you should also inspect the flywheel or driveplate ring gear for damage.

6   Installation is the reverse of removal.

Chapter 6   Emissions control systems

Contents

Specifications

General

Crank angle sensor resistance
  1987 and earlier models (CYL and TDC sensor) ....   0.65 to 0.85 k-ohms
  1988 and later models
    Between any of the paired terminals indicated in the text   ...   350 to 550 ohms
    Throttle angle sensor resistance ....   3.2 to 7.2 k-ohms
Electronic Air Control Valve (EACV) resistance ....   8 to 15 ohms
Intake air temperature sensor resistance ....   1 to 4 k-ohms at room temperature

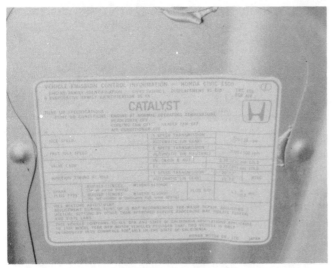

1.6a   The Vehicle Emission Control Information (VECI) label provides essential tune-up specifications like idle speed and fast idle, spark plug types, etc.

1.6b   The Vacuum Hose Routing Diagram tells you what emission control devices the vehicle is equipped with, gives you their approximate locations and provides a vacuum hose routing schematic, which is helpful when you're looking for leaks and disconnected or misrouted hoses

1   General information

Refer to illustrations 1.6a and 1.6b

To prevent pollution of the atmosphere from incompletely burned and evaporating gases, and to maintain good driveability and fuel economy, a number of emission control systems are incorporated. They include the:

Self diagnosis system
Electronic engine controls
Feedback Control system
Exhaust Gas Recirculation (EGR) system
Secondary air supply/air injection system
Fuel evaporative control system
Positive Crankcase Ventilation (PCV) system
Intake air temperature control system
Catalytic converter

The Sections in this Chapter include general descriptions, checking procedures within the scope of the home mechanic and component replacement procedures (when possible) for each of the systems listed above.

Before assuming that an emissions control system is malfunctioning, check the fuel and ignition systems carefully. The diagnosis of some emission control devices requires specialized tools, equipment and training. If checking and servicing become too difficult or if a procedure is beyond your ability, consult a dealer service department. Remember, the most frequent cause of emissions problems is simply a loose or broken vacuum hose or wire, so always check the hose and wiring connections first.

This doesn't mean, however, that emissions control systems are particularly difficult to maintain and repair. You can quickly and easily perform many checks and do most of the regular maintenance at home with common tune-up and hand tools. **Note:** *Because of a Federally mandated extended warranty which covers the emissions control system components, check with your dealer about warranty coverage before working on any emissions-related systems. Once the warranty has expired, you may wish to perform some of the component checks and/or replacement procedures in this Chapter to save money.*

Pay close attention to any special precautions outlined in this Chapter. It should be noted that the illustrations of the various systems may not exactly match the system installed on your vehicle because of changes made by the manufacturer during production or from year-to-year.

A Vehicle Emissions Control Information (VECI) label is attached to the underside of the hood **(see illustration)**. This label contains important

2.1   The ECU on 1988 and later models is located under the carpet at the front of the passenger footwell

emissions specifications and adjustment information. A second label, the Vacuum Hose Routing Diagram, **(see illustration)** provides a vacuum hose schematic with emissions components identified. When servicing the engine or emissions systems, the VECI label and the vacuum hose routing diagram in your particular vehicle should always be checked for up-to-date information.

2   Self diagnosis system – description and code access

Refer to illustration 2.1

Note: *Only engines equipped with PGM-FI are equipped with the self-diagnosis feature. If the vehicle has a PGM-FI light (1985 through 1987 models) or Check Engine light (1988 and later models) on the dashboard, it's equipped with the self-diagnosis system.*

1   To view self-diagnosis information from the ECU memory, you must watch the LED display on the ECU:

  a)   The ECU is located under the passenger seat on 1986 and 1987 models.

b) On 1988 and later models, the ECU is located at the front of the passenger footwell, under the carpet **(see illustration)**.

2   With the ignition ON, the ECU will display four bulbs that flash in a variety of combinations (1985 through 1987 models) or a single flashing light (1988 and later models) indicating the system is operating.

3   When the ECU sets a trouble code, the PGM-FI light (1985 through 1987 models) or the Check Engine light (1988 and later models) will come on and a trouble code will be stored in the memory. The trouble code will stay in the ECU memory until the voltage to the ECU is interrupted. Removing the HAZARD fuse in the main fuse panel for 10 seconds will clear all stored trouble codes. Trouble codes should always be cleared after repairs have been completed. **Caution:** *To prevent damage to the ECU, the ignition switch must be off when disconnecting or connecting power to the ECU (this includes disconnecting and connecting the battery).*

4   The following is a list of the typical trouble codes which may be encountered while diagnosing the computerized system. Also included are simplified troubleshooting procedures. If the problem persists after these checks have been made, more detailed service procedures will have to be done by a dealer service department.

1985 through 1987 models

	LED display	Symptom	Possible cause
1	O O O O (Dash warning light on)	Engine will not start	Check for a disconnected control unit ground connector. Also check for a loose connection at the ECU main relay resistor. Possible faulty ECU.
2	O O O O (Dash warning light on)	Engine will not start	Check for a short circuit in the combination meter or warning light wire. Also check for a disconnected control unit ground wire Possible faulty ECU
3	O O O ✳(1)	System does not operate	Faulty ECU
4	O O ✳(2) O	System does not operate	Faulty ECU
5	O O ✳(2) ✳(1)	Fuel fouled plugs, engine stalls, or hesitation	Check for a disconnected MAP sensor coupler or an open circuit in the MAP sensor wire. Also check for a faulty MAP sensor
6	O ✳(4) O O	System does not operate	Faulty ECU
7	O ✳(4) O ✳(1)	Hesitation, fuel fouled plug or the engine stalls frequently	Check for disconnected MAP sensor vacuum hose
8	O ✳(4) ✳(2) O	High idle speed during warm-up, continued high idle or hard starting at low temperature	Check for a disconnected coolant temperature sensor connector or an open circuit in the coolant temperature sensor wire. Also check for a faulty coolant temperature sensor
9	O ✳(4) ✳(2) ✳(1)	Poor engine response when opening the throttle rapidly, high idle speed or engine does not rev-up when cold	Check for a disconnected throttle angle sensor connector. Also check for an open circuit in the throttle angle sensor wire. Possible faulty throttle angle sensor.
10	✳(8) O O O	Engine does not rev-up, high idle speed or erratic idling	Check for a short or open circuit in the crank angle sensor wire. Spark plug wires interfering with the crank angle sensor wire. Also the crank angle sensor could be faulty.
11	✳(8) O O ✳(1)	Same as above	Same as above
12	✳(8) O ✳(2) O	High idle speed or erratic idling when very cold	Check for a disconnected intake air temperature sensor or an open circuit in the intake air temperature sensor wire. Possible faulty intake air temperature sensor
13	✳(8) O ✳(2) ✳(1)	Continued high idle speed	Check for a disconnected idle mixture adjuster sensor coupler or an open circuit in the idle mixture adjuster sensor wire. Possible faulty idle mixture adjuster sensor.
14	✳(8) ✳(4) O O	System does not operate at all	Faulty ECU
15	✳(8) ✳(4) O ✳(1)	Poor acceleration at high altitude when cold	Check for a disconnected atmospheric pressure sensor coupler or an open circuit in the atmospheric pressure sensor wire. Possible faulty atmospheric pressure sensor.
16	✳(8) ✳(4) ✳(2) O	System does not operate at all	Faulty ECU
17	✳(8) ✳(4) ✳(2) ✳(1)	Same as above	Same as above

1988 through 1990 models

Trouble codes	Circuit or system	Probable cause
Code 0	Faulty ECU	Inspect the number 1 fuse. Replace if necessary. Also check for open circuit in the YEL wire between the # 1 fuse and the combination meter. If no open circuit is found, have the wiring harness checked at a dealer service department or other qualified repair shop.
Code 1 (1 flash)	Oxygen content	Refer to Section 3
Code 3 and 5 (3 or 5 flashes)	Manifold Absolute Pressure	Refer to Section 4
Code 4 (4 flashes)	Crank angle sensor	Refer to Section 5
Code 6 (6 flashes)	Coolant temperature	Have the vehicle checked at a dealership service department
Code 7 (7 flashes)	Throttle angle	Refer to Section 6
Code 8 (8 flashes)	TDC Position	Refer to Section 5
Code 9 (9 flashes)	No. 1 cylinder position (1.6L)	Refer to Section 5
Code 10 (10 flashes)	Intake air temperature	Refer to Section 8
Code 12 (12 flashes)	Exhaust Gas Recirculation System	Refer to Section 16
Code 13 (13 flashes)	Atmospheric Pressure	Have the vehicle checked at a dealership service department
Code 14 (14 flashes)	Electronic Air Control (EACV)	Refer to Section 7
Code 15 (15 flashes)	Ignition output signal	Possible faulty igniter – see Chapter 5
Code 16 (16 flashes)	Fuel injector	See Chapter 4
Code 17 (17 flashes)	Vehicle speed sensor	Have the vehicle checked at a dealership service department
Code 19 (19 flashes)	Lock-up control solenoid valve (automatic transaxle vehicles)	Have the vehicle checked at a dealership service department
Code 20 (20 flashes)	Electric load	Have the vehicle checked at a dealership service department

3   Oxygen sensor (fuel-injected models) – check and replacement

Check

1987 and earlier models

Refer to illustration 3.4

1   Locate the oxygen sensor, which is screwed into the exhaust manifold. Follow the sensor wire back and unplug the electrical connector.
2   Start the engine and allow it to run for two minutes, at 3000 rpm.
3   Raise the engine speed to 4000 rpm and allow the throttle to snap shut (do this at least five times).
4   Raise the engine speed to 5000 rpm, lower it to 2000 rpm then turn the ignition switch to Off. Using a digital voltmeter, promptly measure the voltage between the oxygen sensor side of the electrical connector and ground (**see illustration**). It should be below 0.4-volts.

5   Disconnect the MAP sensor vacuum hose from the throttle body and attach a vacuum pump to the hose. Apply vacuum and check the voltage again. It should be above 0.6-volts.
6   If the oxygen sensor fails either of these two tests, replace it.

1988 and later models

7   Turn the ignition switch to OFF.
8   Remove the HAZARD fuse in the main fuse box (see Chapter 12) for ten seconds to reset the ECU.
9   Check the fuel pressure to make sure it's within specifications (see Chapter 4).
10   If the fuel pressure is okay, warm the engine to normal operating temperature.
11   Block the rear wheels and set the parking brake. Raise the front of the vehicle and support it securely on jackstands.
12   With the engine warmed up, put the transmission in 2nd gear and run the engine at 2000 rpm for 15 minutes. Do not close the throttle at this time.

3.4   When checking the oxygen sensor, use a digital voltmeter to receive accurate low voltage readings

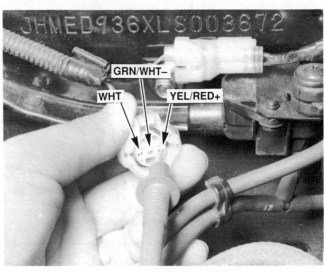

4.7   The MAP sensor is located on the firewall of the engine compartment

13   If the CHECK ENGINE light comes on or the LED flashes code 1, check for poor ground wire connections at the thermostat housing or a loose connector at the oxygen sensor.

14   Unplug the electrical connector at the oxygen sensor and connect a voltmeter between ground and the oxygen sensor connector **(see illustration 3.4).**

15   Warm the vehicle to normal operating temperature, then hold the engine rpm at 4000 for 10 seconds, then allow it to return to idle. The voltage should stay at 0.6-volts while the engine is at 4000 rpm, then it should not drop under 0.4-volts with closed throttle deceleration.

16   If the readings are too high or low, replace the oxygen sensor.

17   If the oxygen sensor tests correctly but code 1 is still present, have the system checked at a dealership service department.

Replacement

Warning: *The electric cooling fan can activate at any time, even when the ignition is in the OFF position. Disconnect the negative battery cable when working in the vicinity of the fan.*

18   Unplug the oxygen sensor electrical connector.

19   Unscrew the oxygen sensor.

20   Apply a small amount of anti-seize compound to the threads of the new oxygen sensor and install it into the exhaust manifold.

21   Plug in the electrical connector.

---

4   Manifold Absolute Pressure (MAP) sensor (fuel-injected models) – check and replacement

Check

1987 and earlier models

1   Check the vacuum hose from the throttle body to the MAP sensor for cracking and general deterioration, replacing it if necessary.

2   Check the electrical connector at the sensor for a snug fit. Check the terminals in the connector and the wires leading to it for looseness and breaks. Repair as required.

3   Any further checks must be performed by a dealer service department or other repair shop, as special tools are required from this point.

1988 and later models

Refer to illustration 4.7

4   Turn the ignition switch to OFF.

5   Remove the hazard fuse in the main fuse box for 10 seconds to reset the ECU.

6   Warm the engine to operating temperature and check to make sure the CHECK ENGINE warning light continues to flash.

7   Turn the ignition Off and disconnect the electrical connector from the MAP sensor **(see illustration).**

8   With the ignition switch ON, measure the voltage between the yellow/red (+) terminal and ground. There should be about five volts.

9   Measure the voltage between the yellow/red (+) terminal and the green/white (-) terminal. There should be about five volts.

10   Measure the voltage between the white (+) and green/white (-) terminals. There should be about five volts.

11   If the voltage readings check out okay, replace the MAP sensor.

12   If these tests don't pinpoint the problem, have the MAP sensor circuit diagnosed by a dealer service department or other repair shop, as special tools are required from this point.

Replacement

13   Disconnect the electrical connector and the vacuum hose from the MAP sensor.

14   Remove the bolts that retain the sensor to the firewall and remove the MAP sensor.

15   Installation is the reverse of removal.

---

5   Crank angle sensor (fuel-injected models) – check and replacement

Check

1987 and earlier models

1   On these models, the crank angle sensor is made up of two individual sensors – a CYL sensor and a TDC sensor. The CYL sensor detects the position of the number one piston as the base for the sequential fuel injection system. The TDC sensor determines the injector timing for each cylinder, as well as sending an engine speed signal to the ECU.

2   To check the CYL sensor, unplug the electrical connector at the distributor and, using an ohmmeter, measure the resistance between the white and red wire terminals in the connector. Compare your reading with the value listed in this Chapter's Specifications.

3   To check the TDC sensor, disconnect the electrical connector at the distributor and, using an ohmmeter, measure the resistance between the brown and blue wire terminals in the connector. Compare your reading with the value listed in this Chapter's Specifications.

1988 and later models

Refer to illustrations 5.8a and 5.8b

4   Turn the ignition switch OFF.

5   Remove the HAZARD fuse in the main fuse box for 10 seconds to reset the ECU.

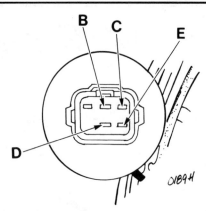

5.8a   Pin designations in the distributor connector on the dual-point fuel injection system

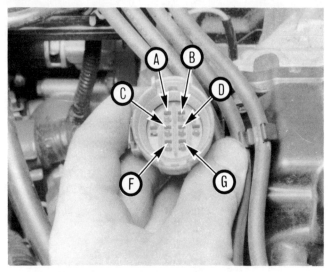

5.8b   Pin designations in the distributor connector on the multi-point fuel injection system

6   Start the engine and make sure the CHECK ENGINE light continues to flash.

7   Stop the engine and disconnect the electrical connector at the distributor.

8   If you're working on a dual-point fuel injection system, measure the resistance between terminals D and E, then B and C **(see illustration)**. If you're working on a multi-point fuel injection system, measure the resistance between terminals C and D, then A and B **(see illustration)**. Compare your readings with the values listed in this Chapter's Specifications.

9   Check for continuity to ground from terminals E, D, B, and C (dual-point fuel injection) or terminal C, D, A and B (multi-point fuel injection). Continuity should exist.

10   If the LED on the ECU flashes Code 9, measure the resistance between terminals F and G. Compare your readings with the values listed in this Chapter's Specifications.

11   Check for continuity to ground from terminals F and G. Continuity should exist.

12   If the test results are correct and the problem still exists, have the distributor checked at a dealership service department.

Replacement

13   If the crank angle sensor failed any of the above tests, the entire distributor must be replaced (at the time of writing no replacement parts were available). Refer to Chapter 5 for the distributor removal and installation procedure.

---

6   Throttle angle sensor (fuel-injected models) – check and replacement

---

Check

1987 and earlier models

1   Locate the throttle angle sensor on the throttle body. Follow the wire harness back and unplug the electrical connector.

2   Measure the resistance between the brown/black wire terminal and the yellow/red wire terminal. Compare your readings with the values listed in this Chapter's Specifications.

3   If the resistance is not as specified, loosen the mounting screws and adjust the position of the switch, then check the resistance again (if shear-head screws are installed, see Step 6). If it still is not within the specified range, replace it.

1988 and later models

4   The throttle angle sensor and circuit on these models must be checked by a dealer service department or other qualified repair shop, as special tools are required.

Replacement

5   Disconnect the electrical connector from the sensor.

6   Remove the screws securing the sensor hold-down plate. If shear-head bolts are installed, it will be necessary to drill a small hole in the center of each screw and remove it with a screw extractor. This is most easily accomplished with the throttle body removed from the vehicle (see Chapter 4).

7   Remove the sensor from the throttle body.

8   Insert the switch (with a new gasket) into the throttle body, aligning the pin on the sensor with the groove in the throttle shaft. On 1987 and earlier models, adjust the switch by turning it against the direction of throttle shaft rotation, all the way, then tighten the screws snugly (but not completely yet).

9   Check the resistance of the sensor as described in Steps 1 through 3, turning the switch as necessary to bring the resistance reading within specification (1987 and earlier models only).

10   Tighten the screws securely. If factory replacement shear-head bolts are being used, tighten them until the heads break off.

11   Reconnect the electrical connector.

---

7   Electronic Air Control Valve (EACV) (1988 and later models) – check and replacement

---

Check

1   Turn the ignition switch OFF.

2   Remove the HAZARD fuse in the main fuse box for 10 seconds to reset the ECU.

3   Start the engine and make sure the CHECK ENGINE light continues to flash. Stop the engine.

4   Locate the EACV. On multi-point systems it's the cylindrical-shaped device mounted on the backside of the intake manifold. On dual-point systems it's located on the left (driver's) side of the intake manifold, near the timing belt cover. Disconnect the electrical connector from the EACV. Measure the resistance with an ohmmeter between the two terminals and compare your reading with the value listed in this Chapter's Specifications.

5   Check for continuity to ground on each terminal. Continuity should not exist.

6   Turn the ignition switch On. Measure the voltage on the wiring harness side of the connector, between the black/yellow (+) wire and the blue/yellow (-) wire.

7   If there is battery voltage, the ECU might be faulty. Have the vehicle checked at a dealer service department or other qualified repair shop.

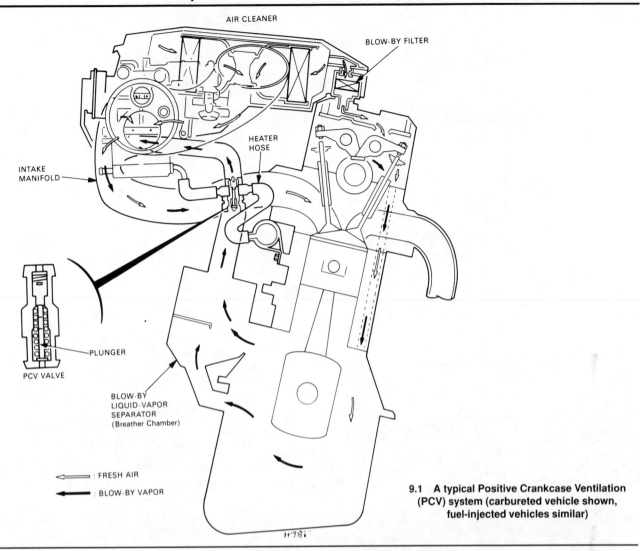

AIR CLEANER

BLOW-BY FILTER

HEATER HOSE

INTAKE MANIFOLD

PLUNGER

PCV VALVE

BLOW-BY LIQUID-VAPOR SEPARATOR (Breather Chamber)

⇐ : FRESH AIR

◀━ : BLOW-BY VAPOR

9.1 A typical Positive Crankcase Ventilation (PCV) system (carbureted vehicle shown, fuel-injected vehicles similar)

8   If there is no voltage, measure the voltage between the black/yellow terminal and ground.

9   If there is no voltage, repair the open circuit in the black/yellow wire between the EACV and the #14 fuse.

10   If there is voltage present, have the vehicle checked at a dealer service department or other qualified repair shop.

Replacement

11   Disconnect the electrical connector from the EACV.

12   Remove the bolts that retain the valve to the intake manifold and remove the EACV from the engine.

13   Installation is the reverse of removal.

8   Intake air temperature (TA) Sensor (fuel-injected models) – check and replacement

Check

1   With the engine cold, disconnect the electrical connector from the TA sensor, which is located on the intake manifold. Using an ohmmeter, measure the resistance between the two terminals on the sensor and compare your reading with the value listed in this Chapter's Specifications.

2   If the test results are incorrect, replace the TA sensor.

3   If the sensor checks out okay but there is still a problem, have the vehicle checked at a dealer service department or other qualified repair shop, as the ECU may be malfunctioning.

Replacement

4   Unplug the electrical connector from the TA sensor.

5   Remove the screws that retain the sensor to the intake manifold and remove the TA sensor.

6   Installation is the reverse of removal.

9   Positive Crankcase Ventilation (PCV) system

Refer to illustration 9.1

1   The Positive Crankcase Ventilation (PCV) system **(see illustration)** reduces hydrocarbon emissions by scavenging crankcase vapors. It does this by circulating fresh air from the air cleaner through the crankcase, where it mixes with blow-by gases and is then rerouted through a PCV valve to the intake manifold.

2   The main components of the PCV system are the PCV valve, a blow-by filter and the vacuum hoses connecting these two components with the engine.

3   To maintain idle quality, the PCV valve restricts the flow when the intake manifold vacuum is high. If abnormal operating conditions (such as piston ring problems) arise, the system is designed to allow excessive amounts of blow-by gases to flow back through the crankcase vent tube into the air cleaner to be consumed by normal combustion.

4   Checking and replacement of the PCV valve and filter is covered in Chapter 1.

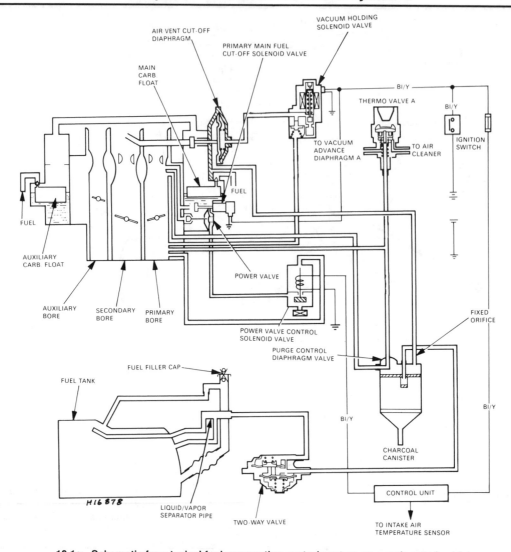

10.1a   Schematic for a typical fuel evaporative control system on a carbureted vehicle

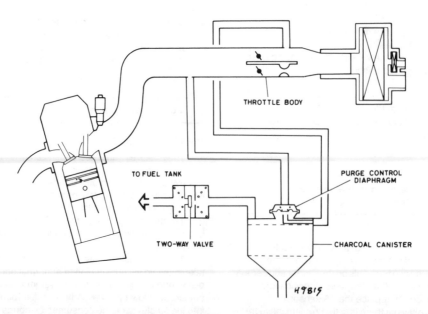

10.1b   Schematic for a typical fuel evaporative control system on a fuel-injected vehicle

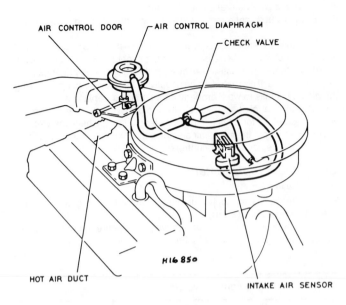

AIR CONTROL DOOR — AIR CONTROL DIAPHRAGM

— CHECK VALVE

H16 850

HOT AIR DUCT

INTAKE AIR SENSOR

11.1 Typical intake air temperature control system

10 Fuel evaporative control system

General description

Refer to illustrations 10.1a and 10.1b

1   The fuel evaporative control system **(see illustrations)** absorbs fuel vapors and, during engine operation, releases them into the engine intake where they mix with the incoming air-fuel mixture.

2   Every evaporative system employs a canister filled with activated charcoal to absorb fuel vapors. The means by which these vapors are controlled, however, varies considerably from one system to another. The following descriptions of typical systems for carbureted and fuel injected vehicles should provide you enough information to understand the system on your vehicle.

Carbureted vehicles

Note: *The following description is not intended as a specific description of the evaporative system on your particular vehicle. Rather, it is intended as a general description of a typical system used on carbureted vehicles. Although the following components are most likely all used on your particular system, there may also be other devices, not included here, which are unique to your system.*

3   The fuel filler cap is fitted with a two-way valve as a safety device. The valve vents fuel vapors to the atmosphere if the evaporative control system fails.

4   Another two-way valve, mounted on the fuel tank, regulates fuel vapor flow from the fuel tank to the charcoal canister, based on the pressure or vacuum caused by temperature changes.

5   After passing through the two-way valve, fuel vapor is carried by vent hoses to the charcoal canister in the engine compartment. The activated charcoal in the canister absorbs and stores these vapors.

6   An air vent cut-off diaphragm, mounted on the carburetor, vents fuel vapors from the float chambers to the charcoal canister when the engine is off.

7   When the engine is running and warmed to a pre-set temperature, a thermo valve on top of the canister closes, allowing a purge control diaphragm valve in the charcoal canister to be opened by intake manifold vacuum. Fuel vapors from the canister are then drawn through the purge control diaphragm valve by intake manifold vacuum.

8   When the engine isn't running, the fuel passages in the main and slow primary fuel metering system are cut off by solenoid valves to prevent the fuel in the float chamber from entering the carburetor bore.

Fuel-injected vehicles

Note: *The following description is not intended as a specific description of the evaporative system on your particular vehicle. Rather, it is a general description of a typical system used on fuel-injected vehicles. Although the following components are most likely all used on your particular system, there may also be other devices, not included here, which are unique to your system.*

9   When fuel vapor pressure in the fuel tank exceeds a pre-set level, a two-way valve on the fuel tank opens and allows the fuel vapors to flow to the charcoal canister.

10   The charcoal canister temporarily stores fuel vapors until they can be purged from the charcoal canister into the engine and burned.

11   Canister purging is controlled by a vapor purge control diaphragm which is opened or closed by a thermo valve. When the engine coolant temperature is below about 131 degrees F, the thermo valve provides no manifold vacuum to the purge control diaphragm. When the temperature exceeds 131 degrees F, the thermo valve directs manifold vacuum to the purge control diaphragm, which admits ported vacuum to the canister and draws fresh air through the canister into a port on the throttle body.

Checking

Note: *Complete checking of the fuel evaporative control system is beyond the scope of the home mechanic. Fortunately, the evaporative control system, like all emission control systems, is protected by a Federally-mandated extended warranty (5 years or 50,000 miles at the time this manual was written). The fuel evaporative system probably won't fail during the service life of the vehicle; however, if it does, the hoses or charcoal canister are usually to blame.*

Hoses

12   Always check the hoses first. A disconnected, damaged or missing hose is the most likely cause of a malfunctioning evaporative system. Refer to the Vacuum Hose Routing Diagram (attached to the underside of the hood) to determine whether the hoses are correctly routed and attached. Repair any damaged hoses or replace any missing hoses as necessary.

Charcoal canister

13   Detach the canister from the firewall.

14   Detach the intake tube hose (refer to the Vacuum Hose Routing Diagram attached to the underside of the hood) and put your finger on the end of the canister inlet fitting.

15   Warm the engine to normal operating temperature, then increase the engine speed to 2500 rpm. If the canister is functioning correctly, air will be drawn into the canister through the inlet tube and you will feel suction. If you don't feel suction, replace the canister.

11 Intake air temperature control system (carbureted models)

General description

Refer to illustration 11.1

1   The air temperature control system **(see illustration)** provides heated intake air during warm-up, then maintains a uniform inlet air temperature of about 100-degrees by mixing warm and cool air. This allows leaner fuel/air mixture settings for the carburetor, which reduces emissions and improves driveability.

2   Two fresh air inlets – one hot and one cold – are used. The balance between the two is controlled by an air control diaphragm, which operates an air control door in the air cleaner.

3   When the underhood temperature is cold, warm air radiating off the exhaust manifold is trapped by a shroud which fits over the manifold and routed up through a hot air duct through the door into the air cleaner. This provides warm air for the carburetor, resulting in better driveability and faster warm-up. As the temperature inside the air cleaner rises, the air control door is gradually closed by the vacuum motor (which, in turn, is controlled by an intake air sensor inside the air cleaner) and the air cleaner draws air through an outside air duct instead. The result is a consistent intake air temperature.

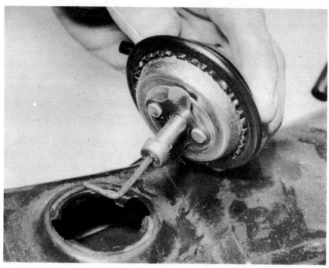

11.9 The air control diaphragm is easy to replace – simply twist it 90-degrees and pull out

Checking

Note: *This check is done with the engine off. Make sure the engine is cold before beginning this test.*

4   Always check the vacuum source and the integrity of all vacuum hoses between the source and the air control diaphragm before beginning the following test. Do not proceed until they're okay.

5   Apply the parking brake and block the wheels.
6   Detach, but do not remove, the air cleaner housing and element (see Chapter 4).
7   Turn the air cleaner housing upside down so the air control door is visible. The door should be open. If it isn't, it might be binding or sticking. Make sure that it's not rusted in an open or closed position by attempting to move it by hand. If it's rusted, it can usually be freed by cleaning and oiling the hinge. If it fails to work properly after servicing, replace it.
8   If the air control door is okay but the motor still fails to operate correctly, check carefully for a leak in the hose leading to it. Check the vacuum source to and from the intake air sensor with a hand vacuum pump. If no leak is found, replace the air control diaphragm

Component replacement
Refer to illustration 11.9

9   To remove the air control diaphragm, twist it 90-degrees and pull straight up **(see illustration).**
10   Installation is the reverse of removal, but be sure the rod on the air control diaphragm engages with the air control door.

---

12   Ignition timing control system

General description
Refer to illustrations 12.1a and 12.1b

1   The ignition timing control system **(see illustrations)** alters ignition timing during and after engine warm-up to reduce emissions, maximize fuel economy and enhance performance.

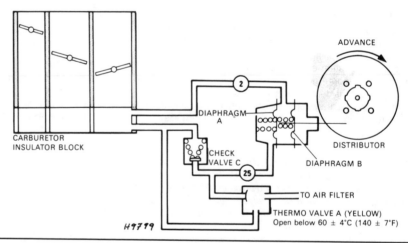

12.1a   Typical ignition timing control system (carbureted models)

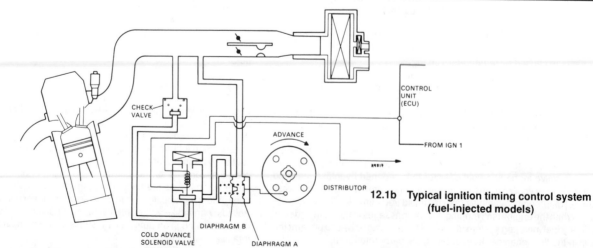

12.1b   Typical ignition timing control system (fuel-injected models)

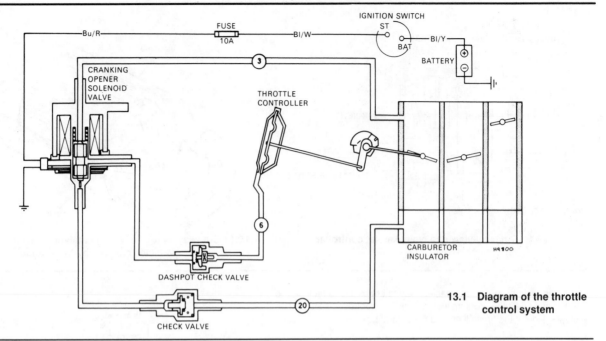

13.1   **Diagram of the throttle control system**

Checking

2   Warm the engine to its normal operating temperature.
3   Attach a tachometer in accordance with the manufacturer's instructions.
4   Detach the hose from the vacuum advance diaphragm on the distributor and attach a vacuum gauge to the hose. If there are two hoses, attach the gauge to the inner hose (closest to the distributor).
5   Start the engine, allow it to idle and verify there is vacuum.
   a) If there is vacuum, go to the next Step.
   b) If no vacuum is indicated on the gauge, check the hose connections between the distributor and the carburetor insulator block for leaks or blockage.
6   Attach a hand vacuum pump/gauge to the hose fitting on the vacuum advance diaphragm and hook up a timing light in accordance with the manufacturer's instructions. Start the engine and apply 20 in-Hg of vacuum. The ignition timing should advance and vacuum should remain steady.
   a) If the timing advances, the system is okay. Detach the tachometer and reattach the vacuum hose.
   b) If the timing doesn't advance and the vacuum doesn't remain steady, the diaphragm is leaking. Replace it (see Chapter 4) and recheck.
   c) If the vacuum remains steady but the timing does not advance, stop the engine and remove the distributor cap. Verify that the breaker plate turns freely by turning it left and right. If there's no evidence of binding, replace the vacuum advance diaphragm (see Chapter 4) and recheck it.

13   Throttle control system

Refer to illustration 13.1

General description

1   To reduce emissions and provide easier starting, a throttle controller **(see illustration)** holds the throttle open slightly to admit extra air during starting, shifting and deceleration.
2   When the engine is running above idle speed, ported vacuum in the carburetor is applied to the throttle controller through a dashpot check valve. On deceleration, this vacuum is bled off through an orifice in the dashpot check valve, gradually diminishing until the throttle closes entirely.

3   When the engine is cranked during start-up, the cranking opener solenoid valve is activated to allow intake manifold vacuum into the diaphragm to ensure the proper throttle opening angle.

Checking

Throttle controller

4   Detach the vacuum hose from the throttle controller, attach a hand vacuum pump to the hose fitting and apply 8 in-Hg vacuum. Engine speed should rise to about 2000 rpm within one minute.
   a) If the speed is lower than specified, widen the adjusting slot in the controller lever with a screwdriver.
   b) If the speed is higher than specified, narrow the adjusting slot in the lever with needle nose pliers.
   c) If the speed can't be adjusted or the diaphragm won't hold vacuum, replace the throttle controller and recheck.

Cranking opener solenoid valve

5   Perform the check described in Steps 4 and 5 above.
6   Ground the coil secondary wire to prevent the engine from starting. Turn the ignition key to Start. The throttle controller arm should retract when you crank the engine. If it doesn't, check all the hoses in the system for damage and proper routing (refer to the Vacuum Hose Routing Diagram on the underside of the vehicle's hood). If all hoses are in good condition and properly routed, take the vehicle to a dealer service department for further checking.

14   Air jet controller

General description

Refer to illustration 14.1

1   The air jet controller **(see illustration)** is an atmospheric pressure sensing device which controls the amount of airflow into the slow and main air jets of the primary carburetor bore and the slow air jet of the secondary carburetor bore.
2   As atmospheric pressure is reduced by increasing altitude, the bellows expands to open the valve in the air jet controller, increasing air flow to the jets to maintain an optimum air/fuel ratio.

Checking

3   A malfunctioning air jet controller normally causes an excessively rich mixture (black smoke coming from the tailpipe) and poor engine performance when operating the vehicle at high altitudes. If you suspect the air jet

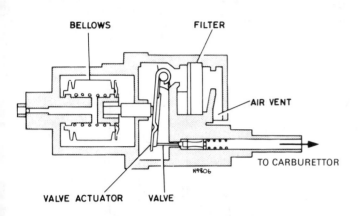

14.1   Cutaway view of a typical air jet controller

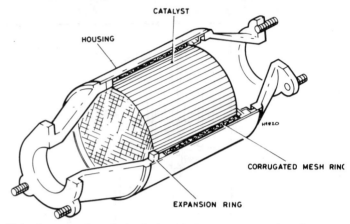

15.1   Cutaway view of a typical catalytic converter used on the vehicles covered by this manual

controller is malfunctioning, the easiest way to check it is to replace the controller and see if the problem is resolved. The controller is located on the engine side of the firewall next to the control box.

15   Catalytic converter

Refer to illustration 15.1
Note: *Because of a Federally mandated extended warranty which covers emissions-related components such as the catalytic converter, check with a dealer service department before replacing the converter at your own expense.*

General description
1   The catalytic converter **(see illustration)** is an emission control device added to the exhaust system to reduce pollutants from the exhaust gas stream. There are two types of converters. The conventional oxidation catalyst reduces the levels of hydrocarbon (HC) and carbon monoxide (CO). The three-way catalyst lowers the levels of oxides of nitrogen (NOx) as well as hydrocarbons (HC) and carbon monoxide (CO).

Checking
2   The test equipment for a catalytic converter is expensive and highly sophisticated. If you suspect that the converter on your vehicle is malfunctioning, take it to a dealer or authorized emissions inspection facility for diagnosis and repair.
3   Whenever the vehicle is raised for servicing of underbody components, check the converter for leaks, corrosion, dents and other damage. Check the welds/flange bolts that attach the front and rear ends of the converter to the exhaust system. If damage is discovered, the converter should be replaced.
4   Although catalytic converters don't break too often, they do become plugged. The easiest way to check for a restricted converter is to use a vacuum gauge to diagnose the effect of a blocked exhaust on intake vacuum.
   a) Open the throttle until the engine speed is about 2000 RPM.
   b) Release the throttle quickly.
   c) If there is no restriction, the gauge will quickly drop to not more than 2 in-Hg or more above its normal reading.
   d) If the gauge does not show 5 in-Hg or more above its normal reading, or seems to momentarily hover around its highest reading for a moment before it returns, the exhaust system, or the converter, is plugged (or an exhaust pipe is bent or dented, or the core inside the muffler has shifted).

Component replacement
5   Refer to the exhaust system removal and installation section in Chapter 4.

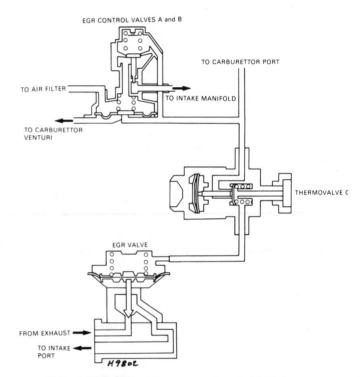

16.2   Typical EGR system on a carbureted vehicle

16   Exhaust gas recirculation (EGR) system

General description
Refer to illustrations 16.2 and 16.3
1   The EGR system reduces oxides of nitrogen by recirculating exhaust gas through the EGR valve and intake manifold into the combustion chambers.
2   On carbureted vehicles, the EGR system **(see illustration)** consists of the EGR valve, a pair of control valves and a thermovalve. The EGR valve, which is operated by ported vacuum via the two control valves, recirculates gases in accordance with engine load (intake air volume). To eliminate recirculation at idle, the vacuum signal is ported above the idle throttle position. During cold engine operation, the thermovalve opens,

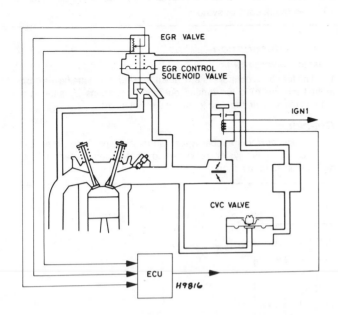

16.3   **Typical EGR system on a fuel-injected vehicle**

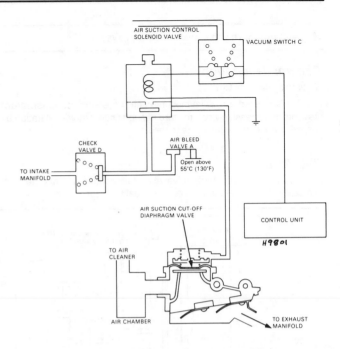

17.1   **Typical secondary air supply system**

bleeding off ported vacuum and keeping the EGR valve closed. When the engine coolant temperature exceeds the set temperature of the thermovalve, it closes and ported vacuum is applied to the EGR valve and control valve A. This opens the EGR valve and allows exhaust gas into the intake manifold. Control valve B is normally closed. When manifold vacuum reaches a set level, the valve opens, allowing venturi vacuum to enter control valve A and the EGR valve.

3   On fuel-injected vehicles, the EGR system (**see illustration**) consists of the EGR valve, the CVC valve, the EGR control solenoid valve, the Electronic Control Unit (ECU) and various sensors. The ECU memory is programmed to produce the ideal EGR valve lift for each operating condition. An EGR valve lift sensor detects the amount of EGR valve lift and sends this information to the ECU. The ECU then compares it with the ideal EGR valve lift, which is determined by data received from the other sensors. If there's any difference between the two, the ECU triggers the EGR control solenoid valve to reduce the amount of vacuum applied to the EGR valve.

Checking

EGR valve
4   Start the engine and allow it to idle.
5   Detach the vacuum hose from the EGR valve and attach a hand vacuum pump in its place.
6   Apply vacuum to the EGR valve. Vacuum should remain steady and the engine should run poorly.
   a) If vacuum doesn't remain steady and the engine doesn't run poorly, replace the EGR valve and recheck it.
   b) If vacuum remains steady but the engine doesn't run poorly, remove the EGR valve and check the valve and the intake manifold for blockage. Clean or replace as necessary and recheck.

EGR system (carbureted vehicles)
7   Detach the vacuum hose from the EGR valve and attach a vacuum gauge to the hose.
8   Start the engine and warm it to its normal operating temperature (wait for the electric cooling fan to come on).
9   Remove the control box from the firewall (it's attached with four bolts), then remove the control box cover (it's held on by four screws). Vacuum at

the EGR hose should be as follows:
   a) At idle, there should be no vacuum. If there is, replace the EGR control valve and check the vacuum hose routing (refer to the Vacuum Hose Routing diagram on the underside of the hood).
   b) At 4500 rpm, there should be 2 to 6 in-Hg of vacuum. If there isn't, check for vacuum at the inlet and outlet of the thermovalve. If there is vacuum at the inlet but none at the outlet, replace the thermovalve. If there is no vacuum at the inlet, check the routing of the vacuum hoses and repair or replace them as necessary.
   c) At 4500 rpm with the vacuum bleed hose pinched, there should be less than 2 in-Hg. If there is more, replace the EGR control valve and check the vacuum hose routing.
   d) During rapid acceleration, there should be 2 to 6 in-Hg. If there isn't, check for vacuum at the thermovalve inlet and outlet. If there's vacuum at the inlet but not at the outlet, replace the thermovalve. If there's no vacuum at the inlet, check the routing of the vacuum hoses and repair or replace them as necessary.
   e) During deceleration, there should be no vacuum.

EGR system (fuel-injected vehicles)
10   Checking the EGR system on fuel-injected vehicles requires special tools and equipment. Take the vehicle to a dealer service department or other qualified repair shop for checking.

17   Secondary air supply/air injection system

General description
Refer to illustration 17.1

1   The secondary air supply system (**see illustration**) is designed to improve emission control performance by introducing fresh air from the air cleaner into the exhaust manifold through the air suction cut-off diaphragm valve.

Checking
2   Checking the secondary air supply system is best left to a dealer service department or other qualified repair shop.

18   Anti-afterburn valve/mixture control system

General description

Refer to illustration 18.1

1   The anti-afterburn valve/mixture control system **(see illustration)** prevents an excessively rich mixture during shifting and deceleration by supplying fresh air to the intake manifold.

Checking

2   Checking the anti-afterburn valve/mixture control system is best left to a dealer service department or other qualified repair shop.

19   Feedback control system

General description

Refer to illustration 19.1

1   The feedback control system **(see illustration)** maintains the proper air/fuel mixture ratio for various operating conditions by altering the amount of extra air supplied to the intake manifold.

Checking

2   This system requires special tools and test equipment for proper diagnosis. Checking the system is best left to a dealer service department or other qualified repair shop.

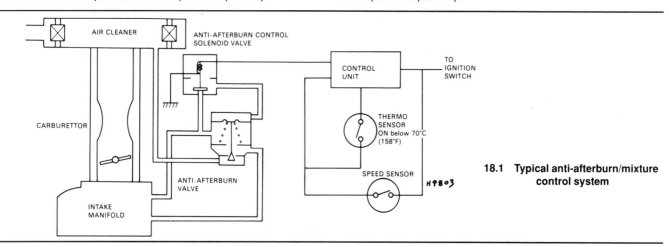

18.1   Typical anti-afterburn/mixture control system

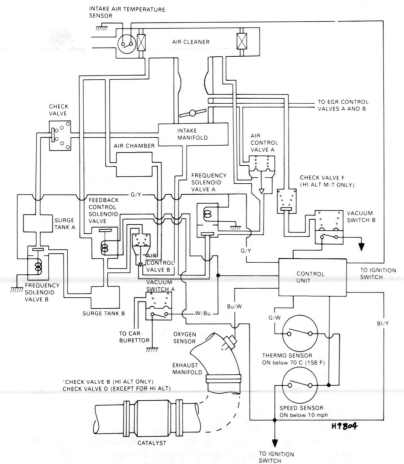

19.1   Typical feedback control system

Chapter 7 Part A   Manual transaxle

Contents

Specifications

Transaxle overhaul

First gear
  Endplay .... 0.001 to 0.007 in (0.03 to 0.18 mm)
  Endplay adjustment .... Selective thrust washers
  Thrust washer thicknesses .... 0.074 to 0.076 in (1.89 to 1.92 mm)
    0.076 to 0.077 in (1.92 to 1.95 mm)
    0.077 to 0.078 in (1.95 to 1.98 mm)

Second, third and fourth gear
  Endplay .... 0.002 to 0.007 in (0.05 to 0.18 mm)
  Spacer collar thicknesses .... 1.103 to 1.104 in (28.01 to 28.04 mm)
    1.104 to 1.105 in (28.04 to 28.07 mm)
    1.105 to 1.106 in (28.07 to 28.10 mm)
    1.106 to 1.107 in (28.10 to 28.13 mm)

Fifth gear
  Endplay .... 0.002 to 0.016 in (0.05 to 0.4 mm)
  Gear or end cover circlip thicknesses .... 0.019 to 0.062 in (0.500 to 1.575 mm) in 0.001 in (0.025 mm) increments
Selector fork-to-synchro sleeve groove clearance .... 0.018 to 0.039 in (0.45 to 1.0 mm)
Blocking ring-to-gear clearance .... 0.016 in (0.40 mm)
Differential pinion gear
  Backlash .... 0.002 to 0.006 in (0.05 to 0.15 mm)
  Backlash adjustment .... Selective thrust washer
  Thrust washer thicknesses .... 0.028 to 0.039 in (0.7 to 1.0 mm) in 0.002 in (0.05 mm) increments

Differential
　　Side clearance .... 0.004 to 0.006 in (0.10 to 0.15 mm)
　　Side clearance adjustment .... Selective circlips
　　Circlip thicknesses .... 0.096 to 0.116 in (2.45 to 2.95 mm) in 0.004 in (0.10 mm) increments

Torque specifications   **Ft-lbs** (unless otherwise indicated)
Countershaft locknut 65
End cover bolts .... 108 in-lbs
Selector arm holder bolts .... 108 in-lbs
Transaxle case-to-flywheel housing 20
Transaxle-to-engine bolts
　　4-speed 33
　　5-speed 50

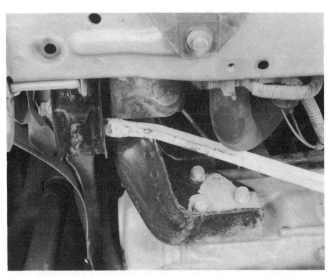

3.1   To check the transaxle mount, insert a large screwdriver or prybar between the mount and the transaxle and pry up

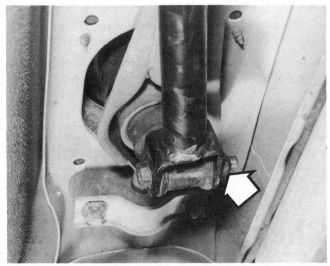

4.2   Remove the nut from the through bolt (arrow), pull out the bolt and detach the shift lever from the remote control rod

1   General information

The vehicles covered by this manual are equipped with either a four- or five-speed manual transaxle or a three speed automatic transaxle. Information on the manual transaxle is included in this Part of Chapter 7. Service procedures for the automatic transaxle are contained in Chapter 7, Part B.

The manual transaxle is a compact, two-piece, lightweight aluminum alloy housing containing both the transmission and differential assemblies.

2   Oil seal replacement

1   Oil leaks frequently occur due to wear of the driveaxle oil seals, and/or the speedometer drive gear oil seal and O-ring. Replacement of these seals is relatively easy, since the repairs can usually be performed without removing the transaxle from the vehicle.

Driveaxle oil seals

2   The driveaxle oil seals are located on the sides of the transaxle, where the driveaxles are attached. If you suspect leakage at the seal, raise the vehicle and support it securely on jackstands. If the seal is leaking, the sides of the transaxle will be coated with lubricant.
3   Remove the driveaxle (see Chapter 8).
4   Using a screwdriver or pry bar, carefully pry the oil seal out of the transaxle bore.

5   If you can't remove the oil seal with a screwdriver or pry bar, you'll have to obtain a special oil seal removal tool (available at auto parts stores).
6   Using a large section of pipe or a large deep socket as a drift, install the new oil seal. Drive it into the bore squarely and make sure it's completely seated.
7   Install the driveaxle. Be careful not to damage the lip of the new seal.

Speedometer cable and driven gear housing

8   The speedometer cable and driven gear housing is located on the transaxle housing. Look for lubricant around the cable housing to determine if the seal and O-ring are leaking.
9   Disconnect the speedometer cable from the transaxle.
10   Using a hook, remove the seal.
11   Using a small socket as a drift, install the new seal.
12   Install a new O-ring on the driven gear housing and reinstall the speedometer cable assembly.

3   Transaxle mount – check and replacement

Refer to illustration 3.1

1   Insert a large screwdriver or prybar between the mount and the transaxle and pry up **(see illustration)**.
2   The transaxle shouldn't move more than about 1/2 to 3/4 inch away from the mount. If it does, replace the mount.

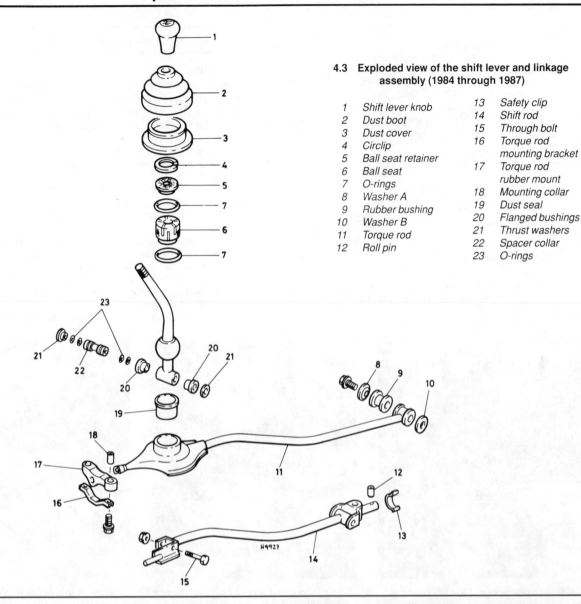

4.3   Exploded view of the shift lever and linkage assembly (1984 through 1987)

1	Shift lever knob	13	Safety clip
2	Dust boot	14	Shift rod
3	Dust cover	15	Through bolt
4	Circlip	16	Torque rod
5	Ball seat retainer		mounting bracket
6	Ball seat	17	Torque rod
7	O-rings		rubber mount
8	Washer A	18	Mounting collar
9	Rubber bushing	19	Dust seal
10	Washer B	20	Flanged bushings
11	Torque rod	21	Thrust washers
12	Roll pin	22	Spacer collar
		23	O-rings

3   To replace the mount, support the transaxle with a jack, remove the nuts and bolts and remove the mount. It may be necessary to raise the transaxle slightly to provide enough clearance to remove the mount.
4   Installation is the reverse of removal.

---

4   Shift lever – removal and installation

Refer to illustrations 4.2, 4.3 and 4.6

1   Raise the vehicle and place it securely on jackstands.
2   Working under the vehicle, remove the through bolt and nut and disconnect the shift lever from the remote control rod **(see illustration)**.
3   Remove the shift lever washers, bushings, spacer collar and O-rings **(see illustration)**.
4   Unscrew and remove the shift lever knob.
5   Remove the center console (see Chapter 11).
6   Pull off the rubber dust boot, remove the circlip and remove the shift lever **(see illustration)**.
7   Remove the ball seat, retainer, O-rings and dust cover.
8   Inspect the parts and replace any that are worn or deformed.
9   Installation is the reverse of removal. Be sure to grease the spacer collar and tighten the pivot bolt securely.

4.6   After you've removed the rubber dust boot, remove the circlip (arrow) and pull out the shift lever

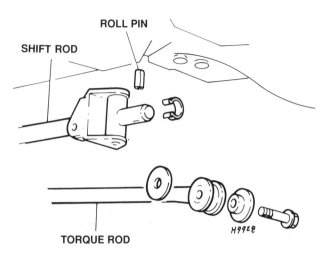

5.4a   **Exploded view of the shift rod and torque rod connections at the transaxle**

5   Transaxle – removal and installation

Removal

Refer to illustrations 5.4a, 5.4b, 5.4c, 5.4d, 5.13a, 5.13b and 5.13c

1   Disconnect the negative cable from the battery.
2   Raise the vehicle and support it securely on jackstands.
3   Drain the transaxle lubricant (see Chapter 1).
4   Disconnect the shift linkage from the transaxle **(see illustrations)**.
5   Disconnect the clutch linkage from the transaxle (see Chapter 8).
6   Detach the speedometer cable and electrical connectors from the transaxle.
7   Remove the exhaust system (see Chapter 4).
8   Remove the starter motor (see Chapter 5).
9   Support the engine from above with an engine hoist, or place a jack (with a block of wood as an insulator) under the engine oil pan. The engine must be supported at all times while the transaxle is out of the vehicle!
10   Remove any chassis or suspension components that will interfere with transaxle removal (see Chapter 10).
11   Disconnect the driveaxles from the transaxle (see Chapter 8).
12   Support the transaxle with a jack, then remove the bolts securing the transaxle to the engine.
13   Remove the transaxle mounts **(see illustrations)**.

5.4b   **To disconnect the shift rod from the transaxle, remove this safety clip, . . .**

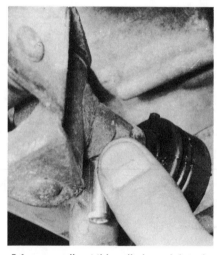

5.4c   **. . . pull out this roll pin and detach the shift rod from the selector shaft**

5.4d   **Remove the retaining bolt from the front end of the torque rod and detach the torque rod from the transaxle**

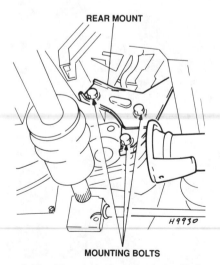

5.13a   **Transaxle rear mount (typical)**

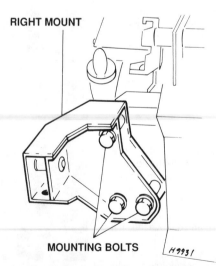

5.13b   **Transaxle right mount (typical)**

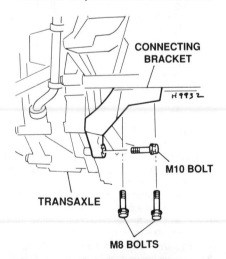

5.13c   **Engine-to-transaxle mounting assembly (typical)**

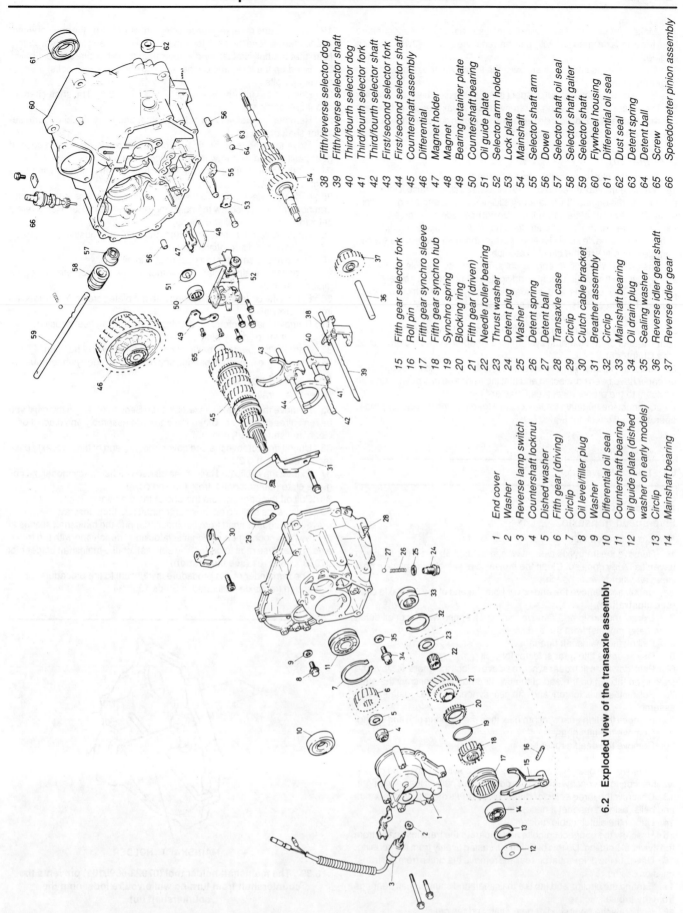

6.2 **Exploded view of the transaxle assembly**

1 End cover
2 Washer
3 Reverse lamp switch
4 Countershaft locknut
5 Dished washer
6 Fifth gear (driving)
7 Circlip
8 Oil level/filler plug
9 Washer
10 Differential oil seal
11 Countershaft bearing
12 Oil guide plate (dished washer on early models)
13 Circlip
14 Mainshaft bearing
15 Fifth gear selector fork
16 Roll pin
17 Fifth gear synchro sleeve
18 Fifth gear synchro hub
19 Synchro spring
20 Blocking ring
21 Fifth gear (driven)
22 Needle roller bearing
23 Thrust washer
24 Detent plug
25 Washer
26 Detent spring
27 Detent ball
28 Transaxle case
29 Circlip
30 Clutch cable bracket
31 Breather assembly
32 Circlip
33 Mainshaft bearing
34 Oil drain plug
35 Sealing washer
36 Reverse idler gear shaft
37 Reverse idler gear
38 Fifth/reverse selector dog
39 Fifth/reverse selector shaft
40 Third/fourth selector dog
41 Third/fourth selector fork
42 Third/fourth selector shaft
43 First/second selector fork
44 First/second selector shaft
45 Countershaft assembly
46 Differential
47 Magnet holder
48 Magnet
49 Bearing retainer plate
50 Countershaft bearing
51 Oil guide plate
52 Selector arm holder
53 Lock plate
54 Mainshaft
55 Selector shaft arm
56 Dowel
57 Selector shaft oil seal
58 Selector shaft gaiter
59 Selector shaft
60 Flywheel housing
61 Differential oil seal
62 Dust seal
63 Detent spring
64 Detent ball
65 Screw
66 Speedometer pinion assembly

14   Make a final check that all wires and hoses have been disconnected from the transaxle, then carefully pull the transaxle and jack away from the engine.

15   Once the input shaft is clear, lower the transaxle and remove it from under the vehicle.

16   While the transaxle is out, inspect the clutch assembly (see Chapter 8). If you want to avoid having to remove the transaxle again in the near future, it's always a good idea to replace worn clutch components – even if they have some service life remaining.

Installation

17   Install the clutch assembly (see Chapter 8).

18   With the transaxle secured to the jack with a chain, raise it into position behind the engine, then carefully slide it forward, engaging the input shaft with the clutch plate hub splines. Do not use excessive force to install the transaxle – if the input shaft does not slide into place, readjust the angle of the transaxle so it is level and/or turn the input shaft so the splines engage properly with the clutch plate hub.

19   Install the transaxle-to-engine bolts. Tighten the bolts securely.

20   Install the transaxle mounts and tighten all fasteners securely.

21   Install any chassis and suspension components which were removed. Tighten all nuts and bolts securely.

22   Remove the jacks supporting the transaxle and engine.

23   Install the various items previously removed, including the starter (see Chapter 5), the exhaust system (see Chapter 4) and the driveaxles (see Chapter 8).

24   Make a final check that all wires, hoses, linkages and the speedometer cable have been connected and that the transaxle has been filled with lubricant to the proper level (see Chapter 1).

25   Connect the negative battery cable. Road test the vehicle for proper operation and check for leaks.

---

6   Transaxle overhaul

Disassembly

Five-speed transaxle

Refer to illustration 6.2

1   Remove the transaxle assembly (see Section 5). Drain the oil, if you haven't already done so. Clean the transaxle assembly and place it on a clean and sturdy work bench.

2   Unbolt and remove the end cover from the end of the transaxle case **(see illustration)**.

3   Extract the circlip and remove the dished spring washer or oil guide plate (later models) from the end cover.

4   Pull off the mainshaft bearing.

5   Drive out the fifth gear selector fork roll pin.

6   Push down the fifth gear synchro sleeve to lock the gears. Relieve the staking on the nut on the end of the countershaft and unscrew the nut.

7   Pull off the selector fork and fifth gear synchro sleeve together as an assembly.

8   Remove the fifth gear synchro hub, then the blocking ring and spring.

9   Remove the fifth gear.

10   Remove the needle roller bearing.

11   Remove the thrust washer.

12   Remove fifth gear, noting the boss faces down. Remove the dished washer, noting its concave side faces down. Use a puller if the gear is tight.

13   Unscrew the three selector detent plugs and extract the coil springs and balls, using a magnet if necessary.

14   Unbolt the clutch cable bracket.

15   Unscrew the connecting bolts and separate the transaxle case from the flywheel housing. Do this by lifting the casing evenly from the housing.

16   Drive out the differential oil seal and remove the circlip from the transmission casing.

17   Expand the circlips and tap the mainshaft and countershaft bearings from the transaxle case.

18   Withdraw the reverse idler gear shaft and the gear.

19   Unscrew the reverse gear selector arm nut, take off the special washer and then remove the selector arm, the detent ball and the detent spring. Note that the ball is of larger diameter than the other three detent balls.

20   Bend up the lock tabs on the three selector fork lock bolts, then remove the bolts.

21   Remove the fifth/reverse selector shaft and dog. The shaft chamfer should be at the top.

22   Remove the first/second selector shaft and then the third/fourth selector shaft and dog.

23   Move the sleeve of the first/second synchro sleeve up into second gear position and withdraw the first/second selector fork.

24   Lift the mainshaft and countershaft from the flywheel housing as a single assembly.

25   Slide the selector arm from side to side to gain access to the selector arm holder bolts. Unscrew the bolts and remove the holder. Remove the selector rod, detent ball and spring.

26   Lift the differential/final drive from the flywheel housing.

27   Remove the differential oil seal.

28   Remove the selector rod dust boot and oil seal.

29   Unbolt the retaining plate and withdraw the speedometer drivegear pinion assembly.

30   Extract the countershaft bearing retainer plate screws. You'll need an impact screwdriver.

31   Remove the countershaft bearings from the flywheel housing.

32   Lift out the oil guide plate.

33   Remove the breather baffle plate from the flywheel housing.

34   Remove the mainshaft bearing and oil seal from the flywheel housing.

Four-speed transaxle

Refer to illustration 6.39

35   Remove the transaxle assembly (see Section 5). Drain the oil, if you haven't already done so. Clean the transaxle assembly and place it on a clean and sturdy work bench.

36   Unbolt and remove the end cover from the end of the transaxle case **(see illustration 6.2)**.

37   Extract the circlip and pull off the dished washer (early models), or oil guide plate (later models), from the end cover.

38   Pull off the bearing from the end of the mainshaft.

39   Relieve the staking on the countershaft nut, then unscrew the nut. To prevent the countershaft from turning, either grip the mainshaft splines at the flywheel housing end using a self-locking wrench and with the transaxle in gear (use rags to protect the splines), or use mainshaft holder tool 07923 – 6890101 **(see illustration)**.

40   The remainder of this procedure is identical to the procedure for the five-speed transaxle described in Steps 13 to 34.

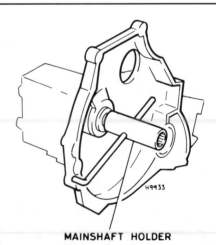

MAINSHAFT HOLDER

6.39   The mainshaft holder tool (07923-6890101) prevents the countershaft from turning while you're loosening the countershaft nut

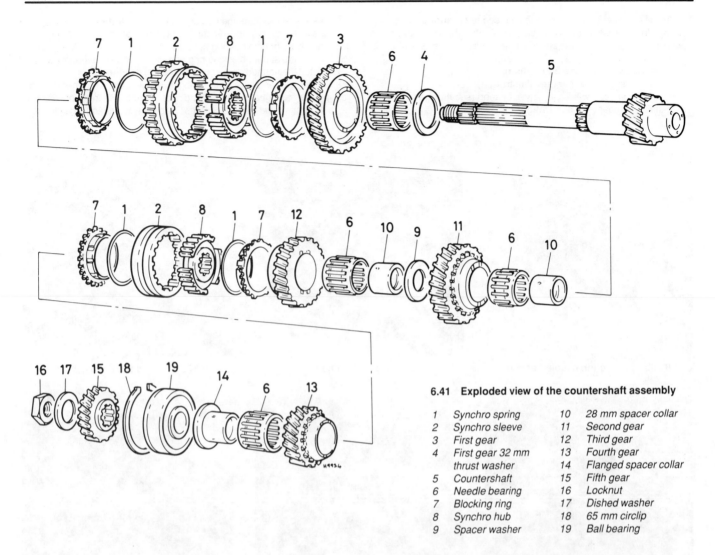

6.41 Exploded view of the countershaft assembly

1	Synchro spring	10	28 mm spacer collar
2	Synchro sleeve	11	Second gear
3	First gear	12	Third gear
4	First gear 32 mm	13	Fourth gear
	thrust washer	14	Flanged spacer collar
5	Countershaft	15	Fifth gear
6	Needle bearing	16	Locknut
7	Blocking ring	17	Dished washer
8	Synchro hub	18	65 mm circlip
9	Spacer washer	19	Ball bearing

Countershaft overhaul (four- and five-speed transaxles)

Refer to illustrations 6.41, 6.56a, 6.56b, 6.57a, 6.57b, 6.58a, 6.58b, 6.58c, 6.59, 6.60, 6.61a, 6.61b, 6.62, 6.63, 6.64, 6.65, 6.66, 6.67, 6.68a, 6.68b, 6.68c and 6.68d

41 Remove the flanged spacer collar **(see illustration)**.
42 Remove fourth gear.
43 Remove the blocking ring and synchro ring.
44 Remove the fourth gear needle bearing.
45 Remove the third/fourth synchro unit.
46 Remove the third gear blocking ring and spring.
47 Remove third gear.
48 Remove the needle bearing and spacer collar.
49 Remove the spacer washer and second gear.
50 Remove the first/second synchro blocking ring and spring.
51 Remove the needle bearing and spacer collar.
52 Remove the first/second synchro unit. The synchro sleeve includes reverse gear.
53 Take off first gear, the blocking ring and the spring.
54 Remove the needle bearing and thrust washer.
55 Clean and inspect all components. Replace as necessary. Lightly oil all parts, then reassemble them as described in the following Steps.
56 Install the thrust washer and needle bearing **(see illustrations)**.

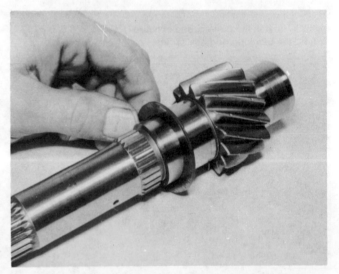

6.56a Install the thrust washer onto the countershaft . . .

57   Install first gear and the blocking ring **(see illustrations)**.
58   Install the first/second synchro unit with reverse, the blocking ring and spring, spacer sleeve and the second gear needle bearing **(see illustrations)**.
59   Install second gear **(see illustration)**.
60   Install the spacer washer **(see illustration)**.
61   Install the spacer collar and needle bearing **(see illustrations)**.
62   Install third gear **(see illustration)**.

63   Install the blocking ring and spring **(see illustration)**.
64   Install the third/fourth synchro unit **(see illustration)**.
65   Install the needle bearing **(see illustration)**.
66   Install the spring, blocking ring and fourth gear **(see illustration)**.
67   Install the flanged spacer collar **(see illustration)**.
68   Apply light pressure to the flanged spacer collar and measure the endplay of each gear **(see illustrations)**. If any measurements are outside the limits listed in this Chapter's Specifications, change the first gear

6.56b . . . and the needle bearing

6.57a   Install first gear . . .

6.57b . . . and the blocking ring

6.58a   Install the first/second synchro unit, the blocking ring, the spring, . . .

6.58b . . . the spacer sleeve . . .

6.58c . . . and the second gear needle roller bearing

6.59   Install second gear

6.60   Install the spacer washer

6.61a   Install the third gear spacer collar . . .

6.61b   . . . and the needle roller bearing

6.62   Install third gear

6.63   Install the blocking ring and spring

6.64   Install the third/fourth synchro unit

6.65   Install the needle roller bearing

6.66   Install the spring, blocking ring and fourth gear

6.67   Install the flanged spacer collar

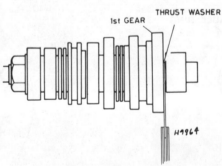

6.68a   Measure the first gear endplay here with a feeler gauge – if it's excessive, change the first gear thrust washer

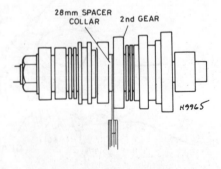

6.68b   Measure the second gear endplay here with a feeler gauge – if it's excessive, change spacer collar

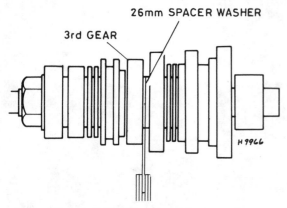

6.68c   Measure the third gear endplay here with a feeler
gauge – if it's excessive, change the spacer collar

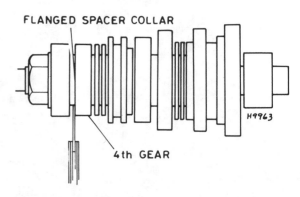

6.68d   Measure the fourth gear endplay here with a feeler
gauge – if it's excessive, change the flanged spacer collar

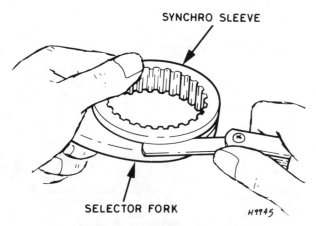

6.73   Measure the clearance between each selector fork and its
respective synchro sleeve groove with a feeler gauge – if the
clearance is excessive, replace the fork

thrust washer, second or third gear spacer collars or the fourth gear
flanged spacer collar, as necessary. Spacer thickness availability is listed
in this Chapter's Specifications.
69   If you're working on the five speed transaxle, place the fifth gear thrust
washer on the mainshaft, followed by fifth gear, the needle roller bearing
and the synchro unit. Apply pressure to the synchro hub and check the fifth
gear endplay. If it exceeds the endplay listed in this Chapter's Specifications, replace the thrust washer.

Component inspection

Refer to illustrations 6.73, 6.74 and 6.76

70   Check the transaxle casing and flywheel housing for cracks, especially around the bolt holes. Clean and reinstall the magnet.
71   Inspect all shafts for grooving or scoring and the gear teeth for chip-
ping or wear.
72   Test the shaft bearings. If they are obviously shaky or rattle when
spun, replace them. Always replace the bearings in the flywheel housing
once they have been removed.
73   Check the clearance of the selector forks in their respective synchro
sleeve grooves **(see illustration)**. If the clearance exceeds the clearance
listed in this Chapter's Specifications, replace the fork.
74   Press each synchro blocking ring onto its gear cone and apply a twisting motion **(see illustration)**. If the ring sticks firmly and has a minimum

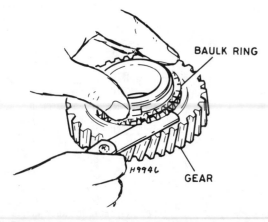

6.74   Press each synchro blocking (baulk) ring onto its gear cone
and apply a twisting motion, then measure the clearance between
the ring and the cone – if the ring doesn't stick firmly or the
ring-to-gear measurement doesn't match the clearance listed in
this Chapter's Specifications, replace the blocking ring

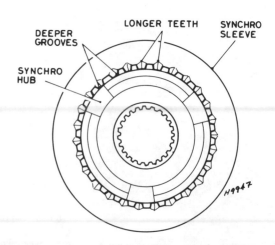

6.76   If you have to disassemble a synchro unit, note that –
because of the master splines – the hub can only be installed
into the sleeve in one of three positions

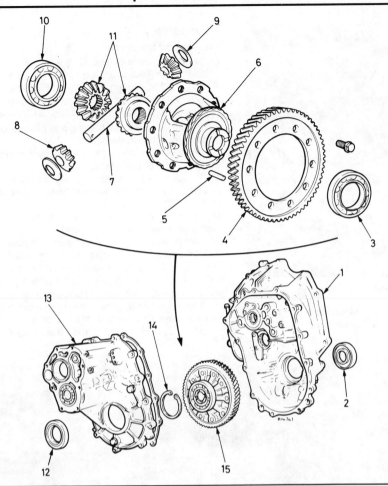

6.81 **Exploded view of final drive/differential**

1   Clutch housing
2   Seal
3   Ball bearing
4   Ring gear
5   Roll pin
6   Carrier
7   Pinion shaft
8   Pinion gear
9   Thrust washer
10   Ball bearing
11   Side gears
12   Seal
13   Transaxle case
14   Snap ring
15   Differential assembly

ring to gear clearance equal to that listed in this Chapter's Specifications, the parts are in good condition. If not, replace the blocking ring.
75   Wear in a synchronizer assembly will already be evident from noisy gear changing. If this is the case, replace the synchro assembly.
76   If you disassemble a synchronizer unit, note that the hub can only be installed into the sleeve in one of three positions because of the master splines **(see illustration)**. Always mark which way round the hub is located in its sleeve before separating the components. No sliding keys are used with this type of synchromesh.
77   To disassemble the countershaft, see Steps 41 through 54. The mainshaft can't be disassembled – the gears are integral with the shaft. If it's worn, replace the entire mainshaft assembly as a single unit.
78   All oil seals and O-rings should be replaced as a matter of course and an new countershaft retaining nut should be used.

Final drive (differential) overhaul

Refer to illustrations 6.81 and 6.88

79   To gain access to the differential, disassemble the transaxle as described in Steps 1 through 40.
80   The differential and final drive components rarely wear out, but it's a good idea to inspect for damaged teeth on the ring gear, pinion and side gear.
81   Before disassembling the final drive/differential assembly, mark the relationship of the ring gear to the differential carrier, and then unscrew the ring gear bolts **(see illustration). Caution:** *These bolts have left-hand threads.*
82   Drive the roll pin out of the differential pinion shaft.
83   Tap the pinion shaft from the carrier.
84   Remove the pinion gears, thrust washers and side gears.
85   Using a suitable puller, remove the differential carrier bearings.
86   Reassembly is the reverse of disassembly. Apply pressure only to the bearing inner tracks.

87   When reinstalling the ring gear, the chamfer on the flange should face towards the differential carrier and the positioning marks should be aligned. Use pinion thrust washers of identical thickness.
88   To check the backlash of the pinion gears, connect the driveaxles, support the differential carrier on V-blocks (positioned under the bearings) and measure the pinion gear backlash with a dial indicator **(see illustration)**. If the measurement is outside the limit listed in this Chapter's Specifications, change the thrust washers. Thickness availability of these washers is provided in the Specifications.

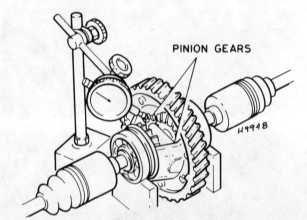

6.88 **To check the backlash of the pinion gears, connect the driveaxles, support the differential carrier on V-blocks and measure the pinion gear backlash with a dial gauge – if the backlash is outside specification, change the thrust washers**

6.89   Flywheel housing bearing components

1	Breather baffle	3	Mainshaft bearing
2	Bearing retainer plate	4	Countershaft bearing

Reassembly

Five-speed transaxle

Refer to illustrations 6.89, 6.92, 6.93a, 6.93b, 6.94, 6.96a, 6.96b, 6.97, 6.98a through 6.98f, 6.100a, 6.100b, 6.101, 6.102, 6.103, 6.104, 6.106a, 6.106b, 6.107a through 6.107f, 6.108, 6.109, 6.110a, 6.110b, 6.112a, 6.112b, 6.113, 6.114a, 6.114b, 6.114c, 6.115, 6.116, 6.117, 6.118a, 6.118b, 6.119, 6.121, 6.122a, 6.122b, 6.122c and 6.124 through 6.130

89   Install the mainshaft bearing and the new oil seal into the flywheel housing **(see illustration)**.

90   Install the breather baffle into the flywheel housing.

91   Install the oil guide plate.

92   Install the countershaft bearing, its retainer plate and tighten the screws securely to the flywheel housing **(see illustration)**. Stake the screw heads.

93   Install the speedometer drive gear assembly and secure it with the plate and screw **(see illustrations)**.

94   Install the shift rod seal and dust boot **(see illustration)**.

95   If the differential bearings are being replaced, lightly drive the new bearing into the transaxle casing to seat the circlip, then drive the differential into the flywheel housing until it's seated.

96   Mate the flywheel housing and transaxle casing and check the clearance between the circlip **(see illustration)** and the differential bearing outer track **(see illustration)**. If it's outside the clearance listed in this Chapter's Specifications, change the circlip thickness. The available

6.92   Install the countershaft bearing and retainer plate and tighten the screws securely to the flywheel housing

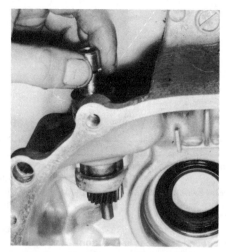

6.93a   Install the speedometer drive gear pinion assembly . . .

6.93b   . . . and secure it with the retaining plate and screw

6.94   Install the shift rod seal and dust boot

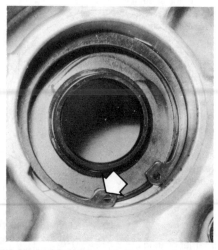

6.96a   The differential bearing circlip

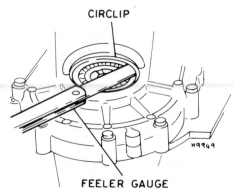

CIRCLIP

FEELER GAUGE

H9949

6.96b   Check the clearance between the differential bearing circlip and the differential bearing outer track with a feeler gauge – if it's excessive, replace the circlip with a thicker one

thicknesses are listed in this Chapter's Specifications.

97   Remove the transaxle case and install the differential into the flywheel housing **(see illustration)**.

98   Insert the selector rod detent spring and ball into their hole in the flywheel housing, depress the ball and insert the selector rod **(see illustrations)**. Install the selector arm to the rod, tighten the lock bolt and bend up on the lockplate tab **(see illustrations)**.

99   With the selector arm correctly located, install the selector arm holder Tighten the holder bolts to the torque listed in this Chapter's Specifications.

100 Install the mainshaft and countershaft simultaneously, with their gears meshed together, into the flywheel housing **(see illustrations)**.

6.97   Install the differential into the flywheel housing

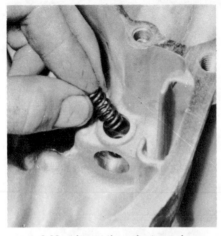
6.98a   Insert the selector rod detent spring . . .

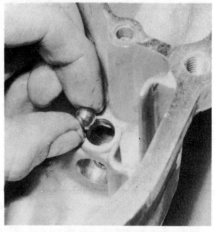
6.98b   . . . and the detent ball into this hole in the flywheel housing . . .

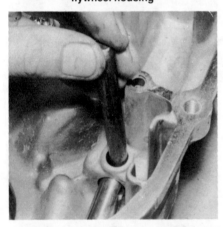
6.98c   . . . then depress the ball with a rod or punch . . .

6.98d   . . . and insert the selector rod into the flywheel housing

6.98e   Install the selector arm on the inner end of the selector rod . . .

6.98f   . . . then push the selector rod all the way into its bore in the housing and secure the selector arm to the rod with the bolt and lockplate

6.100a   With both geartrains held in mesh . . .

6.100b   . . . install the mainshaft and countershaft into the flywheel housing

6.101   Move the sliding sleeve of the first/second synchro into the second gear position and locate the first/second selector fork in the sleeve groove

6.102   Install the third/fourth selector shaft and fork

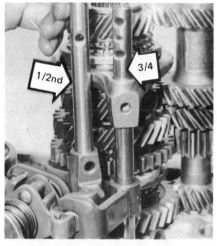

6.103   Install the first/second selector shaft

6.104   Locate the fifth/reverse selector dog and insert the selector shaft through it

6.106a   Using new lockplates, tighten the three selector shaft fork lock bolts . . .

6.106b . . . be sure to bend up the lockplate tab against the side of each bolt – a pair of pliers will work

6.107a   Install the reverse detent spring . . .

6.107b   . . . and the detent ball

6.107c   Install the reverse selector arm, . . .

6.107d   . . . position it correctly over the detent ball, . . .

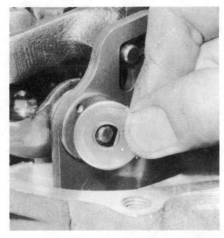

6.107e   . . . install the selector arm special washer . . .

6.107f   . . . and install the retaining nut

6.108   Install the reverse idler gear and shaft

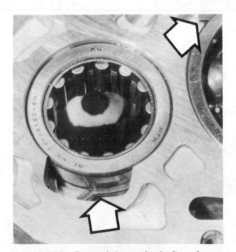

6.109   Spread the mainshaft and countershaft bearing circlips (arrows) and insert the bearings into the transaxle case

6.110a   Apply a thin bead of RTV sealant to the mating surfaces of the transaxle case

101 Move the sliding sleeve of the first/second synchro into the second gear position and locate the first/second selector fork in the sleeve groove (see illustration).

102 Install the third/fourth selector shaft and fork (see illustration).

103 Install the first/second selector shaft (see illustration).

104 Locate the fifth/reverse selector dog and insert the selector shaft through it (see illustration).

105 Verify that the detent grooves on the selector shafts are furthest from the flywheel housing and are also facing towards the outside of the transaxle case.

106 Tighten the three selector shaft fork bolts. Use new lockplates and bend up their tabs by squeezing them with a pair of pliers (see illustrations).

107 Install the reverse detent spring and ball, the reverse selector arm, the special washer and the nut (see illustrations).

108 Install the reverse idler gear and shaft (see illustration).

109 Expand the mainshaft and countershaft bearing circlips using strong circlip pliers and install the bearings into the transaxle case (see illustration).

110 Verify that the positioning dowels are in place in the transaxle case flange and apply a thin bead of RTV sealant to the mating face (see illustration). Install the magnet (see illustration).

6.110b   Install the magnet

6.112a   Mate the transaxle case to the flywheel housing

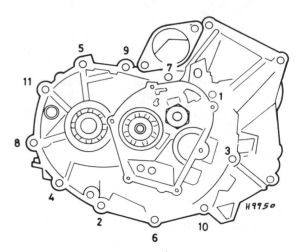

6.112b   Tighten the bolts in the sequence shown

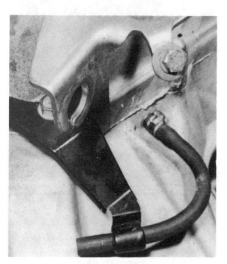

6.113   Install the clutch cable bracket and breather hose brackets

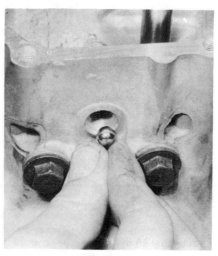

6.114a   Install the selector shaft detent ball . . .

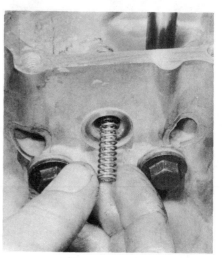

6.114b   . . . the detent spring

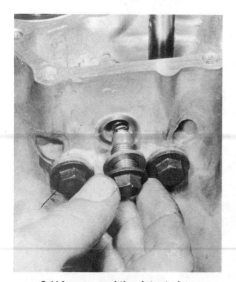

6.114c   . . . and the detent plug

6.115   Install the fifth gear on the countershaft

6.116   Install the dished washer with its concave side toward the gear

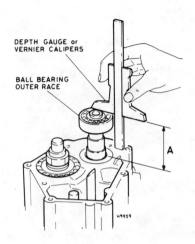

6.117 Measure the fifth gear bearing height (dimension A = height above case)

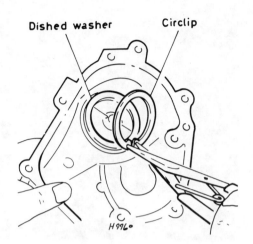

6.118a Remove the circlip and dished washer from the end cover (early models)

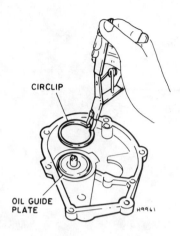

6.118b Remove the circlip and oil guide plate from the end cover (later models)

111 Lightly oil the shaft ends and differential bearing to facilitate the mating of the transaxle case and the flywheel housing.

112 Mate the transaxle case to the flywheel housing, install the connecting bolts and tighten them to the torque listed in this Chapter's Specifications, in the sequence shown (see illustrations).

113 Install the breather hose and clutch cable brackets (see illustration).

114 Install the detent balls, springs and plugs (see illustrations).

115 Install fifth gear on the countershaft so that its boss faces towards the bearing (see illustration).

116 Install the dished washer with its concave side to the gear (see illustration).

117 Install the fifth gear synchro hub and bearing onto the mainshaft. Using a depth gauge, measure height A (see illustration). Take the average of three measurements around the bearing.

118 Remove the bearing and synchro hub from the mainshaft. If you haven't already done so, extract the circlip and remove the dished washer or oil guide plate from the end cover (see illustrations).

119 Place a straightedge across the mounting flange of the end cover and, using the depth gauge, measure dimension B (see illustration). Take the average of three measurements into the circlip seat at equidistant points and subtract the thickness of the straight edge from the measurements.

120 To calculate the thickness of the fifth gear circlip, use the following formula:

Early models with dished washer behind circlip:

$B - A - 0.85$ mm (thickness of dished washer) = thickness of circlip required

Later models with oil guide plate behind circlip:

$B - A - 0.11$ to 0.18 mm (standard clearance) = thickness of circlip required

121 Install the dished washer or oil guide plate to the end cover followed by the circlip (see illustration). Note that it's permissible to use two circlips if necessary to obtain the required thickness.

122 Install the fifth gear thrust washer, the needle roller bearing and fifth

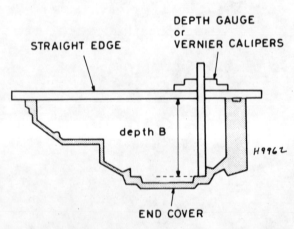

6.119 Place a straightedge across the mounting flange of the end cover and measure dimension B with a depth gauge

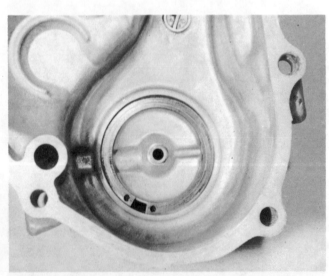

6.121 Install the dished washer (not shown), or oil guide plate (shown) to the end cover, then install the circlip

6.122a   Install the fifth gear
thrust washer . . .

6.122b   . . . the needle roller bearing . . .

6.122c   . . . and fifth gear to the
mainshaft

6.124   Install the fifth gear synchro hub

6.125   Engage the selector fork in the groove of the fifth gear
synchro sleeve and install the sleeve and fork to the shaft as an
assembly – make sure the chamfered side of the sleeve is farthest
from the gear

6.126   Stake the countershaft nut with a hammer and punch

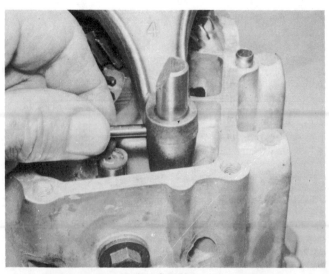

6.127   Insert the roll pin into the fifth gear selector fork

6.128 Install the ball bearing onto the mainshaft with the numbers visible

6.129 Apply RTV sealant to the mating surface of the case; make sure the positioning dowels are in place and install the end cover

gear onto the mainshaft (see illustrations).
123 Install the synchro blocking ring and spring.
124 Install the synchro hub with its recessed side towards fifth gear (see illustration).
125 Engage the selector fork in the groove of the fifth gear synchro sleeve (chamfered side of sleeve furthest from gear) and install the sleeve and fork to the shaft as an assembly (see illustration). Remember that the sleeve will only slide onto the hub on one of three positions due to the location of the master splines. Lock up the geartrains by pushing down on the fifth gear synchro sleeve.
126 Tighten the new countershaft locknut to the torque listed in this Chapter's Specifications. Loosen the nut and then tighten to the torque listed in this Chapter's Specifications for the second time. Stake the nut into the shaft groove (see illustration).
127 Install the fifth gear selector fork roll pin (see illustration).
128 Install the mainshaft ball bearing so the engraved numbers are visible when installed (see illustration).
129 Apply RTV sealant to the mating surface, verify that the positioning dowels are in place and bolt on the end cover (see illustration).
130 Install the back-up light switch (see illustration).
131 Check the selection of all gears by moving the selector shaft.
132 Install the clutch release shaft and bearing (if removed).

Four-speed transaxle

Refer to illustration 6.134

133 Carry out the operations described in Steps 89 through 114.
134 Install the mainshaft bearing onto the mainshaft, and using a depth gauge measure height A (see illustration). Take the average of three measurements around the bearing.

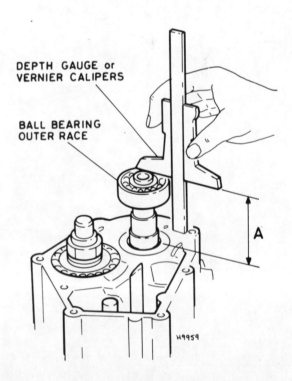

DEPTH GAUGE or VERNIER CALIPERS

BALL BEARING OUTER RACE

A

H9959

6.134 When you install the bearing onto the mainshaft, measure height A with a depth gauge – take the average of three measurements

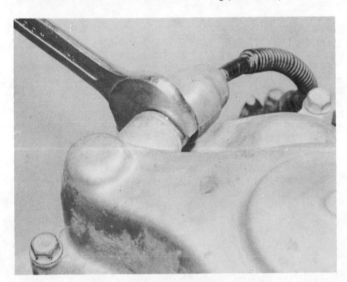

6.130 Install the back-up light switch

135 Remove the bearing from the mainshaft. Extract the circlip and remove the dished washer or oil guide plate from the end cover if not already done.

136 Calculate the thickness of end cover circlip required, using the same procedure as for the fifth gear circlip described in Steps 119 through 121.

137 Lock the countershaft using the same method used during disassembly and screw on a new countershaft locknut. Tighten the nut to the torque listed in this Chapter's Specifications, loosen it, then tighten once more. Stake the nut into the shaft groove.

138 Apply RTV sealant to the mating surface, verify that the positioning dowels are in place and bolt on the end cover.

139 Install the back-up light switch.

140 Check the selection of all gears by moving the selector shaft.

141 Install the clutch release shaft and bearing (if removed).

Chapter 7 Part B   Automatic transaxle

Contents

Specifications

General

Throttle valve cable (carbureted models)
  Dimension X (between cable end and locknut A) . . . .   3-23/64 in (86 mm)
  Throttle valve lever freeplay . . . .   5/64 to 5/32 in (2 to 4 mm)

Torque specifications   **Ft-lbs** (unless otherwise indicated)

Torque converter-to-driveplate bolts
  1984 through 1987   19
  1988 on . . . .   108 in-lbs

1   General information

All vehicles covered in this manual come equipped with either a four-or five-speed manual transaxle or an automatic transaxle. All information on the automatic transaxle is included in this Part of Chapter 7. Information for the manual transaxle can be found in Part A of this Chapter.

Due to the complexity of the automatic transaxles covered in this man-

ual and the need for specialized equipment to perform most service operations, this Chapter contains only general diagnosis, routine maintenance, adjustment and removal and installation procedures.

If the transaxle requires major repair work, it should be left to a dealer service department or an automotive or transmission repair shop. You can, however, remove and install the transaxle yourself and save the expense, even if the repair work is done by a transmission shop.

2   Diagnosis – general

Note: *Automatic transaxle malfunctions may be caused by five general conditions: poor engine performance, improper adjustments, hydraulic malfunctions, mechanical malfunctions or malfunctions in the computer or its signal network. Diagnosis of these problems should always begin with a check of the easily repaired items: fluid level and condition (see Chapter 1), shift linkage adjustment and throttle linkage adjustment. Next, perform a road test to determine if the problem has been corrected or if more diagnosis is necessary. If the problem persists after the preliminary tests and corrections are completed, additional diagnosis should be done by a dealer service department or transmission repair shop. Refer to the Troubleshooting section at the front of this manual for transaxle problem diagnosis.*

Preliminary checks

1   Drive the vehicle to warm the transaxle to normal operating temperature.

2   Check the fluid level as described in Chapter 1:
   a) If the fluid level is unusually low, add enough fluid to bring the level within the designated area of the dipstick, then check for external leaks.
   b) If the fluid level is abnormally high, drain off the excess, then check the drained fluid for contamination by coolant. The presence of engine coolant in the automatic transmission fluid indicates that a failure has occurred in the internal radiator walls that separate the coolant from the transmission fluid (see Chapter 3).
   c) If the fluid is foaming, drain it and refill the transaxle, then check for coolant in the fluid or a high fluid level.

3   Check the engine idle speed. **Note:** *If the engine is malfunctioning, do not proceed with the preliminary checks until it has been repaired and runs normally.*

4   Check the throttle valve cable for freedom of movement. Adjust it if necessary (see Section 3). **Note:** *The throttle valve cable may appear to function properly when the engine is shut off and cold, even though it malfunctions once the engine is hot. Check it at normal engine operating temperature.*

5   Inspect the shift control cable (see Section 4). Make sure that it's properly adjusted and that the linkage operates smoothly.

Fluid leak diagnosis

6   Most fluid leaks are easy to locate visually. Repair usually consists of replacing a seal or gasket. If a leak is difficult to find, the following procedure may help.

7   Identify the fluid. Make sure it's transmission fluid and not engine oil or brake fluid (automatic transmission fluid is a deep red color).

8   Try to pinpoint the source of the leak. Drive the vehicle several miles, then park it over a large sheet of cardboard. After a minute or two, you should be able to locate the leak by determining the source of the fluid dripping onto the cardboard.

9   Make a careful visual inspection of the suspected component and the area immediately around it. Pay particular attention to gasket mating surfaces. A mirror is often helpful for finding leaks in areas that are hard to see.

10   If the leak still cannot be found, clean the suspected area thoroughly with a degreaser or solvent, then dry it.

11   Drive the vehicle for several miles at normal operating temperature and varying speeds. After driving the vehicle, visually inspect the suspected component again.

12   Once the leak has been located, the cause must be determined before it can be properly repaired. If a gasket is replaced but the sealing flange is bent, the new gasket will not stop the leak. The bent flange must be straightened.

13   Before attempting to repair a leak, check to make sure that the following conditions are corrected or they may cause another leak. **Note:** *Some of the following conditions cannot be fixed without highly specialized tools and expertise. Such problems must be referred to a transmission shop or a dealer service department.*

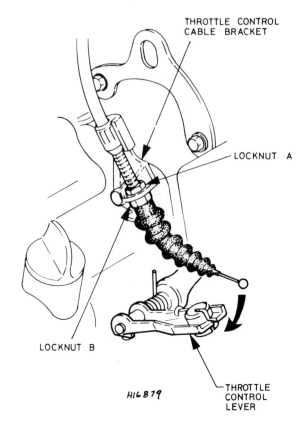

3.2   Detach the throttle valve cable from the throttle valve lever and bracket at the transaxle

Gasket leaks

14   Check the pan periodically. Make sure the bolts are tight, no bolts are missing, the gasket is in good condition and the pan is flat (dents in the pan may indicate damage to the valve body inside).

15   If the pan gasket is leaking, the fluid level or the fluid pressure may be too high, the vent may be plugged, the pan bolts may be too tight, the pan sealing flange may be warped, the sealing surface of the transaxle housing may be damaged, the gasket may be damaged or the transaxle casting may be cracked or porous. If sealant instead of gasket material has been used to form a seal between the pan and the transaxle housing, it may be the wrong sealant.

Seal leaks

16   If a transaxle seal is leaking, the fluid level or pressure may be too high, the vent may be plugged, the seal bore may be damaged, the seal itself may be damaged or improperly installed, the surface of the shaft protruding through the seal may be damaged or a loose bearing may be causing excessive shaft movement.

17   Make sure the dipstick tube seal is in good condition and the tube is properly seated. Periodically check the area around the speedometer gear or sensor for leakage. If transmission fluid is evident, check the O-ring for damage. Also inspect the side gear shaft oil seals for leakage.

Case leaks

18   If the case itself appears to be leaking, the casting is porous and will have to be repaired or replaced.

19   Make sure the oil cooler hose fittings are tight and in good condition.

Fluid comes out vent pipe or fill tube

20   If this condition occurs, the transaxle is overfilled, there is coolant in the fluid, the case is porous, the dipstick is incorrect, the vent is plugged or the drain back holes are plugged.

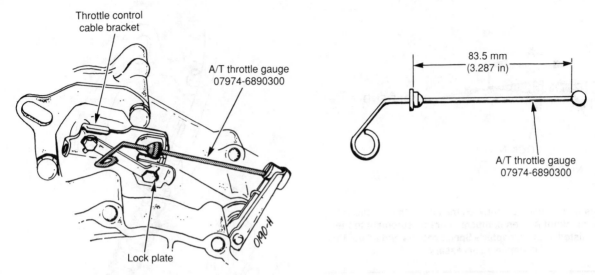

3.5   If you can't obtain this special tool, fabricate your own out of heavy gauge wire

3   Throttle valve cable – adjustment

Carbureted engines

Refer to illustrations 3.2, 3.5, 3.13, 3.15, 3.16 and 3.18

1   Remove the air cleaner assembly (see Chapter 4).
2   Disconnect the throttle valve cable from its bracket and the throttle valve lever **(see illustration)**.

Bracket adjustment

3   Before the cable can be adjusted, the position of the cable bracket should be checked and, if necessary, adjusted.
4   Straighten the lock tabs of the lock plate and remove the bracket bolts. Install a new lock plate, but don't tighten the bolts or bend up the lock tabs yet.
5   Buy or borrow the special tool (07974-6890300) shown in the accompanying illustration, or make a wire gauge of your own with exactly the same dimensions **(see illustration)**.
6   Put the special tool, or your wire gauge, between the throttle valve lever and the bracket.
7   Adjust the position of the bracket so there's no binding between it and

the special tool (a 0 to 0.3 mm tolerance is allowable). Make sure the lever doesn't get pulled toward the bracket side as you tighten the bolts. Tighten the two bolts and bend up the lock plate tabs against the bolt heads.

Throttle valve cable adjustment

8   Check the throttle cable freeplay (see Chapter 4).
9   Start the engine and warm it up. Wait for the electric cooling fan to come on.
10   Check and, if necessary, adjust the idle speed (see Chapter 1).
11   Turn off the engine.
12   Detach the throttle valve cable from the throttle valve lever and bracket on the transaxle **(see illustration 3.2)**.
13   Detach the vacuum hose from the dashpot, connect a vacuum pump and apply vacuum **(see illustration)**. This applied vacuum simulates the normal amount of operating vacuum present at the dashpot during engine operation.
14   Attach a 2-1/2 pound weight to the accelerator pedal. Raise the pedal, then release it. This allows the weight to remove the normal freeplay from the throttle cable.
15   Secure the throttle valve cable with clamps and allow the end of the cable to rest on the battery **(see illustration)**. **Warning:** *Don't let the cable touch the battery terminals.*

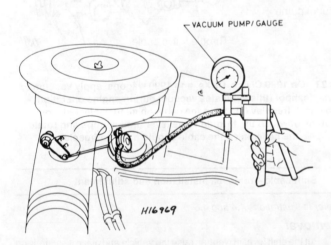

3.13   Use a vacuum pump to actuate the dashpot

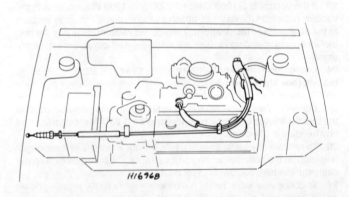

3.15   Before adjusting the throttle valve cable, lay it out like this, clamp it down and put the cable end on top of the battery

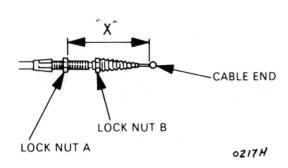

3.16   Measure the distance between the end of the throttle valve cable and locknut A, then compare your measurement to the dimension listed in this Chapter's Specifications and adjust this distance as necessary

16   Measure the distance between the end of the throttle valve cable and locknut A **(see illustration)**. Compare your measurement to the dimension listed in this Chapter's Specifications and adjust this distance as necessary.

17   Insert the end of the throttle valve cable into the slot of the lever. Make sure the cable isn't kinked or twisted, then insert the cable into the bracket and attach it with locknut B. Verify that the cables moves freely by depressing the accelerator pedal.

18   Remove the weight from the accelerator pedal, depress the pedal and verify that the throttle valve lever has the specified amount of freeplay **(see illustration)**.

19   Start the engine and check the synchronization between the carburetor and the throttle valve cable. The throttle valve lever should start to move as engine rpm increases.

   a) If the throttle valve lever starts to move before the engine rpm increases, turn cable locknut A counterclockwise and retighten locknut B.

   b) If the throttle valve lever starts to move after the engine rpm increases, turn cable locknut A clockwise and retighten locknut B.

Fuel-injected engines

Refer to illustration 3.23

20   Make sure the throttle cable freeplay is correct (see Chapter 4).
21   Start the engine and warm it up.
22   Check and, if necessary, adjust the idle speed (see Chapter 1).
23   If the vehicle is a 1989 Civic or CRX, or a 1990 Wagon, detach the vacuum hose from the dashpot, attach a vacuum pump and apply vacuum to the dashpot **(see illustration)**. This applied vacuum simulates the normal amount of operating vacuum present at the dashpot during engine operation.

24   Loosen locknuts A and B of the throttle valve cable at the throttle valve bracket **(see illustration 3.2)**.

25   To check the amount of freeplay (slack) in the throttle valve cable, press down on the throttle valve lever until it stops, hold it down and rotate the throttle linkage bellcrank **(see illustration 3.23)**. There shouldn't be any freeplay in the cable.

26   To remove any cable freeplay, turn locknut A until there's no longer any "slop" in the bellcrank when you rotate it, i.e. the bellcrank tugs on the cable the moment you begin to rotate it.

27   To check your work, rotate the bellcrank while lightly pressing down on the throttle valve lever with your thumb. The lever should start to move at exactly the same time as the bellcrank. If it doesn't, repeat the procedure above.

28   Have an assistant push down the accelerator pedal as far as it will go while you verify that the throttle valve cable moves freely.

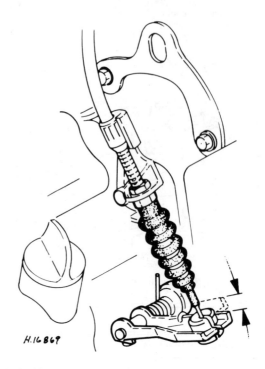

3.18   Measure the amount of freeplay at the throttle valve lever – if it moves before engine rpm increases, turn locknut A counterclockwise and retighten locknut B; if it moves after engine rpm increases, turn locknut A clockwise and retighten locknut B

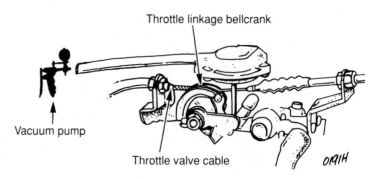

3.23   On 1989 Civics, CRXs, and 1990 wagons, apply vacuum to the dashpot (this simulates vacuum during engine operation) – to check freeplay (slack) in the cable on all fuel injected models, press down on the throttle valve lever until it stops and rotate the bellcrank – the cable should have no freeplay

---

4   Shift cable – removal, installation and adjustment

Refer to illustrations 4.4 and 4.8

Removal

1   Put the shift lever in Neutral, raise the vehicle and place it securely on jackstands.
2   Remove the engine compartment splash pan.

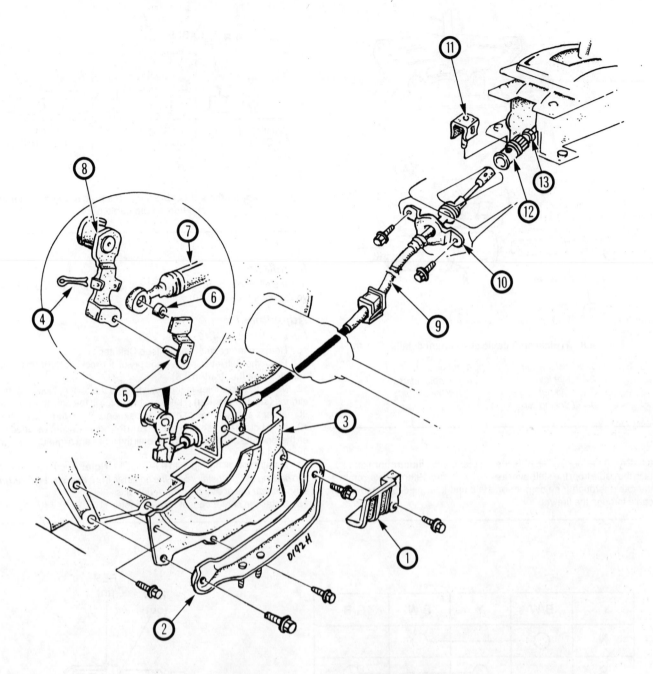

4.4   Exploded view of a typical shift cable assembly

1	Cable bracket	6	Roller	10	Cable bracket
2	Exhaust pipe bracket	7	Shift cable	11	Locking clip
3	Torque converter cover	8	Shift cable lever	12	Cable adjuster
4	Cotter pin	9	Shift cable	13	Locknut
5	Shift cable pin				

3   Remove the front exhaust pipe (see Chapter 4).
4   Remove the torque converter cover **(see illustration)**.
5   Remove the cotter pin from the shift cable pin, pull out the pin and detach the cable from the transaxle. Note how the various parts at the end of

the shift cable fit together. Be careful not to lose any of these parts.
6   If the shift cable assembly is routed through the firewall (1988 and later models), detach the cable bracket from the firewall.
7   Remove the center console (see Chapter 11).

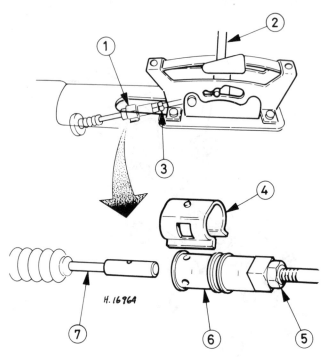

4.8   Typical shift cable adjustment details

1 Locking clip	5 Locknut
2 Shift lever	6 Cable adjuster
3 Locknut	7 Shift cable
4 Locking clip	

8   Pry off the locking clip from the shift cable **(see illustration)** and detach the cable from the shift lever assembly. On pre-1988 models, remove the cable through the floorpan; on 1988 and later models, remove the cable through the firewall.

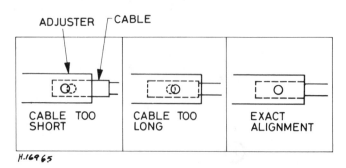

4.12   To adjust the shift cable, align the hole in the adjuster and the hole in the cable pin

Installation

9   Installation is the reverse of removal. Be sure to adjust the cable when you're done (see Step 10).

Adjustment

Refer to illustration 4.12

10   Remove the center console (see Chapter 11).
11   Place the shift lever in Drive and pry off the locking clip from the cable adjuster **(see illustration 4.8).**
12   Verify that the holes in the adjuster and the shift cable are perfectly aligned **(see illustration)**. There are two holes in the adjuster, positioned 90-degrees apart, to permit cable adjustments in 1/4-turn increments.
13   If the hole in the cable and the hole in the adjuster aren't aligned, loosen the locknut and turn the adjuster until the holes are aligned, then tighten the locknut.
14   Install the locking clip onto the adjuster. **Note:** *If you feel the locking clip binding as you install it onto the adjuster, the cable isn't adjusted properly. Repeat the above procedure until it is.*
15   Install the center console (see Chapter 11).

	B/W	Y	B/W	G/B
N	○———————○			
R		○———————○		
P	○———————○			
	ST (IN)	REV (IN)	ST (OUT)	REV (OUT)

0193H

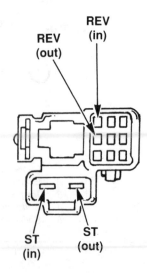

5.2a   Terminal guide and continuity table for the neutral start switch (1984 through 1987 models)

	Neutral safety switch		Back-up light switch	
Terminal Position	11	12	2	3
L				
D_3				
D_4				
N	○———○			
R			○———○	
P	○———○			

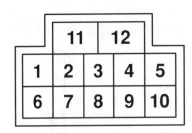

11	12			
1	2	3	4	5
6	7	8	9	10

VIEW FROM
WIRE SIDE

0194H

5.2b Terminal guide and continuity table for the neutral start switch (1988 and later models)

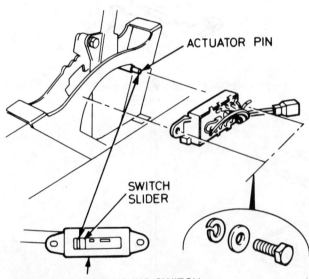

ACTUATOR PIN

SWITCH
SLIDER

NEUTRAL START/BACKUP SWITCH

H14818

5.3 Typical neutral start switch assembly – be sure to put the shift lever in Neutral and position the switch slider onto the actuator pin when installing a new switch

5 Neutral start switch – check and replacement

Refer to illustrations 5.2a, 5.2b and 5.3

1 Try to start the engine in each shift lever position; the starter should operate in Park and Neutral only. If the starter doesn't operate, or operates in any position other than Park or Neutral, check the shift cable adjustment (see Section 4). If the shift cable is properly adjusted and the problem persists, check the Neutral start switch (which also incorporates the back-up light switch).

2 Remove the center console (see Chapter 11) and unplug the connector from the Neutral start switch. With the shift lever in each position, check the connector for continuity **(see illustrations)**.

3 If the continuity isn't as specified, replace the switch. Simply remove the retaining screws and detach the switch from the shift lever mounting bracket **(see illustration)**.

4 When installing the new switch, place the switch slider and shift lever in Neutral; place the switch in position over the actuator pin **(see illustration 5.3)** and tighten the bolts securely.

6 Shift lever assembly – removal and installation

Refer to illustration 6.2

1 Remove the center console (see Chapter 11).

2 Remove the screws from the shift lever knob and remove the knob **(see illustration)**.

3 Remove the gear position indicator panel.

4 Unplug the connector(s) to the neutral start switch, the gear position indicator and, if equipped, the shift lock solenoid.

5 Disconnect the shift cable from the shift lever (see Section 4).

6 Remove the mounting fasteners from the shift lever assembly and remove it.

7 Installation is the reverse of removal. Be sure to adjust the shift cable when you're done (see Section 4).

7 Automatic transaxle – removal and installation

Refer to illustrations 7.4, 7.8, 7.14, 7.16, 7.23, 7.24 and 7.25

Removal

1 Disconnect the cables from the battery and remove the battery (see Chapter 5). **Note:** *Removing the battery tray makes some of the following Steps easier.*

2 Remove the air cleaner housing and intake hose (see Chapter 4).

3 Remove the distributor from the cylinder head (see Chapter 5).

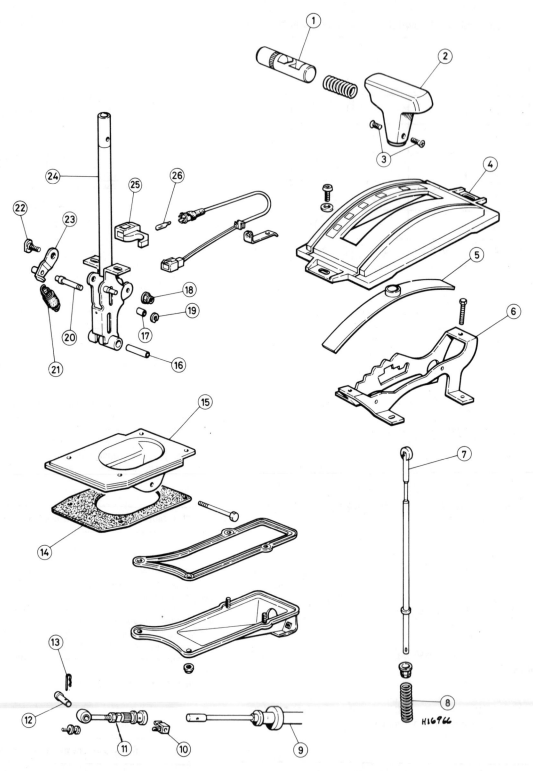

6.2　Exploded view of the shift lever assembly (1984 through 1987 model shown, later models similar)

1	Push button	6	Shift lever	11	Cable adjuster	17	Collar	23	Stop
2	Handle		mounting bracket	12	Control rod pin	18	Nut	24	Shift lever
3	Screws	7	Lock pin rod	13	Locking pin	19	Clip	25	Bulb housing (gear
4	Gear position	8	Lock pin spring	14	Gasket	20	Lock		position indicator)
	indicator panel	9	Shift cable	15	Shift lever bracket	21	Stop spring	26	Bulb
5	Shift lever cover	10	Locking clip	16	Collar	22	Stop bolt		

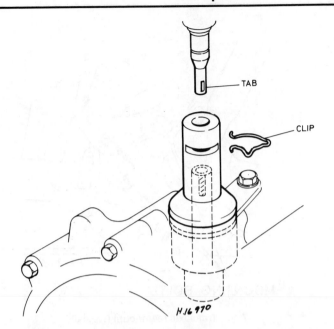

7.4 To disconnect the speedometer cable, remove the retaining clip and pull the cable out of the housing; don't remove the housing itself or the speedometer driven gear may fall into the transaxle housing

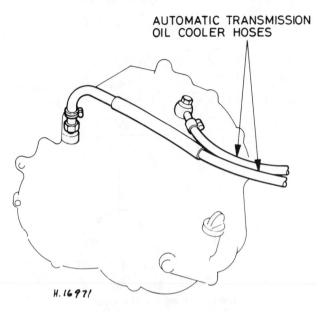

7.8 Detach the cooler hoses for the automatic transmission fluid, plug them to prevent leakage and contamination and wire them up out of the way

4   Disconnect the speedometer cable (see illustration).
5   Mark and detach any vacuum hose(s), or hose clips, from the transaxle.
6   Mark and detach any wiring, including the ground cable(s), from the transaxle.
7   Detach the starter leads and remove the upper mounting bolt from the starter motor (see Chapter 5). The lower mounting bolt is easier to remove after the vehicle is raised.
8   Disconnect the transaxle cooler hoses (see illustration), then plug them to prevent leakage and hang them out of the way with wire.
9   Disconnect the throttle valve cable (see Section 3).
10 Loosen the front wheel lug nuts. Raise the front of the vehicle and sup-

port it securely on jackstands. Remove the front wheels.
11 Remove the engine compartment splash pan and the inner fender liners.
12 Remove the exhaust header pipe (see Chapter 4).
13 Drain the transaxle fluid into a suitable container (see Chapter 1). Reinstall the drain plug.
14 Remove the exhaust pipe bracket and cable holder from the torque converter cover. Remove the torque converter cover (see illustration).
15 Disconnect the shift cable (see Section 4).
16 Mark the relationship of the torque converter to the driveplate so they can be installed in the same position (see illustration).

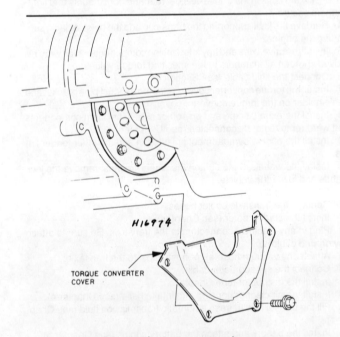

7.14 Remove the torque converter cover

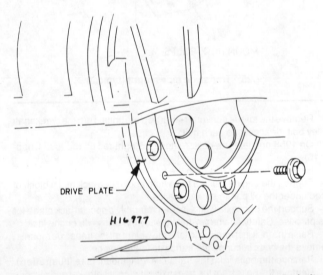

7.16 Before removing the driveplate-to-torque converter bolts, mark the edge of the drive plate to the torque converter to ensure that they're reattached in exactly the same relationship to one another when the transaxle is reinstalled

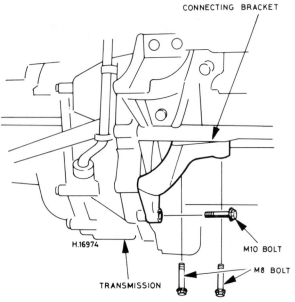

7.23   **Transaxle front mount (typical)**

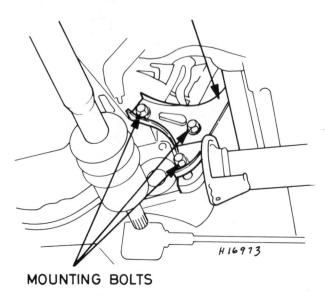

7.24   **Transaxle rear mount (typical)**

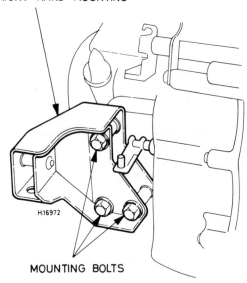

7.25   **Transaxle side mount (typical)**

17   Remove the torque converter-to-driveplate bolts. Turn the crankshaft pulley bolt for access to each bolt.
18   On 1988 and later models, remove the right radius rod (see Chapter 10).
19   Remove the driveaxles from the transaxle (see Chapter 8).
20   Support the engine using a hoist from above or a jack and a block of wood under the oil pan to spread the load.
21   Support the transaxle with a jack – preferably a special jack made for this purpose. Safety chains will help steady the transaxle on the jack.
22   Raise the jack just enough to take the weight off the transaxle mounts. Remove the bolts securing the transaxle to the engine.
23   Remove the bolts from the transaxle front mount **(see illustration)**.
24   Remove the bolts from the transaxle rear mount bracket and remove the bracket **(see illustration)**.
25   Remove the bolts from the transaxle side mount **(see illustration)**.
26   Lower the transaxle slightly, move it back to disengage it from the engine block dowel pins and make sure the torque converter is detached

from the driveplate. Secure the torque converter to the transaxle so it will not fall out during removal. Lower the transaxle from the vehicle.

Installation

27   Prior to installation, make sure that the torque converter hub is securely engaged in the pump.
28   With the transaxle secured to the jack, raise it into position. Be sure to keep it level so the torque converter doesn't slide out.
29   Turn the torque converter to line up the drive studs with the holes in the driveplate. The previously applied matchmarks on the torque converter and the driveplate must line up.
30   Move the transaxle forward carefully until the dowel pins and the torque converter are engaged.
31   Install the transaxle housing-to-engine bolts. Tighten them securely.
32   Install the torque converter-to-driveplate nuts. Tighten the nuts to the torque listed in this Chapter's Specifications.
33   Install the bolts in the transaxle side, rear and front mounts and tighten them securely.
34   Remove the jack supporting the transaxle and the hoist, or jack, supporting the engine.
35   Install the driveaxles and any suspension components which were removed. Tighten all fasteners to the specified torque values.
36   Connect the shift cable (see Section 4).
37   Install the torque converter cover. Install the exhaust pipe bracket and cable holder on the torque converter cover.
38   Install the exhaust pipe and any other exhaust system components that were removed or disconnected.(see Chapter 4).
39   Install the engine compartment splash pan and the inner fender liners.
40   Install the wheels, hand tighten the wheel lug nuts, remove the jack stands and lower the vehicle.
41   Connect the throttle valve cable and adjust it (see Section 3).
42   Connect the transaxle cooler hoses.
43   Install the starter motor (see Chapter 5).
44   Plug in any electrical connectors to the transaxle. Be sure to attach any ground cable(s).
45   Attach any vacuum hose(s), or hose clips, to the transaxle.
46   Connect the speedometer cable.
47   Install the distributor (see Chapter 5).
48   Install the air cleaner housing and intake hose (see Chapter 4).
49   Fill the transaxle with fresh automatic transmission fluid (see Chapter 1).
50   Install the battery and attach the battery cables (see Chapter 5).
51   Start the engine and check for fluid leaks.

Chapter 8 Part A   Clutch and driveaxles

Contents

Specifications

General

Clutch pedal freeplay
   All models except 1984 through 1987 CRX .... 5/8 to 7/8 in
   1984 through 1987 CRX .... 3/8 to 1-1/4 in
Release arm freeplay
   1984 through 1987 .... 3/16 to 1/4 in
   1988 on .... 1/8 to 3/16
Driveaxles
Driveaxle length*
   1984 through 1987
      Left .... 30-7/16 to 30-9/16 in
      Right .... 18-1/2 to 18-11/16 in
   1988 and 1989
      Left
         With dynamic damper .... 30-1/2 to 30-11/16 in
         Without dynamic damper .... 30-7/16 to 30-5/8 in
      Right .... 19 to 19-1/8 in
   1990
      Left .... 31-1/8 to 31-1/4 in
      Right .... 19-1/2 to 19-5/8 in

*Note: *All dimensions listed above are for 2WD models. Driveaxle dimensions for 4WD models are listed in Chapter 8, Part B.*

Torque specifications

	Ft-lbs
Clutch pressure plate bolts	19
Release fork bolt	22
Driveaxle/hub nut	134

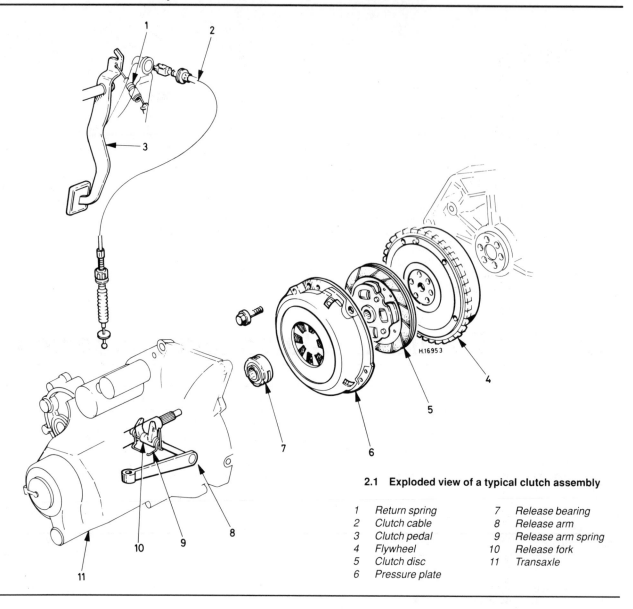

2.1 Exploded view of a typical clutch assembly

1	Return spring	7	Release bearing
2	Clutch cable	8	Release arm
3	Clutch pedal	9	Release arm spring
4	Flywheel	10	Release fork
5	Clutch disc	11	Transaxle
6	Pressure plate		

1   General information

The information in this Chapter deals with the components from the rear of the engine to the the front wheels, except for the transaxle, which is dealt with in the previous Chapter. For the purposes of this Chapter, these components are grouped into two categories: clutch and driveaxles. Separate Sections within this Chapter offer general descriptions and checking procedures for components in each of the two groups. Service procedures related to the 4WD system are included in Part B of this Chapter.

Since nearly all the procedures covered in this Chapter involve working under the vehicle, make sure it's securely supported on sturdy jackstands or on a hoist where the vehicle can be easily raised and lowered.

2   Clutch – description and check

Refer to illustration 2.1

1   All vehicles with a manual transaxle use a single dry plate, diaphragm spring type clutch **(see illustration)**. The clutch disc has a splined hub which allows it to slide along the splines of the transmission input shaft.

The clutch and pressure plate are held in contact by spring pressure exerted by the diaphragm in the pressure plate.
2   The clutch release system is operated by a mechanical release system which includes the clutch pedal, the clutch cable, the clutch release lever and the release bearing.
3   When pressure is applied to the clutch pedal to release the clutch, mechanical pressure is exerted against the outer end of the clutch release lever. As the lever pivots the shaft fingers push against the release bearing. The bearing pushes against the fingers of the diaphragm spring of the pressure plate assembly, which in turn releases the clutch plate.
4   Terminology can be a problem when discussing the clutch components because common names are in some cases different from those used by the manufacturer. For example, the driven plate is also called the clutch plate or disc, the clutch release bearing is sometimes called a throwout bearing, the pressure plate is sometimes called the clutch cover.
5   The following preliminary checks can help you diagnose clutch problems.
   a) Check "clutch spin down time" by running the engine at normal idle speed with the transaxle in Neutral (clutch pedal up – engaged). Disengage the clutch (pedal down), wait several seconds and shift the transaxle into Reverse. If it makes a grinding noise, there's a problem with the pressure plate or the clutch disc.

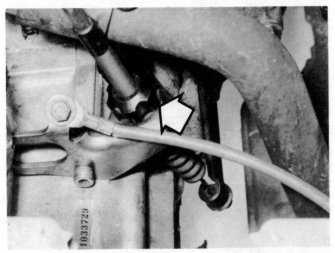

3.2   To remove – or loosen – the clutch cable, back off the cable adjusting nut (arrow)

3.3   Disconnect the clutch cable from the release arm

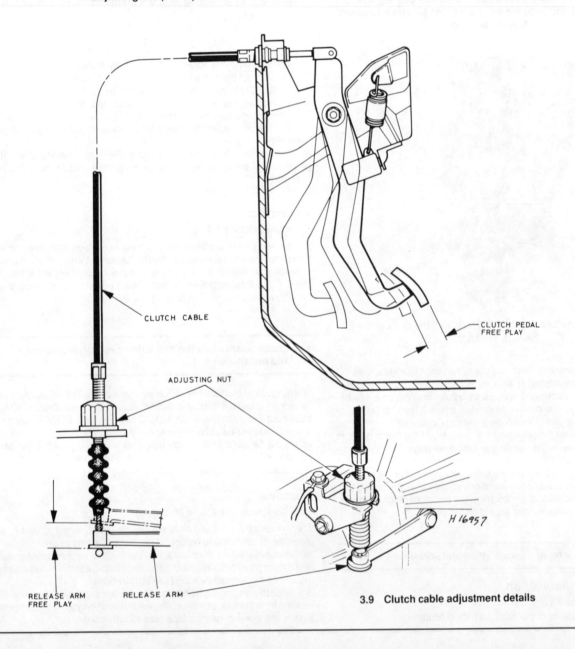

CLUTCH CABLE

ADJUSTING NUT

CLUTCH PEDAL FREE PLAY

RELEASE ARM FREE PLAY

RELEASE ARM

3.9   Clutch cable adjustment details

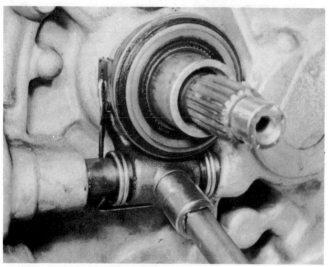

4.2a   Remove the bolt that attaches the release bearing fork to the release shaft and slide the shaft out of the transaxle housing to free the bearing

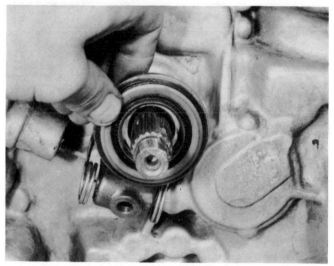

4.2b   Slide the bearing and fork off the transaxle input shaft

4.3   To free the bearing from the fork, pull the ends of the retaining spring out

b) Check for complete clutch release by running the engine (with the parking brake applied to prevent movement) and hold the clutch pedal approximately 1/2-inch from the floor. Shift the transaxle between first gear and Reverse several times. If the shift is hard or the transaxle grinds, component failure is indicated.

c) Visually inspect the pivot bushing at the top of the clutch pedal to make sure there is no binding or excessive play.

d) A clutch pedal that's difficult to operate is most likely caused by a faulty clutch cable. Check the cable, where it enters the housing, for frayed wires, rust and other signs of corrosion. If it looks good, lubricate the cable with penetrating oil. If pedal operation improves, the cable is worn out and should be replaced.

---

3   Clutch cable – removal, installation and adjustment

Removal and installation

Refer to illustrations 3.2 and 3.3

1   Detach the cable from the negative battery terminal.

2   Loosen the cable adjusting nut **(see illustration)**.
3   Disconnect the cable from the release arm **(see illustration)**.
4   Detach the cable from the support bracket.
5   Detach any cable clips in the engine compartment.
6   From inside the vehicle, disconnect the cable from the clutch pedal.
7   Pull the cable assembly through the firewall from the engine compartment side.
8   Installation is the reverse of removal. Be sure to lubricate the clutch pedal end of the cable with moly-based grease. Adjust the cable (see Step 9).

Adjustment

Refer to illustration 3.9

9   Measure the freeplay at the clutch pedal by depressing the pedal by hand from the fully released position to the point at which you can feel resistance **(see illustration)**. Compare your measurement to the freeplay listed in this Chapter's Specifications. If it's outside the specified range, turn the cable adjusting nut to bring it within specification.

---

4   Clutch release bearing and fork – removal, inspection and installation

---

Warning: *Dust produced by clutch wear and deposited on clutch components may contain asbestos, which is hazardous to your health. DO NOT blow it out with compressed air and DO NOT inhale it. DO NOT use gasoline or petroleum-based solvents to remove the dust. Brake system cleaner should be used to flush the dust into a drain pan. After the clutch components are wiped clean with a rag, dispose of the contaminated rags and cleaner in a covered, marked container.*

Removal

Refer to illustrations 4.2a, 4.2b and 4.3

1   Remove the transaxle from the vehicle (see Chapter 7, Part A) and clean the clutch housing as described in the Warning above.
2   Remove the bolt which attaches the release bearing fork to the release shaft **(see illustration)** and slide the shaft out of the transaxle housing to free the release bearing **(see illustration)**.
3   Slide the bearing and fork off the transaxle input shaft. To separate the bearing from the fork, pull the spring ends out, disengaging them from the slots in the bearing locating tabs **(see illustration)**.

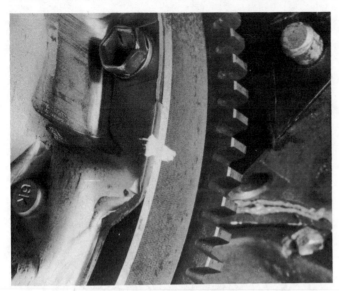

5.5   Index the pressure plate to the flywheel (just in case you're going to reuse the same pressure plate)

5.6   Once the pressure plate bolts are removed and the pressure plate is pulled away from the flywheel, the disc will fall if unsupported, so grasp it firmly, and make sure you don't breathe the dust deposited on the clutch components – it may contain asbestos, which is carcinogenic

the surface appearance. Refer to Chapter 2 for the flywheel removal and installation procedure.

Inspection

4   Check the release fork, release shaft and lever for excessive wear, replacing them if necessary.
5   Inspect the bearing for damage, wear and cracks. Hold the center of the bearing and spin the outer race. If the bearing doesn't turn smoothly or if it's noisy, replace it with a new one. It's common practice to replace the bearing with a new one whenever a clutch job is performed, to decrease the possibility of a bearing failure in the future.

Installation

6   Wipe the old grease from the release bearing, if the bearing is to be reused. Do not clean it by immersing it in solvent; it's packed with grease and sealed at the factory and would be ruined if solvent got into it. Fill the groove in the inner diameter of the bearing with high-temperature grease.
7   Replace the bearing on the release fork, making sure the spring ends completely engage with the bearing locating tabs.
8   Lubricate the release shaft with multi-purpose grease, position the release fork/bearing assembly in the transaxle housing and install the release shaft. Align the hole in the fork with the threaded hole in the shaft and install the bolt and washer. Tighten the bolt to the torque listed in this Chapter's Specifications.
9   Work the release shaft arm by hand to verify smooth operation of the release shaft and bearing. The remainder of installation is the reverse of the removal procedure. Don't forget to adjust the clutch cable (see Section 3).

---

5   **Clutch components – removal, inspection and installation**

Warning: *Dust produced by clutch wear and deposited on clutch components may contain asbestos, which is hazardous to your health. DO NOT blow it out with compressed air and DO NOT inhale it. DO NOT use gasoline or petroleum-based solvents to remove the dust. Brake system cleaner should be used to flush the dust into a drain pan. After the clutch*

components are wiped clean with a rag, dispose of the contaminated rags and cleaner in a covered, marked container.

Removal

Refer to illustrations 5.5 and 5.6

1   Access to the clutch components is normally accomplished by removing the transaxle, leaving the engine in the vehicle. If the engine is being removed for major overhaul, check the clutch for wear and replace worn components as necessary. However, the relatively low cost of the clutch components compared to the time and trouble spent gaining access to them warrants their replacement anytime the engine or transaxle is removed, unless they are new or in near perfect condition. The following procedures are based on the assumption the engine will stay in place.
2   Remove the transaxle from the vehicle (see Chapter 7, Part A). Support the engine while the transaxle is out. Preferably, an engine hoist should be used to support it from above. However, if a jack is used underneath the engine, make sure a piece of wood is positioned between the jack and oil pan to spread the load. **Caution:** *The pickup for the oil pump is very close to the bottom of the oil pan. If the pan is bent or distorted in any way, engine oil starvation could occur.*
3   The clutch fork and release bearing can remain attached to the transaxle housing for the time being.
4   To support the clutch disc during removal, install a clutch alignment tool through the clutch disc hub.
5   Carefully inspect the flywheel and pressure plate for indexing marks. The marks are usually an X, an O or a white letter. If they cannot be found, scribe or paint marks yourself so the pressure plate and the flywheel will be in the same alignment during installation **(see illustration)**.
6   Turning each bolt a little at a time, loosen the pressure plate-to-flywheel bolts. Work in a criss-cross pattern until all spring pressure is relieved. Then hold the pressure plate securely and completely remove the bolts, followed by the pressure plate and clutch disc **(see illustration)**.

Inspection

Refer to illustrations 5.9 and 5.11

7   Ordinarily, when a problem occurs in the clutch, it can be attributed to wear of the clutch driven plate assembly (clutch disc). However, all components should be inspected at this time.

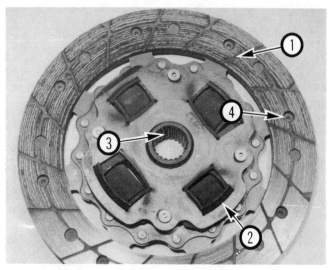

5.9   The clutch disc

1   Lining – this will wear
    down in use
2   Springs – check for cracking
    and deformation
3   Splined hub – the splines must
    not be worn and should slide
    smoothly on the transaxle

    input shaft splines
4   Rivets – these secure
    the lining and will damage
    the flywheel or pressure
    plate if allowed to contact
    the surfaces

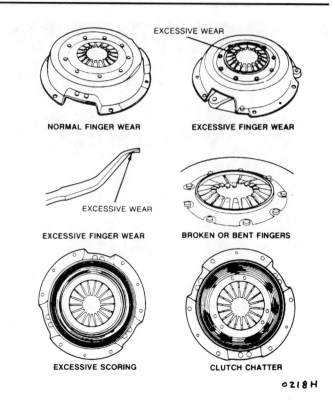

5.11   Replace the pressure plate if excessive wear is noted

5.13   Center the clutch disc in the pressure plate with a clutch alignment tool

8   Inspect the flywheel for cracks, heat checking, grooves and other obvious defects. If the imperfections are slight, a machine shop can machine the surface flat and smooth, which is highly recommended regardless of surface appearance. Refer to Chapter 2 for the flywheel removal and installation procedure.

9   Inspect the lining on the clutch disc. There should be at least 1/16-inch of lining above the rivet heads. Check for loose rivets, distortion, cracks, broken springs and other obvious damage **(see illustration)**. As mentioned above, ordinarily the clutch disc is routinely replaced, so if in doubt about the condition, replace it with a new one.

10   The release bearing should also be replaced along with the clutch disc (see Section 4).

11   Check the machined surfaces and the diaphragm spring fingers of the pressure plate **(see illustration)**. If the surface is grooved or otherwise damaged, replace the pressure plate. Also check for obvious damage, distortion, cracking, etc. Light glazing can be removed with emery cloth or sandpaper. If a new pressure plate is required, new and factory-rebuilt units are available.

Installation

Refer to illustration 5.13

12   Before installation, clean the flywheel and pressure plate machined surfaces with brake cleaner, lacquer thinner or acetone. It's important that no oil or grease is on these surfaces or the lining of the clutch disc. Handle the parts only with clean hands.

13   Position the clutch disc and pressure plate against the flywheel with the clutch held in place with an alignment tool **(see illustration)**. Make sure it's installed properly (most replacement clutch plates will be marked "flywheel side" or something similar – if not marked, install the clutch disc with the damper springs toward the transaxle).

14   Tighten the pressure plate-to-flywheel bolts only finger tight, working around the pressure plate.

15   Center the clutch disc by ensuring the alignment tool extends through the splined hub and into the pocket in the crankshaft. Wiggle the tool up, down or side-to-side as needed to center the disc. Tighten the pressure plate-to-flywheel bolts a little at a time, working in a crisscross pattern to prevent distorting the cover. After all of the bolts are snug, tighten them to the torque listed in this Chapter's Specifications. Remove the alignment tool.

16   Using high-temperature grease, lubricate the inner groove of the release bearing (see Section 4). Also place grease on the release lever contact areas and the transaxle input shaft bearing retainer.

17   Install the clutch release bearing (see Section 4).

18   Install the transaxle and all components removed previously. Tighten all fasteners to the proper torque specifications.

---

6   Pilot bearing – inspection and replacement

1   The clutch pilot bearing, a sealed ball-type bearing pressed into the flywheel, supports the front of the transaxle input shaft. It's greased at the factory and doesn't require additional lubrication. The pilot bearing should

8.2   To prevent the hub from turning while you're breaking the hub nut loose, place a pry bar between two of the wheel studs

8.6   Swing the hub/knuckle assembly out (away from the vehicle) and pull the driveaxle from the hub

be inspected whenever the clutch components are removed from the engine. Because of its inaccessibility, replace it with a new one if you have any doubt about its condition. **Note:** *If the engine has already been removed from the vehicle, disregard the following steps that don't apply.*

2   Remove the transaxle (see Chapter 7, Part A).

3   Remove the clutch components (see Section 5).

4   Inspect for any excessive wear, scoring, lack of grease, dryness or obvious damage. A flashlight will be helpful to direct light into the recess. Turn the inner race of the bearing with your finger. It should rotate smoothly and quietly. Make sure the bearing outer race fits tightly into the flywheel. If the bearing fails to meet any of these criteria, replace it.

5   Remove the flywheel (see Chapter 2, Part A).

6   To remove the old bearing, lay the flywheel on a flat work surface and tap the bearing out with hammer and a soft punch.

7   To install the new bearing, get a solid steel bar, a wooden dowel or a large socket slightly smaller in diameter than the bearing and use it to drive the bearing into place.

8   Install the flywheel (see Chapter 2, Part A).

9   Install the clutch components, transaxle and all other components removed previously, tightening all fasteners properly.

---

7   Starter/clutch interlock switch – check, replacement and adjustment

Check

1   The starter/clutch interlock switch is located near the upper end of the clutch pedal on some models. It has two wires – one coming from the starter relay and one going to ground. When the ignition switch key is turned to the Start position and the clutch pedal is depressed, the starter relay's path to ground is closed by the starter/clutch interlock switch and the starter motor is activated.

2   If the engine won't start when the clutch pedal is depressed, adjust the switch (see Step 6) and try again. If it still won't start, check the switch (see Step 3) and, if necessary, replace it (see Step 5). If the engine starts when the clutch pedal isn't depressed, adjust the switch and try again.

3   If the engine won't start when the clutch pedal is depressed, either there's no voltage from the starter relay to the switch, there's no continuity from the switch to ground, or the switch itself is faulty.

4   Using the wiring diagrams at the end of Chapter 12, check the voltage to the switch with a voltmeter or test light. When you turn the ignition key to the Start position and depress the clutch pedal, there should be voltage in the wire from the starter relay. If there isn't, look for an open or short circuit condition somewhere between the starter relay and the switch. If there is voltage in this wire, check the ground wire side of the switch for voltage. If there's voltage on the ground side as well, the switch should be operating correctly. Try adjusting it (see Step 6). If there's no voltage on the ground side, the switch is bad.

Replacement

5   Unplug the electrical connector, loosen the adjustment nut and remove the switch from its mounting bracket. Installation is the reverse of removal.

Adjustment

6   Loosen the locknut and turn the switch in or out, as necessary, to provide continuity through the switch when the clutch pedal is depressed.

---

8   Driveaxles – removal and installation

Removal

Refer to illustrations 8.2, 8.6 and 8.7

1   Remove the wheel cover, unstake the wheel hub nut and break it loose using a socket and large breaker bar. **Note:** *On some models, you'll have to raise the locking tab on the nut before you can loosen it.* Loosen the wheel lug nuts, raise the front of the vehicle and support it securely on jackstands. Remove the front wheel.

2   Remove the driveaxle hub nut. To prevent the hub from turning, place a pry bar between two of the wheel studs, then loosen the nut **(see illustration)**.

3   Drain the transaxle fluid (see Chapter 1).

4   If you are working on a 1988 or later model, remove the damper fork from the strut assembly and the lower arm.

5   Separate the lower control arm from the steering knuckle (see Chapter 10).

6   Swing the knuckle/hub assembly out (away from the vehicle) until the end of the driveaxle is free of the hub **(see illustration)**. Support the outer end of the driveaxle with a piece of wire to avoid unnecessary strain on the inner CV joint.

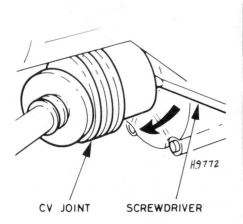

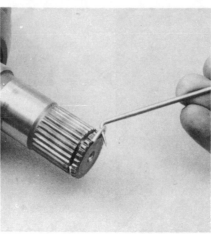

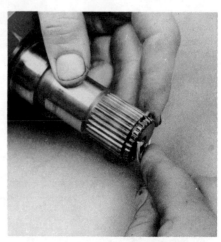

8.7   Use a large screwdriver or a pry bar to pop the inner end of the driveaxle loose from the differential

8.10a   Pry the old spring clip from the inner end of the driveaxle with a small screwdriver or awl

8.10b   To install the new spring clip, start one end in the groove and work the clip over the shaft end, into the groove

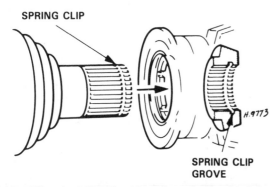

8.10c   When installing the driveaxle, make sure it's fully bottomed and the spring clip pops into place in its groove in the differential – if it's seated properly, you shouldn't be able to pull it out by hand

8   If you're removing the left driveaxle from a 4WD model, pry the inner CV joint from the bearing support of the intermediate shaft with a screwdriver or pry bar until the spring clip pops out of the groove in the intermediate shaft. Pull the driveaxle out of the bearing support. To prevent damage to the intermediate shaft seal, hold the inner CV joint horizontal until the driveaxle is clear of the intermediate shaft.

Installation

Refer to illustrations 8.10a, 8.10b and 8.10c

9   Pry the old spring clip from the inner end of the driveaxle and install a new one. Lubricate the differential seal with multi-purpose grease and raise the driveaxle into position while supporting the CV joints.

10   If you're installing either driveaxle on a 2WD model, or the right driveaxle on a 4WD model, insert the splined end of the inner CV joint into the differential side gear and make sure it bottoms in the differential and the spring clip locks in the differential side gear groove **(see illustrations)**. If you're installing the left driveaxle on a 4WD model, insert the inner end of the driveaxle into the intermediate shaft until the spring clip locks into the intermediate shaft groove.

11   Apply a light coat of multi-purpose grease to the outer CV joint splines, pull out on the strut/steering knuckle assembly and install the stub axle into the hub.

12   Insert the stud of the lower control arm balljoint into the steering knuckle and tighten the nut (see Chapter 10). Be sure to use a new cotter pin. On 1988 and later models, install the damper fork, pinch bolt and nut (see Chapter 10).

7   If you're removing either driveaxle from a 2WD model or the right driveaxle from a 4WD model, carefully pry the inner end of the driveaxle from the transaxle, using a large screwdriver or pry bar positioned between the transaxle and the CV joint housing **(see illustration)**. Support the CV joints and carefully remove the driveaxle from the vehicle.

9.3a   Cut the boot clamps off and discard them

9.3b   Slide the boot down the driveaxle, out of the way

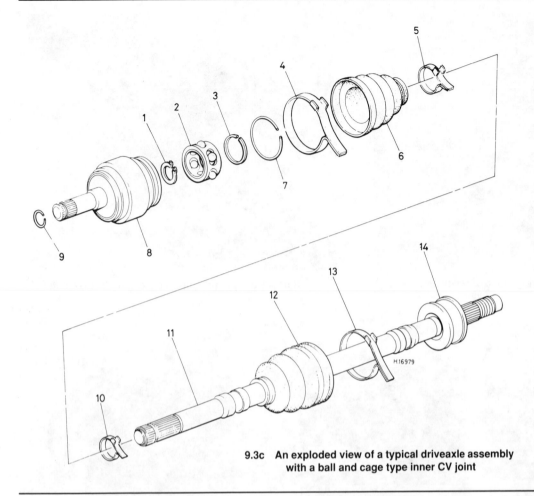

9.3c   An exploded view of a typical driveaxle assembly with a ball and cage type inner CV joint

1	Snap-ring
2	Ball and cage assembly
3	Stop-ring
4	Boot clamp
5	Boot clamp
6	Boot
7	Wire ring
8	Inner CV joint housing/outer race
9	Spring clip
10	Boot clamp
11	Axleshaft
12	Boot
13	Boot clamp
14	Outer CV joint assembly

13   Install the hub nut. Lock the disc as described in Step 2 so it can't turn, then tighten the hub nut securely. Don't try to tighten it to the actual torque specification until you've lowered the vehicle to the ground.

14   Grasp the inner CV joint housing (not the driveaxle) and pull out to make sure the axle has seated securely in the transaxle.

15   Install the wheel and lug nuts, then lower the vehicle.

16   Tighten the lug nuts to the torque listed in the Specifications in Chapter 1. Tighten the hub nut to the torque listed in this Chapter's Specifications. Using a hammer and punch, stake the nut to the groove in the driveaxle. Install the wheel cover (if applicable).

9.4   Paint alignment marks on the outer race, cage, inner race and axleshaft for assembly reference

9   Driveaxle boot replacement and constant velocity (CV) joint overhaul

Note: *If the CV joints are worn, indicating the need for an overhaul (usually due to torn boots), explore all options before beginning the job. Complete rebuilt driveaxles are available on an exchange basis, which eliminates much time and work. If you decide to rebuild a CV joint, check on the cost and availability of parts before disassembling the driveaxle.*

1   Remove the driveaxle from the vehicle (see Section 8).

2   Mount the driveaxle in a vise. The jaws of the vise should be lined with wood or rags to prevent damage to the driveaxle.

Inner CV joint and boot

Ball and cage type
Disassembly

Refer to illustrations 9.3a, 9.3b, 9.3c, 9.4, 9.5, 9.7, 9.9, 9.10a and 9.10b

3   Cut off both boot clamps **(see illustrations)** and discard them. Slide the boot out of the way **(see illustration)**.

4   Mark the inner race, outer race, cage and shaft so they can be reassembled in the same way **(see illustration)**.

9.5   Pry out the wire ring with a screwdriver

9.7   Remove the snap-ring from the end of the axleshaft

9.9   Pry the ball bearings out of the cage with a screwdriver – be careful not to nick or scratch them

9.10a   Align the lands of the inner race with the windows of the cage, . . .

9.10b   . . . then remove the inner race from the cage

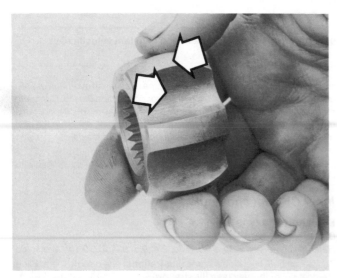

9.11a   Inspect the inner race lands and grooves for pitting and score marks

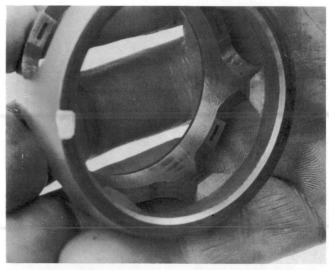

9.11b   Check the cage for cracks, pitting and score marks (shiny spots are normal and don't affect operation)

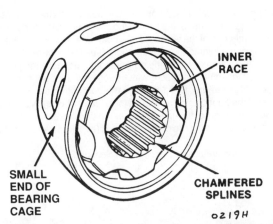

9.12   The chamfered splines on the inner race must face in the same direction as the small end of the cage

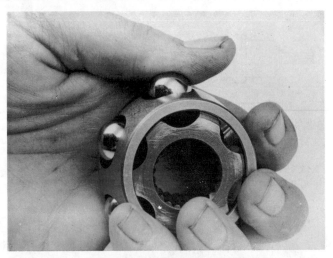

9.13   Press the ball bearings into the cage through the windows using thumb pressure only

5   Pry the wire ring from the outer race (see illustration).
6   Pull the outer race off the inner bearing assembly.
7   Remove the snap-ring from the groove in the axleshaft with a pair of snap-ring pliers (see illustration).
8   Slide the inner bearing assembly off the axleshaft. Remove the stop-ring from the shaft.
9   Using a screwdriver or piece of wood, pry the ball bearings from the cage (see illustration). Be careful not to scratch the inner race, the ball bearings or the cage.
10   Align the inner race lands with the cage windows and pull the race out of the cage (see illustrations).

Inspection
Refer to illustrations 9.11a and 9.11b
11   Clean the components with solvent to remove all traces of grease. Inspect the cage and races for pitting, score marks, cracks and other signs of wear and damage. Shiny, polished spots are normal and will not adversely affect CV joint performance (see illustrations).

Reassembly
Refer to illustrations 9.12, 9.13, 9.14, 9.17, 9.19, 9.20, 9.21a and 9.21b
12   Insert the inner race into the cage with the chamfered splines facing in the same direction as the small end of the cage (see illustration). Verify that the matchmarks are on the same side (it's not necessary for them to be in direct alignment with each other).
13   Press the ball bearings into the cage windows with your thumbs (see illustration).
14   Wrap the axleshaft splines with tape to avoid damaging the boot. Slide the small boot clamp and boot onto the axleshaft, then remove the tape (see illustration).
15   Install the stop-ring into its groove in the axleshaft. Install the inner race and cage assembly on the axleshaft with the larger diameter side or "bulge" of the cage (and the previously applied marks) facing out.
16   Install the snap-ring in the groove. Make sure it's completely seated by pushing on the inner race and cage assembly.
17   Fill the outer race and boot with the correct type and quantity of CV joint grease (normally included with the new boot kit). Pack the inner race and cage assembly with grease, by hand, until grease is worked completely into the assembly (see illustration).
18   Slide the outer race down onto the inner race and install the wire ring.

9.14   Wrap the splined area of the axleshaft with tape to prevent damage to the boot when installing it

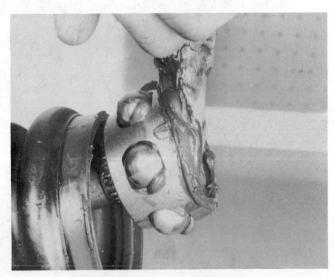

9.17   Pack the inner race and cage assembly full of CV joint grease

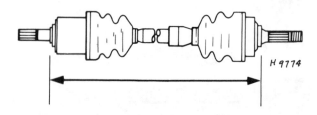

H 9774

9.19   Before tightening the boot clamps, adjust the driveaxle length to the dimension listed in this Chapter's Specifications

19 Wipe any excess grease from the axle boot groove on the outer race. Seat the small diameter of the boot in the recessed area on the axleshaft. Push the other end of the boot onto the outer race and move the race in or out to adjust the joint to the proper length (**see illustration**).

20 With the driveaxle set to the proper length, equalize the pressure in the boot by inserting a dull screwdriver between the boot and the outer race (**see illustration**). Don't damage the boot with the tool.

21 Install the boot clamps as shown (**see illustrations**). Make sure you don't alter the length of the driveaxle assembly while installing the clamps.

22 Install a new spring clip on the stub axle (**see illustrations 8.10a and 8.10b**).

23 Install the driveaxle as described in Section 8.

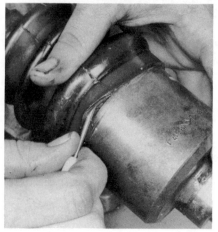

9.20   Equalize the pressure inside the boot by inserting a small, dull screwdriver between the boot and the outer race

9.21a   To install the new clamps, bend the tang down . . .

9.21b   . . . and flatten the tabs to hold it in place

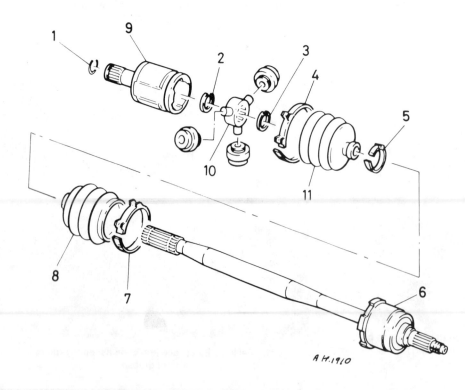

A H.1910

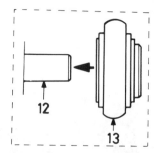

9.24   An exploded view of a typical driveaxle assembly with a tri-pot type inner CV joint

1   Spring clip
2   Snap-ring
3   Stop-ring
4   Boot clamp
5   Boot clamp
6   Outer CV joint assembly
7   Boot clamp
8   Boot
9   Inner CV joint housing/outer race
10 Tri-pot assembly
11 Boot
12 Tri-pot post
13 Roller bearing

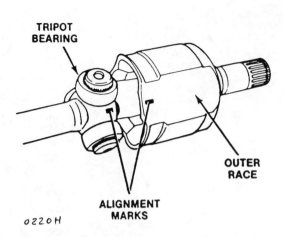

9.25 Scribe or paint alignment marks on the tri-pot assembly and the outer race, then slide the outer race off

9.26 Remove the snap-ring from end of the axleshaft, then mark the relationship of the tri-pot to the axleshaft

Tri-pot type

Disassembly

Refer to illustrations 9.24, 9.25, 9.26 and 9.27

24 Cut off both boot clamps **(see illustration)** and slide the boot towards the center of the driveaxle.

25 Mark or paint alignment marks on the outer race and the tri-pot bearing assembly **(see illustration)** so they can be returned to their original position, then slide the outer race off the tri-pot bearing assembly.

26 Remove the snap-ring from the end of the axleshaft, then mark the relationship of the tri-pot bearing assembly to the axleshaft **(see illustration)**.

27 Secure the bearing rollers with tape, then remove the tri-pot bearing assembly from the axleshaft with a brass drift and a hammer **(see illustration)**. Remove the tape, but don't let the rollers fall off and get mixed up.

28 Remove the stop-ring, slide the old boot off the driveaxle and discard it.

Inspection

29 Clean the old grease from the outer race and the tri-pot bearing assembly. Paint or scribe marks on each bearing roller and its respective shaft to ensure proper reassembly, then carefully disassemble each section of the tri-pot assembly, one at a time, and clean the needle bearings with solvent.

30 Inspect the rollers, tri-pot, bearings and outer race for scoring, pitting or other signs of abnormal wear, which will warrant the replacement of the inner CV joint.

Reassembly

Refer to illustrations 9.31, 9.33, 9.34 and 9.35

31 Wrap the splines of the axleshaft with tape to avoid damaging the new boot, then slide the boot onto the axleshaft **(see illustration 9.14)**. Remove the tape and slide the inner snap-ring into place **(see illustration)**.

32 Align the match marks you made before disassembly and tap the tri-pot assembly onto the axleshaft with a hammer and brass drift.

33 Install the outer snap-ring **(see illustration)**.

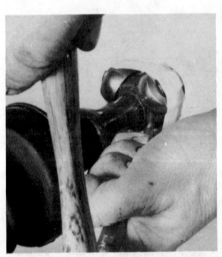

9.27 Secure the bearing rollers with tape and drive the tri-pot off the shaft with a hammer and a brass drift, then remove the stop-ring

9.31 Install the stop-ring on the axleshaft, making sure it seats in its groove

9.33 Install the tri-pot assembly on the axleshaft, making sure the punch marks are lined up, then install the snap-ring

9.34 Use plenty of CV joint grease to hold the needle bearings in place when you install the roller assemblies on the tri-pot and make sure you put each roller in its original position

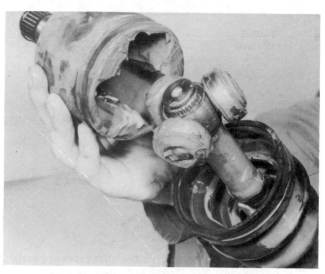

9.35 Pack the outer race with grease and slide it over the tri-pot assembly – make sure the match marks on the outer race and tri-pot line up

34 Apply a coat of CV joint grease to the inner bearing surfaces to hold the needle bearings in place when reassembling the tri-pot assembly **(see illustration)**. Make sure each roller is installed on the same post as before.

35 Pack the outer race with half of the grease furnished with the new boot and place the remainder in the boot. Install the outer race **(see illustration)**. Make sure the marks you made on the tri-pot assembly and the outer race are aligned.

36 Seat the boot in the grooves in the outer race and the axleshaft, then adjust the driveaxle to the proper length **(see illustration 9.19)**.

37 With the driveaxle set to the proper length, equalize the pressure in the boot by inserting a blunt screwdriver between the boot and the outer race **(see illustration 9.20)**. Don't damage the boot with the tool.

38 Install and tighten the new boot clamps **(see illustrations 9.21a and 9.21b)**.

39 Install the driveaxle assembly (see Section 8).

Outer CV joint and boot
Disassembly

40 Following Steps 3 through 10 (ball and cage type joint) or Steps 24 through 28 (tri-pot type joint), remove the inner CV joint from the driveaxle and disassemble it.

41 If the driveaxle is equipped with a dynamic damper, scribe or paint an alignment mark on the axleshaft along the outer edge of the damper (the side facing the outer CV joint), cut the retaining clamp and slide off the damper.

42 Cut the boot clamps from the outer CV joint. Slide the boot off the shaft.

Inspection
Refer to illustration 9.44

43 Thoroughly wash the inner and outer CV joints in clean solvent and blow them dry with compressed air, if available. **Note:** *Because the outer joint can't be disassembled, it is difficult to wash away all the old grease and to rid the bearing of solvent once it's clean. But it is imperative that the job be done thoroughly, so take your time and do it right.*

44 Bend the outer CV joint housing at an angle to the axleshaft to expose the bearings, inner race and cage **(see illustration)**. Inspect the bearing surfaces for signs of wear. If the bearings are damaged or worn, replace the driveaxle.

Reassembly

45 Slide the new outer boot onto the axleshaft. It's a good idea to wrap tape around the splines of the shaft to prevent damage to the boot **(see illustration 9.14)**. When the boot is in position, add the specified amount of grease (included in the boot replacement kit) to the outer joint and the boot (pack the joint with as much grease as it will hold and put the rest into the boot). Slide the boot on the rest of the way and install the new clamps **(see illustrations 9.21a and 9.21b)**.

46 Slide the dynamic damper, if equipped, onto the shaft. Make sure its outer edge is aligned with the previously applied mark. Install a new retaining clamp.

47 Proceed to clean and reassemble the inner CV joint by following Steps 12 through 22 (ball and cage type) or Steps 31 through 38 (tri-pot type), then install the driveaxle as outlined in Section 8.

9.44 After the old grease has been rinsed away and the solvent has been blown out with compressed air, rotate the outer joint assembly through its full range of motion and inspect the bearing surfaces for wear and damage – if any of the ball bearings, the race or the cage look damaged, replace the driveaxle and outer joint assembly

Chapter 8 Part B
Four-wheel drive (4WD) system

Contents

Specifications

General

Left driveaxle length	
1985 through 1987	18-1/4 to 18-9/16 in
1988 and 1989	19-1/8 to 19-1/4 in
1990	19-5/8 to 19-3/4 in
Driveshaft runout limit	0.060 in

Torque specifications

Ft-lbs (unless otherwise specified)

Driveshaft

Flange nut (front and middle tubes)	
Initial torque	94
Final torque	43
Flange-to-driveshaft tube bolts	24
Flange-to-viscous coupler bolts	24
U-joint bolts	24

Transfer

Bearing preload	7 to 10 in-lbs
Companion flange nut	87
Driven gear assembly mounting bolts	20

Rear axle

Companion flange locknut	
1985 through 1987	87
1988 and 1989	130
1990	127
Differential carrier bolts	16
Axle holder nuts (1985 through 1987)	30

1   General information

The rear brakes on 4WD models are identical to the drum brakes used on 2WD models. The only difference is a hole in the middle of the brake backing plate for the axleshaft or driveaxle (see Chapter 9). The rear suspension on 1985 through 1987 4WD models is different from the rear suspension on 2WD models built during those years; the rear suspension on 1988 and later 4WD models is similar to the rear suspension on 2WD models built during this period (see Chapter 10).

This Chapter covers the drivetrain components unique to 4WD models, with the exception of the rear suspension used on 1985 through 1987 models (see Chapter 10).

If a 4WD drivetrain component is similar to a 2WD part, refer to the appropriate Section in Chapter 8, Part A.

2   Intermediate shaft – removal, seal/bearing replacement and installation

Removal

Refer to illustration 2.3

Note: *Removal and installation of the intermediate shaft is straightforward, but replacing the inner seal and bearing in the bearing support requires special equipment available only at a dealer service department or other well-equipped repair shop.*

1   Loosen the left wheel lug nuts, raise the front of the vehicle, place it securely on jackstands and remove the left wheel.
2   Drain the oil from the transaxle (see Chapter 1).
3   Remove the three bearing support bolts **(see illustration)**.
4   Carefully lower the bearing support a few inches and – supporting the intermediate shaft at both ends to prevent damage to the differential oil seal – pull the intermediate shaft and bearing support assembly out of the differential.

Seal and bearing replacement

Refer to illustration 2.5

5   Remove the outer seal and snap-ring from the bearing support **(see illustration)**.
6   Take the intermediate shaft and bearing support assembly to a dealer service department or an automotive machine shop to have the new bearing and seals installed, as a hydraulic press and special fixtures are required perform this job.

Installation

7   Installation is the reverse of removal.

2.3   To detach the bearing support from the engine, remove these three bolts (arrows)

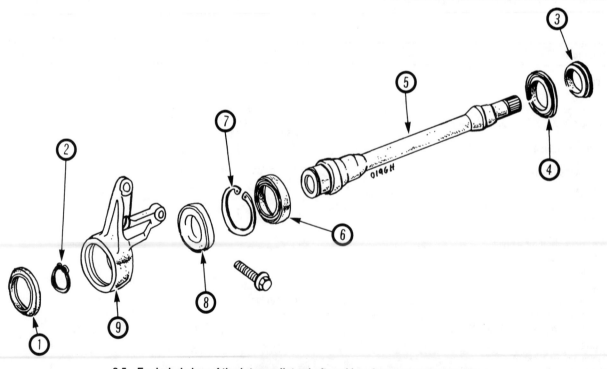

2.5   Exploded view of the intermediate shaft and bearing support assembly

1 Outer seal	4 Bearing support ring	7 Inner snap-ring
2 Outer snap-ring	5 Intermediate shaft	8 Intermediate shaft bearing
3 Intermediate shaft ring	6 Inner seal	9 Bearing support

3   Driveshaft and universal joints – description and check

Description

Refer to illustration 3.1

1   The driveshaft is a series of interconnected tubes which transmit power from the transaxle to the rear differential. On 1985 through 1987 models, the driveshaft consists of three tubes. In 1987, a viscous coupler was added to the front of the middle tube **(see illustration)**. On 1988 and later models, the viscous coupler replaces the middle tube entirely.

2   On 1985 through 1987 models, the differential is an integral part of the solid rear axle. On all models, universal joints (U-joints) at each end provide flexibility. A third U-joint is employed between the middle and rear tubes. A tri-pot CV joint between the front and middle tubes allows the driveshaft to shorten and lengthen as necessary. In 1987, a viscous coupler was installed on the middle tube that connects the front and rear tubes. In 1988, with the introduction of fully independent rear suspension, the middle tube was eliminated. The viscous coupler became, in effect, the middle tube.

3   The driveshaft rides on bearings housed in a pair of center bearing supports, located on each end of the middle tube (or viscous coupling).

4   Up front, an oil seal at the transfer unit prevents leakage of fluid and keeps dirt and contaminants from entering the transaxle. Another seal at the other end protects the pinion gear in the rear differential.

5   The driveshaft assembly itself requires very little service. The universal joints are lubricated for life and must be replaced if problems develop. Tri-pot CV joints can be overhauled and the boots can be replaced. Viscous couplers are sealed units – if it malfunctions, it must be replaced. The driveshaft must be removed from the vehicle for all of these procedures.

On-the-road check

6   Problems with the driveshaft are usually indicated by a noise or vibration while driving the vehicle. A road test should verify if the problem is the driveshaft or another vehicle component:

a)   On an open road, free of traffic, drive the vehicle and note the engine speed (rpm) at which the problem is most evident.

b)   With this noted, drive the vehicle again, this time manually keeping the transaxle in 1st, then 2nd, then 3rd gear ranges and running the engine up to the engine speed noted.

c)   If the noise or vibration occurs at the same engine speed regardless of which gear the transaxle is in, the driveshaft is not at fault because the speed of the driveshaft varies in each gear.

d)   If the noise or vibration decreased or was eliminated, visually inspect the driveshaft for damage, material on the shaft which would effect balance, missing weights and damaged universal joints. Another possibility for this condition would be tires which are out-of-balance.

7   To check for worn universal joints:

a)   On an open road, free of traffic, drive the vehicle slowly until the transaxle is in High gear. Let off on the accelerator, allowing the vehicle to coast, then accelerate. A clunking or knocking noise will indicate worn universal joints.

b)   Drive the vehicle at a speed of about 10 to 15 mph and then place the transaxle in Neutral, allowing the vehicle to coast. Listen for abnormal driveline noises.

Under vehicle inspection

8   If you hear any unfamiliar noises, park the vehicle, block the wheels, raise the vehicle and support it securely on jackstands (only the rear wheels must be raised for all of the following checks except the viscous coupler test, which requires that all four wheels be raised).

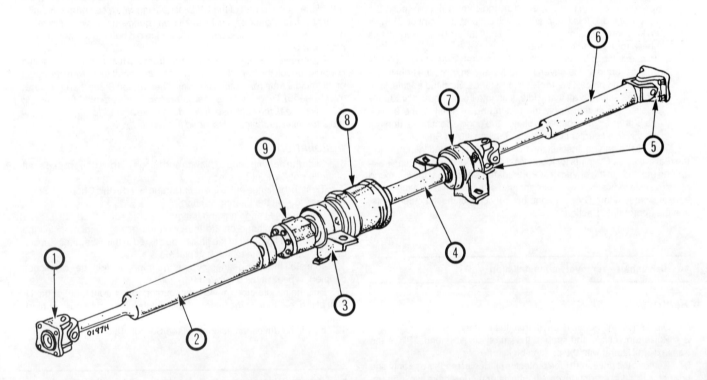

3.1   Driveshaft assembly on 1987 4WD models (1985 and 1986 models have no viscous coupler; 1988 and later models have coupler, but no middle tube)

1	U-joint	4	Middle tube	7	Rear support
2	Front tube	5	U-joints	8	Viscous coupler
3	Front support	6	Rear tube	9	Tri-pot type CV joint

9   Crawl under the vehicle and visually inspect the driveshaft. Since the driveshaft is a balanced unit, it's important that no undercoating, mud, etc. be allowed to stay on it. When the vehicle is raised for service it's a good idea to clean the driveshaft and inspect it for any obvious damage. Also check that the small weights used to originally balance the driveshaft are in place and securely attached. Whenever the driveshaft is removed it's important that it be reinstalled in the same relative position to preserve the balance. Look for any dents or cracks in the tubing. If damage is evident, replace the driveshaft (see Section 4).

10   Look for oil leaks at the front and rear ends of the driveshaft. Leakage at the front indicates a defective transfer seal; leakage at the rear indicates a defective pinion seal. Replacement procedures for these seals are in Sections 9 and 10, respectively.

11   Remain under the vehicle. Have an assistant put the transaxle in Neutral and rotate the driveshaft by turning one rear wheel while you hold the other.

a) Listen to the universal joints – make sure they're operating properly without binding, noise or looseness. Make sure all U-joint flange bolts are tight. Check the U-joints statically by gripping your hands on either side of each joint and trying to twist it, or by lifting up on the driveshaft. Any play is a sign of considerable wear. If a U-joint is worn or damaged, that portion of the driveshaft must be replaced as a unit, as the replacement U-joints are not available.

b) Have your assistant rotate the driveshaft again. Listen to the bearing in each center bearing support. A noisy bearing indicates wear or damage. Check the rubber portion of each bearing support for cracks or splits. If it's damaged, replace it (see Section 5).

c) Listen to each tri-pot CV joint as the driveshaft turns. It shouldn't make any grating or clicking sounds. If it's loose or noisy, or if the boot is leaking, overhaul and, if necessary, replace it (see Section 6).

d) If you have a dial indicator, set it up with the probe touching the center of each driveshaft tube. Have your assistant rotate a wheel while you hold the other wheel. If the indicated runout exceeds the runout listed in this Chapter's Specifications, a U-joint or CV joint is likely worn or damaged (or a driveshaft tube is bent). Repeat this check for each driveshaft tube.

e) To check the viscous coupler, all four wheels must be completely off the ground. If you haven't already done so, raise the front of the vehicle and place it securely on jackstands. Start the engine, wait for it to settle into a steady idle, shift into Low gear and gradually release the clutch. Apply the parking brake firmly. If the engine stalls, the viscous coupler is okay. If the engine continues running, the viscous coupler is defective. Replace it (see Section 8).

12   Turn off the engine. Inspect the front and, on 1988 and later models, the rear driveaxle CV joints for looseness. Also look for oil or grease leaks around the ends of the driveaxles. Parts coated with oil near the inner end of a driveaxle indicates a worn or damaged oil seal. Grease on the same parts indicates a torn CV joint boot. For servicing of these components, see the appropriate Sections.

---

4   Driveshaft – removal and installation

Removal

1   Disconnect the negative cable from the battery.
2   Raise the vehicle and support it securely on jackstands. Place the transaxle in Neutral with the parking brake off.
3   Remove the driveshaft tube protector(s). Earlier models use only one protector, under the front driveshaft tube; later models have two, one under the front tube and another under the rear tube.
4   To ensure the driveshaft is reinstalled in the same position (to preserve its balance), make alignment marks on the front and rear U-joint flanges with a scribe, white paint or a hammer and punch.
5   Remove the rear universal-joint bolts. Turn the driveshaft (or tires) as necessary to bring the bolts into the most accessible position.
6   Remove the bolts holding the front and rear bearing supports and low-

er the center part of the driveshaft assembly from the vehicle.
7   Remove the front universal-joint bolts and lower the front part of the driveshaft assembly from the vehicle.

Installation

8   Raise the rear of the driveshaft into position, checking to be sure the marks are in alignment. If not, turn the rear wheels to match the pinion flange and the driveshaft. Install the bolts for the rear U-joint.
9   Raise the front part of the driveshaft into position and install the bolts for the front U-joint.
10   Raise the middle part of the driveshaft assembly into position and install the bolts for the front and rear bearing supports.
11   Tighten all fasteners to the torque listed in this Chapter's Specifications.
12   Install the driveshaft protector(s).

---

5   Driveshaft support bearings – removal and installation

Removal

1   Remove the driveshaft assembly (see Section 4).
2   Unbolt middle tube (or viscous coupler) from the flange of the front tube.
3   Mark the flange of the front driveshaft tube and the flange nut with a scribe, white paint or a hammer and punch (to ensure the driveshaft's balance is preserved when it's reinstalled), then remove the nut from the flange. **Note:** *You'll need to use a flange holding tool to prevent the tube from turning while you break the nut loose. If you don't have access to a flange holder, install a couple of bolts in two adjacent holes in the flange and insert a prybar between them.*
4   Grasp the front support bearing with one hand and tap lightly on the end of the splined shaft of the CV joint housing with a soft hammer until it clears the bearing support. If the shaft won't budge, use a two or three-jaw puller. If you have to use a puller, discard the old bearing support and replace it with a new unit.
5   To remove the rear support bearing from the middle tube (or viscous coupler), unbolt the front U-joint of the rear driveshaft tube from the flange of the middle tube (or viscous coupler), then repeat Steps 3 and 4. **Note:** *You'll need a flange holding tool to prevent the assembly from turning while you break the nut loose. If you don't have access to such a tool, use the alternative technique described in Step 3.*

Installation

6   Slide the bearing support, flange and flange nut onto the splined shaft of the tri-pot CV joint assembly.
7   Tighten the flange nut to the initial torque listed in this Chapter's Specifications to seat the bearing support.
8   Remove the flange nut and flange.
9   Position the flange on the tube with the marks aligned, install the flange nut and tighten it to the final torque listed in this Chapter's Specifications. Stake the nut to lock it in place.
10   To install the rear bearing support onto the middle tube (or viscous coupler), repeat Steps 6 through 9.
11   Bolt the middle tube (or viscous coupler) to the front tube, or the U-joint of the rear tube to the flange of the middle tube (or viscous coupler). Tighten the bolts to the torque listed in this Chapter's Specifications.
12   Install the driveshaft assembly (see Section 4).

---

6   Tri-pot CV joint – removal, overhaul and installation

Removal

1   Remove the driveshaft (see Section 4).
2   Remove the bolts from the CV joint boot flange.
3   Mark the CV joint housing and front driveshaft tube to ensure proper realignment, then pull the housing off the tube (refer to the illustrations for

tri-pot CV joint overhaul in Chapter 8, Part A). Don't let the rollers fall off the tri-pot posts.

4   Pry the snap-ring off the splined end of the tube, scribe or paint alignment marks on the tri-pot and the splined end of the tube and slide the tripot assembly off the tube. Remove the stopper ring.

5   Pry the locking tabs on the boot clamp open, remove the clamp, remove the boot and remove the boot guard.

Overhaul

6   The tri-pot CV joint assembly on the driveshaft is virtually identical to the tri-pot CV joint assembly on a driveaxle. See Chapter 8, Part A.

Installation

7   Slide the boot guard, boot clamp, boot ring and boot onto the front driveshaft tube.

8   Position the boot on the tube so the raised area of the boot is aligned with the groove in the front tube.

9   Seat the stopper ring in its groove in the front tube.

10 Install the tri-pot assembly onto the splined end of the front tube. Make sure the marks you made during disassembly are aligned.

11 Install the snap-ring in its groove on the splined end of the tube.

12 Thoroughly lubricate the rollers and CV joint housing with moly-based grease. Pack the inside of the boot with an additional amount of grease. Slide the tri-pot and roller assembly onto the joint housing. Again, make sure the marks you made during disassembly are aligned.

13 Attach the boot flange to the joint housing and tighten the bolts securely.

14 Install a new boot clamp and bend the lug of the boot clamp toward the locking tabs.

15 Secure the lug with the locking tabs on the boot.

16 Install the driveshaft assembly (see Section 4).

7   Universal joints – replacement

1   If a universal joint is damaged or worn, the front or rear driveshaft tube to which it's attached, and the U-joint itself, must be replaced as a single assembly. The U-joints can't be rebuilt and they can't be removed from the driveshaft tubes.

2   Remove the driveshaft assembly from the vehicle (see Section 4).

3   To remove the front tube, unbolt the middle tube flange or viscous coupler from the front tube flange, remove the front support bearing (see Section 5) and the tri-pot CV joint (see Section 6).

4   To remove the rear tube, simply unbolt the U-joint from the flange at the rear end of the middle tube (or viscous coupler).

5   To install the front tube, install the front support bearing (see Section 5) and tri-pot CV joint (see Section 6) onto the new tube.

6   To install the rear tube, bolt the rear U-joint to the flange at the rear of the middle tube (or viscous coupler). Tighten the U-joint bolts to the torque listed in this Chapter's Specifications.

7   Install the driveshaft assembly. Tighten the U-joint bolts to the torque listed in this Chapter's Specifications.

8   Viscous coupler – removal and installation

1   The viscous coupler isn't rebuildable. If it's defective (see stall test in Section 3), replace it.

2   Unbolt the viscous coupler from the flange behind the front support bearing.

3   Unbolt the flange behind the rear support bearing from the U-joint flange at the front end of the rear driveshaft tube.

4   Remove the mounting bolts from the viscous coupler.

5   Remove the viscous coupler.

6   Installation is the reverse of removal.

9   Transfer seal – replacement

Refer to illustration 9.3

1   Detach the U-joint at the front end of the front driveshaft tube (see Section 4). Support it out of the way.

2   Hold the companion flange with a flange holding tool and remove the locknut. If you don't have a flange holding tool, thread bolts into two adjacent holes in the companion flange, insert a prybar between them and break the nut loose. Remove the lock-washer and the companion flange. If the companion flange is difficult to pull off, remove it with a two or three-jaw puller.

3   Remove the bolts from the driven gear assembly **(see illustration)**, pull it out of the transfer case and place it in a bench vise.

4   Carefully pry the oil seal out of the driven gear assembly with a screwdriver. Make sure you don't damage the driven gear shaft or the seal bore.

5   Drive a new seal into place with a large socket or a short section of pipe. Make sure the seal seats properly.

6   Coat the inner and outer sealing lips of the seal with grease.

7   Install the companion flange, the lock-washer and the locknut.

8   Temporarily install the driven gear assembly in the transfer case.

9   Tighten the companion flange locknut to the torque listed in this Chapter's Specifications.

10 Remove the driven gear assembly from the transfer case and place it in a bench vise again.

11 Measure the preload of the driven gear bearing. This measurement, which indicates the resistance to rotation generated by the driven gear bearing, is critical. Place a 22mm socket over the companion flange locknut, attach an inch-pound torque wrench and rotate the flange with the wrench handle. Compare your measurement to the preload listed in this Chapter's Specifications. If the indicated preload is less than the specified amount, adjust it by tightening the flange locknut a little at a time. If the indicated preload is more than the specified amount, take the driven gear assembly to a dealer and have a new spacer installed between the two bearings inside. This procedure requires a number of special tools, so it's not recommended to do the job at home.

12 Install the driven gear assembly and tighten the bolts to the torque listed in this Chapter's Specifications.

13 Attach the driveshaft to the companion flange (see Section 4) and tighten the bolts to the torque listed in this Chapter's Specifications.

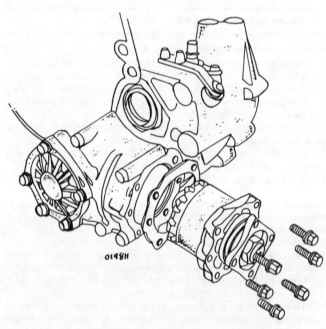

9.3 Mounting details of the driven gear assembly

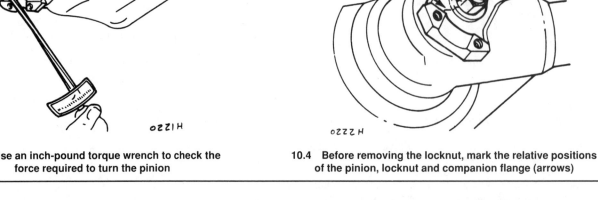

10.3   Use an inch-pound torque wrench to check the force required to turn the pinion

10.4   Before removing the locknut, mark the relative positions of the pinion, locknut and companion flange (arrows)

11   Align the mating marks made before disassembly and install the companion flange. If necessary, tighten the pinion nut to draw the flange into place. Do not hammer the flange into position.

12   Apply non-hardening sealant to the ends of the splines visible in the center of the flange so oil will be sealed in.

13   Install the washer (if equipped) and pinion nut. Tighten the nut carefully until the original number of threads are exposed.

14   Measure the torque required to rotate the pinion and tighten the nut in small increments until it matches the figure recorded in Step 5. In order to compensate for the drag of the new oil seal, the nut should be tightened more until the rotational torque of the pinion slightly exceeds what was recorded earlier, but not by more than 5 in-lbs.

15   Connect the driveshaft (see Section 4) and lower the vehicle.

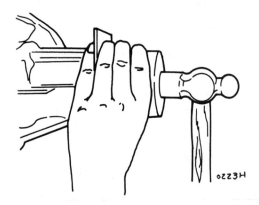

10.10   Use a large socket or a piece of pipe to tap the pinion seal into position

---

11   Rear axle – description and check

Description

1   The rear axle assembly on 1985 through 1987 models is a semi-floating type (the brake drums and rear wheels are mounted directly on the ends of the axleshafts). The differential carrier, which is bolted to the rear axle housing, is a hypoid, bevel type.

2   On 1988 and later models, the rear suspension is fully independent. The differential is mounted solidly to the vehicle and a pair of driveaxles, similar to those used at the front, are employed.

Check

3   Many times a problem is suspected in the rear axle area when, in fact, it lies elsewhere. For this reason, a thorough check should be performed before assuming a rear axle problem.

4   The following noises are those commonly associated with rear axle diagnosis procedures:

   a)   Road noise is often mistaken for mechanical faults. Driving the vehicle on different surfaces will show whether the road surface is the cause of the noise. Road noise will remain the same if the vehicle is under power or coasting.

   b)   Tire noise is sometimes mistaken for mechanical problems. Tires which are worn or low on pressure are particularly susceptible to emitting vibrations and noises. Tire noise will remain about the same during varying driving situations, where rear axle noise will change during coasting, acceleration, etc.

   c)   Engine and transaxle noise can be deceiving because it will travel along the driveline. To isolate engine and transaxle noises, make a note of the engine speed at which the noise is most pronounced. Stop the vehicle and place the transaxle in Neutral and run the engine to the same speed. If the noise is the same, the rear axle is not at fault.

---

10   Pinion seal – replacement

Refer to illustrations 10.3, 10.4 and 10.10

1   Raise the rear of the vehicle and support it securely on jackstands. Block the front wheels to keep the vehicle from rolling off the stands.

2   Disconnect the driveshaft (see Section 4) and fasten it out of the way.

3   Use an inch-pound torque wrench to check the torque required to rotate the pinion **(see illustration)**. Record it for later use.

4   Scribe or punch alignment marks on the pinion shaft, nut and flange **(see illustration)**.

5   Count the number of threads visible between the end of the nut and the end of the pinion shaft and record it for later use.

6   A special flange holding tool can be used to keep the companion flange from moving while the pinion nut is loosened. If the special tool isn't available, try using a large pair of adjustable pliers or insert a couple of bolts into two adjacent holes in the companion flange and place a pry bar between them.

7   Remove the pinion nut.

8   Withdraw the companion flange. It may be necessary to use a two or three-jaw puller engaged behind the flange to draw it out. Don't attempt to pry behind the flange or hammer on the end of the pinion shaft.

9   Pry out the old seal and discard it.

10   Lubricate the lips of the new seal with high-temperature grease and tap it evenly into position with a seal installation tool or a large socket **(see illustration)**. Make sure it enters the housing squarely and is tapped in to its full depth.

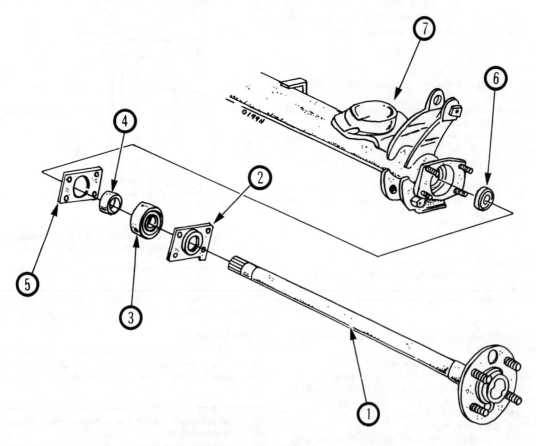

12.4 Rear axleshaft details (1985 through 1987 models)

1	Axleshaft	4	Bearing holder
2	Axleshaft holder	5	Shim
3	Bearing	6	Oil seal
		7	Axle housing

5   Because of the many special tools and critical measurements required, overhaul and general repair of the rear axle assembly on older models is beyond the scope of the home mechanic. So the procedures included in this Chapter are limited to axleshaft removal and installation, seal and bearing replacement, and removal of the entire unit for repair or replacement.

6   On newer models, the procedures covered include rear driveaxle removal and installation; rear driveaxle boot replacement and CV joint overhaul; and rear differential removal and installation.

12 Axleshaft removal, seal replacement and installation (1985 through 1987 models)

Removal

Refer to illustrations 12.4, 12.5 and 12.9

1   Loosen the rear wheel lug nuts. Raise the rear of the vehicle, support it securely and remove the wheel and brake drum (see Chapter 9).

2   Drain the oil from the differential (see Chapter 1).

3   Disconnect the brake line from the wheel cylinder, remove the brake shoes and detach the parking brake cable (see Chapter 9).

4   Remove the nuts from the axleshaft holder **(see illustration)**.

5   Attach a slide hammer with a flange adapter to the axleshaft **(see illustration)** and remove the axleshaft from the axle housing.

6   Rotate the axleshaft bearing. If it feels rough or dry, take the axleshaft

to a dealer and have a new bearing installed. This procedure, which requires a number of special tools, is beyond the scope of the average home mechanic.

Seal replacement

7   Carefully pry out the oil seal with a large screwdriver. Don't scratch or gouge the axle housing bore.

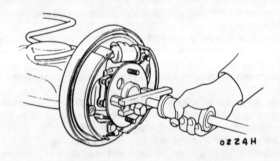

12.5 A flange adapter and slide hammer may be needed to remove the rear axleshaft

8   Using a large socket or piece of pipe with an outside diameter slightly smaller than the outside diameter of the seal, drive the new seal into the axle housing

Installation

9   Apply RTV sealant to the area inside the axle tube where the bearing seats **(see illustration)**.
10   Guide the axle into the axle housing, making sure the splines on the end of the shaft engage with the splines in the differential side gear.
11   Install the nuts on the axle holder and tighten them to the torque listed in this Chapter's Specifications.
12   Connect the brake line to the wheel cylinder, reattach the parking brake cable, install the brake shoes and brake drum (see Chapter 9).
13   Install the wheel, hand tighten the wheel lug nuts, remove the safety stands and lower the vehicle. Tighten the wheel lug nuts to the torque listed in the Chapter 1 Specifications.
14   Bleed the brakes (see Chapter 9).

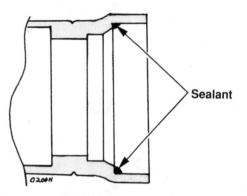

12.9   Apply RTV sealant to the area where the axle bearing seats in the axle housing

13   Differential carrier (1985 through 1987 models) – removal and installation

Removal

1   Loosen the rear wheel lug nuts, raise the vehicle, place it on safety stands and remove the rear wheels.
2   Drain the oil from the differential (see Chapter 1).
3   Mark the relationship of the rear driveshaft U-joint flange and the pinion flange, then disconnect the driveshaft (see Section 4). Hang the driveshaft out of the way with a piece of wire.
4   Remove both axleshafts (see Section 12).
5   Remove the differential carrier bolts.
6   Tap on the bosses around the edge of the carrier with a soft-faced hammer to loosen it. Remove the carrier from the axle housing.
7   Because of the large number of specialized tools necessary to disassemble, inspect and overhaul the carrier, further disassembly is beyond the scope of the average home mechanic. Take the carrier to a dealer service department or other repair shop if it needs to be rebuilt.

Installation

8   Installation is the reverse of removal. Be sure to tighten the differential carrier bolts to the torque listed in this Chapter's Specifications and refill the differential with the type and amount of lubricant specified in Chapter 1.

14   Rear axle assembly (1985 through 1987 models) – removal and installation

Removal

1   Loosen the rear wheel lug nuts, raise the vehicle and support it securely on jackstands placed underneath the frame. Remove the wheels.
2   Support the rear axle assembly with a floor jack placed underneath the differential.
3   Disconnect the driveshaft from the differential pinion shaft flange (see Section 4) and hang the rear of the driveshaft from the underbody with a piece of wire.
4   Disconnect the parking brake cables from the rear brakes (see Chapter 9).
5   Disconnect the flexible brake hose from the junction block on the rear axle housing. Plug the end of the hose or wrap a plastic bag tightly around it to prevent excessive fluid loss and contamination.
6   Disconnect the breather hose from the axle housing.
7   Unbolt the right end of the Panhard rod (see Chapter 10) from the axle housing.
8   Loosen the upper and lower control arm nuts and bolts, but don't remove them yet (see Chapter 10).
9   Remove the coil springs (see Chapter 10).

10   Remove the upper and lower control arm nuts and bolts. Lower the jack and move the axle assembly out from under the vehicle.

Installation

11   Installation is the reverse of the removal procedure. Be sure to tighten all fasteners to the torque values listed in this Chapter's Specifications and the Chapter 10 Specifications, where applicable.

15   Rear driveaxles (1988 and later models) – removal, overhaul and installation

The rear driveaxles on 4WD models are the same as as the front driveaxles (with tri-pot type inner CV joints) on 2WD models. Refer to Chapter 8, Part A, Section 8 for the driveaxle removal and installation procedure, and Section 9 for the driveaxle boot replacement and CV joint overhaul procedure. Refer to Chapter 10 if you need information about any rear suspension components that must be disconnected.

16   Rear differential (1988 and later models) – removal and installation

Removal

1   Raise the rear of the vehicle and support it securely on jackstands. Block the front wheels to prevent it from rolling.
2   Drain the differential lubricant (see Chapter 1).
3   Remove the driveaxles (see Chapter 8, Part A).
4   Mark the relationship of the driveshaft rear flange to the differential companion flange. Remove the driveshaft-to-differential companion flange bolts and nuts and disconnect the driveshaft from the differential. Support the driveshaft with a piece of wire – don't let it hang free.
5   Remove the mounting bolts from the crossmember-to-differential brackets.
6   Support the differential carrier with a floor jack.
7   Remove the bolts from the differential upper bracket and carefully lower the differential and bracket assembly to the ground.
8   Detach the upper differential bracket from the rear differential.
9   Due to the complex nature, critical adjustments and special tools necessary to overhaul the differential assembly, we recommend that you take the unit to a dealer service department or a qualified garage for repairs.

Installation

10   Installation is the reverse of the removal procedure. Be sure to tighten the mounting bolts securely and fill the differential with the recommended lubricant (see Chapter 1).

Chapter 9 Brakes

Contents

Specifications

General

Parking brake lever travel	See Chapter 1
Power brake booster pushrod-to-master cylinder piston clearance (with a vacuum of 20 in-Hg applied to booster)	0.0 to 0.016 in (0.0 to 0.4 mm)

Disc brakes

Brake pad minimum thickness	See Chapter 1
Disc minimum thickness	Refer to minimum thickness cast into rotor
Thickness variation (parallelism)	No more than 0.0006 in (0.015 mm)
Runout limit	0.004 in (0.10 mm)

Drum brakes

Brake lining minimum thickness	See Chapter 1
Drum diameter	Refer to maximum diameter cast into drum

Torque specifications

Ft-lbs (unless otherwise indicated)

General

Brake hose-to-caliper banjo bolt (front or rear)	25
Master cylinder mounting nuts	
1984 though 1987	60 in-lbs
1988 on	132 in-lbs
Brake booster mounting nuts	108 in-lbs

Front disc brake
Caliper guide pin (mounting bolts)
  1984 through 1987 (all models)
    Upper bolt   14
    Lower bolt   13
  1988
    Civic, CRX Std and Si, 2WD Wagon
      Upper bolt   40
      Lower bolt   33
    CRX HF   24
    4WD Wagon   36
  1989 on
    Civic, CRX DX and 2WD Wagon
      Upper bolt   25
      Lower bolt   20
    Civic EX   24
    CRX HF   17
    CRX Si and 4WD Wagon   36
Caliper mounting bracket bolts
  1984 through 1987   56
  1988 on   53

Rear disc brake
Caliper mounting bolts   16
Caliper mounting bracket bolts   28

Rear drum brake
Wheel cylinder nuts . . . .   72 in-lbs
Brake backing plate
  Nuts (1984 through 1987)
    2WD   33
    4WD   30
  Bolts
    1988 and 1989   28
    1990   47

---

1   General information

General

All vehicles covered by this manual are equipped with hydraulically operated power assisted brake systems. All front brake systems are disc type, while the rear brakes are either disc or drum type.

All brakes are self-adjusting. The front and rear disc brakes automatically compensate for pad wear, while the rear drum brakes incorporate an adjustment mechanism which is activated as the brakes are applied, either through the pedal or the parking brake lever.

The hydraulic system is a diagonally split design, meaning there are separate circuits for the left front/right rear and the right front/left rear brakes. If one circuit fails, the other circuit will remain functional and a warning indicator will light up on the dashboard when a substantial amount of brake fluid is lost, showing that a failure has occurred.

Master cylinder

The master cylinder is located under the hood, mounted to the power brake booster, and is best recognized by the large fluid reservoir on top. The fluid reservoir is a removable plastic cup, secured to the master cylinder by a clamp.

The master cylinder is designed for the "split system" mentioned earlier and has separate primary and secondary piston assemblies, the piston nearest the firewall being the secondary piston.

Proportioning valves

The proportioning valve assembly is bolted to the right strut tower. It incorporates two separate valves – one valve for each circuit.

The proportioning valves regulate the hydraulic pressure to the rear brakes during heavy braking to eliminate rear wheel lock-up. Under normal braking conditions they allow full pressure to the rear brake system until a predetermined pedal pressure is reached. Above that point, the pressure to the rear brakes is limited.

The proportioning valve is not serviceable – if a problem develops with the valve, it must be replaced as an assembly.

Power brake booster

The power brake booster, utilizing engine manifold vacuum and atmospheric pressure to provide assistance to the hydraulically operated brakes, is mounted on the firewall in the engine compartment.

Parking brake

The parking brake mechanically operates the rear brakes only. On drum brake models the parking brake cables pull on a lever attached to the brake shoe assembly, causing the shoes to expand against the drum. On models with rear disc brakes, the cables pull on levers that are attached to screw-type actuators in the caliper housings, which apply force to the caliper pistons, clamping the brake pads against the brake disc.

Precautions

There are some general cautions and warnings involving the brake system on this vehicle:

a) Use only brake fluid conforming to DOT 3 specifications.

b) The brake pads and linings may contain asbestos fibers which are hazardous to your health if inhaled. Whenever you work on brake system components, clean all parts with brake system cleaner or denatured alcohol. Do not allow the fine dust to become airborne.

c) Safety should be paramount whenever any servicing of the brake components is performed. Do not use parts or fasteners which are not in perfect condition, and be sure that all clearances and torque specifications are adhered to. If you are at all unsure about a certain procedure, seek professional advice. Upon completion of any brake system work, test the brakes carefully in a controlled area before putting the vehicle into normal service.

If a problem is suspected in the brake system, don't drive the vehicle until it's fixed.

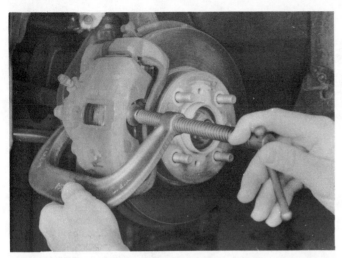

2.5   Using a large C-clamp, push the piston back into the caliper – note that one end of the clamp is on the flat area on the back side of the caliper and the other end (screw end) is pressing on the outer brake pad

2.6a   Before removing anything, spray the caliper and brake pads with brake cleaner to remove the dust produced by brake pad wear – DO NOT blow the dust off with compressed air!

2   Disc brake pads – replacement

Warning: *Disc brake pads must be replaced on both front wheels at the same time – never replace the pads on only one wheel. Also, the dust created by the brake system may contain asbestos, which is harmful to your health. Never blow it out with compressed air and don't inhale any of it. An approved filtering mask should be worn when working on the brakes. Do not, under any circumstances, use petroleum-based solvents to clean brake parts. Use brake cleaner or denatured alcohol only!*

Note: *When servicing the disc brakes, use only high quality, nationally recognized name brand pads Most models have disc brakes at the front wheels only, with drum brakes at the rear. The replacement procedure for the rear drum brake shoes is in Section 5. Some later CRX models have disc brakes at the rear. On these models, use the following procedure for both the front and rear pads.*

1   Remove the cap from the brake fluid reservoir.
2   Loosen the wheel lug nuts, raise the front, or rear, of the vehicle and support it securely on jackstands.
3   Remove the front, or rear, wheels. Work on one brake assembly at a time, using the assembled brake for reference if necessary.
4   Inspect the brake disc carefully as outlined in Section 4. If machining is necessary, follow the information in that Section to remove the disc, at which time the calipers and pads can be removed as well.

Front pads

Refer to illustrations 2.5 and 2.6a through 2.6k

5   Push the piston back into the bore to provide room for the new brake pads. A C-clamp can be used to accomplish this **(see illustration)**. As the piston is depressed to the bottom of the caliper bore, the fluid in the master cylinder will rise. Make sure it doesn't overflow. If necessary, siphon off some of the fluid.

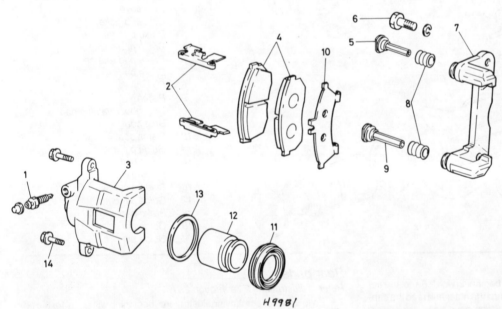

2.6b   Exploded view of the Tokico type front brake assembly

1   Bleeder screw
2   Brake pad retainers
3   Caliper
4   Brake pads
5   Guide pin
6   Caliper bracket bolt
7   Caliper bracket
8   Dust cover
9   Guide pin
10   Brake pad shim
11   Dust boot
12   Piston
13   Piston seal
14   Guide pin bolt

H9981

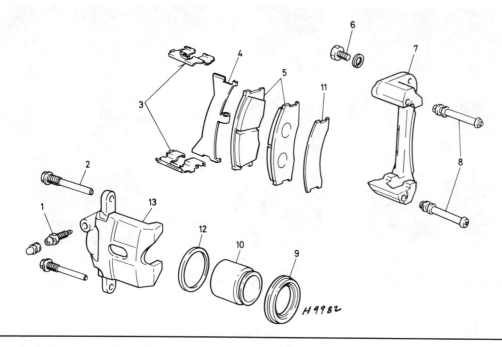

2.6c   Exploded view of the Sumitomo type front brake assembly

1   Bleeder screw
2   Guide pin bolt
3   Brake pad retainers
4   Brake pad retainer plate
5   Brake pads
6   Caliper bracket retaining bolt
7   Caliper bracket
8   Guide pin bushings
9   Dust boot
10   Piston
11   Brake pad shim
12   Piston seal
13   Caliper

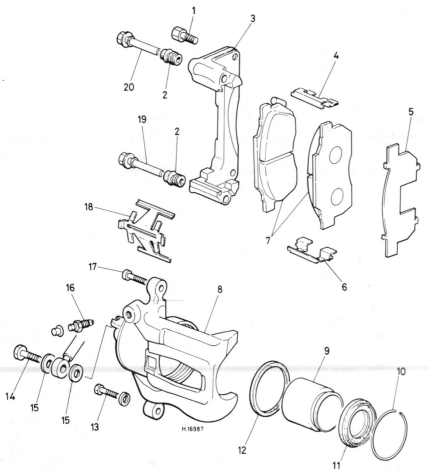

2.6d   Exploded view of the Nissin type front brake assembly

1   Caliper bracket retaining bolt
2   Dust cover
3   Caliper bracket
4   Brake pad retainer
5   Brake pad shim
6   Brake pad retainer
7   Brake pads
8   Caliper
9   Piston
10   Dust boot retaining ring
11   Dust boot
12   Piston seal
13   Guide pin bolt
14   Banjo bolt
15   Sealing washers
16   Bleeder screw
17   Guide pin bolt
18   Brake pad retainer
19   Guide pin
20   Guide pin

6   Follow the accompanying illustrations, beginning with 2.6a, for the actual pad replacement procedure. Be sure to stay in order and read the caption under each illustration. When those Steps have been completed, proceed to Step 8.

Rear pads

Refer to illustrations 2.7a through 2.7f

7   Follow the accompanying illustrations, beginning with 2.7a, for the actual pad replacement procedure. Be sure to stay in order and read the cap-

2.6e   Remove the lower guide pin bolt

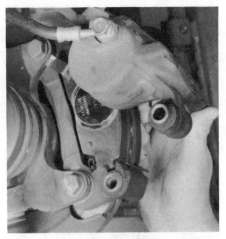

2.6f   Pivot the caliper up

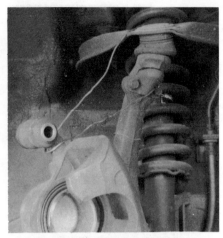

2.6g   Loop a piece of wire over the strut or the upper control arm to support the caliper in this position

2.6h   Remove the brake pad shims

2.6i   Remove the outer brake pad

2.6j   Remove the inner brake pad

2.6k   Remove the brake pad retainers (lower retainer shown, upper retainer similar) – pay close attention to the way these springs are installed before you pry them out

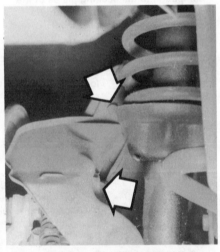

2.7a   Remove the caliper shield bolts (arrows) and the shield

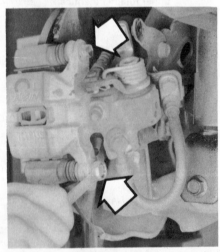

2.7b   Remove the two caliper mounting bolts (arrows) . . .

2.7c . . . and lift the caliper from its mounting bracket – hang the caliper out of the way with a piece of wire – don't let it hang by the brake hose

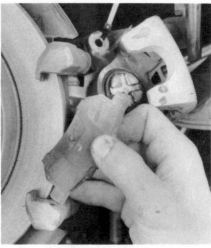

2.7d Remove the outer shim and pad

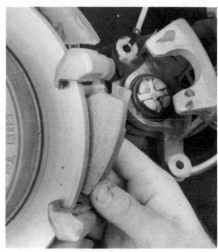

2.7e Remove the inner shim and pad

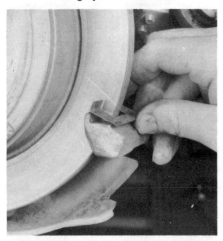

2.7f Remove the brake pad retainers from the caliper (lower retainer shown, upper retainer identical)

2.8 Before installing the brake pads, apply a coat of disc brake anti-squeal compound to the backing plates of the pads – follow the manufacturer's instructions on the label

2.13 To provide enough clearance between the caliper piston and the rotor, back the piston into the caliper bore by rotating it with a pair of needle-nose pliers

tion under each illustration. When those Steps have been completed, proceed to Step 8.

Front or rear pads

Refer to illustration 2.8

8   Apply a thin coat of disc brake anti-squeal compound, in accordance with the manufacturer's recommendations, on the backing plates of the new pads **(see illustration)**.

9   Install the shims onto their respective pads.

10   Install the pad retainers in the caliper mounting bracket. Lubricate the retainers with a thin film of silicone grease.

11   Install the new pads and shims to the caliper mounting bracket.

12   If you're working on a front caliper, install the caliper bolt(s) and tighten them to the torque listed in this Chapter's Specifications, then proceed to Step 15. If you're working on a rear caliper, proceed to the next Step.

Rear pads

Refer to illustration 2.13

13   Retract the piston by engaging the tips of a pair of needle-nose pliers with two of the grooves in the top of the piston and turning it clockwise until it bottoms out **(see illustration)**. Now, rotate the piston out until one of its

grooves is aligned with the tab on the inner brake pad when you install the caliper. You may have to adjust the piston position by turning it back and forth until the tab fits. If the piston dust boot becomes distorted when the piston is turned, turn the piston in the opposite direction to restore the shape of the boot, but make sure the cut-out still lines up.

14   Install the caliper protector.

Front or rear pads

15   Install the wheel and lug nuts, lower the vehicle and tighten the lug nuts to the torque specified in Chapter 1.

16   Check the brake fluid level and add fluid, if necessary (see Chapter 1).

17   Apply and release the brake pedal and (if you replaced rear pads) the hand brake lever several times to bring the pads into contact with the brake discs. Check the operation of the brakes in an isolated area before driving the vehicle in traffic.

---

3   Disc brake caliper – removal, overhaul and installation

Warning: *Dust created by the brake system may contain asbestos, which is harmful to your health. Never blow it out with compressed air and don't*

3.2   The parking brake cable is attached to the rear caliper by a clevis pin that is secured by a cotter pin

3.3a   When you disconnect the brake hose banjo bolt from the caliper, discard the two sealing washers – use new washers at reassembly time

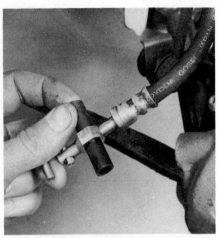

3.3b   Using a piece of rubber hose of the appropriate diameter, plug the brake line fitting

inhale any of it. An approved filtering mask should be worn when working on the brakes. Do not, under any circumstances, use petroleum-based solvents to clean brake parts. Use brake cleaner or denatured alcohol only!.

Note: *If an overhaul is indicated (usually because of fluid leakage), explore all options before beginning the job. New and factory rebuilt calipers are available on an exchange basis, which makes this job quite easy. If you decide to rebuild the calipers, make sure a rebuild kit is available before proceeding. Always rebuild the calipers in pairs – never rebuild just one of them.*

Removal

Refer to illustrations 3.2, 3.3a and 3.3b

1   Loosen – but don't remove – the lug nuts on the front, or rear wheels. Raise the front, or rear, of the vehicle and place it securely on jackstands. Remove the front, or rear, wheels.

2   If you're removing a rear caliper, remove the cotter pin from the clevis pin that connects the parking brake cable to the parking brake lever **(see illustration)**. Pull out the pin and detach the cable.

3   Disconnect the brake line from the caliper **(see illustration)** and plug it to keep contaminants out of the brake system and to prevent losing any more brake fluid than is necessary **(see illustration)**.

4   Remove the caliper guide pin(s) (mounting bolts) and lift the caliper off

its mounting bracket (see Section 2), or (on some models) rotate the caliper up and slide it off the upper guide pin.

Overhaul

Front caliper

Refer to illustrations 3.5, 3.6, 3.8, 3.9, 3.14 and 3.16

Note: *In addition to the illustrations accompanying this Section, refer to the exploded views accompanying Section 2 in this Chapter. The models covered by this book include a number of different caliper assemblies. They're all similar in design, but when you buy a caliper rebuild kit, be sure to tell your dealer or auto parts store the year and model of your vehicle so you don't get the wrong kit.*

5   Place the caliper on a clean workbench. If there are any pad retainers in the caliper, note how they're installed, then remove them. If the dust boot is held in place by a retaining ring, remove it **(see illustration)**. Pry out the dust boot.

6   Before you remove the piston, place a wood block between the piston and caliper to prevent damage as it is removed. To remove the piston from the caliper, apply compressed air to the brake fluid hose connection on the caliper body **(see illustration)**. Use only enough pressure to ease the piston out of its bore. **Warning:** *Be careful not to place your fingers between the piston and the caliper, as the piston may come out with some force.*

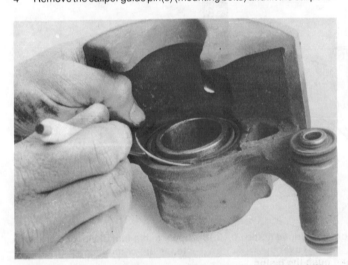

3.5   Use a small screwdriver to remove the dust boot retaining ring (not used on all calipers)

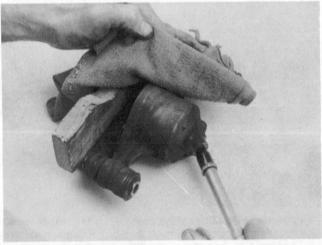

3.6   With the caliper padded to catch the piston, use compressed air to force the piston out of its bore – make sure your hands or fingers are not between the piston and the caliper

3.8   The piston seal should be removed with a plastic or wooden tool to avoid damage to the bore and seal groove – a pencil will do the job

7   Inspect the mating surfaces of the piston and caliper bore wall. If there is any scoring, rust, pitting or bright areas, replace the complete caliper unit with a new one.

8   If these components are in good condition, remove the piston seal from the caliper bore using a wooden or plastic tool **(see illustration)**. Metal tools may damage the cylinder bore.

9   Push the mounting bolt sleeves out of the caliper ears **(see illustration)** and remove the rubber boots from both ends (this doesn't apply to all models). Slide the bushing sleeves out of the caliper ears.

10   Wash all the components in brake cleaner, clean brake fluid or alcohol.

11   To reassemble the caliper, you should already have the correct rebuild kit for the vehicle.

12   Submerge the new piston seal in brake fluid and install it in the lower groove in the caliper bore.

13   If the caliper doesn't use a retaining ring on the piston dust boot, install the boot in the upper groove in the caliper bore.

14   Lubricate the piston with clean brake fluid; carefully slide it through

the new boot, position it squarely in the caliper bore and apply firm (but not excessive) pressure to install it. Make sure the piston boot seats in the groove in the piston **(see illustration)**.

15   If the caliper uses a retaining ring for the piston dust boot, install the new boot and pop the retaining ring into place.

16   Lubricate the sliding bushings and sleeves with silicone-based grease (supplied in the kit) and push them into the caliper ears. Install the dust covers. Also lubricate the caliper upper mounting pin or guide pin bolt with silicone grease **(see illustration)**.

Rear caliper (1990 CRX only)

17   Disassembly of the rear caliper requires special tools not generally available to the home mechanic. If the rear caliper needs to be overhauled, take it to a dealer service department or other repair shop.

Installation

18   Install the caliper by reversing the removal procedure. Remember to replace the copper sealing washer on either side of the brake line fitting (they should be included with the rebuild kit).

19   Bleed the brake system (see Section 10).

20   Install the wheels, hand tighten the wheel lug nuts, remove the safety stands and lower the vehicle. Tighten the wheel lug nuts to the torque listed in the Chapter 1 Specifications.

---

4   Brake disc – inspection, removal and installation

Note: *This procedure applies to both the front and rear brake discs (on vehicles so equipped).*

Inspection

Refer to illustrations 4.2a, 4.2b, 4.3, 4.4a, 4.4b, 4.5a, 4.5b and 4.6

1   Loosen the wheel lug nuts, raise the vehicle and support it securely on jackstands. Remove the wheel and install two lug nuts with 3 mm thick washers under them to hold the disc in place (if the two disc retaining screws are still in place, this will be unnecessary). If you're removing the rear disc, release the parking brake.

2   Remove the front or rear brake caliper (see Section 3). It's not necessary to disconnect the brake hose. After removing the caliper bolts, suspend the caliper out of the way with a piece of wire. Remove the two caliper mounting bracket-to-steering knuckle bolts **(see illustration)** or, on rear calipers, the bracket-to-spindle bolts **(see illustration)**, and remove the mounting bracket.

3.9   On each side of the caliper, push the mounting bolt sleeves through the boot and pull them free, then remove the dust boots (not applicable to all calipers)

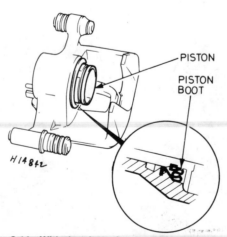

3.14   With the piston boot positioned in the caliper bore, stretch the boot over the bottom of the piston and push the piston into the bore – the folds of the boot should be even, with no distortion or twist

3.16   Apply a thin film of silicone grease to the upper mounting pin

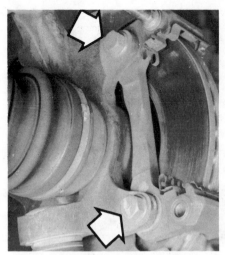

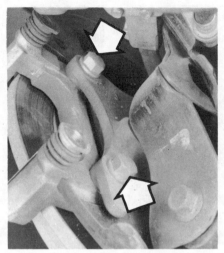

4.2a Before you can remove the front disc, you'll have to remove these caliper mounting bracket-to-steering knuckle bolts (arrows) and the bracket

4.2b To remove the rear disc, remove these caliper mounting bracket-to-spindle bolts (arrows) and the bracket

4.3 The brake pads on this vehicle were obviously neglected, as they wore down to the rivets; the rivets then cut deep grooves into the disc, and now the disc must be replaced

3   Visually inspect the disc surface for scoring or damage. Light scratches and shallow grooves are normal after use and may not always be detrimental to brake operation, but deep scoring (over 0.015 inch) requires refinishing by an automotive machine shop. Be sure to check both sides of the disc **(see illustration)**.

4   If you've noted pulsation during braking, suspect disc runout. To check disc runout, place a dial indicator at a point about 1/2-inch from the outer edge of the disc **(see illustration)**. Set the indicator to zero and turn the disc. The indicator reading should not exceed the specified allowable runout limit. If it does, have the disc refinished by an automotive machine shop.

Note: *You should resurface the discs regardless of the dial indicator reading, as this will impart a smooth finish and ensure a perfectly flat surface, eliminating any brake pedal pulsation or other undesirable symptoms related to questionable discs. At the very least, if you elect not to have the discs resurfaced, remove the glazing from the surface with emery cloth or sandpaper using a swirling motion **(see illustration)**.*

5   It is absolutely critical that the disc not be machined to a thickness less than the minimum allowable thickness. The minimum wear (or discard) thickness is stamped on the disc **(see illustration)**. The disc thickness can be checked with a micrometer **(see illustration)**.

4.4a With two lug nuts (with washers underneath) or the disc retaining screws installed to hold the brake disc in place, rotate the disc and check the runout with a dial indicator – if the reading exceeds the maximum allowable runout limit, the disc will have to be machined or replaced

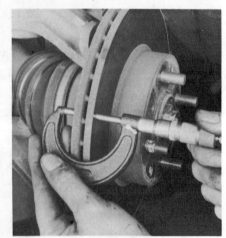

4.4b Using a swirling motion, remove the glaze from the disc with emery cloth or sandpaper

4.5a The minimum allowable thickness is stamped into the disc

4.5b A micrometer is used to measure disc thickness

4.6   If the disc is stuck, thread two bolts into the holes in the disc and tighten them

5.2   If the drum is hard to pull off, thread a pair of 8 mm bolts into the holes provided and press the drum off

Removal

Refer to illustration 4.6

6   Remove the two lug nuts which were put on to hold the disc in place (or the two disc retaining screws, if present) and remove the disc from the hub. If the disc is stuck to the hub and won't come off, thread two bolts into the holes provided **(see illustration)** and tighten them. Alternate between the bolts, turning them a couple of turns at a time, until the disc is free.

Installation

7   Place the disc in position over the threaded studs.

8   Install the caliper mounting bracket, brake pads and caliper over the disc. Tighten the mounting bracket and caliper bolts to the specified torque.

9   Install the wheel, then lower the vehicle to the ground. Depress the brake pedal a few times to bring the brake pads into contact with the disc. Bleeding of the system will not be necessary unless the fluid hose was dis-

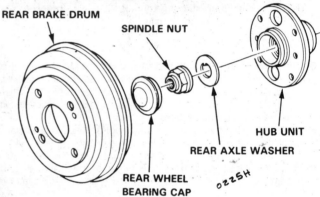

5.3   Exploded view of a typical hub and bearing assembly

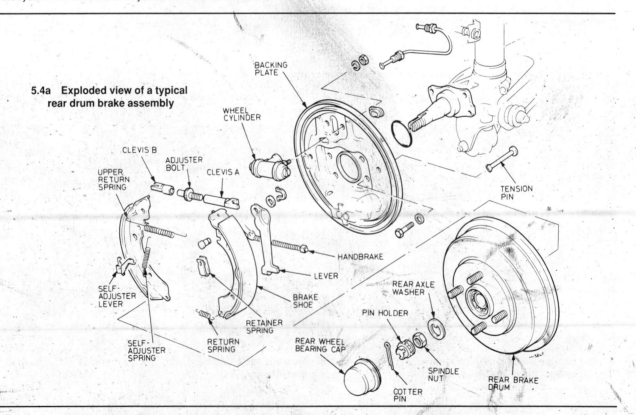

5.4a   Exploded view of a typical rear drum brake assembly

5.4b   Before removing anything, clean the brake assembly with brake cleaner and allow it to dry – position a drain pan under the brake to catch the residue – DO NOT USE COMPRESSED AIR TO BLOW THE DUST FROM THE PARTS!

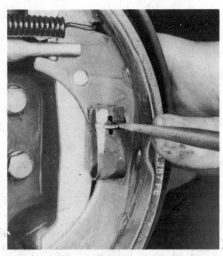

5.4c   Push down on the retainer spring with a screwdriver, then turn the tension pin to align its blade with the slot in the retainer spring – the spring should pop off (repeat this on the other spring)

5.4d   Pull the shoe assembly down and over the spindle

connected from the caliper. Check the operation of the brakes carefully before placing the vehicle into normal service.

5   Drum brake shoes – replacement

Refer to illustrations 5.2, 5.3, 5.4a through 5.4s and 5.5

Warning: Drum brake shoes must be replaced on both wheels at the same time – never replace the shoes on only one wheel. Also, the dust created by the brake system may contain asbestos, which is harmful to your health. Never blow it out with compressed air and don't inhale any of it. An approved filtering mask should be worn when working on the brakes. Do not, under any circumstances, use petroleum-based solvents to clean brake parts. Use brake cleaner or denatured alcohol only!

Caution: Whenever the brake shoes are replaced, the return and hold-down springs should also be replaced. Due to the continuous heating/cooling cycle that the springs are subjected to, they lose their tension over a period of time and may allow the shoes to drag on the drum and wear at a much faster rate than normal. When replacing the rear brake shoes, use only high quality, nationally recognized brand-name parts.

1   Loosen the wheel lug nuts, raise the rear of the vehicle and support it securely on jackstands. Block the front wheels to keep the vehicle from rolling. Remove the rear wheels. Release the parking brake.

2   Remove the brake drum. It should simply pull straight off the hub (2WD models) or axleshaft flange (4WD models). If the drums won't come off, tap them carefully with a soft-faced mallet, or screw a couple of 8.0 mm bolts into the tapped holes **(see illustration)**. If it still won't budge, the

3   Replacing the shoes is a lot easier on 2WD models if you remove the rear wheel bearing cap, spindle nut and washer, and slide off the hub unit **(see illustration)**.

4   Follow the accompanying illustrations (5.4a through 5.4s) for the inspection and replacement of the brake shoes. Be sure to stay in order and read the caption under each illustration. All four rear brake shoes must be

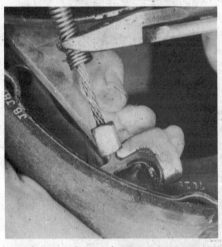

5.4e   Using a pair of diagonal cutting pliers, pull back on the parking brake cable spring and squeeze the pliers just enough to grip the cable, holding the spring in the compressed position (be careful not to cut the cable); unhook the cable end from the parking brake lever

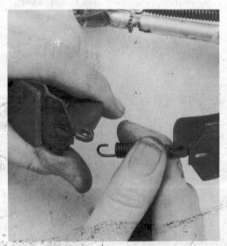

5.4f   With the brake shoe assembly on a clean working surface, unhook the lower return spring from the shoes

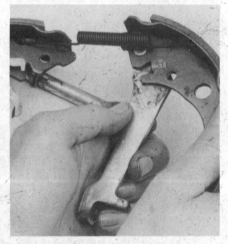

5.4g   Swing the parking brake lever away from the trailing shoe, which will force the adjuster bolt clevis out of its groove in the shoe; the two shoes can now be separated

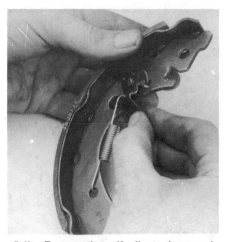

5.4h　Remove the self adjuster lever and spring from the leading shoe

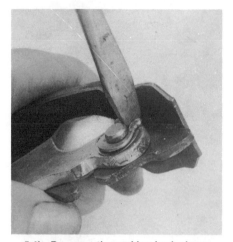

5.4i　Pry open the parking brake lever retaining clip and separate the lever from the shoe; be careful not to lose the wave washer that is under the clip

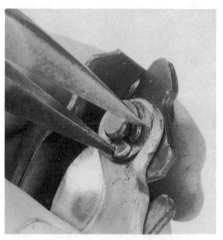

5.4j　Put the new trailing shoe on the lever, place the wave washer over the pin, then install the retaining clip; crimp the ends of the clip together with a pair of needle-nose pliers

5.4k　Clean the adjuster bolt and clevis, then lubricate the threads and ends with high-temperature grease

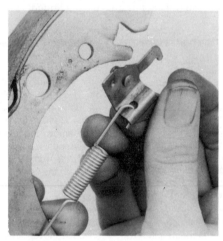

5.4l　Connect the self adjuster lever spring to the leading brake shoe, then insert the pin on the lever into its hole in the shoe

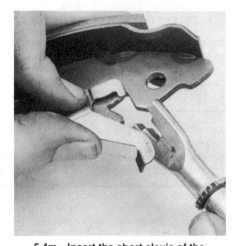

5.4m　Insert the short clevis of the adjuster bolt into its slot in the leading shoe, making sure it catches the self adjuster lever

5.4n　Connect the upper return spring between the two shoes, pry the lower ends of the shoes apart and insert the clevis at the other end of the adjuster bolt into the slot in the shoe; notice the position of the stepped portion of the clevis opening

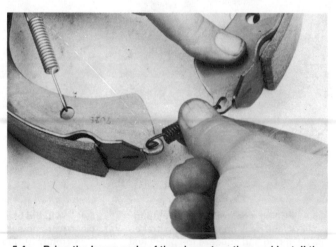

5.4o　Bring the lower ends of the shoes together and install the lower return spring

replaced at the same time, but to avoid mixing up parts, work on only one brake assembly at a time.

5   Before reinstalling the drum it should be checked for cracks, score marks, deep scratches and hard spots, which will appear as small discolored areas. If the hard spots cannot be removed with fine emery cloth or if any of the other conditions listed above exist, the drum must be taken to an automotive machine shop to have it turned. **Note:** *Professionals recommend resurfacing the drums whenever a brake job is done. Resurfacing will eliminate the possibility of out-of-round drums. If the drums are worn so much that they can't be resurfaced without exceeding the maximum allowable diameter (stamped into the drum)* **(see illustration)**, *then new ones will be required. At the very least, if you elect not to have the drums resurfaced, remove the glazing from the surface with sandpaper or emery cloth using a swirling motion.*

6   Install the hub and bearing unit, the washer and a new spindle nut (if removed previously). Tighten the nut to the torque listed in the Chapter 10 Specifications. Install the brake drum.

7   Mount the wheel, install the lug nuts, then lower the vehicle. Tighten the lug nuts to the torque listed in the Chapter 1 Specifications.

8   Make a number of forward and reverse stops to adjust the brakes until satisfactory pedal action is obtained.

9   Check brake operation before driving the vehicle in traffic.

---

6   Wheel cylinder – removal, overhaul and installation

Note: *If an overhaul is indicated (usually because of fluid leakage or sticky operation) explore all options before beginning the job. New wheel cylinders are available, which makes this job quite easy. If you decide to rebuild the wheel cylinder, make sure that a rebuild kit is available before proceeding. Never overhaul one wheel cylinder – always rebuild both of them at the same time.*

Removal
Refer to illustration 6.4

1   Raise the rear of the vehicle and support it securely on jackstands. Block the front wheels to keep the vehicle from rolling.

5.4p   Lubricate the brake shoe contact areas on the backing plate with high-temperature grease

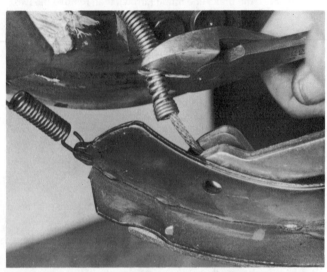

5.4q   Compress the parking brake cable spring, hold it in position and connect the cable end to the parking brake lever

5.4r   Place the brake shoe assembly against the backing plate and slide it up, engaging the upper ends of the shoes in the slots in the wheel cylinder pistons

5.4s   With the brake shoes in position on the backing plate, pass the tension pins through the holes in the backing plate and brake shoes, then install the retainer springs (see illustration 5.4c) – make sure the parking brake cable spring and the lower return spring are seated behind the anchor plate, as shown here

5.5   The maximum diameter is cast into the drum

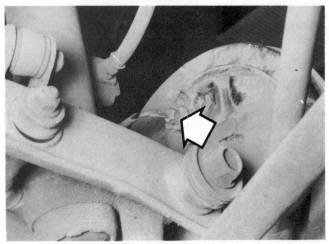

6.4   Unscrew the brake line fitting (arrow), then remove the two mounting nuts or bolts

2   Remove the brake shoe assembly (see Section 5).
3   Remove all dirt and foreign material from around the wheel cylinder.
4   Unscrew the brake line fitting **(see illustration)**. Don't pull the brake line away from the wheel cylinder.
5   Remove the wheel cylinder mounting fasteners.
6   Detach the wheel cylinder from the brake backing plate and place it on a clean workbench. Immediately plug the brake line to prevent fluid loss and contamination. **Note:** *If the brake shoe linings are contaminated with brake fluid, install new brake shoes and clean the drums with brake cleaner.*

Overhaul

Refer to illustration 6.7

7   Remove the bleed screw, dust covers, pistons, piston cups and spring assembly from the wheel cylinder body **(see illustration)**.
8   Clean the wheel cylinder with brake fluid, denatured alcohol or brake system cleaner. **Warning:** *Do not, under any circumstances, use petroleum-based solvents to clean brake parts!*

9   Use compressed air to remove excess fluid from the wheel cylinder and to blow out the passages.
10   Check the cylinder bore for corrosion and score marks. Crocus cloth can be used to remove light corrosion and stains, but the cylinder must be replaced with a new one if the defects cannot be removed easily, or if the bore is scored.
11   Lubricate the new cups with brake fluid.
12   Assemble the wheel cylinder components. Make sure the cup lips face in.

Installation

13   Apply silicone sealant to the mating surface of the wheel cylinder and the brake backing plate, place the cylinder in position and connect the brake line. Don't tighten the fitting completely yet.
14   Install the mounting bolts, tightening them securely. Tighten the brake line fitting. Install the brake shoe assembly.
15   Bleed the brakes (see Section 10).
16   Check brake operation before driving the vehicle in traffic.

---

7   Master cylinder – removal, overhaul and installation

Note: *Before deciding to overhaul the master cylinder, check on the availability and cost of a new or factory rebuilt unit and also the availability of a rebuild kit.*

Removal

Refer to illustrations 7.4 and 7.6

1   The master cylinder is located in the engine compartment, mounted to the power brake booster.
2   Remove as much fluid as you can from the reservoir with a syringe.
3   Place rags under the fluid fittings and prepare caps or plastic bags to cover the ends of the lines once they are disconnected. **Caution:** *Brake fluid will damage paint. Cover all body parts and be careful not to spill fluid during this procedure.*
4   Loosen the tube nuts at the ends of the brake lines where they enter the master cylinder **(see illustration)**. To prevent rounding off the flats on these nuts, the use of a flare nut wrench, which wraps around the nut, is preferred.

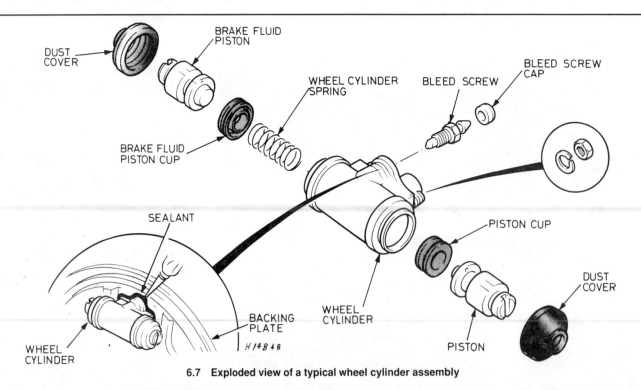

6.7   Exploded view of a typical wheel cylinder assembly

7.4   Use a flare nut wrench to loosen the threaded fittings for the brake lines at the master cylinder

7.6   To detach the master cylinder from the brake booster, remove these two nuts (arrows)

7.8   Exploded view of a typical master cylinder assembly

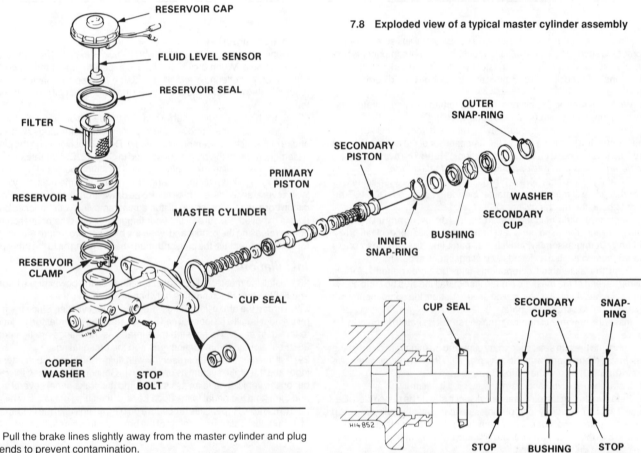

7.9   Order of assembly of the secondary cups, stop plates, bushing and snap-ring

5   Pull the brake lines slightly away from the master cylinder and plug the ends to prevent contamination.

6   Disconnect the electrical connector at the master cylinder, then remove the nuts attaching the master cylinder to the power booster (see illustration). Pull the master cylinder off the studs and out of the engine compartment. Again, be careful not to spill the fluid as this is done.

Overhaul

Refer to illustrations 7.8, 7.9, 7.10 and 7.12

7   Before attempting the overhaul of the master cylinder, obtain the proper rebuild kit, which will contain the necessary replacement parts and also any instructions which may be specific to your model.

8   Loosen the reservoir clamp and pull the reservoir off the master cylinder body (see illustration).

9   Remove the outer snap-ring, followed by the stop plates, secondary cups and bushing (see illustration).

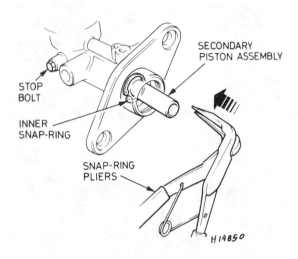

7.10   Push in on the secondary piston assembly and remove the stop bolt and inner snap-ring

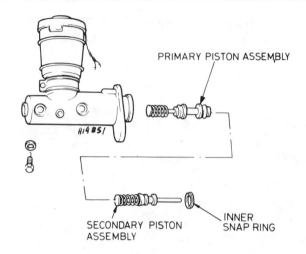

7.12   The master cylinder primary and secondary piston assemblies can be removed from the cylinder once the snap-ring has been removed – it may be necessary to tap the open end of the cylinder on a block of wood to eject the piston assemblies

10   Place the cylinder in a vise and use a punch or Phillips screwdriver to depress the secondary piston assembly until the internal components bottom against the other end of the master cylinder (see illustration). Hold the pistons in this position and remove the stop bolt on the side of the master cylinder.

11   While still holding the pistons in the bottomed position, carefully remove the inner snap-ring (see illustration 7.10).

12   The internal components can now be removed from the cylinder bore (see illustration). Make a note of the proper order of the components so they can be returned to their original locations. **Note:** *The two springs are of different tension, so pay particular attention to their order.*

13   Carefully inspect the bore of the master cylinder. Any deep scoring or other damage will mean a new master cylinder is required. DO NOT attempt to hone the master cylinder.

14   Replace all parts included in the rebuild kit, following any instructions in the kit. Clean all reused parts with brake system cleaner or clean brake fluid only. During assembly, lubricate all parts liberally with clean brake fluid. Be sure to tighten all fittings and connections securely.

15   Push the assembled components into the bore, bottoming them against the end of the master cylinder, then install the stop bolt and a new copper washer. A screwdriver can be used to bottom the components, but be careful not to scratch the bore.

16   Install the new inner snap-ring, making sure it is seated properly in the groove.

17   Lubricate the cup seal, secondary cups and bushing with clean brake fluid. Install them, along with the stop plates, in the master cylinder (see illustration 7.9). Install the snap-ring.

18   Install the reservoir and clamp, tightening it securely.

19   Before installing the new master cylinder it should be bench bled. Because it will be necessary to apply pressure to the master cylinder piston and, at the same time, control flow from the brake line outlets, it is recommended that the master cylinder be mounted in a vise, with the jaws of the vise clamping on the mounting flange.

20   Insert threaded plugs into the brake line outlet holes and snug them down so that there will be no air leakage past them, but not so tight that they cannot be easily loosened.

21   Fill the reservoir with brake fluid of the recommended type (see Chapter 1).

22   Remove one plug and push the piston assembly into the master cylinder bore to expel the air from the master cylinder. A large Phillips screwdriver can be used to push on the piston assembly.

23   To prevent air from being drawn back into the master cylinder, the plug must be replaced and snugged down before releasing the pressure on the

piston assembly.

24   Repeat the procedure until only brake fluid is expelled from the brake line outlet hole. When only brake fluid is expelled, repeat the procedure with the other outlet hole and plug. Be sure to keep the master cylinder reservoir filled with brake fluid to prevent the introduction of air into the system.

25   Since high pressure is not involved in the bench bleeding procedure, an alternative to the removal and replacement of the plugs with each stroke of the piston assembly is available. Before pushing in on the piston assembly, remove the plug as described in Step 22. Before releasing the piston, however, instead of replacing the plug, simply put your finger tightly over the hole to keep air from being drawn back into the master cylinder. Wait several seconds for brake fluid to be drawn from the reservoir into the piston bore, then depress the piston again, removing your finger as brake fluid is expelled. Be sure to put your finger back over the hole each time before releasing the piston, and when the bleeding procedure is complete for that outlet, replace the plug and snug it before going on to the other port.

Installation

26   Install the master cylinder over the studs on the power brake booster and tighten the attaching nuts only finger tight at this time.

27   Thread the brake line fittings into the master cylinder. Since the master cylinder is still a bit loose, it can be moved slightly in order for the fittings to thread in easily. Do not strip the threads as the fittings are tightened.

28   Fully tighten the mounting nuts and the brake fittings.

29   Fill the master cylinder reservoir with fluid, then bleed the master cylinder and the brake system as described in Section 10. To bleed the cylinder on the vehicle, have an assistant pump the brake pedal several times and then hold the pedal to the floor. Loosen the fitting nut to allow air and fluid to escape. Repeat this procedure on both fittings until the fluid is clear of air bubbles. Test the operation of the brake system carefully before placing the vehicle in normal service.

8   Proportioning valve – general information

Refer to illustration 8.1

1   The proportioning valve (see illustration) is mounted on the right side strut tower. Its purpose is to limit hydraulic pressure to the rear brakes under heavy braking conditions to prevent rear wheel lockup.

2   The valve is not serviceable and if a problem is suspected with it, it must be checked by a dealer service department or repair shop equipped with the necessary pressure gauges.

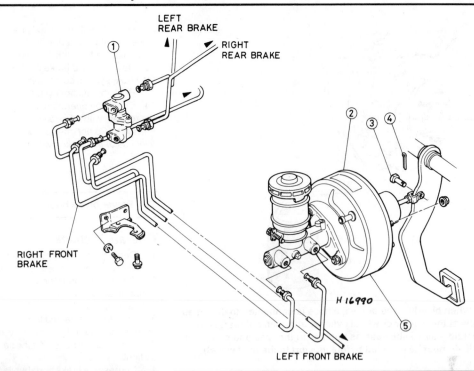

LEFT REAR BRAKE

RIGHT REAR BRAKE

RIGHT FRONT BRAKE

H 16990

LEFT FRONT BRAKE

8.1 Exploded view of a typical proportioning valve and power brake booster assembly

1   Dual proportioning valve
2   Master cylinder
3   Clevis pin
4   Cotter pin
5   Power brake booster

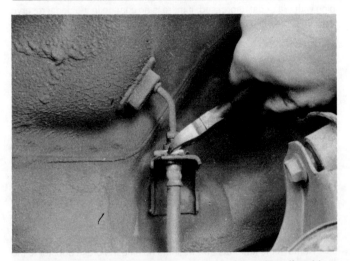

9.4a To disconnect a brake hose, pull off the spring clip with a pair of pliers . . .

3   If the valve is known to be defective, it can be replaced by unscrewing the brake lines (using a flare nut wrench, if available) and unbolting the valve from the strut tower. After the new valve is installed, bleed the complete brake system as described in Section 10.

9   Brake hoses and lines – inspection and replacement

Refer to illustrations 9.4a and 9.4b

1   About every six months the flexible hoses which connect the steel brake lines with the rear brakes and front calipers should be inspected for cracks, chafing of the outer cover, leaks, blisters, and other damage.
2   Replacement steel and flexible brake lines are commonly available from dealer parts departments and auto parts stores. Do not, under any circumstances, use anything other than genuine steel lines or approved flexible brake hoses as replacement items.
3   When installing the brake line, leave at least 0.75 in (19 mm) clearance between the line and any moving or vibrating parts.

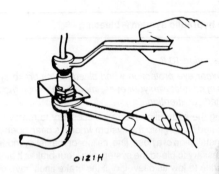

0121H

9.4b . . . then, using a flare nut wrench on the threaded fitting for the metal line and an open end wrench on the hose, break loose the fitting

4   To disconnect a hose and line, first remove the spring clip **(see illustration)**. Then, using a normal wrench to hold the hose and a flare-nut wrench to hold the tube, make the disconnection **(see illustration)**. Use the wrenches in the same manner when making a connection, then install the clip. **Note:** *Make sure the tube passes through the center of the grommet.*
5   When disconnecting two hoses, use normal wrenches on the hose fittings. When connecting two hoses, make sure they are not twisted or strained.
6   Steel brake lines are usually retained along their span with clips. Always remove these clips completely before removing a fixed brake line. Always reinstall these clips, or new ones if the old ones are damaged, when replacing a brake line, as they provide support and keep the lines from vibrating, which can eventually break them.
7   When replacing brake lines be sure to use the correct parts. NEVER use copper tubing! Purchase steel brake lines from a dealer or auto parts store.
8   When installing a steel line, make sure it's securely supported in the brackets and has plenty of clearance between moving or hot components.
9   After installation, check the fluid level in the master cylinder and add fluid as necessary. Bleed the brake system as described in Section 10 and test the brakes carefully before driving the vehicle in traffic.

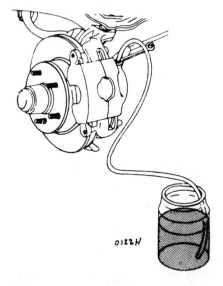

0122H

10.8   When bleeding the brakes, a hose is connected to the bleed screw at the caliper or wheel cylinder and then submerged in brake fluid – air will be seen as bubbles in the tube and container (all air must be expelled before moving to the next wheel)

10   Brake hydraulic system – bleeding

Refer to illustration 10.8

Warning: *Wear eye protection when bleeding the brake system. If the fluid comes in contact with your eyes, immediately rinse them with water and seek medical attention.*

1   Bleeding the hydraulic system is necessary to remove any air that manages to find its way into the system when it's been opened during removal and installation of a hose, line, caliper or master cylinder. It will probably be necessary to bleed the system at all four brakes if air has entered the system due to low fluid level, or if the brake lines have been disconnected at the master cylinder.

2   If a brake line was disconnected only at a wheel, then only that caliper or wheel cylinder must be bled.

3   If a brake line is disconnected at a fitting located between the master cylinder and any of the brakes, that part of the system served by the disconnected line must be bled.

4   Remove any residual vacuum from the brake power booster by applying the brake several times with the engine off.

5   Remove the master cylinder reservoir cover and fill the reservoir with brake fluid. Reinstall the cover. **Note:** *Check the fluid level often during the bleeding operation and add fluid as necessary to prevent the fluid level from falling low enough to allow air bubbles into the master cylinder.*

6   Have an assistant on hand, as well as a supply of new brake fluid, a clear container partially filled with clean brake fluid, a length of 3/16-inch plastic, rubber or vinyl tubing to fit over the bleed screw and a wrench to open and close the bleed screw.

7   Beginning at the left front wheel, loosen the bleed screw slightly, then tighten it to a point where it is snug but can still be loosened quickly and easily.

8   Place one end of the tubing over the bleed screw and submerge the other end in brake fluid in the container **(see illustration)**.

9   Have the assistant pump the brakes slowly a few times to get pressure in the system, then hold the pedal firmly depressed.

10   While the pedal is held depressed, open the bleed screw just enough to allow a flow of fluid to leave the screw. Watch for air bubbles to exit the submerged end of the tube. When the fluid flow slows after a couple of seconds, close the screw and have your assistant release the pedal.

11   Repeat Steps 9 and 10 until no more air is seen leaving the tube, then

tighten the bleed screw and proceed to the right rear wheel, the right front wheel and the left rear wheel, in that order, and perform the same procedure. Be sure to check the fluid in the master cylinder reservoir frequently.

12   Never use old brake fluid. It contains moisture which will deteriorate the brake system components.

13   Refill the master cylinder with fluid at the end of the operation.

14   Check the operation of the brakes. The pedal should feel solid when depressed, with no sponginess. If necessary, repeat the entire process. **Warning:** *Do not operate the vehicle if you are in doubt about the effectiveness of the brake system.*

11   Power brake booster – check, removal and installation

Operating check

1   Depress the brake pedal several times with the engine off and make sure there is no change in the pedal reserve distance.

2   Depress the pedal and start the engine. If the pedal goes down slightly, operation is normal.

Air tightness check

3   Start the engine and turn it off after one or two minutes. Depress the brake pedal several times slowly. If the pedal goes down farther the first time but gradually rises after the second or third depression, the booster is air tight.

4   Depress the brake pedal while the engine is running, then stop the engine with the pedal depressed. If there is no change in the pedal reserve travel after holding the pedal for 30 seconds, the booster is air tight.

Removal

5   Power brake booster units should not be disassembled. They require special tools not normally found in most automotive repair stations or shops. They are fairly complex and because of their critical relationship to brake performance it is best to replace a defective booster unit with a new or rebuilt one.

6   To remove the booster, first remove the brake master cylinder as described in Section 7.

7   Locate the pushrod clevis pin connecting the booster to the brake pedal **(see illustration 8.1)**. This is accessible from under the dash panel in front of the driver's seat.

8   Remove the clevis pin retaining clip with pliers and pull out the pin.

9   Holding the clevis with pliers, disconnect the clevis locknut with a wrench. The clevis is now loose.

10   Disconnect the hose leading from the engine to the booster. Be careful not to damage the hose when removing it from the booster fitting.

11   Remove the four nuts and washers holding the brake booster to the firewall. You may need a light to see these, as they are up under the dash area.

12   Slide the booster straight out from the firewall until the studs clear the holes and pull the booster, brackets and gaskets from the engine compartment area.

Installation

Refer to illustrations 11.14a and 11.14b

13   Installation procedures are basically the reverse of those for removal. Tighten the clevis locknut securely and the booster mounting nuts to the specified torque. Also, be sure to use a new cotter pin on the clevis pin.

14   If the power booster unit is being replaced, the clearance between the master cylinder piston and the pushrod in the vacuum booster must be measured. Using a depth micrometer or vernier calipers, measure the distance from the seat (recessed area) in the master cylinder piston to the master cylinder mounting flange. Next, apply a vacuum of 20 in-Hg to the booster (using a hand vacuum pump) and measure the distance from the end of the vacuum booster pushrod to the mounting face of the booster (including gasket, if used) where the master cylinder mounting flange seats. Subtract the two measurements to get the clearance **(see illustration)**. If the clearance is more or less than specified, loosen the star locknut and turn the adjuster on the power booster pushrod until the clearance

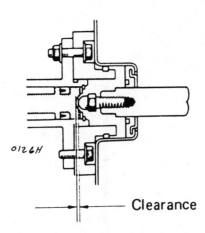

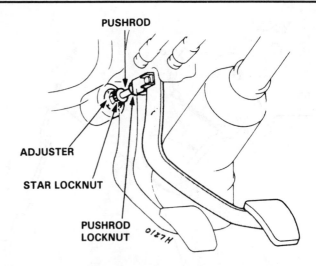

11.14a The booster pushrod-to-master cylinder clearance must be as specified – if there is interference between the two, the brakes may drag; if there is too much clearance, there will be excessive brake pedal travel

11.14b To adjust the length of the booster pushrod, loosen the star locknut and turn the adjuster in or out, as necessary, to achieve the desired setting

is within the specified limit **(see illustration)**. After adjustment, tighten the locknut.

15 After the final installation of the master cylinder and brake hoses and lines, bleed the brakes as described in Section 10.

12 Parking brake – adjustment

Refer to illustrations 12.2 and 12.4

1 Refer to Chapter 11 and remove the console trim around the parking brake lever.

2 Remove the parking brake equalizer cover plate **(see illustration)** to gain access to the equalizer.

3 Block the front wheels, raise the rear of the vehicle and support it securely on jackstands. Apply the parking brake lever until you hear one click.

4 Turn the adjuster nut on the equalizer **(see illustration)** clockwise while rotating the rear wheels. Stop turning the nut when the brakes just

start to drag on the rear wheels.

5 Release the parking brake lever and check to see that the brakes don't drag when the rear wheels are turned. The travel on the parking brake lever should be as listed in the Chapter 1 Specifications when properly adjusted.

6 Lower the vehicle and reinstall the equalizer cover plate and console trim.

13 Parking brake cable(s) – replacement

Refer to illustrations 13.4a, 13.4b and 13.6

1 Block the front wheels and loosen the rear wheel lug nuts. Raise the rear of the vehicle and support it securely on jackstands.

2 On vehicles with rear drum brakes, remove the brake drum(s) (see Section 5).

3 Following the procedure in the previous Section, loosen the equalizer adjuster nut. Remove the cable clamp from the cable housing **(see illustration 12.4)** and unhook the cable from the equalizer.

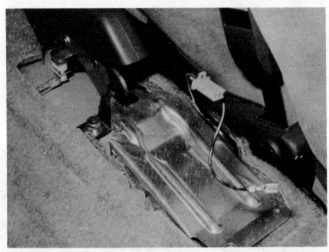

12.2 After removing the console trim, remove the equalizer cover plate

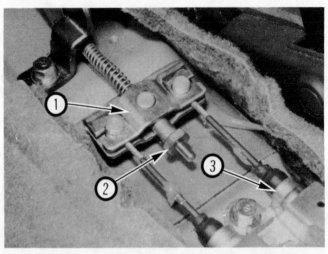

12.4 Parking brake equalizer and adjuster

1 Equalizer 2 Adjuster nut 3 Cable clamp

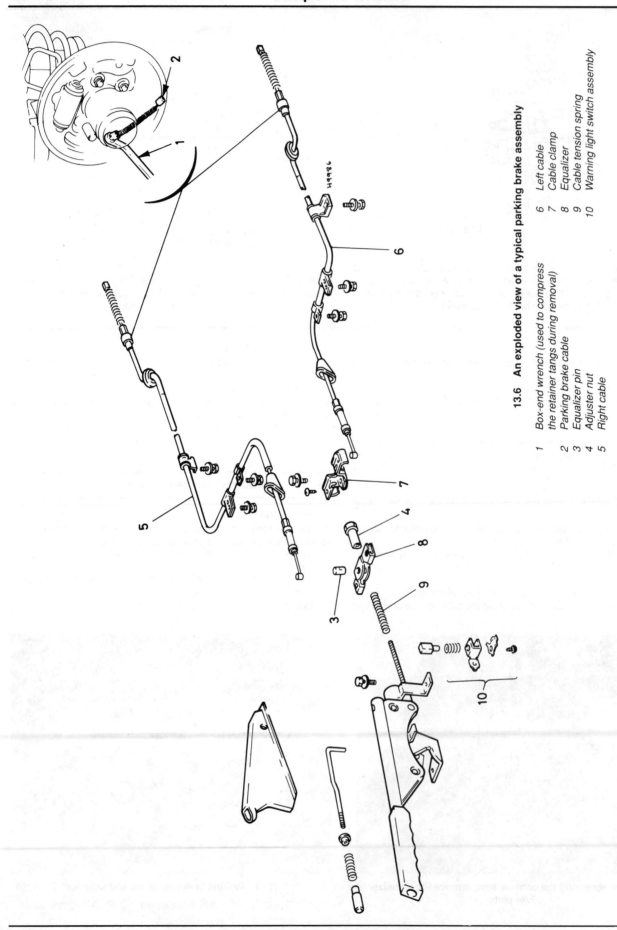

13.6   An exploded view of a typical parking brake assembly

1   Box-end wrench (used to compress the retainer tangs during removal)
2   Parking brake cable
3   Equalizer pin
4   Adjuster nut
5   Right cable
6   Left cable
7   Cable clamp
8   Equalizer
9   Cable tension spring
10   Warning light switch assembly

13.4a   To detach the parking brake cable from a drum brake, remove the brake shoe and grab the cable end with a pair of needle nose pliers and pull it out of its slot in the parking brake lever . . .

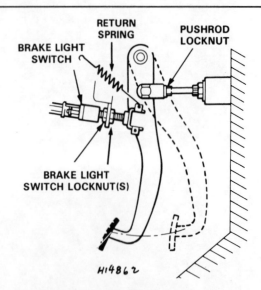

13.4b   . . . then compress the tangs on the retainer by sliding an offset box wrench over the end of the cable onto the retainer, and pull the cable out the inner side of the backing plate

4   On models with rear drum brakes, remove the brake shoes (see Section 5) and disconnect the cable end from the lever on the trailing brake shoe (see illustration). Depress the tangs on the cable housing retainer and pass the cable through the backing plate. You can do this by passing an offset 12mm box end wrench over the end of the cable and onto the retainer (see illustration). This compresses all the tangs simultaneously.

5   On models with rear disc brakes, remove the clip and clevis to disconnect the cable end from the actuator lever on the caliper (see illustration 3.2), then remove the spring clip to free the cable housing from the support bracket.

6   Unbolt the cable housing clamps from the underbody, noting how the cable is routed, then remove the cable from the vehicle (see illustration). It may be necessary to remove the exhaust pipe heat shield bolts at the rear to allow cable removal.

7   If both cables are to be removed, repeat the above steps to remove the remaining cable.

8   Installation is the reverse of the removal procedure. After the cable(s) are installed, be sure to adjust them according to the procedure described in Section 12.

14   Parking brake lever – removal and installation

Refer to illustration 14.3

1   Remove the center console (see Chapter 11).
2   Detach the parking brake cable (see Section 13).
3   Disconnect the electrical connector from the warning light switch (see illustration).
4   Remove the parking brake lever mounting bolts and remove the lever assembly.
5   Installation is the reverse of removal.

15   Brake light switch – check, replacement and adjustment

Check

Refer to illustration 15.1

1   Locate the brake light switch at the top of the brake pedal (see illustration).

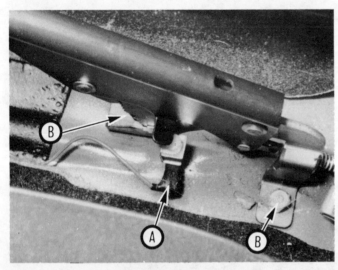

14.3   To remove the parking brake lever, disconnect the electrical connector from the warning light switch (A) and remove the lever mounting bolts (B)

15.1   Typical brake light switch assembly

2   Unplug the switch connector.
3   Check for continuity across the switch terminals with an ohmmeter. When the switch plunger is pushed in, there should be no continuity; when it's released, there should be continuity. If the switch doesn't operate as described, replace it.

Replacement

4   Disconnect the electrical connector from the switch, if you haven't already done so.
5   Remove the locknut on the pedal side of the switch (see illustration 15.1) and unscrew the switch from the bracket.

6   Installation of the brake light switch is the reverse of the removal procedure.

Adjustment

7   Back off the locknut on the connector side of the switch and screw the switch in until the plunger at the end is completely depressed by the brake pedal.
8   Unscrew the switch one-half turn and tighten the locknut.
9   Verify the brake lights operate when the pedal is depressed and go off when the pedal is released.

Chapter 10
Suspension and steering systems

Contents

Specifications

General

Power steering fluid type . . . . See Chapter 1
Vehicle ride height (1984 through 1987 models)
   Hatchback . . . . 24-13/16 to 26 in (631 to 661 mm)
   Sedan . . . . 25 to 26-7/32 in (636 to 666 mm)
   Wagon . . . . 24-15/16 to 26-1/8 in (634 to 664 mm)
   CRX . . . . 24-11/16 to 25-15/16 in (629 to 659 mm)

Torque specifications

Ft-lbs

Front suspension

1984 through 1987

Stabilizer bar clamp bolts	16
Stabilizer bar-to-lower arm bolt and nut	16
Lower arm balljoint nut	32
Lower arm-to-radius arm bolts	28
Steering knuckle-to-strut pinch bolt	47
Strut upper mounting nuts	28
Strut damper rod self-locking nut	32
Radius arm bushing nut	60
Torque tube holder bolts	16
Steering/suspension crossmember bolts	47

1988 on

Strut assembly	
Upper mounting nuts	29
Damper rod nut	22
Damper fork	
Damper fork-to-strut assembly pinch bolt	32
Damper fork-to-lower arm through-bolt nut	47
Radius rod	
Front nut	32
Rear bolts	80
Lower arm inner pivot bolt	43
Steering knuckle-to-lower arm balljoint stud nut	40
Upper arm	
Arm-to-steering knuckle balljoint stud nut	32
Upper arm pivot bolt nuts	22

Rear suspension

1984 through 1987

Panhard rod-to-body bracket bolt	40
Panhard rod-to-axle beam	54
Trailing arm-to-body	47
Hub retaining nut	134
Strut upper mounting nut	16
Strut lower mounting nut	40
Control arm nuts	29
Spindle nuts	33
Swing bearing nuts	33
Stabilizer bar-to-axle beam	54

1988 on

Strut assembly	
Upper mounting nuts	29
Strut-to-lower arm mounting bolt	29
Damper rod self-locking nut	22
Upper arm bushing bracket bolts	29
Lower arm inner through bolt and nut	40
Compensator arm through bolts	47
Trailing arm	
Trailing arm bushing bracket bolts	47
Trailing arm-to-upper arm bolt and nut	40
Trailing arm-to-lower arm bolt	40
Hub retaining nut	134

Steering system

Steering gear mounting bolts	
1987 and earlier	29
1988 on	
Right side bolts	28
Left side bolts	32
Tie-rod end-to-steering knuckle nut	32

1.2   Front suspension on 1984 through 1987 models

| 1 | Strut assembly | 3 | Lower arm | 4 | Radius arm |
| 2 | Steering knuckle | | | 5 | Torsion bar |

1.3 Rear suspension on 1984 through 1987 models (2WD)

1   Panhard rod
2   Strut assembly
3   Beam axle
4   Trailing arm

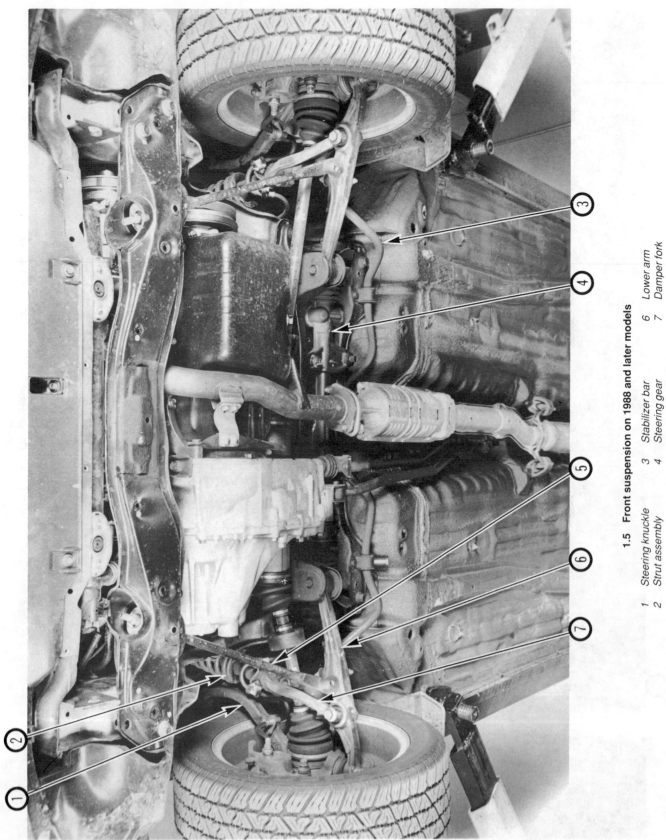

1.5   Front suspension on 1988 and later models

1	Steering knuckle	3	Stabilizer bar	6	Lower arm
2	Strut assembly	4	Steering gear	7	Damper fork
		5	Radius rod		

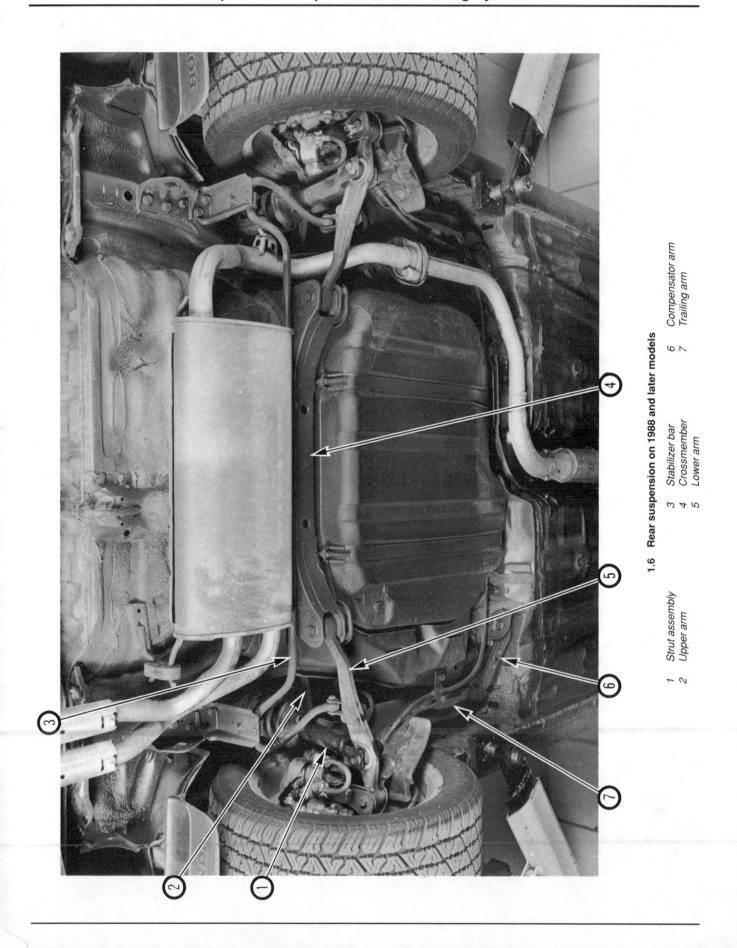

1.6   Rear suspension on 1988 and later models

1	Strut assembly	3	Stabilizer bar
2	Upper arm	4	Crossmember
		5	Lower arm
		6	Compensator arm
		7	Trailing arm

1 General information

Refer to illustrations 1.2, 1.3, 1.5 and 1.6

The vehicles covered by this manual, while similar in many respects, have two different front and three different rear suspension designs.

The front suspension on 1984 through 1987 models **(see illustration)** is a fully independent design which uses MacPherson struts and torsion bar springs.

The rear suspension on 1984 through 1987 two-wheel drive (2WD) models **(see illustration)** is a trailing arm design. It consists of a beam axle laterally located by a Panhard rod and longitudinally located by trailing arms. A pair of strut assemblies attached to the body and the spindles handle suspension and damping. A stabilizer bar is installed inside the right end of the beam axle.

The rear suspension on four-wheel drive (4WD) versions of 1985 through 1987 models has a live axle suspended by a pair of shock absorbers and a pair of coil springs. The axle is laterally located by a Panhard rod and longitudinally located by upper and lower trailing arms.

The front suspension on 1988 and later models **(see illustration)** uses coil-over struts, but is otherwise quite different from conventional Mac-Pherson strut-type suspension designs. The strut plays no part in locating the upper end of the steering knuckle. Instead, the upper end of the steering knuckle is controlled by an upper arm. The inner end of the upper arm is bolted to the body.

The rear suspension on 1988 and later models **(see illustration)** is also a fully independent design. The upper end of a strut is bolted to the body; the lower end is attached to the lower arm. The wheel is located laterally by the lower arm and an upper arm, and longitudinally by the trailing arm. The trailing arm is bolted to the body a few inches away from its forward end, and connected to a compensator arm at the front. This allows the rear wheel toe setting to change as the vehicle negotiates turns, resulting in optimum handling characteristics. The rear suspension on 2WD and 4WD Wagon models is virtually identical, except the lower arm is stouter.

All models use either a manual or power-assisted rack-and-pinion steering gear. The power steering system employs an engine-driven pump connected by hoses to the steering gear.

Frequently, when working on the suspension or steering system components, you may come across fasteners which seem impossible to loosen. These fasteners on the underside of the vehicle are continually subjected to water, road grime, mud, etc., and can become rusted or "frozen," making them extremely difficult to remove. In order to unscrew these stubborn fasteners without damaging them (or other components), be sure to use lots of penetrating oil and allow it to soak in for a while. Using a wire brush to clean exposed threads will also ease removal of the nut or bolt and prevent damage to the threads. Sometimes a sharp blow with a hammer and punch is effective in breaking the bond between a nut and bolt threads, but care must be taken to prevent the punch from slipping off the fastener and ruining the threads. Heating the stuck fastener and surrounding area with a torch sometimes helps too, but isn't recommended because of the obvious dangers associated with fire. Long breaker bars and extension, or "cheater," pipes will increase leverage, but never use an extension pipe on a ratchet – the ratcheting mechanism could be damaged. Sometimes, turning the nut or bolt in the tightening (clockwise) direction first will help to break it loose. Fasteners that require drastic measures to unscrew should always be replaced with new ones.

Since most of the procedures that are dealt with in this chapter involve jacking up the vehicle and working underneath it, a good pair of jackstands will be needed. A hydraulic floor jack is the preferred type of jack to lift the vehicle, and it can also be used to support certain components during various operations. **Warning:** *Never, under any circumstances, rely on a jack to support the vehicle while working on it. Whenever any of the suspension or steering fasteners are loosened or removed they must be inspected and, if necessary, be replaced with new ones of the same part number or of original equipment quality and design. Torque specifications must be followed for proper reassembly and component retention. Never attempt to heat or straighten any suspension or steering components. Instead, replace any bent or damaged part with a new one.*

2 Front strut assembly – removal and installation

Removal

1   Loosen the wheel lug nuts, raise the front of the vehicle, place it securely on jackstands and remove the front wheels.

1984 through 1987 models
Refer to illustrations 2.2 and 2.3

2   Place a floor jack under the lower arm **(see illustration)**. Raise the jack just enough to remove the load from the upper mounting nuts.
3   Detach the brake hose from its bracket on the strut **(see illustration)**.

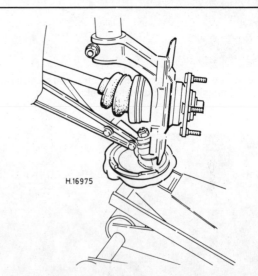

H.16975

2.2   Position a floor jack directly beneath the outer end of the lower arm and raise the steering knuckle and lower arm enough to remove the load from the upper mounting nuts

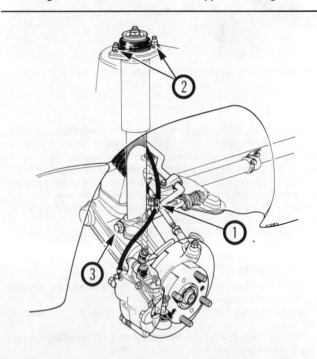

2.3   Strut assembly mounting details (1984 through 1987 models)

1	Brake hose bracket	3	Steering knuckle-to-strut
2	Strut upper mounting nuts		pinch bolt

2.7   Brake hose brackets (arrows) on the strut and steering knuckle (1988 and later models)

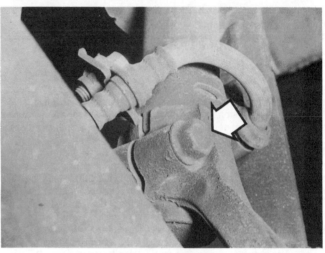

2.8   On 1988 and later models, remove the pinch bolt from the damper fork (arrow)

2.9   Remove the damper fork-to-lower arm through bolt (1988 and later models)

2.10   Remove the strut upper mounting nuts (arrows) and washers (1988 and later models)

4   Remove the steering knuckle pinch bolt at the base of the strut, lower the jack slightly and detach the strut from the steering knuckle. If necessary, tap on the steering knuckle with a hammer to separate the two components. **Warning:** *Make sure the lower arm is properly supported by the jack. It's under a load from the torsion bar, which will react just like a spring if the jack should suddenly slip out from under the lower arm.*

5   Remove the strut mounting nuts and washers from the top of the strut tower inside the engine compartment.

6   Guide the strut out from the fenderwell.

1988 and later models

Refer to illustrations 2.7, 2.8, 2.9 and 2.10

7   Unbolt the brake hose brackets from the strut and the steering knuckle **(see illustration)**.

8   Remove the pinch bolt from the top of the damper fork **(see illustration)**.

9   Remove the damper fork-to-lower arm through bolt **(see illustration)** and pull the damper fork off the lower end of the strut.

10   Remove the strut mounting nuts from the top of the strut tower inside the engine compartment **(see illustration)** and remove the strut assembly. **Warning:** *DO NOT remove the large nut at the top of the strut – it secures the coil spring upper seat and is under great spring pressure.*

Installation

11   Place the strut in position, raise it up until the studs protrude through the holes in the top of the strut tower and install the washers and mounting nuts hand tight. **Note:** *These fasteners should be tightened after the vehicle is on the ground, not while it's raised.*

12   On 1987 and earlier models, attach the lower end of the strut to the steering knuckle. If necessary, raise the knuckle slightly with the floor jack. On 1988 and later models, install the damper fork, using a new nut on the fork-to-lower arm bolt (don't tighten the damper fork-to-lower arm bolt/nut yet). On all models, make sure the alignment tab on the strut is aligned with the slot in the steering knuckle or damper fork. Install the pinch bolt and tighten it to the torque listed in this Chapter's Specifications.

13   On 1988 and later models, place a floor jack under the steering knuckle. Raise the knuckle just enough to lift the vehicle off the safety stand.

14   Tighten the damper fork-to-strut pinch bolt and the new nut on the damper fork-to-lower arm through bolt to the torque listed in this Chapter's Specifications.

15   Attach the brake hose brackets to the strut.

16   Remove the floor jack.

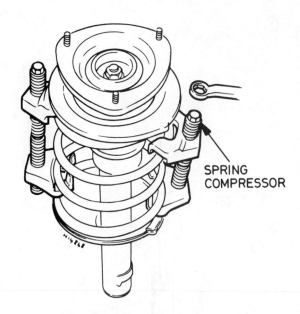

3.4 On 1988 and later models, install the spring compressor in accordance with the manufacturer's instructions and compress the spring until the spring is no longer pressing against the spring seat

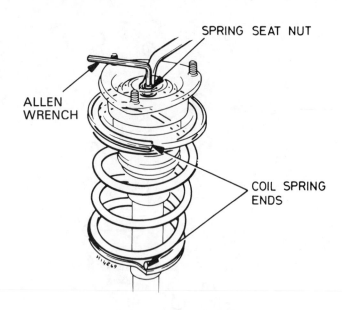

3.5 With the spring compressed, remove the damper rod (spring seat) nut while holding the damper rod with an Allen wrench

17 Install the wheel and lug nuts, lower the vehicle and tighten the lug nuts to the torque listed in the Chapter 1 Specifications.

18 Tighten the upper mounting nuts to the torque listed in this Chapter's Specifications.

3 Strut assembly – replacement

Refer to illustrations 3.4, 3.5, 3.6a and 3.6b

1 Remove the strut assembly from the vehicle (see Section 2).

2 Check the strut/shock absorber for leaking fluid, dents, cracks or other obvious damage. Check the coil spring for chips or cracks which could cause premature failure and inspect the spring seats for hardness or general deterioration. Complete strut assemblies are available on an exchange basis. This eliminates much time and work. So, before disassembling the strut assembly to replace individual components, check on the availability of parts and the price of a complete rebuilt unit. **Warning:** *Disassembling a strut assembly is a potentially dangerous undertaking and utmost attention must be directed to the job at hand, or serious injury may result. Use only a high quality spring compressor and carefully follow the manufacturer's instructions furnished with the tool. After removing the coil spring from the strut or shock, set it aside in a safe, isolated area (a steel cabinet is preferred).*

3 Mount the strut/shock absorber assembly in a vise. Line the vise jaws with wood or rags to prevent damage to the unit and don't tighten the vise excessively.

4 On 1988 and later units, install a spring compressor in accordance with the tool manufacturer's instructions **(see illustration)**. (You can buy a spring compressor at most auto parts stores or rent one from most equipment yards on a daily basis.) Compress the spring far enough to relieve all pressure from the spring seat (if you can wiggle the spring, it's loose enough).

5 Place an offset box wrench on the damper rod nut, insert an Allen wrench in the recessed hex in the damper rod and remove the nut **(see illustration)**.

6 Disassemble the strut assembly **(see illustrations)**. On 1988 and later models, carefully lift the compressed spring from the assembly and set it in a safe place, such as a steel cabinet. **Warning:** *Keep the ends of the*

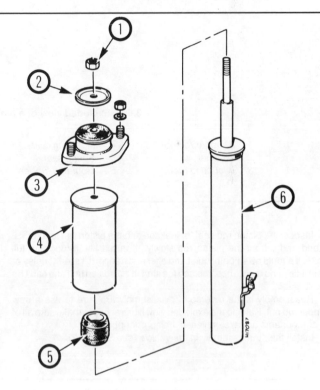

3.6a Exploded view of a typical strut assembly (1984 through 1987 models)

1	Damper rod nut	3	Collar	5	Rubber bump stop
2	Washer	4	Shield	6	Strut

spring facing away from your body! Pay close attention to the order in which you remove the parts. It's a good idea to lay the parts out in their exact relationship to each other on the work bench because everything must be reassembled exactly the same way it came off.

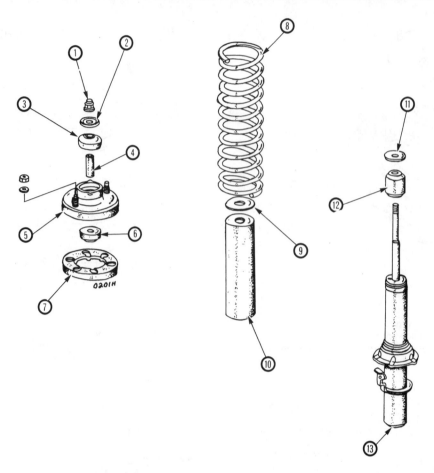

3.6b   Exploded view of a typical strut assembly (1988 on)

1	Damper rod nut	4	Mounting collar	7	Spring insulator	10	Dust cover
2	Washer	5	Spring seat	8	Coil spring	11	Bump stop plate
3	Mounting rubber	6	Mounting rubber	9	Dust cover plate	12	Bump stop
						13	Strut unit

7   Inspect the piston rod seal for leakage and the piston rod for cracks. Extend and retract the piston rod slowly, then quickly, through its full stroke. It should be smooth, quiet and offer resistance. If it's jerky, noisy or offers little or no resistance, replace the strut. It's a sealed unit and can't be rebuilt.

8   Reassembly is the reverse of disassembly. Be sure to use a new damper rod nut. Refer to the exploded view illustrations to make sure all of the components are assembled in their proper positions.

9   Install the strut assembly in the vehicle (see Section 2).

4   Steering knuckle and hub assembly – removal and installation

Removal

1   Remove the wheel cover, if equipped. Loosen the driveaxle nut (see Chapter 8, Part A). Loosen the wheel lug nuts, raise the front of the vehicle and support it securely on jackstands. Remove the wheel and the driveaxle hub nut.

2   Unbolt the brake hose bracket(s) from the strut and/or steering knuckle. Unbolt the brake caliper, hang it out of the way with a piece of wire, remove the caliper mounting bracket and remove the brake disc (see

Chapter 9).

3   Disconnect the tie-rod end from the steering knuckle (see Section 25).

4   On 1984 through 1987 models, separate the radius arm balljoint stud from the bottom of the steering knuckle (see Section 7). On 1988 and later models, separate the lower arm from the balljoint in the bottom of the steering knuckle (see Section 11).

5   On 1984 through 1987 models, remove the pinch bolt from the upper end of the knuckle **(see illustration 2.3)** and tap the knuckle and hub assembly off the lower end of the strut.

6   On 1988 and later models, separate the upper end of the knuckle from the upper arm balljoint (see Section 12).

7   Carefully pull the knuckle and hub assembly off of the driveaxle. Support the driveaxle with a piece of wire to prevent damage to the inner CV joint.

8   Due to the special tools and expertise required to press the hub and bearing from the steering knuckle, the assembly should be taken to a dealer service department or other repair shop to have the bearings replaced, if they're worn.

Installation

9   Apply a light coat of wheel bearing grease to the driveaxle splines. Insert the driveaxle through the splined bore of the hub while guiding the steering knuckle into position.

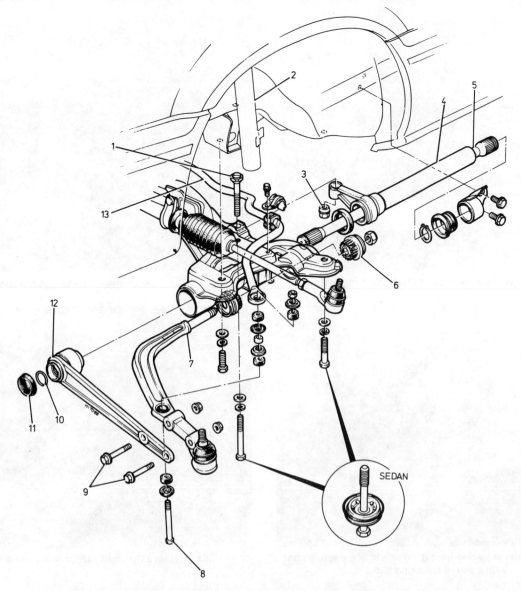

5.3 An exploded view of the front suspension on 1984 through 1987 models

1	Height adjusting bolt	4	Torque tube	7	Radius arm	10	Torsion bar snap-ring
2	Strut unit	5	Torsion bar	8	Stabilizer bar mounting bolt	11	Torsion bar cap
3	Height adjusting nut	6	Radius arm bushing	9	Lower arm bolt	12	Lower arm
						13	Stabilizer bar

10 On 1984 through 1987 models, attach the upper end of the knuckle to the lower end of the strut, making sure the tab on the strut engages with the split in the pinch joint (see Section 2). Install the pinch bolt and tighten it to the torque listed in this Chapter's Specifications.

11 On 1988 and later models, connect the upper end of the knuckle to the upper arm balljoint (see Section 12). Tighten the balljoint stud nut to the torque listed in this Chapter's Specifications.

12 On 1984 through 1987 models, connect the lower end of the knuckle to the radius arm balljoint stud (see Section 7). On 1988 and later models, connect the balljoint on the bottom of the knuckle to the lower arm (see Section 11).

13 Install the brake disc, caliper mount and caliper (see Chapter 9). Attach the brake hose bracket(s).

14 Install the driveaxle nut and tighten it securely.

15 Install the wheel and lug nuts, lower the vehicle and tighten the lug nuts to the torque listed in the Chapter 1 Specifications.

16 Tighten the driveaxle nut to the torque specified in Chapter 8, Part A.

17 Drive the vehicle to an alignment shop and have the front end alignment checked and, if necessary, adjusted.

5 Torsion bar (1984 through 1987 models) – removal, installation and adjustment

Removal

Refer to illustrations 5.3, 5.4a, 5.4b, 5.5, 5.6a, 5.6b

1 Raise the vehicle and place it securely on jackstands.

2 Place a floor jack directly under the lower arm. **Warning:** *The jack will absorb the reaction of the torsion bar during the following removal procedure, so make sure the jack head is centered on the end of the lower arm.*

3 Remove the height adjusting nut **(see illustration)**.

5.4a   Remove the torque tube holder mounting bolts . . .

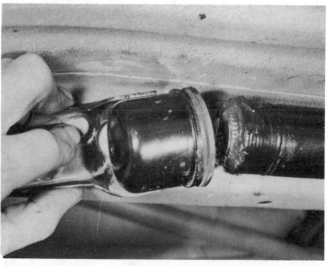

5.4b   . . . and remove the torque tube holder

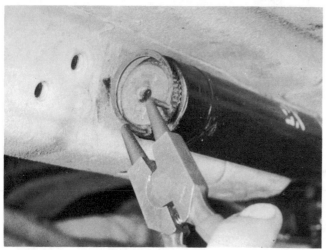

5.5   Remove the snap-ring from the rear end of the torsion bar
with a pair of snap-ring pliers

5.6a   Remove the front cap from the torsion bar . . .

5.6b   . . . tap the torsion bar forward slightly (until the snap-ring
is exposed) and remove the snap-ring from its groove in the front
end of the torsion bar

4   Remove the mounting bolts from the torque tube holder (**see illustration**) and remove the torque tube holder and cap bushing (**see illustration**).
5   Using snap-ring pliers, remove the snap-ring from the rear of the torsion bar (**see illustration**).
6   Remove the cap from the front end of the torsion bar (**see illustration**), then tap the bar forward slightly until the snap-ring is accessible. Moving the lower arm up and down slightly will make the torsion bar bar easier to slide forward. When you can get at the snap-ring, remove it (**see illustration**).
7   There should already be a punch mark or paint mark on the torque tube splines and a cutout or paint mark on the torsion bar splines. If there aren't, paint or scribe alignment marks on the front edges of the tube and the bar to ensure proper reassembly.
8   Using a soft-face hammer, tap the torsion bar out of the lower arm (toward the rear) and remove it from the the torque tube.
9   Remove the torque tube and the torque tube seal.
10   Inspect the torsion bar for cracks and worn splines. If any damage or wear is evident, replace it.

Installation

11   Liberally lubricate the torque tube sliding surfaces, and a new seal, with multi-purpose grease, then position the seal and torque tube on the steering/suspension crossmember.

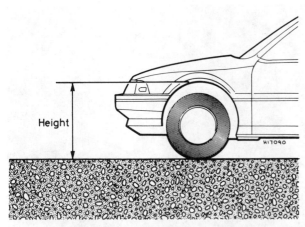

5.24   Ride height is measured between the highest point of the wheel well arch and the ground – compare your measurements to the ride height specified at the beginning of the Chapter and adjust it if necessary

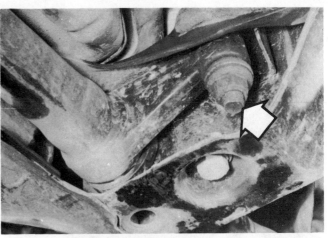

5.27   To adjust ride height, turn the torsion bar height adjusting nut clockwise to increase the height or counterclockwise to decrease it

12   Lubricate the torsion bar splines with grease and insert the bar into the torque tube from the rear.

13   Align the mark on the torque tube splines with the mark on the torsion bar splines.

14   Push the torsion bar through the splined bore of the lower arm until the front snap-ring groove is protruding far enough to install the snap-ring. Note that the cut-out in the torsion bar splines must mate with the projection in the splined bore of the lower arm.

15   Install the snap-ring and the cap on the front end of the torsion bar.

16   Install the other snap-ring on the rear end of the torsion bar.

17   Lubricate the cap bushing with multi-purpose grease and slip it over the rear end of the torsion bar.

18   Install the torque tube holder and mounting bolts. Tighten the bolts securely.

19   Lubricate the height adjusting nut and screw it on finger tight.

20   Install the wheel and lug nuts, lower the vehicle and tighten the lug nuts to the torque listed in the Chapter 1 Specifications. Be sure to adjust the vehicle ride height when you're done (see next Step).

Vehicle ride height adjustment

Refer to illustrations 5.24 and 5.27

21   Fill the fuel tank. Check the tire pressures (see your owner's manual). Make sure they're correct.

22   Place the vehicle on a level surface with the wheels pointed straight ahead. No one must be inside the vehicle.

23   Bounce the vehicle up and down several times to "settle" the suspension.

24   Measure the vertical distance between the highest point of the front wheel well and the ground **(see illustration)** on both sides of the vehicle and record your measurements.

25   Compare your measurements with the dimensions listed in this Chapter's Specifications. If your measurements indicate the vehicle ride height is out of specification, adjust it as follows.

26   Raise the side of the vehicle to be adjusted and place it securely on jackstands.

27   Turn the torsion bar height adjusting nut clockwise (as viewed from below) to increase the height, or counterclockwise to decrease it **(see illustration)**.

Note: *One complete turn of the nut will alter ride height by about 3/16-inch.*

28   After making an approximate adjustment, lower the vehicle, roll it back and forth about half a car's length, bounce the suspension, measure the ride height on both sides, compare your measurements to those listed at the front of this Chapter and, if necessary, raise it up and readjust the ride height nut(s).

29   Repeat this procedure until the ride height is correct.

6   Lower arm (1984 through 1987 models) – removal and installation

Because of the special tools required to remove and install the lower arm, this procedure is beyond the scope of the average home mechanic. If you need to replace the lower arm, have it done by a dealer service department or other qualified repair shop.

7   Radius arm (1984 through 1987 models) – removal and installation

Refer to illustrations 7.3, 7.4 and 7.7

Removal

1   Loosen the front wheel lug nuts, raise the front of the vehicle and place it securely on jackstands. Remove the wheel.

2   Place a floor jack beneath the lower arm. **Warning:** *The jack must absorb the full torque reaction of the torsion bar when the balljoint is released, so make sure the jack is properly located.*

3   Remove the cotter pin from the castle nut on the balljoint stud of the radius arm and remove the nut **(see illustration)**.

7.3   After removing the cotter pin, remove this castle nut which secures the radius arm balljoint stud to the steering knuckle

7.4   Use a balljoint separator to separate the balljoint stud in the radius arm from the steering knuckle

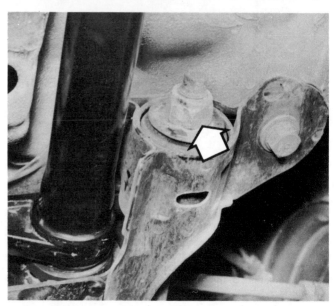

7.7   Remove this self-locking nut from the radius arm stud

4   Using a balljoint separator, separate the balljoint stud from the steering knuckle **(see illustration)**.
5   Unbolt the radius arm from the lower arm **(see illustration 5.3)**.
6   Detach the stabilizer bar from the radius arm (see Section 9).
7   Remove the self-locking nut from the radius arm stud which faces to the rear, through the radius arm bushing **(see illustration)**.
8   Carefully lower the floor jack to relieve the tension on the torsion bar/lower arm assembly and to provide enough clearance to remove the radius arm.
9   Rotate the radius arm down, slide it forward, out of its bushing and remove it.
10   Inspect the radius arm bushings. If they're worn, cracked or torn, replace them. Check the balljoint. If it's worn or damaged, replace the radius arm. The balljoint can't be replaced individually.

Installation

11   Installation is the reverse of removal. Replace all self-locking nuts that don't fit tightly on their respective bolts. Tighten all fasteners to the torque listed in this Chapter's Specifications. Don't tighten the radius arm bushing nut to specification until the vehicle is resting on the ground.

8   Steering/suspension crossmember (1984 through 1987 models) – removal and installation

Refer to illustration 8.10

1   Loosen the wheel lug nuts, raise the vehicle and place it securely on jackstands. Remove the wheels.
2   Remove the steering gear (see Section 27).
3   Place a floor jack directly under the left radius arm balljoint **(see illustration 2.2)**. **Warning:** *The jack must absorb the full torque reaction of the torsion bar when the balljoint is released, so make sure the jack is properly located.*
4   Disconnect the radius arm balljoint from the steering knuckle (see Section 7).
5   Slowly lower the jack until the radius arm is no longer stressed.

6   Repeat Steps 3, 4 and 5 for the right-side radius arm balljoint.
7   Remove the bolts which secure the torque tube holders at the rear end of each torsion bar (see Section 5).
8   Support the engine with an engine hoist or with a floor jack under the oil pan (see Chapter 2). If a floor jack is used, be sure to place a wood block on the jack head to act as a cushion.
9   Remove the nuts and bolts which secure the engine/transaxle assembly to the rear mount (see Chapter 7).
10   Support the center of the steering/suspension crossmember with a floor jack and remove all mounting nuts and bolts **(see illustration)**.
11   Slowly lower the crossmember to the ground and remove it from under the vehicle.
12   Installation is the reverse of removal. Be sure to tighten all fasteners to the torque listed in this Chapter's Specifications.

9   Front stabilizer bar and bushings – removal and installation

Refer to illustrations 9.3 and 9.4

1   Apply the parking brake. Loosen the front wheel lug nuts, raise the front of the vehicle and support it securely on jackstands. Remove the wheels.
2   On 1984 through 1987 models, detach the steering/suspension crossmember from the underside of the vehicle and lower it to the ground (see Section 8). Remove the bolts which attach the stabilizer bar brackets to the crossmember **(see illustration 5.3)**.
3   On 1988 and later models, remove the bolts which attach the stabilizer bar brackets to the underside of the vehicle **(see illustration)**.
4   On 1984 through 1987 models, detach the stabilizer bar link bolt from the radius arm **(see illustration 5.3)**. On 1988 and later models, detach the bar from the lower arm **(see illustration)**. On all models, note the order in which the spacers, washers and bushings are arranged on the link bolt.
5   Remove the bar from under the vehicle.
6   Pull the brackets off the stabilizer bar and inspect the bushings for cracks, hardness and other signs of deterioration. If the bushings are damaged, replace them.
7   Installation is the reverse of removal.

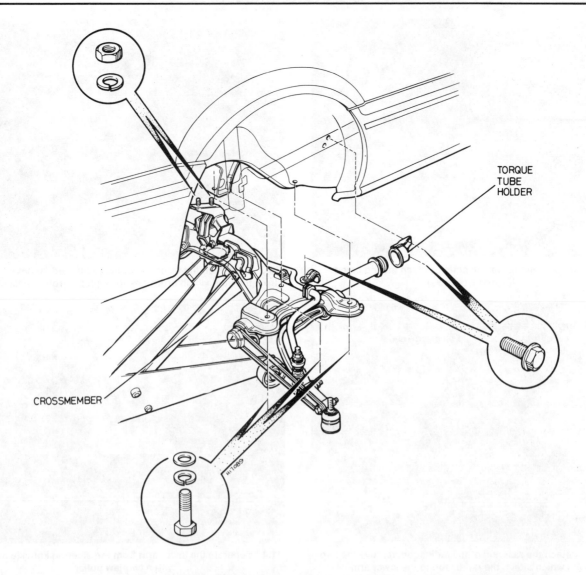

8.10   Installation details of the steering/suspension crossmember

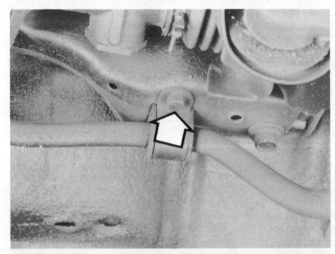

9.3   Stabilizer bar bracket on 1988 and later models (driver's side bracket shown, passenger side bracket similar)

9.4   Stabilizer bar link bolt assembly on 1988 and later models – be sure you note the order in which the various bushings, spacers and washers are arranged

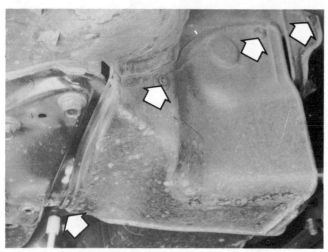

10.2   To remove this splash shield, detach the indicated
fasteners (arrows)

10.3   To detach the front end of the radius rod, remove this nut
from the stud which protrudes through the front crossmember

10.4   To detach the rear end of the radius rod, remove the two
bolts which attach the radius rod to the lower arm

11.4   Separate the lower arm from the steering knuckle balljoint
with a two-jaw puller

10   Radius rod (1988 and later models) – removal and installation

Refer to illustrations 10.2, 10.3 and 10.4

1   Loosen the wheel lug nuts, raise the front of the vehicle and place it
securely on jackstands. Remove the wheel.
2   Remove the plastic splash shield that extends from the wheel well to
the rear of the front crossmember **(see illustration)**.
3   Remove the nut from the front end of the radius rod in the front crossmember **(see illustration)**.
4   Remove the bolts which attach the rear end of the radius rod to the
lower arm **(see illustration)**.
5   Installation is the reverse of removal. Be sure to tighten all fasteners
to the torque listed in this Chapter's Specifications.

11   Lower arm (1988 and later models) – removal and installation

Refer to illustrations 11.4 and 11.5

1   Loosen the front wheel lug nuts, raise the vehicle, place it securely on
jackstands and remove the wheel.
2   Detach the damper fork from the strut assembly (see Section 2).
3   Detach the radius rod from the lower arm (see Section 10).

4   Remove the cotter from the castle nut on the lower balljoint stud.
Loosen the nut. Using a two-jaw puller, separate the lower arm from the
balljoint in the steering knuckle **(see illustration)**.
5   Remove the pivot bolt from the inner end of the lower arm **(see illustration)** and remove the arm.
6   Installation is the reverse of removal.

12   Upper arm (1988 and later models) – removal and installation

Refer to illustrations 12.2 and 12.4

1   Loosen the front wheel lug nuts, raise the vehicle, place it securely on
jackstands and remove the wheel.
2   Remove the upper balljoint nut protector **(see illustration)**.
3   Remove the cotter pin and loosen, but do not remove, the castle nut
from the upper balljoint stud. The nut will prevent the upper arm and the
steering knuckle from separating violently in the next step.
4   Separate the upper arm from the steering knuckle with a special balljoint remover **(see illustration 7.4)**. If you're removing the upper arm because the balljoint is worn out, or if you intend to replace the upper arm with
a new unit, you can use a picklefork-type balljoint separator **(see illustration)**. **Caution:** *Using a picklefork may damage the balljoint dust boot, so
this tool isn't recommended if you plan to reinstall the same upper arm.*

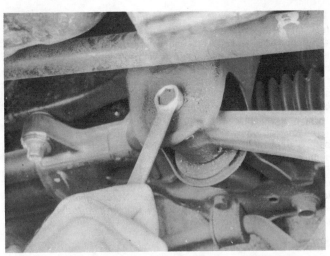

11.5   To remove the lower arm, remove the pivot bolt from the inner end of the arm

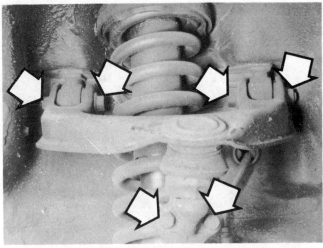

12.2   To remove the upper arm, remove the balljoint stud protector (lower arrows), separate the knuckle from the upper arm and remove the two pivot bolts and nuts (upper arrows)

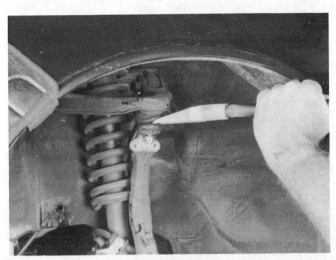

12.4   A picklefork-type balljoint separator can be used, but it may damage the dust boot – apply grease to the end of the tool and the dust boot to minimize damage

5   Remove the upper arm pivot nuts and bolts (see illustration 12.2), the balljoint nut, then remove the upper arm. Note that the heads of the pivot bolts face toward the strut assembly – be sure to install them the same way.
6   Installation is the reverse of removal.

13   Balljoints – replacement

1984 through 1987 models

1   The balljoint in the radius arm isn't removable. If it's worn or damaged, replace the radius arm (see Section 7).

1988 and later models

2   The front suspension on newer models uses two balljoints. The upper balljoint, located in the upper arm, can't be removed. If it's worn or damaged, replace the upper arm (see Section 12).
3   The lower balljoint, located in the steering knuckle, can be removed, but special tools are needed. If it's worn or damaged, remove the knuckle (see Section 4) and take it to a dealer service department or other repair shop to have it replaced.

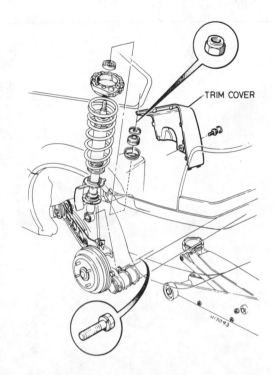

TRIM COVER

14.2   Exploded view of the rear strut assembly on 1984 through 1987 models – note the placement of the floor jack under the beam axle

14   Rear strut assembly – removal and installation

1   Loosen the rear wheel lug nuts, raise the vehicle, place it securely on jackstands and remove the rear wheels.

1984 through 1987 models

Refer to illustrations 14.2, 14.3, 14.4 and 14.6

2   Place a floor jack under the rear axle beam (see illustration) and raise it slightly, so the weight of the axle is firmly supported. **Warning:** *Once you loosen the strut piston rod nut and lower the floor jack, the axle beam will be under considerable force, so make sure it's positioned securely on the floor jack.*

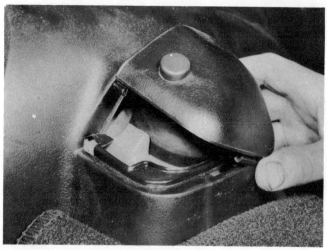

14.3   Remove the trim panel and rubber cap for access to the upper mounting nut

3   From inside the vehicle, remove the trim panel and protective cap **(see illustration)**.

4   Remove the strut upper mounting nut **(see illustration)**. You'll need to prevent the piston rod from turning with an Allen wrench while you're removing the nut. Also remove the big washer and rubber cushion.

5   Slowly lower the floor jack until tension is removed from the coil spring.

6   Unbolt the strut lower mounting bolt **(see illustration)**, lower the jack all the way and remove the strut and spring assembly.

7   If you wish to inspect the strut, refer to Section 3. Be sure to lay out the parts of the strut assembly in order so they're reinstalled in exactly the same order in which they were removed.

8   Installation is the reverse of removal. Make sure the the smaller diameter coils of the spring are at the bottom, and tighten all fasteners to the torque listed in this Chapter's Specifications. **Note:** *Tighten the fasteners securely while the vehicle is raised but don't tighten them to the final torque until it's back on the ground.*

1988 and later models

Refer to illustrations 14.9 and 14.12

9   From inside the vehicle, remove the upper mounting nut access panel in the trim cover **(see illustration)**.

10   Remove the upper mounting nut cover.

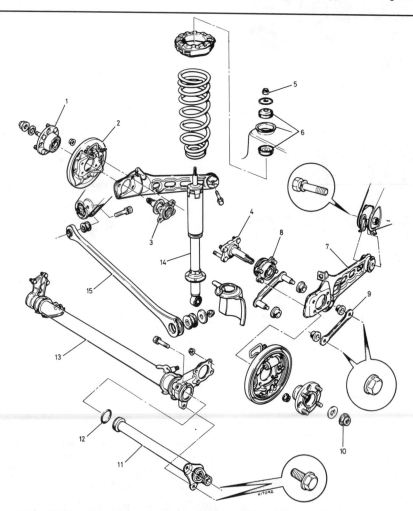

14.4   An exploded view of the rear suspension assembly on 1984 through 1987 models

1	Hub/bearing unit	5	Strut upper mounting nut	9	Control arm	13	Rear axle beam
2	Backing plate	6	Upper mounting cushions	10	Hub unit nut	14	Strut
3	Spindle	7	Trailing arm	11	Stabilizer bar assembly	15	Panhard rod
4	Spindle	8	Swing bearing unit	12	Stabilizer bar seal		

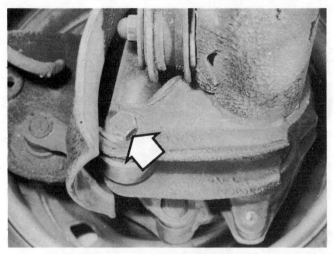

14.6 To detach the lower end of the strut from the axle beam, remove this bolt (arrow)

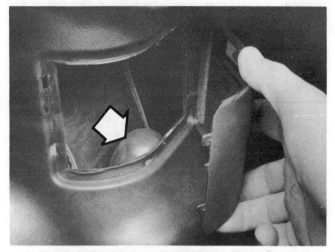

14.9 On 1988 and later models, remove this upper strut mounting nut access cover from the trim panel, remove the protective cover (arrow), then remove the two upper mounting nuts (not visible in this photo)

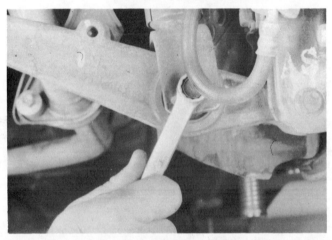

14.12 To detach the lower end of the strut from the lower arm, remove this bolt

11 Remove the upper mounting base nuts.
12 From underneath the vehicle, remove the strut-to-lower arm through bolt (see illustration).
13 Pull the lower arm down and remove the strut assembly
14 Installation is the reverse of removal. Be sure to tighten all fasteners to the torque listed in this Chapter's Specifications.

15 Rear hub and bearing assembly – removal and installation

Refer to illustrations 15.3 and 15.5
Note: *The rear hub and bearing are a single assembly. The bearing is sealed for life and requires no lubrication or attention. If the bearing is worn or damaged, replace the entire hub and bearing assembly.*

1 Loosen the rear wheel lug nuts, raise the vehicle, place it securely on jackstands and remove the rear wheel.
2 Remove the brake drum or disc (see Chapter 9).
3 Unstake the hub retaining nut, unscrew the nut and remove the thrust washer (see illustration).
4 Pull the hub assembly off the spindle. If it's stuck, use a puller to get it off.
5 Install the new hub assembly and thrust washer, tighten the new nut to the torque listed in this Chapter's Specifications, then stake its edge into the groove in the spindle (see illustration).
6 The remainder of installation is the reverse of removal.

15.3 Remove the rear hub nut and thrust washer, then pull the hub unit off

15.5 After tightening the new hub nut to the specified torque, stake it into the groove in the spindle with a hammer and punch

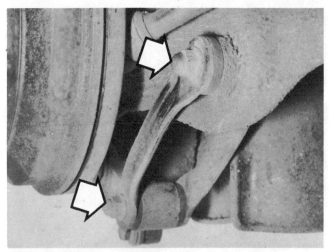

16.5   To remove the right trailing arm, remove these two nuts, pull out the bolts and detach the inner and outer control arms that connect the stabilizer assembly to the trailing arm

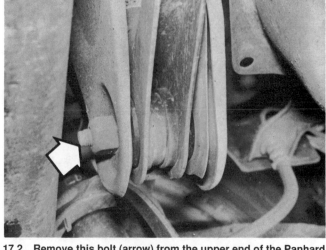

17.2   Remove this bolt (arrow) from the upper end of the Panhard rod (nut in photo is welded in place)

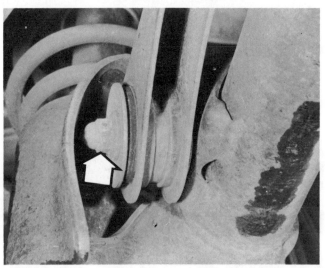

17.3   Remove this nut (arrow) from the Panhard rod's lower mounting stud and slide the rod off the stud

4WD models

8   Loosen the rear wheel lug nuts, raise the vehicle, place it securely on jackstands and remove the wheels.
9   Remove the nuts and bolts which attach the upper and/or lower trailing arms to the body and the axle **(see illustration)**.
10   Installation is the reverse of removal. Be sure to tighten all fasteners to the torque listed in this Chapter's Specifications.

---

17   Panhard rod (1984 through 1987 models) – removal and installation

---

Refer to illustrations 17.2 and 17.3

1   Loosen the rear wheel lug nuts, raise the rear of the vehicle, place it securely on jackstands and remove the wheel.
2   Remove the Panhard rod upper mounting bolt **(see illustration)**.
3   Remove the nut from the lower mounting stud **(see illustration)**, slide the rod off the stud and remove it.
4   Installation is the reverse of removal.

---

18   Rear axle beam (1984 through 1987 models) – removal and installation

---

Refer to illustration 18.5

1   Loosen the rear wheel lug nuts, raise the rear of the vehicle, place it securely on jackstands and remove the wheel.
2   Detach the lower ends of both struts (see Section 14).
3   Detach the Panhard rod from the axle beam (see Section 17).
4   On the left side, remove the rear hub and bearing assembly (see Section 15) and remove the four nuts which attach the brake backing plate, trailing arm and spindle to the axle beam **(see illustration 14.4)**.
5   On the right side, remove the two control arm nuts and remove the inner and outer control arms from the trailing arm and stabilizer bar **(see illustration)**.
6   Remove the four bolts which secure the right spindle/swing bearing unit to the axle beam.
7   Support the axle beam with a floor jack and move it sideways to disengage the spindle studs, then lower the axle beam assembly to the ground.
8   Installation is the reverse of removal. Be sure to tighten all fasteners to the torque listed in this Chapter's Specifications.

---

16   Trailing arm (1984 through 1987 models) – removal and installation

---

2WD models

Refer to illustration 16.5

1   Loosen the rear wheel lug nuts, raise the rear of the vehicle, place it securely on jackstands and remove the wheel.
2   Remove the rear hub and bearing assembly (see Section 15).
3   Detach all brake hose clips from the trailing arm assembly. Disconnect the brake hose from the wheel cylinder or rear caliper and plug it to prevent leakage or contamination (see Chapter 9).
4   Remove the brake backing plate nuts and remove the backing plate **(see illustration 14.4)**.
5   If you're removing the right trailing arm, remove the two control arm nuts and detach the inner and outer control arms from the trailing arm and stabilizer bar assembly **(see illustration)**.
6   Remove the front trailing arm pivot bolt **(see illustration 14.4)** and remove the trailing arm from the vehicle.
7   Installation is the reverse of removal.

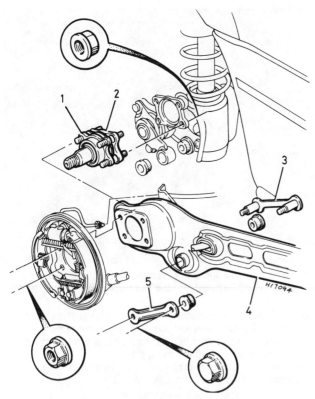

**18.5   Exploded view of the right trailing arm and
related components**

1	Spindle	3	Inner control arm
2	Swing bearing unit	4	Trailing arm
		5	Outer control arm

19   Spindle/swing bearing assembly (1984 through 1987 models) – removal and installation

1   Loosen the rear wheel lug nuts, raise the rear of the vehicle, place it securely on jackstands and remove the rear wheels.

Left spindle

2   Remove the rear axle beam (see Section 18).
3   Pull the spindle out of the brake backing plate and trailing arm **(see illustration 14.4)**. Installation is the reverse of removal.

Right spindle

4   Remove the right rear hub and bearing assembly (see Section 15).
5   Remove the four nuts which attach the brake backing plate and trailing arm to the swing bearing unit.
6   Remove the rear axle beam (see Section 18).
7   Pull the spindle/swing bearing assembly out of the brake backing plate and trailing arm **(see illustration 18.5)**.
8   Installation is the reverse of removal.

Swing bearing

Note: *In the process of removing the swing bearing, it will be destroyed. Therefore, do not have it removed unless you intend to replace it. If you are planning to install a new right spindle, have a new swing bearing pressed on too, because you won't be able to switch the bearing from the old spindle to the new one.*

9   Remove the right spindle/swing bearing assembly (see Steps 4 through 7).
10   Have the swing bearing pressed off the spindle by a dealer service department or other repair shop, and a new bearing pressed on.
11   Installation is the reverse of removal.

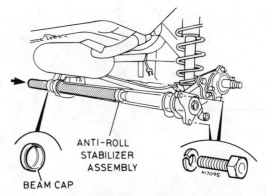

**20.5   Mounting details of the rear stabilizer bar
assembly (1984 through 1987 models) – note the dowel
inserted inside the left end of the axle beam to drive out
the stabilizer bar**

**20.10   To detach the stabilizer bar from 1988 and later models,
remove the stabilizer bar-to-stabilizer link bolt and nut (arrow)
from each end of the lower arm . . .**

20   Rear stabilizer assembly – removal and installation

1   Loosen the rear wheel lug nuts, raise the rear of the vehicle, place it securely on jackstands and remove the rear wheels.

1984 through 1987 models

Refer to illustration 20.5

2   Remove both rear hubs (see Section 15).
3   Remove the brake backing plates (see Chapter 9)
4   On the right side, remove the two nuts and remove the inner and outer control arms from the trailing arm and stabilizer bar **(see illustrations 14.4 and 18.5)**.
5   Extract the cap from the left end of the axle beam **(see illustration)**.
6   Remove the two bolts which attach the stabilizer to the axle beam.
7   Insert a long dowel, such as a broom stick, into the axle beam from the left end and tap out the stabilizer.
8   Installation is the reverse of removal. Be sure to tighten all fasteners to the torque listed in this Chapter's Specifications. Replace any self-locking type fasteners that no longer grip the threads. The two bolts which secure the stabilizer bar to the axle beam should not be tightened until after the control arms have been reinstalled.
9   When you're done, bleed the brakes (see Chapter 9).

1988 and later models

Refer to illustrations 20.10 and 20.11

10   Remove the stabilizer bar-to-stabilizer link nuts and bolts **(see illustration)**.

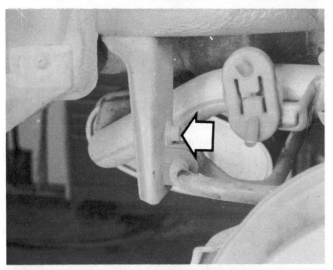

20.11 . . . then remove the stabilizer-to-body clamp bolt (arrow) from each side

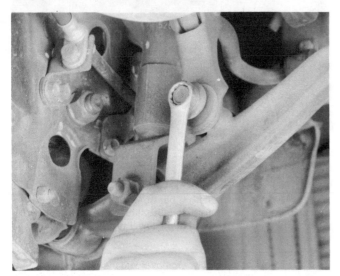

23.6 To remove the lower arm, remove the stabilizer bar link bolt from the lower arm, . . .

11 Remove the stabilizer-to-body clamp bolts **(see illustration)** and re-move the stabilizer bar.

12 Installation is the reverse of removal.

---

21 Shock absorbers (1984 through 1987 4WD models) – removal and installation

---

1 Raise the rear of the vehicle and place it securely on jackstands.

2 Place a floor jack under the axle housing and raise the jack until it's supporting the weight of the housing. **Warning:** *Make sure the axle hous-ing is firmly seated on the floor jack. When the shock absorber is discon-nected from the axle housing, the floor jack must prevent the coil spring from forcing the axle housing down and flying out.*

3 From inside the vehicle, remove the shock absorber access cover in the trim panel **(see illustration 14.9).**

4 Remove the shock absorber cap and, using an Allen wrench to hold the shaft, remove the two upper mounting nuts.

5 Remove the lower mounting bolt and nut and remove the shock **(see illustration 14.6).**

6 To check the shock, slowly move the damper piston rod through a full stroke and note whether it operates smoothly. Listen for any abnormal

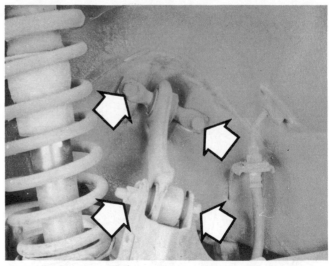

23.2 To remove the upper arm, remove the upper arm-to-trailing arm nut and bolt (arrows) and the two upper arm-to-body bolts

noise. Then jerk the piston rod back and forth two to four inches and note whether it still operates evenly and quietly. Finally, examine the piston rod for signs of wear and inspect the seal for leakage. If any of the above checks reveal a problem, replace the shock.

7 Installation is the reverse of removal. Be sure to tighten all fasteners to the torque listed in this Chapter's Specifications.

---

22 Coil springs (1984 through 1987 4WD models) – removal and installation

---

1 Raise the rear of the vehicle and place it securely on jackstands.

2 Place a floor jack under the axle housing and raise the jack until it's supporting the weight of the housing. **Warning:** *Make sure the axle hous-ing is firmly seated on the floor jack. When the shock absorber is discon-nected from the axle housing, the floor jack must prevent the coil spring from forcing the axle housing down and flying out.*

3 Disconnect the lower end of the shock (see Section 21).

4 Slowly lower the jack until all tension is removed. Remove the coil spring.

5 Installation is the reverse of removal.

---

23 Rear suspension arms (1988 and later models) – removal and installation

---

1 Loosen the rear wheel lug nuts, raise the vehicle, place it securely on jackstands and remove the wheel.

Upper arm

Refer to illustration 23.2

2 Remove the upper arm-to-trailing arm bolt and nut **(see illustration).**

3 Remove the mounting bolts from the upper arm and remove the upper arm.

4 Inspect the bushing for cracking or deterioration. If it's worn, have it pressed out, and a new one installed, by a dealer service department o other repair shop.

5 Installation is the reverse of removal. Be sure to tighten all fasteners to the torque listed in this Chapter's Specifications.

Lower arm

Refer to illustrations 23.6, 23.7 and 23.9

6 Remove the stabilizer link bolt from the lower arm **(see illustration).**

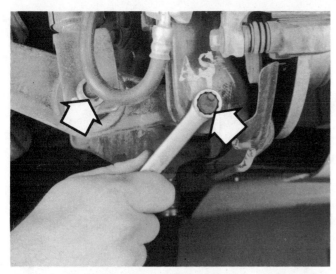

23.7   . . . remove the lower arm-to-trailing arm bolt (arrow) and the strut-to-lower arm bolt (arrow), . . .

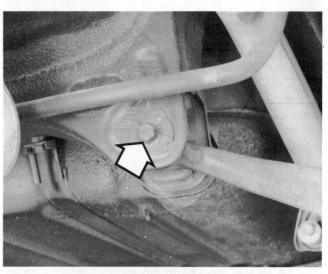

23.9   . . . remove the inner pivot bolt (arrow) and nut from the lower arm and remove the lower arm

23.12   To remove the compensator arm, remove the compensator arm-to-trailing arm bolt (upper arrow) and the compensator arm-to-body nut and bolt (lower arrow)

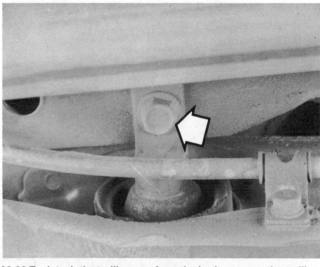

23.20 To detach the trailing arm from the body, remove the trailing arm bushing mounting bolts (inner bolt on right trailing arm shown, outer bolt not visible)

7   Remove the lower arm-to-trailing arm bolt **(see illustration)**.
8   Remove the strut-to-lower arm bolt.
9   Remove the inner pivot bolt and nut from the lower arm **(see illustration)** and remove the lower arm.
10   Inspect the lower arm bushings for cracks and deterioration. If any of them are worn, have them pressed out, and new ones installed, by a dealer service department or other repair shop.
11   Installation is the reverse of removal. Be sure to tighten all fasteners to the torque listed in this Chapter's Specifications.

Compensator arm
Refer to illustration 23.12

12   Remove the compensator arm-to-trailing arm bolt **(see illustration)**.
13   Remove the compensator arm-to-body nut and bolt and remove the compensator arm.
14   Inspect the compensator arm bushings for wear and deterioration. If

either of them need to be replaced, have them pressed out, and new ones installed, by a dealer service department or an automotive machine shop.
15   Installation is the reverse of removal. Be sure to tighten both fasteners to the torque listed in this Chapter's Specifications.

Trailing arm
Refer to illustrations 23.20

16   Disconnect the brake hose from the wheel cylinder or rear caliper and plug the hose to prevent leakage or contamination. Remove the brake drum and brake shoes, or the rear caliper and disc. Disconnect the parking brake cable (see Chapter 9).
17   Remove the rear hub and bearing assembly (see Section 15).
18   Remove the brake backing plate.
19   Detach the upper, lower and compensator arms from the trailing arm (see above).
20   Remove the bolts from the trailing arm bushing **(see illustration)** and remove the streiling arm.

21 Inspect the trailing arm bushing for cracks and deterioration. If it needs to be replaced, have it pressed out, and a new one installed, by a dealer service department or other repair shop.

22 Installation is the reverse of removal. Be sure to tighten all fasteners to the torque listed in this Chapter's Specifications.

24 Steering wheel – removal and installation

Refer to illustrations 24.2 and 24.3

1 Disconnect the cable from the negative battery terminal.
2 Pry off the horn pad emblem **(see illustration)**.
3 Paint or scribe a mark indicating the relationship of the steering shaft to the steering wheel hub and remove the retaining nut **(see illustration)**.
4 Remove the steering wheel by pulling it straight off the shaft (a steering wheel puller isn't required).
5 Installation is the reverse of removal. Be sure to align the index mark on the steering wheel hub with the mark on the shaft when you slip the wheel onto the shaft. Install the mounting nut or bolt and tighten it to the torque listed in this Chapter's Specifications.
6 Connect the negative battery cable.

24.2   To get at the steering wheel retaining nut, pry off the emblem in the horn pad

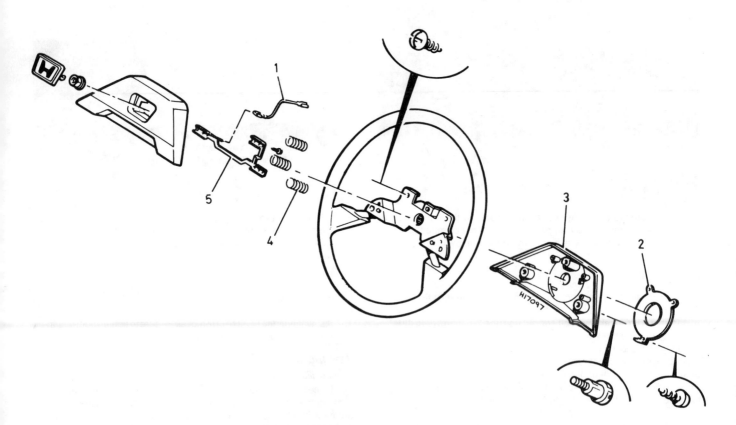

24.3   Exploded view of a typical steering wheel assembly

1	Horn wire	4	Coil spring
2	Slip ring	5	Contact plate
3	Rear cover		

25.2a   Using a backup wrench to prevent the tie-rod end from turning, loosen the jam nut

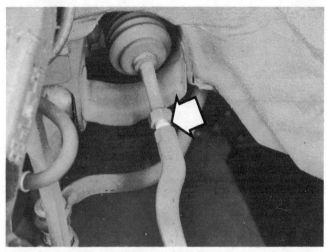

25.2b   Make an alignment mark on the exposed threads, along the edge of the tie-rod end, so the new tie-rod end will be screwed on to the exact same position

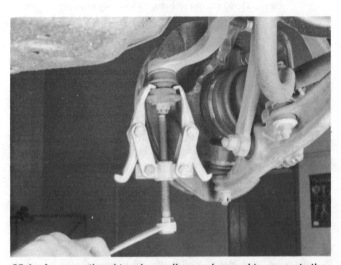

25.4   A conventional two-jaw puller can be used to separate the tie-rod end from the steering knuckle arm

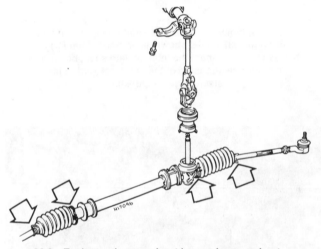

26.3   Each steering gear boot has an inner and outer boot clamp (arrows)

25   Tie-rod ends – removal and installation

Removal

Refer to illustrations 25.2a, 25.2b and 25.4

1   Loosen the wheel lug nuts. Raise the front of the vehicle, support it securely on jackstands and remove the wheel.
2   Hold the tie-rod end with a backup wrench and loosen the jam nut enough to mark the position of the tie-rod end in relation to the threads **(see illustrations)**.
3   Remove the cotter pin and loosen the nut on the tie-rod end stud. Don't completely remove the nut.
4   Separate the tie-rod from the steering knuckle arm with a puller **(see illustration)**. Remove the nut and detach the tie-rod.
5   Unscrew the tie-rod end from the tie-rod.

Installation

6   Thread the tie-rod end on to the marked position and insert the tie-rod stud into the steering knuckle arm. Don't tighten the jam nut yet.
7   Install the castellated nut on the stud and tighten it to the torque listed in this Chapter's Specifications. Install a new cotter pin.
8   Tighten the jam nut securely.

9   Install the wheel and lug nuts. Lower the vehicle and tighten the lug nuts to the torque listed in the Chapter 1 Specifications.
10   Have the alignment checked by a dealer service department or an alignment shop.

26   Steering gear boots – replacement

Refer to illustration 26.3

1   Loosen the lug nuts, raise the front of the vehicle and support it securely on jackstands. Remove the wheel.
2   Remove the tie-rod end and jam nut (see Section 25).
3   Remove the steering gear boot clamps **(see illustration)** and slide the boot off.
4   Before installing the new boot, wrap the threads and serrations on the end of the steering rod with a layer of tape so the small end of the new boot isn't damaged.
5   Slide the new boot into position on the steering gear until it seats in the groove in the steering rod and install new clamps.
6   Remove the tape and install the tie-rod end (see Section 25).
7   Install the wheel and lug nuts. Lower the vehicle and tighten the lug nuts to the torque listed in the Chapter 1 Specifications.

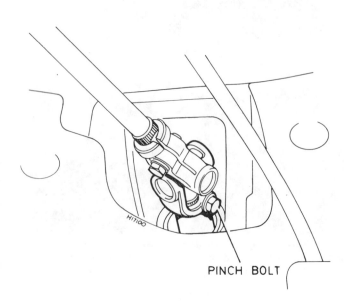

27.3   A typical intermediate shaft pinch bolt (1984 through 1987 model shown, later models similar) – before you disconnect the intermediate shaft, be sure to mark the relationship of the universal joint to the steering gear input shaft

27.5b   . . . and the right (passenger's side) bolts (arrows) and clamp (1990 model shown, all models similar)

2   Place a drain pan under the steering gear (power steering only). Remove the hoses/lines and cap the ends to prevent excessive fluid loss and contamination.
3   Mark the relationship of the intermediate shaft universal joint to the steering gear input shaft and remove the pinch bolt **(see illustration)**.
4   Separate the tie-rod ends from the steering knuckle arms (see Section 25).
5   Support the steering gear and remove the mounting bolts **(see illustrations)**. Lower the unit, separate the intermediate shaft from the steering gear input shaft and remove the steering gear from the vehicle.

Installation

6   Raise the steering gear into position and connect the intermediate shaft, aligning the marks.
7   Install the mounting bolts and washers and tighten them securely.
8   Connect the tie-rod ends to the steering knuckle arms (see Section 25)
9   Install the lower intermediate shaft pinch bolt and tighten it securely.
10   Connect the power steering hoses/lines to the steering gear and fill the power steering pump reservoir with the recommended fluid (see Chapter 1).
11   Lower the vehicle and bleed the steering system (see Section 29).

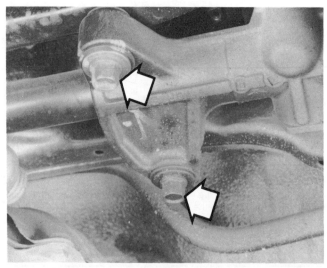

27.5a   To detach the steering gear assembly from the vehicle, remove the left (driver's side) mounting bolts (arrows) . . .

28   Power steering pump – removal and installation

1   Depending on the model, the pump will be easier to remove from above or from underneath the vehicle. If it's down low, raise the vehicle and place it securely on jackstands.
2   Disconnect the fluid hoses at the pump. Note the difference between the pressure and the return hoses. Cap both hoses to prevent leakage or contamination.
3   Remove the pump mounting bolts. If they're different diameters or lengths, note which hole they go to. Remove the pump.
4   Installation is the reverse of removal. Be sure to bleed the power steering system (see next Section) and adjust the drivebelt tension (see Chapter 1).

27   Steering gear – removal and installation

Refer to illustrations 27.3, 27.5a and 27.5b

Note: *This procedure applies to both power and manual steering gear assemblies. When working on a vehicle equipped with a manual steering gear, simply ignore any references made to the power steering system.*

Removal

1   Raise the front of the vehicle and support it securely on jackstands. Apply the parking brake.

29   Power steering system – bleeding

1   Following any operation in which the power steering fluid lines have been disconnected, the power steering system must be bled to remove all air and obtain proper steering performance.

2   With the front wheels in the straight ahead position, check the power steering fluid level (see Chapter 1). If it's low, add fluid until it reaches the Cold mark on the dipstick (1984 through 1987 models) or the lower mark on the reservoir (1988 and later models).

3   Start the engine and allow it to run at fast idle. Recheck the fluid level and add more if necessary to reach the Cold mark on the dipstick.

4   Bleed the system by turning the wheels from side-to-side, without hitting the stops. This will work the air out of the system. Keep the reservoir full of fluid as this is done.

5   When the air is worked out of the system, return the wheels to the straight ahead position and leave the vehicle running for several more minutes before shutting it off.

6   Road test the vehicle to be sure the steering system is functioning normally and noise free.

7   Recheck the fluid level to be sure it is up to the Hot mark on the dipstick while the engine is at normal operating temperature. Add fluid if necessary (see Chapter 1).

30   Wheels and tires – general information

Refer to illustration 30.1

All vehicles covered by this manual are equipped with metric-sized fiberglass or steel belted radial tires **(see illustration)**. Use of other size or type of tires may affect the ride and handling of the vehicle. Don't mix different types of tires, such as radials and bias belted, on the same vehicle as handling may be seriously affected. It's recommended that tires be replaced in pairs on the same axle, but if only one tire is being replaced, be sure it's the same size, structure and tread design as the other.

Because tire pressure has a substantial effect on handling and wear, the pressure on all tires should be checked at least once a month or before any extended trips (see Chapter 1).

Wheels must be replaced if they are bent, dented, leak air, have elongated bolt holes, are heavily rusted, out of vertical symmetry or if the lug nuts won't stay tight. Wheel repairs that use welding or peening are not recommended.

Tire and wheel balance is important to the overall handling, braking and performance of the vehicle. Unbalanced wheels can adversely affect handling and ride characteristics as well as tire life. Whenever a tire is installed on a wheel, the tire and wheel should be balanced by a shop with the proper equipment.

31   Wheel alignment – general information

Refer to illustration 31.1

A wheel alignment refers to the adjustments made to the wheels so they are in proper angular relationship to the suspension and the ground. Wheels that are out of proper alignment not only affect steering control, but also increase tire wear. The only adjustment normally required to the front end is toe-in, although the camber and caster settings should be checked to determine if any of the front end components are worn out or bent **(see illustration)**. On 1988 and later models, the rear toe can also be adjusted.

Getting the proper wheel alignment is a very exacting process, one in which complicated and expensive machines are necessary to perform the job properly. Because of this, you should have a technician with the proper equipment perform these tasks. We will, however, use this space to give

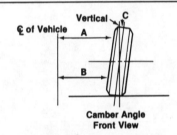

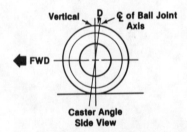

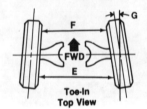

31.1   Front end alignment details – camber (top) and toe-in (bottom). The actual adjustment of these angles is beyond the scope of the home mechanic and must be performed by an alignment shop or service station

A minus B = C (degrees camber)
E minus F = toe-in (measured in inches)
G = toe-in (expressed in degrees)

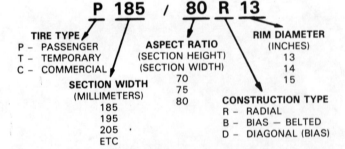

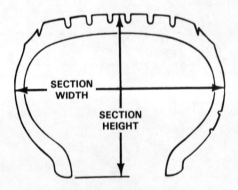

30.1   Metric tire size code

you a basic idea of what is involved with wheel alignment so you can better understand the process and deal intelligently with the shop that does the work.

Toe-in is the turning in of the wheels. The purpose of a toe specification is to ensure parallel rolling of the wheels. In a vehicle with zero toe-in, the distance between the front edges of the wheels will be the same as the distance between the rear edges of the wheels. The actual amount of toe-in is normally only a fraction of an inch. At the front end, toe-in adjustment is controlled by the tie-rod end position on the inner tie-rod. At the rear, it is adjusted by moving the compensator arm, in or out, within its bracket on the body (1988 and later models only. Incorrect toe-in will cause the tires to wear improperly by making them scrub against the road surface.

Camber is the tilting of the wheels from the vertical when viewed from the front or rear of the vehicle. When the wheels tilt out at the top, the camber is said to be positive (+). When the wheels tilt in at the top the camber is negative (-). The amount of tilt is measured in degrees from the vertical and this measurement is called the camber angle. This angle affects the amount of tire tread which contacts the road and compensates for changes in the suspension geometry when the vehicle is cornering or travelling over an undulating surface. Camber isn't adjustable on these vehicles.

Caster is the tilting of the top of the steering axis from the vertical. A tilt toward the rear is positive caster and a tilt toward the front is negative caster. Caster is not adjustable on these vehicles.

Chapter 11   Body

Contents

1   General information

These models feature a "unibody" layout, using a floor pan with front and rear frame side rails which support the body components, front and rear suspension systems and other mechanical components.

Certain components are particularly vulnerable to accident damage and can be unbolted and repaired or replaced. Among these parts are the body moldings, bumpers, the hood and trunk lid (or liftgate) and all glass.

Only general body maintenance practices and body panel repair procedures within the scope of the do-it-yourselfer are included in this Chapter.

2   Body – maintenance

1   The condition of your vehicle's body is very important, because the resale value depends a great deal on it. It's much more difficult to repair a neglected or damaged body than it is to repair mechanical components. The hidden areas of the body, such as the wheel wells, the frame and the engine compartment, are equally important, although they don't require as frequent attention as the rest of the body.

2   Once a year, or every 12,000 miles, it's a good idea to have the underside of the body steam cleaned. All traces of dirt and oil will be removed and the area can then be inspected carefully for rust, damaged brake lines, frayed electrical wires, damaged cables and other problems.

3   At the same time, clean the engine and the engine compartment with a steam cleaner or water soluble degreaser.

4   The wheel wells should be given close attention, since undercoating can peel away and stones and dirt thrown up by the tires can cause the paint to chip and flake, allowing rust to set in. If rust is found, clean down to the bare metal and apply an anti-rust paint.

5   The body should be washed about once a week. Wet the vehicle thoroughly to soften the dirt, then wash it down with a soft sponge and plenty of clean soapy water. If the surplus dirt is not washed off very carefully, it can wear down the paint.

6   Spots of tar or asphalt thrown up from the road should be removed with a cloth soaked in solvent.

7   Once every six months, wax the body and chrome trim. If a chrome cleaner is used to remove rust from any of the vehicle's plated parts, remember that the cleaner also removes part of the chrome, so use it sparingly.

3   Vinyl trim – maintenance

Don't clean vinyl trim with detergents, caustic soap or petroleum based cleaners. Plain soap and water works just fine, with a soft brush to clean dirt that may be ingrained. Wash the vinyl as frequently as the rest of the vehicle.

After cleaning, application of a high quality rubber and vinyl protectant will help prevent oxidation and cracks. The protectant can also be applied to weatherstripping, vacuum lines and rubber hoses, which often fail as a result of chemical degradation, and to the tires.

4   Upholstery and carpets – maintenance

1   Every three months remove the carpets or mats and clean the interior of the vehicle (more frequently if necessary). Vacuum the upholstery and carpets to remove loose dirt and dust.
2   Leather upholstery requires special care. Stains should be removed with warm water and a very mild soap solution. Use a clean, damp cloth to remove the soap, then wipe again with a dry cloth. Never use alcohol, gasoline, nail polish remover or thinner to clean leather upholstery.
3   After cleaning, regularly treat leather upholstery with a leather wax. Never use car wax on leather upholstery.
4   In areas where the interior of the vehicle is subject to bright sunlight, cover leather seats with a sheet if the vehicle is to be left out for any length of time.

5   Body repair – minor damage

See color photo sequence

Repair of minor scratches

1   If the scratch is superficial and does not penetrate to the metal of the body, repair is very simple. Lightly rub the scratched area with a fine rubbing compound to remove loose paint and built up wax. Rinse the area with clean water.
2   Apply touch-up paint to the scratch, using a small brush. Continue to apply thin layers of paint until the surface of the paint in the scratch is level with the surrounding paint. Allow the new paint at least two weeks to harden, then blend it into the surrounding paint by rubbing with a very fine rubbing compound. Finally, apply a coat of wax to the scratch area.
3   If the scratch has penetrated the paint and exposed the metal of the body, causing the metal to rust, a different repair technique is required. Remove all loose rust from the bottom of the scratch with a pocket knife, then apply rust inhibiting paint to prevent the formation of rust in the future. Using a rubber or nylon applicator, coat the scratched area with glaze-type filler. If required, the filler can be mixed with thinner to provide a very thin paste, which is ideal for filling narrow scratches. Before the glaze filler in the scratch hardens, wrap a piece of smooth cotton cloth around the tip of a finger. Dip the cloth in thinner and then quickly wipe it along the surface of the scratch. This will ensure that the surface of the filler is slightly hollow. The scratch can now be painted over as described earlier in this section.

Repair of dents

4   When repairing dents, the first job is to pull the dent out until the affected area is as close as possible to its original shape. There is no point in trying to restore the original shape completely as the metal in the damaged area will have stretched on impact and cannot be restored to its original contours. It is better to bring the level of the dent up to a point which is about 1/8-inch below the level of the surrounding metal. In cases where the dent is very shallow, it is not worth trying to pull it out at all.
5   If the back side of the dent is accessible, it can be hammered out gently from behind using a soft-face hammer. While doing this, hold a block of wood firmly against the opposite side of the metal to absorb the hammer blows and prevent the metal from being stretched.
6   If the dent is in a section of the body which has double layers, or some other factor makes it inaccessible from behind, a different technique is required. Drill several small holes through the metal inside the damaged

area, particularly in the deeper sections. Screw long, self tapping screws into the holes just enough for them to get a good grip in the metal. Now the dent can be pulled out by pulling on the protruding heads of the screws with locking pliers.
7   The next stage of repair is the removal of paint from the damaged area and from an inch or so of the surrounding metal. This is easily done with a wire brush or sanding disk in a drill motor, although it can be done just as effectively by hand with sandpaper. To complete the preparation for filling, score the surface of the bare metal with a screwdriver or the tang of a file or drill small holes in the affected area. This will provide a good grip for the filler material. To complete the repair, see the Section on filling and painting.

Repair of rust holes or gashes

8   Remove all paint from the affected area and from an inch or so of the surrounding metal using a sanding disk or wire brush mounted in a drill motor. If these are not available, a few sheets of sandpaper will do the job just as effectively.
9   With the paint removed, you will be able to determine the severity of the corrosion and decide whether to replace the whole panel, if possible, or repair the affected area. New body panels are not as expensive as most people think and it is often quicker to install a new panel than to repair large areas of rust.
10   Remove all trim pieces from the affected area except those which will act as a guide to the original shape of the damaged body, such as headlight shells, etc. Using metal snips or a hacksaw blade, remove all loose metal and any other metal that is badly affected by rust. Hammer the edges of the hole inward to create a slight depression for the filler material.
11   Wire brush the affected area to remove the powdery rust from the surface of the metal. If the back of the rusted area is accessible, treat it with rust inhibiting paint.
12   Before filling is done, block the hole in some way. This can be done with sheet metal riveted or screwed into place, or by stuffing the hole with wire mesh.
13   Once the hole is blocked off, the affected area can be filled and painted. See the following subsection on filling and painting.

Filling and painting

14   Many types of body fillers are available, but generally speaking, body repair kits which contain filler paste and a tube of resin hardener are best for this type of repair work. A wide, flexible plastic or nylon applicator will be necessary for imparting a smooth and contoured finish to the surface of the filler material. Mix up a small amount of filler on a clean piece of wood or cardboard (use the hardener sparingly). Follow the manufacturer's instructions on the package, otherwise the filler will set incorrectly.
15   Using the applicator, apply the filler paste to the prepared area. Draw the applicator across the surface of the filler to achieve the desired contour and to level the filler surface. As soon as a contour that approximates the original one is achieved, stop working the paste. If you continue, the paste will begin to stick to the applicator. Continue to add thin layers of paste at 20-minute intervals until the level of the filler is just above the surrounding metal.
16   Once the filler has hardened, the excess can be removed with a body file. From then on, progressively finer grades of sandpaper should be used, starting with a 180-grit paper and finishing with 600-grit wet-or-dry paper. Always wrap the sandpaper around a flat rubber or wooden block, otherwise the surface of the filler will not be completely flat. During the sanding of the filler surface, the wet-or-dry paper should be periodically rinsed in water. This will ensure that a very smooth finish is produced in the final stage.
17   At this point, the repair area should be surrounded by a ring of bare metal, which in turn should be encircled by the finely feathered edge of good paint. Rinse the repair area with clean water until all of the dust produced by the sanding operation is gone.
18   Spray the entire area with a light coat of primer. This will reveal any imperfections in the surface of the filler. Repair the imperfections with fresh filler paste or glaze filler and once more smooth the surface with sandpaper. Repeat this spray-and-repair procedure until you are satisfied that the surface of the filler and the feathered edge of the paint are perfect.

Rinse the area with clean water and allow it to dry completely.

19   The repair area is now ready for painting. Spray painting must be carried out in a warm, dry, windless and dust free atmosphere. These conditions can be created if you have access to a large indoor work area, but if you are forced to work in the open, you will have to pick the day very carefully. If you are working indoors, dousing the floor in the work area with water will help settle the dust which would otherwise be in the air. If the repair area is confined to one body panel, mask off the surrounding panels. This will help minimize the effects of a slight mismatch in paint color. Trim pieces such as chrome strips, door handles, etc., will also need to be masked off or removed. Use masking tape and several thicknesses of newspaper for the masking operations.

20   Before spraying, shake the paint can thoroughly, then spray a test area until the spray painting technique is mastered. Cover the repair area with a thick coat of primer. The thickness should be built up using several thin layers of primer rather than one thick one. Using 600-grit wet-or-dry sandpaper, rub down the surface of the primer until it is very smooth. While doing this, the work area should be thoroughly rinsed with water and the wet-or-dry sandpaper periodically rinsed as well. Allow the primer to dry before spraying additional coats.

21   Spray on the top coat, again building up the thickness by using several thin layers of paint. Begin spraying in the center of the repair area and then, using a circular motion, work out until the whole repair area and about two inches of the surrounding original paint is covered. Remove all masking material 10 to 15 minutes after spraying on the final coat of paint. Allow the new paint at least two weeks to harden, then use a very fine rubbing compound to blend the edges of the new paint into the existing paint. Finally, apply a coat of wax.

6   Body repair – major damage

1   Major damage must be repaired by an auto body shop specifically equipped to perform unibody repairs. These shops have the specialized equipment required to do the job properly.

2   If the damage is extensive, the body must be checked for proper alignment or the vehicle's handling characteristics may be adversely affected and other components may wear at an accelerated rate.

3   Due to the fact that all of the major body components (hood, fenders, etc.) are separate and replaceable units, any seriously damaged components should be replaced rather than repaired. Sometimes the components can be found in a wrecking yard that specializes in used vehicle components, often at considerable savings over the cost of new parts.

7   Hinges and locks – maintenance

Once every 3000 miles, or every three months, the hinges and latch assemblies on the doors, hood and trunk (or liftgate) should be given a few drops of light oil or lock lubricant. The door latch strikers should also be lubricated with a thin coat of grease to reduce wear and ensure free movement. Lubricate the door and trunk (or liftgate) locks with spray-on graphite lubricant.

8   Bumpers – removal and installation

Refer to illustrations 8.4a and 8.4b

1   Detach the bumper cover (if equipped).

2   Disconnect any wiring or other components that would interfere with bumper removal.

3   Support the bumper with a jack or jackstand. Alternatively, have an assistant support the bumper as the bolts are removed.

4   Remove the mounting bolts and detach the bumper **(see illustrations)**

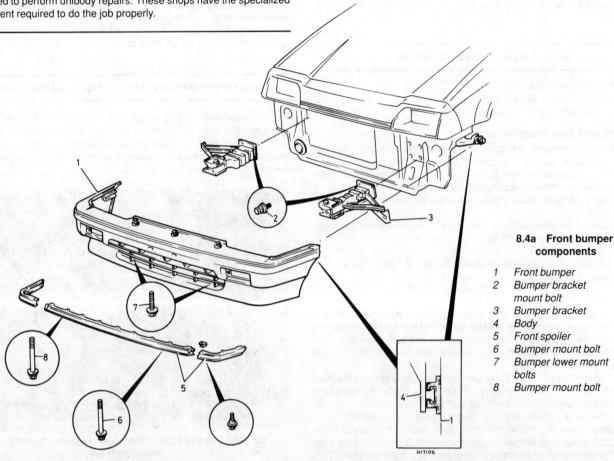

8.4a   Front bumper components

1   *Front bumper*
2   *Bumper bracket mount bolt*
3   *Bumper bracket*
4   *Body*
5   *Front spoiler*
6   *Bumper mount bolt*
7   *Bumper lower mount bolts*
8   *Bumper mount bolt*

H17106

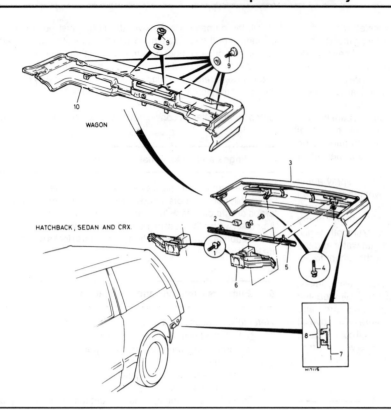

WAGON

HATCHBACK, SEDAN AND CRX.

8.4b Rear bumper components

1   Bumper bracket mount bolt
2   Rubber cushion (not fitted to
    all models)
3   Rear bumper
4   Bumper mount bolt
5   Rear bumper beam (not fitted
    to all models)
6   Bumper bracket
7   Rear bumper
8   Body
9   Bumper mount screws
10 Rear bumper

5   Installation is the reverse of removal. Tighten the retaining bolts securely.
6   Install the bumper cover and any other components that were removed.

9   Hood – removal, installation and adjustment

Refer to illustration 9.2
Note: *The hood is heavy and somewhat awkward to remove and install – at least two people should perform this procedure.*

Removal and installation

1   Use blankets or pads to cover the fenders. This will protect the body and paint as the hood is lifted off.
2   Scribe or paint alignment marks around the bolt heads or nuts to ensure proper alignment during installation **(see illustration)**.
3   Disconnect any cables or wire harnesses which will interfere with removal.
4   Have an assistant support the weight of the hood. Remove the hinge-to-hood nuts or bolts and shims.
5   Lift off the hood.
6   Installation is the reverse of removal. Be sure to reinstall the shims in their original locations.

Adjustment

7   Fore-and-aft adjustment of the hood is done by adding either removing shims between the hinge and body or moving the hood after loosening the hinge-to-body bolts or nuts (some models use both methods).
8   Scribe a line around the entire hinge plate so you can judge the amount of movement.
9   Loosen the bolts or nuts and add or remove shims or move the hood into correct alignment. Move it only a little at a time. Tighten the hinge bolts or nuts and carefully lower the hood to check the alignment.
10   If necessary after installation, the entire hood latch assembly can be adjusted up-and-down as well as from side-to-side on the firewall so the hood closes securely and is flush with the fenders. To do this, scribe a line around the hood latch mounting bolts to provide a reference point. Then

loosen the bolts and reposition the latch assembly as necessary. Following adjustment, retighten the mounting bolts.
11   Finally, adjust the rear edge of the hood until it's flush with the fenders using shims under the hinge plates.
12   The hood latch assembly, as well as the hinges, should be periodically lubricated with white lithium-base grease to prevent sticking and wear.

10   Hood release latch and cable – removal and installation

1   The hood latch may be adjusted by moving it within the limits of its elongated bolt holes so that the hood shuts smoothly and precisely.
2   The hood cable is not adjustable, but may be changed after disconnecting it from the latch and release lever and withdrawing it through the firewall into the engine compartment.

**9.2   Make marks around the hood hinge and bolts before
loosening them**

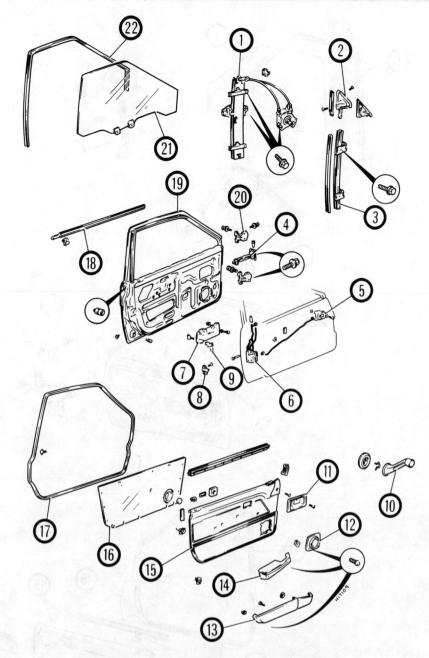

11.4a   Exploded view of the front door – Wagon models

1	Regulator	7	Outside door handle	13	Door pocket	18	Outer moulding
2	Front sash	8	Striker	14	Arm rest	19	Door
3	Front channel	9	Lock cylinder	15	Door panel	20	Door hinge
4	Detent rod	10	Regulator handle	16	Plastic shield	21	Glass
5	Inside door handle	11	Inside handle trim plate	17	Weatherstrip	22	Glass run channel
6	Latch assembly	12	Speaker cover				

11   Door – removal, installation and adjustment

Refer to illustrations 11.4a and 11.4b

Removal

1   Remove the door trim panel (see Section 12). Disconnect any wire harness connectors and push them through the door opening so they won't interfere with door removal.

2   Place a jack or jackstand under the door or have an assistant on hand to support it when the hinge bolts are removed. **Note:** *If a jack or jackstand is used, place a rag between it and the door to protect the door's painted surfaces.*

3   Scribe around the door hinges.

4   Remove the check strap pin and hinge-to-door bolts, then carefully lift off the door **(see illustrations)**.

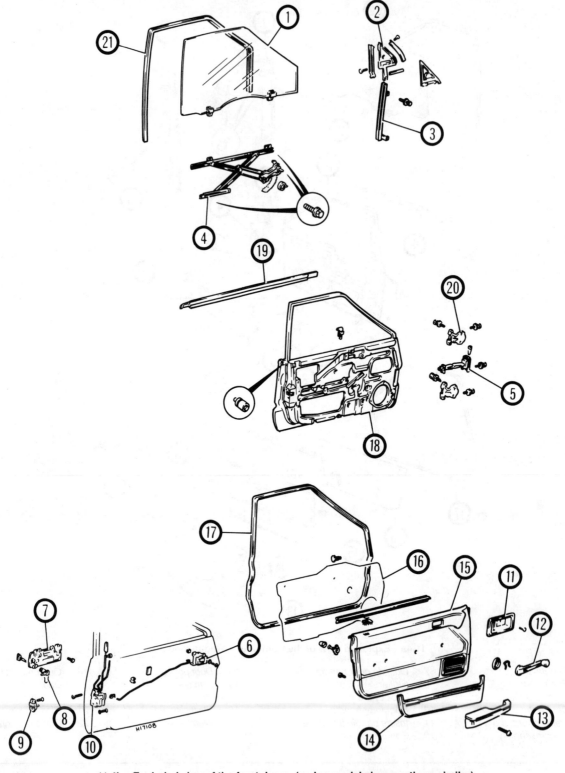

11.4b   Exploded view of the front door – (sedan model shown, others similar)

1	Glass	7	Outside door handle	12	Regulator handle
2	Front sash	8	Lock cylinder	13	Arm rest
3	Front channel	9	Striker	14	Door pocket
4	Regulator	10	Latch assembly	15	Door panel
5	Detent rod	11	Inside handle trim plate	16	Plastic shield
6	Inside door handle				

17	Weatherstrip
18	Door
19	Outer moulding
20	Door hinge
21	Glass run channel

12.2a Remove the trim panel screws (arrows)

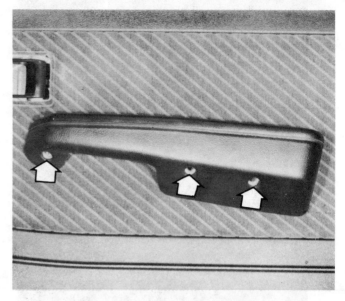

12.2b Remove the arm rest retaining screws (arrows)

Installation and adjustment

5 Installation is the reverse of removal.
6 Following installation of the door, check the alignment and adjust it if necessary as follows:
  a) Up-and-down and forward-and-backward adjustments are made by loosening the hinge-to-body bolts and moving the door as necessary.
  b) The door lock striker can also be adjusted both up-and-down and sideways to provide positive engagement with the lock mechanism. This is done by loosening the mounting bolts and moving the striker as necessary.

12 Door trim panel – removal and installation

Refer to illustrations 12.2a, 12.2b, 12.3a, 12.3b, 12.6, 12.8a and 12.8b
1 Disconnect the negative cable from the battery.
2 Remove all door trim panel retaining screws **(see illustration)** and door pull/armrest assemblies **(see illustration)**. **Note:** *On some CRX models, only the upper part of the armrest on the front and rear doors is removed.*
3 Remove the screw behind the door handle and remove the trim plate **(see illustration)**. On models equipped with manual window regulators, use a rag to release the spring clip on the regulator **(see illustration)**. On

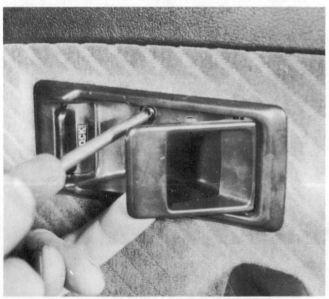

12.3a Lift the door handle out partially to access the screws holding the door handle trim plate

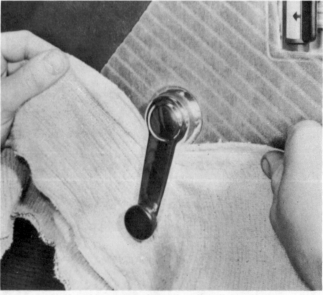

12.3b Use a rag to force the clip off the shaft

This photo sequence illustrates the repair of a dent and damaged paintwork. The procedure for the repair of a hole is similar. Refer to the text for more complete instructions

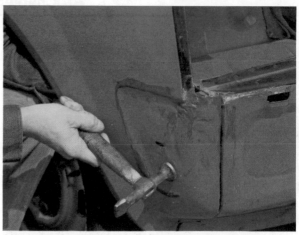

After removing any adjacent body trim, hammer the dent out. The damaged area should then be made slightly concave

Use coarse sandpaper or a sanding disc on a drill motor to remove all paint from the damaged area. Feather the sanded area into the edges of the surrounding paint, using progressively finer grades of sandpaper

The damaged area should be treated with rust remover prior to application of the body filler. In the case of a rust hole, all rusted sheet metal should be cut away

Carefully follow manufacturer's instructions when mixing the body filler so as to have the longest possible working time during application. Rust holes should be covered with fiberglass screen held in place with dabs of body filler prior to repair

Apply the filler with a flexible applicator in thin layers at 20 minute intervals. Use an applicator such as a wood spatula for confined areas. The filler should protrude slightly above the surrounding area

Shape the filler with a surform-type plane. Then, use water and progressively finer grades of sandpaper and a sanding block to wet-sand the area until it is smooth. Feather the edges of the repair area into the surrounding paint.

Use spray or brush applied primer to cover the entire repair area so that slight imperfections in the surface will be filled in. Prime at least one inch into the area surrounding the repair. Be careful of over-spray when using spray-type primer

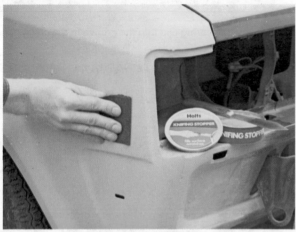

Wet-sand the primer with fine (approximately 400 grade) sandpaper until the area is smooth to the touch and blended into the surrounding paint. Use filler paste on minor imperfections

After the filler paste has dried, use rubbing compound to ensure that the surface of the primer is smooth. Prior to painting, the surface should be wiped down with a tack rag or lint-free cloth soaked in lacquer thinner

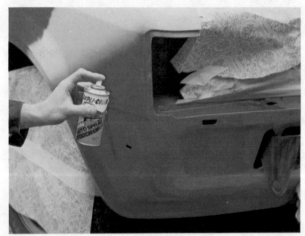

Choose a dry, warm, breeze-free area in which to paint and make sure that adjacent areas are protected from over-spray. Shake the spray paint can thoroughly and apply the top coat to the repair area, building it up by applying several coats, working from the center

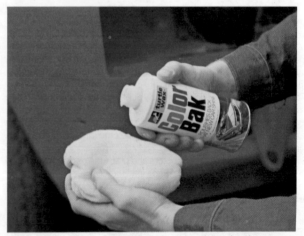

After allowing at least two weeks for the paint to harden, use fine rubbing compound to blend the area into the original paint. Wax can now be applied

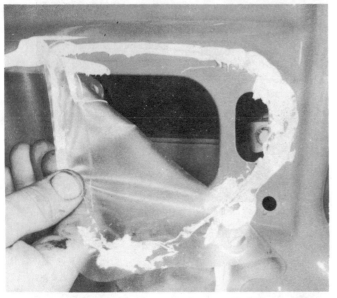

12.6   Carefully peel back the plastic cover. The putty can be reused to seal the plastic cover on reassembly

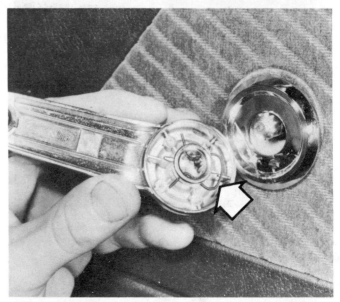

12.8a   Slide the spring clip into the groove in the crank handle

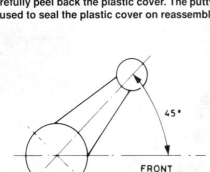

12.8b   Install the crank handle so it's at a 45-degree angle with the window closed

power regulator models, pry out the control switch assembly and unplug it.
4   Insert a putty knife between the trim panel and the door and disengage the retaining clips. Work around the outer edge until the panel is free.
5   Once all of the clips are disengaged, detach the trim panel, unplug any wire harness connectors and remove the trim panel from the vehicle **(see illustrations 11.4a and 11.4b)**.
6   For access to the inner door, carefully peel back the plastic cover **(see illustration)**.
7   Prior to installation of the door panel, be sure to reinstall any clips in the panel which may have come out during the removal procedure and remain in the door itself.
8   Plug in the wire harness connectors and place the panel in position in the door. Press the door panel into place until the clips are seated and install the armrest/door pulls. Install the manual regulator crank handle **(see illustrations)** or power window switch assembly.

---

13   Door latch, lock cylinder and handle – removal and installation

---

Inside door handle

Refer to illustration 13.2a and 13.2b
1   Remove the door trim panel and plastic shield (see Section 12).

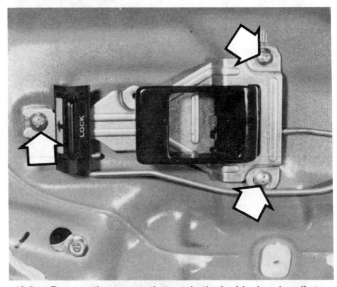

13.2a   Remove the screws that retain the inside door handle to the door

2   Remove the inside door handle retaining screws, disconnect the latch rod and rotate the handle out of the door **(see illustrations)**.
3   Installation is the reverse of removal.

Outside door handle

4   Remove the door trim panel and plastic shield (see Section 12).
5   Disconnect the operating rods attached to the outside door handle.
6   Remove the door handle retaining nuts or bolts and detach the handle from the door **(see illustration 13.2b)**.
7   Installation is the reverse of removal.

Latch

Refer to illustration 13.10
8   Remove the inside door handle (see Section 13).
9   Disconnect the operating rods from the latch.
10   Remove the three latch retaining screws located in the end of the door **(see illustration)**.
11   Detach the latch assembly from the door.
12   Installation is the reverse of removal.

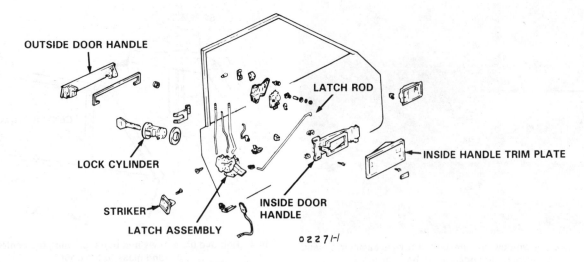

13.2b Door handle, latch and lock cylinder details

13.10 Use a Phillips screwdriver to remove the three latch retaining screws from the end of the door

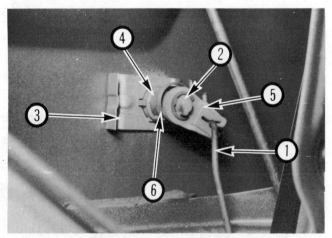

13.15 Door lock cylinder mounting details

1 Operating rod
2 Lock arm-to-lock cylinder circlip
3 Lock cylinder-to-door retaining clip
4 Lock cylinder
5 Lock arm

Lock cylinder

Refer to illustration 13.15

13 Remove the door trim panel and plastic shield (see Section 12).
14 Remove the outside door handle (see Steps 4 through 7).
15 Disconnect the operating rod, remove the retaining clip and withdraw the lock cylinder from the door (**see illustration**).
16 Installation is the reverse of removal.

---

14 Door window glass – removal, installation and adjustment

Removal and installation

Refer to illustrations 14.3a, 14.3b, 14.4 and 14.5

1 Remove the door trim panel and plastic shield (see Section 12).
2 Remove the inside door handle (see Section 13).
3 Lower the window so the rear mounting bolt can be reached through the access hole in the door (**see illustration**), then remove the front bolt (**see illustration**).

14.3a Lower the window to expose the window channel rear bolt through the access hole

14.3b   The other window channel bolt (arrow) is easily accessed through the opening in the door

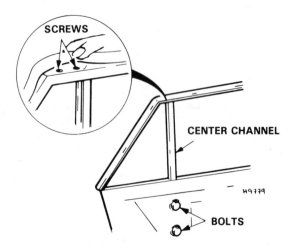

14.4   Remove the screws and bolts retaining the center channel and glass to the door

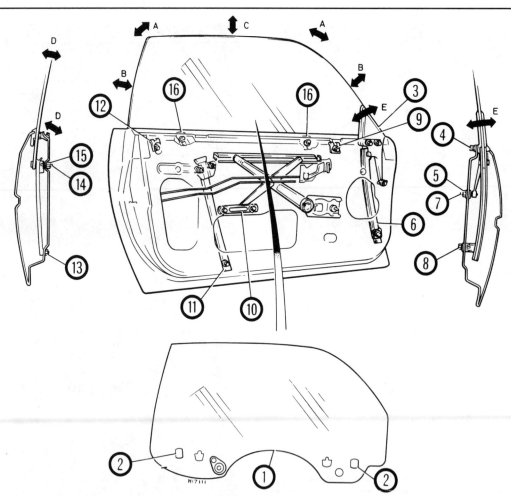

14.7   Window glass adjustment details

1	Glass	6	Front channel	12	Upper stopper	B	Forward\backward
2	Glass stopper	7	Adjuster	13	Nut		adjustment
3	Front sash	8	Bolt	14	Adjuster	C	Vertical adjustment
4	Bolt	9	Upper stopper	15	Locknut	D	Window-to-weatherstrip
5	Locknut	10	Regulator roller guide	16	Stabilizers		seal adjustment
		11	Door glass guide	A	Inclination adjustment	E	Front sash angle adjustment

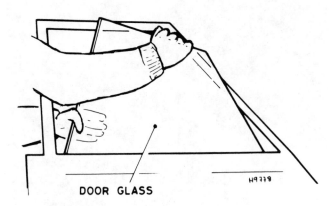

14.5   Lift the glass up out of the door while tilting it in

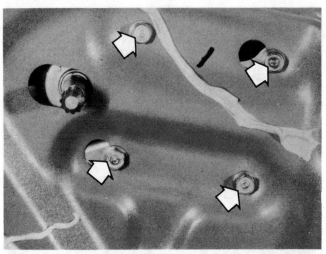

15.4a   Remove the four regulator bolts that are located near the regulator crank.

4   On rear doors, remove the retaining screws and bolts and detach the center channel and stationary glass **(see illustration)**.
5   Lift the door glass up and out of the door window slot, then tilt it and remove it from the door **(see illustration)**.
6   Installation is the reverse of removal.

Adjustment

Refer to illustration 14.7

7   Locate the adjusters on the door **(see illustration)**. Use an open end wrench and a screwdriver to vary the position of the door glass. Adjustment is largely a matter of trial and error until a uniform fit and seal of the glass has been achieved. The various adjustments are as follows:

  a Inclination adjustment – Alter the position of the regulator roller guide so that the glass moves vertically and has a uniform fit all around when closed.
  b Forward/backward adjustment – Move the door glass guide forward or backward until the rear edge of the glass when raised with the door closed is approximately 0.39 in (10.0 mm) from the weatherstrip retainer.
  c Vertical adjustment – Alter the position of the upper stoppers.
  d Window-to-weatherstrip seal adjustment – Use the door glass guides adjusters as necessary to achieve the correct position of the glass and the weatherstrip seal. Mark the position of the guide bolts otherwise the forward and backward adjustments will be upset.
  e Front sash angle adjustment – Loosen the front sash locknut and move the sash to follow the contour of the glass. Tighten the locknut when finished.

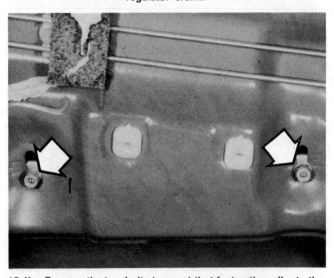

15.4b   Remove the two bolts (arrows) that fasten the roller to the door (located directly above the aperture).

15   Door window glass regulator assembly – removal, installation and adjustment

Refer to illustrations 15.4a and 15.4b

1   Remove the door trim panel and plastic shield (see Section 12).
2   Remove the inside door handle (see Section 13).
3   Remove the door window glass (see Section 14).
4   Loosen the front stopper bolt. Remove the retaining bolts **(see illustrations)** and withdraw the regulator mechanism through the access hole in the door. On power window models, unplug the electrical connector.
5   Prior to installation, lubricate all contact surfaces with multi-purpose grease. Installation is the reverse of removal.
6   To adjust the glass position, refer to Section 14.

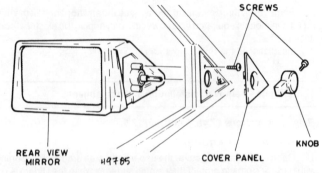

16.1   Exterior mirror mounting details

16   Outside mirror – removal and installation

Refer to illustrations 16.1 and 16.2

1   Remove the screw, pull off the knob, then pry off the cover panel **(see illustration)**. On some later models it may be necessary to remove the door trim panel (see Section 12) for access.

16.2   Remove the three mounting screws

17.4a   Remove the mounting stud from the support strut by unscrewing it from the frame with an open end wrench

17.4b   Remove the cup that covers the mounting bolt on the lower end of the support strut, then remove the bolt

17.5   Remove the bolts (arrows) from the hinges

2   Remove the three mounting screws **(see illustration)** and lift the mirror off. On models equipped with power mirrors, unplug the electrical connector.
3   Installation is the reverse of removal.

---

17   Liftgate – removal, installation and adjustment

Refer to illustrations 17.4a, 17.4b and 17.5

Removal and installation

1   Open the liftgate and cover the upper body area around the opening with pads or cloths to protect the painted surfaces when the liftgate is removed.
2   Disconnect all cables and wire harness connectors that would interfere with removal of the liftgate.
3   Paint or scribe around the hinge flanges.
4   While an assistant supports the liftgate, detach the support struts **(see illustrations)**.
5   Remove the hinge bolts and detach the liftgate from the vehicle **(see illustration)**.
6   Installation is the reverse of removal.

Adjustment

7   After installation, close the liftgate and make sure it's in proper alignment with the surrounding body panels. Adjustments are made by moving the position of the hinge studs in the slots. To adjust it, loosen the hinge nuts and reposition the hinges either side-to-side or fore-and-aft the desired amount and retighten the nuts.
8   The engagement of the liftgate can be adjusted by loosening the lock striker bolts, repositioning the striker and retightening the bolts.

---

18   Dashboard finish panels – removal and installation

Refer to illustrations 18.4a, 18.4b, 18.4c and 18.7

1   Disconnect the negative cable at the battery.
2   Remove the steering wheel (see Chapter 10).
3   Remove the access panel from under the steering column by removing the screws.
4   Remove the glovebox and the undertray – if equipped **(see illustrations)**.
5   Remove the ashtray.
6   Remove the radio (see Chapter 12).

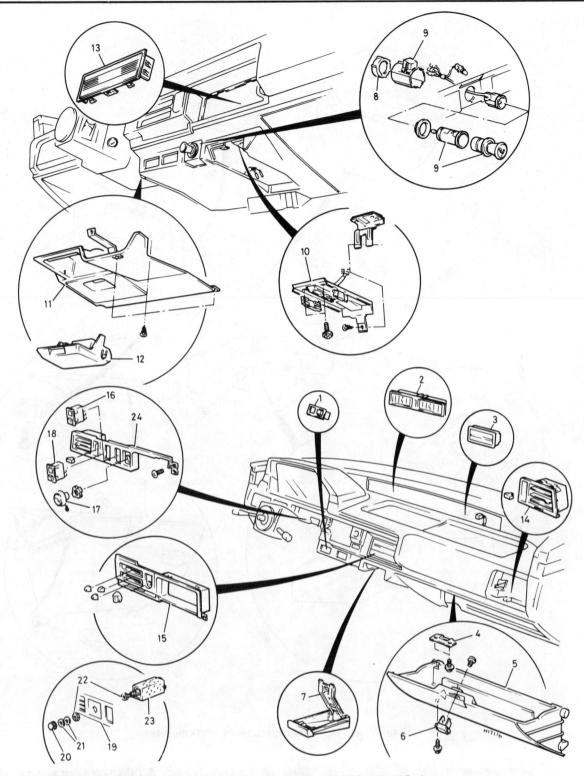

18.4a   Typical dashboard attachments – Hatchback and Sedan

1	Headlight wiper switch	8	Ringnut	14	Side air vent	20	Knob
2	Center air vent	9	Cigarette lighter assembly	15	Heater control face plate	21	Washers
3	Clock	10	Ashtray holder	16	Rear defroster switch	22	Ring nuts
4	Striker	11	Dash lower panel	17	Choke knob	23	Dashlight brightness
5	Glove box	12	Coin box	18	Rear fog light switch		control switch
6	Latch	13	Radio panel	19	Side panel	24	Side face panel
7	Ashtray						

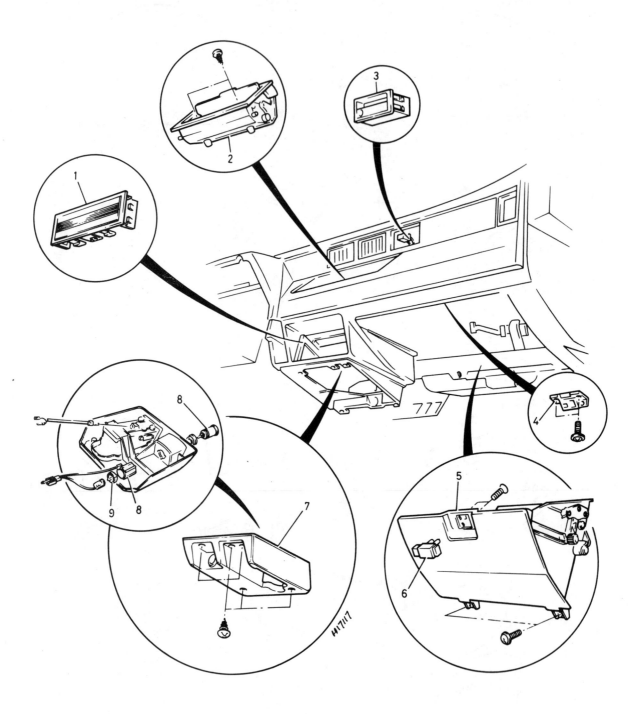

18.4b   Typical dashboard attachments – CRX models

1	Radio panel	4	Striker	7	Center lower panel
2	Center compartment	5	Glove box	8	Cigarette lighter assembly
3	Clock	6	Latch	9	Ring nut

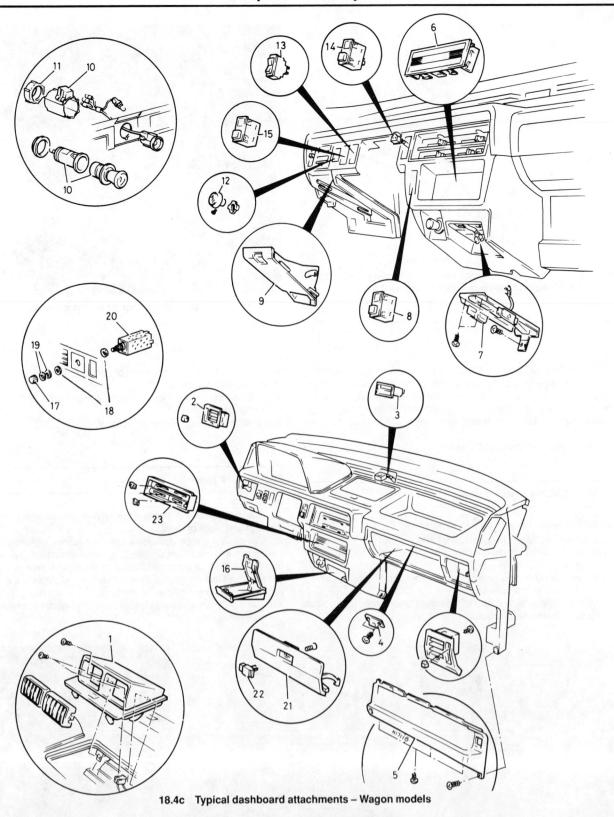

18.4c Typical dashboard attachments – Wagon models

1	Pop-up center air vent	7	Ashtray holder	13	Sunroof switch	19	Washers
2	Side air vent	8	Headlight wiper switch	14	Rear defroster switch	20	Dashlight brightness control
3	Clock	9	Coin box	15	Rear fog light switch		switch
4	Striker	10	Cigarette lighter assembly	16	Ashtray	21	Glove box lid
5	Undertray	11	Ring nut	17	Knob	22	Latch
6	Radio panel	12	Choke knob	18	Ring nuts	23	Heater control face plate

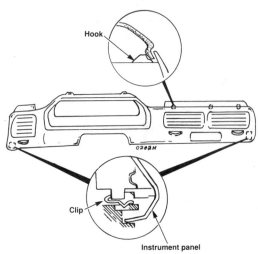

18.7   Use a dull screwdriver or a special upholstery tool to pry the hooks and the clips on the instrument panel

19.4a   Lift the rear lid off the console.

7   Remove the finish panels. **Note:** *The finish panels are fastened to the dashboard with screws, locking tabs, or side clips. Use caution when removing panels with locking tabs being careful not to break the plastic pieces off.* Use a dull screwdriver or upholstery remover to pry the tabs up. Use the same type of tool to remove the instrument panel clips **(see illustration)**.
8   Installation is the reverse of removal.

19   Center console – removal and installation

Refer to illustrations 19.4a, 19.4b, 19.4c and 19.4d
1   Disconnect the negative cable at the battery.
2   Remove the shift lever (automatic transmission) or shift handle (manual transmission).
3   If the vehicle is equipped with a front console, remove the mounting screws and lift out the console box.
4   Pry up the center cap and rear lid **(see illustration)**, then remove the retaining screws **(see illustrations)**.

5   Lift the console up partially, disconnect the electrical connector for the radio speaker balance control.
6   Lift the console over the handbrake lever and shift handle or shift lever assembly and remove it from the car.
7   Installation is the reverse of removal.

20   Seatbelt check

1   Check the seatbelts, buckles, latch plates and guide loops for obvious damage and signs of wear.
2   Check that the seatbelt reminder light comes on when the key is turned to the Run or Start positions. A chime should also sound.
3   The seatbelts are designed to lock up during a sudden stop or impact, yet allow free movement during normal driving. Make sure the retractors return the belt completely when the buckle is unlatched.
4   If any of the above checks reveal problems with the seatbelts, replace parts as necessary.

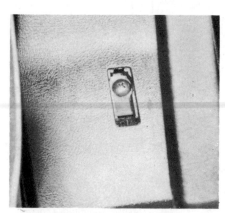

19.4b   Remove the screw directly under the emergency brake handle

19.4c   Remove the screws located on the side of the console

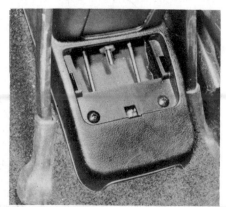

19.4d   Remove the console rear retaining screws.

Chapter 12 Chassis electrical system

Contents

1   General information

The electrical system is a 12-volt, negative ground type. Power for the lights and all electrical accessories is supplied by a lead/acid-type battery which is charged by the alternator.

This chapter covers repair and service procedures for the various electrical components not associated with the engine. Information on the battery, alternator, distributor and starter motor can be found in Chapter 5.

It should be noted that when portions of the electrical system are serviced, the negative battery cable should be disconnected from the battery to prevent electrical shorts and/or fires.

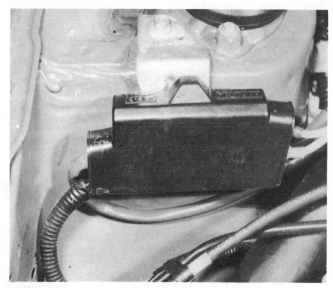

3.1a   On early models, the engine compartment fuse box is mounted to the right shock tower

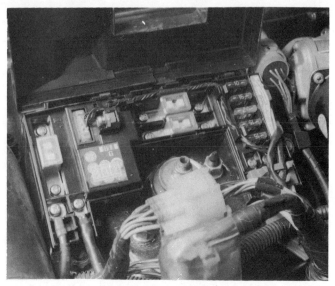

3.1b   On later models, the engine compartment fuse box is next to the battery

2   Electrical troubleshooting – general information

A typical electrical circuit consists of an electrical component, any switches, relays, motors, fuses, fusible links or circuit breakers related to that component and the wiring and connectors that link the component to both the battery and the chassis. To help you pinpoint an electrical circuit problem, wiring diagrams are included at the end of this book.

Before tackling any troublesome electrical circuit, first study the appropriate wiring diagrams to get a complete understanding of what makes up that individual circuit. Trouble spots, for instance, can often be narrowed down by noting if other components related to the circuit are operating properly. If several components or circuits fail at one time, chances are the problem is in a fuse or ground connection, because several circuits are often routed through the same fuse and ground connections.

Electrical problems usually stem from simple causes, such as loose or corroded connections, a blown fuse, a melted fusible link or a bad relay. Visually inspect the condition of all fuses, wires and connections in a problem circuit before troubleshooting it.

If testing instruments are going to be utilized, use the diagrams to plan ahead of time where you will make the necessary connections in order to accurately pinpoint the trouble spot.

The basic tools needed for electrical troubleshooting include a circuit tester or voltmeter (a 12-volt bulb with a set of test leads can also be used), a continuity tester, which includes a bulb, battery and set of test leads, and a jumper wire, preferably with a circuit breaker incorporated, which can be used to bypass electrical components. Before attempting to locate a problem with test instruments, use the wiring diagram(s) to decide where to make the connections.

Voltage checks

Voltage checks should be performed if a circuit is not functioning properly. Connect one lead of a circuit tester to either the negative battery terminal or a known good ground. Connect the other lead to a connector in the circuit being tested, preferably nearest to the battery or fuse. If the bulb of the tester lights, voltage is present, which means that the part of the circuit between the connector and the battery is problem free. Continue checking the rest of the circuit in the same fashion. When you reach a point at which no voltage is present, the problem lies between that point and the last test point with voltage. Most of the time the problem can be traced to a loose connection. **Note:** *Keep in mind that some circuits receive voltage only when the ignition key is in the Accessory or Run position.*

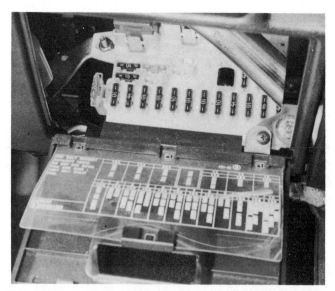

3.1c   The passenger compartment fuse box is accessible after pulling down the hinged access cover under the driver's side of the dashboard

Finding a short

One method of finding shorts in a circuit is to remove the fuse and connect a test light or voltmeter in its place to the fuse terminals. There should be no voltage present in the circuit. Move the wiring harness from side-to-side while watching the test light. If the bulb goes on, there is a short to ground somewhere in that area, probably where the insulation has rubbed through. The same test can be performed on each component in the circuit, even a switch.

Ground check

Perform a ground test to check whether a component is properly grounded. Disconnect the battery and connect one lead of a self-powered test light, known as a continuity tester, to a known good ground. Connect the other lead to the wire or ground connection being tested. If the bulb goes on, the ground is good. If the bulb does not go on, the ground is not good.

Continuity check

A continuity check is done to determine if there are any breaks in a circuit – if it is passing electricity properly. With the circuit off (no power in the circuit), a self-powered continuity tester can be used to check the circuit. Connect the test leads to both ends of the circuit (or to the "power" end and a good ground), and if the test light comes on the circuit is passing current properly. If the light doesn't come on, there is a break somewhere in the circuit. The same procedure can be used to test a switch, by connecting the continuity tester to the switch terminals. With the switch turned On, the test light should come on.

Finding an open circuit

When diagnosing for possible open circuits, it is often difficult to locate them by sight because oxidation or terminal misalignment are hidden by the connectors. Merely wiggling a connector on a sensor or in the wiring harness may correct the open circuit condition. Remember this when an open circuit is indicated when troubleshooting a circuit. Intermittent problems may also be caused by oxidized or loose connections.

Electrical troubleshooting is simple if you keep in mind that all electrical circuits are basically electricity running from the battery, through the wires, switches, relays, fuses and fusible links to each electrical component (light bulb, motor, etc.) and to ground, from which it is passed back to the battery. Any electrical problem is an interruption in the flow of electricity to and from the battery.

O228H

3.3   To test for a blown fuse, pull it out and inspect it for an open (1), then, with the fuse installed and the circuit activated, connect a test light across the terminals (2)

3   Fuses – general information

Refer to illustrations 3.1a, 3.1b, 3.1c and 3.3

The electrical circuits of the vehicle are protected by a combination of fuses, circuit breakers and fusible links. The two fuse blocks are located under the instrument panel on the left side of the dashboard and in the engine compartment **(see illustrations)**.

Each of the fuses is designed to protect a specific circuit, and the various circuits are identified on the fuse panel itself.

Miniaturized fuses are employed in the fuse block. These compact fuses, with blade terminal design, allow fingertip removal and replacement. If an electrical component fails, always check the fuse first. A blown fuse is easily identified through the clear plastic body. Visually inspect the element for evidence of damage **(see illustration)**. If a continuity check is called for, the blade terminal tips are exposed in the fuse body.

Be sure to replace blown fuses with the correct type. Fuses of different ratings are physically interchangeable, but only fuses of the proper rating should be used. Replacing a fuse with one of a higher or lower value than specified is not recommended. Each electrical circuit needs a specific amount of protection. The amperage value of each fuse is molded into the fuse body.

If the replacement fuse immediately fails, don't replace it again until the cause of the problem is isolated and corrected. In most cases, the cause will be a short circuit in the wiring caused by a broken or deteriorated wire.

4   Circuit breakers – general information

Circuit breakers protect components such as power windows, power door locks and headlights.

On some models the circuit breaker resets itself automatically, so an electrical overload in a circuit breaker protected system will cause the circuit to fail momentarily, then come back on. If the circuit does not come back on, check it immediately. Once the condition is corrected, the circuit breaker will resume its normal function. Some circuit breakers must be reset manually.

5   Relays – general information

Several electrical accessories in the vehicle use relays to transmit the electrical signal to the component. If the relay is defective, that component will not operate properly.

The various relays are grouped together in several locations. Some can be found attached to or near the dashboard fuse box. Others are in the engine compartment, near the battery.

If a faulty relay is suspected, it can be removed and tested by a dealer service department or a repair shop. Defective relays must be replaced as a unit.

6   Multi-function (turn signal/hazard/dimmer) switch – check and replacement

Check

Refer to illustrations 6.2a, 6.2b and 6.2c

1   Disconnect the electrical connector that leads to the Multi-function switch (Refer to steps 5 through 8).
2   Use an ohmmeter to check for continuity between the terminals on the Multi-function switch **(see illustrations)**. Refer to the tables and carefully position the switch (OFF, ON, LOW, INT, etc.) and check that for each setting the terminals that are connected by two circles and a line have continuity between them. For example, on 1984 through 1987 models, with the hazard switch in the OFF position and the turn signal switch in the neutral position, there should be continuity between the IG2 terminal and the RELAY IN terminal.
3   Check each switch and each step in order.
4   If the switch does not exhibit continuity on a particular circuit, replace the switch.

Replacement

Refer to illustration 6.7, 6.8a, 6.8b, 6.9 and 6.10

5   Disconnect the negative cable from the battery.
6   Remove the steering wheel (see Chapter 10).

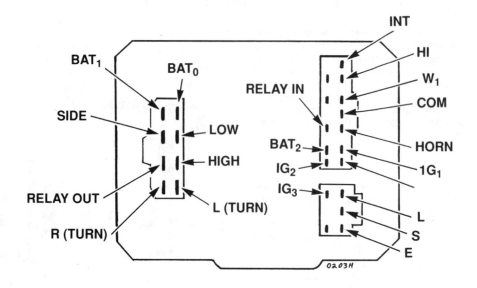

FRONT WIPER SWITCH

SWITCH POSITION		TERMINAL					
WIPER	MIST	HI	LO	E	COM	IG_1	INT
OFF	OFF		O—————O	O			
	ON	O		O			
INT	OFF		O———O		O	O———O	
	ON	O		O		O——O	
LO	OFF		O—O				
	ON	O——————O					
HI	OFF	O——————O					
	ON	O——————O					

FRONT WASHER SWITCH

SWITCH POSITION	TERMINAL	
	W_1	IG_1
OFF		
ON	O———O	

HAZARD/TURN SIGNAL SWITCH

SWITCH POSITION		TERMINAL					
HAZARD	TURN SIG.	BAT_2	IG_2	RELAY IN	RELAY OUT	R (TURN)	L (TURN)
OFF	R		O———O	O——O			
	NEUTRAL		O———O				
	L		O———O		O——O		O
ON		O———O		O——O——O			

HEADLIGHT SWITCH

SWITCH POSITION		TERMINAL		
	BAT_1	SIDE	BAT_0	HEAD
OFF				
	O———O			
	O———O		O———O	

DIMMER SWITCH

SWITCH POSITION	TERMINAL		
	HEAD	HIGH	LOW
HIGH	O———O		
LOW	O———————O		

PASSING LIGHT SWITCH

SWITCH POSITION	TERMINAL	
	BAT_0	HIGH
OFF		
ON	O———O	

REAR WIPER SWITCH

SWITCH POSITION	TERMINAL		
	L	S	E
OFF	O———O		
ON	O———————O		

REAR WASHER SWITCH

SWITCH POSITION	TERMINAL	
	IG_3	W_2
OFF		
ON	O———O	

6.2a   Continuity test tables and switch terminal locations for the Multi-function switch used on 1984 through 1987 models.

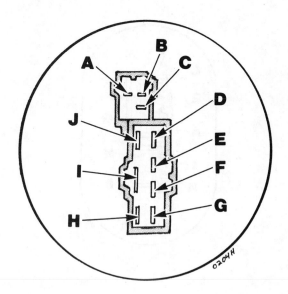

LIGHTING/DIMMER/PASSING SWITCH

SWITCH POSITION		TERMINAL				
		D	E	G	I	J
LIGHTING SWITCH	OFF					
		O——————O				
				O——————O		
DIMMER SWITCH	LOW			O——————O		
	HIGH			O——————O——————O		
PASSING SWITCH	OFF					
	ON				O——————O	

TURN SIGNAL SWITCH

SWITCH POSITION	TERMINAL		
	A	B	C
R	O——————————O		
NEUTRAL			
L	O——————O		

6.2b   Continuity test tables and switch terminal locations for the lighting and turn signal switches used on 1988 and later models

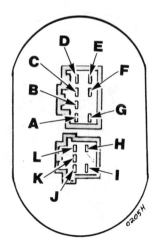

FRONT

SWITCH POSITION	TERMINAL						
	A	B	C	D	E	F	G
OFF	O————————————————————————O					O	
INT	O		O——————O			O	
LO	O———O						O
HI		O					O
Mist switch ON		O					O
Washer switch ON				O——————O		

REAR

SWITCH POSITION	TERMINAL				
	H	I	J	K	L
OFF			O——————O		
ON			O————————————O		O
Washer switch ON	O——————O		O————————————O		O

6.2c   Continuity test tables and switch terminal locations for the windshield washer/wiper switch used on 1988 and later models

6.7   Lift the cancelling sleeve off the steering shaft (arrow)

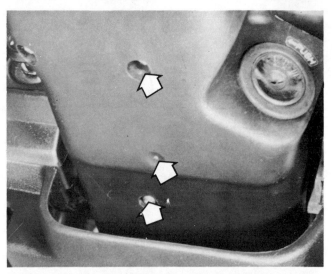

6.8a   Remove the screws from the steering column covers and be sure to mark the screws that are of different lengths

6.8b   Carefully remove the retaining ring

6.9   Remove the two combination switch screws

7   If equipped, lift off the direction indicator cancelling sleeve from the steering shaft **(see illustration)**.
8   Remove the steering column cover retaining screws **(see illustration)** and retaining ring **(see illustration)** and remove the covers.
9   Remove the two screws from the steering column to detach the combination switch **(see illustration)**.
10   Disconnect the electrical connectors and remove the combination switch from the steering column **(see illustration)**.
11   Installation is the reverse of removal. **Note:** *When installing, make sure the cancelling sleeve is fully depressed in the OFF position.*

---

7   Ignition switch/key lock cylinder – check and replacement

Check

1   Remove the dashboard lower panel.
2   Disconnect the electrical connectors from the ignition switch.

1984 through 1987

3   Turn the ignition key to position I and hook up an ohmmeter or continuity tester between the ACC (white/red wire) and BAT (white wire) terminals on the ignition switch side of the connector. There should be continuity.

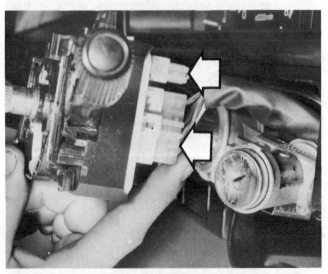

6.10   Disconnect the electrical connectors (arrows) from the backside of the combination switch

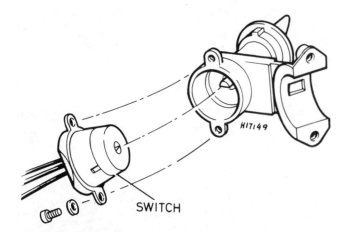

7.13   The ignition switch is held to the housing by two screws

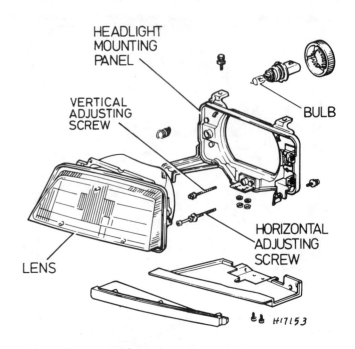

8.4a   A typical bulb-type headlight assembly – exploded view

4   Turn the ignition key to position II and hook up an ohmmeter or continuity tester between the ACC (white/red wire) and BAT (white wire) terminals in the ignition switch side of the connector, then connect the tester between the 1G1 (black/yellow wire) and IG2 (black/yellow wire) terminals. Lastly, connect the tester between the BAT (white wire) and the IG1 (black/yellow wire) terminals. There should be continuity at all connections.
5   Turn the ignition key to position III and hook up an ohmmeter or continuity tester between the BAT (white wire) terminal and the IG1 (black/yellow wire) terminal. Then connect the tester between the IG1 (black/yellow wire) terminal and the ST (black/white wire) terminal. There should be continuity at all connections.

1988 on
Note: *The electrical connectors for the ignition switch are located on the dash fuse box and the main wire harness.*

6   Turn the ignition key to position I and hook up an ohmmeter or continuity tester between the ACC terminal (white/red wire – located on the four-prong connector) and BAT-B terminal (white/black wire – located on the five-prong connector). There should be continuity.
7   Turn the ignition key to position II and perform the following checks:
   a) Hook up an ohmmeter or continuity tester between the ACC terminal and IG2-B terminal (blue/white wire – located on the five-prong connector). There should be continuity.
   b) Hook up the tester between the IG2-B terminal and the BAT-B terminal. There should be continuity.
   c) Connect the tester between the BAT-A terminal (White wire – located on the five-prong connector) and the IG1 terminal (black/yellow wire – located on the four-prong connector). There should be continuity.
   d) Connect the tester between the IG1 terminal and the IG2-A terminal (yellow wire – located on the four-prong connector). There should be continuity.
8   Turn the ignition key to position III and perform the following checks:
   a) Connect an ohmmeter or continuity tester between the BAT-A terminal and the IG1 terminal. There should be continuity.
   b) Connect the tester between the IG1 terminal and the ST terminal (black/white wire – located on the four-prong connector). There should be continuity.
9   Reconnect the electrical connectors and install the dashboard lower panel.

Replacement
Ignition switch
Refer to illustration 7.13
10   Disconnect the negative cable from the battery.
11   Remove the steering column covers (see Section 6) and the lower dash panel.

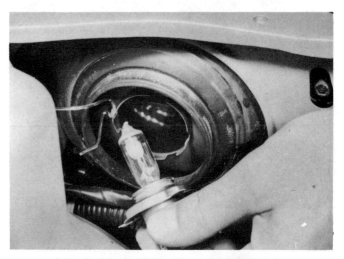

8.4b   Pull the bulb from the headlight assembly

12   Make sure the ignition switch is in the 0 position.
13   Unplug the ignition switch electrical connector, remove the two retaining screws and lift the switch from the steering column **(see illustration)**.
14   Installation is the reverse of removal. When placing the switch in position, make sure the recess on the switch is aligned with the projection on the lock.

Ignition lock cylinder – 1984 through 1987
Note: *These models are not equipped to release the key lock cylinder from the housing. The ignition lock cylinder (key lock cylinder and the housing) must be removed as a complete unit from the steering column.*
15   Remove the steering column covers (see Section 6).
16   Disconnect the electrical connector at the ignition switch.
17   Center punch the two shear screws and drill their heads off with a 3/8 inch drill bit.
18   Remove the lock cylinder from the steering column.
19   Install the new ignition lock cylinder with new shear bolts. **Note:** *Be sure the ignition switch projection lines up with the hole in the steering column.*
20   Tighten the shear screws until the heads twist off.

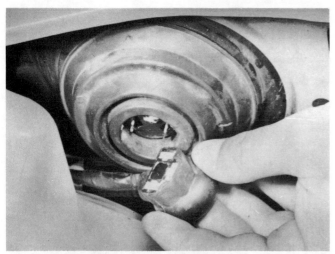

8.7   Disconnect the electrical connector from the back of the headlight (sealed beam type shown)

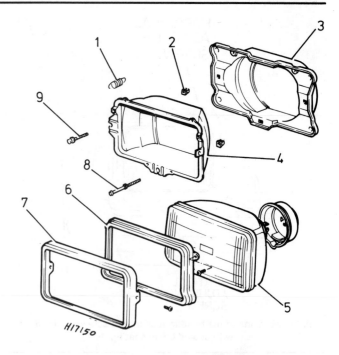

H17150

8.8   Sealed beam type headlight assembly – exploded view

1	Spring	6	Retaining ring
2	Nylon nut	7	Headlight trim
3	Headlight mounting panel	8	Vertical adjustment screw
4	Mount ring	9	Horizontal adjustment screw
5	Sealed beam		

Ignition key lock cylinder – 1988 on

Note: *On 1990 automatic transaxle Civics and Wagons, the key lock cylinder does not separate from the housing. Refer to the previous proce- dure (Steps 15 through 20) to remove the lock cylinder and housing assembly from the steering column.*

21   Remove the steering wheel (see Chapter 10) and the steering column covers (see Section 6).
22   Turn the ignition key to position I.
23   Press the pin located on the top of the lock cylinder housing and pull the lock cylinder out.
24   To install the cylinder, turn the key to the 0 position and align the lock cylinder with the housing.
25   Turn the key almost to the I position and insert the lock cylinder until the pin touches the body.
26   Now turn the key to the I position, push the pin and insert the lock cylinder into the housing until the pin "clicks" into place.

8   Headlights – removal and installation

Refer to illustrations 8.4a, 8.4b, 8.7 and 8.8
1   Disconnect the negative cable from the battery.

Bulb-type (aerodynamic) headlights

Warning: *The halogen gas filled bulbs used on these models are under pressure and may shatter if the surface is scratched or the bulb is dropped. Wear eye protection and handle the bulbs carefully, grasping only the base whenever possible.*
2   Open the hood.
3   Reach behind the headlight assembly and disconnect the electrical connector.
4   Pry back the spring clips or grasp the bulb locking ring and turn it counterclockwise to remove it **(see illustration)**. Lift out the bulb **(see illustration)**.
5   Installation is the reverse of removal.

Sealed beam headlights

6   Open the hood
7   Disconnect the electrical connector at the rear of the headlight **(see illustration)**.
8   Remove the trim and retaining ring and carefully remove the headlight **(see illustration)**. Do not disturb the adjusting screws or the headlight aim will be altered.
9   Installation is the reverse of removal.

9   Headlights – adjustment

Refer to illustration 9.1
Note: *The headlights must be aimed correctly. If adjusted incorrectly they could blind the driver of an oncoming vehicle and cause a serious accident or seriously reduce your ability to see the road. The headlights should be checked for proper aim every 12 months and any time a new headlight is installed or front end body work is performed. It should be emphasized that the following procedure is only an interim step which will provide tempo- rary adjustment until the headlights can be adjusted by a properly equipped shop.*
1   Headlights have two spring-loaded adjusting screws, one on the bot- tom controlling up-and-down movement and one on the side controlling left-and-right movement (see the accompanying illustration and illustra- tion 8.4a).
2   There are several methods of adjusting the headlights. The simplest method requires a blank wall 25 feet in front of the vehicle and a level floor.
3   Position masking tape vertically on the wall in reference to the vehicle centerline and the centerlines of both headlights.
4   Position a horizontal tape line in reference to the centerline of all the headlights. **Note:** *It may be easier to position the tape on the wall with the vehicle parked only a few inches away.*
5   Adjustment should be made with the vehicle sitting level, the gas tank half-full and no unusually heavy load in the vehicle.
6   Starting with the low beam adjustment, position the high intensity zone so it is two inches below the horizontal line and two inches to the right of the headlight vertical line. Adjustment is made by turning the adjusting screw at the top or bottom of the headlight to raise or lower the beam. The adjusting screw on the side should be used in the same manner to move the beam left or right.
7   With the high beams on, the high intensity zone should be vertically centered with the exact center just below the horizontal line. **Note:** *It may not be possible to position the headlight aim exactly for both high and low*

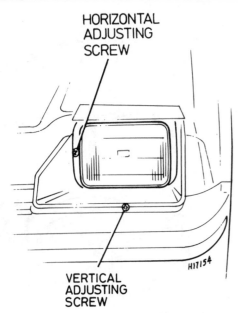

9.1   Locations of the headlight adjusting screws on models with sealed beam headlights

beams. *If a compromise must be made, keep in mind that the low beams are the most used and have the greatest effect on safety.*
8   Have the headlights adjusted by a dealer service department or service station at the earliest opportunity.

10   Bulb replacement

Refer to illustrations 10.1a, 10.1b, 10.2, 10.3a, 10.3b, 10.3c and 10.4
1   The lenses of many lights are held in place by screws, which makes it a simple procedure to gain access to the bulbs **(see illustrations)**.
2   On some lights the lenses are held in place by clips. The lenses can be removed either by unsnapping them or by using a small screwdriver to pry them off **(see illustration)**.
3   Several types of bulbs are used. Some are removed by pushing in and turning them counterclockwise **(see illustrations)**. Others can simply be unclipped from the terminals or pulled straight out of the socket.

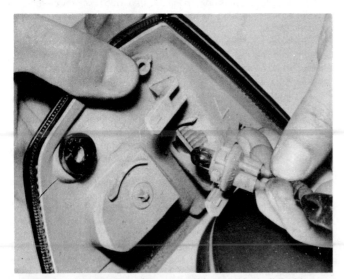

10.1b   . . . pull off the lens assembly, turn the bulb holder counterclockwise and detach the bulb holder from the lens – the bulb pulls straight out of the bulb holder

10.1a   To replace a side marker bulb, remove these two screws (arrows) . . .

4   To gain access to the instrument panel lights **(see illustration)**, the instrument cluster will have to be removed first (see Section 12).

11   Radio and antenna – removal and installation

Refer to illustrations 11.6a and 11.6b
1   Disconnect the negative cable from the battery.

Radio

2   Remove the front console or dashboard trim panel, depending on where the radio is mounted (see Chapter 11).
3   Remove the radio and mounting plate screws, lower the radio, unplug the electrical connector and antenna lead, then pull the radio out of the dashboard.
4   Installation is the reverse of removal.

Antenna

5   On manual antenna models, disconnect the antenna lead at the radio (see above). On power antenna models, extend the antenna and disconnect the cable from the antenna motor.

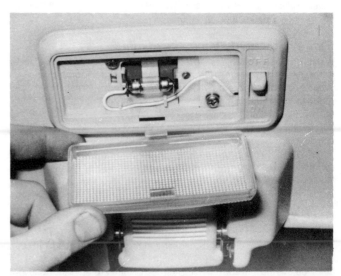

10.2   Pry off the interior light lens for access to the bulb, which can be unclipped from the terminals

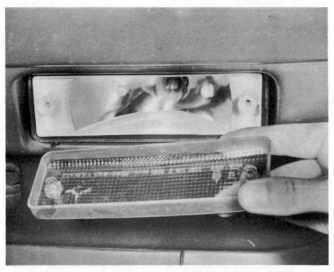

10.3a   To remove the front turn signal bulb, remove the screws, pull off the lens, then push in on the bulb and turn it counterclockwise 1/4-turn

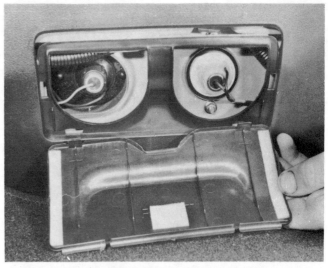

10.3b   Remove the cover inside the vehicle for access to the tail light bulbs

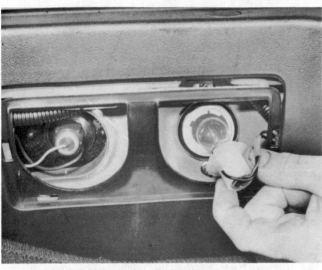

10.3c   Pull the tail light bulb holder from the housing after twisting it counterclockwise

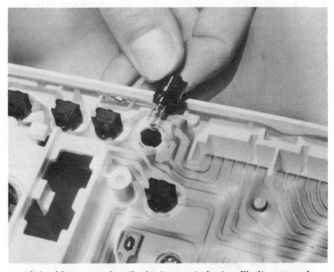

10.4   After removing the instrument cluster, flip it over and replace the bulbs by rotating them and pulling them out

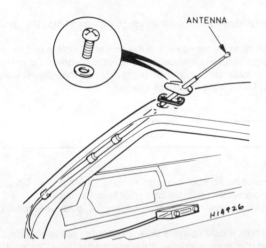

11.6a   After attaching a string or wire to the lead (to make installing the new one easier), remove the antenna screws and pull the assembly out of the body pillar

11.6b   Remove the antenna mounting screws

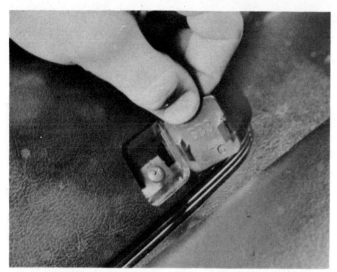

12.4a   The blanking plates are located on top of the instrument cluster hood . . .

12.4b   . . . and at the bottom – 1988 and later Civics don't have blanking plates or screws at the bottom

6   Connect a piece of string or thin wire to the antenna lead **(see illustration)** (at the radio end) or the cable (at the motor end). Remove the mounting screws **(see illustration)** and pull the antenna and lead out of the body pillar.

7   Fasten the wire or string to the lead or cable of the new antenna. Lower the antenna into place while pulling the new lead or cable into the pillar with the wire or string.

8   Disconnect the string or wire and connect the antenna lead or cable to the radio or motor. Install the antenna mounting screws.

12   Instrument cluster – removal and installation

Refer to illustrations 12.4a, 12.4b, 12.8, 12.9a and 12.9b

1   Disconnect the negative cable from the battery.

2   Remove the steering wheel (see Chapter 10).

3   Remove the steering column upper and lower covers (see illustrations 6.8a and 6.8b).

4   Pry out the blanking plates which cover the screws in the instrument cluster hood **(see illustrations)**.

5   Remove the screws from the instrument panel hood.

6   On some models it will be necessary to remove the instrument cluster switches (the dashlight brightness controller and the rear window defogger switch) by prying up at the bottom of each with a screwdriver. Pull the switches out and unplug the electrical connectors.

7   Remove the remaining screws from the instrument panel and remove the instrument panel.

8   Remove the four retaining screws **(see illustration)** and pull the instrument cluster out partially.

9   Pull the cluster out and unplug the electrical connector **(see illustration)**. Disconnect the speedometer cable **(see illustration)** to free the cluster.

10   The instrument cluster can now be easily serviced or the bulbs changed (see Section 10).

11   Installation is the reverse of removal.

13   Speedometer cable – replacement

1   Disconnect the negative cable from the battery.

2   Remove the instrument cluster from the dashboard (see Section 12) and disconnect the speedometer **(see illustration 12.9b)**.

3   Working under the dashboard, remove the undercover panel and release the speedometer cable grommet and boot from the firewall.

12.8   Remove the four screws that retain the instrument cluster

4   Feed the speedometer cable through the firewall into the engine compartment.

5   Working at the transaxle, pull the boot up the cable and extract the spring clip that retains the speedometer cable. **Caution:** *Do not remove the bolt or lockplate or the pinion might drop into the transmission.*

6   Installation is the reverse of removal.

14   Horn – check and replacement

Check

1   Remove the front bumper to gain access to the horn (see Chapter 11).

2   Disconnect the electrical connector from the horn.

3   Use fused jumper wires to apply battery voltage to the terminals of the horn.

4   The horn should sound. If the horn does not sound, replace it.

5   If the horn sounds, remove the steering wheel (see Chapter 10) and turn it over.

6   Check for continuity between the contact ring and hub core on the steering wheel with the horn switch pressed.

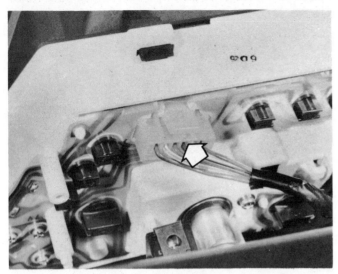

12.9a Disconnect any electrical connectors from the back of
the instrument cluster

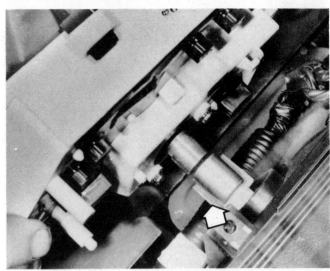

12.9b Push down on the plastic retainer clip and disconnect the
speedometer cable from the cluster

7   If there is no continuity, repair the horn switch.
8   If there's continuity, the problem is likely in the wiring between the
switch and horn or the battery and the horn. Look for loose and corroded
connections.

Replacement

9   Remove the front bumper (see Chapter 11).
10   Disconnect the electrical connectors from the horn.
11   Remove the nut that retains the horn to the chassis and remove the
horn.
12   Installation is the reverse of removal.

**15   Windshield wiper/washer switch and motor – check
and replacement**

Check

1   If the windshield wipers don't work, check the following:
  a) Check for looseness and corrosion at the wiper motor connections.
     Also check the fuse or circuit breaker.
  b) Connect a jumper wire between the wiper motor and ground, then
     retest. If the motor now works, repair the wiper motor ground con-
     nection.
  c) If the motor still doesn't work, turn on the wipers and check for volt-
     age at the wiper motor's electrical connector. If there's voltage at
     the motor, remove the motor (see below) and check it off the vehicle
     with fused jumper wires from the battery. If the motor now works,
     check the wipers for binding linkage. If the motor still doesn't work,
     replace it.
  d) If there's no voltage at the motor, check the switch (see Section 6).
     If the switch is OK, there's most likely a problem in the wiring.
2   If the windshield washer won't work, check the following
  a) Check the washer fluid level. If it's OK, turn on the washer pump
     with the ignition switch on but the engine off. Listen for the sound
     of the pump operating.
  b) If you can't hear the pump operating, check the pump motor. On
     most models, the motor is integral with the washer fluid reservoir.
     To test it, disconnect the electrical connector and hook up fused
     jumper wires from the battery. If the motor now works, the problem
     is in the switch or the wiring. See Section 6 to test the switch.
  c) If you can hear the pump operating but no fluid is being expelled
     from the washer nozzles, trace the hoses and lines between the

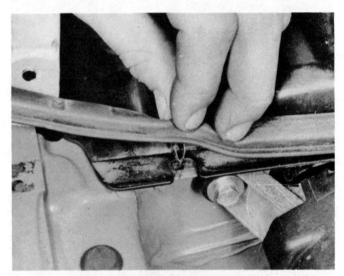

15.5 Be careful not to separate the clips from the rubber
weatherstrip when removing it

pump and nozzles to be sure there's none kinked, damaged or dis-
     connected.
  d) If the hoses and lines are OK, disconnect a hose as close to a
     nozzle as possible and operate the washer again. If a strong
     stream of fluid is expelled from the end of the hose, the nozzle is
     probably clogged. Often, nozzles can be unclogged by inserting a
     pin or paper clip into the hole in the end. If this doesn't unclog the
     nozzle, replace it.
  e) If there's no fluid being expelled from the hose, trace it back to the
     pump and disconnect it there. Operate the washer again. If a strong
     stream of fluid is expelled from the pump, there's a clog in the line
     between the pump and nozzle(s). If no fluid is being expelled from
     the pump, but you can hear it operating, replace the pump.

Replacement

Refer to illustrations 15.5, 15.6, 15.7, 15.8a and 15.8b

3   Disconnect the negative cable from the battery.
4   Remove the retaining nuts and detach the wiper arms.
5   Open the hood and remove the rubber weatherstrip from the cowl
area **(see illustration)**.

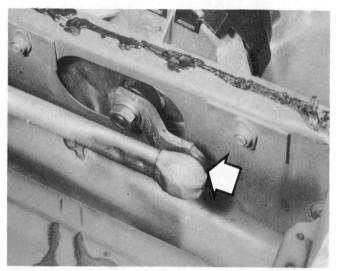

15.6   Use a screwdriver to separate the linkage (arrow) from the wiper motor arm

15.7   Remove the plastic boot (arrow) from the windshield wiper motor

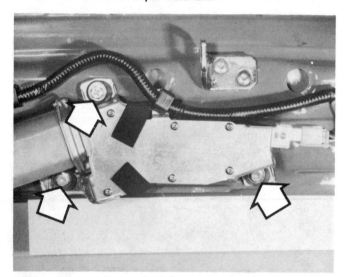

15.8a   Remove the wiper motor mounting bolts (arrows) (early model shown)

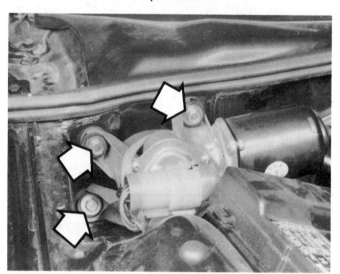

15.8b   Remove the wiper motor mounting bolts (arrows) (later model shown)

6   Disconnect the linkage from the ball connector **(see illustration)** on the wiper motor arm.

7   Remove the plastic boot (if equipped) from the windshield wiper motor **(see illustration)**.

8   Unplug the electrical connector, remove the retaining bolts and lift the wiper motor from the engine compartment **(see illustrations)**.

9   Prior to installation, lubricate the contact points of the wiper linkage with multi-purpose grease. Installation is the reverse of removal.

16   Power door lock system – description and check

The power door lock system operates the door lock actuators mounted in each door. The system consists of the switches, actuators and associated wiring. Since special tools and techniques are required to diagnose the system, it should be left to a dealer service department or a repair shop. However, it is possible for the home mechanic to make simple checks of the wiring connections and actuators for minor faults which can be easily repaired. These include:

  a) Check the system fuse and/or circuit breaker.
  b) Check the switch wires for damage and loose connections. Check the switches for continuity.

  c) Remove the door panel(s) and check the actuator wiring connections to see if they're loose or damaged. Inspect the actuator rods (if equipped) to make sure they aren't bent or damaged. Inspect the actuator wiring for damaged or loose connections. The actuator can be checked by applying battery power momentarily. A discernible click indicates that the solenoid is operating properly.

17   Power window system – description and check

The power window system operates the electric motors mounted in the doors which lower and raise the windows. The system consists of the control switches, the motors (regulators), glass mechanisms and associated wiring.

Because of the complexity of the power window system and the special tools and techniques required for diagnosis, repair should be left to a dealer service department or a repair shop. However, it is possible for the home mechanic to make simple checks of the wiring connections and motors for minor faults which can be easily repaired. These include:

  a) Inspect the power window actuating switches for broken wires and loose connections.
  b) Check the power window fuse and/or circuit breaker.

c) Remove the door panel(s) and check the power window motor wires to see if they're loose or damaged. Inspect the glass mechanisms for damage which could cause binding.

18   Cruise control system – description and check

The cruise control system maintains vehicle speed with a vacuum actuated servo motor located in the engine compartment, which is connected to the throttle linkage by a cable. The system consists of the servo motor, clutch switch, brake switch, control switches, a relay and associated vacuum hoses.

Because of the complexity of the cruise control system and the special tools and techniques required for diagnosis, repair should be left to a dealer service department or a repair shop. However, it is possible for the home mechanic to make simple checks of the wiring and vacuum connections for minor faults which can be easily repaired. These include:

a) Inspect the cruise control actuating switches for broken wires and loose connections.
b) Check the cruise control fuse.
c) The cruise control system is operated by vacuum so it's critical that all vacuum switches, hoses and connections are secure. Check the hoses in the engine compartment for tight connections, cracks and obvious vacuum leaks.

19   Wiring diagrams – general information

Refer to illustration 19.4

Since it isn't possible to include all wiring diagrams for every year covered by this manual, the following diagrams are those that are typical and most commonly needed.

Prior to troubleshooting any circuits, check the fuse and circuit breakers (if equipped) to make sure they're in good condition. Make sure the battery is properly charged and check the cable connections (Chapter 1).

When checking a circuit, make sure that all connectors are clean, with no broken or loose terminals. When unplugging a connector, do not pull on the wires. Pull only on the connector housings themselves.

Refer to the accompanying table for the wire color codes applicable to your vehicle. **Note:** *When a circled number appears on an auxiliary diagram a corresponding number will be found on the main wiring diagram identifying the point where the circuits connect.*

Bl	Black
Y	Yellow
Bu	Blue
G	Green
R	Red
W	White
Br	Brown
O	Orange
Lb	Light blue
Lg	Light green
P	Pink
Gr	Grey
Sw	Switch
Pl	Pilot light

19.4   Wiring diagram color codes

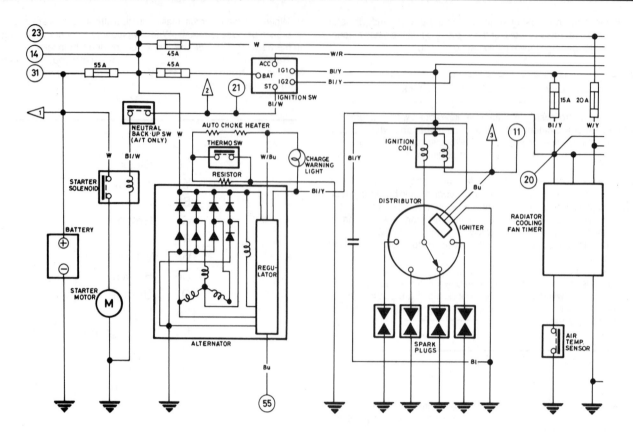

Main wiring diagram – Hatchback and Sedan (1984 through 1987)

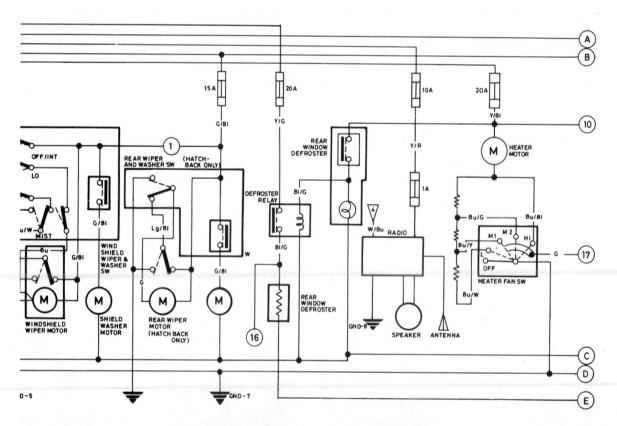

Main wiring diagram – Hatchback and Sedan (continued)

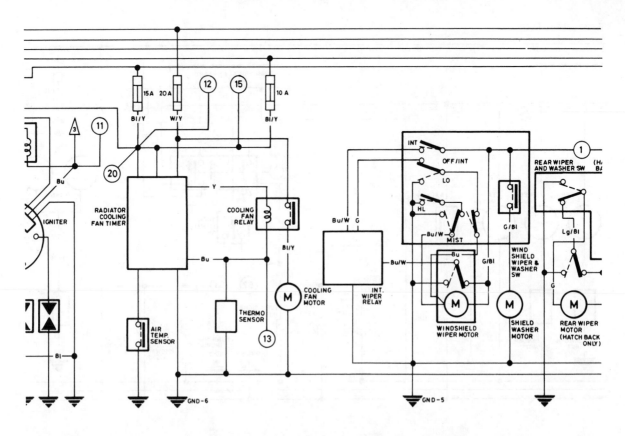

Main wiring diagram – Hatchback and Sedan (continued)

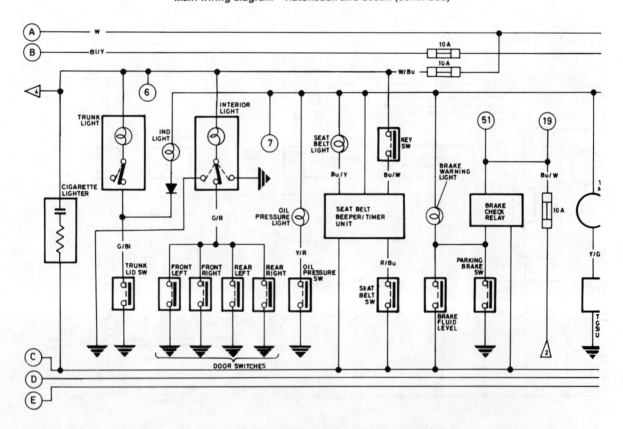

Main wiring diagram – Hatchback and Sedan (continued)

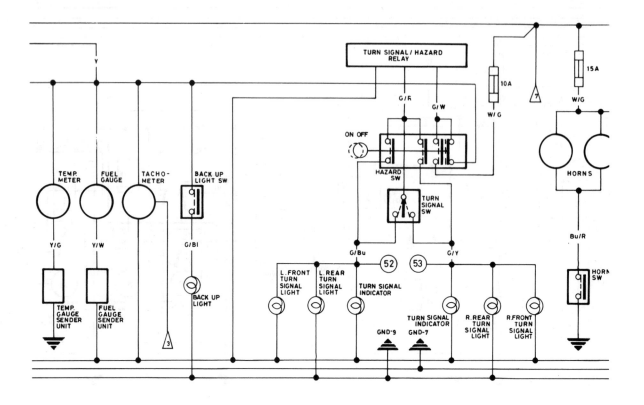

Main wiring diagram – Hatchback and Sedan (continued)

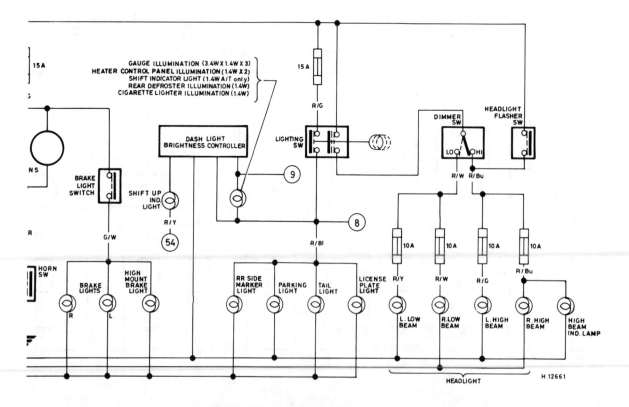

Main wiring diagram – Hatchback and Sedan (continued)

AIR CONDITIONER CIRCUIT (Carb)

CLOCK CIRCUIT

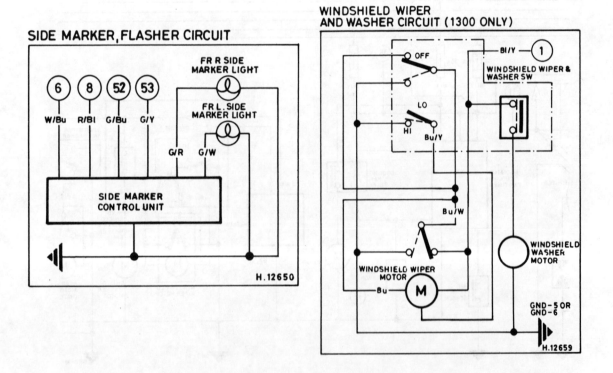

Auxiliary wiring diagram – Hatchback and Sedan (continued)

SIDE MARKER, FLASHER CIRCUIT

WINDSHIELD WIPER
AND WASHER CIRCUIT (1300 ONLY)

Auxiliary wiring diagram – Hatchback and Sedan (continued)

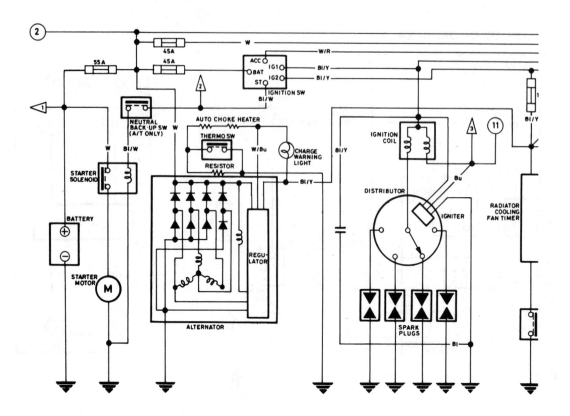

Main wiring diagram – Wagon (1984 through 1987)

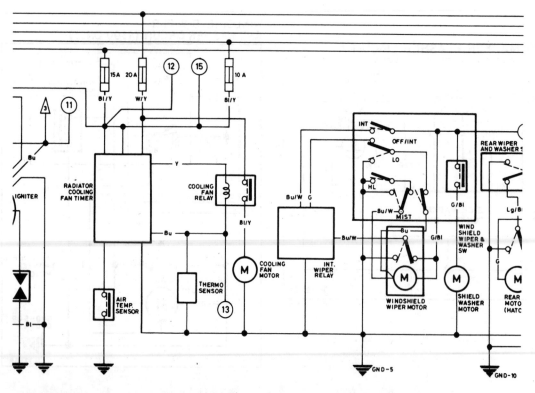

Main wiring diagram – Wagon (continued)

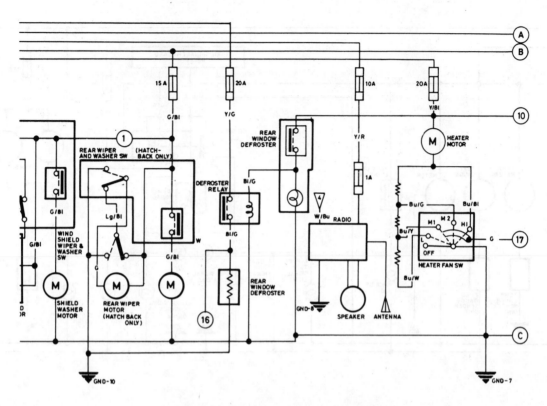

Main wiring diagram – Wagon (continued)

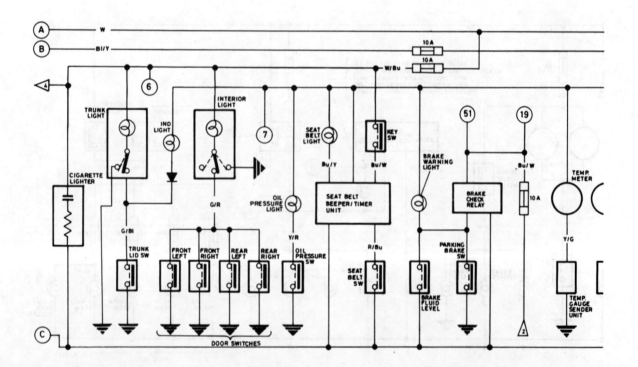

Main wiring diagram – Wagon (continued)

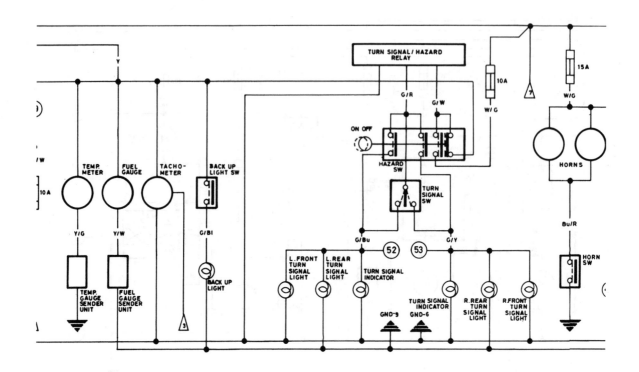

Main wiring diagram – Wagon (continued)

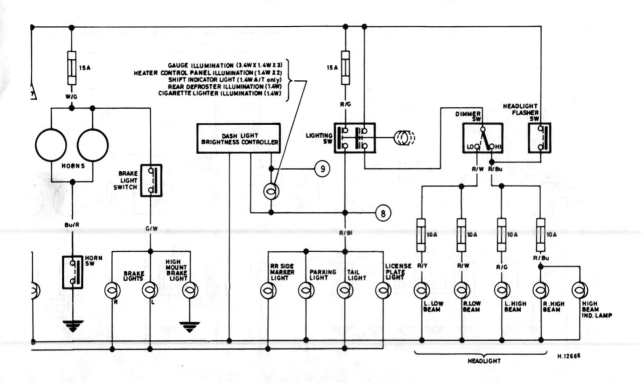

Main wiring diagram – Wagon (continued)

AIR CONDITIONER CIRCUIT

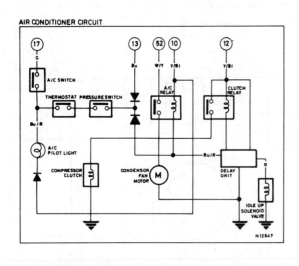

SIDE MARKER, FLASHER CIRCUIT

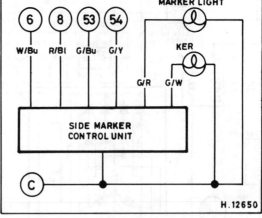

SUNROOF CIRCUIT

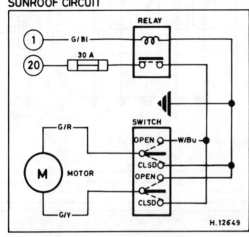

TAILGATE OPENER CIRCUIT

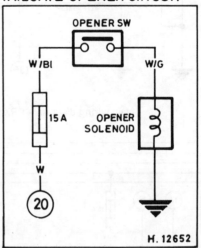

CLOCK CIRCUIT

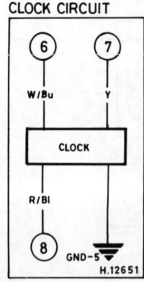

4 WD CIRCUIT

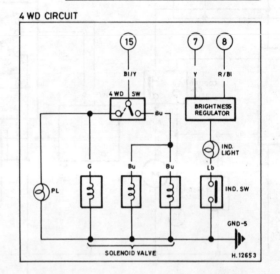

Auxiliary wiring diagram – Wagon (continued)

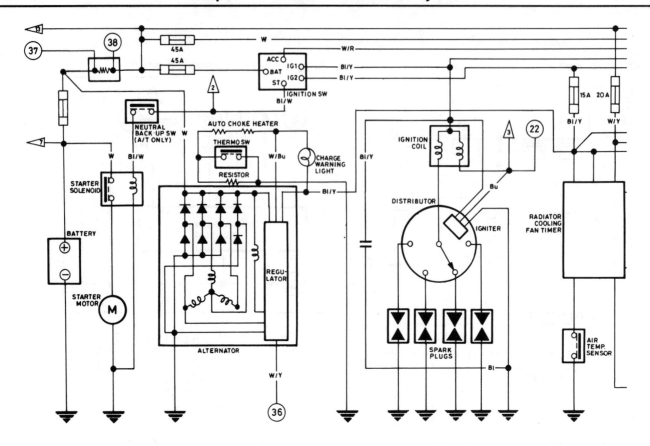

Main wiring diagram – CRX (carbureted models) (1985 through 1987)

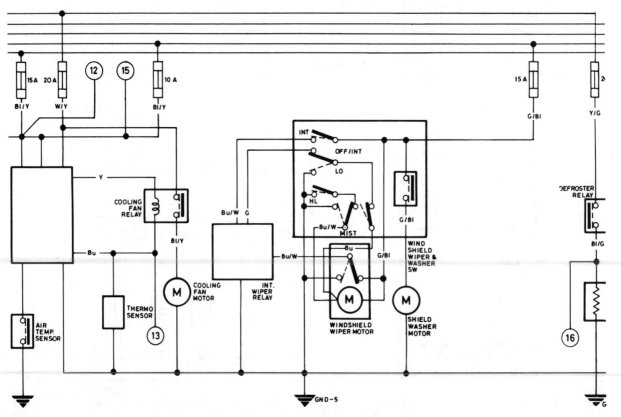

Main wiring diagram – CRX (carbureted models) (continued)

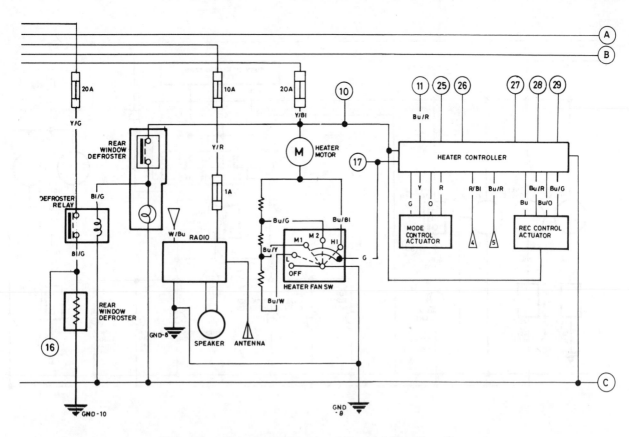

Main wiring diagram – CRX (carbureted models) (continued)

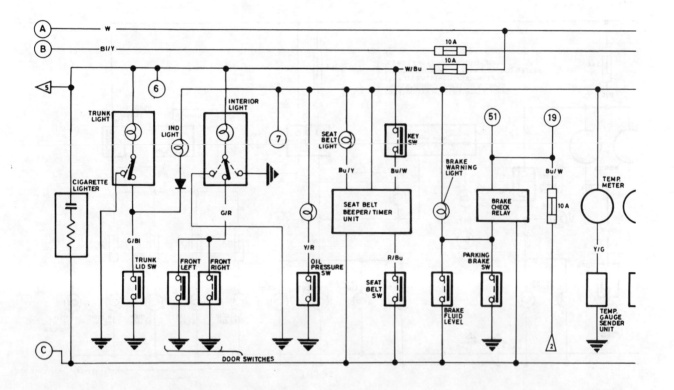

Main wiring diagram – CRX (carbureted models) (continued)

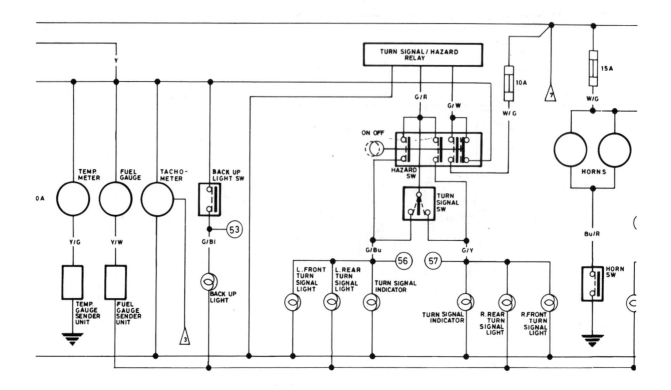

Main wiring diagram – CRX (carbureted models) (continued)

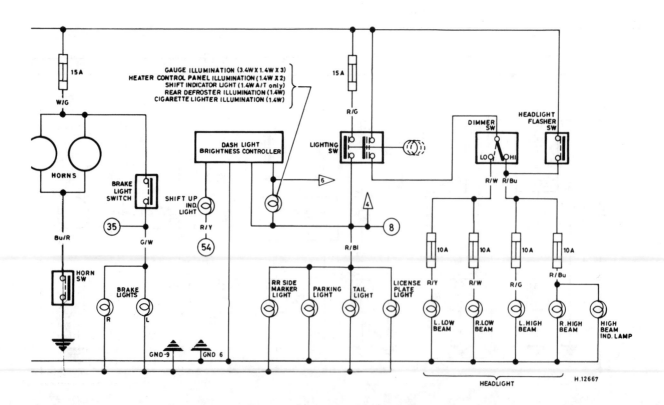

Main wiring diagram – CRX (carbureted models) (continued)

AIR CONDITIONER CIRCUIT (Std)

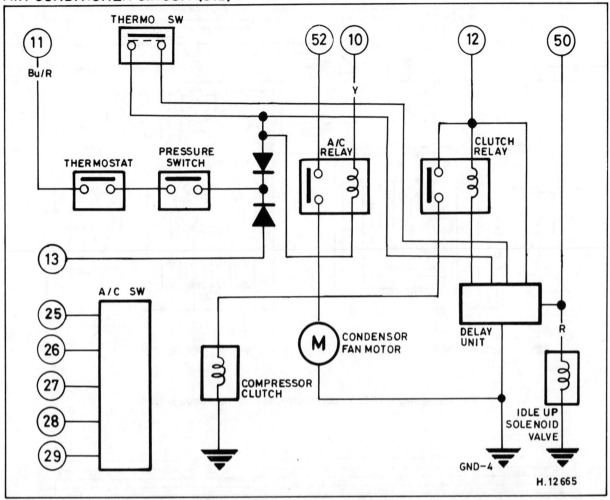

AIR CONDITIONER CIRCUIT (HF)

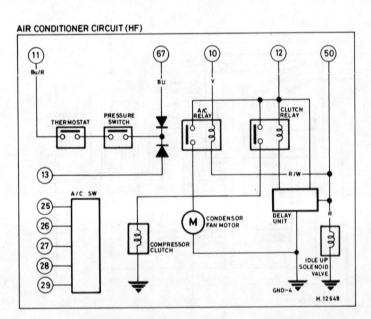

CLOCK CIRCUIT

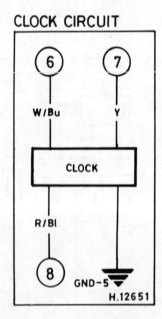

Auxiliary wiring diagram – CRX (carbureted models) (continued)

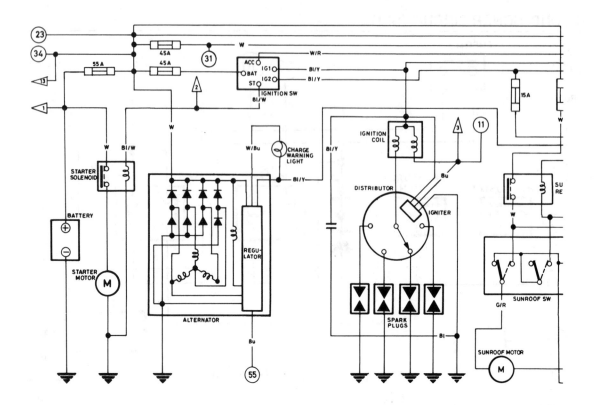

Main wiring diagram – CRX (fuel injected models) (1985 through 1987)

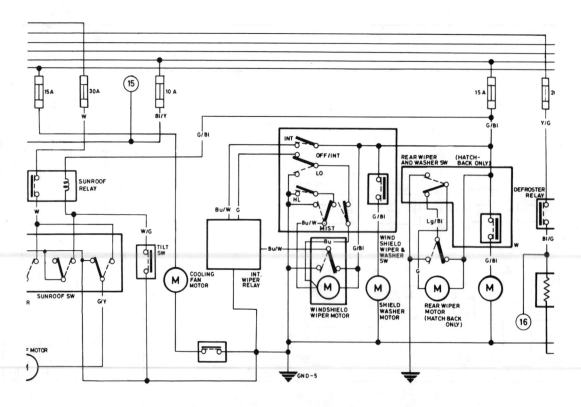

Main wiring diagram – CRX (fuel injected models) (continued)

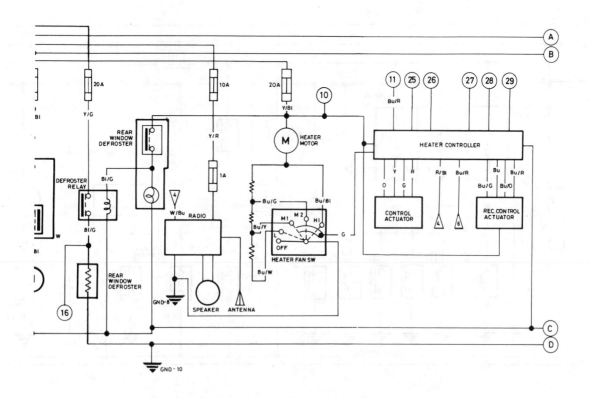

Main wiring diagram – CRX (fuel injected models) (continued)

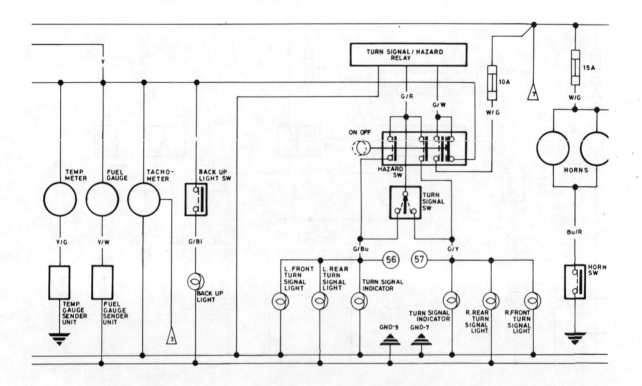

Main wiring diagram – CRX (fuel injected models) (continued)

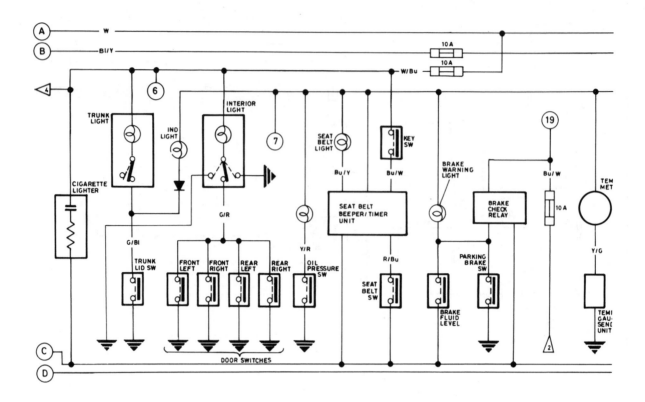

Main wiring diagram – CRX (fuel injected models) (continued)

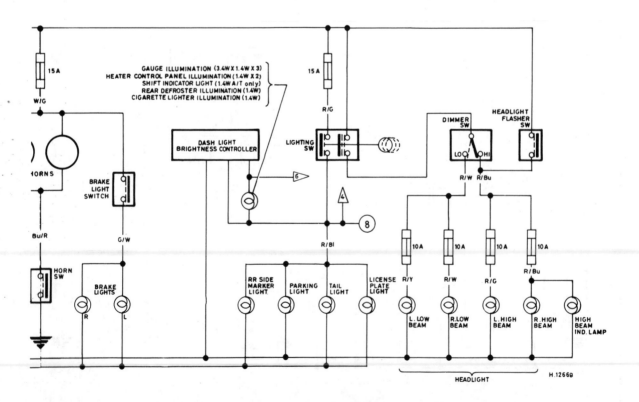

Main wiring diagram – CRX (fuel injected models) (continued)

CLOCK CIRCUIT

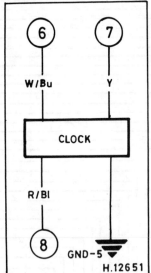

H.12651

SIDE MARKER, FLASHER CIRCUIT

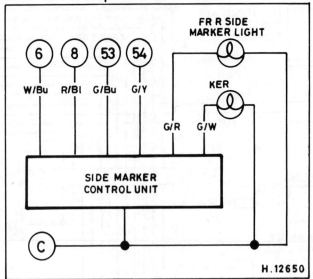

H.12650

AIR CONDITIONER CIRCUIT

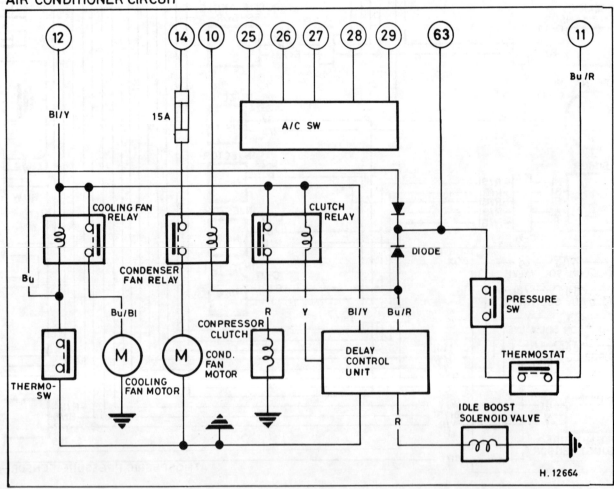

H.12664

Auxiliary wiring diagram – CRX (fuel injected models) (continued)

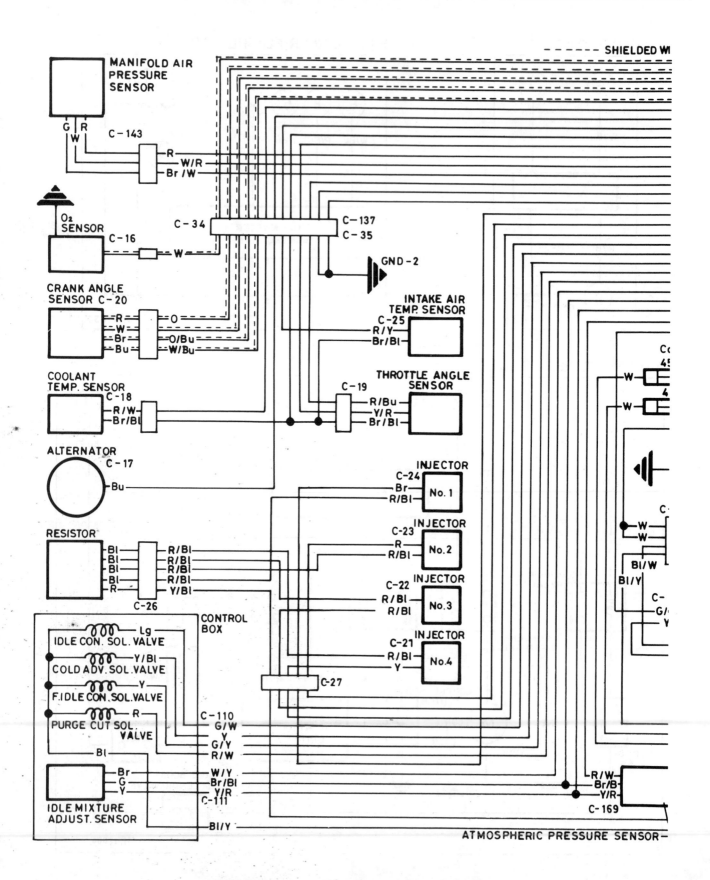

Fuel injection system wiring diagram (1985 through 1987)

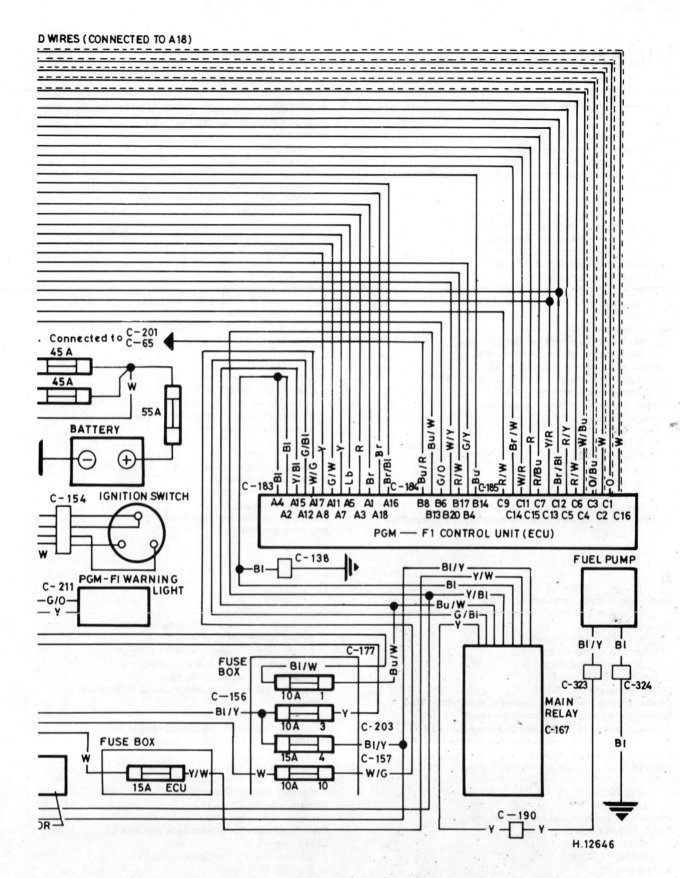

Fuel injection system wiring diagram (continued)

Index

Index

Index

Index